MAN'S ROLE IN THE SHAPING OF THE EASTERN MEDITERRANEAN LANDSCAPE

PROCEEDINGS OF THE INQUA/BAI SYMPOSIUM ON THE IMPACT OF ANCIENT MAN ON THE LANDSCAPE OF THE EASTERN MEDITERRANEAN REGION AND THE NEAR EAST GRONINGEN / NETHERLANDS / 6 - 9 MARCH 1989

Man's Role in the Shaping of the Eastern Mediterranean Landscape

Edited by
S. BOTTEMA, G. ENTJES-NIEBORG & W. VAN ZEIST
Biologisch-Archaeologisch Instituut, Groningen

A.A. BALKEMA / ROTTERDAM / BROOKFIELD / 1990

Published by

A.A.Balkema, P.O.Box 1675, 3000 BR Rotterdam, Netherlands
A.A.Balkema Publishers, Old Post Road, Brookfield, VT 05036, USA

ISBN 90 6191 138 9 ✓

Man's Role in the Shaping of the Eastern Mediterranean Landscape, Bottema, Entjes-Nieborg & van Zeist (eds)
© 1990 Balkema, Rotterdam. ISBN 90 6191 138 9

Table of contents

Man's Role in the Shaping of the Eastern Mediterranean Landscape, Bottema, Entjes-Nieborg & van Zeist (eds)
© 1990 Balkema, Rotterdam. ISBN 90 6191 138 9

Preface

The present volume is the outcome of a symposium entitled 'The impact of ancient man on the landscape of the Eastern Mediterranean region and the Near East', held in Groningen, The Netherlands, from 6 to 9 March 1989. The symposium was organized jointly by the Regional Subcommission for the Study of the Holocene of the Circum-Mediterranean Area of the International Union for Quaternary Research (INQUA) and the Biologisch-Archaeologisch Instituut of the State University of Groningen. The symposium also formed part of the scientific events organized within the framework of the celebration of the 375th anniversary of the Groningen University.

In 1980, at a similar meeting of the INQUA Circum-Mediterranean Subcommission and the Biologisch-Archaeologisch Instituut, the evidence for climatic change in the Eastern Mediterranean was the central theme. This time we thought it appropriate to focus upon the effects of human interference with the environment, bearing in mind that it can be difficult to differentiate between climate-induced and human-induced changes.

The theme of the 1989 symposium touches upon one of the most urgent problems of mankind, namely that of the rapidly deteriorating environment, the disastrous consequence of the unscrupulous exploitation of the world's natural resources. To what extent can the study of the impact of ancient man upon his environment be of any use in finding a way out of the present threat? One should not over-estimate the possible role of palaeo-environmental studies in this respect, because solutions to the present environmental crisis are primarily political and economic issues. However, we may learn from the lessons of the past, and that not only from examples of irreversible destruction inflicted by ancient man. There are also examples of how man succeeded in keeping environmental damage to a minimum with comparatively simple means, and of the regeneration of nature after periods of large-scale and intensive degradation.

The Eastern Mediterranean has a long history of human interference with the landscape. It was ten thousand years or so ago that agriculture, inevitably with implications for the environment, developed in this region, and more than any other part of the world the Eastern Mediterranean has been the scene of the rise of early civilizations. It is from the cooperation between archaeology, zoology, botany, geomorphology, pedology and other disciplines that a picture should arise of the conditions and processes which shaped the 'cultural' landscape of the area under consideration.

With a view to ensuring a wide coverage of the fields contributing to the reconstruction of palaeoenvironmental conditions, a number of scholars were invited to present a so-called 'major paper' on a well defined subject. In addition, the other members of the INQUA Circum-Mediterranean Subcommission were encouraged to prepare a contribution of relevance to the theme of the symposium. The response was very satisfactory, so that we had a full three days of discussion meetings.

This volume contains the revised and in some instances expanded texts of most of the papers read at the symposium. Two papers by scholars who were unable to attend the conference are included. Editorial changes in the manuscripts essentially remained confined to the linguistic editing of part of the contributions. In the discussion sessions of the symposium the papers were grouped according to geographic region. For the proceedings we have opted for a grouping largely according to discipline. The section 'Man-environment interactions' may need some explanation. Although in all chapters the effects of human interference with the environment are the subject of the discussion, the contributions under this heading give greater prominence to ancient man himself.

The papers published in this volume cover a broad range of studies on the relations between man and the biological and physical environment. Some of the results are quite contrasting. Thus, in Jordan human mismanagement led to the virtual depletion of natural resources as early as the 7th millennium bc (Ch. 1). On the other hand, for modern Crete a rapid regeneration of the vegetation after a drastic decline in pasturage has been observed (Ch. 28). Geomorphic changes in the landscape, such as slope erosion and correlative valley alluviation, are usually the unintentional side-effects of human activity. Besides, there is evidence of active shaping of the landscape by ancient man, in the form of structural remains of desert agriculture in the southern Levant (Ch. 8) and in the measures taken by the inhabitants of the Israeli coast to maintain functioning harbours (Ch. 9). Various papers testify to the value of palynology as a tool for tracing and measuring the inroads made by ancient man on the vegetation. Unfortunately, we have as yet been unable to demonstrate palynologically the activities of Neolithic man in the Near East (Ch. 19), although at least locally his impact must have been quite considerable (Ch. 1). Shifts in the proportions of domestic animals in archaeological faunal assemblages are interpreted to reflect lowered carrying capacity associated with overgrazing (Ch. 17) and expanding agriculture (Ch. 16). The Yemen Highlands are an example of combined cultural and natural causes leading to the virtual desertion of an area (Ch. 3).

The Symposium and the publication of the proceedings have been made possible through financial support from the International Union for Quaternary Research (INQUA), the Koninklijke Nederlandse Akademie van Wetenschappen, the Lustrum Fund of the State University of Groningen on the occasion of its 375th anniversary, and the Biologisch-Archaeologisch Instituut. The organizers of the symposium and the editors of the proceedings wish to express their thanks to the respective institutions.

Thanks are also due to those who assisted in the preparation of the present volume. Linguistic revisions were carried out by Ms A.C.Bardet. Mr H.R.Roelink adapted various drawings for publication. Mr W.Haaima and Mr G.Tamminga of the Centrale Fotodienst of the Groningen University took care of the photographic reduction of a great number of illustrations.

The preparation of the camera-ready typescripts was executed by the editors, in particular by G. Entjes-Nieborg.

Biologisch-Archaeologisch Instituut   Sytze Bottema
State University of Groningen   Gertie Entjes-Nieborg
The Netherlands   Willem van Zeist

Man-environment interactions

Man's Role in the Shaping of the Eastern Mediterranean Landscape, Bottema, Entjes-Nieborg & van Zeist (eds)
© 1990 Balkema, Rotterdam. ISBN 90 6191 138 9

The impact of Neolithic subsistence strategies on the environment: The case of 'Ain Ghazal, Jordan

1

Ilse Köhler-Rollefson & Gary O. Rollefson
Department of Anthropology, San Diego State University, Calif., USA

ABSTRACT: Archaeological and palaeobiological evidence from the Neolithic settlement of 'Ain Ghazal (Jordan) suggests that its inhabitants experienced a dramatic narrowing of their resource base during the 2,000 years of occupation. It is proposed that the type of subsistence strategy considered as the hallmark of Neolithic culture, i.e. the combination of sedentary goat husbandry and crop cultivation, was initially productive, but gradually set into motion a spiraling cycle of environmental degradation in the surroundings of the site which eventually resulted in the dispersal of the population into smaller and economically specialized social groups. To illustrate this hypothesis the spatial requirements for Neolithic subsistence strategies, including goat husbandry, crop cultivation and wood utilization are calculated for the various stages of 'Ain Ghazal's development. It is concluded that the widespread abandonments of large sites that occurred at the end of the 7th millennium throughout the Levant may be the consequence of human mismanagement of natural resources and the depletion of catchment zones rather than of climatic change.

1 INTRODUCTION

The area around the former Neolithic settlement of 'Ain Ghazal at the northeastern out-skirts of Amman in Jordan presently conjures up few visions of the former abundance of natural resources that must have once been available to nurture and sustain one of the world's largest known early farming communities. While herds of sheep and goats can occasionally be seen grazing on the degraded pasturage of the open spaces not yet devoured by urban sprawl, the general impression is of a frugal, almost barren setting.

Yet we know from the analysis of faunal remains that during the early part of the pre-ceramic Neolithic period 'Ain Ghazal's inhabitants had access to an extremely diverse wildlife. They exploited over 40 vertebrate taxa, many of which are associated with more boreal and temperate climates, such as badger, marten, squirrel, and red fox, and which imply a dense and to some extent arboreal type of vegetation. The postholes of buildings constructed during this period demonstrate that large trees with substantial diameters were growing in the vicinity. On the other hand the biological remains of the early Pottery Neolithic period indicate that by then the range of animal species exploited had been drastically reduced; building techniques had been adapted to utilize progressively smaller tree trunks and to finally omit any use of constructional timber.

Can these developments which appear to reflect a gradual diminishing of both plant and animal resources in the catchment area be explained solely, or even partially, as repercussions of climatic changes? We suggest the alternative hypothesis that this first sustained, large-scale human sedentism constituted an enormous drain on a rich but sensitive eco-system that gradually and irretrievably lost its integrity. In previous papers

3

we have centered on the environmental consequences of such human activities as crop cultivation and plaster production; while those results will be summarized here, the prime focus of this paper will be on the effects of the close association between humans and goats on the brittle environment of the Fertile Crescent's marginal zones.

2 THE OCCUPATIONAL HISTORY OF 'AIN GHAZAL

Located on the slopes of the Wadi Zarqa at an elevation between 700 and 740 m, the site is lodged between the modern 250-300 mm isohyets (Anonymus). The deepest archaeological deposits, near the center of the site, extend to more than 3.5 m below the surface. It is estimated that more than 10% of the site had been destroyed before investigations began.

Five seasons of excavations were conducted at 'Ain Ghazal between 1982 and 1988 (Rollefson 1984, 1985; Rollefson and Simmons 1986, 1987; Rollefson, Kafafi and Simmons in press). Systematic soil and flotation samples were taken to augment information from artifacts, architecture, and macrofaunal remains obtained through using 0.5 cm screening of all excavated sediments.

27 radiocarbon dates chronicle the sequence of developments at 'Ain Ghazal, which comprised three major cultural periods: the Pre-Pottery Neolithic B (PPNB) (ca 7,250-6,000 bc), a Final Aceramic Neolithic (PPNC) (ca 6,200-?5,500 bc), and the Yarmoukian phase of the early Pottery Neolithic period (ca ?5,500-?5,000 bc).

2.1 Pre-Pottery Neolithic B (PPNB)

More than 200 sq m and over 300 cu m of PPNB cultural deposits have been sampled, and C-14 dates provide temporal benchmarks for four of the six or more observable major phases of occupation in the PPNB at 'Ain Ghazal. Although in most aspects these deposits are typical of the PPNB in the southern Levant (lithic technology and typology, architecture, palaeobotany, etc.) several features merit special mention here.

By the middle of the 7th millennium 'Ain Ghazal had sustained an expansion to about 4-5 ha, but shortly after 6,500 bc the village grew rapidly to about twice that size, and possibly included an enclave to the east across the Zarqa river. In addition to substantial resources provided by goats that were well on their way to full domestication (Köhler-Rollefson in press a,b), and agricultural and wild plant resources, the hunting of wild animals provided nearly half of the meat consumed during the early parts of the PPNB (Köhler-Rollefson et al. 1988). More than 17% of the bone fragments are from small mammals and non-mammals (Table 1), some of which are highly niche-specific and can be considered as gauges of past environmental conditions.

Taxa such as the vole, squirrel, marten and badger are adapted to woodland habitats. The European hedgehog and the goshawk are of boreal origin. The Egyptian mongoose, the long-eared hedgehog, the chukar partridge are representatives of steppic environments. Two species of duck suggest the existence of a local wetland habitat and even standing water in the region (Gillespie unpubl.). Interestingly, in view of the proximity of the river Zarqa, fish remains are extremely rare, although the remains of the sweet water crab (Potamos potamion) are relatively frequent. These ecologically specialized taxa are complemented by a number of animals with a wide ecological tolerance, among them the hare, wild cats, aurochs, and the red fox.

PPNB residents at 'Ain Ghazal relied on a secure agricultural base. Sickle blades accounted for nearly a tenth of the chipped stone tool inventory, and grinding stones were numerous (Rollefson and Simmons 1988). PPNB flotation samples have yielded 24 taxa of seed producing plants (Donaldson unpubl.; Neef unpubl.; cf. Donaldson in Rollefson et al. 1985). The most prominent plants, in descending order of frequency, were field peas, lentils, emmer and einkorn wheat, domestic two-row hulled barley, and chickpeas. Pistachio, fig, almond, horsebean, and vetch

Table 1. List of vertebrate taxa identified at 'Ain Ghazal (1982-1985 seasons).

MAMMALS

Erinaceus europaeus	European Hedgehog
Hemiechinus auritus	Long-eared Hedgehog
Lepus capensis	Brown Hare
Sciurus anomalus	Persian Squirrel
Spalax leucodon	Blind Mole-Rat
Microtus sp.	unid. vole
Meriones sp.	unid. large gerbilline
Mus musculus	House Mouse
Rattus cf. rattus	cf. Black Rat
Vulpes vulpes	Red Fox
Vulpes rüppelli	Sand Fox
Canis lupus	Wolf
Canis familiaris	Dog
Martes foina	Beech Marten
Meles meles	Eurasian Badger
Herpestes ichneumon	Egyptian mongoose
Felis sylvestris	European wildcat
Felis caracal	Caracal lynx
Equus cf. hemionus	unid. equid
Sus scrofa	wild boar
Bos primigenius	aurochs
Bos taurus	domesticated cattle
Gazella sp.	gazelle
Capra aegagrus	Bezoar goat
Capra hircus	domesticated goat

AMPHIBIANS

Bufo viridis	Green Toad

FISH

Barbus sp.	fresh-water catfish

BIRDS

cf. Anas	unid. marsh duck
cf. Aythya	unid. diving duck
Neophron percnopterus	Egyptian Vulture
Circus sp.	unid. harrier
Accipiter gentilis	Goshawk
Accipiter small sp.	unid. sparrowhawk
Buteo buteo	Common Buzzard
Aquila cf. rapax	cf. Steppe Eagle
Aquila chrysaetos	Golden Eagle
unid. Accipitrid	unid. hawk
Alectoris chukar	Chukar Partridge
Coturnix coturnix	Quail
cf. Otis tarda	cf. Great Bustard
cf. Chlamydotis undulata	cf. Houbara Bustard
Columba livia	Rock Dove
cf. Asio sp.	unid. owl
Corvus corone	Hooded Crow
Corvus small sp.	unid. small crow
Corvus corax	Common Raven

REPTILES

Testudo cf. graeca	Small tortoise
Agama sp.	unid. small agamid
Varanus griseus	Desert Monitor
Ophisaurus apodus	Glass Lizard
cf. Malpolon monspessulanus	Montpellier Snake
Viperidae, large unid. sp.	large viper

were present as wild dietary constitutents. Some of the "weedy" taxa may have had pharmaceutical or other non-dietary uses for the population.

2.2 Final Aceramic Neolithic period (PPNC)

Shortly after 6,200 bc the character of the archaeological evidence alters radically at 'Ain Ghazal, suggesting that major socio-economic adjustments had taken place in a relatively short time. From the 200 sq m of PPNC deposits sampled

so far, it is clear that there were fundamental changes in lithic technology and typology, architecture, faunal inventory, and human burial practices (Rollefson and Simmons 1988). Nevertheless, other aspects of the chipped stone industry and architectural embellishment argue for some degree of cultural continuity, supporting geological evidence of an unbroken continuation of occupation at 'Ain Ghazal.

Economically, the period witnessed an increased reliance on goats, which compose nearly 70% of the sample (Table 2), and possibly domestic cattle and pig, while

Table 2. The animal remains from the 1984 season at 'Ain Ghazal in their stratigraphic context (n = number of identified specimens).

Species	PPNB		PPNC		Yarmouk	
	n	%	n	%	n	%
Ovicaprid	1591	53.1	549	68.4	209	71.3
Gazella	401	13.4	79	9.8	19	6.4
Bos	364	12.2	47	5.9	27	9.2
Sus	205	6.8	105	13.1	32	10.9
Equus	-	-	9	1.1	4	1.4
Vulpes	128	4.3	1	0.1	-	-
Sm.Carnivore	61	2.0	-	-	-	-
Felid	38	1.3	1	0.1	-	-
Canid	7	0.2	1	0.1	-	-
Meles	6	0.2	-	-	-	-
Lepus	57	1.9	1	0.1	-	-
Insectiv.	12	0.4	-	-	1	0.3
Rodent	10	0.3	3	0.4	-	-
Bird	55	1.8	-	-	-	-
Turtle	53	1.8	5	0.6	1	0.3
Reptile	6	0.2	2	0.3	-	-
Total	2994	99.9	803	100.0	293	99.9

small vertebrates only represent 1.7% of the faunal remains. The number of identified species narrows dramatically to 12, although to some extent this could be a result of the smaller absolute number of bones recovered from the PPNC. Interestingly, two taxa which were not present in the large PPNB assemblage suddenly occur. They are a medium sized equid (probably Equus hemionus), and the desert monitor lizard (Varanus sp.), which is represented by the vertebrae of one individual (Köhler-Rollefson et al. 1988).

Unfortunately, none of the flotation samples from PPNC deposits produced any macrobotanical remains, so little can be said of the agricultural side of the economy. The absolutely small numbers of sickle blades and grinding stones (Rollefson and Simmons 1986) may hold clues for some changes in this aspect of subsistence.

In terms of wood utilization, it is noteworthy that in house construction posts had been replaced by stone piers and interior walls (cf. Banning and Byrd 1984, 1987; Rollefson and Simmons 1986). A parallel development can be observed in the nature of hearth and firepit residues: charcoal is present only in minute amounts and particle size; the character of the ash deposits is consistent with fires fueled by dung or low-intensity fuels instead.

2.3 The Yarmoukian phase

Approximately 300 sq m of the latest phase of occupation have been exposed, and although it appears that the settlement underwent an in situ transition from the aceramic to the ceramic Neolithic, by the middle of the Yarmoukian period 'Ain Ghazal witnessed a complete realignment in terms of settlement strategy, subsistence base, and social and cultural composition.

In regards to animal exploitation, the trend apparent in the PPNC is intensified: goat husbandry increases further in importance to over 70%; in addition pig and cattle contribute to a 90% reliance on domestic animals. While gazelle hunting continues to decline, equids slightly expand their share. Small mammals and non-mammalian taxa are virtually non-existent in the archaeological record.

The agricultural base of the Yarmoukian inhabitants remains obscure, for as was the case with PPNC sediments, flotation samples have not been productive in terms of macro-botanical remains. Based on the small samples of chipped stone tools from the 1984 and 1985

Table 3. Site size and population estimates for various times at 'Ain Ghazal (cf. Rollefson and Köhler-Rollefson in press)

	Site size	population	No. of families
7250 bc	2.0 ha	572-604	95-100
6750 bc	4.5 ha	1287-1359	215-226
6250 bc	9.5 ha	2717-2869	450-478
5750 bc	12.5 ha	3575-3775	596-629

seasons, sickle blades were scarce (1.6% of the tool inventory), and ground stone artifacts were also relatively rare (Rollefson and Simmons 1988: Table 4).

3 THE EFFECTS OF GOAT HUSBANDRY

From the very beginning of 'Ain Ghazal's archaeological record, goats compose the predominant faunal resource, but initially they represented only one of many species exploited. Over the next 2,000 years the relationship between them and humans strengthened into an almost exclusive alliance that can certainly be regarded as successful for its two partners. However, their gain in numbers can be inferred to have affected other components of the original ecosystem, crowding out certain species and thereby decreasing biological diversity.

The goat, also known as the "black plague of the Middle East", has born the brunt of the blame for the present degraded state of much of the circum-Mediterranean vegetation today. On the other hand, the idea that already in Neolithic times goats could have had a major impact on the environment stretches the imagination of most people. However, a few simple calculations about the size of 'Ain Ghazal's human population, the number of goats likely to have been kept by them, and their forage requirements demonstrate that the demands of goat keeping on the plant resources of the area were substantial, especially when it is considered that they were in strong competition with agricultural and energy needs of the human population.

3.1 Human population estimates

A variety of procedures is avail-able to estimate population sizes of archaeological sites (Hassan 1978), and each of these methods has its critics. The application of such procedures is particularly difficult in the case of 'Ain Ghazal, for only about 1% of the settlement has been excavated intensively for each of the three major cultural periods, and only a few test probes have sampled the limits of domestic construction of the site (Rollefson and Simmons 1986, 1987). There is also little information on the homogeneity of the architectural density during any phase of occupation, although where excavations have exposed relatively broad horizontal areas, houses appear to have been consistently quite close together in the PPNB and PPNC periods. During the Yarmoukian period dwellings appear to have been somewhat more dispersed.

The following calculations (Table 3) are based on Van Beek's study of a modern tell site in Yemen (Van Beek 1982). It has to be strongly emphasized here that the figures in Table 3 (and numbers resulting from subsequent calculations based on these figures) are not to be taken as valid in their absolute terms. They do however provide a useful relative scale to assess the consequences of sustained population growth.

Based on Van Beek's figures of 286-302 people per hectare at Tell Marib (Van Beek 1982) the PPNB population at 'Ain Ghazal can be assumed to have more than doubled by the end of the first 500 years of occupation (225%) and doubled again by 6,250 bc (211%). The growth rate began to level off in the next 500 years (132%) during the PPNC period, and while the earliest Yarmoukian population was probably roughly equal to that of the latest PPNC group, the apparent decrease in the number of Yarmouk-

Table 4. Cultivation requirements based on population estimates

	number of families	hectares
7250 bc	97	190-200
6750 bc	220	430-452
6250 bc	464	900-956
5750 bc	612	1,191-1,258
Total		2,712-2,866

ian structures suggests that the permanent population at the settlement was beginning to dwindle. We estimate that the site was finally abandoned as a permanent settlement in the last century or two of the 6th millennium, changing to a temporary, perhaps seasonal camp.

Using the population estimates derived in Table 3, it is possible to investigate the scale of human needs on the environment in terms of the acreage necessary for farming.

Table 4 reflects the increasing depletion of productive farmland in the vicinity of 'Ain Ghazal. We suggest that the figures are cumulative in view of the terrain and liability of soils to wind and rain erosion (Rollefson and Köhler-Rollefson in press). It may be inferred that by the middle of the PPNC period (ca 5,750 bc) the farmers had to travel at least three kilometers from the settlement to reach the edge of most of the arable fields.

Soil loss was accelerated by the removal of trees from the surrounding countryside for timbers in house construction and for the enormous fuel requirements to manufacture plaster used in the floors and wall surfaces of the dwellings at 'Ain Ghazal (Table 5).

Although natural reforestation would normally be expected to replace at least a good portion of the depleted wooded areas around 'Ain Ghazal, the growing demands for agricultural acreage and the effects of browsing by goats (see below) may have removed forever the trees from the surrounding landscape within a ca 3 km radius from the center of the settlement by Middle PPNC times (cf. Rollefson and Köhler-Rollefson in press).

Table 5. Tree consumption for architectural purposes (60% for plaster manufacture and 40% for structural timber) at 'Ain Ghazal (from Rollefson and Köhler-Rollefson in press)

	Number of houses	Depleted trees	hectares
7250 bc	126	1,260	72.4
7150 bc	157	1,570	89.7
7050 bc	188	1,880	107.5
6950 bc	219	2,190	125.1
6850 bc	250	2,500	142.9
6750 bc	283	2,830	161.7
6650 bc	346	3,460	197.7
6550 bc	409	4,090	233.7
6450 bc	472	4,720	269.7
6350 bc	535	5,350	305.7
6250 bc	600	6,000	342.9
6150 bc	637	3,882+	218.4+
6050 bc	674	4,044+	231.1+
5950 bc	711	4,266+	243.8+
5850 bc	748	4,488+	256.5+
5750 bc	787	4,722+	269.8
Total consumption		57,192	3268.2

(Note that fuel requirements for other domestic activities such as cooking are not considered here).

3.2 The size of the goat population and forage requirements

Based on varying premises about the number of goats that every family of six would consume per year, goat populations were estimated according to Table 6. Calculations are based on the assumption of a 30% annual off-take rate (cf. Dahl and Hjort 1976:208), i.e. that for every goat consumed two additional individuals of breeding stock would have to be kept.

Table 6. Estimated goat populations for various times at 'Ain Ghazal, based on "Low" (2), "High" (12), and "Medium" (6) annual consumption.

	Number of families	goat consumption low	medium	high
7250 bc	97	582	1,746	3,492
6750 bc	220	1,320	3,960	7,920
6250 bc	464	2,784	8,352	16,704
5750 bc	612	3,672	11,016	22,032

The "Low Goat" consumption estimate refers to a "herd" of six
goats for each family, of which two
juveniles are available as meat for
each family each year. The "High
Goat" estimate is a herd of 36
goats per family, providing 12
juveniles annually for inclusion
in the diet. The "Medium Goat"
column refers to a herd of 18
goats, which yields six juveniles
each year for the family's consumption. [Occasionally a senile goat
would also be available for slaugh-
ter.] If in the PPNB period (7,200-
6,000 bc) we accept that 50% of the
meat protein came from wild animals, and in the PPNC period that a
considerable amount of meat was
available from domesticated cattle
and pigs, any of the "low", "high",
and "medium" figures are conservative, and it is convenient to use
the "medium" category as acompro-
mise.

It is obvious that even a relatively low concentration of goats
in the vicinity of 'Ain Ghazal
would have far surpassed the density of any goat population in the
wild. Modern wild goat populations
in Pakistan range in densities between 0.8 and 4.1 individuals per
sq km (Schaller 1977:109). On the
Greek island of Theodorou 97 goats
lived on 68 ha (equal to 143 animals per sq km) and had seriously
altered the composition of the
vegetation (Schaller 1977, quoting
Papageorgiou 1974).

The carrying capacity for the
type of vegetation found presently
around 'Ain Ghazal, but in a non-
degraded condition, has been estimated to be about 1 sheep/ha
(Huss 1977). Since sheep and goats
have approximately the same live
weight, it is legitimate to equate
this with a carrying capacity of
one goat/ha. Based on the premise
that of the total number of goats
kept per family, about 50% would be
juvenile and hence require only
about half the amount of pasturage
of an adult individual, this would
translate into an equation of 1.5
ha supporting 2 goats.

3.3 The feeding behaviour of goats

Although goats feed upon a variety
of plants, including tender grasses
and forbs, browse composes much of
their diet (Sampson 1952). Different from most other domestic ruminants such as cattle and sheep,
goats like to eat the young sprouts
and leaves of ligneous plants (Le
Houérou 1977). While they cannot
damage mature trees above a certain
height, they prevent the regrowth
and establishment of seedlings. It
is exactly for this reason that
goats are successfully employed for
brush control and clearing. For
instance, it is recommended that
"to destroy dense stands of sprout-
ing brush 2 or 3 goats are grazed
per acre the first year, and the
number is decreased as the browse
is thinned out" (Sampson 1952).
These qualities of the goat are
benefits in tropical areas, and may
even initially have aided Neolithic
farmers in clearing land for cultivation. But in a semi-arid environment they are bound to develop into
a serious liability, in this case
preventing any regeneration of the
tree stands cut down by 'Ain Ghazal's inhabitants for house
construction and fuel.

Quite apart from the problems
associated specifically with the
goat, under semi-arid conditions
any sedentary type of animal husbandry (without strictly enforced
deferred rotation grazing systems)
will lead to over-grazing and the
degeneration of range land. According to range management scientists
(e.g. Huss 1977) all types of vegetation need to be protected from
grazing during at least two periods
per year: on emergence from dormancy and on entering dormancy. De-
foliation, i.e. grazing, during
these periods will lead to the
death of plants, and effect the reduction of palatable vegetation and
replacement by less palatable or
toxic plants that are avoided by
animals.

At present we do not know if the
goats herded by the 'Ain Ghazal
people had been domesticated from
local wild populations, i.e. if
they composed part of the native
fauna. Goat remains are extremely
rare in pre-Neolithic deposits in
the Levant, and they were totally
absent during the late Pleistocene
and even the early Neolithic from
the area to the east of 'Ain Ghazal
(Garrard et al. 1988).
If goats were indeed a relatively

9

Table 7. Pasturage requirements (in hectares) of goat herds at 'Ain Ghazal based on "low", "medium" and "high" consumption. (The numbers in brackets reflect the radius in kilometers from the center of the site).

	low	medium	high
7250 bc	437(1.2)	1,310(2.0)	2,619 (2.9)
6750 bc	990(1.8)	2,970(3.1)	5,945 (4.4)
6250 bc	2,088(2.6)	6,264(4.5)	12,528 (6.3)
5750 bc	2,529(2.8)	8,262(5.2)	16,524 (7.3)

recent or human introduction to the area, then their impact must have been especially dramatic, since the vegetation would not yet have developed any adaptive responses to grazing pressure by this particular species, such as the production of toxins and other chemical substances that reduce their digestibility (Nyerges 1980).

3.4 Interaction between goat husbandry and agriculture

When calculating the spatial requirements of the 'Ain Ghazal inhabitants to produce food for their burgeoning numbers, it is important to realize that rotating land use between crop cultivation and animal husbandry, which is often practised in temperate zones, would not have been an option for them. One of the results of an ethnographic and ecologic study of an agro-pastoral community in southern Jordan, living in an ecological setting similar to that of 'Ain Ghazal, was that agricultural land left fallow is of practically no value as pastureland (Köhler-Rollefson 1988). The clearing of land for cultivation always entails the destruction of the perennial sclerophyllous vegetation that constitutes prime pasturage and that is available throughout the year; these plants do not regenerate during the fallowing periods, and all that can be found on fallow are inpalatable plants and, possibly, a short-lasted flush of ephemerals during the rainy season. Hence any land that has once been cultivated is (in the absence of concerted measures to attain regeneration) eliminated as productive pasture.

In addition, the combination of agriculture and goat husbandry within close proximity usually generates other problems as well: goats, with their independent character and tendency to disperse widely (in contrast to sheep), in many cases constitute a grave danger to crops and often appear to wait just for that one moment of diverted attention on the part of their herder to invade and subsequently destroy cultivated fields. In most agricultural areas of the circum-Mediterranean, goat keeping is hence strictly forbidden (cf. Köhler-Rollefson 1988). Neolithic goats, which had not been subjected to generations of human selection for docility and conforming behaviour, most likely presented even greater problems.

The implications of Table 7 take on greater clarity when regarded in view of the agricultural and wood exploitation requirements of the 'Ain Ghazal inhabitants as mentioned above. The pasturage requirements for goats must be considered as additional territorial needs for at least most of the annual round when land under cultivation was unavailable for browsing and grazing.

3.5 Implications for the Neolithic economy

The southern Levantine economy that grew increasingly dependent on an integrated agricultural and pastoral foundation in the aceramic Neolithic period can have been assumed to have had two evident consequences. On one hand, goat husbandry "predisposed" areas of uncultivated land for later agricultural expansion. In this narrow aspect, the combination of herding and farming was self-serving, for as goat were kept away from the fields they "prepared" areas for eventual colonization by the removal of brush and saplings/seedlings (aided by the deforestation for fuel and building construction). But this progression also set into motion an irreversible destruction of the habitats enjoyed by the wild animals so important to the early residents of 'Ain Ghazal. This deterioration could be compensated for only by an increasing reliance on larger numbers of goats and on other domesticated species (cattle and pigs).

The second consequence of the integrated agro-pastoral economy devolved from the first. As goats and other domesticates grew in dietary importance, social adjustments to the conflicting demands of animal husbandry and farming became increasingly necessary. As the figures in Tables 4 and 7 indicate, the range of goat pasturage at the beginning of the 'Ain Ghazal settlement was well within a one-day radius from the site (even at the "High Goat" level). By 6,250 bc herds had to be taken for a five kilometer trek each day at the "Low Goat" level and almost seven kilometers each day (one-way) at a "Medium Goat" level. By the middle of the PPNC period (5,750 bc), herds of goats must have stayed away from the main settlement for most of the year, regardless of herd size, suggesting that a significant portion of the 'Ain Ghazal human population was no longer a permanent part of the settlement.

The latter consequence is of considerable interest, for the archaeological record of Jordan indicates that the non-farmable regions of the eastern steppe and desert regions began to experience more intensive expoitation just at the time when settlement patterns in the more mesic regions became severely disturbed (Rollefson in press a). Thus Garrard et al. (1988) note that small quantities of domesticated cereals turn up at Jilat 7, on the eastern edge of the steppe, in the mid 7th millennium, and that the earliest evidence of domesticated ovicaprids in the Azraq region appears several centuries later.

Furthermore, although exotic materials such as shells and obsidian at 'Ain Ghazal reflect long-distance contacts throughout the history of its occupation (Rollefson 1987), the appearance of a raw material called "Dhabba marble" (a green colored limestone) from the eastern steppe region suddenly occurs in the last half of the 7th millennium and increases in popularity in the PPNC period, indicating the growing familiarity of the 'Ain Ghazal inhabitants with this area.

The picture that emerges from these and other examples (cf. Rollefson 1988, in press b) suggests that the later aceramic peoples of the southern Levant accomodated the strains of the integrated pastoral/ farming economy by segregating the two elements into separate and complementary facets. We propose that by the middle of the Yarmoukian phase of the Pottery Neolithic period the socio-economic character of the populations in the southern Levant had altered considerably from the conditions that held through much of the 7th millennium. The region consisted of small agricultural communities, with groups of domesticated cattle and pigs, who traded their resources with pastoral nomads whose goats (and perhaps sheep) converted the otherwise unusable vegetal resources of the steppe and desert to animal meat and secondary products.

4 SUMMARRY

At 'Ain Ghazal we appear to witness the rise and subsequent fall of a symbiotic association between two species which was so successful that it quickly exceeded its territory's carrying capacity. The equilibrium could only be restored by eliminating one of the affiliates from their ecological niche, in this case the goat, from the vicinity of 'Ain Ghazal.

Goat husbandry had represented an ingenious response to the gradual depletion of game that we can infer to have occurred around early human settlements. Of the plethora of animal species available to Neolithic people, goats were intuitively selected because, from the human point of view, they were endowed with many advantages over other ungulates: they do not voluntarily leave their home territories; they imprint easily onto humans, they are tameable, even docile, and they are of a reasonable size in terms of meat yield per individual animal.

While goat domestication might have seemed like an ideal answer to the growing scarcity of faunal resources, and their availability undoubtedly contributed to human population growth, their rising numbers exerted strains on the environment which at first were imperceptible but steadily gained momentum: they prevented the replenishment of arboreal resources, and instead of articulating with cultivation they competed with it spatially. Their pasture requirements increased not only in proportion to their numbers, but the gradual decline of the carrying capacity due to year-round grazing had to be compensated for.

The effect of the Neolithic goat invites certain comparisons to the ecological disaster that occurred in the U.S. only in the last century when white settlers unleashed their herds of cattle and sheep onto the Western ranges which had previously only supported wild ungulate herds. Although the forage crop at first seemed inexhaustible, within half a century or less of uncontrolled grazing the ranges became seriously impoverished, and extensive grass stands had yielded to mesquite brush and prickly pear (Sampson 1952:361). The boom in livestock numbers turned into a devastating bust in which thousands of animals died of starvation.

Clearly, before goat husbandry could become an economic option that was as productive in the long run as it obviously has been in the Middle East, humans needed to accommodate for the requirements and drawbacks of their chosen commensals and, in order to "milk" the full benefits of this association, they had to adapt their own lifestyles. The seasonal removal of the herds from the village to exploit pastures further afield, i.e. semi-sedentism, was one of the first steps they took, possibly as early as the PPNC. Since keeping goats purely for meat is obviously extremely uneconomic in terms of labour and energy consumption, one wonders at what point in time milk exploitation became a factor. Eventually a whole codex of complicated

grazing rules and regulations was to be developed by the pastoralists in the Arabian peninsula and Syria, the Hema system of range conservation (Draz 1969), an Arabic precursor to Western range management science. But its establishment was posssible only after many trials and errors; it represented the end result of countless human attempts to grapple with the ecological legacy of their Neolithic forefathers who first domesticated ungulates.

REFERENCES

Anonymus.
   Summary of Climatological Data for the period 1965-1977. Monograph of the Meteorological Directorate, Statistics Division, Amman.
Banning, E. and B.Byrd 1984.
   The architecture of PPNB 'Ain Ghazal, Jordan. BASOR 255:15-20.
Banning, E. and B.Byrd 1987.
   Houses and the changing residential unit: domestic architecture at PPNB 'Ain Ghazal, Jordan. Proc. Prehist. Soc. 53:309-325.
Dahl, G. and A.Hjort 1976.
   Having Herds. Stockholm: Department of Social Anthropology.
Draz, O. 1969.
   The "HEMA" system of range reserves in the Arabian peninsula, its possibilities in range improvement and conservation projects in the Near East. Rome: FAO Report, FAO/PL:PFC/13.
Donaldson, M. unpubl.
   The preliminary analysis of plant remains from the 1984 'Ain Ghazal excavations.
Garrard, A., A.Betts, B.Byrd, S.Colledge and C.Hunt 1988.
   Summary of palaeoenvironmental and prehistoric investigations in the Azraq Basin. In A.Garrard and H.Gebel (eds.), The Prehistory of Jordan. BAR International Series 396.
Gillespie, W. unpubl.
   Small mammals, amphibians, reptiles, and birds from 'Ain Ghazal: materials from the 1982, 1984, and 1985 excavations.
Hassan, F. 1978.
   Demographic archaeology. In M. Schiffer (ed.), Advances in archaeological method and theory, Vol. I, p.49-103. New York,

Academic Press.

Huss, D. 1977.
Some range management principles and practices for the Near East. Cairo: FAO.

Köhler-Rollefson, I. 1988.
The aftermath of the Levantine Neolithic Revolution in the light of ecological and ethnographic evidence. Paléorient 14:87-94.

Köhler-Rollefson, I. in press a.
Jordanian goat husbandry from a diachronic perspective. In O. Labianca (ed.), Ancient Mediterranean foodsystems.

Köhler-Rollefson, I. in press b.
Changes in goat exploitation at 'Ain Ghazal between the early and late Neolithic: A metrical analysis. In O.Aurenche et al. (eds.), Préhistoire du Levant II.

Köhler-Rollefson, I.,
W.Gillespie and M.Metzger 1988.
The fauna from Neolithic 'Ain Ghazal. In A.Garrard and H.Gebel (eds.), The Prehistory of Jordan, p.423-430. BAR International Series 396.

Le Houérou, H.N. 1977.
Plant sociology and ecology applied to grazing lands research, survey and management in the Mediterranean basin. In W.Krause (ed.), Application of Vegetation Science to Grassland Husbandry, p.213-276. The Hague, Junk.

Neef, R. unpubl.
A preliminary note on the botanical material of 'Ain Ghazal, 1984.

Nyerges, E. 1980.
Traditional pastoralism. Expedition 22:36-41.

Papageorgiou, N. 1974.
Population Energy Relationships of the Agrimi (Capra aegagrus cretica) on Theodorou Island, Greece. PhD thesis, Michigan State University.

Rollefson, G. 1984.
'Ain Ghazal: An early Neolithic community in highland Jordan, near Amman. BASOR 255:3-14.

Rollefson, G. 1985.
The 1983 season at the early Neolithic site of 'Ain Ghazal. National Geographic Research 1: 44-62.

Rollefson, G. 1987.
Local and external relations in the Levantine PPN period: 'Ain Ghazal (Jordan) as a regional center. In A.Hadidi (ed.),

Studies in the History and Archaeology of Jordan III, p.29-32. Amman, Department of Antiquities.

Rollefson, G. 1988.
Stratified burin classes at 'Ain Ghazal: implications for the "Desert Neolithic" of Jordan. In A.Garrard and H.Gebel (eds.), The Prehistory of Jordan, p.437-449. BAR International Series 396.

Rollefson, G. in press a.
The aceramic Neolithic of the Levant: The view from 'Ain Ghazal. In O.Aurenche et al. (eds.), Préhistoire du Levant II.

Rollefson, G. in press b.
The late aceramic Neolithic of the Levant: A Synthesis. In O. Aurenche et al. (eds.), Préhistoire du Levant II.

Rollefson, G.,
Z.Kafafi and A.Simmons in press.
The 1985 season at 'Ain Ghazal: preliminary report. Annual of the Department of Antiquities of Jordan.

Rollefson, G. and
I.Köhler-Rollefson in press.
The collapse of Early Neolithic settlements in the Southern Levant. In Proceedings of the Second Symposium on Upper Paleolithic, Epipaleolithic, and Neolithic Populations of Europe and the Mediterranean Basin.

Rollefson, G. and A.Simmons 1986.
The Neolithic Village of 'Ain Ghazal, Jordan: Preliminary report on the 1984 season. BASOR Supplem. 24:147-164.

Rollefson, G. and A.Simmons 1987.
The Neolithic village of 'Ain Ghazal, Jordan: Preliminary report on the 1985 Season. BASOR Supplem. 25:93-106.

Rollefson, G. and A.Simmons 1988.
The Neolithic settlement at 'Ain Ghazal. In A.Garrard and H.Gebel (eds.), The Prehistory of Jordan, p.393-421. BAR International Series 396.

Rollefson, G., A.Simmons,
M.Donaldson, W.Gillespie,
Z.Kafafi, I.Köhler-Rollefson,
E.McAdam and S.Rolston 1985.
Excavation at the Pre-Pottery Neolithic B (PPNB) village of 'Ain Ghazal (Jordan), 1983. Mitteilungen der Deutschen Orient Gesellschaft 117:69-116.

Sampson, A. 1952.
Range Management. Principles and

Practice. New York: John Wiley.
Schaller, G. 1977.
Mountain Monarchs. Chicago: The
University of Chicago Press.
Van Beek, G. 1982.
A population estimate for Marib:
A Contemporary Tell village in
North Yemen. BASOR 248:61-67.

Man's Role in the Shaping of the Eastern Mediterranean Landscape, Bottema, Entjes-Nieborg & van Zeist (eds)
© *1990 Balkema, Rotterdam. ISBN 90 6191 138 9*

The effects of irrigation agriculture: Bronze and Iron Age habitation along the Khabur, Eastern Syria

2

Hartmut Kühne
Institut für Archäologie, Freie Universität Berlin, Berlin

ABSTRACT: Recent archaeological research in the Lower Khabur area of northeastern Syria focusses on Bronze and Iron Age habitation. Ancient agriculture in the area must have been based primarily on irrigation, the precipitation regime being unfavourable for rain-fed agriculture. In the Early Bronze Age (ca 3000-2000 BC) and probably also in the Middle Bronze Age (ca 2000-1500 BC) local irrigation systems seem to have existed. In the period ca 1275-1075 BC, under firm and well-organized Middle Assyrian control, large-scale irrigation agriculture fed by regional canals developed. Agriculture in the Lower Khabur area flourished again in the 9th to 7th centuries BC, under Neo-Assyrian supremacy.

1 IRRIGATION AGRICULTURE

Irrigation agriculture in the Near East has been practised since the Neolithic. The earliest evidence of an irrigation system was discovered at Choga Mami, some 110 km east of Baghdad, near the Iraqi-Iranian border. It is dated to the sixth millennium BC, to the Samarran Phase of the Pottery Neolithic Period (Oates and Oates 1976). It is widely accepted that irrigation agriculture formed the basis of the urbanization process in Mesopotamian civilization, which in turn led to the first "Hochkultur", characterized by the introduction of writing and the use of the cylinder seal as an expression of advanced division of labour, craft specialization and administration (Nissen 1988). Various aspects of the beginning of irrigation agriculture and of its effect on prehistoric and historical society have been discussed by Boserup (1965), Harris (1969), Smith (1972), Oates (1972, 1980), Adams (1972), Flannery (1976), and others. These works give a general outline of the development of agriculture in relation to natural conditions and society in the ancient Near East. At the same time

the need for more historical data, raised on a local and/or regional basis, emerges.

Before discussing the effects of irrigation, a brief thought may be devoted to the preconditions for irrigation. There are five important ones which come to mind:

1. the necessity of irrigation, generally caused by the climatic situation and the environment;

2. favourable natural conditions for building an irrigation system;

3. the technical know-how for building it;

4. the "financial" means;

5. a stable, powerful government, or at least a community to carry out such an enterprise and to maintain it once it has come into use.

The possible effects are listed below in the form of advantages and disadvantages, their importance varying only according to the scale of the irrigation works.

Advantages
- agricultural intensification
- improved transportation system
- larger yields
- stabilization of income
- more regular settlement pattern
- occupation and exploitation of otherwise remote areas

- population increase
- stabilization of government, society and culture

Disadvantages
- salinization
- lack of floods
- environmental change

Even without listing all features it cannot be overlooked that the advantages outnumber the disadvantages in quantity and quality. At least superficially the disadvantages appear to be minor effects, although in the long run they may be disastrous.

It is obvious that the encountered features form a causal chain, leading to what may be generalized as "more civilization". On the negative side, they lead to deforestation and unwarranted exploitation of soils, flora and fauna, so that salinization, desiccation and devastation are the long-term (or sometimes the surprisingly short-term) consequences.

2 TELL SCHECH HAMAD

In this paper the effects of irrigation within a certain area and historical time range (3000-500 BC) are to be investigated. Until very recently any basic information on the subject in the fields of archaeology, history, (palaeo)botany, (archaeo)zoology, geomorphology and agriculture for this area has been very scanty. This situation may be explained by the lack of archaeological research, but even more by the lack of an interdisciplinary approach to the problems. Moreover, such questions were not even raised.

Being an archaeologist, I will restrict myself to field-archaeological and historical observations. But having initiated an interdisciplinary project in the area I will use some of the arguments and results my colleagues have arrived at so far.

The Khabur is the largest tributary of the Euphrates, carrying water throughout the year and with an average discharge of 50 cu m/sec. Its spring consists of thirteen karst depressions, one of the largest karst springs in the world. Geographically the Khabur region

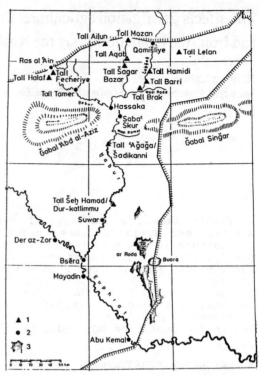

Fig. 1. Map of the Khabur region in northeastern Syria (Ergenzinger 1988). 1. Ancient site; 2. Modern town; 3. Salt-pan.

can be divided into two parts, the Upper Khabur, between Ras al-'Ain and Hassake, and the Lower Khabur, between Hassake and its junction with the Euphrates (Fig. 1). Included in the "Khabur region" is the fan-shaped area of its tributaries north of Hassake, draining a large part of the southern Turkish Taurus range. The river itself marks the western edge of this triangular area, flowing at first in a southeasterly direction to Hassake. Because of the volcano Kaukab, just east of Hassake, and because of a southward-stretching volcanic ridge, the river is diverted to a straight southward course which it maintains until its confluence with the Euphrates. The course of the river passes through three zones of precipitation. The spring lies in a zone of 300 to 400 mm average annual precipitation, the town of Hassake and a narrow zone up to 80 km south of it receive between 300 and 200 mm rainfall. The area south

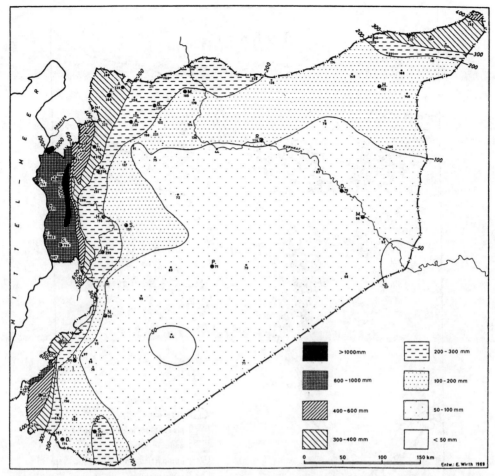

Fig. 2. Mean annual precipitation in the dry years 1958-1960
(Wirth 1971, Map 4).

of this line gets less than 200 mm precipitation. The area of the tributaries barely extending south of Kamishli, which might be regarded as a fourth zone, receives between 400 and 600 mm precipitation (Wirth 1971:Map 3).

According to a division of agricultural zones defined by the Food and Agriculture Organization of the United Nations and based on "intensity and reliability of rainfall", the Khabur region would meet the criteria of four types of zones (FAO 1982; Hopfinger in press). In other words, over a distance of roughly 300 km the Khabur passes through three zones of precipitation and four agricultural zones.

How sensitive the agricultural zones are to the intensity and reliability of rainfall is amply demonstrated in years of drought (Wirth 1971:Map 4; cf. Fig. 2). There are extreme shifts of the zones of precipitation to the north. The whole valley of the Khabur is then situated in the zone of less than 200 mm rainfall. Therefore it has been argued elsewhere (Kühne in press a) that the general geoclimatic and agronomical conditions along the Khabur necessitate a regional irrigation system. It is exactly this reason why the Syrian government is planning large water reservoirs, a dam and a regional canal project (Hopfinger 1984; cf. Fig. 3).

Archaeological research in the Khabur region has been fairly limited. Several explorers and travel-

17

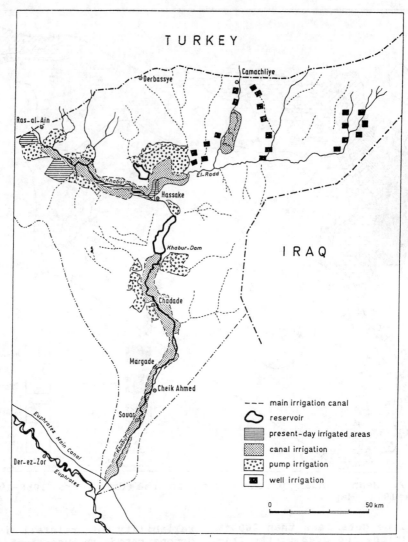

Fig. 3. Map of the planned Khabur irrigation project
(Hopfinger 1984).

lers passed through the area during the second half of the last and the early part of this century, but only a few took a closer interest. From their observations the pioneering work of Oppenheim (1899-1900, 1931, 1943-1962), Sarre and Herzfeld (1911-1920), Poidebard (1934) and Mallowan (1947) ensued. But no systematic survey was made until the "Tübinger Atlas des Vorderen Orients" took up this challenge for the Lower Khabur in 1975 and 1977. The main points of interest for the TAVO were the historical periods of the Bronze and Iron Age (roughly between 3000 and 500 BC), the cuneiform sources of which mention a large number of villages and towns along the river. A fairly complete inventory of nearly 130 sites along the river banks was worked out (Kühne 1974-1977, 1978-1979), covering a time range between the Aceramic Neolithic (around 7000 BC) to the present. As a result of this survey, excavations were undertaken at Tell Schech Hamad in 1978 (Kühne 1984, 1986) and continued yearly since 1980. In 1983 an interdisciplinary programme was launched, endeavouring to reconstruct the environmental conditions of the main settlement period of this site, the Assyrian Period, between 1300 and 500 BC.

Tell Schech Hamad thus became the first systematic excavation along the Lower Khabur. Because of irrigation plans of the Syrian government, a number of rescue excavations have been started in the northern third of the Lower Khabur. Among them is the excavation of Tell Bderi, under the direction of the present author, sponsored and financed by the Free University of Berlin and carried out by Peter Pfälzner (1988a) as field director. This site is situated about 100 km north of Tell Schech Hamad, also on the east bank. It was included in the interdisciplinary programme, as well as Tell 'Agaga, situated about 70 km north of Tell Schech Hamad on the west bank and excavated by As'ad Mahmoud, the director of the National Museum at Deir ez-Zor (Mahmoud 1984; Mahmoud et al. 1988). Thus, the interdisciplinary programme operating from these three base camps, was based on regional data.

None of the numerous sites on the Upper Khabur has been excavated so far, except Tell Halaf and Tell Fakhariyah (McEwan et al. 1958). Archaeological activity after the Second World War has concentrated on the sites situated in the fertile plains of the fan-shaped area of the Khabur tributaries. Several surveys were undertaken, one of which has been published (Meijer 1986), and excavations were carried out in Tell Brak (Oates 1987), Tell Barri (Pecorella and Salvini 1984), Tell Leilan (Weiss 1983), Tell Hamidiya (Eichler et al. 1985), and Tell Mozan (new excavation, directed by G.Bucellati).

Even during the first campaign in Tell Schech Hamad, the Assyrian name of the site had emerged from a Middle Assyrian archive: Dur-katlimmu (Röllig 1978). This name was already known from other Assyrian sources, mainly the Assyrian annals, which describe the town as one of the military stations along the river. After ten successive excavation seasons, the local function and development of this town is quite well understood

(Kühne in press b). It may be summarized briefly as follows: Surface finds indicate a small, village-type settlement as early as in the Late Chalcolithic (late 4th millennium). It was continuously occupied throughout the Early and Middle Bronze Age until the Middle Assyrian period. Then, in the 13th century BC, King Salmanassar I of Assyria seems to have enlarged the settlement area; he fortified the place and established it as a provincial administration centre. The intramural settlement then covered an area of about 15 ha. During a period of political weakness of the Assyrians in the 11th and 10th centuries BC the town was taken over by the Aramaeans. It eventually returned to Assyrian supremacy in the 9th century BC. In the late 8th and during the 7th century BC the intramural settlement was enlarged to 55 ha. Adding the extramural settlement area of another 50 ha, the Assyrian town of Dur-katlimmu now covered an area of over 100 ha. Apparently, the town became a military base camp in addition to its former function. One century after the downfall of the Assyrian empire the enlargement was given up and the intramural settlement was reduced again to its original 15 ha.

Using conventional demographic factors (150 persons per ha of intramural settlement area) the population of Dur-katlimmu must have increased from 2250 in the 13th century BC to about 9000 in the 7th century BC (including the extramural settlement). At the end of the 6th and in the 5th century BC the population apparently dwindled to its original size of about 2250 persons. In comparison, the nearby modern village of Garibe has 2200 inhabitants. Economically, this population has reached the limits of the area's agricultural potential in spite of modern pump irrigation (Hopfinger in press).

What caused this Assyrian extension and how was it supported? It was this question which led to the above-mentioned interdisciplinary research. At present Tell Schech Hamad is situated about 50 km south of the 200 mm isohyet. This line is generally accepted as the border between rain-fed and irrigation agriculture. The sensitivity of the

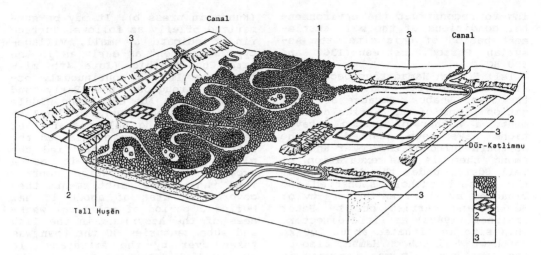

Fig. 4. Reconstruction of the surroundings of the Assyrian town of Dur-katlimmu (Frey and Kürschner in press). 1. Floodplain of the Khabur with Populetum euphraticae forest (Populus euphratica, Platanus orientalis, Tamarix spp.) and reedswamps (Phragmites australis, Typha sp.); 2. Irrigated field systems, partly on alluvial soil; 3. Upland with desert vegetation (Hammadetea salicornicae) and steppe vegetation (Artemisietea herbae-albae mesopotamica).

area to precipitation can be felt physically by driving from Tell Schech Hamad up north to Tell 'Agaga and Tell Bderi. But as mentioned above, in years of drought the whole valley of the Khabur moves into the zone below the 200 m isohyet. This means that irrigation is of essential importance to settled people in the area.

Because of the climatic sensitivity of the area, it is obvious that even small oscillations could have far-reaching consequences for the economy of the area, for the subsistence of the people. Recent investigations by our botanical and palynological colleagues have resulted in the statement that no dramatic changes of climate have taken place (Gremmen and Bottema in press; Frey and Kürschner in press). The present natural vegetation is highly degraded due to deforestation, cultivation and overgrazing, but it is basically not different from the ancient vegetation. However, in Assyrian times the landscape must have looked quite different (Fig. 4). Within the 1.5 to 2 km wide river alluvium, several river beds can be reconstructed (Ergenzinger and Kühne in press; Frey and Kürschner in press) with marshy soils and

rich vegetation of reeds, shrubs and a considerable amount of gallery forest, providing a natural habitat for the animals, whose bones were found in the excavation (Becker in press). Generally, this reconstruction must be correct, but some doubts remain, especially in view of the climatic sensitivity of the area. We must perhaps look for different indicators, which could be provided by the cuneiform texts of the 13th century, discovered at Tell Schech Hamad. This archive consists mainly of economic texts, loans and receipts concerning grain and cattle. Röllig (1987) concluded that the relation between seed corn and yield fluctuated between 1:1 and 1:9, averaging 1:3 or 1:4. Röllig suggests that this fluctuation is associated with rain-fed agriculture. This argument is taken up by Hecker (in Frenzel 1987), who adds some data from Nuzi to arrive at the conclusion that climate in the 13th century BC was moister than today, so that rain-fed agriculture was possible in the area of Tell Schech Hamad/Dur-katlimmu.

This suggestion is in contrast with the results Brentjes (1982, 1988) arrived at. He derived the climatic development from sea-level oscillations and related the

20

achieved optima and pessima to historical events. This leads him to postulate that especially the end of the second millennium BC was a climatic pessimum in the Eastern Mediterranean region, causing the migration of the sea people, the downfall of the Hittite and Babylonian empires and a weakening of the Assyrian empire. In the first millennium BC the provisioning of the postulated increase of population in the region of the Khabur created an even larger problem. Brentjes (1982, 1988) and Hecker (in Frenzel 1987) agree that climate then was a little moister than today. Even so, Dur-katlimmu may have been situated at best at the periphery of rain-fed agriculture. The larger population was even more in need of a guaranteed subsistence. Any crop failure must have been a catastrophe. To support a population of 9000 three times as much grain as is harvested today was needed. For growing that amount of grain crop additional water would be required. Where, then, did the water come from?

In 1983, an artificial depression, 2.4 km east of Tell Schech Hamad, was discovered (Kühne 1984). It had been noticed already by Van Liere and Lauffray (1954-1955) and must be interpreted as an ancient canal. It can easily be distinguished in the landscape, because there is no other regular depression of this size. It was surveyed at three points, viz. near Hassake, Shaddada and Marqada. Disregarding the dams, the depression is 8-6 m wide and 1-3 m deep.

The first impression of a local system for irrigating the area of Dur-katlimmu soon proved to be wrong. Airphotos showed longer sections of two canals still visible along both sides of the Khabur. It was possible to verify most of these on the ground (Ergenzinger 1987). The western canal (Fig. 5) can be traced from the Upper Khabur down to the junction with the Euphrates with its head south of the Ras al-'Ain, near the mouth of Wadi Girgib. It amounts to a length of about 250 km. The eastern canal cannot be traced along the Upper Khabur (Fig. 5). This is due to a southern ridge of the volcano Kaukab which also causes the river to change its direction. It was not

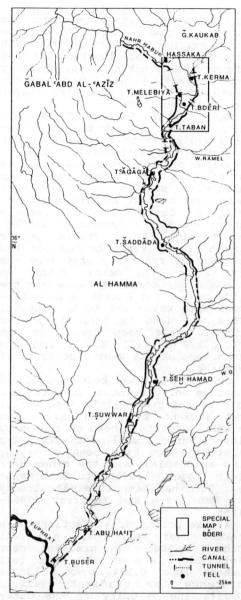

Fig. 5. Map of the Assyrian canals (Ergenzinger 1987).

possible for the builders of the canals to penetrate this ridge. A natural configuration of several rapids near Tell Kerma, south of Hassake, seems to indicate the head of the canal (Ergenzinger 1987; Ergenzinger et al. 1988). Later investigations suggested that the water from the river Gaggag, northeast of Hassake, had been diverted

21

to the canal, bypassing the volcano Kaukab in the east (Ergenzinger and Kühne in press). Thus, the eastern canal reaches a length of about 220 km, down to the junction of the Khabur with the Euphrates, where it most probably joined a canal on the north bank of the Euphrates (Geyer and Monchamber 1987).

The canal-builders had to deal with a number of obstacles. Numerous wadis had to be crossed, most probably by earth dams, since no remains of constructions such as stone dams or bridges have been discovered so far. Earth dams must have been subject to frequent damaging or destruction. It appears therefore that a number of settlements very near to crucial points of the canal were founded for the purpose of regularly observing and maintaining the canals (Kühne in press a). Another obstacle was the wide gypsum and limestone mountainnous area which had to be crossed. This was done by tunnelling. Two tunnels have been traced in the vicinity of Tell Bderi, and one large one on the west side south of Hassake.

Subsystems have been traced in patches only. Branches of subcanals can be observed fairly frequently, but ancient field irrigation has almost completely been destroyed by later agricultural activity. Two field systems have been surveyed, one at Shaddada and the other near Tell 'Agaga, leading to Tell Maraza. Both had been observed already by Van Liere and Lauffray (1954-1955).

At two points drill sections were taken: near Tell Bderi and Tell Schech Hamad. The gradient near Tell Bderi was 0.09%; near Tell Schech Hamad 0.17%. Over a longer distance the gradient averaged 0.35%. The velocity of the water was 2.5-3.5 cu m/sec. The loss of water by seepage through the canal bed must have been about 400 l/sec, which amounts to about 13% on a distance of 200 km. This figure probably has to be doubled because of water seepage on the slopes. The discharge of the Khabur averaged 50 cu m/sec (see above) prior to modern motor pumping. Given this figure, about 10% of the Khabur water was diverted into the canals.

To construct these canals must have been a major task. Their main function must have been that of irrigation. Van Liere and Lauffray (1954-1955) calculated that the four canals had irrigated about 30,000 ha between Ras al-'Ain and Tell Schech Hamad (they assumed that the eastern canal had ended at Tell Schech Hamad). According to our calculations, the irrigable land around Tell Schech Hamad/Durkatlimmu was tripled by the use of the canals in comparison to modern pumping irrigation, thus providing means of subsistence for a population three times as large as today's. Thus, the above-estimated figure of 9000 inhabitants for ancient Dur-katlimmu is almost exactly met by a completely different approach.

Another function of the canals may have been traffic routes. Ergenzinger and Kühne (in press) have said that the size of the canals and the size of Babylonian towbarges fit well, according to Salonen (1939). The necessary power to tow a load of 10 tonnes upstream along a canal was less than 600 Newton, less than two horses can pull. Thus, a cheap means of transportation of heavy goods was available. Tow-barge navigation on the Khabur, on the other hand, can be ruled out because the reconstructed vegetation and environmental situation would not allow for a towpath.

The most crucial point is the dating of the canals. A trench through the dam of the canal near Tell Schech Hamad revealed no architectural remains. Only two sherds of Late Roman/Byzantine brittle ware were found in the second layer. The lower layers were sterile. On the surface of the area around the excavation 32 sherds were collected. Later on, another 20 sherds in the adjacent areas were sampled. The oldest sherds belong to the chaff-tempered Assyrian ware, the largest amount of pottery is Late Roman sandy ware, and some sherds are glazed Islamic ware. These assemblages suggest a date for the construction of the two canals and their first functioning in the Neoassyrian period, in the 8th or 7th century BC. The canals were continuously used until the Mongol raid in the 13th century AD, which totally devastated the Khabur valley (Ergenzinger et al.

1988:122).

The Assyrians are well-known as constructors of long-distance irrigation canals, the tradition starting as early as the 14th century BC. If Reade (1978) is right in stating that "there is evidence that Sanherib and some other Assyrian kings built canals almost anywhere that it seemed practicable to do so", then we need not even wonder why there is no written evidence so far on the Khabur canals. It may be an Assy-rian understatement to the effect that they regarded the construction of the Khabur canals as an everyday task.

3 THE EFFECTS OF IRRIGATION
  AGRICULTURE

To come finally to the effects of irrigation agriculture on the Khabur, it has to be stressed that, to judge these effects, our data are as yet rather scanty and unreliable. It has been argued elsewhere (Ergenzinger et al. 1988) that the most indicative effects of irrigation would be reflected in the settlement pattern, but the archaeological evidence is very poor. For although we assume the existence of these older irrigation works, we cannot trace them on the ground, and even if we could, we often cannot date them. It has to be considered also that earlier irrigation works have been destroyed in the course of repairing them or building new ones.

Of major importance is also the reconstruction of the history of climate. It has been demonstrated above, that the Lower Khabur valley is a very sensitive area to minor climatic changes. As was shown also, there are few data, and worse than that, it seems that there are few if any methods of reconstructing regional climatic fluctuations. The analysis of molluscs from Tell Schech Hamad (Reese in press) and Tell Bderi may shed some light on this problem. In other fields the situation is no better: little is known for example about the effects of irrigation agriculture on soils in this particular area and time range (Van Liere 1965; Mousli 1979). An investigation of the soils and a classification have been carried out during the last

two seasons by the pedologist U. Smettan (Figs. 6 and 7) within the environs of Tell Schech Hamad, in order to estimate the agronomic potential of the Assyrian town of Dur-katlimmu. According to her results, the agronomic soil potential around Tell Schech Hamad to be irrigated by the ancient canal amounts to about 500 ha, not sufficient to nourish 9000 people. Other areas north and south of the wadis limiting this potential must have been included in the catchment area of Dur-katlimmu. These and other data make it worthwhile to re-evaluate the relationship between the canal and the development of settlements as an indicator of irrigation agriculture. It has to be kept in mind that our general assumption is that the settlements had to rely on irrigation because the climate never was sufficiently favourable for rain-fed agriculure to be carried out without risk.

From the beginning of the Early Bronze Age (roughly 3000 BC) down to the end of the Middle Bronze Age (around 1500 BC) only local systems of irrigation seem to have existed along the Lower Khabur, concentrating in the northern part of it while the southern part remained rather remote. In the Early Bronze Age the alignment of settlements at Tell Kerma, Tell Raga'i and Tell Ga'bi on the east bank, Tell Mullamatar and Tell Gudede on the west bank, or Hirbat al-Banat, Tell Snetle and Hirbat Snetle a little further south, could be interpreted as an indicator of local irrigation systems. The fact that these sites were settled almost exclusively during that period, could underline the reliance on such local irrigation works. On the other hand, centres in the steppe, such as Tell Malhat ed-Deru, Tell Mu'azzar, Tell Matiyaha, Tell Murtiya south of the Jebel 'Abd al-'Aziz, and - just to mention a couple north and west of the Jebel 'Abd al-'Aziz - Tell Mabtuh-West and Tell Huera which also flourished almost exclusively during the Early Bronze Age, existed without irrigation (so far no traces of irrigation works have been discovered).

It cannot be denied that these two assumptions are contradictory to a certain extent. Why should the settlements on the Khabur need

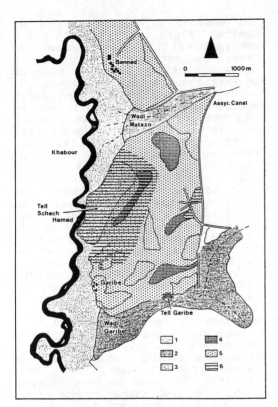

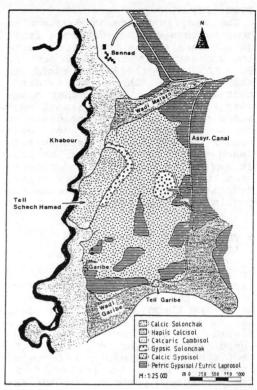

Fig. 6. Classification of soils around Tell Schech Hamad, according to U. Smettan. 1. Floodplain sediment of loamy clay; 2. Wadi sediment of sandy and argillaceous loam; 3. Tell deposits of silt and loam; 4. Silt on argillaceous loam; 5. Silt on sand and gravel; 6. Neo-Assyrian pottery sherds.

Fig. 7. Classification of soils around Tell Schech Hamad, according to U. Smettan.

local irrigation systems while the settlements in the steppe existed on rain-fed agriculture? One could argue that the settlements on the Khabur used the natural resources for irrigation to exclude any risk. This does not explain the existence of the settlements in the steppe south of the Jebel 'Abd al-'Aziz. A solution is offered by climatologists, suggesting a moister climate in the third millennium BC (Brentjes 1982:471). At the end of the Early Bronze Age, both the settlements in the steppe and those along the river declined, possibly because the climate became drier (Brentjes) and because of political factors which coincided with this development (Moorgat-Correns 1972; Kühne 1976).

In the Middle Bronze Age (roughly between 2000 and 1500 BC) the situation is much more difficult to explain. The settlement pattern along the Khabur does not show any characteristic alignment betraying a possible irrigation system. Moreover it lacks any true centres although on the grounds of written evidence one has to assume that they existed. One can only speculate that local irrigation works did exist.

Taking the cuneiform sources into account, two canals (Isim Jahdunlim, Igi.Kur (Groneberg 1980:299, 291)) are mentioned in connection with place names (Dur-Jahdunlim (Groneberg 1980:60)) which have to be located near the junction of the Khabur with the Euphrates and along the Euphrates. Only one canal - if it is one - is mentioned along the Khabur; its name is Khabur-ibal-bugas, situated between Dur-Isarlim and Dur-Igitlim (Groneberg 1980:59, 284). If Röllig (1978:420) is right in assuming that Dur-Igitlim could be the Old-Babylonian place name of Dur-katlimmu/Tell Schech Hamad, a local or possibly a regional irrigation system may be indicated. The problem is where to locate Dur-Isarlim. According to the archaeological evidence there is not too much choice: Tell Asamsani and Tell Radgami in the northern vicinity; ... is to be identified with ... (Kühne 1980; Nashef 1983). Nashef in the north bears very close resemblance. ... Tell Abu Bata ... which is probable to be ... with Tell ... gar (Kühne ...). Possibly a local system. ... could be modern Tell Damu just mentioned Tell Bderi, Tell ... Tell Radgam, Tell ... or Tell Nam... can be ...

[handwritten note:] 03/03/2015 — To do: DSA, Matlab appointment, Fieldwork meeting, Research Project Proposal, Check Bank account

identified. ... katlimmu and Tell 'Agaga/... Lacking these arguments is Tell Hassake, but it should be added because of historic-geographical arguments which indicate identity with Magarisi (Kühne 1980). Kessler (1987) suggests Tell Abu Bakr which is situated opposite Tell Hassake. Otherwise a surprisingly small number of settlements of that period can be mapped (Ergenzinger et al. 1988:122, Fig. 6). It has been argued that one should expect more numerous settlements if a regional

irrigation system had existed.

By now, more and important information is available. In one of these small settlements, Tell Bderi, which had been a centre during the preceding Mitannian period, Assyrian inscribed cylinders have been excavated in 1987 and 1988 (Pfälzner in press). An eponym dates them to the reign of king Tiglat-pilesar I (1112-1074 BC). It is possible to identify Tell Bderi with a hitherto unknown place, namely Dur Assur-kitte-lisir [the reading was provided by S. ...l; Pfälzner (1988b) used the ... reading Dur Assur-napistir-...). The person in honour of ... the place was named, is a ...ce of a local dynasty of Tabe-... The town should be the same as ... Babylonian Tabatum (Groneberg ...:243).

...here remains little doubt now ... both should be identified with ...rn Tell Tabun which lies only ... km south of Tell Bderi (Kühne ...80; Nashef 1983; Kessler 1987). ...e texts of Tell Bderi leave no ...ubt that Dur Assur-kitte-lisir ...as a small, dependent settlement ...f Tabete. The importance of this ...nformation lies in the fact that ...or the first time a glimpse is ...ffered of the extent of the territory of such subcentres. Calculating that the catchment of these subcentres may have been about 15 km in radius and applying it to the map, a very interesting statement is possible: the three centres Magarisi, Tabete and Sadikanni controlled the northern half of the Lower Khabur in regularly arranged districts. The area between Sadikanni and the next centre further south, Qatni, is characterized by a mountainous ridge north of modern Saddada. This explains the longer distance between these two districts. The distance between the districts of Qatni and Dur-katlimmu is regular again. South of Dur-katlimmu no Assyrian settlement was found (Fig. 8).

Historically this observation is of great importance. It proves that the Lower Khabur valley was under firm and well organized Middle Assyrian administration, the centre of which, with a governor (bel pahete) was Dur-katlimmu. As for the settlement pattern, one cannot expect more centres; the subdivi-

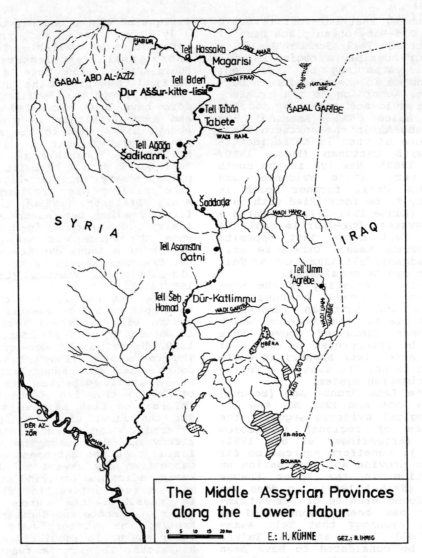

Fig. 8. Middle Assyrian administrative centres along the Lower Khabur, according to H. Kühne.

sion is complete. Yet to be found are the smallest settlements, hamlets and the like, some of which will certainly have been overlooked in the survey. The well-established Middle Assyrian administration of the Lower Khabur, beginning with the reign of King Salmanassar I and ending with the reign of King Tiglat-pilesar I (1273-1074 BC), is a strong argument in favour of the postulated canal and of large-scale irrigation agriculture. The canal would have to be reconstructed from near Tell Kerma in the north, down to Dur-katlimmu (Ergenzinger et al.

1988:118). The agricultural potential may well have been the motive for King Assur-bel-kala's unsuccessful attempt to regain the area from the Aramaeans and for the Assyrian kings of the late 10th and 9th century BC, Adad-nirari II, Tukulti-ninurta II and Assurnasirpal II, to campaign along the Khabur and to firmly re-establish their supremacy.

The need to construct this canal may have been caused also by the climate - this would be an argument in favour of the suggested pessimum (cf. Brentjes 1982, 1988). In con-

26

nection with this hypothesis one hitherto unknown site has to be considered, Tell Umm 'Aqrebe. This site is situated about 40 km east of Tell Schech Hamad, within the steppe, on a straight route to the capital Assur. The surface collections leave no doubt about a settlement during the Middle Assyrian period. The specific pottery found there even argues in favour of a function similar to that of the above-mentioned subcentres (Pfälzner 1986). But when the area suffered severe drought, how could the population in a place with this geographic position possibly survive?

The most important function of the site was surely one of a traffic station with some additional administrative tasks. Considering its position on the direct route to the capital Assur this makes sense. It certainly was not an agricultural centre, as a neighbouring site became in Neoassyrian times. For survival there is plenty of groundwater right beneath the surface (even today) which is quite sufficient for drinking water and possibly some irrigation agriculture to feed a few families in Tell Umm 'Aqrebe.

Tell Umm 'Aqrebe favours the hypothesis of a climatic pessimum (Brentjes 1982, 1988); it does not strengthen the idea of dry farming (Röllig 1978, 1987; Hecker 1987). But mostly it confirms the reconstruction of a tight and well-established Middle Assyrian administration on the Lower Khabur region.

Summarizing, the Bronze Age habitation along the Lower Khabur (and probably along the Upper Khabur as well) must have been based primarily on irrigation agriculture. During the Early and Middle Bronze Age local irrigation systems seem to have prevailed. It cannot be excluded, though, that, especially in the south of the Lower Khabur, a larger irrigation system connected with the Euphrates existed. Politically the Lower Khabur was dependent on Mari and Hana in the Middle Bronze Age, both situated in the southeast, on the Middle Euphrates. In the first half of the Late Bronze Age (the Mitanni period) the Lower Khabur does not seem to have been settled densely.

During the second half of the Late Bronze Age, the Middle Assyrian period, the Lower Khabur was under firm Assyrian control. The well-organized administration favours the postulation of a regional irrigation system, extending to near Tell Schech Hamad/Dur-katlimmu.

The Neo-Assyrians took advantage of the well-prepared and organized settlement pattern along the Lower Khabur that their predecessors had left. After a period of weakness in the late 11th and 10th century BC, during which the Aramaeans settled down in all the centres, they re-established their supremacy in the 9th century and kept it until the downfall of the Assyrian empire at the end of the 7th century BC.

Even if there had been no dating evidence at all for the canals, the settlement pattern in the 9th to 7th centuries BC strongly suggests a regional irrigation system. The regular arrangement of the towns and villages, much closer together in the northern half than in the southern half of the valley, the newly established sites south of Dur-katlimmu in that remote part of the Lower Khabur, and the settlement clusters in the steppe east of the Khabur could not be explained without a flourishing agriculture, with high yields to support a growing population, the cause of which must have been large-scale irrigation. This in turn must have strengthened the communities as it did the provincial centres, as is known from the excavations in Tell 'Agaga/Sadikanni and Tell Schech Hamad/Dur-katlimmu (Ergenzinger et al. 1988).

The cluster of settlements east of Tell Schech Hamad/Dur-katlimmu has to be emphasized. There is no reason to believe that the former route to the Assyrian heartland no longer existed. Along this route and centring around Tell Umm 'Aqruba and Gilib al-'Amah an astonishing number of hamlets was recognized in the field, strongly suggesting a colonization of the steppe. It cannot be imagined that this rather unattractive area would have been chosen for agricultural acitivity if the climate had been as unfavourable as before.

The agricultural richness of the Lower Khabur is amply demonstrated by the settlement pattern of the later Hellenistic, Roman, Byzantine and Islamic periods. It was based on large-scale irrigation, provided by regional canals which were constructed first by the Assyrians and probably destroyed by the Mongols. Lacking a firm administration, the area was taken over by nomadic Arab tribes, who became sedentary only a generation ago and took up motor-pumping irrigation.

REFERENCES

Adams, R.McC. 1972.
  Patterns and urbanization in early southern Mesopotamia. In P.J.Ucko, R.Tringham and G.W.Dimbleby (eds.), Man, settlement and urbanism, p.735-547. London, Duckworth.
Becker, C. in press.
  Die Tierknochen aus Tall Seh Hamad - Die mittelassyrischen Funde aus Raum A, Gebäude P. In H.Kühne (ed.), Die rezente Umwelt von Tall Seh Hamad und Daten zur Umweltrekonstruktion der Assyrischen Stadt Dur-katlimmu. Berichte der Ausgrabung Tall Seh Hamad/Dur-katlimmu 1.
Boserup, E. 1965.
  The conditions of agricultural growth. London: Allen and Unwin.
Brentjes, B. 1982.
  Holozän-Geologie und Archäologie, Gedanken und Fragen zur Korrelation der Resultate zweier Wissenschaften. In J.L.Bintliff and W. van Zeist (eds.), Palaeoclimates, palaeoenvironments and human communities in the Eastern Mediterranean region in Later Prehistory, p.453-484. BAR International Series 133.
Brentjes, B. 1988.
  Die "dunklen Jahrhunderte" der frühen Eisenzeit und die Kulturgeschichte Mittelasiens. Hallesche Beiträge zur Orientwissenschaft 12:5-24.
Eichler, S, V.Haas, D.Steudler, M.Wäfler and D.Warburton 1985.
  Tall Al-Hamidiya 1. Vorbericht 1984. Orbis Biblicus et Orientalis, Series Archaeologica 4.
Ergenzinger, P.J. 1987.
  Big hydraulic structures in ancient Mesopotamia in North-East Syria. Die Erde 118:33-36.
Ergenzinger, P.J., W.Frey, H.Kühne and H.Kürschner 1988.
  The reconstruction of environment, irrigation and development of settlement on the Habur in North-East Syria. In J.L.Bintliff, D.A.Davidson and E.G.Grant (eds.), Conceptual Issues in Environmental Archaeology, p.108-128.
Ergenzinger, P.J.
  and H.Kühne in press.
  Ein regionales Bewässerungssystem aus Neuassyrischer Zeit am Habur. In H.Kühne (ed.), Die rezente Umwelt von Tall Seh Hamad und Daten zur Umweltrekonstruktion der Assyrischen Stadt Dur-katlimmu. Berichte der Ausgrabung Tall Seh Hamad/Dur-katlimmu 1.
FAO 1982.
  Regional Study on Rainfed Agriculture and Agroclimatic Inventory of Eleven Countries in the Near East Region. Food and Agriculture Organization of the United Nations, Near East Regional Office/Land and Water Development Division: 85-97.
Flannery, K.V. 1976.
  The Ecology of Early Food Production in Mesopotamia. In A.P. Vayda (ed.), Environment and Cultural Behavior.
Frenzel, B. 1987.
  Bericht der Projektgruppe "Terrestrische Paläoklimatologie". Jahrbuch der Akademie der Wissenschaften und der Literatur, Mainz.
Frey, W. and H.Kürschner in press.
  Die aktuelle und potentielle natürliche Vegetation im Bereich des Unteren Habur. In H.Kühne (ed.), Die rezente Umwelt von Tall Seh Hamad und Daten zur Umweltrekonstruktion der Assyrischen Stadt Dur-katlimmu. Berichte der Ausgrabung Tall Seh Hamad/Dur-katlimmu 1.
Geyer, B.
  and J.-Y.Monchambert 1987.
  Prospection de la Moyenne Valleé de l'Euphrat: rapport préliminaire 1982-1985. MARI, Annales de Recherches Interdisciplinaire 5:293-344.
Gremmen, W.H.E. and S.Bottema in press. Palynological investigations in the Syrian Gazinra. In H.Kühne (ed.), Die rezente Umwelt von Tall Seh Hamad und Daten zur Umweltrekonstruktion der Assyrischen Stadt Dur-katlimmu. Berichte der Ausgrabung Tall Seh Hamad/Dur-katlimmu 1.

Groneberg, B. 1980.
Die Orts- und Gewässernamen der altbabylonischen Zeit. Répertoire Géographique des Textes Cunéiformes Bd. 3. Beihefte zum Tübinger Atlas des Vorderen Orients Reihe B Nr. 7/3.

Harris, D.R. 1969.
Agricultural systems, ecosystems and the origins of agriculture. In P.J.Ucko and G.W.Dimbleby (eds.), The domestication and exploitation of plants and animals, p.3-15. London, Duckworth.

Hopfinger, H. 1984.
Ein neues Staudamm- und Bewässerungsprojekt am nordostsyrischen Khabour: Grundzüge und Probleme seiner Planung. Geographische Zeitschrift 72/3: 189-195.

Hopfinger, H. in press.
Wirtschaft- und sozialgeographische Untersuchungen zur aktuellen Landnutzung in Gariba/Tall Seh Hamad. In H.Kühne (ed.), Die rezente Umwelt von Tall Seh Hamad und Daten zur Umweltrekonstruktion der Assyrischen Stadt Dur-katlimmu. Berichte der Ausgrabung Tall Seh Hamad/Dur-katlimmu 1.

Kühne, H. 1976.
Die Keramik vom Tell Chuera.

Kühne, H. 1974-1977.
Zur historischen Geographie am Unteren Habur. Vorläufiger Bericht über eine archäologische Geländebegehung. Archiv für Orientforschung 25:249-255.

Kühne, H. 1978-1979.
Zur historischen Geographie am Unteren Habur. Zweiter vorläufiger Bericht über eine archäologische Geländebegehung. Archiv für Orientforschung 26:181-195.

Kühne, H. 1980.
Zur Rekonstruktion der Feldzüge Adad-Nirari II, Tukulti-Ninurta II und Assurnasirpal II im Habur-Gebiet. Baghdader Mitteilungen 11:44-70.

Kühne, H. 1984.
Tall Seh Hamad/Dur-katlimmu 1981-1983; Tall Seh Hamad/Dur-katlimmu 1984. Archiv für Orientforschung 31:166-178.

Kühne, H. 1986.
Tall Seh Hamad/Dur-katlimmu, the Assyrian Provincial Capital in the Mohafazat Deir az-Zor. Les Annals Archéologiques Arabes Syriennes, special volume: Histoire de Deir ez-Zur et ses Antiquités.

Kühne, H. in press a.

Ein Bewässerungssystem des Ersten Jahrtausends v.Chr. am Unteren Habur. In Les Techniques et les Pratiques Hydro-Agricoles traditionelles en Domaine Irrigué. Bibliothèque Archéologique et Historique.

Kühne, H. in press b.
Gedanken zur historischen und städtebaulichen Entwicklung der assyrischen Stadt Dur-katlimmu. Festschrift für Adnan Bounni.

Kühne, H. (ed.) in press c.
Die rezente Umwelt von Tall Seh Hamad und Daten zur Umweltrekonstruktion der Assyrischen Stadt Dur-katlimmu. Berichte der Ausgrabung Tall Seh Hamad/Dur-katlimmu 1.

Liere, W.J.van
and J.Lauffray 1954-1955.
Nouvelle Prospection Archéologique dans la Haute Jezireh Syrienne. Les Annales Archéologique Arabes Syriennes 4-5:129-148.

Liere, W.J.van 1965.
Classification and Rational Utilisation of Soils. Food and Agriculture Organization of the United States, Report No. 2075, Rome.

Mahmoud, A. 1984.
Neo-Assyrian Sculptures from Sadikanni (Tall 'Agaga). Assur IV:67-70.

Mahmoud, A., R.Bernbeck, H.Kühne, P.Pfälzner and W.Röllig 1988.
Die Ausgrabung auf dem Tall 'Agaga/ Sadikanni 1982. Damaszener Mitteilungen 3:141-184.

Mallowan, M.E.L. 1947.
Excavations at Brak and Chagar Bazar. Iraq 9.

McEwan, C.W., L.S.Braidwood, H.Frankfort, H.G.Güterbock, R.C.Haines, H.J.Kanor and C.H.Kraeling 1958. Soundings at Tell Fakhariyah. Oriental Institute Publications LXXIX.

Meijer, D.J.W. 1986.
A Survey in Northeastern Syria. Uitgaven van het Nederlands Historisch-Archaeologisch Instituut te Istanbul LVIII.

Moortgat-Correns, U. 1972.
Die Bildwerke vom Djebelet el Beda in ihrer Räumlichen und Zeitlichen Umwelt. Berlin: De Gruyter.

Mousli, O.M. 1979.
Evaluation and Classification of Gypsiferous Soils and their Suitability for irrigated Agriculture. Food and Agriculture

Organization of the United States, World Soil Resources Reports 50.

Nashef, K. 1982.
Die Orts- und Gewässernamen der mittelbabylonischen und mittelassyrischen Zeit. Répertoire Géographique des Textes Cunéiformes Bd. 5. Beihefte zum Tübinger Atlas des Vorderen Orients Reihe B Nr. 7/5.

Nashef, K. 1983.
Babylonia and Assyria in the Second Half of the Second Millennium B.C. Tübinger Atlas des Vorderen Orients, map no. B III 7.

Nissen, H.-J. 1988.
The early history of the Near East - 9000-2000 B.C.

Oates, D. and J.Oates 1976.
Early irrigation agriculture in Mesopotamia. In G. de G.Sieveking, I.H.Longworth and K.E.Wilson (eds.), Problems in Economic and Social Archaeology, p.109-135.

Oates, J. 1972.
Prehistoric settlement patterns in Mesopotamia. In P.J.Ucko, R.Tringham and G.W.Dimbleby (eds.), Man, settlement and urbanism, p.299-310. London, Duckworth.

Oates, J. 1980.
Land use and population in prehistoric Mesopotamia. In Colloques Internationaux du CNRS no. 580: Archéologie de l'Iraq du debut de l'époque néolithique à 333 avant notre Ere.

Oates, D. 1987.
Excavations at Tell Brak 1985-1986. Iraq 49:175-191.

Oppenheim, Max, Freiherr von, 1899-1900. Vom Mittelmeer zum Persischen Golf. 2 Vols.

Oppenheim, Max, Freiherr von, 1930. Der Tell Halaf.

Oppenheim, Max, Freiherr von (ed.) 1943-1962. Tell Halaf, Vol. I-IV.

Pecorella, P.E. and M.Salvini 1984. Tell Bakhri/Kahat. Archiv für Orientforschung 31:114-118.

Pfälzner, P. 1986.
Aspekte mittelassyrischer Keramikproduktion und Provinzverwaltung im 'Agiggebiet und am Unteren Habur. Unpublished Masterthesis.

Pfälzner, P. 1988a.
Tall Bderi 1985. Bericht über die erste Kampagne. Damaszener Mitteilungen 3:223-386.

Pfälzner, P. 1988b.
Tall Bderi. Syrian Archaeology Bulletin 1,2.

Pfälzner, P. in press.
Preliminary report on the excavation of Tall Bderi 1987. Les Annales Archéologiques Arabes Syriennes.

Pfälzner, P. in press.
Preliminary report on the excavation of Tall Bderi 1988. Les Annales Archéologiques Arabes Syriennes.

Poidebard, A. 1934.
La Trace de Rome.

Reade, J. 1978.
Studies in Assyrian Geography. Revue d'Assyriologie 72:47-72, 157-180.

Reese, D.S. in press.
Marine and fresh-water shells and an Ostrich eggshell from Tall Seh Hamad. In H.Kühne (ed.), Die rezente Umwelt von Tall Seh Hamad und Daten zur Umweltrekonstruktion der Assyrischen Stadt Dur-katlimmu. Berichte der Ausgrabung Tall Seh Hamad/Dur-katlimmu 1.

Röllig, W. 1978.
Dur-katlimmu. Orientalia 47:419-430.

Röllig, W. 1987.
Zur Landwirtschaft am Unteren Habur im 2. Jahrtausend v.Chr. Unpublished manuscript, read at the 34th Rencontre Assyriologique International, Istanbul.

Sarre and Herzfeld 1911-1920.
Reise in Euphrat- und Tigrisgebiet. Vol. I-IV.

Smith, P.E.L. 1972.
Land-use, settlement patterns and subsistence agriculture: a demographic perspective. In P.J.Ucko, R.Tringham and G.W.Dimbleby (eds.), Man, settlement and urbanism, p.409-426. London, Duckworth.

Salonen, A. 1939.
Die Wasserfahrzeuge in Babylonien (nach sumerisch-akkadischen Quellen). Stuida Orientalia, Ed. Societas Orientales Fennica Vol. VIII,4.

Weiss, H. 1983.
Excavations at Tell Leilan and the origins of north Mesopotamian cities in the third millennium B.C. Paléorient 9:39-52.

Wirth, E. 1971.
Syrien. Eine geographische Landeskunde. Darmstadt.

Man's Role in the Shaping of the Eastern Mediterranean Landscape, Bottema, Entjes-Nieborg & van Zeist (eds)
© *1990 Balkema, Rotterdam. ISBN 90 6191 138 9*

Man, land and climate: Emerging interactions from the Holocene of the Yemen Highlands

Francesco G. Fedele
Institute of Anthropology, University of Naples, Italy

ABSTRACT: The prehistoric succession in the eastern Yemen Highlands (2000-2200 m above sea level), comprising "mesolithic", neolithic, and Bronze Age cultures, is described, alongside the standard depositional sequence for the region. Village-dwelling, cattle-breeding, aceramic neolithic groups are correlated with a mid-Holocene paleosol (5280-4000 cal. BC) indicating a high watertable in upland valleys and abundant vegetation. Subsequent Bronze Age farmers mainly living off caprines and sorghum (ca 2900-1800 cal. BC) may have exerted excessive economic pressure on a fragile ecosystem tending towards desiccation. That peaked when renewed tectonic uplift lowered the watertable and altered the landscape geometry. Cultural and climatic causes of environmental deterioration were escalated by tectonic interference, leading to the widespread desertion of today.

1 THE REGION AND THE PROBLEM

Regional survey and site excavations in the eastern Highlands of Yemen, above 2000 m in altitude, have begun to provide a basis for reconstructing Holocene sequences in a part of the Arabian Peninsula whose prehistoric archaeology and environmental history were unknown until a few years ago. In this paper I will summarize and discuss some of the results of the Italian Archeological Mission to the Yemen Arab Republic (MAIRAY, IsMEO, Rome), which has been working in that country since 1983 under a bilaterial cooperation agreement.

The core of North Yemen is high-mountain country. The Yemen and Asir Highlands form the backbone relief of the southwestern Arabian Peninsula, the Asir being the mountain ranges of western Saudi Arabia (Fig. 1). This mountain system corresponds within the peninsula to highly peculiar eco-zones, which are more African in character than Middle Eastern. But these rugged mountains only represent one physiographic division of Yemen, as this country has impres-

sive landscape diversity, manifest in other equally important physiographic and ecologic zones.

To the south and west, Yemen is bounded by the Indian Ocean and that torrid inlet, the Red Sea, along which rifting and tectonic uplifting are still creating a narrow coastal plain, the Tihamah. Imposing escarpments contour the massive mountain block of the Yemen Highlands, ranging in elevation from 2000 to 3600 m and chaotically dissected. In addition to past volcanism and rifting, during the Oligocene-Miocene and Pleistocene periods, the uplifting of the Highlands still is a cause of tectonic instability (Fedele in press c).

The uplands are scarred by wadis (widian in Arabic) or seasonal streams, which disappear into the vast stretches of stony-grassy semi-desert and sandy desert to the north and east. This is the margin of the "empty quarter" or Rubᶜ al-Khali, one of the harshest deserts in the world. The eastern Highlands of Yemen fall off onto the sand-covered Ramlat Sabᶜatayn Desert, a lobe of the Rubᶜ al-Khali.

The Highlands belong today in the

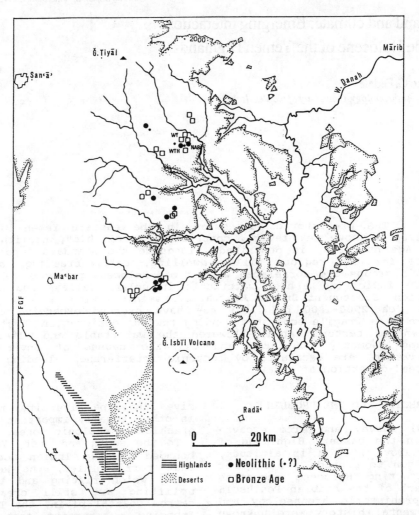

Fig. 1. Map of the central part of the eastern Highlands of North Yemen, emphasizing the Wadi Danah drainage and the 2000 metre contour line. The main prehistoric sites are plotted; NAB = An-Nagid al-Abyad, WTH = Wadi at-Tayyilah, WY = Wadi Yana'im. Inset map shows he Asir-Yemen Highlands in the southwestern part of the Arabian Peninsula (F.G. Fedele 1989).

belt of monsoonal rains, but the eastern part of the mountains is less strongly affected and here a sub-arid regime normally obtains. Some monsoonal influence can be perceived as far north and inland as the higher Asir (Whitney 1982). In the eastern Yemen Highlands, southern monsoon winds are responsible for a major rainfall season from July to September, during which 200-400 mm of orographic rain in the form of frequent thunderstorms can fall on the eastern Highlands. At the beginning of this season, wadis are usually turned by heavy outpours into raging torrents. However, completely dry years are known to occur as well (Blume 1976; Kopp 1981; Fein and Stephens 1987).

From this short description it should be clear that the landscape history of Yemen must owe a great deal to the interplay of rainfall, aridity, and tectonics. Investigations of this interplay and the superimposed activities of prehistoric man have begun, through a comparative study of man-environment relationships across the environmental spectrum of the region, from coast to plateau to desert, and obivously through time. The undertaking is far from completion, however, and several ecological compartments still await deeper inspection.

2 LAND AND CLIMATE

2.1 Depositional sequences in North Yemen

In this paper I intend to confine myself to the Holocene of our main study area in the eastern Highlands, at an altitude of 2000-2200 m above sea level. Information from other areas will be used where relevant. The study area lies about 50 km southeast of the North Yemen capital, San'a', and includes the upper and middle reaches of the Wadi Danah drainage. This is the wadi system which flows down to Marib, the famous ancient Sabaean capital on the desert margin.

The whole eastern Highlands region now has very low population densities, both of humans and animals. In contrast, the archaeological maps we have constructed for the Neolithic and Bronze Age, although incomplete (Fig. 1), point to higher population densities than today. Thus it is immediately apparent that the recent desertion contrasts with the situation during an earlier part of the Holocene, up to at least the 3rd millennium BC. (All dates in this paper are calendar dates, unless otherwise indicated.)

In an attempt at understanding the "double helix" of landscape variation and human action, an assessment will be made of the mutual effects of landscape and humans (see sections 3 and 4). Distinguishing between the differential roles of physiographic and climatic changes within the "landscape" factor will be more difficult. The landscape background and its changes will be considered first.

In the eastern Highlands a generalised sedimentary sequence is emerging, whose most complete occurrences have been studied in the An-Nagid al-Abyad and Wadi at-Tayyilah valleys, 60 km southeast

of San'a' (Marcolongo and Palmieri 1986, 1988; Fedele in prep.). In this area as well as elsewhere in the Highlands, Holocene terraces on the lower slopes are mainly composed of re-deposited aeolian silt, intergrading lower down in the sequence with alluvial sediments. From bottom to top, the standard sequence is the following (Fig. 2), varying in thickness from 1 to 4 metres:

I. the lowermost of 4 distinct strata, which represent different depositional conditions, is a conglomerate indicating high-energy transport of a torrential type;

II. a complex of sandy-silty-clayey units follows, alluvial and then more colluvial in origin; there is lateral variation to evaporitic deposits near former springs (travertine or calcareous sinter); an alternating wet-dry regime seems to be indicated;

III. complex II is topped by a dark grey band, more or less truncated at the top, rich in organic matter and accumulated $CaCO_3$ (Fig. 3); this is a B-type horizon of a paleosol, which I called the Thayyilah paleosol, from Wadi at-Tayyilah (Fedele 1986, 1988; see below);

IV. finally, complex IV consists of aeolian silt and slope-wash lenses of sand and gravel, largely affected by aeolian deflation; today hammada surfaces are common, as well as exfoliation of desert varnish from rock faces.

The Thayyilah paleosol appears to represent a useful pedostratigraphic marker over a wide area (Fedele, unpublished survey data). It was dated on humic acids to 5750±500 BP (Rome, unpubl.; Marcolongo and Palmieri 1986). This date calibrates to about 5280-4000 BC according to the "Radiocarbon" 1986 curves (Pearson et al. 1986) and compares well with dates for organic-rich units of pedogenetic origin in similar sequences from Saudi Arabia (see section 2.2 below). Both information from central Arabia and our own observations point to the occurrence of a weak and variable, but widespread, pedogenetic event around the 6th millennium BC (cf. Roberts 1982). Our report of this event from the uplands of the Arabian Peninsula lends support to the contention

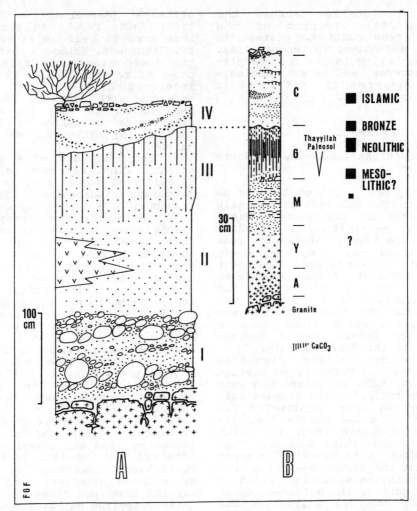

Fig. 2. Late Quaternary depositional sequences in the eastern Highlands of North Yemen, NAB-WTH area (cf. Fig. 1). A: Generalised lithostratigraphic profile (see 2.1) (Marcolongo and Palmieri 1988). B: Stratigraphy of site WTHiii on the Wadi at-Tayyilah, according to the 1984-1986 excavations; lithostratigraphic members and cultural horizons to the right profile (F.G. Fedele 1989).

that what we see here is a signal of a regional oscillation that is climatic in origin.

2.2 Regional comparisons

The eastern Highlands sequence is clearly comparable with situations reported from further north in the Arabian Peninsula (e.g. McClure 1978), and particularly with the sequence from western Saudi Arabia briefly described by Whitney

(1982). In the high mountainous region of the Asir, tufa deposits were formed in the streambeds and near former springs about 8000-3800 BC (ca 7500-3000 radiocarbon years BC). Aeolian silt layers were then formed on the lower slopes, during an early to middle Holocene period when there was enough rainfall to support hillslope and floodplain vegetation and to serve as aeolian sediment traps. Final stream dissection began about 4300 BC (ca 3500 radiocarbon years BC) (Whitney

1982).

Between the 8th and 5th millennia BC, according to different lines of evidence (Garrard et al. 1981; Luz 1982; Roberts 1982; Rognon 1982), humid or "pluvial" conditions obtained in central and southern Arabia. In the core of the peninsula, south of a certain latitude (28° north, vide Roberts 1982), a long-term climatic trend towards aridity was interrupted by several oscillations of rainfall and perhaps temperature, and a rapid progression of rain increases resulted in a phase variously called Mid-Holocene Pluvial, Holocene Subpluvial, or Neolithic Wet Phase (cf. Brice 1978).

The problems connected with this period were discussed at length during a meeting held at Groningen in 1980, with contrasting results (Bintliff and van Zeist 1982:242-246), the early-middle Holocene southern "pluvial" was "undoubtedly a product of a climatic regime markedly different from that of the present day, in which the intertropical convergence zone (ITCZ) lay around 10° north of its modern position". The Asir-Yemen Highlands receive their moisture from southerly monsoon winds which, during the mid-Holocene "interstadial", may have been deflected more often into this area than today (Whitney 1982). The present arid climate became established about 3000-2500 BC.

It is important to note that the model of a mid-Holocene pluvial is essentially based on lacustrine episodes so far detected in low-lying desert settings. The details of stream discharge in the Arabian uplands are virtually unknown, and our own research in Yemen has yet to produce quantitative information. But, in purely climatic terms, one is tempted nevertheless to correlate the dark grey Thayyilah paleosol of the Yemem Highlands with the Holocene phase characterized by milder and moister conditions than today (Fedele 1988; de Maigret et al. 1988).

The latter part of this period may have been marked in Yemen by a series of oscillating moist and dry spells, coinciding perhaps with the time when the monsoon regime settled into its modern pattern. By the beginning of the 3rd millen-

nium BC, whether or not the "Indus wet phase" (Brice 1978:351-356) was effective in the west, a new cycle of severe desiccation was developing in central and southern Arabia as well as elsewhere in the tropical belt (cf. Ritchie et al. 1985). As the data from upland Yemen seem to accord well with the general environmental sequence emerging for parts of tropical Arabia, I feel inclined to favour a certain climatic control for the most general Holocene changes, as discussed above with reference to the widely held ideas on the climatic change in the Arabian region. But in North Yemen it is equally clear that importance cannot be accorded to climate change alone.

At least in our main study area, some geomorphological facts were superimposed upon climatic effects. Somewhere between strata III and IV of the generalised succession of Fig. 2, one may place a sharp renewal of riverbed erosion (Fig. 5). As it coincides with conditions of increasing aridity, downcutting at this point is most likely explained by relief rejuvenation due to tectonic causes. The results of regional geomorphological mapping (Marcolongo and Palmieri 1988; and unpublished data) support this contention.

Pronounced stream erosion following the formation of the Thayyilah paleosol seems to characterize the whole Wadi Danah basin, which represents a large sector of the eastern Highlands and the one where high population density prior to the 2nd millennium BC is best documented. A change in the basin geometry because of differential tectonic uplift is apparent throughout our study area, and geologically speaking it looks like a recent event or series of events. A sill (i.e. a parallel magmatic intrusion) connected with the latest block faulting is currently being dated by the K-Ar method.

3 CULTURAL EVIDENCE: THE NEOLITHIC

A separate line of evidence is provided by the cultural record. One of the main results of the Italian Mission's work between 1983-1987 has been the building up

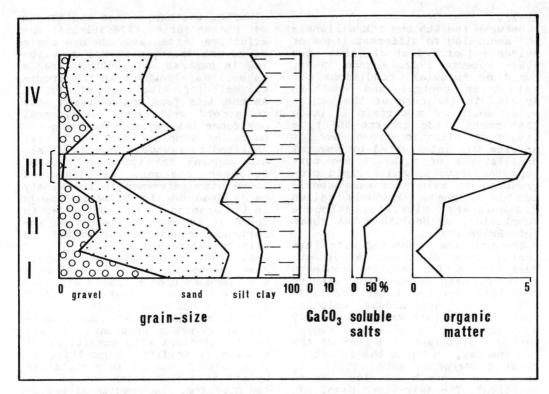

Fig. 3. Sediment analysis of an exposure on the lower Wadi at-Tayyilah;
cf. Fig. 2 A (adapted from Marcolongo and Palmieri 1988).

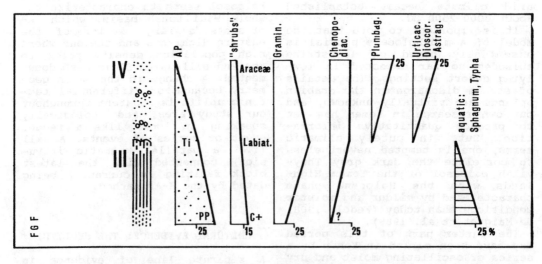

Fig. 4. Preliminary pollen analysis of samples from the lower Wadi at-
Tayyilah sequence. AP = arboreal plants; C+ = Calluna, Epilobium,
Lycopsis and Najadaceae; PP = Pinus silvestris and Pseudotsuga; T =
Tiliaceae (redrawn by author from data in Lentini 1988).

36

of the first prehistoric sequence for North Yemen. Without going into unnecessary archaeological detail, we can simply speak of a "neolithic" phase, bracketed between a later or Bronze Age, which is comparatively well known, and an earlier phase, which at the moment I would suggest considering "mesolithic".

These stadial labels are obviously tentative. Unsatisfactory as they are south of the Fertile Crescent, they are still practical insofar as they convey a basic idea of the stratigraphic position and cultural contents of the units involved. In view of some archaeological similarities with eastern Africa, the neolithic and "mesolithic" phases may better be grouped under a designation such as the Late Stone Age of Yemen, in accordance with the African terminology (e.g. Phillipson 1977:22-23).

The Neolithic is the centrepiece of the Holocene prehistory of the Highlands. A dozen or so sites attributable to this phase are known (Fedele in prep.). In 1984-1986 we managed to test one of them extensively through open-area excavation, strict spatial and stratigraphic control, and total recovery by 4-mm screening. This appears to have remained the only such experiment in southwestern Arabia (Fedele 1986; and in prep.).

The cultural data point to the existence of village-living,cattle-breeding communities, with no apparent knowledge of pottery or bone tools. They have been tentatively described as representing an upland-adapted tradition specific to southwestern Arabia (Fedele 1988). A sizeable sample of animal bone has been collected by use of on-site consolidation, in spite of the heavy damage caused by sun-cracking, wind abrasion and salinization. This faunal sample is the only direct source of information on the Neolithic economy.

The agricultural capacity is not known, but the integration of these groups into a tropical high-altitude ecosystem appears to have been efficient. Stone artefacts show both small and large, heavy-duty equipment, while some rabot-like scrapers and other stout tool types probably indicate the habi-

tual processing of wood. Useful information about the spatial organisation of one settlement is also available. In addition to substantial elliptical huts built with large stone blocks, smaller and often flimsy structures made from organic materials have been brought to light, suggesting rather complex villages (Fedele 1986; de Maigret et al. 1988).

In the area where most work has been done, the Hawlan et-Tiyal, these settlements are correlated with the Thayyilah paleosol, or more exactly the period of geomorphic stability with which it is broadly associated. According to topography, soil and sediment evidence, and a preliminary palynological test, we have taken our data to indicate the presence of some vegetation cover, as well as high watertable conditions in many valleys (Marcolongo and Palmieri 1986, 1988).

The palynological test (Lentini 1988; see Fig. 4) is obviously preliminary and by itself inconclusive. Conifer pollen can travel very long distances in tropical wind systems (Beug pers. comm.; cf. Hooghiemstra 1988), but some at least of the pollen in the relevant samples (e.g. Typha, Sphagnum) provide sufficient indication that the Thayyilah paleosol supported greater vegetation cover than today, including some humidity-loving species. The relative abundance of humic colloids in the paleosol supports this reconstruction. Confirmatory evidence can also be found in cattle husbandry, as the development of cattle pastoralism requires suitably watered pastures, ideally within walking distance of the settlements.

Our available data would thus suggest that selected parts of the pediment slopes and wadi terraces were mantled with grass and scrub vegetation, possibly interspersed with tree stands. To what extent this picture can be generalised throughout the Yemen Highlands is unknown.

There have been dating problems, including confusion over charcoal samples sent to a radiocarbon laboratory, but through the paleosol correlation, I would date the florescene of these neolithic groups to the 6th-4th millennia BC.

4 CULTURAL EVIDENCE: BEFORE AND AFTER THE NEOLITHIC

The most extensively tested site, though shallow (80 cm on the average), has turned out to be stratified. The findings from the deeper levels of this site, WTHiii on Wadi at-Tayyilah, include pits, charcoal patches, and a tiny faunal sample of Bos material (de Maigret et al. 1988). A measurable radius falls in the overlap zone of wild and domestic cattle (Fedele 1988; C. Grigson pers. comm.). If importance can be attached to a single outstanding find - a figurine of unbaked clay (Fedele 1986; de Maigret et al. 1988) - this phase is apparently correlated with Pre-Pottery Neolithic B (PPNB) adaptions in the Levant.

According to this hypothesis a date in the 7th or 8th millennium BC is suggested. From a general standpoint our data, though very scanty, may point to local antecedents of the neolithic groups already illustrated. Tentatively speaking, the concept of a mesolithic or incipient neolithic phase for Yemen is perhaps permissible.

This is all we know at the moment of the early and middle Holocene part of the North Yemen sequence. When we come to post-neolithic times, the picture for a certain area of the Yemen Highlands becomes clearer. In the eastern Highlands the neolithic herders were superseded by - or evolved into - Bronze Age farmers, radiocarbon-dated to the 3rd and early 2nd millennium BC (de Maigret 1988a; radiocarbon dates, see Fedele in press b). Village life has been reconstructed, so far, from three excavated sites in the Hawlan at-Tiyal district and a number of ruins in the Wadi Danah basin (de Maigret et al. in press).

These Bronze Age farmers lived essentially off caprines and sorghum. They made pottery, apparently related to the advanced Early Bronze tradition of Palestine and Syria. Grain impressions in pottery indicate the cultivation of wheat, barley and millet (Costantini 1984). An equid bone, possibly from a donkey, was pieced together from fragments found at Wadi Yanaʿim, site 1 (WYi). Animals associated with Bronze Age settlements mainly include sheep or indeterminate caprines (about 90-95 percent of finds), followed by cattle, pig, gazelle, wild or domestic cat, and the above mentioned equid (Fedele in press a).

This information suggests a caprine-based, mixed-farming economy, likely to be the cause of increasing stress to the immediate environment. The diminutive size of sheep and perhaps cattle may well reflect some climatic and/or nutritional stress. As microstratigraphy and sedimento-climatic correlations at site WTHiii suggest a slight increase of slope erosion prior to the onset of full aridity, the possibility of excessive human pressure, on an increasingly fragile landscape tending towards desiccation, cannot be ruled out.

At about the same time, somewhere between the 4th and first millennium BC, a site in the Ramlat Sabʿatayn Desert of Yemen, indicates the presence of hunting groups exploiting wild equids (onagers?) and gazelles. This site, HARii near Wadi Harib, is the only one so far discovered in the desert (Di Mario 1986; Di Mario et al. in press).

The pastoralists of the uplands may thus be contrasted with persistent hunting groups in the desert periphery. Different economic strategies may have been used side by side in the various ecological zones of Yemen, as is supported by a recent survey of the Tihamah coastal areas (Tosi 1986). Whether such economies represented complementary segments of the same sociocultural group, or else independent cultural entities ("cultures") of their own, is impossible to tell. But as a hypothesis, the possibility can be borne in mind of the development of specialised, complementary social units within an overall cultural and demographic continuum, encompassing the Bronze Age and perhaps the Neolithic.

5 HUMAN AND ENVIRONMENTAL ROLES

This admittedly coarse-grained story of man-environment interactions in North Yemen (Fig. 5) is expected to improve as more and better information becomes available. But I believe we have a good

	LAND	CLIMATE & BIOME	MAN
TODAY		Hammada surface Slope wash, deep watertable	Monsoonal, subarid/arid with flash floods	Widespread desertion Sabaean kingdom
1500 BC	IV	Stream dissection Tectonic crisis, uplifting Lowered watertable Tectonic instability	Increasing aridity Calcification Monsoon fluctuations	Bronze Age: caprine-and-sorghum farming ? Neolithic
3000				
3500	III	Thayyilah Paleosol: pedogenesis, c.5300-4000 BC Stabilised slopes and terraces, some vegetation, shallow watertable Stream stability & slight aggradation	Holocene Subpluvial: maximum Holocene rainfall	Neolithic: cattle pastoralism (hunting in desert?) "Mesolithic"
6000				
8000	II	Aeolian silt Tufa deposits	Alternating moist-dry	? "Mesolithic"
>9000	I	Torrential deposits	?	?

Fig. 5. North Yemen, eastern Highlands: an interim synopsis of man, land, and climate interrelationships during the Holocene. I-IV: main lithostratigraphic members as in Fig. 2 A dates to the left are approximate, in calendar years BC (F.G. Fedele 1989).

case of tectonic control over the final collapse of agricultural fertility. In certain areas of the Hawlan at-Tiyal, late Holocene fault-controlled block movements have been responsible for a lowering of the watertable, adding to the impoverishment of soils which had been already affected by climatic desiccation. The process must have reached its terminal stage around 2000 BC.

Tectonic changes and their attendant effects on hydrology should be regarded as a major factor of biome depletion and settlement and economic shift. At a slightly later time it must have contributed decisively to the abandonment of a number of areas in the eastern Highlands. Even small-scale structural changes in the land were enough to alter the delicate balance on which the conditions favourable to farming

depended. The long-term climatic trends towards aridity, far less severe in the mountains than in the low-lying parts of the Arabian Peninsula, and overforaging by domestic livestock, may not have led alone to the eventual desertion of the region.

A few centuries later, sometime in the later part of the 2nd millennium BC, a new way of life was firmly established in the lowlands alongside the desert sand-sea. This was the cultural pattern based on large dams built to capture the seasonal flood from the mountains, and connected by caravans to long-distance trade systems, a way of life concomitant with the rise of state societies around 1000 BC.

Thus in upland and interior Yemen, climate may have shaped the potential for a certain type of landscape, but within these imposed limits the actual configuration of the ecosystem, its opportunities and lack of them, were dictated by other factors - tectonics and man. Man's role is rather h.rd to assess, however, and one cannot be quite sure where to pick out evidence of human mismanagement in the North Yemen sequence.

If as a heuristic hypothesis we suppose that climatic and tectonic causes of environmental deterioration were escalated by human interference, I would predict that even a limited stress placed on the local biome by browsing and mixed-feeding animals may have reached a critical peak during the 3rd or early 2nd millennium BC. At the time when the Bronze Age techno-economic system was already probably coping with spreading desiccation, renewed tectonic activity resulted in the termination of the shallow groundwater conditions. Wadi erosion and the removal of thin fertile soils could only add to the uncertainties of living in the mountains. Although the exact chronology of these facts has to be determined, the overall sequence seems to be valid.

Man's role must have been overshadowed by the role of tectonics, the geomorphological changes connected with the perennial instability of the land itself. The ultimate control of human behaviour at the population level must probably be attributed to the land (Fedele in press c). This may sound a rather negative conclusion insofar as the impact of ancient man on the landscape seems to have been no more than a contributing factor in the overwhelming environmental drama. While aware of this, I generally prefer to take a nuanced view of man's impact on the environment, with a number of grades and modes between man being full actor or full victim, across a continuum of ecological possibilities.

6 ACKNOWLEDGEMENTS

Special thanks are due to A. de Maigret and the other colleagues in the Italian Archaeological Mission, in particular B. Marcolongo, A.M. Palmieri and M. Tosi. H.-J. Beug, C. Grigson and H.J. Bruins have provided literature or comments, though the use here made of this information is my responsibility alone. Jill Morris has kindly revised my English text and typed most of the manuscript.

7 REFERENCES

Bintliff, J.L. and W.van Zeist (eds.) 1982. Palaeoclimates, Palaeoenvironments and Human Communities in the Eastern Mediterranean Region in Later Prehistory. BAR International Series 133.

Blume, H. 1976. Saudi Arabien. Tübingen, Basel: Erdmann.

Brice, W.C. (ed.) 1978. The environmental history of the Near and Middle East since the last ice age. London, New York: Academic Press.

Costantini, L. 1984. Plant impressions in Bronze Age pottery from Yemen Arab Republic. East and West 34:107-115.

Di Mario, F. 1986. The 'Neolithic' in the Ramlat Sabʿatayn Desert. In A.de Maigret et al. 1986. Archaeological activities in the Yemen Arab Republic, 1986. East and West 36: 414-418.

Di Mario, F. et al. in press. The western ar-Rubʿ al-Khali 'Neolithic': new data _rom the Ramlat Sabʿatayn (Yemen Arab Republic). Ann. Ist. Univ. Orient. Napoli 39.

Fedele, F.G. 1986. Excavations and researches in the Eastern Highlands. In A.de Maigret et al. 1986. Archaeological activities in the Yemen Arab Republic, 1986. East and West 36: 396-400.

Fedele, F.G. 1988. North Yemen: the Neolithic. In W.Daum (ed.), Yemen, 3000 years of art and civilisation in Arabia Felix, p.34-37. Innsbruck, Pinguin-Verlag; Frankfurt/Main, Umschau-Verlag.

Fedele, F.G. in press a. Bronze Age faunal collections from North Yemen. In A.de Maigret et al., The Bronze Age culture of Hawlan at-Tiyal and Al-Hada (Yemen Arab Republic), Vols. 1-2, Chapter III/7. Rome: IsMEO.

Fedele, F.G. in press b.
Radiocarbon dates. In A.de Maigret et al., The Bronze Age culture of Hawlan at-Tiyal and Al-Hada (Yemen Arab Republic), Vols. 1-2, Chapter III/8. Rome: IsMEO.

Fedele, F.G. in press c.
Fossil volcanism and archaeology: the North Yemen Highlands. In C.Albore Livadie and F.Widemann (eds.), Volcanology and archaeology. Louvain-la-Neuve, PACT/Conseil de l'Europe.

Fedele, F.G. in preparation.
Wadi et-Tayyilah, site 3 (WTHiii), a stratified neolithic settlement in the eastern Highlands. In In A.de Maigret et al. (eds.), The paleolithic and neolithic cultures of the Yemen Arab Republic. Rome, IsMEO.

Fein, J.S. and
P.L. Stephens (eds.) 1987.
Monsoons. Chichester: John Wiley.

Garrard, A.N., C.P.D.Harvey
and V.R.Switsur 1981.
Environment and settlement during the Upper Pleistocene and Holocene at Jubba in the Great Nefud, northern Arabia. Atlal 5:137-148.

Hooghiemstra, H. 1988.
Palynological records from northwest African marine sediments: a general outline of the interpretation of the pollen signal. Philosophical Transactions of the Royal Society London B318:431-449.

Kopp, H. 1981.
Agrargeographie der Arabischen Republik Jemen. Erlangen, Erlanger Geographische Arbeiten, Sonderband 11.

Lentini, A. 1988.
Preliminary pollen analysis of paleosoil (sic) horizon in the Yala area. In A.de Maigret (ed.), The Sabaean archaeological complex in the Wadi Yala (Eastern Hawlan at-Tiyal, Y.A.R.): a preliminary report, p.52-53. Rome, IsMEO.

Luz, B. 1982.
Palaeoclimatic interpretation of the last 20,000 yr record of deep-sea cores around the Middle East. In J.L.Bintliff and W.van Zeist (eds.) 1982. Palaeoclimates, Palaeoenvironments and Human Communities in the Eastern Mediterranean Region in Later Prehistory, p.41-65. BAR International Series 133.

Maigret, A. de 1988a.
The Yemini Bronze Age. In W.Daum (ed.), Yemen, 3000 years of art and civilisation in Arabia Felix, p.38-40. Innsbruck, Pinguin-Verlag; Frankfurt/Main, Umschau-Verlag.

Maigret, A. de 1988b.
The Sabaean archaeological complex in the Wadi Yala (Eastern Hawlan at-Tiyal, Y.A.R.): a preliminary report. Rome: IsMEO.

Maigret, A. de,
F.G.Fedele and F.Di Mario 1988.
Lo Yemen prima del regno di Saba. Le Scienze 40, 234:12-23.

Maigret, A. de et al. in press.
The Bronze Age culture of Hawlan at-Tiyal and Al-Hada (Yemen Arab Republic), Vols. 1-2. Rome: IsMEO.

Marcolongo, B. and A.M.Palmieri
1986. Palaeoenvironmental conditions in the areas of Wadi at-Tayyilah and Baraqis: preliminary report. In A.de Maigret et al. 1986. Archaeological activities in the Yemen Arab Republic, 1986. East and West 36:461-464.

Marcolongo, B. and A.M.Palmieri
1988. Environmental modification and settlement conditions in the Yala area. In A.de Maigret (ed.) The Sabaean archaeological complex in the Wadi Yala (Eastern Hawlan at-Tiyal, Y.A.R.): a preliminary report, p.45-51. Rome, IsMEO.

McClure, H.A. 1978.
Ar-Rub' al-Khali. In S.S.Al-Sayari and J.G.Zötl (eds.), Quaternary period in Saudi Arabia, vol. 1, p.252-263. Wien, New York, Springer Verlag.

Pearson, G.W., J.R.Pilcher,
M.G.L.Baillie, D.M.Corbett and F.Qua 1986.
High precision 14C measurement of Irish oaks to show the natural 14C variation from AD 1840 to 5210 BC. Radiocarbon 28/2B:911-934.

Phillipson, D.W. 1977.
The later prehistory of Eastern and Southern Africa. London: Heinemann.

Ritchie, J.C.,
C.H.Eyles and C.V.Haynes 1985.
Sediment and pollen evidence for an early to mid-Holocene humid period in the eastern Sahara. Nature 314:352-355.

Roberts, N. 1982.
Lake levels as an indicator of

Near Eastern palaeo-climates: a
preliminary appraisal. In J.L.
Bintliff and W.van Zeist (eds.)
1982. Palaeoclimates, Palaeoenvironments and Human Communities
in the Eastern Mediterranean
Region in Later Prehistory,
p.235-271. BAR International
Series 133.

Rognon, P. 1982.
Modifications des climats et des
environnements en Afrique du Nord
et au Moyen Orient depuis 20.000
B.P. In J.L.Bintliff and W.van
Zeist (eds.) 1982. Palaeoclimates, Palaeoenvironments and Human
Communities in the Eastern Mediterranean Region in Later Prehistory, p.67-102. BAR International Series 133.

Tosi, M. 1986.
Survey and excavations on the
coastal plain (Tihamah). In A.de
Maigret et al. 1986. Archaeolo-
gical activities in the Yemen
Arab Republic, 1986. East and
West 36:400-414.

Whitney, J.W. 1982.
Geologic evidence of late Quaternary climate change in western
Saudi Arabia. In J.L.Bintliff
and W.van Zeist (eds.) 1982.
Palaeoclimates, Palaeoenvironments and Human Communities in
the Eastern Mediterranean Region
in Later Prehistory, p.231-233.
BAR International Series 133.

Ancient man's impact on the Mediterranean landscape in Israel – Ecological and evolutionary perspectives

4

Zev Naveh
Technion, Israel Institute of Technology, Haifa, Israel

ABSTRACT: The final stages of the geological and biological evolution of Mediterranean landscapes in Israel coincided with the major stages of the biological and cultural evolution of Mediterranean man from the Acheulian food gathering Homo erectus to the intensive food collecting epipaleolithic Natufian and the food producing neolithic Homo sapiens. In these closely coupled physical, biological, and cultural processes of co-evolutionary feedback relations the use of fire became a major driving force in the creation of the semi-natural and agricultural landscapes. This landscape genesis can be described as multivariate biogenic, pedogenic and anthropogenic functions in which human land use impacts became an integral part of the controlling physical and biotic state factors and flux potentials, modifying the dependent soil and vegetation variables of the landscape ecotopes and adding human artifacts.

1 INTRODUCTION

This paper differs in several aspects from all others presented in this volume:

1) It deals chiefly with those ancient human impacts in the Pleistocene for which there is not sufficient archeological and geomorphological evidence.

2) It treats these impacts from an evolutionary and ecological point of view, not as linear, one directional cause-effects of human disturbances, but as mutual-caused processes of co-evolution of Mediterranean people and their landscapes.

According to Stebbins (1982) co-evolution is the simultaneous evolution of two genetically independent, but ecologically interdependent lines via biological and cultural templates.

From Middle Pleistocene onwards, the final stages of the geological and biological evolution of Mediterranean landscapes coincided with the major phases of human biological and cultural evolution in this region. Broadening our conception of co-evolution, we can consider these closely coupled processes of human evolution and the gradual conversion of natural landscapes and their vegetation into semi-natural and agricultural landscapes as a co-evolutionary process.

3) I refer to landscapes not only within the geomorphological context, but regard these in a more holistic way as total space/time defined concrete ecological, geographical and cultural systems, and as the living space of our Total Human Ecosystem (Naveh 1982a; Naveh and Lieberman 1984).

This Total Human Ecosystem had its early beginning in the Near East already several hundred thousand years before the neolithic revolution. However, from this period, tectonics and erosion have obliterated most archeological evidences of human activities. No ash deposits of forest and brush fires and sparse floral remains have been detected in open in situ habitations. Even recent, sophisticated flotation methods have not provided large samples of vegetal relics in shallow and eroded Mediterranean upland soils, especially in terra rossa in which preservation is very poor. It should be realized that in these specific climatic and edaphic conditions, most of the ashes of forest and brush fires are washed away by the first heavy rains, and their remnants become intimately mixed with the thin upper layer of humus-rich terra rossa and rendzina soils (Naveh 1973). Some of these slopes underwent severe geological erosion and morphotectonic upheavals and even in the caves, most traces of hearths and fire have probably been erased by erosion and by changes in sea level, followed by sedimentation.

But even if there were more cultural artifacts and vegetal remains from open sites, river terraces and caves, we still would not be able to trace back in a mechanistic way these gradual, long-lasting processes of mutual feedback relations, leading to co-evolution. We can also not trace back in a mechanistic way the processes of plant speciation and sudden appearance of new genera and taxa, as well as the subtle changes in the cortex and in the nervous system, in conscience and in behaviour patterns leading from the Acheulian food gathering Homo erectus of the Upper Jordan Rift Valley to the intensive food collecting epipaleolithic Natufian and finally to the food producing neolithic Homo sapiens of Mt. Carmel. But nevertheless nobody of us will deny that such a biological and cultural evolution has taken place in the Pleistocene.

In my reasoning, I have relied therefore not only on relevant archeological findings, but on deductions from our ecological studies (Naveh 1973, 1975; Naveh and Dan 1973; Naveh and Whittaker 1979; Kutiel and Naveh 1987) and on comparisons with contemporary gatherer-hunter economies in California (Lewis 1973) and Western Australia (Hallam 1979) in similar ecological conditions.

The following is a condensed version of what has been recently presented in more detail elsewhere (Naveh 1984; Naveh and Kutiel 1989). It can be considered also an expansion of the study by Pignatti (1983) on man-vegetation relations in the Mediterranean, emphasizing its important role in the evolution of new habitats and in stimulating the evolution of the Mediterranean flora. It collaborates the findings by Di Castri (1981) that humans have co-evolved with these ecosystems and co-evolutionary features are present in a number of ecological and cultural characters of this region.

This process of co-evolution can be sub-divided into three major phases, corresponding roughly with major cultural stages in the Pleistocene.

2 THE EARLY PHASE OF CO-EVOLUTION

There is a tendency among paleoecologists to regard paleolithic man chiefly as a hunter and to belittle his influence on environment and vegetation. Thus, for instance, Pons and Quézel (1985:35), in reviewing man's impact in the Mediterranean, claimed: "Early man was a hunter and a gatherer and had relatively little influence on natural vegetation." But, as stated rightly by Leaky and Lewin (1979), it would be foolish to ignore the lessons that contemporary societies of hunters and gatherers could teach us. On the basis of the importance of plants in their diets and economies, the time spent on food collecting, and the tools used (mostly wood and therefore perishable), they concluded that it would be more accurate to refer to these people, as well as to their paleolithic ancestors, as gatherer-hunters and not as hunter-gatherers. This applies most probably also to the earliest human populations in Israel, in the Upper Jordan Rift Valley, whose lithic Acheulian assemblages show still African similarities or even origin (Bar-Yosef 1984).

The close interaction between the creation and maintenance of anthropogenic environments with the cultural traits of such paleolithic gatherer-hunters has been emphasized also by Rindos (1984) in his co-evolutionary treatment of the origin of agriculture. He considered their interrelations with the plants near their habitations as the first step of "incidental domestication".

Even if the interference of these widely scattered populations with

Table 1. Production and nutrition accumulation of wheat plants grown in pots with soil from burned and unburned pine forest of Mt. Carmel (Kutiel and Naveh 1987).

		Burned	Unburned	Ratio
Dry weight (g/sq m)	shoots	1142	197	5.8
	roots	709	158	4.5
Shoot:root ratio		2.2	1.2	1.8
Dry weight spikes (g/sq m)		512	39	13.0
No. of seeds m^{-2}		13740	1102	12.05
Seed weight (g/sq m)		128	11	11.6
Nutrient accumulation	N	0.6	0.2	3.0
	P	0.2	0.02	10.0
	Mg	0.6	0.08	7.5
	K	0.2	0.04	5.0
	Ca	0.9	0.1	9.0
	Zn	0.02	0.005	4.0
	Fe	0.3	0.06	5

the vegetation canopy, its litter, humus and upper soil layer was only very slight and patchy, it could have, in the long run, far-reaching implications on plant evolution and vegetation dynamics and on the landscape as a whole.

The destruction of plants, the formation of gaps in the closed tree cover for food and fuel, the clearing of land for habitation and the trampling of paths, the digging for bulbs and earth animals and the disposing of human and kitchen waste, all these intentional and unintentional activities are creating favourable regeneration niches sensu Grubb (1977) for herbaceous plants. Many of these evolved presumably during the Pleistocene in this region as opportunistic, so-called ruderals, which could take best advantage of the improved light, fertility, and moisture regimes. Among these are grasses, such as Avena sterilis and Hordeum spontaneum, which served as progenitors for our cereals and which are responding vigorously to nitrogen and phosphate for early growth and reproduction (Naveh 1982b). The same is true also for many legumes, Compositae and other progenitors of pulses and vegetables.

In representative sites of 1000 sq m on Mt. Carmel we found that relatively small grassy patches and their ecotones, scattered between dense stands of maquis trees and shrubs can contribute hundred and more herbaceous species and of these at least two thirds have edible parts or are of other human uses.

The pollen samples from the lowest F bed of the Carmel Tabun cave, attributed by Horowitz (1979) to Upper Acheulian-Yabrudian layers, and containing Scabiosa prolifera, Compositae and Gramineae, are characteristic of such gregariously distributed nitrophilous plants which can still be found on grassy openings near this cave.

In addition to other, more or less catastrophic natural perturbations and to increasing drought, fire, caused by volcanic activities and by lightning, acted as a strong selection force in these Mediterranean landscapes. This was most probably true during the drier interpluvials in which the Mediterranean climate patterns became established. It created favourable conditions for the germination of light-demanding woody plants, such as Pinus halepensis and most chamaephytes, as well as for the abovementioned herbaceous plants, facilitating their spreading over larger areas.

Our studies showed these herbaceous fire followers serve as an efficient sink for the post-fire flush of nutrients released in the first winter, which cause a manifold increase in their vegetative growth and in reproduction (Table 1).

In Western Galilee, and in recent wild-fires on Mt. Carmel, we could observe the striking proliferation of ruderal fire followers, especially of Hordeum spontaneum and Pipthaterum miliaceum from small islands and waste heaps into the burned pine-oak forest. Whereas the annual plants are crowded out after a few years by the vigorously rege-nerating woody plants, a few peren-nial species, especially Pipthate-rum miliaceum, remain in the semi-shaded woody cover and survive for many years until the next fire. The latter is a shade-tolerant perenni-al grass which can also make best use of the above-mentioned, man-created, tree-shrub-grass ecotones and edge habitats. Its stout bun-ches produce many millet-like seeds which can be easily collected by cutting or combing the panicles. A closely resembling North American species Oryzopsis hymenoides is called "Indian rice" because its seeds were gathered by the Indians of California and the dry South-west.

We can therefore assume that positive feedback couplings between such wildfires in the Pleistocene and these colonizing ruderal plants, especially Cerealia, could have caused their spreading in space and time far beyond man-in-duced forest gaps and ecotones. This would most probably not have escaped the sharp eyes of the paleolithic gatherer-hunters. They must have realized that they could improve their diet from the inva-ding grasses, legumes, bulbs and tuberous plants. In addition, game, especially gazelle, was attracted to these grasses and the lush re-generating woody plants. It is therefore very likely that man came to use fire as the first extra-somatal energy source, not only for heating, cooking, tool making and socialization, but also as his first vegetation and land-scape management tool. This was suggested already by Sauer (1965), the eminent geographer, who regard-ed speech, tools and fire as the "tripods of cultural evolution". He also pointed to volcanism in the Eastern Mediterranean and the Jordan Rift Valley as the first source of such fires and to their cultural importance for food col-lecting and hunting.

In fact, the earliest archeologi-cal evidence of human use of fire in Israel is from such volcanic land of the Upper Jordan Rift Val-ley, from a Late Acheulian assem-blage near Jisr Banat, where Stekelis (1960) found splinters of burned bone together with bifaces and flake cleavers made of basalt.

3 THE MAJOR PHASE OF CO-EVOLUTION

During the Early Upper Pleistocene, the special character of Early Mediterranean-Levant stone cultures emerged, exhibiting adaptation to their environment (Bar-Yosef 1984). This period marks the beginning of the major phase of co-evolution. The gradual intensification of human interference was accompanied, most probably, also by more sophis-ticated use of fire by Mousterian gatherer-hunters and Neanderthal-oids. These, according to Perles (1977), brought the mastering of fire to perfection and produced torches to carry and set fire.

The Tabun cave of Mt. Carmel bears evidence of human use of fire by reddened earth and mixed ashes from hearths, and also of the ac-cumulation of fine ash deposits (Jelinek 1981). This ash could have been blown inside the cave from burning of the woody vegeta-tion, surrounding it.

During the last pluvial, pre-agricultural landscape modification reached apparently its peak through intensive, broad spectrum utiliza-tion of coastal and upland plant and animal resources by prospering epipaleolithic cultures, such as the Natufian of Mt. Carmel.

As described in more detail by Bar-Yosef (1984), the Natufians used carefully prepared, tiny sharp microliths to hunt game, especially gazelle, which may have been at-tracted to the freshly-burned open forest and brush-fire "pastures". They used flint sickles to cut wild grasses, and mortars and pestles as pounding tools in the preparation of staple food from roasted cereals and acorns. They constructed houses and developed a complex and rich communal, cultural and spiritual life, which may have had many common features with Pre-European Indians of Central and Southern Coastal California. These were the most advanced pre-agricultural In-dians, living in comparable ecolo-gical conditions and using pre-scribed burning as a major manage-ment tool which maintained a dyna-mic flow equilibrium between the woody and herbaceous vegetation layers. We can therefore assume that also the Natufians set cooler fires and in much shorter cycles than the natural ones, and on smaller patches, creating thereby mosaics of different regeneration stages and also frequently burned fire corridors and grassy fields.

The colonization of such man- and fire-induced open and drier sites by desert and rock dwelling rodents, like Acomys russatus, and Gerbillus dasyurus, should therefore not necessarily be interpreted as a result of climatic changes, as suggested by Tchernov (1975).

4 THE FINAL PHASE OF CO-EVOLUTION

It seems most probable that the Natufians and other epipaleolithic cultures served as important links in the transition from intensive food collection to food production and the domestication of plants and animals. The creation of early agricultural ecosystems and their concrete, space/time defined landscape units or ecotopes, can be regarded as the culmination of the co-evolution. In this process, burning and creation of favourable ash seedbeds for the above-mentioned herbaceous fire followers acted probably as a major cultural trigger.

The most favourable sites for incipient agriculture were the deep and fertile soils of broad wadis and coastal valleys, covered by dense oak and pistachio forests. These tall trees could be felled, as shown by Iversen (1971) with the help of flint axes, which have been found also in the Sefunim cave of Mt. Carmel (Ronen 1984). The ashes of the burned trees, together with the dried brushwood could serve for reseeding of those species which were found most suitable. In this way the neolithic slash-and-burn cultivation by the first European farmers, described by Narr (1956), was preceeded by several thousand years in the Levant.

According to Pons and Quézel (1985) such early slash-and-burn agriculture in Quercus pubescens forests is indicated in Southern France about 9000 years ago by charcoal findings, the decrease of oak pollen and a simultaneous increase in Labiatae, Leguminosae,

Plantago and other species, considered to be weeds of cereal cultivation.

5 THE FINAL FORMATION OF THE AGRO-PASTORAL LANDSCAPE

With the gradual conversion of the semi-natural landscape into the agro-pastoral Mediterranean landscape in the Early Holocene, this unique mutual adaptation and co-evolution of physical, biological and cultural features was replaced gradually by unilateral human dominance. It was initiated by the narrowing of the broad spectrum neolithic agriculture into field crop and animal husbandry. This caused the destruction of the pristine vegetation canopy in the lowlands and foothills and led to severe soil erosion (Dan and Yaalon 1971). It culminated several thousand years later, with the invention of iron tools, enabling the uprooting of trees and shrubs on the slopes. The invention of the sophisticated agro- and hydro-engineering methods of terracing of arable slopes by the Phoenicians and Israeli led to a stable, rich and higly diverse culture, lasting for many centuries. But throughout historical times, their maintenance or negligence determined the fate of these uplands for good and for worse.

6 DISCUSSION AND CONCLUSIONS

I have attempted to show in this paper that ancient man's impact on the landscape cannot be judged solely by the few archeological and paleo-ecological remains in the Pleistocene and by the catastrophic geomorphological events of erosion, sedimentation and aggradation in the Holocene. They must be evaluated within a much broader evolutionary, ecological and anthropological context and within different scales of spatio-temporal and conceptual hierarchies. For this purpose, a holistic landscape-ecological approach and the realization of mutual-causal cybernetic feedback effects between man and landscape seemed to be most appropriate.

In this way, the description of

the evolution of the man-modified semi-natural landscape has to include not only the dimensions of physical space, but also the cultural dimensions of conceptual space (the "noosphere" - sensu Teilhard de Chardin (1966)). This conceptual space is the realm of human mind, feelings, imagination, perception and conception. Man seems to be the only animal on earth to have fully developed such a conceptual space (Jantsch 1975).

The semi-natural, man-modified "cultural" landscape contains therefore more than the sum of the measurable and quantifiable parameters in which space-time dimensions are expressed and also more than the geological, archeological and paleontological findings from which we endeavour to trace man's early history. For these reasons we have to embark upon some speculations on the impact of man's noospheric conceptual space on his Pleistocene and early Holocene Total Human Ecosystem.

In the gradual transformation of both man and his landscape ecotopes, the mastering of fire was coupled by positive feedback loops with the accumulation and exchange of noospheric information, the further sophistication of group hunting and gathering technologies and the evolving of more complex interactions and community patterns. Such amplifying couplings have been called "multiplier effects" by Renfrew (1972) in his description of the emergence of Aegean civilizations. The prominent role of fire as such a multiplier effect has been verified in the thorough study by Perles (1977) as follows: "Mankind could have become evolved into Homo habilis without fire, but it would never have become Homo sapiens without fire."

Subtle, small-scale effects and therefore of "small numbers" in space, but of large, geological numbers in time, were induced by widely dispersed, but long-lasting human activities and disturbances. These may have been of no lesser impact on the landscape than shorter-lasting geomorphological events of large spatial scale. These subtle, small-scale events could have interacted through positive feedback coupling with such large-scale events as fire and climatic desiccation.

For these reasons I cannot agree with those Mediterranean ecologists who do not acknowledge the importance of human impact before the neolithic revolution because of the small number populations and the lack of large numbers evidence.

The complex and closely interwoven processes of landscape genesis can be described as multivariate landscape state factor equations of biogenic and pedogenic functions, based on Jenny's (1961) functional-factorial approach:

$$LE_{s,v,a\cdots} =$$
$$f(P,R,C_{dr},fi^{O}gr \cdots T>100\ 000)$$

where $LE_{s,v,a\cdots}$ represent the dependent landscape ecotope variables of soil, vegetation, animals, and other, unidentified variables, as a function of the initial geological and physiographic landscape state factors, represented by soil parent material (P) and by relief (R), and the driving flux potentials of climate (C) and living organisms (O) with their most important evolutionary forces of drought (dr) and fire (fi) as major climatic, and grazing (gr) as major biotic selection stress factors, together with other, unidentified factors (...), acting through geological times (T) of more than hundred thousand years.

The dynamic role of man and his impact on the landscape through time can be treated as part of this multivariate state factor equation. Thus, in the course of the above-described co-evolution in the Pleistocene, the paleolithic gatherer-hunter ($H_{gath-hun}$) became a more and more independent state factor of his Total Human Ecosystem and therefore these "natural" biopedogenic functions became also gradually "cultural" anthropogenic functions, each lasting for more than ten thousand years. In these, man became the driving force, modifying the dependent ecotope variables and adding human-made artifacts (har) and using prescribed burning (bu) as one of his major tools for the conversion of natural ecotopes into semi-natural ones. This co-evolutionary process was coupled by positive (deviation amplifying) feedback loops of more and more efficient energy conversion of fire, wild plants and animals, with

the biological and cultural evolution of Homo sapiens:

$$LE_{s,v,a,har}\cdots = f(H_{gath-hun,bu}, P, R, C_{dr}, fi^O_{gr}\cdots \atop T>10\ 000).$$

In the early Holocene, agro-
pastoral man ($H_{agr-past}$) gained
complete dominance over his Total
Human Ecosystem, by burning, cutting, land clearing, cultivating,
terracing, planting, grazing and
building. Thereby, he changed not
only the dependent ecotope variables, but also the controlling
state factors of organisms, relief,
soil parent material and even climate and hydrology. These anthropogenic functions occurred in land-
use cycles, lasting for several
hundred years. They can therefore
be expressed by the following
general equation:

$$LE_{v,s,ar}\cdots = f(H_{agr-past} P, R, C, O \ldots T>100).$$

We are not yet able to quantify
these equations and all its parameters. But this may be achieved in
the future with the help of artificial intelligence computer software
using fuzzy set systems, which
allow approximate reasoning and
quantitative analyses with linguistic and qualitative values (Negotia
1985).

But even in their present state,
these multivariate equations can
serve as models for interdisciplinary studies. They demonstrate
clearly the futility of one-sided,
deterministic approaches in which
certain factors are singled out as
the sole explanation of complex,
closely interwoven physical, biological and cultural processes.

REFERENCES

Bar-Yosef, O. 1984.
    Near East. Neue Forschungen zur
    Altsteinzeit:232-298.
Dan, J. and D.H.Yaalon 1971.
    On the origin and nature of the
    paleopedological formations in
    the central coastal fringe areas
    of Israel. In D.H.Yaalon (ed.),
    Paleopedology: Origin, nature and
    dating of paleosols, p.245-260.
    Jerusalem, Israel Universities
    Press.
Di Castri, F. 1981.
    Mediterranean-type shrublands of
    the world. In F.di Castri, F.W.
Goodall and R.L.Specht (eds.),
    Ecosystems of the world 11-
    Mediterranean-type shrublands,
    p.1-52. Amsterdam, Elsevier.
Grubb, P.J. 1977.
    The maintenance of species rich-
    ness in plant communities and
    the importance of the regenera-
    tion niche. Biol. Rev. 52:107-
    145.
Hallam, S.J. 1979.
    Fire and hearth. A study of abo-
    riginal usage and European usur-
    pation in Southwestern Australia.
    Canberra: Australia Inst. of
    Aboriginal Studies.
Horowitz, A. 1979.
    The Quaternary of Israel. New
    York: Academic Press.
Iversen, I. 1971.
    Forest clearance in the Stone
    Age. In P.R.Ehrlich, J.P.Holdren
    and R.W.Holm (eds.), Man and the
    ecosphere, p.26-31. San Fransis-
    co, Freeman and Comp.
Jantsch, E. 1975.
    Design for evolution. New York:
    Braziller.
Jelinek, A.J. 1981.
    Middle Paleolithic of the Tabun
    Cave. In Colloques internationaux
    598: Préhistoire du Levant, p.
    265-283. Paris, CNRS.
Jenny, H. 1961.
    Derivation of state factor equa-
    tions of soils and ecosystems.
    Soil Sci. Proc.:385-388.
Kutiel, P. and Z.Naveh 1987.
    The effect of fire on soil nu-
    trients of Pinus halepensis
    forests in Israel. Plant and Soil
    104:269-274.
Leaky, R.E. and R.Lewin 1979.
    People of the lake. New York:
    Avon Books.
Lewis, H.T. 1973.
    Pattern of Indian burning in
    California: Ecology and ethnohis-
    tory. Anthropological Papers 1.
    Ramona, California: Ballena
    Press.
Narr, K.J. 1965.
    Early food producing populations.
    In W.L.Thomas (ed.), Man's role
    in changing the face of the
    earth, p.134-151. Chicago, The
    University Press.
Naveh, Z. 1973.
    The ecology of fire in Israel.
    An. Tall Timbers Fire Ecol. Conf.
    Tallahassee, Florida:131-170.
Naveh, Z. 1975.
    The evolutionary significance of
    fire in the Mediterranean region.

Vegetatio 9:199-206.

Naveh, Z. 1982a.
Landscape ecology as emerging branch of human eco-system science. Adv. Ecol. Res. 12:189-232.

Naveh, Z. 1982b.
The dependence of the productivity of a semi-arid Mediterranean hill pasture eco-system on climatic fluctuations. Agriculture and Environment 7:47-61.

Naveh, Z. 1984.
The vegetation of the Carmel and Nahal Sefunim and the evolution of the cultural landscape. In A.Ronen, The Sefunim prehistoric sites, Mount Carmel, Israel. BAR International Series 230.

Naveh, Z. and J.Dan 1973.
The human degradation of Mediterranean landscapes in Israel. In F.di Castri and H.A.Mooney(eds.), Mediterranean-type ecosystems, origin and structure. Heidelberg -Berlin-New York, Springer Verlag.

Naveh, Z. and R.H.Whittaker 1979.
Structural and floristic diversity of shrublands and woodlands in Northern Israel and other Mediterranean areas. Vegetatio 14: 301-309.

Naveh, Z. and A.S.Lieberman 1984.
Landscape ecology - theory and applications. New York-Heidelberg -Berlin-Tokyo, Springer Verlag.

Naveh, Z. and P.Kutiel 1989.
Changes in the Mediterranean vegetation of Israel in response to human habitation and land use. In G.M.Woodwell (ed.), The earth in transition. Patterns and processes of biotic impoverishment. New York, Cambridge Press.

Negotia, C.V. 1985.
Expert systems and fuzzy set systems. Menlo Park, California: Benjamin Cummings Publishing Co.

Perles, C. 1977.
Préhistoire du feu. Paris:Masson.

Pignatti, S. 1983.
Human impact on the vegetation of the Mediterranean. In W.Holzner, M.J.A.Werger and I.Ikusima(eds.), Man's impact on vegetation, p. 151-162. The Hague, Junk.

Pons, A. and P.Quézel 1985.
The history of the flora and vegetation and past and present human disturbance in the Mediterranean. In C.Gommez-Campo (ed.), Conservation of Mediterranean plants, p.25-43. The Hague, Junk.

Renfrew, C. 1972.
The emergence of civilization. London: Methuen.

Rindos, D. 1984.
The origin of agriculture. An evolutionary perspective. New York-London-Toronto, Academic Press.

Ronen, A. 1984.
The Sefunim prehistoric sites, Mount Carmel, Israel. BAR International Series 230.

Sauer, C.O. 1961.
Sedentary and mobile bands in early societies. In S.L.Washburn (ed.), Social life of early man, p.256-266. Viking Publ. in Anthropology 31.

Stebbins, M. 1960.
The paleolithic deposits of Jisr Banat Yaqub. Bull. Res. Conc. Israel, Sect. G. Geo-sciences 9: 346-367.

Teilhard de Chardin, P. 1966.
Man's place in nature. London: William Collins.

Tchernov, E. 1985.
Rodent fauna and environmental changes in the Pleistocene of Israel. In Praksh and P.K.Gosh (eds.), Rodents in desert environments, p.331-362. The Hague, Dr. W.Junk.

Geomorphology/Sedimentology

© 1990 Balkema, Rotterdam. ISBN 90 6191 138 9

Human-induced landscape change in South and Southwest Turkey during the later Holocene

5

Neil Roberts
Department of Geography, Loughborough University, Leicester, UK

ABSTRACT: The environmental history of South and Southwest Turkey is used to illustrate the changing relationship between soi erosion (via alluvial chronologies), vegetation cover and composition (via palynology), and human settlement and land use (via archaeology and historical geography). Each of these data sources has a different spatial and temporal resolution, which may help explain apparent discrepancies such as exist, for example, between pollen- and archaeologically-based land-use histories at Söğüt-Balboura. Cyclical, progressive and steady-state models are evaluated for each component of landscape change. It is concluded that there is a need for more studies of environmental history which are regionally based and multi-disciplinary.

1 DATA SOURCES AND THEIR INTERPRETATION

Since the mid Holocene, and possibly earlier, human agency has transformed the natural landscapes of the Eastern Mediterranean. Amongst the most important components of the landscape are human occupance, the soil, and vegetation, and the history of each of these can be reconstructed using well established techniques. For the early and mid Holocene, human occupance of the Eastern Mediterranean region is known almost exclusively through archaeology, either from survey data or from site excavation. For the later Holocene, archaeological data are supplemented by archival records of settlement, society and economy (Wagstaff 1985), from which more comprehensive historical geographies may be reconstituted. Vegetation history is known primarily through palynology (van Zeist and Bottema 1982), but may also draw on the historical desriptions of classical or Ottoman writers (Rowton 1967; Thirgood 1981). In the same way the changing state of the soil, and particularly erosion and siltation, can be reconstructed by his-torical accounts on the one hand and by proxy methods such as alluvial chronologies on the other.

Each of these methods has strengths and weaknesses. Archaeological surveys will only provide a partial picture of settlement patterns, because of differential site destruction and burial, linked to geomorphological and other processes (Hammond 1978; Vita-Finzi 1978). This distortion is usually greater for more ancient than for more recent time periods, so that our record of Roman sites is more complete than it is for Neolithic ones. On the other hand, archaeological and historical chronologies are well established and relatively precise; indeed artefacts or built structures are often important in establishing environmental chronologies (e.g. Roberts 1979).

Pollen analysis has been of great importance in unravelling the vegetation of land-use history of the Near East. It has revealed, for instance, well-defined clearance phases in some regions, for example Southwest Turkey, but not yet in others such as western Iran and eastern Turkey (Bottema and Woldring this volume). However, there are many uncertainties concerning

the interpretation of pollen diagrams, involving pollen productivity and representation, the importance of the streamborne component,
and other factors (Tauber 1965;
Andersen 1973; Pennington 1979;
Edwards 1979; Jacobson and Bradshaw
1981). When these factors are considered, the absence of clearance
phases or indeed any abrupt changes
in the pollen diagrams from Lakes
Van and Urmia may be explained not
so much by a distinctive land-use
history, as by the fact that they
are derived from cores taken in
very large lakes (van Zeist and
Woldring 1978; Bottema 1986). This
has caused pollen to be recruited
from a wide area and in consequence
these diagrams present a spatially
blurred pattern of local land-use
changes. The large catchment area
for the Van pollen profile is indicated by the presence of significant amounts of pine pollen (Fig.
3), despite the nearest pine
forest being more than 150 km away
from the lake. In contrast, the
diagrams from Beyşehir, which include a very marked Late Holocene
clearance phase, are based on cores
taken not in the middle of Lake
Beyşehir, but in a marsh at its
southwestern corner (van Zeist et
al. 1975). This site is likely to
have recruited its pollen from a
much smaller catchment area and
presumably reflects localised
clearance, farming and arboriculture (Roberts 1982:240).

A second problem associated with
studies of both erosion/deposition
and vegetation changes is temporal
resolution. Although in theory individual radiocarbon dates may
have a precision of less than a
century, in practice the radiometric time scale for Eastern Mediterranean environmental histories
is currently at least an order of
magnitude less precise than the
chronology available for cultural
histories. Individual sediment
cores or sections rarely have more
than two or three radiocarbon
dates, and core tops are usually
assumed to date to the present day,
although this need not be the case
in recently drained lakes and
marshes. Additionally, there may be
problems of contamination by old or
young carbon, while radiocarbon
dates older than ca 2200 years need
to be calibrated when comparison is

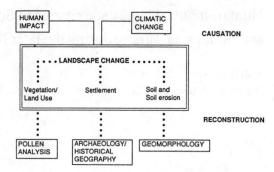

Fig. 1. Conceptual framework for
evaluating components of landscape
change.

being made with historical chronologies (Olsen 1986). Linear interpolation between dates assumes
constant sediment accumulation, but
where a clearance phase is recorded
accumulation rates are likely to
have varied considerably, and in
some cases the duration of the
phase to have been overestimated.

Degraded hillslopes are widespread in the Eastern Mediterranean
region, but on their own they rarely provide data on the origin or
age of erosion. Soil erosion histories have instead been reconstructed mainly from sites of net
deposition, including valley fills
(Vita-Finzi 1979; van Andel and
Zangger this volume) and estuaries
(Bintliff 1981). Small lake basins
can also be relatively effective
sediment traps (Dearing 1986) but
their potential as records of erosion has so far hardly been investigated in the Eastern Mediterranean region. In any case, using
sediment yield as a surrogate for
soil loss tends to underestimate
true erosion rates and does not
take account of sediment storage
within the drainage basin. Late
Holocene alluviation/erosion cycles
are clearly in evidence in the
circum-Mediterranean region, but
they may be caused by shifts in
climate or tectonism as well as
human-induced land-use change
(Wagstaff 1981).

This catalogue of difficulties
does not invalidate our attempts
at landscape reconstruction but it
should remind us that each source
of data has a different spatio-
temporal resolution and rather dif-

ferent methodological characteristics. These differences are further emphasised by the fact that each type of data is furnished by a different specialist, most often from archaeology, palaeoecology and geomorphology. This division can be regrettable in that human occupance, vegetation and soil are functionally and historically interrelated elements of the landscape (Fig. 1). Thus, agriculture is both determined by the distribution of different soil types and in turn is capable of modifying the nature of the soil, for example by erosion. Similarly human activities have been responsible for major vegetation changes, via burning, tree felling and so forth, while soil condition and vegetation are closely interdependent. Although specialists from different disciplines can and do collaborate, truly integrated projects investigating the landscape history of a particular part of the Near East are, as yet, far from being the norm. Yet if we are to move beyond our initial objective of establishing the nature and timing of human impact on the landscape, then integrated multidisciplinary field research becomes essential.

2 TEMPORAL MODELS OF LANDSCAPE CHANGE

One important objective of palaeoenvironmental research is to test different models of environmental change, especially the response of ecosystems to human-induced disturbance. Oldfield (1983) has discussed three of the principal models, namely cyclical, progressive and steady-state (Fig. 2). CYCLICAL or harmonic models have been used to explain variations over a wide range of temporal scales especially those in climate. Glacial-interglacial fluctuations in climate are commonly considered to follow cycles, as are some shorter term climatic fluctuations (e.g. Aaby 1976). Settlement in the Near East, where states and civilisations have a long antiquity, has also been viewed as following a cyclical or quasi-cyclical pattern through time. Across environmentally marginal land, such as the semi-arid limit to dry farming, settle-

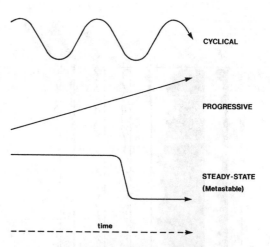

Fig. 2. Temporal models of environmental/cultural change.

ment has waxed and waned in response to periods of politico-economic stability and instability and to climatic variations. In some better watered areas, clearance of the forest for settlement and farming has been followed by abandonment and regeneration of secondary woodland, in a rather different cycle of landscape change. One of the key distinguishing features of cyclical environmental changes is that they must be reversible (viz. not only from condition A to condition B, but also back again). Thus in the case of clearance phases, it must be possible for forest to regenerate after abandonment, as occurred in the area southwest of Beyşehir, and not be prevented by factors such as soil degradation.

PROGRESSIVE models of landscape change are, by contrast, unidirectional and more or less linear in their progression from one condition to another (Fig. 2). The succession to climax model of ecological change following abandonment of agricultural land is one obvious example which falls in this category. Depending on the timescale of observation, progressive models may be nested within cyclical ones, so that the apparently progressive transition from glacial steppe to post-glacial woodland in fact forms part of a longer cyclical alternation between the two during the Pleistocene. Progressive models are very commonly used to describe human impact on the landscape, with

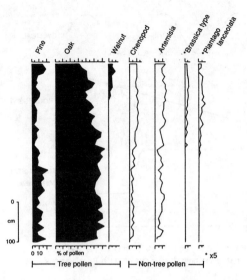

Fig. 3. Pollen diagram from Lake Van, East Turkey (based on van Zeist and Woldring 1978). The section shown covers about the last 5000 years.

the second half of the Holocene being viewed as a period during which a cultural landscape of fields and farms came progressively to replace a natural one of forest and grassland.

While this may be broadly valid over whole regions (e.g. the whole Near East) and over a Holocene time frame, at smaller spatial and shorter temporal scales this apparently progressive transition may be revealed as the cumulative superimposition of numerous local non-progressive changes. These may be cyclical, or they may involve episodic shifts between a series of METASTABLE STEADY-STATES. In the latter case, prolonged periods of landscape stability are broken by relatively short, unstable transition phases when the ecosystem as a whole is marked by positive rather than by negative feedback (Oldfield 1983). These unstable transition phases are usually the product of external disturbance such as abrupt climate change, major fire, or culturally caused deforestation, and they are often characterised by increases in soil erosion and sediment flux of at least one order of magnitude (e.g. Knox 1972; Davis 1976). Adjustment of the environ-

mental system will eventually lead to another metastable equilibrium state, but this will form a new landscape rather then a return to the old one. In this case, unlike that of forest regeneration discussed above, controlling parameters will have changed to the point whereby environmental change is not reversible. The most obvious and important of these controlling parameters is the soil which, if it has been subject to erosion and degradation, may no longer support the original vegetation cover. In this case the new, stable state may only be stable in the sense that one component of the environmental system has been exhausted.

Distinguishing between progressive and episodic (metastable) records of landscape change requires the selection of appropriate sites for palaeoenvironmental investigation. The Lake Van pollen record, for example, shows a gradual decrease in oak and a gradual increase in cultigens and weeds such as walnut, brassicas and ribwort plantain during the Late Holocene (Fig. 3). However, for the reasons discussed above, this sequence cannot be used as supporting evidence for progressive landscape change except at the broadest regional scale, because of the large catchment area from which pollen was recruited. In the next section of the paper, an attempt will be made to test the validity of these three different models based on a region with a more detailed palaeoenvironmental and cultural record, namely South and Southwest Turkey.

3 LANDSCAPE HISTORY IN SOUTH AND SOUTHWEST TURKEY

3.1 Konya-Beyşehir

This region comprises three contrasting eco-physiographic zones, namely the coastal plains and slopes, the Toros Mountain Belt, and the interior Anatolian Plateau. The Konya Basin of south central Turkey provides an example of the last of these zones. It lies at the agro-climatic limit for dry farming, but because it is adjacent to the montane belt it receives surface water from inflowing rivers which can be used for irrigation

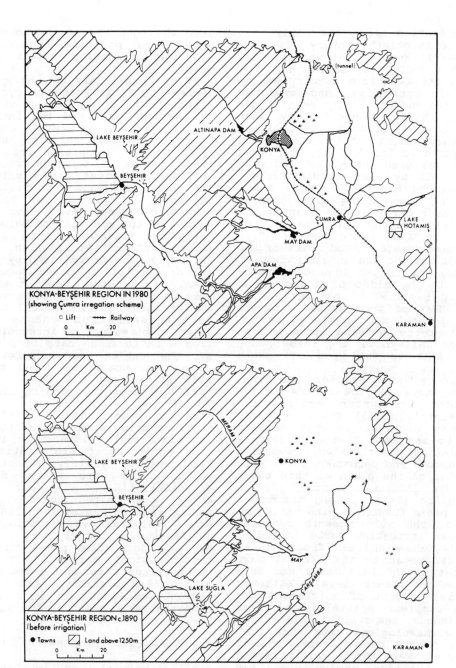

Fig. 4. 20th-century landscape transformation in the western Konya Basin.

agriculture. Irrigation, however, requires an organised system of water diversion, distribution, and drainage which may be threathened both by environmental problems such as soil salinization and by socio-political ones such as competition for resources with migrant pastoralists. A productive irrigation system operates along the alluvial margins of the Konya Basin at the present day, but this has only been

57

in operation since the early part of the twentieth century (Huntington 1911; Money 1919; Oehler 1938; Roberts 1980). Population has followed the twentieth century expansion in agriculture and many new villages and towns have been founded. In the nineteenth century, when the Ottoman system of political and military administration was at the low point of its decline, the Konya Basin was used not by settled farmers, but by semi-nomadic Türkmen tribes who had their summer camps (yaylas) here along with grazing for their herds of sheep and goat. Travelling along the edge of the plain in 1800, Leake bemoaned "... the same uninterrupted level of the finest soil, quite uncultivated. It is painful to behold such desolation in the midst of a region so highly favoured by nature" (1824: 94). Most of the settled villages were located not on the plain but in the better watered and more protected valleys of the Toros Mountain Belt to the west and south (Fig. 4).

Some centuries earlier, the Konya Plain was again the centre of important irrigation agriculture. Hütteroth's (1968) study of early Ottoman archival records enabled him to map late sixteenth century population distribution, revealing widespread and permanent rural settlement of the plain at this time. In the fifteenth century de la Broquière (1433) passed through a fine plain furnished with villages, and in the mid-sixteenth century, complex irrigation works including canals, dams and artificial lakes carried water to the central part of the plain (Beldiceanu and Beldiceanu-Steinherr 1968). Although earlier records of settlement are less complete spatially and less continuous temporally, historical and archaeological data show that still further back in time parts of the plain were intensively utilised for irrigation agriculture, for example during the period of Roman imperial rule (French 1970; Sherratt 1972). It is therefore not difficult to envisage Holocene settlement in south central Turkey following a cyclical pattern, with population expanding onto the dry but potentially fertile Konya Plain during times of political and economic stability, and retreating into the security of the mountains when central political organisation and the irrigation system broke down.

It has previously been suggested (Roberts 1982:239) that a cyclical alternation of population between the montane belt and the interior plains may help to explain the apparent lack of correlation between the Beyşehir Occupation phase and major historical events (Bottema and Woldring 1984; this volume). The pollen diagrams from Southwest Beyşehir do not record only a single clearance event over the course of the mid to late Holocene, but rather a series of them of different intensities (pollen zones 2b, 3a, 3d and 4) followed by partial or complete woodland regeneration. On the other hand, there is some uncertainty about the chronology of these quasi-cyclical clearance/regeneration phases. For example, based on the interpolation from a radiocarbon date of 3265 yr BP, the end of the main Beyşehir Occupation phase is dated to ca 2185 yr BP (ca 235 BC) and the period between then and ca 1550 yr BP (AD 400) was one of forest regeneration. However this is difficult to reconcile with archaeological and historical evidence for intensive agricultural exploitation of the Yeşilköy valley, whence the pollen cores were taken, during classical times. At least three major Roman sites surround this marshy valley (Ramsey 1902:260 ff.; Hall 1968:72 ff.), suggesting that at least the latter part of the Beyşehir Occupation phase dates to the classical period. This also demonstrates that during the Roman period, and possibly others, settlement was widespread in both the mountain valleys and on the plains.

3.2 The Lycian Toros Belt

Similar partial conflict between records of settlement and vegetation emerges in the Lycian part of the Toros Mountain Belt (Figs. 5 and 6). This is a region of alluvial intermontane valleys with some small lakes, often karstic, lying at elevations around 1000 m above sea level, and set between mountains reaching over 3000 m. Cores have been taken towards the edges

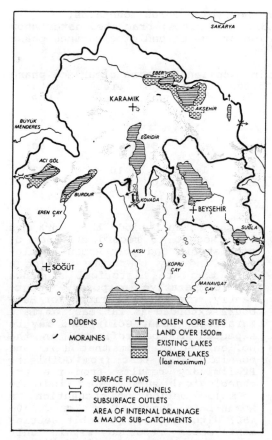

Fig. 5. Relief and drainage,
Southwest Turkey.

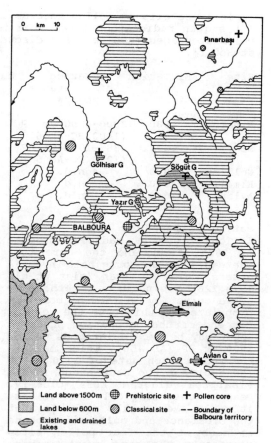

Fig. 6. Part of the Lycian Toros
Mountain Belt, showing pollen and
selected archaeological sites.

of five of these partly drained
lakes or marshes and analysed by
palynologists from the Biologisch-
Archaeologisch Instituut in Groningen. In consequence, this area has,
by Near Eastern standards, an unusually detailed spatial coverage
of late Holocene pollen diagrams,
whose records of land use and vegetation should primarily reflect
changes which took place within the
local region rather than further
afield. Four of the five resulting
pollen diagrams record a major
phase in clearance followed by
farming with arboriculture, and
even the fifth - Avlan Gölü - weakly records some human disturbance,
presumably at a distance from the
site. There are important contrasts
in the major cultigens recorded at
the other four sites; walnut
(Juglans) and manna-ash (Fraxinus
ornus) are strongly represented at

Elmali, suggesting extensive exploitation of these crops on the
surrounding plain, while cereal-
type pollen is at high values for
Söğüt and Gölhisar, presumably as a
result of wheat and barley cultivation. Olive pollen is also rather
strongly represented at these
latter two sites as well as at
Pinarbaşi, a topic whose significance is discussed further below.

Chronologies for these cultural
impact, on the landscape are somewhat imprecise, as only two of the
pollen cores have been dated
directly by radiocarbon (Table 1).
Söğüt and Pinarbaşi indicate broadly similar dates as start of clearance, around 3000 yr BP (1400 cal.
BC), but the occupation phase is
inferred to have ended earlier at
Söğüt than at Pinarbaşi. However
it should be noted that the Söğüt

59

Table 1. Details of pollen records in the Lycian Toros mountains.
* based on radiocarbon dates from individual sites; bracketed dates show
calibrated ages (see text for discussion of age of end of clearance phase
at Söğüt).

Site	Elevation (m)	Duration of Clearance phase*	Maximum pollen % during clearance phase				
			olive	walnut	manna ash	cereal-type	total NAP
Pinarbaşi	980	3000-1350 yr BP (1400 BC-AD 600)	5	1.5	1	2	45
Söğüt	1393	2885-1900 yr BP (1250 BC-AD 50)	5	5	5	10	60
Gölhisar	930	n.d.	5-15	1	2	10	67
Elmali	930	n.d.	1	20	10	3	62
Avlan	1043	n.d.	<1	<1	<1	1.5	18

dating is based on linear interpolation between a radiocarbon date of 2885 yr BP and the core top, whereas, as the original investigators point out (van Zeist et al. 1975:126) a sine wave for the age-depth curve may in fact be more appropriate. In this case the age for the end of the occupation phase at Söğüt may be recalculated as nearer 1500 yr BP (AD 450), which matches the radiocarbon date of 1370 yr BP (AD 580) for the same event in the Pinarbaşi diagram more closely. Despite chronological limitations, it would seem highly probable that the clearance and cultivation phase at each of the four pollen sites represents the same event, corresponding to what has been termed the Beyşehir Occupation phase (Bottema and Woldring this volume).

The occupation phase was clearly widespread rather than localised within Southwest Turkey, specifically within the Lycian Toros Belt. Consequently there must be historical-archaeological evidence of settlement to match the pollen record of cultural landscape change. As noted above, archaeological survey data are frequently selective and are not equally informative about different cultural phases. For example, settlement in the Elmali Plain has been studied in some detail for the Neolithic and Chalcolithic periods (Eslick 1978) but is less well known for some other archaeological phases. A more promising area for comparison of cultural and palaeoecological records is around the classical city of Balboura, whose hinterland has been the subject of recent field survey (Coulton 1988). Although focussing

on the Roman period, this work has also sought to record evidence of prehistoric and post-Roman settlement, and may therefore provide a more complete historical sequence for comparative purposes. Importantly, the Roman territory of Balboura extended as far east as Lake Karalitis (Söğüt Gölü), and may be expected to be reflected in the pollen record from that lake and possibly also that from Gölhisar. Preliminary results from the archaeological survey work indicate a major period of occupation in Roman-Late Roman times (ca AD 0-450) with fourteen probable settlement sites recorded within only part of Balboura's territory. There was an apparent decline in settlement during the following two centuries and more or less complete abandonment by AD 700, after which the area lacked permanent settlement for many centuries (Coulton 1988:15). During the nineteenth and early twentieth centuries the area around Söğüt was occupied only in summer by pastoralists whose winter villages lay on the Pamphylian Plain around Antalya (de Planhol 1958:208 ff.). The pollen record suggests that this traditional system of semi-nomadism may have operated here more or less unbroken from the Byzantine era to late Ottoman times. Archaeological and historical data are therefore in good agreement with palynological evidence for land abandonment and woodland regeneration during the first millennium AD, and in particular with the revised chronology for the end of the Beyşehir Occupation phase discussed above.

On the other hand, pollen and

archaeological data are in less good agreement about dating the onset and duration of the Beyşehir Occupation phase. Archaeological survey has revealed at least one prehistoric site with pottery of the fifth/fourth and third millennia BC. Such earlier prehistoric clearance phases are not obviously present in pollen diagrams from the Lycian Toros, although they are recored elsewhere in the Toros Mountain Belt (van Zeist et al. 1975). After occupation during the early first millennium BC there is a gap in evidence of settlement until the late first millennium BC when the classical city of Balboura was founded (Coulton 1988). This conflicts with palynological data which indicate an onset of clearance during the late second millennium BC (based on calibrated radiocarbon dates), with occupation continuing effectively unbroken until Roman times. It is evidently not possible to reconcile these different data sources without further field research. On the other hand, the Beyşehir Occupation phase is now well known in pollen diagrams from Southwest Turkey, so that there must be a possibility of archaeological survey data being biased by cultural superimposition of later occupation phases on earlier ones. This phenomenon of earlier occupation phases being archaeologically "invisible" is known from many projects which archaeological and palaeoecological sources have been used together to provide an integrated landscape history (e.g. Shaugh Moor, Southwest England: Balaam et al. 1982).

Archaeological and pollen data may also be combined and brought to bear on another problem, namely the question of olive cultivation. Significant amounts of olive pollen are recorded at Söğüt, Pinarbaşi and several other pollen sites in Southwest Turkey. Because these sites lie at or above the modern altitudinal limit for olive cultivation (900-1000 m above sea level), it has been suggested pollen was of long-distance airborne origin from the coastal Eu-Mediterranean zone (Bottema and Woldring this volume). It is known that olive pollen is produced abundantly and well dispersed by the wind. On the other hand, high olive pollen values are not recorded in other nearby diagrams, such as Elmali (Table 1), while it may be noted that the intermontane valleys of Lycian Toros are separated from coastal olive groves by high mountains. Additionally, archaeological survey round Balboura has revealed large stone weights with perforated loops at the top, which, if found in other contexts, would be interpreted as part of olive presses. These weights have been found at five classical sites lying, along with associated agricultural land, at elevations up to 1600 m above sea level (Coulton 1988:15). In combination, these two pieces of independent data represent rather convincing evidence for local olive cultivation. Of course the corollary of this is that climatic conditions must have been more favourable to olive growth during the classical period than they are at the present day. Certainly the agro-ecological skills of farmers familiar with olive cultivation at lower elevations would have helped minimise frost damage to the trees. None the less, with local lapse rates of ca 0.6°C per 100 m and an upward shift in the limit to olive cultivation of 500 m or more, it is probable that winter and spring temperatures, in particular, were in the order of 2-3°C higher than today.

4 SOIL CHANGE AND WOODLAND REGENERATION

The Beyşehir Occupation phase involved a full cycle from woodland clearance, through farming to abandonment back to woodland once again. This was achieved because of the ability of trees to regenerate in most of the areas which had been cleared. By the end of the first millennium AD, the Toros Mountain Belt was once again a predominantly wooded landscape. On the other hand, the species composition of the secondary woodland shows some significant shifts from that prior to the Beyşehir Occupation phase. In particular pine, which declined markedly as a result of clearance, frequently became the dominant pollen type following regeneration. At Söğüt, for example, juniper and deciduous oak were co-dominant with

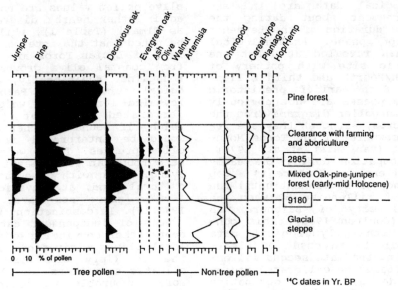

Fig. 7. Pollen diagram from Söğüt Gölü (based on van Zeist et al. 1975).

pine in the early mid-Holocene forest, but were virtually absent from secondary woodland (Fig. 7). At other sites, such as Beyşehir and Pınarbaşı, the pine-cedar ratio shifted in favour of the former in the post-occupation period. Long-distance transport alone could not account for the high pine values recorded during the late Holocene, and a number of hypotheses may be suggested to explain the apparently advantaged position of pine in relation to other trees.

1. It is part of a long-term cycle in which pine becomes dominant in the later part of interglacials, related to soil maturation, etc. (cf. Andersen 1969).

2. Climate change, such as the probable cooling described above in relation to olive cultivation.

3. Soil degradation during and after the occupation phase.

4. The role of livestock, in particular goats, potentially leading to the reduction or even elimination of those trees and shrubs preferred for browse.

While pastoralism almost certainly continued after the end of the Beyşehir Occupation phase, it is not clear how this might have hindered reforestation by coniferous trees such as cedar and juniper (Juniperus excelsa). Goats and other small livestock may have had a more important role in controlling the development of the understorey layer including shrubs such as Quercus cerris and Q. calliprinos. The Oro-Mediterranean pine woods of Southwest Turkey have been managed over many centuries, with the deciduous oak understorey being cut and used for fuel-wood and animal fodder. Over time this has reduced the deciduous oak component to the point where it has become rare in this region (Akman et al. 1979:213 ff.). The limited contribution of oak to pollen rain has increased the apparent dominance of other taxa, including pine. Similarly, it is hard to envisage a simple linkage between climate change and any increase in pine pollen. A fall in temperature after ca AD 500 would tend to favour cedar, juniper and fir as well as Black pine (Pinus nigra), at the expense of Pinus brutia and deciduous oak (Quercus cerris) which prefer lower altitudes. Of course, both livestock and climate might have been important, but operating in conjunction with other factors rather than on their own. The other principal factor to be considered is soil change, and particularly soil degradation through erosion. South and Southwest Turkey include areas whose soils have suffered from erosion, and while most of these continue to experience soil loss at the present-day, it is clear that at least some of this erosion is of considerable antiquity. Perhaps the best clue to the age of the onset of accelerated erosion comes from alluvial fills which, as elsewehre in the circum-Mediterranean basin, have been deposited in historial times, notably from the late Roman to the medieval period (Vita-Finzi 1969). Rivers draining the mountain belt of Southwest Turkey, such as the Küçük and Büyük Menderes (Maeander) rivers, extended their deltas seawards by many kilometres during the classical period, slowing down again in medieval and Ottoman times (Eisma 1978; Marchese 1986). Hillslope erosion may have begun earlier than this, notably at the onset of the Beyşehir Occupation phase, but with the eroded soils temporarily stored as colluvium before being evacuated downstream by rivers after the land was abandoned.

It is important to note that erosion has occurred differentially depending on soil erodibility, and hence on relief and geology. A good example of this process, and its possible influence on vegetation composition, is in the Lycian Toros between Burdur and Elmali. This region receives sufficient precipitation for it to lie within the eco-climatic limit of the Oro-Mediterranean forest zone (van Zeist et al. 1975: Fig. 6). On the other hand, maps of actual forest distribution show a large swathe of land here without trees, the 'cuvette steppique d'Elmali' (Yeni Türkiye Atlasi 1977: reproduced as Fig. 1 in Bottema and Woldring 1984). This region contains extensive badland terrain, developed on Tertiary rocks, especially on highly erodible Eocene flysch and Neogene marls (M.T.A. 1963). On these highly degraded soils, tree growth is no longer possible, although prior to the onset of accelerated erosion they would surely have been capable of supporting a cover of woodland vegetation. While a chronology for erosion of Neogene and flysch soils remains uncertain, it is reasonable to suspect that this coincided in large part with the Beyşehir Occu-

pation phase recorded so clearly in pollen diagrams from this region.

Following abandonment, reforestation was only possible on the more resistant upland soils, notably those developed on hard Mesozoic limestone. Historial sources confirm that many other soils remained bare of forest, the semi-nomadic Yürük, for example, traditionally utilizing the open vegetation of the flysch east of Söğüt, in preference to the calcareous massifs which were deficient in both water and grazing (de Planhol 1958:225). The preventing of woodland regeneration on degraded flysch soils around Söğüt would have disadvantaged juniper, while the decline in oak would probably have resulted from the combination of understorey clearance, discussed above, together with the maintenance of many alluvial environments as grassland rather than allowing their reversion to woodland. Deciduous oak is generally intolerant of calcareous soils, and full woodland develops best in this region on deep alluvial soils (Akman et al. 1979:190; van Zeist et al. 1975:65). On the Mesozoic limestone, pine is better able to survive on part degraded soils than cedar (Akman et al. 1979:240,270), which helps to explain the shift towards pine in the post-clearance Oro-Mediterranean forest. It seems probable, therefore, that selective erosion of soils during and after the Beyşehir Occupation phase made a significant contribution to the character of the regenerating woodland, in particular by reducing habitat and hence species diversity.

5 CONCLUSION

Vegetation and land-use histories from different regions within South and Southwest Turkey broadly conform to a cyclical model of landscape change. One major period of regional clearance, the Beyşehir Occupation phase, was followed by woodland regeneration over most of the Toros mountain zone, prior to modern, twentieth-century deforestation. Smaller amplitude cycles of disturbance and recovery occurred earlier in the Holocene, although their spatial impact was more loca-

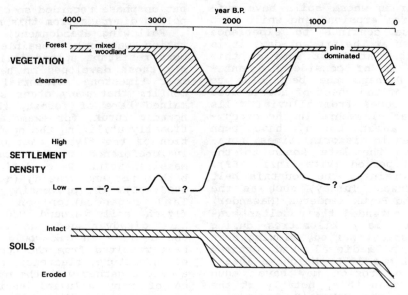

Fig. 8. Simplified sequence of Late Holocene changes in the Söğüt-Balboura area based on existing palynological, archaeological and geomorphic data.

lised. Settlement history was clearly also cyclical in both the montane zone and the interior plateau during the later Holocene with periods of an organised agricultural landscape alternating with phases in which the land was allowed to revert to natural or semi-natural vegetation and was used primarily for semi-nomadic pastoralism. In the environmentally favoured coastal zone, the history of settlement may have been more continuous and less cyclical than in the mountains. Where archaeological and historical records of settlement history exist adjacent to pollen coring sites, as at Söğüt-Balboura, they show excellent agreement with vegetation changes for the last two thousand years. For earlier periods, and particularly for the earlier first millennium BC, discrepancies between palynological and archaeological data over the intensity and age of human occupance and impact, point to the need for further, preferably integrated studies of landscape history.

Soil changes, by contrast, are less easily reversed, and their history is consequently less one of cycles of erosion than of a series of metastable equilibrium states

(Fig. 8). This is particularly true of highly erodible Tertiary marls and flysch, which have become permanently degraded to create badland landscapes. Selective erosion of different soil types has in turn influenced the type and species composition of the vegetation which recolonised land after its abandonment, in some cases making a return to woodland impossible, and in others favouring pine forest at the expense of other tree species. Reconstruction of total landscape history requires close collaboration between different disciplinary specialists within the same geographical region (Birks et al. 1988). Only when this occurs does it become possible to establish causal linkages beyween the various components of landscape change and to establish which models describing cultural-environmental interactions are most appropriate.

6 ACKNOWLEDGEMENTS

The author is grateful to Anne Tarver for cartographic and to Val Pheby and Ruth Austin for secretarial assistance. Dr Jim Coulton provided valuable information on Balboura and its territory.

REFERENCES

Aaby, B. 1976.
Cyclic climatic variations in climate over the past 5500 years reflected in raised bogs. Nature 263:281-284.

Akman, K.,
M.Barbéro and P. Quézel 1979. Contribution à l'étude de la végétation forestière d'Anatolie méditerranéenne (deuxième partie). Phytocoenologia 5:189-276.

Andel, Tj.H. van and E.Zangger
this volume. Landscape stability and destabilisation in the prehistory of Greece.

Andersen, S.Th. 1969.
Interglacial soil and vegetation development. Meddedelser fra Dansk Geologisk Forening 19:90-102.

Andersen, S.Th. 1973.
The differential pollen productivity of trees and its significance for the interpretation of a pollen diagram from a forested region. In H.J.B.Birks and R.G. West (eds.), Quaternary Plant Ecology, p.109-115. Oxford, Blackwell.

Balaam, N.D.,
K.Smith and G.J.Wainwright 1982. The Saugh Moor project: fourth report - environment, context and conclusion. Proceedings of the Prehistoric Society 48:203-278.

Beldiceanu, N.
and I. Beldiceanu-Steinherr 1968. Recherches sur la province de Qaraman au XVIe siècle. Leiden: Brill.

Bintliff, J.L. 1981.
Archaeology and the Holocene evolution of coastal plains in the Aegean and Circum-Mediterranean. In D.Brothwell and G.Dimbleby (eds.), Environmental aspects of coasts and islands, p.11-31. BAR International Series 94.

Birks, H.H., H.J.B.Birks,
P.E.Kaland and D.Moe (eds.) 1988. The Cultural Landscape - Past, Present and Future. Cambridge: Cambridge University Press.

Bottema, S. 1986.
A Late Quaternary pollen diagram from Lake Urmia (northwestern Iran). Review of Palaeobotany and Palynology 47:241-261.

Bottema, S. and H. Woldring 1984.
Late Quaternary vegetation and climate of southwestern Turkey II. Palaeohistoria 26:123-149.

Bottema, S. and H.Woldring
this volume. Anthropogenic indicators in the pollen record of the Eastern Mediterranean.

Broquière, B. de la 1433.
Travels to Palestine and return from Jerusalem overland (1432-1433). Hafod.Tr. T.Johnes (1807).

Coulton, J.J. 1988.
Balboura survey. Annual report of the British Institute of Archaeology at Ankara 40:13-15.

Davis, M.B. 1976.
Erosion rates and land use histories in southern Michigan. Environmental Conservation 3:139-148.

Dearing, J. 1986.
Core correlation and total sediment influx. In B.E.Berglund (ed.), Handbook of Holocene palaeoecology and palaeohydrology, p.247-272. Chichester, John Wiley.

Edwards, K.J. 1979.
Palynological and temporal inference in the context of prehistory, with special reference to the evidence from lake and peat deposits. Journal of Archaeological Science 6:255-270.

Eisma, D., 1978.
Stream deposition and erosion by the eastern shore of the Aegean. In W.C.Brice (ed.), The environmental history of the Near and Middle East since the last Ice Age, p.67-81. London, Academic Press.

Eslick, C.M. 1978.
The Neolithic and Chalcolithic pottery of the Elmali plain, southwestern Turkey. Unpubl. PhD thesis, Bryn Mawr College.

French, D.H. 1970.
Notes on site distribution in the Çumra area. Anatolian Studies 20: 139-148.

Hall, A.S. 1968.
Notes and inscriptions from eastern Pisidia. Anatolian Studies 18:57-92.

Hammond, F.W. 1978.
Regional survey strategies: a simulation approach. In J.F.Cherry, C.Gamble and S.Shennan (eds.), Sampling in contemporary British archaeology, p.63-86. BAR International Series 50.

Huntington, E. 1911.
The Karst country of southern Asia Minor. Bulletin of the American Geographical Society 43:91-

106.

Hütteroth, W.-D. 1968.
Landliche Siedlungen im südlichen Inner-Anatolien in den letzten vierhundert Jahren. Göttinger Geographische Abhandlungen 46.

Knox, J.C. 1972.
Valley alluviation in south-western Wisconsin. Annals, Association of American Geographers 62: 401-410.

Jacobson, G.L. and R.H.W.Bradshaw 1981. The selection of sites for palaeovegetation studies. Quaternary Research 16:80-96.

Leake, W.M. 1824.
Journal of a tour in Asia Minor. London: John Murray.

Marchese, R.T. 1986.
The Lower Maeander Flood Plain. A regional settlement study. BAR International Series 292.

Money, R.I. 1919.
The irrigation of the Konya Basin. Geographical Journal 54: 298-303.

M.T.A. 1963.
1:500.000 Geological Map of Turkey. Konya Sheet.

Oelher, Th. 1938.
Die wasserwirtschaftlichen Grundlagen für die Bewasserung der Konya-Ebene. Deutsche Wasserwirtschaft 11:333-338,12:375-380.

Oldfield, F. 1983.
Man's impact on the environment: some recent perspectives. Geography 68:245-256.

Olsson, I.U. 1986.
Radiometric dating. In B.E.Berglund (ed.), Handbook of Holocene palaeoecology and palaeohydrology, p.273-312. Chichester: John Wiley.

Planhol, X. de 1958.
De la plaine pamphyliènne aux lacs pisidiens. Nomadisme et vie paysanne. Paris: Bibliothèque Archéologique et Historique de l'Institut Français d'Archéologie d'Istanbul III.

Pennington, W. 1979.
The origin of pollen in lake sediments: an enclosed lake compared with one receiving inflow streams. New Phytologist 83:189-213.

Ramsay, W.M. 1902.
Pisidia and the Lycaonian frontier. Annual of the British School in Athens 9:243-273.

Roberts, N. 1979.
The location and environment of Knossos. Annual of the British

School in Athens 74:231-241.

Roberts, N. 1980.
Late Quaternary geomorphology and palaeoecology of the Konya Basin, Turkey. Unpubl. PhD thesis, London University.

Roberts, N. 1982.
Forest re-advance and the Anatolian Neolithic. In M.Bell and S. Limbrey (eds.), Archaeological aspects of woodland ecology, p. 231-246. BAR International Series 146.

Rowton, M.B. 1967.
The woodlands of ancient western Asia. Journal of Near Eastern Studies 26:261-277.

Sherratt, A.G. 1972.
Socio-economic and demographic models for the Neolithic and Bronze Ages of Europe. In D.L. Clarke (ed.), Models in Archaeology, p.477-542. London, Methuen.

Tauber, H. 1965.
Differential pollen dispersal and the interpretation of pollen diagrams. Danmarks Geologiske Undersøgelse II 89:1-69.

Thirgood, J.V. 1981.
Man and the Mediterranean forest: a history of resource depletion. London.

Vita-Finzi, C. 1969.
The Mediterranean Valleys. Cambridge: Cambridge University Press.

Vita-Finzi, C. 1978.
Archaeological sites in their setting. London: Thames and Hudson.

Wagstaff, J.M. 1981.
Buried assumptions: some problems in the interpretation of the 'Younger Fill' raised by recent data from Greece. Journal of Archaeological Science 8:247-264.

Wagstaff, J.M. 1985.
The evolution of Middle Eastern landscapes. An outline to AD 1840. London: Croom Helm.

Yeni Türkiye Atlasi 1977.
Ankara: M.S.B. Harita Genel Müdürlügü.

Zeist, W. van and S.Bottema 1982.
Vegetational history of the Eastern Mediterranean and the Near East during the last 20,000 years. In J.L.Bintliff and W.van Zeist (eds.), Palaeoclimates, palaeoenvironments and human communities in the Eastern Mediterranean region in later prehistory, p.277-321. BAR International Series 133.

Zeist, W.van and H.Woldring 1978.
   A Postglacial pollen diagram from
   Lake Van in East Anatolia. Review
   of Palaeobotany and Palynology
   26:249-276.
Zeist, W.van,
   H.Woldring and D.Stapert 1975.
   Late Quaternary vegetation and
   climate of southwestern Turkey.
   Palaeohistoria 17:53-143.

Man's Role in the Shaping of the Eastern Mediterranean Landscape, Bottema, Entjes-Nieborg & van Zeist (eds)
© 1990 Balkema, Rotterdam. ISBN 90 6191 138 9

Late Holocene geomorphic evolution of the Beşige-Troy area (NW Anatolia) and the environment of prehistoric man

6

Ilhan Kayan
Department of Geography, Ege University, Izmir, Turkey

The western coastline of the Biga peninsula in the south of the Canakkale strait (Dardanelles) (Fig. 1) extends in a north-south direction along the western edge of a low plateau of 50-60 m elevation. The profile of the coastline is predominantly steep and cliffy. Beşige is only a small coastal plain in the northern section of this cliff coast. The plain extends eastward and inland between the plateau ridges on Neogene shallow marine sediments (mostly limestone, sandstone, mudstone).

There is no main stream coming to the plain and bringing much alluvium to form the coastal flat. Therefore the plain is filled with mostly colluvial foot-hill deposits and coastal sediments. The Beşige plain is separated by a low threshold from the Karamenderes floodplain in the east. The ruins of the ancient city of Troy occur on the eastern edge of the floodplain.

During ancient times, Beşige occupied a convenient position as a natural harbour along the Aegean coast, closest to the site of Troy. Therefore, this small coastal plain is being searched by archaeologists for findings related to ancient Troy. Yassitepe and Sivritepe, on the edge of a low plateau in the north of the plain are important archaeological sites here.

It is known that prehistoric man had different natural resources from the present. For example, many heaps or layers of shells (mostly oyster) which were found at Sivritepe or Yassitepe, and Troy also, were explained as food remains in these occupation sites. However, the present coastal environment is not very suitable for shell-fish exploitation. This means that the geography was different in prehistoric times.

For understanding such relations in the Beşige area, we first carried out geomorphological research. Present geomorphology was delineated by detailed field work using large-scale topographical maps and aerial photographs. Then, in order to determine the nature and depth of the sedimentary environments, we performed hand-boring drill studies in each sedimentary-geomorphic unit throughout the plain, penetrating to a maximum depth of 7 m from the surface. By studying the three-dimensional shapes of the sedimentary units deposited in each environment, and with radiocarbon datings from some organic-rich layers, we made precise palaeogeomorphic reconstructions of the Beşige plain covering the Holocene (the last 10,000 years). As a result of this study, the geomorphic evolution of the Beşige plain and the potential of the landscape at each stage for prehistoric and historical man can be outlined as follows:
- Following the last glacial regression, the sea level rose rapidly by about 100 m during the early Holocene and reached the present position around 6000 years ago. Beşige must have been a bay extending about 2 km toward the east from the present coastline at the end of this rapid rising of the sea, because coastal sedimentary deposits rich in shallow-marine shells extend to the innermost edge of the Beşige plain. The cores cut them under the alluvial-colluvial

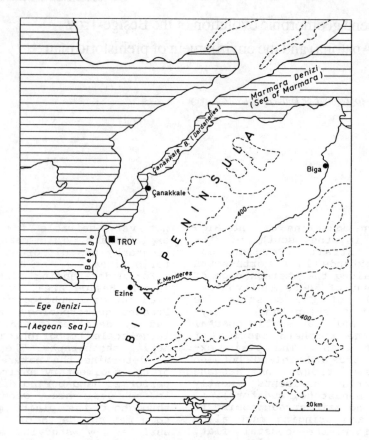

Fig. 1. Map of the Beşige-Troy area.

foothill deposits almost at the present sea level.
- Since then, the sea level has not changed much. A coastal barrier must have been formed along the mouth of the "Beşige Bay" in the course of time, during the same stage of high sea level. It seems that the barrier first developed in sea water, and the inner part of the bay turned into a lagoon. The people who lived at Yassitepe and Sivritepe consumed plenty of shallow-marine or lagunal seafood, such as oysters, during this period, about 5000 years before present.
- Some evidence indicates that the sea level fell by about 1.5-2 m around 3500-3000 years before present. Hence the lagoon was filled with mostly colluvial foothill deposits and the barrier widened during this period. According to this geomorphic interpretation, it is possible that Beşige was a sheltered, convenient natural harbour for the Achaean navy during the famous Trojan War about 3250 years ago.
- Since that time, the sea level has slowly risen again to the present position. But a well-formed barrier maintained the coastline and preserved the lagoon from ingression of the sea. Then the present low coastal part of the Beşige plain has formed slowly by accumulation of eolian sand and dust mostly coming from the land side with the dry summer winds, and partly by coastal sedimentation. It seems that the coastal geomorphic process has been very slow in Beşige for three to four thousand years.

Man's Role in the Shaping of the Eastern Mediterranean Landscape, Bottema, Entjes-Nieborg & van Zeist (eds)
© *1990 Balkema, Rotterdam. ISBN 90 6191 138 9*

The effect of man on geomorphological processes based upon evidence from the Levant and adjacent areas

7

Paul Goldberg
Institute of Archaeology, The Hebrew University, Jerusalem, Israel

Ofer Bar-Yosef
Department of Anthropology, Harvard University, Cambridge, Mass., USA

ABSTRACT: Evidence of geomorphic changes in the vicinity of archaeological sites, dating from the Late Palaeolithic to the Byzantine period, is reviewed. In arid and semi-arid portions of the southern Levant, sequences of wadi alluviation and down-cutting are the main geomorphological processes. In the more humid parts, colluvial deposits that interfinger with or cover archaeological material, seem to be typical. In the early part of the Holocene, climatic fluctuations played the major role in shaping the Levantine landscape, whereas during the last five millennia human interference with the environment has become the decisive factor.

"In the rudest stages of life, man depends upon spontaneous animal and vegetable growth for food and clothing, and his consumption of such products consequently diminishes the numerical abundance of the species which serves his uses. At more advanced periods, he protects and propagates certain esculent vegetables and certain fowls and quadrupeds, and, at the same time, wars upon rival organisms which prey upon these objects of his care or obstruct the increase of their numbers. Hence the action of man upon the organic world tends to subvert the original balance of its species, and while it reduces the numbers of some of them, or even extirpates them altogether, it multiplies other forms of animal and vegetable life" (George P. Marsh 1864:3).

1 INTRODUCTION

In the anthropological/botanical literature we very often encounter statements such as these: "It is now generally agreed that the Mediterranean region has suffered more than other regions in the world from landscape decay and desiccation, not because of adverse climatical changes.., but as a result of man's misuse of this landscape...." (Naveh and Dan 1973).

One should keep in mind that the above assertion was written after our modern industrial civilisation had already become aware of the ecological damages to their immediate environment. However, we ought to ask at the outset, what is the hard evidence for human-induced landscape changes in the Levant and if there is, when do the earliest signs of anthropogenic modification appear? These two questions form the main parts of this paper. In order to answer them we will attempt to summarize the evidence for Holocene geomorphic changes for this region and present some background information of Holocene palaeoenvironments in which to judge these geomorphic changes.

The geographic region covered by this study includes large portions of the Southern Levant (Fig. 1). Intensive archaeological surveys (Betts 1985; Bruins 1986; Cohen and Dever 1981; Garrard et al. 1986, 1987; Goring-Morris 1987; S.Rosen 1987) along with other palaeo-environmental work (e.g., Baruch 1986; Leroi-Gourhan and Darmon 1987; Thompson et al. 1985) over the past two decades has led to the accumulation of a sizable body of infor-

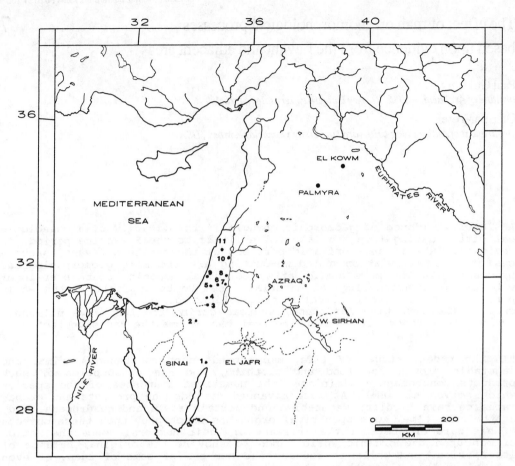

Fig. 1. The geographic distribution of sites and regional studies mentioned in the text: 1. Biqat'Uvda; 2. Nahal Ressisim; 3. Nahal Be'er Sheva (Shiqmim); 4. Tel Lachis area; 5. Hatoula (Nahal Soreq); 6. Abu Gosh; 7. Jericho; 8. Salibiya depression (Netiv Hagdud and Gilgal); 9. Ganei HaTa'arukhah (Tel Aviv); 10. Beit She'an (Munhatta); 11. Yiftahel.

mation, which is still quite frag-mentary.

2 GEOMORPHIC CHANGES IN THE HOLOCENE

Holocene geomorphic changes in the Levant are primarily represented by sequences of wadi alluviation and downcutting in the drier southern and central portions of the region. Geomorphic changes in the Central Levant are less well known due to the limited number of detailed sur-veys and to the masking effects of modern agricultural activities. We attempt to summarize some of these geomorphic changes, starting in the south and working northward.

The archaeological chronology adopted in the following pages is approximate, with the temporal sub-divisions given in Table 1 (Bar-Yosef 1987; Avi-Yonah and Stern 1977).

2.1 The Negev Region

2.1.1 Biqa'at Uvda and Nahal Issaron

The Early Bronze (EB) and Middle Bronze (MB) Age sites in Biqa'at Uvda are located at the contact between the western slopes of the

Table 1.

Pre-Pottery Neolithic A (PPNA)	10,300-9,300 BP	
Pre-Pottery Neolithic B (PPNB)	9,300-8,000 BP	
Pottery Neolithic (PN)	8,000-6,500 BP	
Chalcolithic	6,500-5,300 BP	
Early Bronze Age (EB)	3,300-2,150 BC*	
Middle Bronze Age (MB)	2,150-1,500 BC	
Late Bronze Age (LB)	1,500-1,200 BC	
Iron Age	1,200- 586 BC	
Persian and Hellenistic	586- 37 BC	
Roman	37 BC-324 AD	
Byzantine	324-640 AD	
Early Arab	640-1099 AD	
Crusader	1,099-1,291 AD	

*N.B.: BC refers to calendar years

eastern hilly ridge and the plain. Very little accumulation of colluvial-alluvial deposits was reported from the excavations of these sites (Goring-Morris and Gopher 1983). In contrast, the Pre-Pottery Neolithic B (PPNB) layers in Nahal Issaron were totally covered and the top PPN layer was clearly disturbed by flowing water and muddy deposits (Fig. 2). In chronological terms, this means that the main period of deposition and subsequent erosion took place in post-PPNB times, pro

bably during the 6th and perhaps during the 5th millennia BC.

2.1.2 Nahal Resisim

A series of stepped landforms occurs in Nahal Resisim, a wadi which drains the Negev Highlands and flows into Nahal Nizzana, one of the major drainages of the Western Negev (Figs. 1 and 2; see also Cohen and Dever 1981). The uppermost bench is situated ca 8-10 m

Fig. 2. Photograph of the PPNB site of Nahal Issaron showing the location of the site and its burial by the alluvial fan (Photograph courtesy N. Goring-Morris).

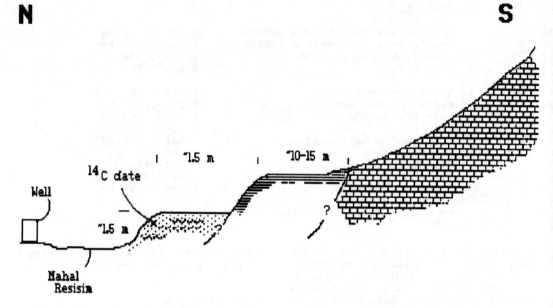

Fig. 3. Generalized sketch of terraces at Nahal Resissim

above the wadi and varies in width from 10-30 m. It is covered with abundant artifacts that appear to date from the Middle Bronze Age (MB). There are no exposures of this terrace and thus it is not possible to determine the nature of the materials which underlie the silty surface cover. The latter is similar to loessial silts which are widespread in the Negev, and may represent accumulations of colluvial slope wash. In any case, this loessic material clearly pre-dates the MB material which covers the surface.

Below this and adjacent to the present-day wadi channel is a smaller terrace, about 5 m wide and 1.5 m high (Fig. 3). Good exposures reveal interbedded soft stony silts and compact well-sorted gravels. Byzantine pottery occurs on the surface and was recovered from a depth of 10-25 cm below it. Pieces of charcoal also were recovered from these depths and were dated to 4515±410 BP (QC 831; uncalibrated), which corresponds roughly to the EB Period. This discrepancy of ca 3,000 years may be explained in several ways. It may indicate two periods of deposition, a marked one corresponding to the EB Period in which most of the 1.5 m of alluvium

was deposited and a lesser and later one of 10-20 cm which accumulated during the Byzantine Period; material at the contact of both deposits would naturally be somewhat mixed. Alternatively, Byzantine pottery could have been worked down into the upper surface of a primarily EB deposit by anthropogenic activities such as cultivation (there are many Byzantine agricultural fields in the area). Lastly, the 1.5 m thick deposit could be entirely Byzantine in age and stray pieces of charcoal derived from the nearby occupation could have been incorporated into this deposit. This latter explanation is doubtful since it does not seem likely that whole pieces of charcoal could have remained intact after having been translocated. The widespread occurrence of Byzantine wadi fill throughout the Western Negev and Eastern Sinai (see Nahal Be'er Sheva/Shiqmim below) would lend support to the first hypothesis.

2.1.3 Nahal Be'er Sheva/Shiqmim

Nahal Be'er Sheva is one of the principal drainages in the Negev, having a catchment of ca 3,300 sq

74

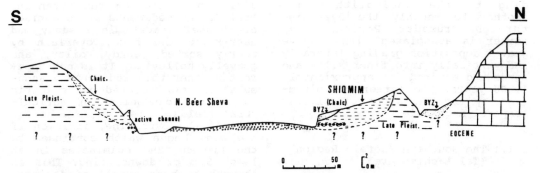

S N

Chalc.

Late Pleist.

N. Be'er Sheva

active channel

? ? ?

SHIQMIM
(Chalc)

BYZ.

BYZ.

Late Pleist.

? ? ?

EOCENE

0   50
        m

2
0 m

Fig. 4. Cross-section of Nahal Be'er Sheva at the Chalcolithic site of Shiqmim

km (including that of Nahal Besor). It originates in the Judean Mountains near Arad and flows about 50 km westward where it joins with Nahal Besor which continues to the Mediterranean Sea. Good exposures of Pleistocene and Holocene alluvial sediments replete with prehistoric and archaeological sites can be found especially in its lower reaches, near the confluence with Nahal Besor (Fig. 1) (Goldberg 1986, 1987). Well-exhibited in the interfluve area are ca 18-20 m of interstratified clayey silts, silts and sand which contain Upper-Palaeolithic sites in the middle of the fill and Epi-Palaeolithic sites near the eroded top.

The Chalcolithic village of Shiqmim is situated in the Nahal Be'er Sheva, about 3 km upstream from the confluence with Nahal Besor (Levy 1987). Unlike many other Chalcolithic sites in the area which are found scattered over the Upper Pleistocene sediments described above, Shiqmim is located on a bench next to the Nahal Be'er Sheva channel itself, about 15 m below the level attained by the late Pleistocene sediments (Fig. 4). Recent excavations (1987) show that the site rests upon at least ca 3 m of moderately sorted, well-rounded and bedded gravels. Quarrying operations in the Nahal Be'er Sheva adjacent to the site retrieved a large basalt bowl and demonstrated that the gravels that form the base of the current wadi bed both continue with depth for at least another 3 m and extend some 150 m to the south side of the wadi.

Additional geological trenching shows that locally at the base of the site, particularly in a northward direction away from the channel, finer grained, moderately sorted, flood plain silts interfinger with the cultural deposits over a thickness of about 1 to 2 m. The remainq 2-3 m of cultural deposits are interfingered with whole and collapsed mudbrick, and colluvium derived from these materials.

Temporal brackets for the "Chalcolithic fill" - particularly the lower, gravelly part of the sequence - are lacking. Though radiocarbon dates for charcoal collected from the site are pending initial dates indicate that the occupation of the Upper Village took place between about 6,150 and 5,750 BP whereas the Lower Village appeared to be occupied somewhat later, between about 5,250 and 5,050 BP (Levy and Alon 1985). In any case, from published data it would appear that the Chalcolithic Period lasted no longer than about 1,500 radiocarbon years, from ca 6,500 to ca 5,000 BP.

In the lower reaches of the site, adjacent to Nahal Be'er Sheva is a ca 1.5 m step consisting of massively bedded powdery silts (Goldberg 1987). Excavations show that these rest unconformably upon and are eroded into the Chalcolithic gravels underlying the site. These silts are widespread over the Western Negev and Southern Shefela regions of Israel (Rosen 1986a) and contain Byzantine pottery. Radiocarbon dates suggest that they accumulated over the interval of ca 650 to 1,750 BP (Goldberg 1986).

Thus, evidence at Shiqmim reveals two alluvial phases, one correspon-

ding to the Chalcolithic and
another to roughly the Byzantine
through Crusader Periods. The
former is associated with massive
gravel deposition grading laterally
and vertically into finer silts and
sands and endured for approximately
1,200 years. The latter is epitom-
ized by massive silts of similar
temporal magnitude.

2.1.4 The Southern Shefela Region (Tel Lachish Area)

A Holocene alluvial sequence for
Nahal Lachish in the south-central
Shefela Region of Israel was recently described by Rosen (1986a,b,
c) (Fig. 1). This area lies in the
foothill region and receives about
350 mm of annual precipitation; the
vegetation is Mediterranean maquis.

In several exposures along the
Nahal Lachish, Rosen recognized
four alluvial units, each dated by
the pottery that is incorporated
into the sediment. The basal unit
is comprised of well-rounded channel gravels or lateral floodplain
sediments with EB pottery. The
clayey fine fraction was suggestive
of ponding or low velocity flows in
the dry season; weak soil development is denotative of a stable land
surface. Rosen tentatively assigned
this unit to a climate somewhat
moister than today's and with a
higher water table than at present.

Overlying this are laminated
clayey and sandy silts, and sands
representing rapid flood plain aggradation during the MB I. This depositional episode "may be related
to rapidly fluctuating rainfall
patterns interspersed with drought
leading to soil stripping from the
hillslopes" (Rosen 1986b: 56,57).
An erosional episode ensued, spanning the MB II through Late Bronze
Age (LB) and tied to drier conditions and a lower watertable.

During the Iron Age renewed deposition occurred, marked by angular, poorly sorted gravels and
sandy silts which Rosen ascribes to
short-distance transport, such as
colluviation of hillslope and tell
materials following the destruction
of the site and abandonment, leading to neglect of agricultural
fields and soil erosion.

Post Iron Age downcutting was
followed by renewed deposition

during or following the Byzantine
Period. The sediments are comprised
of channel gravels in a sandy mud
matrix at the base, overlain by
poorly sorted, sandy, silty, and
gravelly colluvium. It is not apparent whether this sedimentary accumulation was related to climatic
change or abandonment of agricultural fields.

After the Byzantine, incision of
the wadi began which continues to
the present and culminates in at
least 5 m of downcutting. This is
thought to be a result of desiccation and devegetation (Rosen 1986b,
citing Vita-Finzi 1969).

Further downstream along Nahal
Lachish (near Tel 'Erani), as well
as in Nahal Shiqma to the south-
southwest, Rosen (1986b) found
remnants of a 2-6 m thick terrace
accumulation consisting of poorly
sorted gravels overlain by massive
and bedded silts. Chalcolithic/EB
pottery was found in both localities.

2.1.5 The Salibiya Depression, Lower Jordan Valley

The Salibiya Depression in the
lower Jordan Valley is situated
approximately 13 km north of Jericho, between the base of the Samarian foothills in the west, and a
small rise 2 km to the east upon
which is found the PPNA site of
Gilgal I (Noy et al. 1980) (Figs. 1
and 5). It slopes eastward toward
the main part of the Jordan Rift
Valley. The area is arid and receives ca 150 mm of rainfall annually,
falling entirely in winter. The
stratigraphic sequence based upon
the distribution of prehistoric
sites in their stratigraphic and
palaeogeographic contexts around
the time of the Pleistocene/Holo-
cene transition can be briefly summarized as follows (Schuldenrein
1984; Schuldenrein and Goldberg
1981):

The retreat of Lake Lisan (the
Pleistocene ancestor of the Dead
Sea) some time around 14,000 years
ago (Schuldenrein and Goldberg
1981; Hovers and Bar-Yosef 1987)
was accompanied by successive prehistoric occupations, with younger
sites found generally at progressively lower elevations within the
basin: Epi-Palaeolithic sites

Fig. 5. Photograph of the Salibiya depression looking west from the ridge of Gilgal. The PPNA site of Netiv Hagdud is next to the water tower, at the apex of an alluvial fan at the base of the hills. The fine grained sediments of the toe of the fan (foreground) bury Early-Late Natufian sites and encase the PPNA site of Salibiya IX. The active badlands are post PPNA (and Chalcolithic?) in age.

(Kebaran and Geometric Kebaran, ca 17,000-13,500 BP) are found above -180 m whereas early and later Natufian sites (ca 12,500-10,500 BP) are found at -218 m and -230 m, respectively. These latter sites tend to be situated in subaerially eroded gullies and pockets that were developed on the Lisan marls as Lake Lisan retreated.

This erosion was halted by the deposition of pinkish brown silts that filled in this partially eroded terrain and post-date the early Neolithic (PPNA) sites of Salibiya IX (Bar-Yosef 1980), Gilgal I (Noy et al. 1980) and Netiv Hagdud (Bar-Yosef et al. 1980). These silts represent the finer sediments that accumulated at the distal end of the alluvial fan produced by Wadi Baqar. Localized in the lowermost few centimetres of these silts and clearly overlying Late Natufian sites are in situ masses and pieces of algal tufa that formed from water seeping out of small, localized depressions. Consequently the sediments coarsen westward in the direction of Netiv Hagdud where the fan is quite conglomeratic. Coarse boulders and gravel also partially cover the settlement of Netiv Hagdud, thereby indicating roughly continual deposition after the PPNA. Ten samples of charcoal from Netiv Hagdud indicate a range of ^{14}C dates from 10,230 to 9,400 BP, mostly concentrated between 9,700 to 9,500 BP.

The deposition of silts and the gravels described above covered the PPNA site though firm dating of this is not possible. A date contemporary or just after the Chalcolithic (ca 6,500 BP) is feasible since a massive Chalcolithic building is situated in the topmost coeval alluvial fan sediments in Wadi Fazael about 7 km to the north. If this is correct, then Post-Chalcolithic time is characterized by erosion and the formation of the badlands that typify the Salibiya Depression today.

2.1.6 Sites in the Galilee, Judea and the Coastal Plain

Numerous archaeological sites are found throughout much of the more

77

Fig. 6. Photograph of the PPNB site Yiftahel (excavated by Y. Garfunkel), showing plastered floors covered by occupational debris and capped by colluvial reddish brown clay derived from nearby slopes such as the one in the background (Photograph courtesy of Israel Department of Antiquities).

humid northern parts of Israel, but most of these are not associated with alluvial erosional and depositional sequences. Rather, they generally exhibit archaeological material that interfingers with or has been covered by colluvial materials. We present here a very eclectic sample of some of the more prominent sites.

The site of Ganei HaTarukhah is situated along the coastal plain near Tel-Aviv, a few km east of the coast. Here, a Chalcolithic site was overlain by a clay layer and successive deposits containing Proto-Urban, EB and MB I pottery; this is followed by sterile and post-MB I sediments (Horowitz 1979; Ritter-Kaplan 1984). On the basis of the stratigraphy and somewhat scanty pollen counts, Horowitz interpreted the Chalcolithic through Early Bronze Age strata to have been deposited under swampy conditions during a more humid climate. After the EB drier conditions returned accompanied by a lowering of the groundwater table.

At the contact between the Upper Shefela and the base of the Judean Mountains is the Natufian-Khiamian site of Hatoula (Lechevalier and Ronen 1985) (Fig. 1). Situated at the base of a rolling hill the site exhibits ca 2.5 m of cultural deposits which are capped by ca 30 cm of partially disturbed clayey colluvium, material which originally was much thicker before recent afforestation. Some of the cultural layers also show colluvial intercalations. The date of the post-occupation colluviation could not be determined.

A somewhat similar picture is apparent at the PPNB site of Abu Ghosh, which is situated in the Judean Hills, about 12 km west of Jerusalem at an elevation of ca 700 m (Lechevallier 1978) (Fig. 1). Overlying the architectural remains are a dark yellowish brown loamy stony layer ca 50 cm thick, which is in turn capped by a dark brown 30-50 cm thick loam mixed with lithic material and Byzantine pottery. Though the origin of the stony fraction is not completely clear (Farrand, in Lechevallier 1978) the fine fraction is certainly colluvially reworked terra rossa.

The site of Yiftahel is located in the Lower Galilee about 8 km west of Nazareth at an elevation of 145 m above sea level (Garfinkel 1987) (Fig. 1). Its stratigraphic altitude is similar to that at Hatoula being situated along the contact zone between rolling limestone hills and clayey alluvium of Nahal Yiftahel. In the area of the PPNB settlement about 2 m of cultural debris has been covered by at least 1.5 m of red brown clayey colluvium derived from the slopes to the east (Fig. 6). This material is partially contemporaneous with the EB I village that is found ca 50 m to the south.

3 EVALUATION

In accordance with the aims of the symposium, we shall try in this section to evaluate the geomorphic and palynological evidence presented above in order to differentiate between the imprint of climatic fluctuations on the varied Levantine environments, and those caused by humans. We will stress the former in the first part of this discussion and the latter in the second part.

Our working assumptions are twofold:

1. Late Pleistocene and Early Holocene climatic fluctuations are registered independently in ice cores, deep-sea cores, and to a certain extent in lake levels and palynological records. Modelling of climatic fluctuations for this time interval in terms of Milankovitch forcing is accessible in the literature (e.g., Kutzbach 1983) and these changes have been partially tested against palynological and lake levels records.

2. The former impact of humans should be directly related to the degree and complexity of social organization. Social evolution in the Near East was studied by many archaeologists since at least the mid-19th century. With progress in prehistoric research in recent years we can conjecture several relationships between humans and their immediate or more remote environments. At first, we would expect hunter-gatherers to have used fires as part of their subsistence strategies, as known from Australian and Northwest American examples

(Lewis 1982), but unfortunately direct evidence for such practices in the prehistoric Levant is still missing. Secondly, a more decisive role is expected from village societies when wood became extensively used for building and for combustion. Finally, the introduction of domesticated plants including grain cultivation and planting fruit trees, as well as the introduction of domesticated animals should have had their impact on the environment. The emergence of urban societies should have brought about a marked increase in deforestation, and potential overgrazing caused by increased herding.

Sorting out the impact of either natural of human agencies, especially during the period when both seem to be highly interwoven, is not an easy task, and we are fully aware that the following assertions are open to criticism. However, within the framework of this symposium, we believe that taking such a stand would lead to fruitful discussions.

As noted above, Holocene geomorphic changes are for the most part presented by alluviation and erosion in the arid and semi-arid regions, while in the more moist locations, colluvial mantles seem to be more typical. Moreover, whereas distinct and extensive alluvial phases are associated with the Chalcolithic and Byzantine periods, other depositional episodes seem to be sprinkled in space and time.

The occurrence of Holocene alluvium however, does not necessarily translate itself into human destabilization of the landscape, by hypothetical partial or total destruction of the vegetation cover. We see for example, several similar aggradational and erosional phases that are widespread over the Negev during the Late Pleistocene (Goldberg 1986). The interpretations of such episodes are problematic in themselves but usually focus on climatic and tectonic mechanisms, though natural oscillations of the fluvial system have also been cited (Andres 1980). Climatic interpretations range from dry=deposition/wet =erosion, to the opposite (Goldberg 1984). Accordingly, any of the above explanatory scenarios could apply to Holocene alluviation as

well, though the Chalcolithic terrace at Shiqmim seems reasonably interpreted in terms of deposition during a wetter climate (see Levy 1987). In any case, because of the small size of Pleistocene prehistoric sites and populations, most researchers would agree that Pleistocene alluvial cycles (at least) are not anthropogenically related.

Another point worth stressing is the lithology of the alluvial units and whether the latter are composed of locally derived material or that which has been transported along slopes or from upstream. In the case of the Jordan Valley sequence (Salibiya), for example, the reddish alluvium certainly indicates a terra rossa source in the Samarian Hills to the west. In the western Negev area on the other hand, the loess-like silts of both Chalcolithic and "Byzantine" alluvia probably represent

1) externally derived aeolian dust that was pene-contemporaneously being washed out of the atmosphere and transported over short distances along slopes,

2) remnants of late Pleistocene alluvial silts that were being eroded by gullying and sheetwash. Aeolian addition is supported by the occurrence of aeolian silt (true loess) that overlies Chalcolithic sites on the Har Harif plateau of the Negev Highlands to the southeast. Thus, the situation in the drier areas of the southern Levant is unlike that which is typically cited for Holocene alluvium in the eastern Mediterranean, where valley filling is a result of the stripping of pre-existing soil-covered slopes. It is interesting to note that in Nahal Resisim at least, Byzantine check dams are both built upon and appear to be contemporaneous with fluvially reworked loessial deposits. This suggests that the silts were already accumulating before the dams were built.

In addition, an alluvial sequence consisting of successive depositional units may have different implications from that where the alluvial units are expressed as distinct morpho-stratigraphic entities, such as terraces. The former might imply a ubiquitous depositional mode for the fluvial system, in which an overall trend

80

Table 2.

Age (BP)	Zone	Depth (m)	Interpretation
4,500	C2	0-8	Decrease in AP possibly due to human interference or drier conditions
7,400-4,500	C1	8-15	High tree pollen values with fluctuations. Oak less dominant; marked presence of olive and pistachio. Establishment of present-day vegetation
10,000-7,400	B	24-15	Increase in open vegetation and decrease in oak. Increase in climatic dryness and rise in temperature
14,000-10,000	A2	31-24	Increase in oak; climatic amelioration with increase in precipitation and low winter temperatures

of alluviation is punctuated by minor phases of relative stability. The second case on the other hand, implies major shifts in the wadi regime, from depositional to erosional modes (and vice versa) reflecting a variety of options, such as changes in climate or base level. The former case (e.g., Lachish) may indeed point to continued destabilisation of the slopes but again, direct evidence is needed to establish this.

If the landscape changes discussed above are indeed induced by human activities such as clearance (e.g., tree cutting, slash-and-burn) then some of these activities should be reflected in the palaeobotanical evidence.

In the Hula Basin there is the often cited pollen diagram of Tsukada which has been interpreted by van Zeist and Bottema (1982) as shown in Table 2 (only the later part of the core is considered here). Thus, according to their interpretation late Pleistocene and early Holocene vegetational changes are predominantly climatically induced, whereas those of the last 4,500 years seem to be related to human modifications.

In the nearby Sea of Galilee (Kinneret), Baruch (1986) studied a 5-m-long core that spans the past 5,300 years. Although this core covers essentially only the second half of the Holocene, he concluded that the natural vegetation existed in the area until the end of the fourth millennium BC and that vegetational changes were a reflection of human induced conditions and not climatic ones. [This is in contrast to Horowitz' (1979) interpretation for two cores from the Hula.] We see for example, a sharp drop in AP values between ca 3,700 and 2,400 years ago (zone X2), ostensibly as a result of human activity, such as clearing. Such activities are even better expressed by the increase in the relative frequency of olive during the Hellenistic through Byzantine periods, about 2,400 to 1,400 years ago. Furthermore, Baruch (1986:46) notes: "The evolution of the forest of the Lake Kinneret area as from the middle of the 1st millennium AD and onwards, as may be inferred from the pollen record of the lake, seems to reflect the effects of continuous human interference with the natural vegetation. This must have been mainly in the form of grazing and limited tree cutting....". Thus, according to these data and interpretations, the botanical record has been conspicuously and almost irreversibly influenced by anthropogenic effects only during the past ca 3,700 years, most notably during the period 2,400 to 1,400 BP. This is somewhat more recent than the 4,500 years given by van Zeist and Bottema for Tsukada's Hula diagram. In either case, anthropogenic impacts seem to date to the latter part of the Holocene and not earlier.

Changes in sedimentation rates in the Kinneret core also reflect the inferred changes in vegetation. Interpolations using the radiocarbon dates for this core (which are somewhat problematical but certainly within the correct order of magnitude; Thompson et al. 1985) show a marked increase in the upper part of the core, corresponding to the last ca 3,000 years:

Depth (cm)	Corr. 14C date	Rate of sedimentation (cm/1000 years)
0		140
143	1020	117
278	2170	102
358	2955	48
468	5217	

Also of note is the relative increase of non-siliceous algae in the interval 300-40 cm, which apparently represents the initial stages of eutrophication and enrichment of nutrients (Stiller et al. 1983-1984). Thus, both the pollen and algae evidence point to human induced modifications only ca 3,000 years ago.

Estimates of the same order of magnitude were given by Gophna et al. (1986-1987) for the central coastal plain region of Israel. Using conservative estimates for population, and for areas of agriculture, pasture, and wood supply, they concluded that:

- During the Chalcolithic and EB Ia periods, populations and exploitation areas were too small to have a significant effect on the vegetation; there was ample opportunity for the vegetation to recover after abandonment.
- However, during EB Ib and EB II periods, population increases were associated with expanded cultivation and grazing.
- During the Intermediate Bronze Age (2,200 to 2,000 BC), settlements were again reduced in size and forest recovery could take place.
- The growth of large towns during the Middle Bronze Age led to discernible damage of the vegetation at this time.
- Finally, they note: "it may be presumed that during the time span between the Chalcolithic period and the Middle Bronze Age some of the forest areas underwent changes characterized by full or partial deforestation, followed by recovery. In spite of these fluctuations, a maximum of only about 25%

of the total region could have been affected. This maximum was reached during the Middle Bronze Age" (Gophna et al. 1986-1987:81).

Finally, we wish to remark that even if human induced vegetational changes can be documented for only the past 3,000 years or so, there is still no direct evidence to show that such changes were responsible for the geomorphic transformations that were described above. If we assume that some of the vegetation was removed by burning it is not unreasonable to expect that some traces of charcoal would be found in both the alluvial or colluvial units, as has been recounted from Australia (Blong and Gillespie 1978) where prehistoric burning practices are well known. If remains of charcoal are present in the Holocene they are rare or at least have yet to be reported.

It is evident that in the future much more work is needed to clearly document the relationship between human utilisation and possible exploitation of the landscape and its geomorphic responses. Until now, inferences relating the two have been indirect. Some suggestions for future work should include:

- Detailed microstratigraphic study of buried sediment and soil profiles to detect the likelihood of human interference. Recent work using micromorpholoy (study of soils and sediments in thin section) has demonstrated the possibility of recognizing such soil features as cultivation, burning and tree-uprooting (Courty et al. 1989; Macphail and Goldberg in press). If we never look for such features we will never find them.
- Detailed palynological study of additional cores from lakes in the region with tight chronological control. Such cores would not only furnish palaeobotanical information but also detailed estimates of sedimentation rates, crude approximations of which were presented for the Kinneret core. In such cores, we might also look out for charcoal as an indicator of forest clearance. In appropriately chosen cores (e.g., near the mouths of wadis) charcoal may be readily apparent.
- Following the direction of Rosen (1986c), it would be profitable to examine closely exposures

of alluvial and colluvial sequences in proximity to tells where archaeological traces of human activities are both abundant and interpretable. Such an approach might also clarify the apparent differences from north to south in the nature of Holocene depositional sequences.

In addition to purely climatic considerations, Holocene landscape evolution must also be evaluated in terms of the evolution of human societies and their activities during this time span. It is our contention that the successful emergence of farming societies in the "Levantine Corridor" (Bar-Yosef and Belfer-Cohen in press), which stretches from the middle Euphrates through the Damascus Basin into the Jordan Valley and the Trans-Jordanian Plateau as far south as southern Jordan, could have occurred only under optimal climatic conditions. By this we mean a slight increase in precipitation and its optimal distribution over the region. As known from other sources, temperatures were rising to reach the climatic optimum during the fifth millennium bc. Pollen evidence from the Huleh and the Ghab, as well as the faunal record from drier places like the Lower Jordan Valley, indicate wetter conditions during the eighth and seventh millennia bc (demonstrating for example, the presence of a fresh water body; Bar-Yosef in press). However, given the small number of known Early Neolithic village sites (Pre-Pottery Neolithic A or Mureybet IB-III), we suggest that the impact of human communities on the environment was minimal and can be defined as local. When an area was exhausted beyond the daily reach of the sedentary community, the entire village could be moved. It is also not impossible that flexible social structure and partial sedentism (e.g., nine months in a base camp) enabled a better exploitation of the environments causing only restricted increased erosion as a result of local intensive deforestation. Such is perhaps the explanation for the abandonment of sites like Netiv Hagdud or Jericho; interestingly, a protective wall built against flooding and alluviation may provide a reasonable explanation of an intriguing archaeo-logical phenomenon (Bar-Yosef 1986).

The seventh millennium bc (uncalibrated radiometric chronology) provided amplified evidence for increased precipitation (such as lakes in the Arabian peninsula or pollen records across the northern Near East). Village societies practising cultivation continued to expand and a few large sites are 10-14 hectares in size (Abu Hureyra, Beisamoun, Ain Ghazal, Basta). During this period goats and sheep (but mainly goats) were introduced and herded in the Levant. The current evidence points to the Zagros (and perhaps parts of the Taurus) as their origin but it should be stressed that their distribution in farming societies was uneven and mainly confined to the "Levantine Corridor". Moreover, there are sites with ample evidence (in the form of carbonized plant remains) for the practice of cultivation together with continued hunting (e.g., Nahal Oren, Yiftahel). Thus, regardless of the exact role of goats in causing environmental destruction of a particular locale (e.g., Ain Ghazal, see Köhler-Rollefson and Rollefson this volume), even when accompanied with increased deforestation, the result appears to be only localized human impact.

The following 1,000 to 1,500 years (sixth and fifth millennia bc) are the most intriguing during the Holocene for the Eastern Mediterranean. The archaeological evidence demonstrates the presence of farmers and herders not only along the "Levantine Corridor" but also in the coastal plain and the fringes of the Syro-Arabian desert, especially in oases (e.g., Azraq). It probably represents the time of emergence of truly herding societies which eventually became dependent on the farming communities. However, the drastic change in settlement pattern does not detract from the impression one gains from sifting through the literature about a relative decrease in site numbers from northern Syria all the way to southern Sinai. It seems that both climatic fluctuation and the social collapse of the PPNB societal structure contributed to this situation. The climatic improvement is seen in the natural restoration of the forests (during the early Chalcolithic) and the feasibility of having sedentary farming and herding communities on the edge of the deserts. Only a kind of climatic stability (optimal distribution of annual rains) would account for their success along the valley of Be'er Sheva, where the vegetation was mainly similar to today's (Kislev 1987). We should keep in mind that this period saw the emergence of complex city states in Mesopotamia, the invention of early writing, the exploitation of copper mines in many places including Oman and the two sides of the Arava Valley. Thus, the fourth millennium bc denotes the major change in the impact of humans on the environment: exploitation of the environment increased at the time of the emergence of complex social structures when control over other human communities in far away areas began. Faunal records indicate the virtually complete disappearance of wild game hunting in the Levant while it undoubtedly continued in the Zagros, the Taurus, and western Anatolia. Deforestation increased and one may infer the impact of humans on their environment as reaching the level of regional destruction.

During the Bronze and Iron Ages the two are closely interwoven and much finer chronological control over deep-sea records or palynological cores from remote lakes is needed in order to sort them out. It seems that during the late Roman, Byzantine and Early Arab periods there are indications for climatic improvement, although like in the Bronze-Iron Age, many of the alluvial accumulations might have resulted from agricultural activities and from the need in dry areas like the Negev to increase the amount of runoff (Bruins this volume).

Finally, we should bear in mind that the evidence for the "Little Ice Age" in Europe comes from various independent sources. The direct relationship between the European palaeoclimatic sequence and that from the Near East is becoming clearer over the years (e.g., Bottema 1987). One is therefore tempted to suggest that this cooling period had its effects in the Near East as reflected in the palaeolevels of the Dead Sea (Klein 1982), for example. Unfortunately, most of the historians and archaeologists working in the Near East are not interested in the climate of the last millennium (though see Kedar 1985) and thus the available information is sparse and doubtful.

To sum up, while during the early part of the Holocene climatic fluctuations played the major role in shaping the Near Eastern landscape, it was during the last five millennia that human intervention increased and in some cases became the decisive factor in changing the environment. This shift could not have been done without the evolution of a complex structure where the demand for products motivated the emergence of pastoral societies, mining activities, agricultural operations, and transportation across land masses and seas.

REFERENCES

Andres, W. 1980.
On the paleoclimatic significance of erosion and deposition in arid regions. Zeitschrift für Geomorphologie, Suppl.-Bd. 36:113-122.
Avi-Yanoh, M. and E.Stern 1977.
Encyclopedia of Archaeological Excavations in the Holy Land. Oxford: Oxford University Press.
Baruch, U. 1986.
The late Holocene vegetational history of Lake Kinneret (Sea of Galilee), Israel. Paléorient 12/2:37-48.
Bar-Yosef, O. 1980.
A figurine from a Khiamian site in the lower Jordan Valley. Paléorient 6:193-99.
Bar-Yosef, O. 1986.
The walls of Jericho: an alternative interpretation. Current Anthropology 27:157-162.
Bar-Yosef, O. 1987.
Prehistory of the Jordan Rift. Israel Journal of Earth Science 36:107-119.
Bar-Yosef, O. in press.
PPNA sites in the Jordan Valley. Paléorient.
Bar-Yosef, O., A.Gopher and A.N.Goring-Morris 1980.
Netiv Hagdud: A "Sultanian" mound in the Lower Jordan Valley. Paléorient 6:201-206.

Bar-Yosef, O. and A.Belfer-Cohen
in press. The origins of sedentism and farming communities in
the Levant. Journal of World
Prehistory 3.

Betts, A. 1985.
Black Desert Survey Jordan: third
preliminary report. Levant 17:29-
52.

Blong, R.J. and R.Gillespie 1978.
Fluvially transported charcoal
gives erroneous 14C ages for recent deposits. Nature 271:739-
741.

Bottema, S. 1987.
Chronology and climatic phases in
the Near East from 16,000 to
10,000 B.P. In O.Aurenche, J.Evin
and F.Hours (eds.), Chronologies
in the Near East, p.295-310. BAR
International Series 379.

Bruins, H.J. 1986.
Desert Environment and Agricul-
ture in the Central Negev and
Kadesh-Barnea during Historical
Times. Nijkerk: Midbar Founda-
tion.

Bruins, H.J. (this volume)
The impact of man and climate on
the Central Negev and northeastern Sinai deserts during the
Late Holocene.

Cohen, R. and W.G.Dever 1981.
Preliminary report of the third
and final season of the "Central
Negev Highlands Project". BASOR
243:57-77.

Courty, M.A., P.Goldberg
and R.I.Macphail 1989.
Soils, Micro-morphology and
Archaeology. Cambridge: Cambridge
University Press.

Garfinkel, Y. 1987.
Yiftahel: A Neolithic village
from the seventh millennium B.C.
in Lower Galilee, Israel. Journal
of Field Archaeology 14:199-212.

Garrard, A.,
B.Byrd and A.Betts 1986.
Prehistoric environment and
settlement in the Azraq Basin: an
interim report on the 1984 season. Levant 18:5-24.

Garrard, A., A.Betts,
B.Byrd and C.Hunt 1987.
Prehistoric environment and
settlement in the Azraq Basin: an
interim report on the 1985 season. Levant 19:5-25.

Goldberg, P. 1984.
Late Quaternary history of Qadesh
Barnea, Northeastern Sinai. Zeitschrift für Geomorphology 28:193-
217.

Goldberg, P. 1986.
Late Quaternary environmental
history of the Southern Levant.
Geoarchaeology 1:224-244.

Goldberg, P. 1987.
The geology and stratigraphy of
Shiqmim. In T.E.Levy (ed.),
Shiqmim I, Studies concerning
Chalcolithic Societies in the
Northern Negev Desert, Israel
(1982-1984), p.35-44. BAR Inter-
national Series 356.

Gophna, R., N.Lipschitz
and S.Lev-Yadun 1986-1987.
Man's impact on the natural vegetation of the Central Coastal
Plain of Israel during the Chalcolithic Period and the Bronze
Age. Tel-Aviv 13-14:71-84.

Goring-Morris, A.N. 1987.
At the Edge. BAR International
Series 361.

Goring-Morris, A.N. and A.Gopher
1983. Nahal Issaron: A Neolithic
settlement in the Southern Negev.
Israel Exploration Journal 33:
149-162.

Horowitz, A. 1979.
The Quaternary of Israel. New
York: Academic Press.

Hovers, E. and O.Bar-Yosef 1987.
Prehistoric survey of eastern
Samaria: a preliminary report.
Israel Exploration Journal 37:
77-87.

Kedar, B.Z. 1985.
The Arab conquests and agriculture: a seventh-century apocalyp-
se, satellite imagery, and palynology. Asian and African Studies
19:1-15.

Kislev, M. 1987.
Chalcolithic plant husbandry and
ancient vegetation at Shiqmim.
In T.E.Levy (ed.), Shiqmim I,
Studies concerning Chalcolithic
Societies in the Northern Negev
Desert, Israel (1982-1984),
p.251-563. BAR International
Series 356.

Klein, C. 1982.
Morphological evidence of lake
level changes, western shore of
the Dead Sea. Israel Journal of
Earth Science 31:67-94.

Köhler-Rollefson, I. and
G.O.Rollefson (this volume)
The impact of Neolithic subsistence strategies on the environment: the case of 'Ain Ghazal.

Kutzbach, J.E. 1983.
Monsoon rains of the Late Pleistocene and Early Holocene:
patterns, intensity and possible

causes of change. In A.Street-Perrott, M.Beran and R.A.S.Ratcliffe (eds.), Variations in the Global Water Budget, p.379-389. Dordrecht, Reidel.

Lechevallier, M. 1978.
Abou Gosh et Beisamoun. Mém. Trav. Prat. Cent. Rech. Préhist. Franc. Jerusalem no. 2.

Lechevallier, M. and A.Ronen 1985.
Le site Natoufien-Khiamien de Hatoula, près de Latroun, Israel. Cah. Cent. Rech. Franç. Jerusalem no. 1.

Leroi-Gourhan, A.
and F.Darmon 1987.
Analyses palynologiques de sites archéologiques du Pléistocène final dans la Vallée du Jourdain. Israel Journal of Earth Science 36:65-72.

Levy, T.E. (ed.) 1987.
Shiqmim I, Studies concerning Chalcolithic Societies in the Northern Negev Desert, Israel (1982-1984). BAR International Series 356.

Levy, T.E. and D.Alon 1985.
Shiqmim: A Chalcolithic village and mortuary centre in the Northern Negev. Paléorient 11:71-83.

Lewis, H.T. 1982.
Fire technology and resource management in the Aboriginal North America and Australia. In N.M.Williams and E.S.Hunn (eds.), Resource Managers: North American and Australian Hunter-Gatherers, p.45-68. Boulder, Westview Press.

Macphail, R.I. and P.Goldberg
in press. The micromorphology of tree subsoil hollows: their significance to soil science and archaeology. Proceedings International Working Meeting on Soil Micromorphology, San Antonio, July 1988.

Marsh, G.P. 1864.
Man and Nature: or, Physical Geography as Modified by Human Action. New York: Scribner.

Naveh, Z. and J.Dan 1973.
The human degradation of Mediterranean landscapes in Israel. In F.di Castri and H.A.Mooney (eds.), Ecological Studies, Analysis and Synthesis 7:373-389.

Noy, T., J.Schuldenrein
and E.Tchernov 1980.
Gilgal, a Pre-Pottery Neolithic A site in the Lower Jordan Valley. Israel Exploration Journal 30:63-82.

Ritter-Kaplan, H. 1984.
The impact of drought on Third Millennium B.C. cultures on the basis of excavations in the Tel Aviv Exhibition grounds. Zeitschrift Deutsch. Paläst.-Ver. 100:2-8.

Rosen, A. 1986a.
Quaternary alluvial stratigraphy of the Shephela and its paleoclimatic implications. Geological Survey of Israel, Report GSI/25/86.

Rosen, A. 1986b.
Environmental change and settlement at Tel Lachish, Israel. BASOR 263:55-60.

Rosen, A. 1986c.
Cities of Clay. Chicago: University of Chicago Press.

Rosen, S. 1987.
Demographic trends in the Negev Highlands: Preliminary results from the emergency surveys. BASOR 266:45-58.

Schuldenrein, J. 1984.
Unpublished Ph.D.dissertation, University of Chicago.

Schuldenrein, J.
and P.Goldberg 1981.
Late Quaternary palaeoenvironments and prehistoric site distributions in the Lower Jordan Valley: A preliminary report. Paléorient 7:57-71.

Stiller, M., A.Ehrlich, U.Pollinger, U.Baruch and A.Kaufman 1983-1984. The late Holocene sediments of Lake Kinneret (Israel) - Multidisciplinary study of a five meter core. Geological Survey of Israel, Current Research:83-88.

Thompson, R., G.M.Turner, M.Stiller and A.Kaufman 1985.
Near East paleomagnetic secular variation recorded in sediments from the Sea of Galilee (Lake Kinneret). Quaternary Research 23:175-188.

Vita-Finzi, C. 1969.
Mediterranean Valleys. Cambridge: Cambridge University Press.

Zeist, W.van and S.Bottema 1982.
Vegetational history of the Eastern Mediterranean and the Near East during the last 20,000 years. In J.L.Bintliff and W.van Zeist (eds.), Palaeoclimates, Palaeoenvironments and Human Communities in the Eastern Mediterranean Region in Later Prehistory, p.277-323. BAR International Series 133.

Man's Role in the Shaping of the Eastern Mediterranean Landscape, Bottema, Entjes-Nieborg & van Zeist (eds)
© *1990 Balkema, Rotterdam. ISBN 90 6191 138 9*

The impact of man and climate on the Central Negev and northeastern Sinai deserts during the Late Holocene

8

Hendrik J. Bruins
Jacob Blaustein Institute for Desert Research, Ben-Gurion University of the Negev, Sede Boqer Campus, Israel

ABSTRACT: Extensive remains of ancient desert agriculture appear in the central Negev and adjacent region of northeastern Sinai. Thousands of check-dams were built in numerous valleys (wadis). Countless little stone mounds dot thousands of hectares of hilly uplands. These ancient constructions built in the landscape to enable rain-fed farming based on run-off water, date to several historical periods, i.e. the Iron Age and particularly to Nabatean, Roman, Byzantine and Early Arab times. These man-made structures had a positive impact on the landscape: increased water storage in the terraced wadis, increased sedimentation and subsequent soil depth in the arable fields, protection against erosion and greening the desert. Also climate had an apparent effect on the desert landscape. Stream channel sedimentation occurred during relatively wet periods and wadi-bed erosion took place in relatively dry phases: Roman fill deposit, Incision (ca AD 700-1200), Major sedimentation (ca AD 1200-1700), Incision (ca 1700-today). The respective impact of man and climate has to be investigated in each catchment area, and the effect of either factor may be superimposed on top of the other.

1 INTRODUCTION

The habitation and development of arid regions can often be regarded as a challenge to man, particularly in dry areas devoid of exotic rivers or other external water resources. The meagre rainfall amounts and consequent low natural carrying capacity of arid lands pose special problems in terms of water and food supply. It is, therefore, quite remarkable how, in ancient times, man was capable to settle in the arid parts of the Near East. It seems reasonable to assume that useful lessons may be learned from past man-desert relationship. Hence the impact of ancient man on the arid lands in the Near East deserves to be investigated. Both benign and adverse anthropogenic effects upon the landscape in ancient times (Gibson 1982) ought to be taken into account in modern arid-zone planning. In environmental archaeological investigations it is important to separate human influence on the landscape from climatic effects. The impact of man and climate may often be intertwined in an intricate way, difficult to disentangle. The present paper addresses these problems as encountered in the central Negev and northeastern Sinai deserts.

2 PHYSICAL ENVIRONMENT

The Sinai and Negev constitute the landbridge between the continents of Africa and Asia (Fig. 1), situated at the northern edge of the huge Saharo-Arabian desert belt. The areas under consideration, the central Negev and northeastern Sinai, are situated at a distance of some 100 km from the southeastern corner of the Mediterranean Sea and about 120 km northwest from the Red Sea tip near Elat. The region forms part of a planetary desert, benignly influenced in the winter season by rain-bringing depressions, usually from the west. The present climate in the studied areas is characterized by a hot dry summer lasting from May to October, with maximum temperatures occasionally reaching 40 degrees Celsius. The winter is rather cool with occasional frost at ground-level. The average annual temperature is about 18 degrees C. The average rainfall varies around 100 mm per year, spread over some 26 rainy days from October to April. Inter-annual rainfall variations are large.

The central Negev and north-eastern Sinai are hilly areas, ranging in altitude from about 200 to 1000 m. The landscape is largely composed of Late Cretaceous and Early Tertiary marine, carbonate rocks. Loessial dust, generally reworked, forms a prominent consti-tuent of the soils, which are very shallow and stony on the hillslopes and usually much thicker in the valleys (Yaalon and Dan 1974; Bruins 1986). The vegetation in the area (Danin 1983) is largely Irano-Turonian in composition, albeit with clear Saharo-Arabian influen-ces.

3 ANCIENT LAND-USE

A useful way to indicate the aridi-ty of dry regions has been develop-ed by UNESCO (1979). The degree of aridity or bioclimatic dryness depends on the relative amounts of water gained from rainfall (P) and lost by evaporation and transpira-tion (ETP = mean annual evapotran-spiration). Bioclimatic aridity can thus be expressed in terms of the ratio P/ETP. On the basis of this aridity index UNESCO (1979) has defined and delimitated the arid zones:

Hyper-arid zone, P/ETP ratio smaller than 0.03;

Arid zone, P/ETP ratio ranges from 0.03 - 0.20;

Semi-arid zone, P/ETP ratio ranges from 0.20 - 0.50.

Land-use in the hyper-arid zone of the inner desert is entirely restricted to oases. The arid zone has been used traditionally by nomads for extensive livestock rearing, but is too dry for normal rain-fed agriculture. However, in the central Negev an ingenious

Fig. 1. The location of the Negev and Sinai as a landbridge between Africa and Asia (after Bruins 1986:6).

system of agriculture has been developed in antiquity, based upon local rainfall and surface runoff (Evenari et al. 1971, 1982; Bruins 1986; Bruins et al. 1987). The central Negev and northeastern Sinai have at present a P/ETP ratio of about 0.07, which shows that the area is located at the dry edge of the arid zone, close to the hyper-arid zone.

The main principles of runoff agriculture can be illustrated in the following way. An important food crop like wheat needs some 300 mm of water for a reasonable yield. The average annual rainfall in the area is only 100 mm, which is far too low. However, the hilly landscape in the area converts rainfall into surface runoff, during rainfall events of suffi-cient duration and intensity. The runoff waters naturally concen-trate in the valleys due to the force of gravity, eventually flow-ing into the ephemeral stream chan-nels. These wadis may contain soils largely composed of redeposited loess, very suitable for agricul-ture, provided there is sufficient water. However, the infiltration rate of the runoff floodwaters into the loessial soils is rather slow, rapidly decreasing to just 3 mm/hour (Evenari et al. 1971, 1982). A significant part of the runoff,

88

therefore, flows further downstream before it can infiltrate in wadi-fields designated for agriculture.

At some stage in antiquity, man began to build little check-dams in the wadis to arrest more of the runoff waters for agriculture. During a significant rainstorm, the runoff floodwaters will cascade down the terraced wadis, filling each terrace until the level of the check-dam. If these check-dams are 20 cm high, each terraced field will be ponded by 20 cm (= 200 mm) of runoff water during a flood. Since the ponded water cannot flow away it has time and opportunity to infiltrate into the loessial soil, where it is stored. Together with the 100 mm of direct rainfall, the total amount of rainfall + runoff = 300 mm, the required amount to grow wheat. This simplified example leaves aside factors such as inter-annual rainfall variation, rainfall effectivity in relation to catchment size, depression storage, and evaporation, but it demonstrates the principle of runoff agriculture in arid regions.

4 CONCISE ARCHAEOLOGICAL HISTORY OF RUNOFF AGRICULTURE IN THE AREA

There is no direct evidence as yet when runoff agriculture was first practised in the central Negev desert. Dating of check-dams and other agricultural structures is often difficult (Mayerson 1960). The area was settled quite extensively during the Early Bronze Age (3rd millennium BC) and Middle Bronze Age I (ca 2200-2000 BC), but no runoff-farming structures have so far been dated to these periods (Cohen 1986). The relation between dwelling remains and check-dams seems to become firmer in certain Iron Age sites (ca around 1000 BC) (Aharoni et al. 1960; Cohen 1976; Bruins 1986). After an apparent gap in habitation, runoff farming was again practised in the central Negev highlands by the Nabateans, perhaps beginning in the latter part of the 1st century AD (Negev 1982).

The peak of runoff-agricultural development in the central Negev and northeastern Sinai (Photo 1) was reached during the Byzantine period when six desert cities, founded by the Nabateans (Negev 1983), flourished in the region. Various systems of runoff farming were practised, i.e. the Terraced Wadi System (Photo 1), Hillside Conduit System and Diversion System (Bruins 1986; Bruins et al. 1986). This rainwater-harvesting desert civilization formed the southeastern border of the Byzantine Empire (Gihon 1967; Negev 1981). After the Muslim-Arab conquest of the Negev in AD 636, the situation obviously changed, but runoff farming by a settled population continued for some time into the Early Islamic period.

5 ANCIENT CHECK-DAMS IN THE VALLEYS

The amount of structures built by ancient man in the hilly desert landscape of the central Negev, in order to "harvest" runoff for drinking water (cisterns) and runoff agriculture is quite extraordinary. In a region with very few springs indeed, virtually everything depended on runoff rainwater. Thousands of check-dams were constructed in numerous wadis. Kedar (1967) made a survey of the areal extent of the fields terraced for runoff farming in ephemeral stream channels, using aerial photographs. Excluding the Sinai, which Kedar did not include in his survey, the runoff farming district in the central Negev hills encompasses an area of about 200,000 hectares (Fig. 2). Within this region Kedar (1967) made a calculation of the total area of runoff-agricultural fields and he arrived at a figure of 4000 hectares. A detailed archaeological survey in the western part of the central Negev was carried out by Haiman (1989), who concluded that the area of runoff-agricultural fields for that particular region is much higher than calculated by Kedar (1967).

A detailed investigation of runoff-farming fields in three little wadis at Horvat Haluqim, a site largely attributed to the Early Iron age (Cohen 1976), demonstrates the considerable effort made by ancient man to practise runoff-agriculture in the desert (Bruins 1986). A total of 72 ancient check-dams were counted in these little wadis of first to second order. The

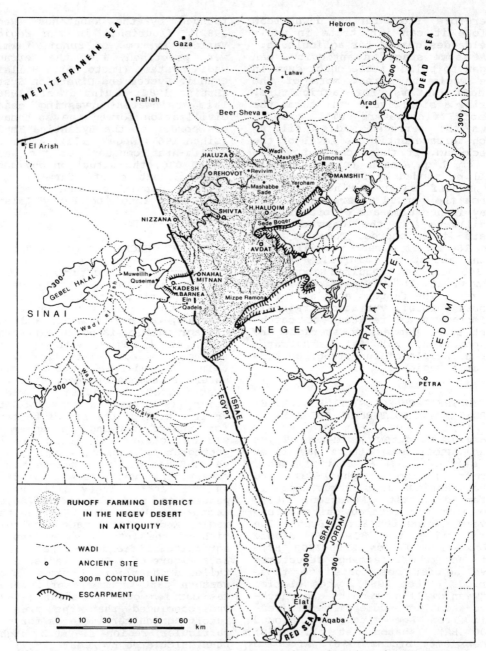

Fig. 2. The location of the runoff farming district in the Negev
(after Bruins 1986:8).

average length of the dams is 17.1 m (= width of the fields). The average length of the terraced fields (in between two check-dams) is 15.4 m. The smallest check-dam is 5.5 m long, the largest 32.5 m. The total length of all the check-dams in the three little wadis is 1233.6 m, and the total area of all the terraced fields is just over 2 hectares. A large amount of energy and work had to be invested indeed to obtain a mere 2 hectares of agricultural fields. As the com-

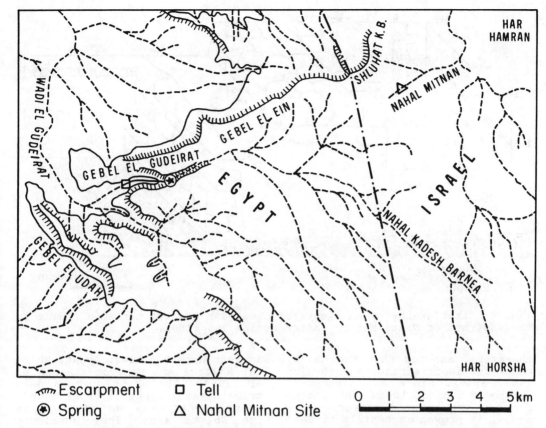

Escarpment   □ **Tell**
   ⊛ **Spring**   △ **Nahal Mitnan Site**

0   1   2   3   4   5 km

Fig. 3. Location of Nahal Mitnan and the catchment area of Wadi el Gudeirat, including the position of the spring of Ein el Gudeirat, and the tell (after Bruins 1986:106).

bined catchment area of the three wadis is about 36 ha, the ratio between runoff receiving area (terraced fields) and runoff producing area is about 1:17 (Bruins 1986). This figure for Horvat Haluqim is very near the average ratio of 1:18 for runoff farms in the central Negev (Kedar 1967).

An excavation in ancient agricultural terraces at Nahal Mitnan in the western central Negev (Fig. 3), not far from the border with Sinai, revealed the stratigraphy of both the check-dam and the sediments (Bruins 1986, 1989). The check-dam is composed of two separate sections (Fig. 4). It seems likely that the five stone courses of the lower dam were not constructed at one time. First the two lower courses may have been built. Terracing the wadi with check-dams enhanced alluvial sedimentation and

checked stream channel erosion. The subsequent aggradation of the wadi bed lowered the relative height of the check-dam above the terraced field. Less runoff water was retained as a result. This necessitated the building of additional stone courses, in order to keep up with the level of alluvial sedimentation. At some stage a new section of the dam was built about 0.5 to 1.5 m upstream from the older part, which rendered the entire construction more durable from a hydro-architectural point of view (Bruins 1986, 1989).

An excavated farmstead next to the terraced wadi of Nahal Mitnan has been dated by Haiman (1982) to Late Byzantine-Early Islamic times. The neat and careful construction of the excavated check-dam seems similar to the precise architecture of the nearby farmstead. It is,

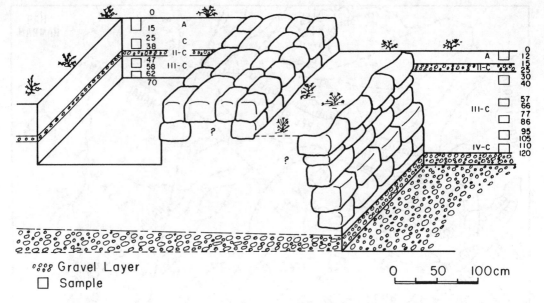

Fig. 4. Stratigraphy of an excavated check-dam and two terraced fields in the wadi-bed of Nahal Mitnan (after Bruins 1986:100).

°⁰₈₈ Gravel Layer
☐ Sample

0   50   100cm

therefore, assumed that the nearby check-dam is of similar age (Bruins 1986, 1989). Since no independent dating was possible on the check-dam and the related terrace sediments, it proved impossible to date the different stages of check-dam additions and subsequent sediment accumulation. The ancient terraced fields are at present filled with sediments to the uppermost part of the check-dams. No erosion has apparently occurred in this terraced part of Nahal Mitnan since the fields were abandoned by the ancient farmers, probably in Early Islamic times.

6 ANCIENT MAN-MADE STONE MOUNDS ON THE HILLSLOPES

Apart from numerous check-dams built in the wadis, also the hillslopes were effected by man in antiquity. Conduits were constructed on hillslopes to channel runoff water to agricultural fields (Hillside Conduit System) as well as to cisterns. Quite extraordinary is the fact that numerous little stone mounds, sometimes in combination with gravel strips and conduits, are found on thousands of hectares of uplands in the vicinity of four

ancient desert cities: Avdat, Shivta, Nizzana and Rehovot (Shanan et al. 1958). The above authors describe several types of stone mounds in the Avdat area and one type in the Shivta area. They attribute these stone mounds to gravel clearing of hillslopes and uplands in order to increase the amount of surface runoff destined for the fields below (Tadmor et al. 1958). Other theories have also been advanced. The name given to these stone heaps by the Bedouin, teleilat el-'anab, meaning grape mounds, has given rise to speculation that grapes were grown here on the hillslopes in ancient times (Mayerson 1959, 1960).

The inherent agricultural problems in such an explanation were outlined by Kedar (1964). He considered the enhancement of soil erosion as the main purpose for building these mounds, so that more soil would accumulate in the terraced wadi-fields. In Kedar's view the stone mounds "were created when man decided to speed up the processes of natural erosion. In order that the slopes should supply him with runoff water and soil, he opened the desert pavement and broke the crust that covers the softened soil underneath. He thus

92

created new conditions for the erosive forces which from now on could wash down the soft soil onto the wadi grounds. This process was originated only by active intervention of man. To lay bare the soil and then allow it to be washed off unhampered into the canals which directed it onto the cultivated plots below, our ancient farmers had to rake together or pick up the stones that formed the hamada cover, and the logical thing to do was to heap them into mounds. The mounds, then, had an origin but not a function. They served no purpose in themselves in ancient agriculture, they were simply dumps of material to be cleared from the ground. They were the by-product of man's endeavour to create cultivable land where the probability of runoff would be highest when it rained somewhere in the area - to bring together soil and water, the two fundamental elements of agriculture, at the most favourable spot. This interpretation is borne out by the invariable correlation of fields of mounds above and cultivable plots below" (Kedar 1957:185).

It seems reasonable to suppose that stone clearance brought about an initial increase in soil erosion. However, a new soil crust will form quickly on the disturbed surface after the first rains, so that the effect of stone clearance on soil erosion appears rather limited. An exposed soil surface, on the other hand, is likely to loose more soil by erosion, even with a crust, than a soil protected by a stone cover.

While Kedar placed the emphasis on soil "harvesting", Shanan (1975) experimentally studied the effect of stone clearance on water "harvesting". He measured that stone clearance brings about an increase in average annual runoff production of 24% on 10% slopes and of nearly 50% on steeper 20% slopes in the present, rather gentle rainfall regime of the central Negev (Shanan et al. 1969; Shanan 1975). These experimental results are as yet most convincing that the prime reason for stone clearance and the subsequent building of stone mounds was to enhance runoff production from the slopes.

Experimental studies were conducted in the Negev highlands by Yair et al. (1978) on the partial area contribution of runoff. It was found in certain geomorphological situations, that a specific part of the slope received more often runoff water than the wadi below. Yair and Shachak (1987) subsequently designed mini-catchments on the hillslope in which they planted a number of different tree species. The initial results appear to be successful. In order to trap the runoff water each tree is partially surrounded downslope by a little semi-circular checkdam built of local stones found on the slope. If Yair and Schachak (1987) are able today to grow trees on certain parts of the hillslopes on runoff water, the ancient farmers may also have been successful to grow grapevines on the slopes? The grapevine theory put forward for the stone mounds by Mayerson (1959, 1960) on philological grounds, first rejected by the "scientists" as unrealistic from an agricultural point of view, may, on new scientific evidence (Yair and Shachak 1987), have to be reconsidered for at least some of the stone mounds. A "scholarly" warning was already sounded by Negev (1983:209), "Ich glaube, dass die moderne Wissenschaft dazu neigt, Tradition und Erinnerungsvermögen der Beduinen zu unterschätzen. Nur den Beduinen verdanken wir die Erhaltung uralter Ortsnamen, wie Abde für Oboda, Khalasa für Elusa, Isbeita für Sobota und andere".

It does still seem unlikely, however, that most of the hundreds of thousands of stone mounds, which do not have a shape to retain runoff waters, could enhance the growth of grapevines on the hillslopes. The majority of the stone mounds seem best explained as being the result of stone clearance to increase runoff production from the hillslopes (Shanan 1975), whereby soil may have been a by-product (Kedar 1957). In view of the lack of concensus and the new results by Yair and Shachak (1987), it seems, nevertheless, worthwhile to renew archaeological and experimental investigations on the ancient man-made stone mounds.

7 VALLEY CHANGES IN WADI EL GUDEIRAT (NORTHEASTERN SINAI)

Some 9 km to the southwest of Nahal Mitnan lies the valley of Ein el Gudeirat (Fig. 3; Photo 2), situated in northeastern Sinai. A prominent regional spring arises in this valley, which has been associated with biblical Kadesh-Barnea (Cohen 1981). Although upper tributaries of Wadi el Gudeirat were terraced in the past for run-off farming, the investigated section of the valley of Ein el Gudeirat was used for irrigation farming with water from the spring (Bruins 1986).

The Late Quaternary history of the area was investigated by Goldberg (1984), who focussed on the Late Pleistocene and found evidence for several depositional and erosional episodes in Wadi el Gudeirat. Goldberg remarked that the reason for these alternating periods have yet to be fully clarified, but initial indication points to deposition during wetter intervals and erosion during drier periods (Goldberg 1984).

The Late Holocene valley history of Ein el Gudeirat could be deciphered in considerable detail (Bruins 1986), due to the presence of various archaeological remains, i.e. Tell el Gudeirat (Cohen 1981) (Photo 2), a number of aquaduct remnants and the presence of charcoal material suited for radiocarbon dating (Bruins and Mook 1987). The detected periods of Late Holocene stream channel sedimentation and erosion (Bruins 1986) can be summarized as follows:

ROMAN FILL DEPOSIT. Aggradation may have taken place in Roman times, as suggested by Goldberg (1984) on the basis of a radiocarbon date in a fill deposit (1755± 105 BP). The precise time-range of this depositional period is unknown, due to lack of data.

INCISION DURING THE EARLY ISLAMIC PERIOD. Downcutting took place after the 7th century AD and prior to the next aggradational period, which began around 1200 AD.

MAIN FILL DEPOSIT (LATE CRUSADER -MAMLUK-EARLY OTTOMAN PERIOD). The most remarkable sedimentation period during the Late Holocene occurred from about AD 1200-1700, when progressive filling raised the wadi bed by some 4 metre.

INCISION SINCE THE LATE OTTOMAN PERIOD UNTIL TODAY. Downcutting and stream channel erosion lowered the wadi bed by some 4 metre since about AD 1700.

7.1 Assessment of possible anthropogenic relationships

The arid zone has traditionally been used by nomadic and semi-nomadic pastoralists for extensive livestock rearing. Archaeological remains in the central Negev were attributed by Rosen (1987) to Byzantine nomadism. The rather one-sided economy of specialized pastoralism meant that nomads could never exist on their own without adjacent sedentary societies (Khazanov 1984). Pastoral nomads produce a luxury product, meat, for which they need a market in settled societies. They sell or exchange their animals for farming produce and other goods, as cereals constitute the staple food of many pastoralists (Marx 1982). The dependency of pastoral nomads on sedentary farmers might suggest that pastoralism declined with the departure of the farmers from the central Negev in Late Byzantine and Early Arab times. Hardly anything is known, however, about the Late Holocene history of pastoralism in the central Negev and northeastern Sinai. The impact of ancient pastoralists on the landscape cannot be assessed, therefore.

Photo 1. A tributary wadi in northeastern Sinai, situated in the catchment area of Wadi el Gudeirat, upstream from the valley oasis of Ein el Gudeirat. The wadi was probably terraced for runoff farming in the Byzantine period. Local Bedouin farm the ancient terraced fields, which were not affected by erosion (after Bruins 1986:184).

Photo 2. The valley oasis of Ein el Gudeirat in northeastern Sinai, just downstream from the main outlet of the spring. The tell appears in the centre of the photo (after Bruins 1986:119).

Most archaeological remains in the area belong to the Bronze Age, Iron Age, or Byzantine-Early Arab period (Haiman 1982, pers. comm.). This conclusion is substantiated by radiocarbon dates from northeastern Sinai (Bruins 1986; Bruins and Mook 1987). Historical documents studied by Mayerson (1963) seem to indicate the absence of runoff farming southwest of Shivta in the late 4th century AD. The latter city constituted the border of the oecumene or settled area, whereas the inner desert began southwest of Shivta, according to the narrative of Nilus the Ascetic. However, by the Late Byzantine period the habitated area had extended itself west and south for a considerable distance, as indicated by the itinerarium of Antoninus of Placentia (ca AD 570) as well as by the Nizzana papyri (Mayerson 1963).

Hence there is no apparent relationship between the agricultural history in the catchment area of Wadi el Gudeirat and the Roman fill, although the latter is poorly dated. Sedentary runoff farming finally ceased in the central Negev and northeastern Sinai during the Early Arab period, perhaps in the 8th century AD. Could this have led to incision in the valley of Ein el Gudeirat? The possible deterioration of abandoned runoff-farming terraces in the tributaries of Wadi el Gudeirat might have supplied more sediment to the valley of Ein el Gudeirat, situated downstream, causing perhaps aggradation rather than incision.

There seem to be no historical and archaeological data about any land-use in the area in the period from AD 1200-1700. It appears difficult, therefore, to invoke a human cause to explain the most remarkable accumulation of valley sediments during the Late Holocene in the above period. Sedimentation ceased from about 1700 and since then erosion appears to have been the dominant process in the stream channel, which has cut some 4 metre in the previously deposited sediments. There is no knowledge of any change in land-use, if at all, in the desert of northeastern Sinai around 1700, when the geomorphic regime in the stream channel of Wadi el Gudeirat changed from depositional to erosive (Bruins 1986).

7.2 Time relationships with palaeoclimatic trends

ROMAN FILL DEPOSIT. Although the Roman fill has not been well dated, it is noteworthy that a dramatic rise occurred in the level of the Dead Sea from ca 100 BC-AD 40, which is understood to reflect an increase in rainfall (Klein 1982).

INCISION (ca AD 700-1200). Evidence of widespread drought in the eastern Mediterranean during the 7th and 8th centuries AD is quoted by Lamb (1977:428). Red loams, containing Byzantine artifacts, are covered by coastal dunes in the central coastal plain of Israel (Issar 1968), which is understood to indicate increased aridity following the Byzantine period (Issar and Tsoar 1987).

MAIN FILL DEPOSIT (ca AD 1200-1700). Well-dated and detailed proxy-climatic data are available for the region from about 1100. These data have been derived from lake-level variations in the Dead Sea (Klein 1981) and from tree rings of a Juniperus phoenicea tree which grew on Gebel Halal in northern Sinai from 1185-1968 (Waisel and Liphschitz 1968). From 1170-1700 the climate was generally wetter than usual, especially for the periods 1170-1320, 1360-1430, and 1470-1650 (Klein 1981).

INCISION (ca 1700-today). From 1700-1880 the climate was very dry, but became more moist at the end of the 19th century and during the first decades of the 20th century. The present century can be regarded as relatively dry.

8 CONCLUSIONS

There seems to be a rather convincing time-coincidence between climatic variations and alternating periods of stream channel deposition and erosion in the valley of Ein el Gudeirat, which was not terraced for runoff agriculture. These alternating periods during the Late Holocene seem to have a duration of several hundred years each. Wadi-bed sedimentation tends to occur during a relatively wet climatic period. Wadi-bed incision and erosion seem to be prevalent during a relatively dry climatic period (Bruins 1986).

Preliminary conclusions of a similar nature were reached by Goldberg (1984) for Late Pleistocene alluvial sequences in the same area. It should be noted, however, that the periods of deposition and sedimentation distinguished by Goldberg (1984) for the Late Pleistocene seem to have a duration of many thousands of years. The Late Holocene record, described above, is of a much finer time resolution. The recording mechanisms in the environment of both climate and landscape history are usually neither continuous nor sufficiently detailed. Parameters as rainfall intensity and duration, for example, cannot usually be obtained from proxy-climatic indicators.

Many questions, therefore, remain unanswered and possible causes can only be suggested: "More rainfall may lead to a differential increase in vegetation: a slight increase on the hillside catchment and a much more dramatic increase in the stream channels, due to different soil depths and moisture storage capabilities on the hillslopes and valleys, respectively. Such a development might help to slow down silt laden runoff streams in the wadis, thereby perhaps inducing aggradation. This is, however, but one aspect of the complex and intricate reaction of the landscape to more rainfall... More research is needed to unravel the intricate processes that cause aggradation and incision in relation to wet and dry periods, respectively" (Bruins 1986:192-193).

There exists no apparent time-relationship between the known human history in the catchment area of Wadi el Gudeirat and the detected periods of wadi-bed sedimentation and incision. The impact of climatic variations, although not yet understood in terms of climo-geomorphic processes, appears to have been the likely cause. In other wadis, terraced by man for runoff farming purposes, the picture is usually quite different. Here the impact of man on the stream channel history has to be taken very much into account. The respective effect of both man and climate has to be investigated in each catchment area and the effect of either factor may be super-imposed on top of the other. In general terms it can be stated that the impact of man on the desert landscape of the central Negev and northeastern Sinai has been quite considerable. Hundreds of thousands of stone mounds were built on the hillslopes and thousands of check-dams were constructed in numerous wadis for the purpose of runoff agriculture. These man-made constructions in the landscape definitely caused sedimentation in the terraced wadis. In the course of time, even after their abandonment by the ancient farmers, many terraced wadis did not suffer erosion (Photo 1), whereas many non-terraced wadis often appear today in a badly eroded state, sometimes completely stripped of sediments and soils. The impact of ancient man, therefore, on the desert landscape of the region can be regarded as very positive. The ancient man-made constructions contributed to erosion control in the terraced valleys and enlarged the regional carrying capacity. Thus instead of desertification and erosion, ancient man stabilized the soils in the wadis, increased their thickness and succeeded in greening the desert through rainwater-harvesting techniques.

REFERENCES

Aharoni, Y., M.Evenari, L.Shanan and N.H.Tadmor 1960. The ancient desert agriculture of the Negev. V. An Israelite settlement at Ramat Matred. Israel Exploration Journal 10:23-36, 97-111.

Bruins, H.J. 1986. Desert environment and agriculture in the central Negev and Kadesh-Barnea during historical times. Nijkerk: Midbar Foundation.

Bruins, H.J. 1989. Ancient agricultural terraces at Nahal Mitnan. Atiqot (in press).

Bruins, H.J., M.Evenari and U.Nessler 1986. Rainwater-harvesting agriculture for food production in arid zones: the challenge of the African famine. Applied Geography 6:13-32.

Bruins, H.J.,
M.Evenari and A.Rogel 1987.
Runoff farming management and
climate. In L.Berkofsky and M.G.
Wurtele (eds.), Progress in
desert research, p.3-14. Totowa
(NJ), Rowman and Littlefield.
Bruins, H.J. and W.G.Mook 1987.
Radiocarbon dating in the north-
eastern Sinai desert (Ein el
Gudeirat, Kadesh-Barnea). In
H.T.Waterbolk and W.G.Mook
(eds.), Proceedings of the 2nd
international symposium on ar-
chaeology and 14C. PACT, Council
of Europe (in press).
Cohen, R. 1976.
Excavations at Horvat Haluqim.
Atiqot 11:34-50.
Cohen, R. 1981.
Excavations at Kadesh-Barnea,
1976-1978. Biblical Archeologist
44:93-107.
Cohen, R. 1986.
The settlement of the central
Negev in the light of archaeology
and literary sources during the
4th-1st millennium B.C.E. PhD
Thesis, The Hebrew University of
Jerusalem.
Danin, A. 1983.
Desert vegetation of Israel and
Sinai. Jerusalem: Cana Publish-
ing House.
Evenari, M.,
L.Shanan and N.H.Tadmor 1971.
The Negev - The challenge of a
desert. Cambridge (MA): Harvard
University Press 1982. Second
enlarged edition.
Gibson, M. 1982.
The breakdown of ancient desert
civilizations. In UNITAR, Alter-
native strategies for desert
development and management. Vol.
4. Desert Management p.1227-
1237. Pergamon Press.
Gihon, M. 1967.
The Negev frontier. In M.Gihon
and S.Applebaum (eds.), The 7th
international congress of Roman
frontier studies. Tel Aviv: Tel-
Aviv University Printing Press.
Goldberg, P. 1984.
Late Quaternary history of Qadesh
Barnea, northeastern Sinai. Zeit-
schrift für Geomorphologie N.F.
28:193-217.
Haiman, M. 1982.
Nahal Mitnan. Israel Exploration
Journal 32:265-266.
Haiman, M. in press.
Agricultural settlements of Ramat
Barnea in the Late Byzantine

period. Atiqot.
Issar, A.S. 1968.
Geology of the central coastal
plain of Israel. Israel Journal
of Earth Sciences 17:16-29.
Issar, A.S. and H.Tsoar 1987.
Who is to blame for the deserti-
fication of the Negev, Israel?
In Proceedings of the Vancouver
Symposium, The influence of
climatic change and climatic
variability on the hydrologic
regime and water resources. IAHS
Publ. no.168:577-583.
Kedar, Y. 1957.
Water and soil from the desert:
Some ancient agricultural
achievements in the central
Negev. The Geographical Journal
123:179-187.
Kedar, Y. 1964.
More about the teleilat el-'anab
in the Negeb. Bulletin of the
American Schools of Oriental
Research 176:47-49.
Kedar, Y. 1967.
The ancient agriculture in the
Negev mountains. Jerusalem:
Bialik Institute (in Hebrew).
Khazanov, A.M. 1984.
Nomads and the outside world.
Cambridge: Cambridge University
Press.
Klein, C. 1981.
The influence of rainfall over
the catchment area on the fluctu-
ations of the level of the Dead
Sea since the 12th century.
Israel Meteorological Research
Papers 3:29-58.
Klein, C. 1982.
Morphological evidence of lake
level changes, western shore of
the Dead Sea. Israel Journal of
Earth Sciences 31:67-94.
Lamb, H.H. 1977.
Climate - Present, past and
future. Vol. 2. Climatic history
and the future. London: Methuen.
Marx, E. 1982.
New trends in the study of pas-
toral nomads. Nomadic Peoples
10:65-68.
Mayerson, Ph. 1959.
Ancient agricultural remains in
the central Negeb: The Teleilat
el-'Anab. Bulletin of the
American Schools of Oriental
Research 153:19-31.
Mayerson, Ph. 1960.
The ancient agricultural remains
of the central Negeb: Methodol-
ogy and dating criteria. Bulle-
tin of the American Schools of

Oriental Research 160:27-37.

Mayerson, Ph. 1963.
The desert of southern Palestine according to Byzantine sources. Proceedings of the American Philosophical Society 107:160-172.

Negev, A. 1981.
Les Nabateans au Negev. Le Christianisme au Negev. La vie économique et sociale a l'époque Byzantine. Le Monde de la Bible 18:4-46.

Negev, A. 1982.
Numismatics and Nabataean chronology. Palestine Exploration Quarterly 114:19-128.

Negev, A. 1983.
Tempel, Kirchen und Zisternen. Stuttgart: Calwer Verlag.

Rosen, S. 1987.
Byzantine nomadism in the Negev: Results from the emergency survey. Journal of Field Archaeology 14:29-42.

Shanan, L. 1975.
Rainfall and runoff relationships in small watersheds in the Avdat region of the Negev desert highlands. PhD Thesis, The Hebrew University of Jerusalem.

Shanan, L.,
M.Evenari and N.H.Tadmor 1969.
Ancient technology and modern science applied to desert agriculture. Endeavour 28:68-72.

Shanan, L.,
N.Tadmor and M.Evenari 1958.
The ancient desert agriculture of the Negev. II. Utilization of runoff from small watersheds in the Abde (Ovdat) region. Ktavim 9:107-129.

Tadmor, N.H., M.Evenari,
L.Shanan and D.Hillel 1958.
The ancient desert agriculture in the Negev. I. Gravel mounds and strips near Shivta. Ktavim 8:127-151.

Unesco 1979.
Map of the world distribution of arid regions. MAB Technical Notes 7. Paris, Unesco.

Waisel, Y. and N.Liphschitz 1968.
Dendrochronological studies in Israel. II. Juniperus Phoenica of north and central Sinai. La-Yaaran 1:2-22 (in Hebrew, with English summary, p.63-67).

Yaalon, D.H. and J.Dan 1974.
Accumulation and distribution of loess-derived deposits in the semi-arid and desert fringe areas of Israel. Zeitschrift für Geo-morphologie N.F. 20:91-105.

Yair, A.,
D.Sharon and H.Lavee 1978.
An instrumented watershed for the study of partial area contribution of runoff in the arid zone. Zeitschrift für Geomorphologie N.F. 29:71-82.

Yair, A. and M.Shachak 1987.
Studies in watershed ecology of an arid area. In L.Berkofsky and M.G.Wurtele (eds.), Progress in desert research, p.145-193. Totowa (NJ), Rowman and Littlefield.

Man's Role in the Shaping of the Eastern Mediterranean Landscape, Bottema, Entjes-Nieborg & van Zeist (eds)
© *1990 Balkema, Rotterdam. ISBN 90 6191 138 9*

Man-instigated coastal changes along the Israeli shore of the Mediterranean in ancient times

9

Avner Raban
Center for Maritime Studies, University of Haifa, Israel

ABSTRACT: The first phase of urbanism along the Israeli Mediterranean coastline took place some 4000 years ago. This settling process coincided with the final phase of the post-glacial transgression and isostatic movements that established the coastline roughly at its present location. This newly established "status quo" initiated a series of coastal processes of wave erosion, long-shore sand movements and depositions, and a rapid process of siltation of estuaries and other natural havens. The new settlers had to take measures in order to keep their harbours functioning by altering the natural processes, or harnessing them for improving the quality of their havens. The archaeological and geomorphological studies at and around these ancient coastal sites have enabled us to reconstruct some of these projects; riverine siltation was controlled by damming the lower parts of river courses and altering their outlets. Navigable channels were cut in the rocky segments of the shore on the lee side of natural promontories, leading to inner harbour basins behind the newly created coastal sandbars. The drainage system of the coastal plain was perfected by rock-cut passages for rivers - directing their discharge in a way that would keep havens silt-free. Later, the long-shore currents were directed through flushing channels along artificial free-standing moles and rocky promontories. Wave-carried sand was trapped within artificial confines and used as a constructive component in building wide breakwaters and enabling the down-current shore to remain silt-free. Seasonal beaches were stabilized and protected by retaining groynes and seawalls. Coastal sand dunes were stabilized by artificial cover and great efforts were made to control the additional sand, in order to maintain functioning harbours. Most of the changing populations of the coast carried these measures on through the ages until later antiquity.

1 INTRODUCTION

The present Mediterranean coastline of Israel presents a slightly curved line, turning from SW-NE in its southern part to a meridional course in its northern section. Only in one place, the "Nose" of Mount Carmel, is there a Cretaceous range reaching into the sea, defining the south edge of the bay of Haifa. The rest of the coastline is well defined by long-shore, low ridges of aeolianites dating to the Pleistocene. In some places these ridges are buried under sand dunes or gapped by river outlets (Nir 1982, 1985).

The aeolianite ridges contain interbedded strata of gray sand, red loam and calcarenite (Gvirtzman et al. 1984), which represent sequences of different climatic, topographic and other environmental conditions during the varying land-sea relations throughout the Pleistocene. The fluctuating sea level of this geological period shifted the coastline to the east and west of the present one and created a series of such ridges, some of which are now submerged on the continental shelf and others, parallel to the present coastline, are on the coastal plain. The main source of beach sediments is the quartzite sand originating from the Nile delta and carried by the long-shore current. These sediments are deposited on the shore by the breaking waves, creating beaches and sandbars (Nir 1988). At present only few rivers are of perennial waterflow with sufficient energy for keeping their outlets from being blocked by coastal sandbars during the summer season. The absence of tidal fluctuation in this part of the Mediterranean (with daily amplitude not exceeding 30 cm), the lack of topographic gradient for the river courses across the coastal plain and the long summer drought are the main reasons for this phenomenon. The post-glacial transgression which raised the erosional baselevel and hampered the drainage system of the coastal plain produced marshy lagoons and seasonally inundated areas in the low basins between the long-shore kurkar (aeolianite) ridges, which slowly filled with clay and silt brought from the hilly hinterland by the rivers' winter floods. In places where the coastal ridge was low, buried below the sand or gapped by Pleistocene river courses, the wave-carried sand was deposited in the gaps and quantities were even carried farther inland by the prevailing westerly winds, creating sand dunes and sand fields within the coastal plain (Bakler 1988; Nir 1989). These topographic characteristics of the Holocene processes are predominant in the western part of the coastal plain, mostly between the two inshore kurkar ridges (Fig. 1). It is quite obvious that such characteristics of the coastline and its immediate hinterland were most unfavourable for either maritime activity or coastal human habitation. Lacking bays, coves, capes, offshore islands or any other type of sheltered water, the Israeli coastline could hardly offer natural havens other than the temporarily existing estuaries (of the lower courses) of the coastal rivers during the rapidly rising sea level of the early Holocene. Once this last transgressional trend slowed down, due to the stabilization of post-glacial climate, these estuaries soon were silted up and their outlets blocked (Fig. 2).

This process of siltation, the

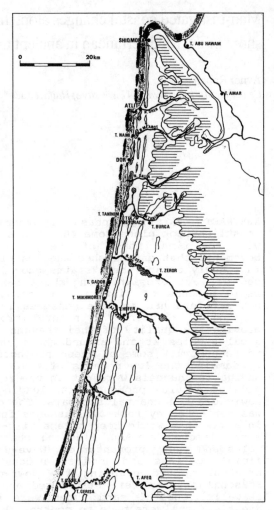

Fig. 1. Typical series of kurkar ridges along the coastline south of Haifa.

affected gradient of the draining system of the coastal plain and the continuous process of petrification of long-shore sand ridges, all contributing towards the creation of coastal marshes, would make this area poorly suited for agricultural use and hardly accessible by either long-shore or cross-country trade routes. These harsh facts were known and fully comprehended by the people who came to settle this area since at least the late 3rd or early 2nd millennium BC.

We know almost nothing about the settlers and the settlements along this shore during the Early Bronze

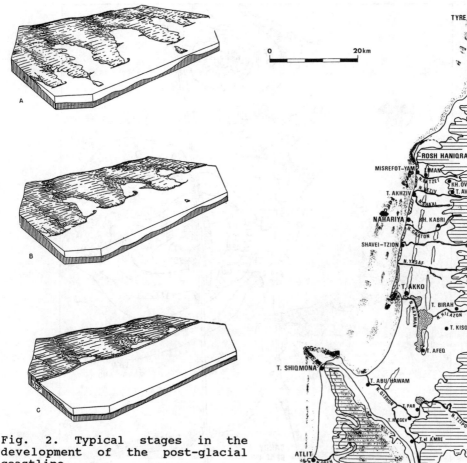

Fig. 2. Typical stages in the development of the post-glacial coastline.

Fig. 3. Location of the sites on the north coast of Israel.

Age, due to almost total absence of archaeological data from this period at the present coastline. Among dozens of ancient urban sites along this coast, none was settled as such during the urban phases of EB II-IV (2900-2100 BC), with the single exception of Ashkelon in the south, where pottery of these periods was recently found (Stager pers. comm.) Of earlier periods we do have village sites in currently submerged areas up to 12 m below Mediterranean sea level (Galili and Weinstein-Evron 1985; Raban 1983a). Some of these sites were submerged as a result of recent tectonic faulting (Galili et al. 1988), others may have been submerged during the eustatic transgression of the Postglacial. If so, it seems that this rise of sea level continued along the Levantine coast

until the Early Bronze Age and maybe even later, until some 4000 years before present (Raban 1985a). At the present stage of research, we know about the inhabitants of these prehistoric coastal villages that they fished with nets and harvested the sea floor for molluscs, using free diving (breath-holding) techniques (Galili 1987). It is also clear that they were aware of the shallow water table and the interface phenomenon, which enabled them to extract fresh water from shallow hand-dug wells (Raban and Galili 1985). But how man has

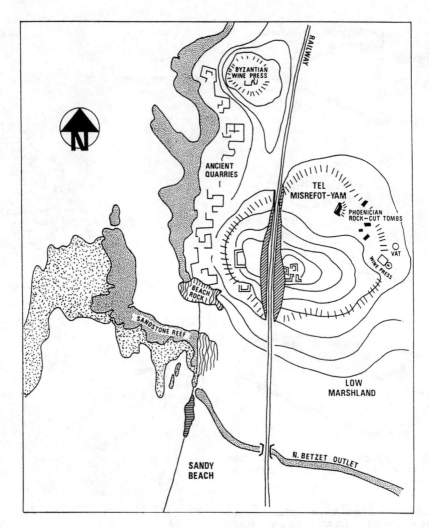

Fig. 4. Plan of the coastal features at Misrefot-Yam.

coped with the problems characteristic of the Israeli coast of the
Mediterranean, we know only for the
time since this coastline became
relatively stable and much the same
as it is nowadays, some 4000 years
ago.

2 KEEPING ESTUARIES SILT-FREE

Many of the towns which were first
settled along the Israeli shore
around 4000 years ago are at sites
near what was, at that time, a
tidal river outlet. Along some 200
km of shoreline there are about
twenty such sites. The currently

sand-filled estuaries of the MBIIa
period disguise the ancient features in most cases. Yet in many
instances the topographic outlines
of the time when these urban sites
were settled, can be traced (Raban
1987a,b). Among these sites one can
follow the measures taken by the
settlers in order to either prevent, slow down or intercept the
siltation and blocking process of
the nearby, protected body of water
that enabled them to keep up their
maritime activities and to offer
services to seaborne trade.

At the site of Misrefot-Yam (Fig.
3), located on the coastal kurkar
ridge to the north of the nowadays

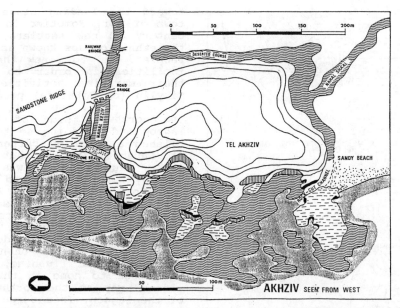

Fig. 5. Reconstruction of the ancient, human-instigated topography at Akhziv.

sand-filled river gap of Nahal Betzet, a rock-cut outlet was artificially dug through the abrasion platform at the foots of the settlement to the west. This artificial channel, some 8-10 m wide and over 30 m long, with its outlet facing north, away from the weather, could be used for keeping a free flow of water from the sand-blocked lagoon on the lee side of the settlement and as a navigable channel for vessels using this body of water as a safe haven (Fig. 4). A few kilometres further south, a similar location was selected for the harbour site of Akhziv, at the outlet of the river Keziv. At Akhziv the artificial alteration of the natural features was even more complex. Finding out that this particular river carried large loads of pebbles, silt and mud from the hilly hinterland during the winter floods, the people of Akhziv built a dam across the inland tip of its estuary and cut the river an alternative course to the sea on the north side of their town, across the low coastal kurkar ridge. To the southwest of the settlement, at the north edge of the 300-m-wide estuary, they dug a 3-m-wide navigable channel, which would give marine vessels access

to the lagoon behind the blocking sand-bar and to leeward of the town walls (Fig. 5). Similar measures were taken at other sites along the coast, such as Michmoret, which is located on the northern edge of the ancient estuary of Nahal Alexander in the Sharon Plain, and maybe also at nowadays land-locked sites such as Akko, Tell Abu Hawam, Yaffo and Tel Poleg (Raban 1985a).

3 FREE CIRCULATION OF WATER IN ANCHORAGES

With the amounts of wave-carried sand along the coast of Israel every body of water even partially protected from the full force of the surge, will soon be silted up and be a terminal deposition site for the wave load. Such natural processes may be prevented only if an ample flushing current is either naturally or artificially operating through the confined area of water. These facts seem to have been fully comprehended by the coastal inhabitants at least since the Late Bronze Age.

At Dor, just north of the ancient estuary of Nahal Dalia, a series of close-by rocky islets offered a natural haven on their lee side. This

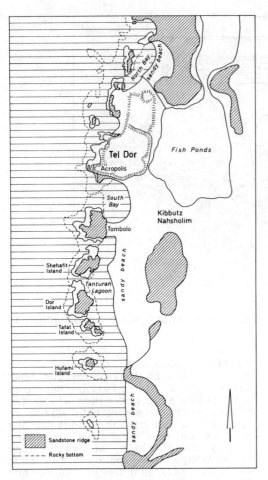

Fig. 6. Plan of Dor and its present-day coastal area.

toward the landing stages of the town of Dor. Sometime in the 13th century BC new settlers, part of the ethnic groups known as the "Sea People", had to renew the harbour facilities in order to maintain their maritime activities. These Sikyliu (or Sikalaia) people cut a channel across the rocky shelf at the northwest side of the long lagoon and in doing so they established a flushing current within it (Raban 1987b). At that time the inner, eastern lagoon was probably already blocked off from the main one. So the Late Bronze Age quays were located along the south side of the town, at the north end of the main lagoon (Fig. 7). A further rise of the sea level during the preceding centuries changed this well-controlled flushing, enabling the surge to come in through the widened gap at the northwest side of the lagoon. This surge soon deposited quantities of sand at the beach on the opposite side and a blocking tombolo to the south. This natural process, first instigated by human activity, brought about the present topographic situation, in which the northern part of the original Bronze Age lagoon is separated from the rest of it by a tombolo and has turned into a wide bay, unsuited for a harbour.

The same principle of rock-cut flush channels was to be used later at Dor, during the Hellenistic and Roman periods, on the northern side of the town (Raban and Galili 1985), as well as in other Levantine harbours, such as Tyre, Sidon, Akko and Caesarea (Raban 1988).

4 ARTIFICIAL DRAINAGE OF THE COASTAL PLAIN

From the above description of the post-glacial characteristic features of the coastal plain, one might understand the necessity of perfecting or even artificially remodelling the natural drainage system in order to avoid the development of coastal marshes, the creation of hydromorphic soils and the gradual salinization of the cultivated basins. A survey of the lower courses of the rivers crossing the central part of the coastal plain of Israel, between Haifa and Tel Aviv, shows that this is proba-

unique natural feature along the Israeli coastline enabled people to locate their port town at the north end of this lagoon, which was then connected to another lagoon on the eastern side of the urban site (Fig. 6).

The eastern lagoon was of the type of haven described above for Misrefot-Yam, Akhziv and Michmoret and was first used as such in the same period, MBIIa (Raban and Galili 1985). Yet, extensive wave erosion around the islets protecting the lagoon to the south eventually produced an opening for incoming wave-carried sand to be deposited in the lagoon, gradually creating sand bars and tombolos between the islets and the main shore and blocking the navigational passage

Fig. 7. Reconstruction of the coastal topography at Tel
Dor around 1200 BC.

bly what the ancient settlers did.
The main kurkar ridge along the
coast (T-2; see Gvirtzman et al.
1984) was dissected by artificially
cut channels, either deepening the
original river courses or creating
new ones. These artificial water
passages functioned successfully,
as is attested by the fact that in
most cases no hydromorphic soils
were found in the low basins east
of them (Butrimovitz 1971). In some
cases the rock-cut channels were
made purely for better drainage of
the coastal plain (Nir 1959), but

in at least one case they were wide
and deep enough (almost to sea
level) to carry river navigation
all the way to the nearby settlement.

This is the case with the rock-
cut passage, almost 20 m deep and
7-8 m wide, across the ridge on
which Tel Poleg is situated. This
MBIIa town is located on a kurkar
ridge, some 1.5 km away from the
present shore. Whereas there is a
gap of more than one kilometre in
the coastal cliff, at the outlet
and ancient estuary of Nahal Poleg,

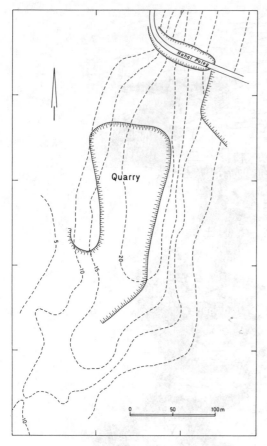

Fig. 8. Plan of the MBII site and rock-cut passage at Tel Poleg (after Gophna 1973).

there was no adequate natural passage or even topographic depression in the main ridge to the east for this river to cross through. The artificial passage radically changed the local topography, connecting the lower course of the river with the marshy depression on

the east side of the main ridge, thus creating a perennially-controlled lagoon lake in this depression. This body of fresh water, with a navigable approach from the open sea, not only controlled the water table of the surrounding plain, but also gave additional importance to the settlement at Tel Poleg and some other MBIIa sites along its shore (Gophna and Ayalon 1980, 1982). The relation between the fortification lines of Tel Poleg and the rock-cut passage may suggest that both were made by the same people, early in the second millennium BC (Gophna 1973; Fig. 8). As a matter of fact, all other rock-cut passages were associated with nearby sites of that period. This is the case with the rock-cut passage for Nahal Hame'arot and the MBIIa site at Tel Nami, the rock-cut passage for Nahal Dalia and the agricultural territory of Dor, and the passage of Nahal Oren with the nearby MBII site at Atlit (Raban 1987a).

5 CONSTRUCTIVE USE OF WAVE-CARRIED SAND

As discussed above, the coastal inhabitants of Palestine were well aware of the delicate equilibrium of wave erosion versus sand deposition and they took measures to control these natural processes, a thing that has often been neglected in the recent past (Nir 1988). In one case the coastal inhabitants not only managed to control the shifting sand and to keep it out of their anchorages and harbour basins, but also to channel the sand into constructive use. This case is the construction of the free-standing moles and breakwaters of Sebastos. The great artificial

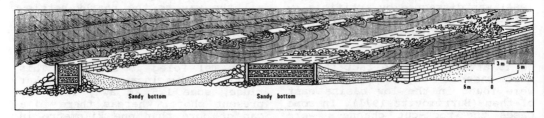

Fig. 9. Schematic block diagram across the main breakwater of Sebastos (the harbour of Caesarea) during the initial phase of its construction.

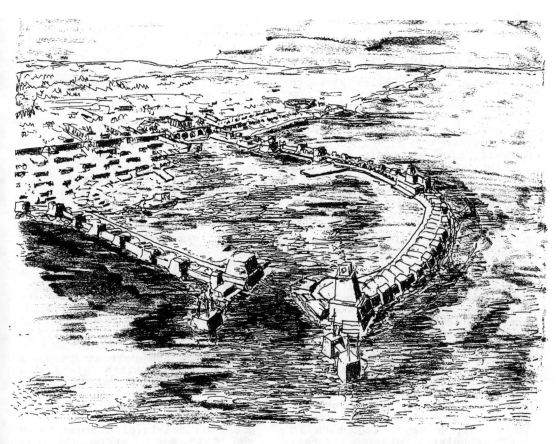

Fig. 10. Artist's rendering of the Herodian harbour of Caesarea.

harbour of Caesarea (named Sebastos) was built by the Jewish King Herod between 21 and 10 BC (Josephus, Jewish Wars I.410-414; Jewish Antiquities XV.331-338). An artificial basin of still water off a straight coastline was created by laying moles, 60-70 m wide and almost 1000 m long, on the floor of the open sea. These moles were constructed to serve multiple purposes: breaking the wave energy, absorbing this energy and projecting some of it back into the open sea, carrying storage facilities for the goods and boarding hostels for the sailors, and having mooring berths with loading and unloading platforms. Recent underwater research of these moles, which have subsided tectonically by 5-6 m since antiquity, has proved that this daring feat of engineering was made possible through intimate knowledge of the local coastal processes.

The vast moles were built by sinking wooden-framed caissons of conglomerate mixed with hydraulic cement (Oleson 1985) in lines onto the sea floor, thus forming walls of large chambers up to the contemporary sea level. The surge, which would constantly flood the top of these walls, would deposit its load of sand in the chambers and eventually fill them up to sea level (Fig. 9). Then the sea and its winter storms were left to do the job of filling-in the moles (this process may have taken 3-4 years (Raban 1985b)), and when completed the above water superstructures were built by human hands. By trapping over 100,000 cu m of sand in this way, the harbour engineers not only saved a large portion of building material that otherwise would have had to be quarried on land and carried to the site in barges, but they also reduced the risk that their basin under construction would silt up before its flushing system could be made operational.

It seems as if similar attempts to slow down sand deposition by "storing" significant quantities of it, had taken place some 1800 years earlier, when the MBII people of Akko quarried the sandbar that was gradually blocking their estuarine harbour at the outlet of the Na'aman (Belus), digging over a million cubic metres of sand to be used for the fortification of their town. Given the present annual rate of new sand supply in this part of the Haifa bay, a few generations may have passed before this sand deficit had been replenished and the beach had been restored (Carmel et al. 1984). This calculation might account for the otherwise unexplained fact that at Akko five such ramparts were built one on top of the other within a period of less than 300 years (Dothan 1976; Raban 1983b).

Finally, the marine engineers of Herod added to the great moles of the harbour at Caesarea a unique external feature to which Josephus referred as "prokumatia" (toward the waves), a hapax legomenon in Greek vocabulary. This was a subsidiary breakwater, a rather humble structure that hardly reached sea level and was segmented by a series of openings (Fig. 10). If we properly comprehend the genius of these ancient engineers, it looks as though the sole purpose of the "prokumatia" was to cause breaking of the waves some 20-30 m away from the seawall of the main moles, in much the same way it was done when these moles were built (see above). Yet, here the openings would allow the rip current to carry away much of the deposited sand (maybe there was more sand in the settling zones behind the subsidiary breakwater during summer time and less during the winter?) leaving the space between the two structures deep enough to properly serve as a wave absorber.

REFERENCES

Bakler, N. 1988.
Regional Geology. In Z.Herzog, G.Rapp and O.Negbi (eds.), Excavations at Tel Michal, Israel, p.198-202. Minneapolis, University of Minnesota Press.
Butrimovitz, Y. 1971.
About the artificial passages in the eastern kurkar ridge of the Carmel coastal plain. Menashe County Press (in Hebrew).
Carmel, Z.,
D.L.Imman and A.Golik 1984.
Transport of Nile sand along the southeastern Mediterranean coast. Proceedings 19th Coastal Engineering Conference, ASCE:1282-1290.
Dothan, M. 1976.
Akko: interim excavation report, first season, 1973/4. BASOR 224: 1-48.
Galili, E. 1987.
A Late Pre-Pottery Neolithic B site on the Sea Floor at Atlit, Mitekufat Haeven. Journal of the Israel Prehistoric Society 20:50-71.
Galili, E. and
M.Weinstein-Evron 1985.
Prehistory and paleoenvironments of submerged sites along the Carmel coast of Israel. Paléorient 11/1:37-52.
Galili, E., M.Weinstein-Evron and A.Ronen 1988.
Holocene sea-level changes based on submerged archaeological sites off the northern Carmel coast in Israel. Quaternary Research 29:36-42.
Gophna, R. 1973.
The Middle Bronze Age II fortifications at Tel Poleg. Eretz Israel 11:111-119 (in Hebrew).
Gophna, R. and E.Ayalon 1980.
Survey of the Central Coastal Plain, 1978-1979, settlement pattern of the MBIIa. Tel-Aviv 7:147-151.
Gophna, R. and E.Ayalon 1982.
A fortified MBIIa site at Ain Zurekiyeh in the Poleg Basin. Tel-Aviv 9:69-78.
Gvirtzman, G., E.Shachnai, N.Bakler and S.Ilani 1984.
Stratigraphy of the kurkar group (quaternary) of the coastal plain of Israel. Geological Survey of Irsael, Current Research 1983-1984:70-82.
Nir, D. 1959.
Artificial outlet of Mount Carmel valleys through the coastal "kurkar" ridge. Israel Exploration Journal 9: 46-54.

Nir, Y. 1982.
Israel and Sinai, coastal morphology. In M.L.Schwartz (ed.), Encyclopedia of Beaches and Coastal Environment, p.86-98. Stroudsburg, Hutchinson Ross.

Nir, Y. 1985.
Israel. Chapter 70 in E.C.F.Bird and M.L.Schwartz (eds.), The World's Coastlines, p.505-511. New York, Van Norstrand Reinhold.

Nir, Y. 1988.
Sedimentological aspects of the Israel and Sinai Mediterranean Coasts. GSI 39/88, Jerusalem (in Hebrew).

Nir, Y. 1989.
Beaches and Dunes. In A.Raban, The Harbours of Caesarea Maritima. Vol. 1, The site and the excavations, p.21-25. BAR International Series 491.

Oleson, J.P. 1985.
Herod and Vitruvius: preliminary thoughts on harbour engineering at Sebastos, the harbour of Caesarea Maritima. In A.Raban (ed.), Harbour Archaeology, p.165-172. BAR International Series 257.

Raban, A. 1983a.
Submerged prehistoric sites off the Mediterranean coast of Israel. In P.M.Masters and N.C.Fellming (eds.), Quaternary Coastlines, p.215-232. London, Academic Press.

Raban, A. 1983b.
The Biblical port of Akko on Israel's coast. Archaeology 38/1: 60-61.

Raban, A. 1985a.
The ancient harbours of Israel in Biblical times. In A.Raban (ed.), Harbour Archaeology, p.11-44. BAR International Series 257.

Raban, A. 1985b.
Caesarea Maritima 1983-1984. International Journal of Nautical Archaeology 14/2:155-177.

Raban, A.1987a.
Alternated river courses during the Bronze Age along the Israeli coastline. In Déplacements des lignes de rivage en méditerranée d'après les données de l'archéologie, p.173-199. Paris, CNRS.

Raban, A. 1987b.
The Harbour of the Sea People at Dor. Biblical Archaeologist 50/2: 118-126.

Raban, A. 1988.
Coastal processes and ancient harbour engineering. In A.Raban (ed.), Archaeology of coastal changes, p.185-208. - BAR International Series 404.

Raban, A. and E.Galili 1985.
Recent maritime archaeological research in Israel: a preliminary report. International Journal of Nautical Archaeology 14/4:321-356.

Man's Role in the Shaping of the Eastern Mediterranean Landscape, Bottema, Entjes-Nieborg & van Zeist (eds)
© *1990 Balkema, Rotterdam. ISBN 90 6191 138 9*

Anthropogenic irrigation sediments, Dakhla Oasis, Egypt

10

Ian A. Brookes
Department of Geography, York University, Toronto, Ont., Canada

ABSTRACT: A traditional system of irrigation agriculture is described from Dakhla Oasis, Egypt (25.5°N, 29°E). Field cultivation in this hyper-arid, wind-swept lowland, has traditionally been based on wind-blown soil parent material artificially trapped by windrows and irrigated in a reti-culated system by water raised from wells by animal-powered water wheels (saqiya). Distinctive bodies of stratified sediment, called "irrigation deposits", have thus formed, up to 5 m thick and 1 sq km in area. Free drainage of irrigation water through these mainly sandy materials in-hibits salinization. Patches of these deposits have grown around and downslope from wells, to be abandoned when sufficient water can no longer be lifted to the cultivated surface. The process is renewed in adjacent areas with favourable water supply, and has resulted in the growth of a mosaic of irrigation deposits over Dakhla Oasis since intro-duction of the water wheel in Roman times. Since the 1950s, this tradi-tional water- and soil-conserving system of land use has been in decline, through replacement by irrigation from deep wells feeding large canals which cross low-lying areas. This has led to salinization, despite recent deceleration of development and efforts to draw off excess water into detention lakes. On the northwest and east outskirts of Dakhla, the ex-tensive level floors of extinct lakes are being mechanically developed into large arable tracts also irrigated from deep wells. Salinization is predictable there also, with counter-productive effects on food produc-tion for a rapidly growing Egyptian population.

1 INTRODUCTION

Many tropical desert soils require only irrigation before they demon-strate a high natural fertility, which, at optimal insolation and temperature levels, is reflected in high crop yields. Irrigation may, however, adversely affect crop growth when it leads to soil sali-nization, particularly in the level or gently sloping terrain favourable to the organization of water delivery networks. A concise review of arid-land irrigation and its problems is given by Stanhill (1986). Expanded technical treat-ments are given in Yaron et al. (1973) and Shainberg and Shalhevet (1984).

This paper draws attention to a system of irrigation agriculture practiced in a desert environment among the most hostile to farming to be found anywhere. Under this system salinization appears tradi-tionally to have been combatted by purposeful accretion of soil parent materials, so that cultivation took place "Above the Salt". This system is presently in decline, under modernization pressures. While studies are at an early stage and results are preliminary, they suggest that abandonment of small-scale sediment accretion in favour of large-scale irrigation and mechanization of agriculture may rapidly lead to extensive saliniza-tion, which will defeat the objec-tive of increased food production.

Fig. 1. Dakhla Oasis region, south-central Egypt. Large format Camera Photograph showing major physiographic regions and extent of agricultural land (dark tone in lowland, which included some abandoned or uncultivated moister land). Towns are Mt: Mût, Q: El-Qâsr, Bt: Balât. Latitude, longitude and scale approximate.

2 THE STUDY AREA

Dakhla Oasis is situated in the Western Desert of Egypt, about 325 km west of Luxor, centered at approximately 25.5°N, 29°E. The oasis occupies a shale-floored lowland encompassed by the 140 m contour, and extends roughly 70 km WNW to ESE and up to 20 km N to S (Fig. 1). On the south, the oasis is bordered by a sandstone cuesta and plain at 140-160 m, and to the north by a 300 m escarpment forming the southern edge of the Libyan Plateau at 450-550 m. The region is among the driest on earth, with a mean annual rainfall less than 1 mm. Records for the period 1938-1967 show measurable rainfall of 11 mm in 1942 and 1 mm in 1956 (Shahin 1985:472-473). Potential evapotranspiration calculated by the Penman method is about 2250 mm, an average of 6.1 mm per day (Shahin 1985:226, 273). Temperatures range from 12.3°C (mean January) to 30.8°C (mean July), with an annual mean of 22.8°C. Traditional agriculture was supported by groundwater tapped by wells dug to a shallow aquifer (less than 200 m depth) within the Nubia Group sandstones which underlie the lowland shales (Beadnell 1901). This aquifer was last significantly recharged by local rainfall during an early Holocene pluvial, between 9500 and 4500 years BP (Sonntag et al. 1980; Brookes in press a). Deeper sandstone aquifers at 750 m to 1500 m depth, last significantly recharged by local rainfall between 20,000 and 40,000 years BP (Sonntag et al. 1980), have been tapped by drilled wells since the late-1950s.

Preliminary studies of the geomorphology and Quaternary geology of the Dakhla region are reported in Brookes (in press b). Seven Pleistocene sedimentary formations reflect humid climatic episodes tentatively dated to between about 200,000 and 20,000 years BP. These formations, derived from sources bordering the lowland to the north and south, were probably never very thick (perhaps less than 5 m) in the lowland, and have therefore been largely removed from it by intensive wind erosion in the intervals between the humid ones. Consequently, over large areas of the lowland red shale bedrock is either exposed or may form the substrate of the very recent sediments discussed here. The early Holocene pluvial saw lacustrine sediments deposited in basins around the borders of the oasis (Brookes in press a). Their absence from the lowland proper is best explained by intense late Holocene deflation.

3 IRRIGATION DEPOSITS

The sediments of concern here are termed "irrigation deposits" for reasons which will be clear when their genesis is discussed. First, their character will be described. These deposits cover large areas of the Dakhla lowland as an irregular mosaic of growing and diminishing patches, up to 5 m thick, and from a few hectares to about 1 sq km in area. Where their base is visible they rest on wind-scoured bedrock, various Quaternary sediments, or on the lower flanks of defunct wells. Typically, they are topographically expressed as level-topped plinths (Fig. 2a) with steep depositional or erosional edges above various types of surrounding terrain.

Structurally, the sediments consist of both regular and irregular sequences of three bedding types (Fig. 2b):

(i), 15-50 cm subhorizontal beds with horizontal or low-angle cross-stratification. These alternate with or are frequently parted by (ii) 10-20 cm horizontal wavy or rippled parallel beds;

(iii), less frequent, 50-100 cm planar, high-angle, cross-stratified beds, bounded horizontally by types (i) and (ii).

Inclined bedding in type (iii) shows consistent dips towards southerly points, which, with its structural character, points to an aeolian origin. Yardangs in bedrock and Quaternary sediments of various ages indicate that this has been the dominant (and the prevailing) wind direction in this region for hundreds of thousands of years (Brookes in press b). Each bedding type, moreover, is penetrated by mainly vertical, sandy root casts (cf. Klappa 1980), typically up to 2 cm in diameter, with a few up to 5 cm. In a yardang exposure in western Dakhla an intact mold of an Acacia trunk penetrates bedding

Fig. 2a. Northeast edge of plinth of irrigation sediments, 5 km SE of Balât, showing sub-horizontal stratification in yardang flanks. Plinth rises in distance approximately 8 km to palm and Acacia on right skyline, near which an intact 1st-century Roman period temple and early Byzantine architecture are buried by the sediments.

Fig. 2b. Flank of yardang in irrigation deposits, 9 km SW of El-Qâsr. Tabular bedding type (iii) 1 m thick in mid-section, between interbedded types (i) and (ii). Uppermost blocky layer is well dredgeate.

Fig. 2c. Windward side of yardang in irrigation deposits, 15 km SW of El-Qâsr, shwoing mold of Acacia trunk (left of scale). Scale bars 10 cm.

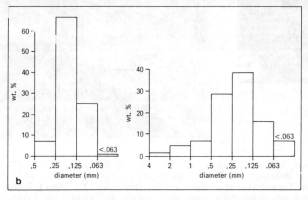

Fig. 3. a) Granulometry of irrigation deposits from (left) 15 km SW of el-Qâsr and (right) 7.5 km SSE of el-Qâsr. Predominant are sub-angular, sub-discoidal/spherical grains of recycled irrigation deposits, with less abundant subrounded, spherical quartz grains. Scale 1 mm. b) Photomicrograph of 0.5-1.0 mm fraction of irrigation deposits from 7.5 km SSE of el-Qâsr.

type (iii), indicating that the sediment accumulated in a coppice dune (Fig. 2c). Root casts point to an anchoring mat of grasses and woody shrubs. Overall, the structure of these sediments points to accumulation over level topography by sand sheet growth (bedding type (i)), sedimentation from slowly flowing or still water (bedding type (ii)), and by avalanching on slip faces of medium and large aeolian ripples (bedding type (iii)), with all accumulation assisted by vegetation.

Texturally, the sediments are dominated by very fine to medium,

moderately to well sorted sand (Fig. 3b), with finer grains dispersed in pore spaces and concentrated in some laminae within bedding type (ii). Lithologically, they are very diverse, including varying proportions of local and far-travelled quartz, local shale and limestone, as well as various Quaternary sediments and recycled grains of older irrigation deposits (Fig. 3a). Gypsum, halite, and calcite, introduced in aeolian dust and translocated in infiltrating soil water, contribute to the tough consistency of the deposits.

In addition to the genetic in-

117

Fig. 4. a) Narrow aqueduct up to 3 m above deflation surface, 8.5 km S of Balât. Scale in foreground in centimetres. b) Irrigation deposits (in vertical shaded sections) overlain by well dredgeate (loping from summit), 7 km SSW of El-Qâsr. c) Potsherd in situ in irrigation deposits. Scale in cms (upper).

ference drawn from structural features, keys to the environment of sediment accumulation lie in several observations of the association of the deposits with agricultural features. First, severe deflation of the deposits has occasionally left in relief more indurated aqueducts (Fig. 4a). Depending on their place in the hierarchy or original irrigation channels, these range in width from several metres to about 30 cm, and from modern analogy, were hoed into shape from field soil material, acquiring a firmer consistency by waterlogging and salt concentration. Second, even where severely eroded, the deposits are clearly associated with ancient and modern wells, either downslope from a well-head, or around and level with it (Fig. 4b). Third, potsherds are occasionally seen in

the deposits (Fig. 4c), and are abundant where lag concentrates litter deflation surfaces, indicating human use of the aggrading sediment. Fourth, observation of the present-day artificially assisted accretion and cultivation of sediments around the margins of higher sediment patches provides a uniformitarian basis for a genetic explanation.

4 PREVIOUS STUDIES

In Kharga Oasis, 140 km east of Dakhla, sediments similar to those described above were termed "historic well deposits" by Caton-Thompson and Gardner (1932), in opposition to Beadnell's (1909) conclusion that they are lacustrine. Again, their association with

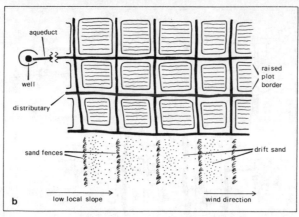

Fig. 5. a) View across expanding margin of irrigation deposits in linear system 5 km E of Balât. Trees line aqueduct which waters darker established plots, with light, fresh sands in foreground accumulating between sand fences over wind-scoured shale surface. b) Schematic plan of linear irrigation system, with plots ≈ 4 m square.

sherds (dating from not older than 300 BC to not younger than AD 600), and with wells and ancient field systems, was decisive. The mode of deposition was inferred to be by aeolian sand drift into vegetated pools of overflowed irrigation water.

Recently, Haynes (1983, 1984, 1985) has followed up that early study, drawing a similar but more detailed conclusion on the origin of these deposits, but a different one on their age. At a site south of Kharga town, where Caton-Thompson and Gardner had made their most

detailed observations, Haynes (1985:280) inferred the accumulation of "at least 10 m of eolian sand and agricultural soil" by 1400 BC, "and another 8 m was deposited by 600 BC". He viewed the sediment as accumulated from sand drifting across vegetated fields.

5 GENESIS OF IRRIGATION DEPOSITS IN DAKHLA

Two patterns of traditional cultivation, outside village orchards and gardens, have so far been

119

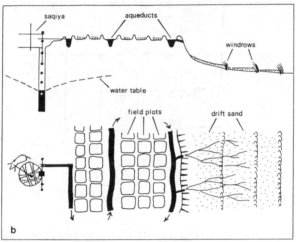

Fig. 6. a) View across expanding edge of irrigation deposits, with higher
established plot to left, 8 km SSW of Balât. b) Schematic plan and profile of rectilinear irrigation system.

recognized in Dakhla Oasis, based
on the type of well and its location with respect to fields irrigated from it. Both belong to the
"reticulated" type of distribution,
in which delivery of water is completely, rather than partially,
controlled (Heathcote 1983:192). In
the first pattern (Fig. 5) the well
is located along a spring line or
in a defunct natural spring mound.
A master aqueduct leads water from
it to be tapped along its length by
smaller ones which laterally feed a
rectangular pattern of small ridged
plots. In this pattern, vertical

accretion of sediment is restricted
by the height of the water level in
the master aqueduct. Horizontal expansion, on the other hand, is
limited only by the availability of
water to the borders of the cultivated area.

The second pattern (Fig. 6) sees
water delivered to a well-head,
whence it is distributed to fields
via an aqueduct which winds around
and through the cultivation in a
generally rectangular pattern.
Here, vertical sediment accretion
is limited more by the rate of
water delivery to the surface. Con-

120

versely, accretion increases the lift required. The increase in elevation of the accreting surface increases the area to which water can be delivered under gravity flow through the aqueduct network, until crop demand outpaces water supply.

Two questions now need to be addressed: how is sediment accumulated? How is water raised? Observations of present-day practice show that, in order to induce sediment accumulation, leafy or grassy windrows are laid or planted across the wind at intervals of a few metres. These form "sand fences" in the lee of which the trapped sand is levelled and borders are raised, in preparation for irrigation then planting (Fig. 5a, b). Commonly fodder alfalfa is planted which nitrogenates the soil, and this can be grazed after harvest by sheep and goats. Dung not collected for fuel, as well as subsurface plant material, is later hoed in as a fertilizing mulch. Irrigation water deconstitutes sand-size grains of cemented mud and shale particles to yield silt and clay, while bacterial activity reduces the sulphate of gypsum.

A few centimetres of new soil has thus been created from materials which, without this controlled accretion, would either have blown through the region or accumulated in irregular hummocks around vegetation - not where it was needed. Notwithstanding the clear intent of current practice to stabilize drift sand for cultivation around the borders of cultivated plots, a question can be raised as to the role the sand fences might play in protecting cultivated plots from deflation. Contrary to this it can be stated that no contemporary cases have been observed where this intention is obvious. Soil not protected by a crop cover retains ghost patterns of field borders and aqueducts several decades after abandonment, according to local information on land-use history, so that deflation appears not to be a significant problem during the life of a body of this sediment.

However, Haynes (pers. comm. in 1988) received local reports of a soil protective role for grassy fences in Kharga, which may reflect a necessity to combat soil loss by the stronger winds channelled

north-south through the axis of this depression, and (or) the preponderance of more erodible, far-travelled quartz sand in Kharga, in contrast to that of sand-size mud grains in Dakhla. Future comparison may prove instructive.

In erosional exposures of older irrigation deposits in Dakhla the absence of raised plot borders may be explained in several ways:

(a) plot borders were not raised in earlier times,

(b) they were infilled or levelled by soil-preparation procedures prior to annual planting,

(c) they were deflated in fallow intervals.

Continuity of bedding type (ii) indicates water flow over wide areas. Bedding type (iii) indicates occasionally thick sand drift, presumably over fallowed or abandoned land.

To raise water, the water-wheel was used, and is today, although to a rapidly decreasing extent. This animal-powered, gear-driven device (Fig. 7), of the type also known as the bucket chain or pot garland, in Egypt as saqiya (Oleson 1984), was introduced into Egypt in late Ptolemaic times (1st century AD) but probably was not used in Upper Egypt or Nubia until Roman times, in the 2nd century (Adams 1977). Lack of this efficient water-lifting device in Egyptian oases in earlier times (presumably, only the levered shaduf was available) severely limited settlement between the late Old Kingdom (ca 2200 BC), when Dakhla was an important economic and political entity with its own governor, and Ptolemaic times, when, after a long hiatus, archaeological evidence for similar importance again becomes abundant (Mills in press).

Prior to the Naguib-Nasser revolution of 1952-1953, wells were dug as deep as 200 m using a derrick-mounted, windlass-powered auger and cutter to penetrate the sandstone aquifer beneath the surface shale (Beadnell 1901). The average daily yield of 805 such shallow wells in Dakhla in 1953 was 315 cu m per well. A small number (7) of deeper wells had been drilled between 1941 and 1951, to depths of 220-350 m, and yielded 1670 to 8705 cu m per day (Seddik and Shafei 1979). If artesian pressure was insufficient

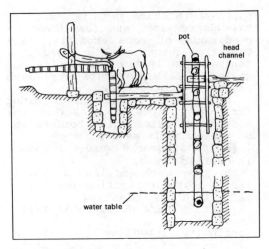

Fig. 7. Section through saqiya,
modified after Adams (1977).

to deliver adequate quantities of
water from wells to master aqueducts, the saqiya was used to lift
it to them. Unfortunately, direct
archaeological and historical information on the use of the saqiya
is scant. Beadnell (1901) reported
it almost unknown in Dakhla in
1899. Known and presumed Roman-
period aqueducts, occasionally huge
(20 m wide by 5 m deep), nevertheless cross waterless desert 1-2 km
from today's closest cropland, and
deserve future study in regard to
their capacity and hierarchical
structure.

Saqiya pots have a capacity of
approximately 3 l and cannot be
spaced too closely along the rope
suspended around the vertical
wheel, because the draft animal
will not be able to lift the weight
of water in the rising pots. I
timed the rate of pot-emptying into
the head channel at one saqiya
(being very rapidly turned by a
young man proud to demonstrate his
strength!) at 3 per second, amount-
ing to a maximum of ca 9 l per
second (assuming the pots completely emptied as they swung over the
top of the wheel, which is unlikely
at this rate). At, say, 5 l per
second over a 12-hour day, 20 mm of
water can be delivered to a 1 hectare plot, not accounting for evaporative and transmission losses en
route. This amounts to 8 times the
winter, and double the summer daily

potential evaporation (Shahin 1985:
226,273).

Raised in this fashion, water is
distributed in the two patterns
described earlier. As mentioned, as
the cultivated surface rises, the
water must be lifted higher (the
saqiya is raised). Of course, the
soil surface will not rise as
rapidly if soil accretion measures
are dropped; most material arriving
at the surface of a rising sediment
plinth will drift across it. Again,
with an irrigated standing crop in
the plots, water drained through
the sediment will moisten surrounding areas and inhibit sand drift.
Whether or not it rises, however,
continued water withdrawal will
form a cone of depression around
the well, which, because of the
limit on pot spacing, will progressively decrease the rate of water
delivery. Clearly, then, a limit is
reached to expansion of the cultivated area, which must ultimately
be abandoned.

6 CULTIVATION, SEDIMENT, AND SALT

The important point to be extracted
from this description of traditional irrigation agriculture in Dakhla
Oasis is that salt does not accumulate in these freely draining ac-
creted soils. It does, however, accumulate over adjacent lower areas
as water containing dissolved salts
seeps through the flanks of the
raised plinths. Drainage in those
areas is impeded where topography
is level; even more so where they
are confined between surrounding
plinths. Salts are thus concentrated there and initially form efflo-
rescences then rock-hard crusts
with rough microtopography marked
by swollen domes and cone structures.

Salinization adjacent to abandoned cultivation does not, however,
impede the shift of soil accretion
practices. As long as the cones of
depression around abandoned wells
are avoided, accretion can be
started anew over the salinized
substrate. As soil patches grow, as
they are abandoned and deflated,
and as they shift location over
time, large areas become mantled
with variable thicknesses of these
irrigation deposits in various
stages of growth and decay.

Archaeological studies in Dakhla Oasis have identified settlements, ranging from towns to individual farms, whose agricultural base is inferred to have been founded in irrigation by the water-wheel. These fall into the Roman, Romano-Byzantine, Byzantine, and Islamic periods of the regional historical sequence (Mills in press). Hand in hand, geoarchaeological studies have identified irrigation deposits around former well-heads and down-slope over former cultivated areas associated with these occupations. Potsherds, usually found deflated from the deposits, but occasionally in situ, provide at least maximum ages for them. That is, the deposits cannot be older than the pottery, but can be younger, if old pottery was incorporated into them. It is not known, however, what proportion of sherds is contemporary with the deposits: many were probably collected from older cultural waste and spread on fields, either to improve tilth or (and?) to inhibit aeolian sand accumulation by enhancing saltation across a rougher surface. Continuing studies may illuminate the chronology of irrigation deposits.

For present purposes it is more urgent to recognize that traditional agricultural techniques, practiced with varying intensity over two millennia in an environment as harsh as any ever occupied by farming people, managed not merely to accomodate the natural environment, but turned one of its most hostile elements - drifting sand - into a life-sustaining resource. Begun as a Roman colonial "megaproject", the demise of which probably resulted from a combination of over-exploitation of groundwater, deterioration of maintenance, and soil salinization, the technology of water-wheel irrigation of artificially trapped drift sand sustained reduced populations in Dakhla into modern times.

7 IMPLICATIONS FOR DEVELOPMENT

Times, as usual, are changing. Revolutionized Egypt adopted a plan to convert the Western Desert oases into "The New Valley", to help feed the rapidly growing population in the Nile Valley (Ezzat 1974). Wells were drilled through Nubia sandstone aquifers at depths up to 1500 metres, in which groundwater was last recharged 20,000 to 40,000 years ago. Water gushed to the surface under artesian pressure, feeding large unlined canals, backhoed geometrically across the level areas of Dakhla's lowland. Large cones of depression formed around these wells, cutting off water from traditional shallow ones and forcing abandonment of land and some smaller settlements. These deleterious effects were recognized by the late 1960s, forcing more careful development. Today, discharge from wells is regulated, and excess water led to small detention lakes, but this has been too late to prevent severe efflorescent salinization of some level land, particularly east of Mût (Fig. 8a).

Whereas agricultural and population expansion has been slowed in Dakhla itself, beyond its borders they are driving developments which raise concern. There, beginning in the mid-1980s, the extensive level floors of extinct lakes, tentatively assigned a Late Pleistocene age (Fig. 8b), are being backhoed and bulldozed to form new agricultural areas, complete with grid-iron, concrete block villages. Water from deep wells is to be distributed to large fields in regulated amounts, but careful water management and system maintenance will be necessary in order to avoid salinization of fields and canal borders. Predictions are hazardous, but comparison of this extensive, energy-intensive system with the traditional system of smaller-scale cultivation "Above the Salt" undermines confidence in its outcome.

8 ACKNOWLEDGEMENTS

This research is part of a broader study of geomorphology and Quaternary geology contributing to the Dakhla Oasis Project. I thank the project's cosponsors, The Society for the Study of Egyptian Antiquities and Royal Ontario Museum, both of Toronto, for logistical, technical and financial support. Major project funding has come from The Social Sciences and Humanities Research Council of Canada, while The Natural Sciences and Engineer-

Fig. 8. a) Salt efflorescence over level land east of Mût. b) Containment dike (left) and perimeter canal (right) under construction in irrigation project at Zayât, 90 km E of Mût. Materials are Late Pleistocene lake sediments over sandstone. Bulldozer at left for scale.

ing Research Council of Canada and York University have additionally supported my work. At York University, the Cartographc Office drafted the line drawings and Secretarial Services word-processed the manuscript. Photographs were reproduced from transparencies by Exhibit and Design Services, Royal Ontario Museum. The Large Format Camera photo was generously supplied by C.S. Breed, U.S. Geological Survey. The comments of C. Vance Haynes Jr., University of Arizona, on a draft were very useful in preparing the final version.

REFERENCES

Adams, W.Y. 1977.
Nubia: Corridor to Africa. Penguin Books.
Beadnell, H.J.L. 1901.
Dakhla Oasis: its topography and geology. Report for 1899. Cairo: Geological Survey of Egypt.
Beadnell, H.J.L. 1909.
An Egyptian Oasis: an account of the oasis of Kharga in the Libyan Desert. London: John Murray.
Brookes, I.A. in press a.
Early Holocene basinal sediments of the Dakhleh Oasis region,

south-central Egypt, and their paleoclimatic significance. Quaternary Research.
Brookes, I.A. in press b.
Quaternary geology and geomorphology of the Dakhleh Oasis region, south-central Egypt: an interim report. In A.J.Mills (ed.), The Dakhleh Oasis Project, Interim Reports, Vol. 1. Toronto, Royal Ontario Museum.
Caton-Thompson, G. and E.W.Gardner 1932. The prehistoric geography of Kharga Oasis. Geographical Journal 80:369-409.
Ezzat, M. 1974.
Exploitation of ground water in El Wadi El Gedid project area (New Valley): Part II - Hydrologic conditions in Dakhla-Kharga area. Cairo, Ministry of Agriculture and Land Reclamation, Executive Agency, for Desert Projects.
Haynes, C.V. Jr. 1983.
Quaternary studies, Western Desert, Egypt and Sudan, 1975-1978. National Geographic Society Research Reports 15:257-293.
Haynes, C.V. Jr. 1984.
Western Desert Quaternary Studies: preliminary report on the 1984 field season. Mimeo.
Haynes, C.V. Jr. 1985.
Quaternary studies, Western

Desert, Egypt and Sudan, 1979-
1983 field seasons. National
Geographic Society Research Re-
ports 19:269-341.
Heathcote, R.L. 1983.
The Arid Lands: their use and
abuse. New York: Longmans.
Klappa, C.F. 1980.
Rhizoliths in terrestrial car-
bonates: classification, recog-
nition, genesis, and significan-
ce. Sedimentology 27:613-629.
Mills, A.J. in press.
The Pharaonic period in the
Dakhleh Oasis. In A.J.Mills
(ed.), The Dakhleh Oasis Project,
Interim Reports, Vol. 1. Toronto,
Royal Ontario Museum.
Oleson, J.P. 1984.
Greek and Roman Mechanical Water
Lifting Devices: the history of a
technology. Toronto: University
of Toronto Press.
Seddik, M.M. and S. Shafei 1979.
Water resources and land reclama-
tion in Egypt. In A.Bishay and
W.G.McGinnies (eds.), Advances in
Desert and Arid Land Technology
and Development, Vol. 1, p.201-
210. New York, Harwood Academic
Publishers.
Shahin, M. 1985.
Hydrology of the Nile Basin.
Developments in Water Science 21.
New York, Elsevier.
Shainberg, I. and J. Shalhevet
(eds.) 1984. Soil Salinity under
Irrigation: processes and manage-
ment. New York: Springer.
Sonntag, C. et al. 1980.
Isotopic identification of
Saharian groundwaters, groundwa-
ter formation in the past.
Palaeoecology of Africa 12:159-
171.
Stanhill, R. 1986.
Irrigation in arid lands. Philo-
sophical Transactions of the
Royal Society of London A316:261-
273.
Yaron, B., E.Danfors
and Y.Vaida (eds.) 1973.
Arid Zone Irrigation. New York:
Springer.

Man's Role in the Shaping of the Eastern Mediterranean Landscape, Bottema, Entjes-Nieborg & van Zeist (eds)
© 1990 Balkema, Rotterdam. ISBN 90 6191 138 9

Changes in the Mediterranean ecosystem during antiquity   11
A geomorphological approach as seen in two examples

Helmut Brückner
Geographisches Institut, Universität Düsseldorf, FR Germany

ABSTRACT: By examples from Basilicata (Southern Italy) and Attika (Greece) the effects of the human impact on the ecologically unstable Mediterranean environment in historical times are demonstrated. Phases of soil eorsion on the slopes and in upper regions and correlative alluviation in the valley bottoms are connected with periods of intensive settlement, deforestation and agriculture. The conclusions are derived from geomorphological evidence, radiocarbon dating of palaeosols, archaeological finds and historical sources.

1 INTRODUCTION

Since Vita-Finzi's classical book "The Mediterranean Valleys" was published in 1969 discussion about the cause of the "historical fills" has not ceased. Thick Holocene river terraces and extraordinary delta growth since antiquity are recorded in many Mediterranean countries (cf. the synopsis in Brückner 1986). Two basically different interpretations are given: one favouring man (e.g. Brückner 1983, 1986), the other one climate (e.g. Hempel 1984, 1987, 1988) as being the main morphodynamic agent.

In the following, two examples are given to demonstrate the human impact on the ecosystem of the Mediterranean subtropics which is vulnerable in many aspects. The Italian example is taken from an area with an easily erodable bedrock (Calabriano clays), the Greek one from a limestone and schist region is much more resistant to surface erosion. The geomorphological approach used here is the identification of the sediments in the valley bottoms which are correlative to the erosion processes on the hill slopes and in the hinterland (Photos 1 and 5). These alluvial fills contain mostly artefacts and/or intercalated palaeosols. If the former can be identified ar-

chaeologically and the latter are radiocarbon dated, a good chronostratigraphy can be established which is then interpreted with regard to the specific settlement history of the region.

2 A CASE STUDY FROM BASILICATA

In Basilicata (the former province of Lucania in southern Italy) the alluviation of the valleys and the seaward progradation of the shoreline occurred in several phases: in the late Pleistocene/early Holocene (Sediment 1), in Graeco-Roman times (Sediment 2), in the Middle Ages (Sediment 3) and in the 19th and early 20th centuries (Sediment 4). Fig. 2 shows a synoptical profile which is representative of the middle and lower courses of the Lucanian rivers (Bràdano, Basento and Cavone (Fig. 1, Photos 1 and 2). The profiles are described in detail by Brückner (1983, 1986) and Neboit (1983, 1984). From their research the following conclusions can be drawn:

The first phase of sedimentation was climatically/eustatically caused (Versilian transgression). With the rising sea level of the Tarentinian Gulf the lower river courses were drowned, a ria-type coast developed and Sediment 1 was

Fig. 1. The study area in southern Italy with the main rivers.

deposited in the valley bottoms. Its graded bedding from coarse pebbles to loam indicates a natural cause. An embedded fossil yielded a radiocarbon age of 7250±140 BP (Table 1:GY-4299). On its top a very dark greyish brown Borowina soil developed (profile: A_h-M_{Ca}-M, colour: 10 YR 3/2) which yielded radiocarbon ages between 5090 and 4410 cal. BC (Table 1: BR PS 1,

GY-4304, Palaeosol A). Whether or not the samples GY-4302 and CA PS 1A from the third and second millennia BC, respectively, are from the same palaeosol or from a younger one cannot be decided since there is no topographic continuity between the sites. The charcoal (GY-4298) within Sediment 1 with ages between 2450 and 2040 cal. BC also indicates that this prehistorical sediment consists of two separate layers.

Sediment 2 is prominent. Its facies (exclusively fine grains, palaeosol sediments, missing graded bedding) is different from Sediment 1. It mainly consists of reworked bedrock material from the hinterland and the valley slopes (Calabriano clays). Embedded charcoal yielded calibrated radiocarbon ages between the first and fourth centuries BC (Table 1). Within Sediment 2 archaeological remains from the Great Greek Era and in the uppermost part late Roman roofing tiles were found (Fig. 2, Photo 3). The olive grey to dark greyish brown palaeosol (5 Y 5/2 - 2.5 YR 4/2) on its top is much less developed than Palaeosol A (feldspar grains are

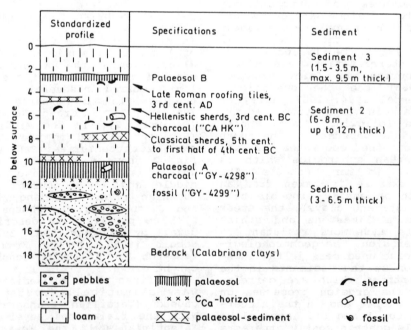

Fig. 2. The main Holocene terrace of the rivers Bràdano, Basento and Cavone (synoptical profile).

Photo 1. Caselike valley of the Cavone (at Feroleto near Pisticci) with the main Holocene terrace at its base being dissected by the present river (middle part). The slopes in the background show erosion features with outcrops of bedrock (Calabriano clays) in some parts and maquis vegetation in others.

Photo 2. Holocene terraces of the Bràdano (near Montescaglioso). Exposed by a former cut-bank of the river the main terrace shows palaeosols and palaeosol sediments within the loamy accumulations. In the left part the second Holocene terrace is visible, which incises into the first one.

Photo 3. Detail of the Cavone terrace at Feroleto with remains from the Great Greek Era: sherds and bricks of a destroyed farmstead plus a charcoal layer (where the scale indicates "65 cm").

still visible in thin sections). It formed between 72 and 400 cal. AD (Table 1, Palaeosol B).

Thus, Sediment 2 (which may reach a thickness of up to 12 m) formed during classical antiquity. It can be correlated to periods of intensive settlement, deforestation and agriculture when southern Italy became part of the Greek world, followed by the Roman Empire. Colo-nization of Magna Graecia led to the foundation of many cities (cf. Tàranto, Metaponto) from the 8th century BC onward and to an intensified occupation of the interior by the Lucanians and other native groups. In the hinterland of Metaponto hundreds of farms existed alreaby by 550 BC (Adamesteanu 1974). The ear of grain on coins symbolizes the importance of agri-

129

Photo 4. A coin of Metaponto
(Magna Graecia) portraying an ear
of grain. This underlines the
significant role agriculture played
(replica near the entrance of the
antiquarium at Tavole Palatine).

culture in those times (Photo 4).

Strabo and Columelia (cf. Ranieri
1972) mentioned latifundia with extensive land use at the height of
the Roman Empire. But already in
the 1st century AD Seneca (cf. Ranieri 1972) wrote about Lucanian
woods and at the beginning of the
second half of the 3rd century AD
and during the whole late Roman
Empire, the Lucanian hill country
must have been covered once again
by wood. The radiocarbon dates of
Palaeosol B and the late Roman
tiles in the uppermost part of Sediment 2 indicate that the ecosystem stabilized, i.e. soil erosion
decreased and pedogenesis increased, simultaneously with the
decay of the Roman Empire.

Sediment 3 is probably linked to
the Middle Ages when - after a time
of depopulation and desertion following the Roman Era - the Lucanians began settling on hilltops and
cultivating the land once again.
The building-up of this sediment
ended in the 11th/12th or 14th/15th
centuries probably because of tectonic uplift or political changes
(Brückner 1983). Thereby the main
Holocene terrace of the Lucanian
valleys - consisting of Sediments
1, 2 and 3 - is finished. Incised
into it is a second Holocene terrace (Sediment 4, 4-8 m thick, Photo
2) which most probably formed as
the result of deforestation caused
by population pressure since the
middle of the 19th and in the early
20th centuries (Tichy 1962).

To summarize, the Lucanian case
study shows that - except for Sediment 1 - the phases of sedimentation in the valley bottoms can be
correlated very well to periods of
intensive settlement, devegetation
and agriculture.

3 A CASE STUDY FROM ATTIKA

An archaeological survey comprising
the valleys of Charaka, Hagia Photini and Thimari at the southern
tip of Attika led to the detection
of an area which was densely populated and intensively cultivated
with olive groves during the Classical Period, i.e. the 5th and 4th
centuries BC (Lohmann 1983, 1985,
1987). We know from literary evidence that Attika was famous for
its excellent and costly olive oil
which was exported in large quantities to meet the enormous demand
for grain of the urban masses. The
cheaper grain was imported from the
Pontus region (i.e. the Ukraine).

At Charaka as well as in other
parts of Attika the lower slopes of
the mountains and hills were almost
completely terraced with stone
walls, 0.80-1.40 m thick and up to
1.60 m high, for the cultivation of
olives (Lohmann 1983, 1985, 1987).
These agricultural terraces bear
clear witness of the enormous investment during the 5th and 4th
centuries BC by the rural population. Lohmann measured, mapped and
described these terraces in detail.
He concludes that the extent to
which the countryside, the so-called chora of the polis of Athens,
was cultivated indicates a dramatic
shortage of land caused by over-
population. Just so it seems
obvious that this development of
the country - which as by no means
resticted to agricultural terraces
but included large farmhouses as
well as roads, mule tracks, dams
and embankkment walls in the numerous rivers - could not have been
accomplished without the labour of
slaves.

The technical reasons for terracing the slopes even in limestone
areas are not yet definitely revealed. Protection against soil
erosion seems not necessary for the
olive trees but rather for the
undercrops. The purpose may also
have been the amelioration of the

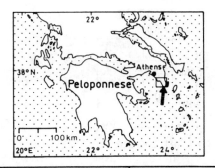

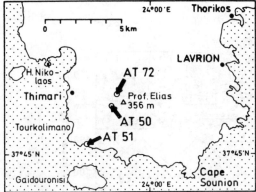

Fig. 3. The study area in southern Attika (with archaeological sites mentioned below).

water budget of the soil in this semi-arid environment.

How did the intensive cultivation effect the ecosystem? Which morphological testimonies of this human impact are found? In Greece this question is all the more interesting since it is here that according to Hempel (1984, 1987, 1988) the factor climate was the motor for the transformation of the ecosystem. The author attributes only few and relatively thin accumulations to human influence and all the others to prehistorical natural events. Schneider (1987) came to similar results for the Sparta Basin. On the other hand, the Olympia terraces of the Alpheios, covering the sites of the historical Olympic Games with a 10-m-thick alluvium since AD 500, is attributed to the abandonment of fields and the neglect of agriculture with the decline of civilisation (Büdel 1977).

For the study area in southern Attika (Fig. 3) it is important to note that erosion was differential and selective. There are sites where the terrace walls are totally preserved - nothing seems to have changed since the 5th and 4th centuries BC. But there are also once terraced slopes where hardly any of the old walls can still be recognized. The former is predominantly the case in limestone areas where surface runoff is reduced because of karstification, the latter in schists which are much more easily erodable (see also Photo 7).

Where the Rhevma Livadonas leaves its limestone canyon and enters the Charaka Plain some of the classical agricultural terraces are still preserved testifying the intensive cultivation during that period. The rhevma (= torrential river) then passes 500 m east of a small late Roman settlement described by Eliot (1962) before it flows into the Aegean Sea (Photo 5).

The correlative sediments were deposited in the lower course of the rhevma (Photo 6, Fig. 3, site AT 51). North of the bridge of the coastal road to Cape Sounion and 120 m before the river mouth a 2.50-m-thick historical fill is exposed for 16 m at the eastern rhevma bank (Fig. 4, bottom). It is a typical torrential deposit, clearly layered with sudden changes between coarse and fine grained sediments. Unlike the Pleistocene debris cones they are not cemented. The angular to subangular pebbles (up to 65 cm long) consist by 75% of marble and limestone; the others are ankerite, quartz, marlstone and small pieces of schists. The matrix is sand. Clay and loam only exist in few lenses and towards the top; the majority of this material was transported directly into the sea.

The whole sediment contains fragments of ancient pottery (Table 2: AT 51 A-O). The datable ones of the lower and middle layers are from classical times (5th and 4th centuries BC) or even older. The only exception is AT 51 F; however, it is not sure whether the sherd was in situ, it may also have rolled down from the top. On the surface (now a vineyard) late Roman fragments occur, some of which may have been ploughed out of the uppermost layer.

This stratigraphy is confirmed at another site close by. In a pit 25

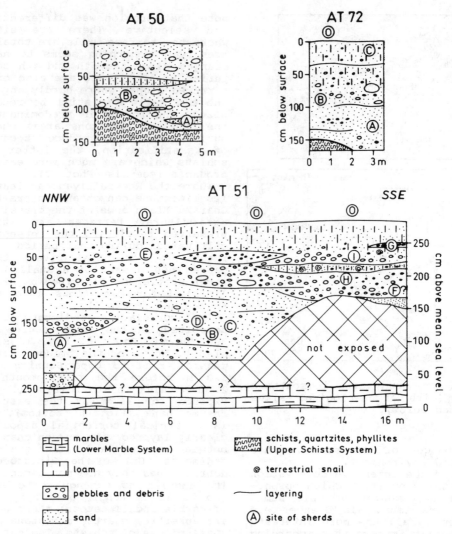

Fig. 4. Historical valley fills in southern Attika. Site AT 51: lower course of Rhevma Livadonas, sites AT 50 and AT 72: terraces of torrential creeks at the foot of Mt. Prophet Elias (description of sherds in Table 2).

m upstream and in 3 m distance from the western rhevma bank, a large wall fragment of an amphora, probably classic, was found 1 m below the surface (AT 53), whereas late Roman pottery only occurs on the surface (AT 55/2). Therefore, it is most probable that the building-up of this historical terrace started during or after the Classical Era and terminated in late Roman times. Since intercalated palaeosols are missing a further differentiation is not possible.

Profiles in little rhevmata at the foot of Mt. Prophet Elias principally show an analogous situation (Fig. 3, Fig. 4 top). Here the bedrock consists of schists which more easily tend to erosion than limestones or marbles. Therefore, the classical agricultural terraces once covering the slopes are mostly eroded. It is in the valley bottoms that the correlative accumulations are found. As in the case of Rhevma Livadonas, the archaeological remains within the alluvium date to

Table 1. Radiocarbon dates from the alluvial fills of rivers from Basilicata. Calibration according to van der Plicht and Mook (in press), (*) according to Kromer et al. (1986); 1 sigma confidence level.

sediment, soil	river	sample	radiocarbon age	calibrated radiocarbon age
Sediment 3	- no radiocarbon dates			
Palaeosol B	Cavone	CA PS 1B	1880±40 BP[1]	72-142 cal. AD
				and 166-200 cal. AD
	Cavone	CA PS 4A	1730±40 BP[1]	246-346 cal. AD
	Bràdano	BR PS 4	1690±40 BP[1]	262-286 cal. AD
				and 332-400 cal. AD
Sediment 2	Bràdano (charcoal)	Gianpasquale	2160±160 BP[2]	390-10 cal. BC
	Cavone (charcoal)	CA HK	2290±40 BP[1]	280-262 cal. BC
				and 400-364 cal. BC
Palaeosol A?	Cavone	CA PS 1A	3350±40 BP[1]	1550-1538 cal. BC
				1690-1610 cal. BC
				and 1734-1722 cal. BC
	Bràdano	GY-4302	3910±110 BP[3]	2250-2210 cal. BC
				2510-2280 cal. BC
				and 2580-2530 cal. BC
Palaeosol A	Bràdano	GY-4303	5700±120 BP [3]	4420-4410 cal. BC
				and 4720-4460 cal. BC
	Bràdano	BR PS 1	6100±60 BP[1]	5090-4910 cal. BC(*)
Sediment 1	Bràdano (charcoal)	GY-4298	3760±110 BP[3]	2340-2040 cal. BC
				and 2450-2440 cal. BC
	Basento (fossil)	GY-4299	7250±140 BP[3]	not calibrated

[1] Brückner 1982, 1983, 1986
[2] Cotecchia et al. 1969
[3] Neboit 1983, 1984

the 5th and 4th centuries BC (AT 50 A/2, AT 72 A) or even earlier (AT 50 B) whereas late Roman pottery only occurs in the uppermost parts of the sediment or on its surface (AT 72 C/3, C/4, AT 72 O).

From the evidence presented here we may definitely conclude that in southern Attika the Holocene river terraces and valley bottom fills are anthropogenic. Man's impact on the vulnerable ecosystem by terracing the slopes during the Classical Era caused soil eorsion in the terraced areas (especially where schists form the bedrock) and as correlative process the alluviation of lower river courses, valley bottoms and even of lower parts of the slopes (Photo 7). The clearing of the vegetation and cultivation of the land exposed the soil to the heavy rainfall dynamics which are typical for the semi-arid environment (between 1955 and 1987 the meteorological station at the airport of Athens once recorded nearly one third (113 mm) of the annual precipitation (378 mm) within 24 hours).

The denudation and successive alluviation probably started already during the 5th and 4th centuries BC, continued with decreasing intensity in the late Roman Era and then ceased. Thus the accumulation of these historical fills reflects well the settlement history of this region.

Southern Attika was relatively densely inhabited in the Classical Period with a sharp decline at the

Photo 5. The Charaka Plain with Rhevma Livadonas. The torrential river passes the limestone canyon (background), then follows the line where the trees grow and leaves the photo in its bottom right corner. During the Classic Era parts of the slopes at the back were terraced for olive tree plantations (erosion and denudation area in the background, accumulation area in the foreground).

Photo 6. The historical fill in the lower course of Rhevma Livadonas (detail of Photo 5, bottom right part) consisting of 2.50 m of sediment with sherds on top of the bedrock (marbles, foreground) (cf. Fig. 4, bottom).

Photo 7. Grave terrace of the latest 4th cent. BC (Phontini No. 3). The alluviation was selective: the southeast corner is still completely visible (with scale: 1.60 m) whereas the southwest corner is covered by an accumulation, upto 1.50 m thick (foreground). The sediments were eroded from the nearby slopes (inclination up to 10°).

end of this epoch. The region was left almost uninhabited for several centuries until late Roman times when the Attic countryside was re-occupied to a certain extent. Besides a small late Roman agricultural settlement at Charaka, a little cloister at Hagia Photini and perhaps a few scattered, isolated farmsteads, the greater part of the region was in use by shepherds for transhumance during the winter.

Even these modest activities died out before the Middle Ages and the whole region was left practically unpopulated until these days (Lohmann 1983, 1985, 1987). The cessation of the sedimentation in late Roman times clearly demonstrates the soil conserving effect of the secondary vegetation like maquis and garrigue which subsequently developed on hill slopes and in valleys.

Table 2. Finds of an archaeological survey in the historical fills from southern Attika (cf. Figs. 3 and 4).

AT 50 - historical fill of a little rhevma at the southwest foot of Mt. Prophet Elias

AT 50 A/1	wall fragment of an amphora, thin-walled ware	Archaic-Classic
AT 50 A/2	wall fragment of a lecanis	Classic (5th-4th cent. BC)
AT 50 B	rim fragment of a bowl	Bronze Age, early Helladic I (2500-2250 BC)

AT 51 - archaeological finds within and on top of the accumulations of Rhevma Livadonas, lower course near the river mouth

AT 51 A	thin-walled ware, traces of black glaze	Iron Age (7th-3rd cent. BC)
AT 51 C	wall fragment	presumedly Classic (5th-4th centuries BC)
AT 51 F	wall fragment	late Roman (4th-7th cent. AD)
AT 51 G	wall fragment	presumedly Classic
AT 51 I	wall fragment	probably Classic
AT 51 O/1	amphora handle, yellow slipped ware	4th cent. BC
AT 51 O/2	wall fragment, amphora?	presumedly Classic
AT 51 O/3	wall fragment of an amphora	not datable (late Roman possible)
AT 51 B,D,E,H and O/4 (seven fragments)		undatable

AT 53, 55 - same as AT 51, but 25 m upstream

AT 53	wall fragment, of an amphora	probably Classic
AT 55/1	household pottery, fragment	presumedly Classic
AT 55/2	wall fragment	late Roman

AT 72 - alluvial fills at the conjunction of several little creeks northwest of Mt. Prophet Elias

AT 72 A/1	fragment of a roof tile	Classic
AT 72 A/2	fragment of a roof tile, with traces of black glaze, very thick (2.9 cm)	Classic
AT 72 A/3	wall fragment, amphora?, traces of yellow slip	Classic, 4th cent. BC
AT 72 B	fragment, roof tile?	undatable
AT 72 C/1	handle fragment, skyphos, black glaze	Classic, 5th cent. BC
AT 72 C/2	thin-walled ware	presumedly Classic
AT 72 C/3	wall fragment of an amphora	late Roman
AT 72 C/4	fragments	possibly late Roman
AT 72 O/1	wall fragment, amphora?	probably late Roman
AT 72 O/2	fragment of a bee hive	late Roman?
AT 72 O/3	fragment of a roof tile	not Classic, perhaps late Roman
AT 72 O/4	wall fragment	late Roman
AT 72 O/5		undatable

4 CONCLUSION

The examples of southern Italy and Greece show accelerated rates of erosion and correlative alluviation in historical times. The long history of settlement in an ecologically unstable environment (Mediterranean subtropics with heavy rainfall dynamics, easily erodable unconsolidated sedimentary rocks, steep relief in the hinterland) were the main reasons why the impact of man on nature had catastrophic results (badlands in the interior elevations and on valley slopes, enormous accumulations in the valleys and coastal plains). A comparison of the periods of increased delta growth and/or valley alluviation in different Mediterranean countries (cf. Brückner 1986:Fig. 7) shows a clear diachronism. The phases of ecological instability (erosion and alluviation) on the one hand and of stability (pedogenesis) on the other can often be correlated with phases of progression and regression of settlements, respectively. Compared with that, the effects of climatic changes or tectonics were subordinate in historical times.

ACKNOWLEDGEMENTS

Dr H. Lohmann, Bochum (FRG), was an excellent guide in Attika and identified the sherds mentioned in Table 2 on the sites. Radiocarbon dating of the samples was carried out by Dr B. Kromer, Heidelberg (FRG). Dr J. van der Plicht, Groningen (the Netherlands), calibrated all radiocarbon dates.

REFERENCES

Adamesteanu, D. 1974.
La Basilicata antica - storia e monumenti. Cava dei Tirreni.
Brückner, H. 1982.
Ausmaß von Erosion und Akkumulation im Verlauf des Quartärs in der Basilicata (Süditalien). Zeitschrift für Geomorphologie N.F. Suppl.-Bd. 43:121-137.
Brückner, H. 1983.
Holozäne Bodenbildungen in den Alluvionen süditalienischer Flüsse. Zeitschrift für Geomorphologie N.F. Suppl.-Bd. 48:99-116.
Brückner, H. 1986.
Man's impact on the evolution of the physical environment in the Mediterranean Region in historical times. Geo-Journal 13/1:7-17.
Büdel, J. 1977.
Klima-Geomorphologie. Berlin, Stuttgart.
Cotecchia, V.,
G.Dai Pra and G.Magri. 1969.
Oscillazioni tirreniane e oloceniche del livello mare nel Golfo di Tàranto, corredate da datazioni col metodo del radiocarbonio.

Geol. Applicata e Idrogeol. IV: 93-148.
Eliot, C.W.J. 1962.
Coastal Demes of Attika. Phoenix Suppl. 5:127-130.
Hempel, L. 1984.
Geoökodynamik im Mittelmeerraum während des Jungquartärs; Beobachtungen zur Frage "Mensch und/ oder Klima" in Südgriechenland und auf Kreta. Geoökodynamik 5: 99-140.
Hempel, L. 1987.
The "Mediterraneanization" of the climate in Mediterranean countries - a cause of the unstable ecobudget. Geo-Journal 14/2:163-173.
Hempel, L. 1988.
Jungquartäre Erosion und Akkumulation im Landschaftshaushalt Griechenlands. Geographische Rundschau 40/4:12-18.
Kromer, B. et al. 1986.
Radiocarbon calibration data for the 6th to the 8th millennia BC. Radiocarbon 28/2B:954-960.
Lohmann, H. 1983.
Atene - eine attische Landgemeinde Klassischer Zeit. Hellenika Jahrbuch 1983:98-117.
Lohmann, H. 1985.
Landleben im klassischen Attika. Ergebnisse und Probleme einer archäologischen Landesaufnahme des Demos Atene. Jahrbuch der Ruhr-Universität Bochum:71-96.
Lohmann, H. 1987.
Zur Prosopographie und Demographie der attischen Landgemeinde Atene. Stuttgarter Kolloquium zur historischen Geographie des Altertums, Geographica Historica 5.
Neboit, R. 1983.
L'Homme et l'érosion. Faculté des Lettres et Sciences humaines de l'Université de Clermont-Ferrand II, Nouv. Sér. 17.
Neboit, R. 1984.
L'Homme agent de l'évolution du milieu physique. 25e Congrès International de Géographie, Paris 1984, Actes du Congrès:23-26.
Plicht, J. van der
and W.G. Mook in press.
Calibration of radiocarbon ages by computer. Radiocarbon.
Ranieri, L. 1972.
Basilicata. In R.Almagià and E. Migliorini (eds.), Le Regioni d'Italia 15. Torino.
Schneider, Ch. 1987.
Studien zur jüngeren Talgeschich-

te im Becken von Sparta (Peloponnes). Münstersche Geographische Arbeiten 27:189-198.

Tichy, F. 1962.
Die Wälder der Basilicata und die Entwaldung im 19. Jahrhundert. Vorgänge, Ursachen und Folgen. Heidelberger Geographische Arbeiten 8.

Vita-Finzi, C. 1969.
The Mediterranean Valleys. Cambridge, Cambridge University Press.

Man's Role in the Shaping of the Eastern Mediterranean Landscape, Bottema, Entjes-Nieborg & van Zeist (eds)
© 1990 Balkema, Rotterdam. ISBN 90 6191 138 9

Landscape stability and destabilisation in the prehistory of Greece

12

Tjeerd H. van Andel & Eberhard Zangger
Department of Earth Sciences, University of Cambridge, UK

ABSTRACT: Vita-Finzi's model for the late Quaternary history of stream erosion and alluviation in the Mediterranean presented in 1969 has greatly influenced views on prehistoric human land use in Greece. Here we summarize the results of three major regional studies (southern Argolid, Thessaly, Plain of Argos) of this subject in selected areas of Greece. Comparison of the three data sets and the literature indicates a single, early ubiquitous event, followed by marked regional differences, but leaves little doubt that the cause of soil erosion since the middle Holocene has been human activity. In three regions, major erosion and valley alluviation occurred about 1,000 years after the onset of widespread Neolithic land use; the date depends on the time large scale Neolithic land clearing began. From about the 3rd century BC to 3rd century AD, soil erosion is evident in the southern Argolid and probably the Thessalian plain and is indicated in the literature elsewhere in Greece, such as Elis, Euboea and the area of Olympia. In other areas, isolated erosion phases occurred during the 1st millennium BC. Medieval erosion and alluviation affected all regions, but apparently at somewhat different times depending on local conditions. Except for the Neolithic phase, local conditions appear to have been dominant in the stabilization and destabilization of the landscape, and a simple universal stratigraphy is impossible to construct.

INTRODUCTION

A growing concern regarding the impact of human interference in the global environment is inspiring increasing study of biological and physical processes causing global change. Many of these studies have tended to focus on establishing a baseline for the last hundred thousand years of the natural (and mainly climatic) variation. Public awareness of the issue, on the other hand, is being stimulated mainly by such human-induced events as the greenhouse effect, water pollution, drought, or catastrophic soil erosion. Either view yields an incomplete perspective; although the human factor has long been merely an overprint on a complex sequence of events ultimately driven by climate, well before the industrial revolution its impact has become significant and measurable.

Research on the late Quaternary climatic history, with a marked emphasis on the oceans, has major successes, but global changes of the last 8,000 years on land, the time when natural processes and human activity began to interact in a significant way, have attracted less attention and much less understanding has been achieved. Still, only for this interval do we possess the chronological means to resolve those rapid, even "catastrophic" natural environmental changes that are increasingly suspected.

Although for different reasons, the study of the human impact on global change and the demonstration of catastrophic change both present great difficulties, the first because of the complexity of the terrestrial environment, the second because it demands high-resolution dating. Tectonics, the geology of the substrate, vegetation successions, volcanism, sedimentation and erosion, and sea level changes combine into a system of such temporal and spatial complexity that a case history approach rather than modeling based on processes or on inferences from a global history seems for the time being to be the best strategy.

Key features of the Holocene history on land

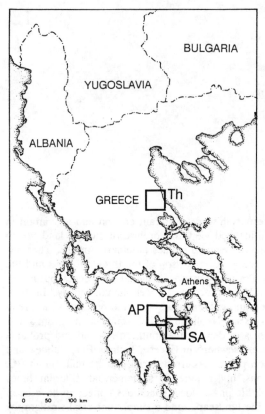

Fig.1. Location of three case histories discussed in the text. SA: Southern Argolid; AP: Argive plain; Th: Larissa basin, Thessaly.

are the many sequences of soil erosion and river valley aggradation, both often seen as consequences of farming and animal husbandry. Alternatively, increases and decreases in precipitation, tectonic uplift and subsidence, and sea level changes have been invoked. An understanding of these events on the long timescale of human prehistory and early history usefully complements the traditional view of the causes and consequences of soil erosion resting on the experience of the 20th century.

This paper is a summary of ten years of research in the Holocene history slope erosion and valley aggradation and their probable relation to prehistoric agriculture in Greece (Figure 1), carried out by our group, then at Stanford University in California. Greece is well suited to this undertaking because its subhumid to semiarid climate renders it sensitive to climatic change and human interference alike, and its agricultural

history is comparatively well known. Two of the case histories reported below were supported by the U.S. National Science Foundation, the third by the German Archaeological Institute in Berlin and Athens, and all three by Stanford friends of the programme.

EARLY MODELS OF LATE QUATERNARY SOIL EROSION AND VALLEY AGGRADATION IN THE MEDITERRANEAN

In 1969 Claudio Vita-Finzi, having added over a period of several years a large body of his own evidence to existing data on the Late Quaternary history of stream deposition in the Mediterranean, presented a simple model that has been widely used, especially among archaeologists (Vita-Finzi 1969). He recognized two major phases of alluviation, the Older and the Younger Fill, often easily distinguished by colour and texture; the Older Fill tends to red tones, the Younger one to browns and greys. During each phase sediments filled the valleys and stream channels cut in a preceding erosional phase. Renewed erosion which continues today in most valleys of the Mediterranean ended the Younger Fill. Vita-Finzi held climatic factors responsible for both aggradation phases. Archaeological data seemed to place the Younger Fill between late Roman (ca. 400 AD) and early modern times, while the Older Fill was thought to be of late Pleistocene to early Holocene age (ca. 50,000 - 10,000 bp). Subsequently, this model was widely applied in Greek archaeology by Bintliff (1976a, b, 1977) who modified it by placing the Older Fill in a pluvial phase of the early or middle last glacial on the assumption that it required a much higher rainfall than the present one. Like Vita-Finzi he attributed the Younger Fill to climate changes which he placed between the middle of the first millennium AD and late Medieval time.

The validity of such a simple model for a region as large and diverse in terms of geology, tectonic state, vegetation, climate and human history as the Mediterranean appears a priori suspect, and conflicting data and contrary points of view soon emerged (e.g. Butzer 1969; Davidson 1971, 1980; Eisma 1964, 1978; Kraft et al. 1975, 1977; Raphael 1968, 1973, 1978). Large differences in the proposed ages and numbers of alluviation events, and the wide range of causes invoked

Fig.2. Drainage systems of the Southern Argolid. Shaded: northern boundary mountains (after van Andel and Sutton 1987: Figure 5).

Cherry et al. 1988) incorporated geological studies into their programmes, although thus far little has been published. As a result the latest Quaternary soil and alluviation record in Greece is now much better known.

Similar studies have been carried out elsewhere in the Mediterranean, but a comprehensive review of the subject is beyond the scope of this paper. It should be noted, however, that Vita-Finzi's model, although now obsolete, has triggered so much study of Late Quaternary alluviation in the Mediterranean, that it must be regarded as highly fertile and rewarding.

Below we shall summarize three comprehensive studies carried out in the southern Argolid, the Argive plain, and the eastern Peneios basin in Thessaly which have shaped our current views expressed in the final sections of this paper.

FIRST CASE HISTORY AND MODELS - THE SOUTHERN ARGOLID

The Southern Argolid (Figure 2) is a small peninsula separated from the rest of the Argolis by a high transverse limestone and flysch range (van Andel and Sutton 1987). The northern half of the area is marked by steep limestone ridges, bare except for local remnants of red, gravelly, consolidated Pleistocene fans. The intervening valleys are filled with alluvium. Bedrock in the southern part consists of softer Late Cenozoic marls and conglomerates and is deeply dissected, although the uplands locally retain remnants of the once deep woodland soils. Rain falls mainly in the winter months with an annual total of ca. 500 mm. The streams are consequently ephemeral except for a few that are fed by large springs. According to local informants the others only flow approximately once every 10-15 years. The numerous drainages are small; most measure no more than 10 km² and the largest a mere 70 km². Modern stream channels deeply incise the valley floors; older terraces occur discontinuously.

The Quaternary of the peninsula was mapped in detail (Pope and van Andel 1984) from aerial photos and field study. Three basic depositional facies were recognized: (1) a chaotic, often very coarse, ill-sorted gravel in which the fine fraction supports the coarse material, a feature typical of debris flows; (2) well bedded and sorted sands and gravels of streamflood origin, and (3) sandy overbank loams. These facies combine in various

implied that, in contrast to Vita-Finzi's perception of regional stratigraphic uniformity, there might have been considerable local variation, and that both aggradation phases might comprise units of several ages. In a detailed analysis of the Younger Fill Wagstaff (1981) demonstrated the complex history of late Holocene alluviation and suggested an anthropogenic rather than a climatic origin.

It is obvious that an overly simplified or even erroneous model of alternating soil erosion and landscape stabilization, when applied to the record of Greek prehistoric and historic land use, would be capable of generating considerable confusion and misunderstanding. Concerned about this possibility, one of us (vA) initiated in 1978 a series of studies of soil erosion and valley alluviation in an archaeological context. The first of these was integrated in a detailed archaeological survey of the Southern Argolid conducted by Stanford University between 1979 and 1984 (Jameson et al. in press; van Andel and Runnels 1987). Other investigations followed in areas selected for their different geological settings and land use histories as the complexity of the late Pleistocene and Holocene soils and alluviation units became clear and their relation to the local history of land use gained credibility. During the past decade other archaeological surveys (e.g. Boeotia: Bintliff and Snodgrass 1985; Melos: Renfrew and Wagstaff 1982; and Nemea:

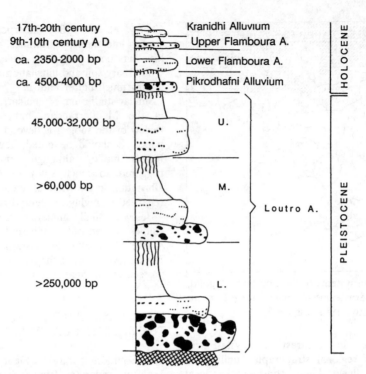

17th-20th century		Kranidhi Alluvium	
9th-10th century A D		Upper Flamboura A.	
ca. 2350-2000 bp		Lower Flamboura A.	
ca. 4500-4000 bp		Pikrodhafni Alluvium	
45,000-32,000 bp		U.	
>60,000 bp		M.	Loutro A.
>250,000 bp		L.	

Fig.3. Late Pleistocene and Holocene alluvium and soil stratigraphy, Southern Argolid (after van Andel et al. 1984: Fig. 4). Beds with large pebbles are debris flows, those with bands of small ones streamflood deposits; loams are blank. Wavy vertical lines indicate soils; length of line proportional to soil maturity. Bed thickness roughly proportional to thickness of unit.

ways to form the late Quaternary depositional units of the area.

Debris flows are evidence of catastrophic, sheet-wise slope erosion and occur when a reduction in plant cover, due either to decreased rainfall or to human activity, renders them vulnerable. Streamflood deposits, on the other hand, form when gully erosion is enhanced by increased precipitation or when livestock or humans damage the existing protective vegetation.

Each depositional unit marks a period of erosion of slopes and headwaters that caused valley aggradation, and each ends with a soil profile indicating a period of slope stability combined with non-deposition or erosion in the valleys. The semi-arid soils have a thin, rarely preserved A horizon and a distinct B horizon which, with increasing age, turns darker red in colour, acquires a higher clay content and blocky structure, and develops a lower, calcareous zone (B_{ca} horizon). The latter evolves with time from carbonate flecks and stringers via well developed carbonate nodules to a thick, hard calcareous

bank. The age-related characteristics of these soils (Birkeland 1984; Harden 1982) are useful in establishing their relative ages and in correlating depositional units from one drainage to another for the construction of composite stratigraphic sections.

Prehistoric and historic settlement maps for 26 intervals from Middle Palaeolithic to Modern, when placed accurately on the soil and alluvia map, together with imbedded sherds and radiocarbon and uranium disequilibrium dates (Pope and van Andel 1984: table 3), date the composite stratigraphic section (Figure 3).

The oldest Pleistocene alluvium dates to ca. 300,000 bp; two more units follow between ca. 100,000 and 35,000 bp (Pope et al. 1984), whereas four alluviation phases mark the last 5,000 years of the Holocene. All Pleistocene units combine debris flows and streamflood deposits, but those of the Holocene consist of either debris flows (Pikrodhafni and Upper Flambouro units) or streamflood deposits (Lower Flambouro and Kranidhi units). What triggered the infrequent but

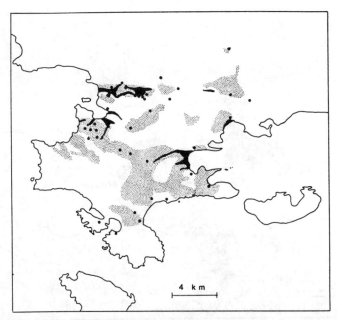

Fig. 4. Settlement and alluviation of the Final Neolithic and Early Bronze Age in the Southern Argolid. Shading indicates deep woodland soils; Pikrodhafni Alluvium of the late 3rd mill. B C shown in black. Dots are sites. Modified from van Andel et al. (1986: Figs. 7 and 8).

voluminous Pleistocene alluviations is difficult to say because the low resolution of the dating does not permit a correlation with indices of changing climate. Their absence during the last glacial maximum and the Holocene climatic improvement, however, suggests that erosion and aggradation are not related in a simple way to major climatic changes.

In the aggregate the Holocene deposits are far thinner than those of the Pleistocene and their regional distributions vary greatly. All but the last one have well-developed soil profiles which indicate prolonged quiescence between alluviations. Evidently slope erosion events were brief compared to times of stability; the Lower Flambouro unit is bracketed by dates that allow a duration of at most a few centuries.

The onset of frequent slope destabilisation came some 500-1000 years after the Southern Argolid had become settled by agriculturists (Runnels and van Andel 1987). Although farming was introduced here in the Early Neolithic, settlement remained restricted to a single site until the mid-4th millennium BC, when numerous small farms spread across the deep woodland soils of the lower hills and some valleys. Evidence for soil erosion, however, does not appear until the late

3rd millennium when Pikrodhafni debris flows, indicating extensive sheet erosion of slopes, covered the valley floors of the drainages occupied by Early Bronze Age settlers (Figure 4). Thus, the initial clearing of woodland cannot be held responsible, and van Andel et al. (1986) attributed the debris flows to gradual intensification of land use with shorter fallow, or to expansion onto steeper, less stable slopes. In either case, a temporary increase in summer or autumn rains (before the vegetation had freshened) might have acted as a trigger, but such short-lived climate changes are not easily detected in the record.

After a decrease in settlement in the early 2nd millennium the Mycenaean period brought renewed widespread use of the same soils, this time entirely without soil erosion, probably because of soil conservation measures such as terracing and gully check dams. These measures seem to have been effective; not even the nearly complete post-Mycenaean depopulation of the 11th - 10th centuries BC brought renewed erosion, perhaps because in the absence of tillage or grazing the natural vegetation was rapidly restored. Good soil management apparently continued throughout the following centuries of recolonization which culminated in the late 5th

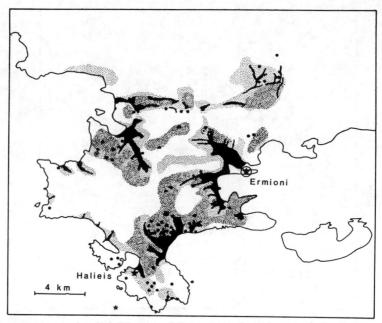

Fig. 5. Settlement, land use, and alluviation in the Classical/Hellenistic (black dots; ca. 325-250 BC) and Early Roman (circled; 1st cen. BC -3rd cen. AD) periods in the Southern Argolid. Large starred sites are cities. Dark stippling: deep woodland soils; light stippling: Pleistocene (Loutro) and middle Holocene (Pikrodhafni) alluvium; Black: Lower Flambouro alluvium resulting from Hellenistic and Early Roman soil erosion event. Modified from van Andel et al. (1986: Figs. 10, 11).

and 4th centuries BC in a major expansion of olive cultivation onto poorer and often steep Pleistocene fans and alluvia accompanied by dense settlement (Figure 5). In the last centuries BC, however, extensive well-sorted and stratified streamflood deposits formed in the valley bottoms (Lower Flambouro unit). This event coincided with a sharp decrease in site numbers during a historically well-documented period of rural economic decline. Comparison with practices in currently economically depressed areas of Greece shows that farmers tend to withdraw to their best soils and turn over the more distant or poorer fields to pasturage (van Andel et al. 1986). Even in prosperous times, fallow fields and olive orchards are used for grazing but shepherds take care to maintain terrace walls and dams damaged by livestock. Under economic stress, however, this is not the case, and the modern southern Argolid shows that in a few decades terrace walls tumble, gully erosion strips the stored soil, and streamflood deposits rapidly accumulate. A wetter climate, potential cause of streamflood alluviation, has

sometimes been postulated for the end of the first millennium, but the evidence is weak and the observations do not require it. Prosperity returned in Late Roman time (3rd through 6th century AD) and with it extensive exploitation of all usable lands, but no erosion and alluviation occurred, indicating that soil management was practiced successfully. Another depopulation began early in the 7th century, but the landscape remained stable, presumably because of rapid colonization by maquis.

In the 9th century AD upland and headwater areas away from the sea were resettled and extensive aggradation of the valleys below the new settlements took place (Upper Flambouro). These debris flows suggest careless clearing of the steep slopes without proper attention to soil conservation. Stabilization returned a few centuries later. The final alluviation phase (Kranidhi unit) began in early modern times; it is localized and of different ages in different valleys and continues today in several drainages. Its relation to local economic conditions is clear; terraces are allowed to decay because of land speculation related to a booming tourist industry or land is carelessly cleared (with bulldozers) for new crops and causes erosion.

There is thus good reason to attribute the frequent (but quantitatively minor) series of alluviation events of the middle and later Holocene mainly to human land use, although brief, minor climate changes may have contributed.

Interestingly, the onset of major woodland clearance in the late Neolithic was not followed by soil erosion until much later; one is inclined to attribute this delay to low soil disturbance and long fallow. Soil management was eventually learned and the landscape became stable, even at times of nearly complete depopulation, because the natural vegetation (maquis) is capable of rapidly stabilizing fields and terraces. Without soil management, however, extensive rapid clearing of steep slopes and coarse soils is inevitably followed by severe erosion and debris flows.

Once the landscape is under control, maintenance has its price and economic recessions may render this price too high. Neglect follows, and uncontrolled grazing may cause extensive damage to terraces and check dams, producing gully rather than sheet erosion and the deposition of streamflood deposits in the valleys.

SECOND CASE HISTORY - THE ARGIVE PLAIN

The model presented above, not being amenable to further testing in the Southern Argolid, required the study of appropriately different areas. The Southern Argolid was in the past, as it is today, a remote and rural sector of Greece. Widespread farming started late and throughout the history of the region great political and cultural events were muted there. Natural environmental changes also have been on a small scale; the area does not possess large rivers or wide plains nor is it very active tectonically.

Thus we undertook in 1984 a parallel study, again backed by a good archaeological data base, in a region closer to the heartland of Greek history, where human exploitation began sooner and on a larger scale. The rivers of the Argive plain are larger as is the sediment supply, and its drainage basin is well integrated, but it is close enough to the Southern Argolid to possess a comparable climatic, vegetation and geological

history. Despite its proximity the Argive plain contrasts with the Southern Argolid geomorphologically as well as archaeologically. It was thus well suited to test whether the models of landscape destabilisation developed in the Southern Argolid possessed a wider applicability.

From a purely archaeological perspective a reconstruction of the Holocene landscape of this historically rich area has long been needed to establish the environmental context of its great Bronze Age sites. Current views of the Bronze Age in the Argive plain (e.g. Carpenter 1966; Kraft 1972; Bintliff 1977; Kilian 1978) rest on a somewhat narrow factual base because palaeo-environmental and palaeogeographical studies in the area (Boblaye and Virley 1883; Lehmann 1931, 1937; Kraft 1977; Reisch 1980) are so sparse.

The Argive plain and the Southern Argolid have both been used by Bintliff (1977) to support his version of Vita-Finzi's scheme of Older and Younger Fill. In his view the Argive plain was a swamp of no economic importance until about 2000 years ago. At that time the Younger Fill, his only Holocene phase of soil erosion, began to blanket the wet lowlands, and when this phase ended about 200 years ago the soil had been provided that now supports the thriving agriculture of the region.

The Argive plain is a coastal basin of tectonic origin, about 243 km² in area, and bordered by the steep, barren slopes of mountain ranges rising to 400-700 meter. Many Pleistocene alluvial fans about 1-3 km wide fringe the central plain; their mature, deep red, calcareous soils indicate a long lasting surface stability. In the central part of the plain these Pleistocene palaeosols are buried under a Holocene alluvium which has been supplied by the ephemeral Inakhos River on the western margin of the plain. In contrast to the small drainages and short streams of the Southern Argolid, the Argive plain has a unified drainage system of 1167 km² (Lehmann 1937); almost all of the material eroded in this large area is deposited near the present coast where it has caused significant progradation of the shore.

The differences in depositional environment between the Argive plain and the Southern Argolid demand a different approach that relies especially in the coastal zone on about 150 drill holes ranging in depth from 4 - 30 m, rather than on aerial photos and natural outcrops (Finke 1988). Man-made outcrops also abound in this densely populated area and were used as well. Cross

145

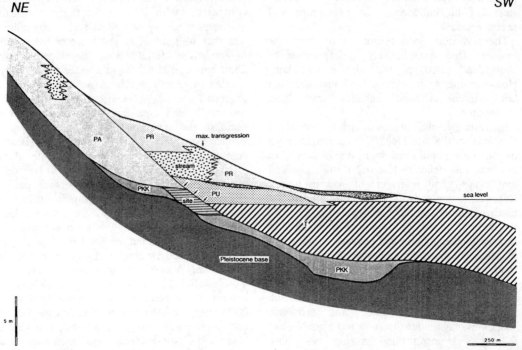

Fig. 6. Genetic classification of the soils in the Argive plain and their distribution. Most central plain soils formed on Bronze Age alluvium. The margin of the plain consists of Pleistocene alluvial fans while young overbank loams occur along the Inakhos river. The coastal zone has gone through alternating dry and wet stages in the Holocene and the present soils there have formed on recent marsh and lake deposits. Modified from Finke (1988: Fig. 18).

sections based on the drill data reveal major phases of landscape destabilisation and their impact in the coastal zone. Such cross sections (Figure 6) constitute the core of the following discussion. The Pleistocene red beds provide a distinct marker at the base of the Holocene deposits. This Pleistocene surface was formed during the last glacial when sea level was ca. 120 m below present and the Argive plain extended 10 km farther south (Finke 1988). A dark brown, clay-rich and organic A-horizon, full of roots, developed under its plant cover (unit PKK). It represents the early and middle Holocene land surface. Locally, abundant charcoal and pottery fragments indicate occupation of this surface. Evidence for a Middle Neolithic site was found in two auger cores at 5.5 m below the present surface (Figure 6). The unit is preserved only where the Pleistocene is buried under younger alluvium.

The first Holocene deposit (unit PA) is a coarse,

rather poorly sorted, consolidated alluvium sedimentologically quite similar to Pleistocene fan deposits. However, since it covers the Middle Neolithic site (Figure 6), it must have been deposited after 5000-4000 BC. During a following phase of landscape stability there was time for an A horizon to form on the alluvium and it was resettled. Subsequently, the postglacial sea level rise shifted the coastline far inland of the present shore until during the maximum transgression at about 2500 BC the Neolithic site and parts of the later alluvium were eroded.

The most extensive environmental changes occurred during the Early Bronze Age (Early Helladic II). Aggradation, especially in the coastal zone, covered the old surface with 1-3 m of floodplain deposits which today form the surface of most of the plain (Figure 7). These Early Bronze Age deposits, easily identified by their reddish brown colour (Munsell 7.5YR), high degree of consolidation, relatively thick clay films,

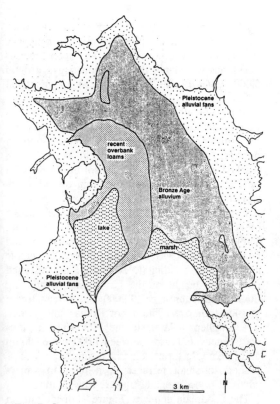

Fig. 7. Cross-section showing Holocene landscape changes of the southern part of the Argive plain. The Pleistocene base is covered at many places with a thick A horizon (PKK) which contains sherds in its upper part. A Middle Neolithic site is asscociated with this soil and was dated by ceramics and radicarbon method at 6200 BP. The first Holocene alluvium (PA) postdates the site but was deposited before the peak of the postglacial transgression (4,500 B P). Site and alluvium (PA) were eroded during the sealevel rise (arrows). Early Bronze Age alluviation (PU) resulted in a progradation of the coast (T = marine deposits). The final stage of deposition (PR) was triggered by man-made diversion of a stream in the Mycenaean period. After Finke (1988: Fig. 30).

and ubiquitous Early Helladic pottery, are most extensive on the inner plain and along streams.

This Early Helladic phase of sediment aggradation followed immediately upon the peak of the marine transgression and increased the deposition rate at the coast so much that it exceeded the combined rates of coastal erosion

and sea level rise. A rapid progradation of the shore began which extended in places halfway to the present coast (Figure 6).

A subsequent interval of surface stability lasted long enough for an A horizon to form on the Early Helladic II alluvium. This time of quiescence lasted until late in the Bronze Age (Late Helladic IIIB) when alluviations (Figure 6: PR) associated with natural and man-made shifts of an ephemeral stream on the east side of the plain buried the lower town of Tiryns under several meters of alluvium (Finke 1988; Zangger 1989).

No alluviations of regional extent have affected the Argive plain since the end of the Bronze Age. Unsorted black colluvium was deposited near Argos in Classical times and may be a result of landslides after fires. Everywhere the ruins of Classical and Hellenistic houses are found less than one meter below the present surface, demonstrating that deposition during the last 2,000 years has not exceeded one meter.

In conclusion, the present appearance of the Argive plain was shaped mainly by three regional phases of soil instability in the Middle to Late Neolithic, the Early Helladic II and the Late Helladic IIIB. All subsequent landscape changes have been minor in impact and extent.

Although the geological record is silent regarding the causes of the three soil erosion phases, the timing of the two most extensive ones between 5000 and 2000 BC is significant. It is not likely that the transgression itself would have increased the rate of sediment supply; its impact would have been limited essentially to the shore zone. The increasing population of the Argive plain, on the other hand, an expansion of land clearing and such innovations as the introduction of the plough could not fail to result in deforestation, seasonally unprotected slopes, and ultimately soil erosion.

The Holocene history of the Argive plain proposed here is quite different from Bintliff's reconstruction (1977). Where he assumed that alluviations took place only during the last 2,000 years, we have placed the main erosional events in the Bronze Age, leaving a single meter of deposits for the last 2000 years. The plain clearly never was in its entirety a swamp, although prior to the over-exploitation of groundwater since the middle of this century, the water table was much higher and small lakes and bogs did locally exist. The soils that are the source of the current prosperity of the Argive plain were also available to

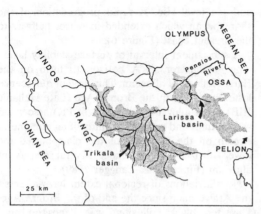

Fig. 8. The Peneios River system in northern Greece.

prehistoric farmers and exploited by them since the early Bronze Age.

THIRD CASE HISTORY - THE PENEIOS PLAIN IN THESSALY

The third case study of soil stability and destabilization in Greece was to be carried out in an inland basin far from the influence of the sea and changing sea levels. Most important would be a much earlier start of extensive woodland clearing and farming. The Larissa basin in Thessaly, part of the eastern Peneios drainage, meets these requirements including essential insulation from sea level changes (Demitrack 1986). A detailed study of its late Pleistocene and Holocene depositional history was undertaken since 1981 (Demitrack 1986). The archaeological background comes mainly from Halstead (1977, 1981, 1984). The Thessalian plain (Figure 8), one of the largest in Greece, is divided into an eastern (Larissa) and a western (Trikala) basin by a low NW-SE trending ridge. The Peneios River, rising far to the northwest in the high Pindos range, crosses both basins and, joined by several tributaries, finds its way to the Aegean Sea through narrow gorges across the Pilion-Ossa-Olympus coastal massif. The region is tectonically active; along its northern margin subsidence takes place on a number of normal faults.

In the Larissa basin itself the rainfall is low (ca. 520 mm), but the surrounding mountains receive up to 800 mm, and the main rivers flow all year. Trees are rare at the present time, but originally the basin was covered with an open, mixed-deciduous woodland; deforestation began around 5,000 bp (Bottema 1979; van Zeist and Bottema 1982).

Numerous alluvial fans fringe the northern rim of the Larissa basin and river alluvium blankets its central and southern parts. Fans and floodplain deposits have formed in several stages, each marked at the top by a palaeosol indicative of a period of quiescent non-deposition, during which stream incision took place.

The earliest dated Pleistocene sequence consists of no fewer than eight fan units (Old Red Fan: Table 1) separated by soils. It ended around 54,000 bp and was followed by much tectonic activity. Fan building (New Red Fan) resumed during the height of the last glacial, continuing intermittently until ca. 14,000 bp, when stream incision took over. The minor Rodia Fans formed a few millennia later. In the Holocene the fans were reactivated twice between 7,000 and 6,000 bp and in early historical times. Present deposition is limited to small terraces in a few fan valleys where it is occasionally triggered by faulting.

The floodplain deposits (Figure 9) divide into an older, higher group (Schneider's "Niederterrasse"; 1968) of Late Pleistocene and Middle Holocene age, and a historical pair deposited from 5 to 15 m below the Niederterrasse. The earliest, most extensive of the deposits of the higher floodplain (the Agia Sophia Alluvium) belongs to the middle of the last glacial (ca. 40,000-27,000 bp) and is topped by a mature palaeosol. Not until 14,000 - 10,000 bp did deposition resume (the Mikrolithos Alluvium), and another break followed in the Early Holocene. The construction of the higher floodplain ended with the Middle Holocene Girtoni Alluvium.

The present floodplain formed in two stages, both of which can be dated with the aid of archaeological data. The earlier one appears to involve Classical, Hellenistic and perhaps Roman sites, but without further work its precise age cannot be established. The late stage dates to the last 200 years.

Neolithic and Bronze Age settlements are numerous in the Larissa basin; most are conspicuous habitation mounds (magoules) resting on old land surfaces. In the Early Neolithic (8,000-7,000 bp) settlements were built upon the late Pleistocene Agia Sophia Soil which had already

Table 1 - Sequence and Age of Alluvia, Fans, and Soils in the Larissa Basin, Thessaly (after Demitrack, 1986)

Period	Age (yrs)	Alluvium unit	Fan unit	Soil unit
Latest Holocene	<200 (?)	Modern Peneios alluvium	Modern fan	Peneios Group soils
Late Holocene	historical (?)	Pre-modern Peneios alluvium	New Deleria fan	Deleria soil
Middle Holocene	7000-6000 bp	Girtoni alluvium	Old Deleria fan	Girtoni Soil
Early Holocene				
Latest Pleistocene	14,000-10,000 bp	Mikrolithos alluvium	Rodia fan	Noncalcareous Brown soil
	30,000-14,000 bp		New Red fan	Gonnoi Group soils
Late Pleistocene	27,000-8,000 bp			Agia Sophia soil
	42,000-27,000 bp	Agia Sophia alluvium		
Middle Late Pleistocene	125,000-<54,000 bp		Old Red fan	Rodia Group soils

been eroded down to its calcareous B_{ca} horizon. The Noncalcareous Brown Soil surface existed at the time but was not settled until the Middle Neolithic (7,000-6,500 bp). The Girtoni Soil on the eponymous Middle Holocene alluvium was not occupied until the Late Neolithic (6,500-6,000 bp). Early mounds on this surface are buried at the edges under up to 1.5 m of Girtoni Alluvium, and the soil profile is evidence of slow, continuous aggradation. Evidently the surface was being farmed well before deposition (during spring floods?) had ceased. The formation of the Girtoni Alluvium is thus placed in the Middle to Late Neolithic, about 1,000 years after the high Thessalian floodplain began to be farmed. All Bronze Age sites (since ca. 5,000 bp), however, are on top of the Girtoni Soil.

As Demitrack (1986) has shown in more detail, the causes of alternating phases of fan and floodplain deposition and soil formation in this area involve distant events in the source areas of streams and sediments as well as local ones in the basin and at the Peneios River mouth. Climate, vegetation neotectonics and human exploitation have each played a not always clear role. Contrary to the Southern Argolid, there is evidence for climatic impact on alluviation in the later Pleistocene, but the true cause-and-effect relations are not really clear. For example, the beginning of the dry glacial maximum (Bottema 1979; van Zeist and Bottema 1982) coincides fittingly with the cessation of aggradation in the floodplain and the onset of a long period of soil formation (Agia Sophia Soil).

On the floodplain deposition is resumed (Mikrolithos Alluvium) during the shift from dry late glacial to more humid postglacial conditions (van Zeist and Bottema 1982). Fan activity along

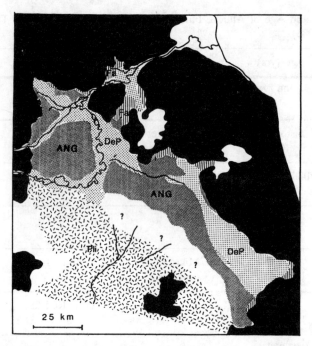

Fig. 9. Map of the late Quaternary soils of the Larissa basin, eastern Thessaly. ANG: Agia Sophia, Noncalcareous Brown, and Girtoni soils of the palaeo-floodplain; DeP: Deleria and Peneios Group soils; FA: late Pleistocene fan soils; Pli: Pliocene sediments of the Middle Thessalian hills; black: pre-Pliocene bedrock. Modified from Demitrack (1986: Fig. 6).

the northern basin margin, on the other hand, continues during the glacial maximum (New Red Fans) and latest glacial (Rodia Fan). Tectonics, in the form of basinward downfaulting, caused alternating deposition and incision while soils formed during quiet times.

To us the human factor is of greatest interest. The Girtoni aggradation, beginning like the Pikrodhafni Alluvium in the Southern Argolid about 1,000 years after the first occupation of the floodplain, strongly suggests a correlation between human land use and the Holocene resumption of soil erosion and floodplain aggradation. There is no evidence that the early settlers exploited the slopes of the Thessalian plain (Halstead 1984) to any great degree, a conclusion in accord with evidence from the pollen record that only minor clearing of their open oak woodland took place at this time (Bottema 1979). Thus the soil erosion that produced the aggradation must have occurred on the older levels of the floodplain itself. That such erosion

is possible on the nearly level palaeo-floodplain is clear because the Neolithic settlements on the Agia Sophia surface, where examined, rest on a truncated soil profile. During the interval between the first exploitation of the floodplain and the onset of the Girtoni alluviation, the density of settlements and presumably of population increased steadily (Halstead 1977, 1984), suggesting that here as in the Southern Argolid soil erosion was not caused by initial clearing but was the result of a later process, perhaps more intensive farming practices such as a shortening of fallow, deeper turning of the soil, or better removal of weeds. Alternatively, the use of the surrounding hill slopes for grazing may have resulted in slow woodland degradation and increased gully erosion. Climatic variations not resolvable with the available pollen record may have contributed; the fact that the early Holocene soil is non-calcic, the middle Holocene one calcic on essentially the same substrate, suggests such a possibility.

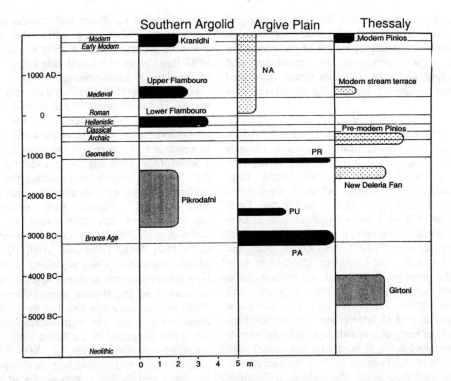

Fig. 10. Comparison of stratigraphic columns from the Southern Argolid, Argive Plain and Peneios basin (Thessaly) studies. Intensity of shading decreases with decreasing quality of dating; length of blocks represents approximate aggregate thickness of each unit. The last 2,000 years in the Argive plain accumulated only 1 metre of deposit. Pre-modern and Modern Peneios units are not adequately dated.

HOLOCENE SOIL EROSION AND ALLUVIATION IN GREECE - A CURRENT PERSPECTIVE

In the preceding pages we have presented summaries of three studies of Late Pleistocene and Holocene slope erosion and stream aggradation in Greece that are, to our knowledge, among the most comprehensive available today.

They cast little light on late Pleistocene alluviation history, because details sufficient to resolve individual phases are scarce and a reliable chronology of adequate resolving power is not available. The most comprehensive sequence comes from Thessaly (Schneider 1968; Demitrack 1986); its complexity, a function of changes in climate and consequently vegetation, slope stability, runoff, and neotectonic activity, may well be typical of the period. We do not see similar complexity in the threefold division of the

Middle and Late Pleistocene in the Southern Argolid (Pope and van Andel 1984; Pope et al. 1984), but this may be more apparent than real, given the fragmentary outcrop record. Useful as it has been in its time, Vita-Finzi's (1969) definition of the Older Fill appears to be only another name for "Middle and Late Pleistocene alluvium" without stratigraphical or palaeo-environmental significance.

Neither the Thessalian nor the Argolid sequence can be correlated with the glacial-interglacial or stadial-interstadial climatic changes of the Pleistocene, suggesting that our northwestern European sense for the geomorphological impact of ice age climatic changes needs adjustment when dealing with the late Quaternary history of the eastern Mediterranean.

For the Holocene much new evidence has been obtained since Vita-Finzi introduced the concept of the Younger Fill. The chronological and environmental resolving power of the methods has

151

increased considerably and the understanding of depositional and post-depositional processes has deepened. The stratigraphic use of palaeosols has added a new dimension to chronology and correlation, and several studies closely integrated with the results of archaeological surveys now exist.

The Holocene soil erosion/valley aggradation event histories of the Southern Argolid, the Argive plain and the Larissa basin of eastern Thessaly (Figure 10) agree only in the broadest sense, even if allowance is made for sometimes large uncertainties in the dating. All three experienced a time of landscape stability during the Early Holocene, followed by widespread soil erosion some time after the first spread of settlement and farming. In two of the three (Argive plain and Thessaly) these first Holocene alluviations were also the most extensive and voluminous ones; although not always the thickest deposits, their regional extent and effect on the landscape exceeded that of all later phases. In the Southern Argolid the early phase, although quite massive, is overshadowed by (and mostly buried under) later sediments of the Hellenistic-Early Roman phase.

After this first event the individual histories diverge. The Southern Argolid lacks the deposits of the Late Bronze Age observed in the Argive plain and Thessaly, but has instead two extensive aggradation phases late in the 1st millennium BC and in Medieval times. They may correspond to the pre-modern and modern Peneios alluvia in Thessaly, but the dating of those events is uncertain. The Argive plain, on the other hand, has remained essentially stable since the Bronze Age.

Figure 10 also demonstrates just how brief individual erosion phases can be. The common occurrence of pottery fragments in Argive plain sediments or the accurate positioning of sites of known age in the Southern Argolid sometimes allow very close bracketing of an event. In one instance the maximum time available for the deposition of 4.8 m of sediment was 50 years (event PR, LHIII-B2), and the entire Lower Flambouro event did not last more than 2-3 centuries. On close examination, the age of phases of apparently long duration often turns out to be poorly constrained, and some of those may also have been quite brief.

Thus the model proposed as a result of the Southern Argolid data appears to be upheld in some of its parts and not rejected in others. The

appearance of significant soil erosion and valley aggradation rather long after the onset of extensive Neolithic land clearing appears to hold in all three areas, the actual date being a function of the time of initial clearing.

For other parts of Greece, data regarding the earliest Holocene phase of soil erosion and valley aggradation is sparse. Genre (1988) suspects alluviation on Euboea before ca. 4,000 bp, and in Macedonia L. Faugères (in Delibrias 1978) noted a widespread loam deposit post-dating ca. 7500 B P. It is tempting to see especially the latter as evidence for soil erosion after the first Neolithic land clearing, although early settlement in Macedonia was less dense than in Thessaly (Jarman et al. 1982) and major deforestation came much later there (Wijmstra 1969). During the Middle Neolithic brown woodland soils of the type preferred in the southern Argolid were used extensively in the Nemea basin (Cherry et al. 1988) and subsequently lost, but the time of this erosion event has not been established and it may have happened in the Bronze Age.

Reports on Bronze Age (ca. 5,000-3,000 bp) soil erosion and alluviation are also rare. Davidson and Tasker (1982) suggested that soil erosion on Melos may have begun in late Mycenaean time, but if so it was localized. The southeastern Argive plain around Tiryns shows that problems of catastrophic deposition did arise locally (being successfully solved by stream management), but in general soil erosion seems not to have been a problem during the second millennium BC, almost certainly because of the extensive use of terracing and checkdams.

Considerably more data, although often poorly constrained chronologically or even geologically, exists for historic times. The Hellenistic - Early Roman phase of erosion and aggradation of the last few centuries BC seems to have been fairly widespread. In Elis Raphael (1968, 1978) dates it between ca. 350 BC and 300 AD. Dufaure (1976) placed the apparent analogue in the Alpheus basin above Olympia in the 2nd - 6th centuries AD, but his dating for this earlier one of his two phases is not robust. Hempel (1982, 1984) noted alluvium of this age in the southern Peloponnese and Crete. On the Ionian coast Eisma (1978) dated major alluviation in the Küçük Menderes valley between 500 and 100 BC, but in the adjacent Büyük Menderes valley the main phase fell between 100 and 300 AD. Anecdotal references to the burial of Classical, Hellenistic, and Early Roman structures under alluvium abound, but the dating tends to be inexact.

We view the last few centuries BC as a time of widespread although not ubiquitous destabilisation of the Greek landscape. This does not mean, however, that the preceding Archaic and Classical periods enjoyed complete freedom of soil erosion and valley aggradation problems. Genre (1988) and Rust (1978) have presented persuasive arguments for two brief, bothersome events of alluviation at Eretria on Euboea between 720 and 680 BC and again at the end of the 5th and beginning of the 4th century BC. As at Tiryns, the remedy for those problems consisted of quite sophisticated engineering works. Rust (1978) and Genre (1988) hold deforestation of upstream areas responsible for these local catastrophes. Local soil erosion also took place on Crete and in the southern Peloponnese between 700 and 200 BC (Hempel, 1982, 1984). On Melos, an historic alluviation phase began perhaps as early as the start of the first millennium BC (Davidson and Tasker, 1982).

Deposits of the later 1st and the 2nd millennium AD have been noted in many places. Büdel (1965) and later Dufaure (1976) described major alluviation at Olympia between the 7th and 14th centuries AD. Renault-Miskovsky (1983) described alluvial loams emplaced on Naxos between the 3rd and 7th centuries AD. The Melian erosion phase cited above reached its climax about 500 AD.

Major soil erosion and valley aggradation comparable to and synchronous with the Upper Flambouro of the Southern Argolid has been described by Genre (1988) for central and northern Euboea in the 9th to 12th centuries AD. L. Faugères (in Delibrias 1978) mentions alluviation in Macedonia from the 9th century AD onward. Wagstaff (1981), in his critical analysis of Vita-Finzi's "Younger Fill", cites many other cases extending from the 9th century AD (Middle Byzantine) to the Turkish period to support his argument that slope destabilisation and valley aggradation were episodic and occurred at different times and with different intensities in different places. This dispersal across time and space argues against a climatic cause, for example the Little Ice Age favored by some, and lends strength to Wagstaff's suggestion (and ours) that human interference with slope equilibrium has been at fault.

This view contrasts with that of Vita-Finzi (1969) who attributed the Older as well as the Younger Fill to climatic changes. Hassan (1985) also placed strong emphasis on climatic factors in the destabilisation of slopes and aggradation of valleys in semi-arid and arid climates. Brückner (1986) and Genre (1988), on the other hand, after thorough consideration of other possible forcing factors, came to the conclusion that in historic times neither climate nor changes in the relative levels of land and sea induced the observed soil erosion and alluviation events, and opted instead for the human factor.

Still, climate and sea level changes are obviously credible factors in Aegean Holocene geomorphology and should not be casually dismissed. A thorough discussion of the natural (and human-induced) surface processes operating in subhumid and semi-arid landscapes is beyond our scope; we refer to Hassan (1985), Nir (1983) and Thornes (1987) for more detail. That we regard these factors of at best minor importance rests on the following argument. Except for neotectonic uplift/subsidence where such activity is well documented, changes of sea level and stream base level have been small in the Aegean (a few meters) during the period considered here. As regards climatic changes (which may well have been significant), hard evidence for them is entirely lacking, and they are commonly invoked by reference to northwest European Holocene climatic history, an inappropriate analogue. When postulating climate or relative sea level changes as causes of landscape destabilisation in the Aegean, the burden of proof rests on the proposer and such proof has, to our knowledge, never yet been satisfactorily presented.

Perusal of the literature suggests to us two further general comments. The first is the casual or at least ill-defined use of the unqualified terms erosion and erosional phase for soil and slope erosion as well as for the erosion accompanying the incision of streams. Since slope erosion is often associated with stream aggradation and stream incision with slope stability, such indiscrimate use is confusing.

There also appears to be a widespread belief that valley aggradation and coastal accretion are independent processes that need not or even cannot be concurrent. This is not true. Schumm (1977, 1981; Schumm et al. 1984; Patton and Schumm 1981), summarizing the extensive experimental and observational literature on stream behavior and drainage basin evolution, has pointed out that the response of a drainage system to a change in conditions is complex. A single cause, e.g. increased slope erosion, can set off a chain of down-valley consequences, and may evoke different responses in different parts of the valley. Major slope destabilisation in the upper reaches of a drainage often produces aggradation which begins at the mouth of the stream where it is associated with coastal accretion, and proceeds upward with time.

CONCLUSION AND PROSPECT

In summary, the evidence that can be brought to bear on the problem of natural versus human-induced landscape destabilisation in the Aegean, although still limited, appears to us to point firmly in the direction of a dominant impact of human activity.The chronology, alas, remains less certain than one might wish, and this is even more true for our understanding of those processes of soil erosion and alluviation that relate to land use practices. Some inferences come from the small drainages of the Southern Argolid (van Andel et al. 1986), but much more is needed. We further suspect that the soil preferences of early farmers were not strong and played only a secondary role in land use patterns. It appears that the brown woodland soils of later Cenozoic marls and shales and those of Holocene valley bottoms provided preferred land for cereals to the present day, while the coarser deposits of alluvial fans and slopes were not exploited widely until the introduction of large scale olive culture in the Late Bronze Age (Runnels and Hansen 1986). Beyond this broad generalization, however, we see little evidence pointing towards a large influence of soil quality on land use until very recently. It has been water more than soil that appears to have controlled land use and settlement patterns from the early Neolithic to the 19th century. Many problems remain, such as our lack of knowledge of the time of introduction of terrace agriculture, or the important question of how much the aggregate soil erosion of the Holocene has really stripped the land. A reasonably secure estimate for the Southern Argolid (van Andel in Jameson et al. in press) suggests that it amounted there to ca. 40 cm removed from the mountains and less than 100 cm in easily erodable terrain, and so was insignificant compared to the impact of the Pleistocene. More such estimates are urgently needed, but for the time being, it seems excessive to label historic soil erosion in Greece as "catastrophic" as Brückner (1986) has suggested.

REFERENCES

Bachmann, G.H. and Risch, H. 1978. Late Mesozoic and Paleogene development of the Argolis Peninsula (Peloponnese). Interunion Geodynamics Commission, Scientific Reports 38: 137-160.

Bannert, D. and Bender, H. 1968. Zur Geologie der Argolis-Halbinsel (Peloponnes, Griechenland). Geologica et Palaeontologica 2: 151-162.

Bintliff, J.L. 1976. Sediments and settlement in southern Greece. In D.A. Davidson and M.L. Shackley (eds.), Geoarchaeology, p. 267-275. Duckworth, London.

Bintliff, J.L. 1976. The plain of western Macedonia and the Neolithic site of Nea Nikomedia. Proceedings of the Prehistoric Society 42: 241-262.

Bintliff, J.L. 1977. Natural Environment and Human Settlement in Prehistoric Greece. British Archaeological Reports, Supplementary Series 28 (i, ii), Oxford.

Bintliff, J.L. and Snodgrass, A.M. 1985. The Cambridge/Bradford Boeotian Expedition; The first four years. Journal of Field Archaeology 12: 125-161.

Birkeland, P.W. 1984. Soils and Geomorphology. Oxford University Press, Oxford.

Boblaye, E.P. and Virley, T. 1883. Expédition Scientifique de Morée. Section des Sciences Physiques II, 1, Géographie; 2, Géologie. Paris, 1832-1836.

Bottema, S. 1979. Pollenanalytical investigations in Thessaly, Greece. Palaeohistoria 21: 19-40.

Brückner, H. 1986. Man's impact on the evolution of the physical environment in the Mediterranean region in historical times. Geo-Journal 13: 7-17.

Büdel, J. 1965. Aufbau und Verschüttung Olympias. Mediterrane Flußtätigkeit seit der Frühantike. Deutsche Geographische Tagung, Heidelberg 1963, Tagungsberichte und Wissenschaftliche Abhandlungen: 179-183.

Butzer, K.W. 1969. Changes in the land. Review of C. Vita-Finzi "The Mediterranean Valleys", Science 165: 52-53.

Carpenter, R. 1966. Discontinuity in Greek Civilisations. Cambridge University Press, Cambridge.

Cherry, J.F., Davis, J.L., Demitrack, A., Mantzourani, E., Strasser, T.F. and Talalay, L.E. 1988. Archaeological survey in an artifact-rich landscape: A Middle Neolithic example from Nemea, Greece. American Journal of Archaeology 92: 159-176.

Davidson, D.A. 1971. Geomorphology and prehistoric settlement of the plain of Drama. Revue de Géomorphologie Dynamique 20: 22-26.

Davidson, D.A. 1980. Erosion in Greece during the first and second millennia B.C. In R.A. Cullingford and D.A. Davidson (eds.), Timescales in Geomorphology, p. 143-158.

Davidson, D. and Tasker, C. 1982. Geomorphological evolution during the late Holocene. In C. Renfrew and J.M. Wagstaff (eds.), An Island Polity - The Archaeology of Exploitation in Melos, p. 82-94. Cambridge University Press, Cambridge.

Delibrias, G. (ed.). 1978. Evolution des paysages sur les rives nord-méditerranéennes au course du Post-glaciaire. 6° R.A.S.T., Orsay.

Demitrack, A. 1986. The Late Quaternary Geologic History of the Larissa Plain, Thessaly, Greece - Tectonic, Climatic and Human Impact on the Landscape. Unpublished PhD-dissertation, Stanford University, Stanford, California.

Dufaure, J.J. 1976. La terrasse holocène d'Olympie et ses équivalents méditerranéens. Bulletin de l'Association Géographique Française 433: 85-94.

Eisma, D. 1964. Stream deposition in the Mediterranean area in historical times. Nature 203: 1061.

Eisma, D. 1978. Stream deposition and erosion by the eastern shore of the Aegean. In W.C. Brice (ed.), The Environmental History of the Near and Middle East since the Last Ice Age, p. 67-81. Academic Press, London.

Finke, E. 1988. Landscape Evolution of the Argive Plain (Greece): Paleoecology, Holocene Depositional History and Coastline Changes. Ph D -dissertation, Stanford University, Stanford. University Microfilm International, publication number 88-26140, Ann Arbor, Michigan: xiii + 209p.

Genre, C. 1988. Les alluvionnements historiques en Eubée, Grèce; Caractères principaux, chronologie, signification. Actes de la Table Ronde "Géomorphologie et Dynamique des Bassins Versants Elementaires en Régions Méditerranéennes":229-258. Etudes Méditerranéennes 12, Poitiers.

Halstead, P. 1977. Prehistoric Thessaly: The submergence of civilisation. In J.L. Bintliff (ed.), Mycenaean Geography, p. 23-29. University Library Press, Cambridge.

Halstead, P.L.J. 1981. Counting Sheep in Neolithic and Bronze Age Greece. In I. Hodder, G. Isaac and N. Hammond (eds.), Pattern of the Past: Studies in Honour of David Clarke, p. 307-339. Cambridge University Press, Cambridge.

Halstead, P.L.J. 1984. Strategies for Survival: An Ecological Approach to Social and Economic Change in the Early Farming Communities of Thessaly, Northern Greece. Unpublished Ph D-dissertation, Cambridge University.

Harden, J.W. 1982. A quantitative index of soil development from field descriptions: Examples from a chronosequence in central California. Geoderma 28: 1-28.

Hassan, F.A. 1985. Fluvial systems and geoarchaeology in arid lands: With examples from North Africa, the Near East, and the American southwest. In J.K. Stein and W.R. Farrand (eds.), Archaeological Sediments in Context, 53-68. University of Maine, Orono.

Hempel, L. 1982. Jungquartäre Formungsprozesse in Südgriechenland und auf Kreta. Forschungsbericht des Landes Nordrhein-Westfalen 3114.

Hempel, L. 1984. Geoökodynamik im Mittelmeerraum während des Jungquartärs. Beobachtungen zur Frage "Mensch und/oder Klima?" in Südgriechenland und auf Kreta. Geoökodynamik 5: 99-104.

Jameson, M.H., Runnels, C.N. and van Andel, T.H. (in press). A Greek Countryside: The Southern Argolid from Prehistory to the Present Day. Stanford University Press, Stanford.

Jarman, M.R., Bailey, G.N. and Jarman, H.N. 1982. Early European Agriculture. Cambridge University Press, Cambridge.

Kilian, K. 1978. Ausgrabungen in Tiryns 1976. Archäologischer Anzeiger 4: 449-470.

Kraft, J. C. 1972. A Reconnaisance of the Geology of the Sandy Coastal Areas of Eastern

Greece and the Peloponnese. Techn. Rep. No. 9, ONR N0014-69-A0407, College of Marine Studies. Newark, Delaware.

Kraft, J. C., Aschenbrenner, S. E. and Rapp, G. 1977. Paleogeographic reconstructions of coastal Aegean archaeological sites. Science 195: 941-947.

Kraft, J.C., Rapp, G. Jr. and Aschenbrenner, S.E. 1975. Late Holocene paleogeography of the coastal plain of the Gulf of Messenia, Greece, and its relationship to archaeological setting and coastal change. Bulletin of the Geological Society of America 86: 1191-1208.

Lehmann, H. 1931. Zur Kulturgeographie der Ebene von Argos. Zeitschrift der Gesellschaft für Erdkunde zu Berlin: 38-59.

Lehmann, H. 1937. Argolis - Landeskunde der Ebene von Argos und ihrer Randgebiete. Herausgegeben vom Deutschen Archäologischen Institut, Athen.

Nir, D. 1983. Man, A Geomorphological Agent. Reidel, Dordrecht.

Patton, P.C. and Schumm, S.A. 1981. Ephemeral stream processes: implications for studies of Quaternary valley fills. Quaternary Research 15: 24-43.

Pope, K.O., Runnels, C.N. and Ku, T.-L. 1984. Dating Middle Palaeolithic red beds in southern Greece. Nature 312: 264-266.

Pope, K.O. and van Andel, Tj.H. 1984. Late Quaternary alluviation and soil formation in the southern Argolid: Its history, causes and archaeological implications. Journal of Archaeological Science 11: 281-306.

Raphael, C.N. 1968. Geomorphology and Archaeology of the Northwest Peloponnese. Unpublished PhD-dissertation, Louisiana State University.

Raphael, C.N. 1973. Late Quaternary changes in coastal Elis. Geographical Review 63:73-89.

Raphael, C.N. 1978. The erosional history of the plain of Elis in the Peloponnese. In W.C. Brice (ed.), The Environmental History of the Near and Middle East since the Last Ice Age, p. 52-66. Academic Press, London.

Reisch, L. 1980. Pleistozän und Urgeschichte der Peloponnes. Unpublished Habilitation at Erlangen University.

Renault-Miskovsky, J. 1983. Les connaissances actuells sur la végétation et les climats du Quaternaire en Grèce d'après les données des analyses polliniques. Les Cyclades, Table Ronde: 99-109. Editions du C.N.R.S., Lyon.

Runnels, C.N. and Hansen, J. 1986. The olive in the prehistoric Aegean: The evidence for domestication in the Early Bronze Age. Oxford Journal of Archaeology 5: 299-308.

Runnels, C.N. and van Andel, T.H. 1987. The evolution of settlement in the southern Argolid, Greece. Hesperia 56: 303-334.

Rust, U. 1978. Die Reaktion der fluvialen Morphodynamik auf anthropogene Entwaldung östliches Chalkis (Insel Euboea, Griechenland). Zeitschrift für Geomorphologie, Supplement Band 30: 183-203.

Schneider, H.E. 1968. Zur Quartärgeologischen Entwicklungsgeschichte Thessaliens (Griechenland). Beiträge zur Ur- und Frühgeschichtlicher Archäologie des Mittelmeerischen Kulturraumes 6: 1-127. Habelt, Bonn.

Schumm, S.A. 1977. The Fluvial System. Wiley, New York.

Schumm, S.A. 1981. Evolution and response of the fluvial system: sedimentological implications. Society of Economic Paleontologists and Mineralogists, Special Publication 31: 19-29.

Schumm, S.A., Harvey, M.D. and Watson, C.C. 1984. Incised Channels: Morphology, Dynamics and Control. Water Resources Publication, Littleton, Colorado.

Thornes, J.B. 1987. The paleoecology of erosion. In J.W. Wagstaff (ed.), Landscape and Culture, p. 37-55. Blackwell, Oxford.

van Andel, T.H., Runnels, C.N. and Pope, K.O. 1986. Five thousand years of land use and abuse in the southern Argolid, Greece. Hesperia 55: 103-128.

van Andel, T.H. and Runnels, C.N. 1987. Beyond the Akropolis - A Rural Greek Past. Stanford University Press, Stanford, California.

van Andel, T.H. and Sutton, S.B. 1987. Landscape and People of the Franchthi Region. In T.W. Jacobsen (ed.), Excavations at Franchthi Cave, Greece. Fasc. 2. Indiana University Press, Bloomington.

van Zeist, W. and Bottema, S. 1982. Vegetational history of the eastern Mediterranean and the Near East during the last 20,000 years. In J.L. Bintliff and W. van Zeist (eds.), Palaeoclimates, Palaeoenvironments and Human Communities in the Eastern Mediterranean Region in Later Prehistory, p. 277-321. British Archaeological Reports, International Series 133.

Vita-Finzi, C. 1969. The Mediterranean Valleys: Geological Changes in Historical Times. Cambridge University Press, Cambridge.

Wagstaff, J.M. 1981. Buried assumptions: Some problems in the interpretation of the "Younger Fill" raised by recent data from Greece. Journal of Archaeological Science 8: 247-264.

Zangger, E. 1989. Prehistoric Soils in the Argive Plain. First Joint Archaeological Congress (abstracts), p. 93-94. Baltimore.

Wijmstra, T.A. 1969. Palynology of the first 30 metres of a 120 m deep section in northern Greece. Acta Bot. Neerlandica 18:511-527.

Man's Role in the Shaping of the Eastern Mediterranean Landscape, Bottema, Entjes-Nieborg & van Zeist (eds)
© 1990 Balkema, Rotterdam. ISBN 90 6191 138 9

Trace metal accumulation in soils on and around ancient settlements in Greece

13

John L. Bintliff, C. Gaffney & A. Waters
Department of Archaeological Sciences, Bradford University, UK

B. Davies
Department of Environmental Sciences, Bradford University, UK

A. Snodgrass
Museum of Classical Archaeology, Cambridge University, UK

1 INTRODUCTION

Modern evidence suggests that wherever people live or work metal concentrations in nearby soils rise, the metals are bound in chemical forms which are often not susceptible to diminution by leaching, and the resultant accumulations can still be detected several centuries later. This suggests the possibility that much more ancient settlement could also be associated with unusual and localised accumulations of certain metals in soil. Other soil properties, notably soluble phosphorus content and magnetic susceptibility, are commonly studied as an aid in archaeological research, together with other changes in soil properties revealed by cropmarks visible in air photographs. The success of these methods suggests that changes which are imposed on the soil mantle can be identified many hundreds of years, even millennia later.

The objective of a recent investigation was to determine whether certain pre-Industrial archaeological sites in Greece were characterised by unusual accumulations of trace metals in soil. Several metals were selected. COPPER and LEAD compounds have been used since later prehistory as has ZINC when alloyed with copper (brass) even though metallic zinc was not known in Europe until the 15th century. Nickel is a modern metal and there is no reason to suppose it should have accumulated in ancient sites other than around copper ore workings. MANGANESE was used in the ancient world to bleach glass but the metal was not isolated until the 19th century; its soil chemis-

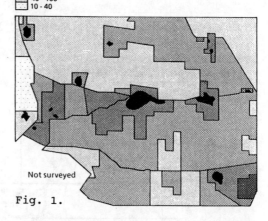

A TYPICAL BOEOTIAN DENSITY PLOT
In the northern sector, the ground slopes steadily from north to south; in the southern it is virtually level

- SITE
- Urban periphery
- 600 + sherds per hectare
- 100 - 600
- 40 - 100
- 10 - 40

Not surveyed

Fig. 1.

try suggests it is not a good candidate for an archaeological marker but it is a useful indicator of pedological conditions. However all of these elements may concentrate in animal and human faeces.

The samples were collected during the 1986 and 1987 field seasons of the Bradford and Cambridge Boeotian Expedition. Since 1979 the Boeotia Survey has systematically field-walked over 40 sq km of countryside in the central Greek province of Boeotia (Bintliff and Snodgrass 1988a). Ancient habitation sites have been identified from concentrations of surface artefacts (essentially pottery and tile) and by mapping 'offsite' background densities of ancient artefacts between these sites in order to trace past human activity such as field manur-

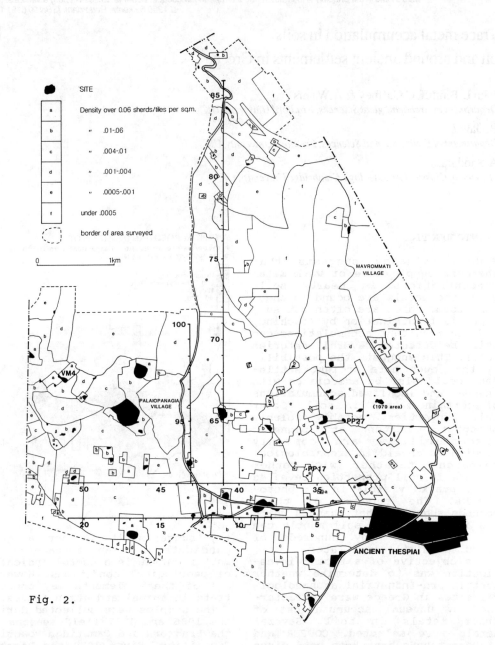

SITE

a	Density over 0.06 sherds/tiles per sq.m.
b	" .01-.06
c	" .004-.01
d	" .001-.004
e	" .0005-.001
f	under .0005

border of area surveyed

0 _____ 1km

MAVROMMATI VILLAGE

VM4

PALAIOPANAGIA VILLAGE

(1979 area)

PP27

PP17

ANCIENT THESPIAI

Fig. 2.

ing and work stations in the cultivated landscape (see the sector mapped in Fig. 1 with offsite density variations). It should be pointed out that our geomorphological researches suggest that the vast majority of this landscape has not been buried by eroded material since the time of the sites being considered in this paper, i.e. Hellenistic times; however it has generally suffered topsoil erosion

into localised lowlying depressions. In other words we consider this to be a truncated relict landscape.

2 TRACE METAL SURVEY

2.1 Regional survey

In order to provide regional baseline data for trace metal analysis and to seek evidence for any long-distance trends, surface soil samples were collected along several long transects (Fig. 2). Two east-west lines of transect were established, 500 m apart but in parallel, and both ran for 4 km west from the edge of the ancient city of Thespiae. At right-angles two further transects, running north-south, were set up, running for 2 and 5 km respectively. Samples were taken at 200 m intervals.

2.2 On site survey

A series of surface sites was chosen for each of which a grid of soil samples was taken for trace metal analysis. They included the ancient city of Thespiae, the medieval village at VM 4, and Greco-Roman rural villa sites at TPW 2, PP 17, PP 27, VM 64, VM 89 and VM 95. In most cases complementary information was available from geophysics (for structural evidence), magnetic susceptibility (reflecting habitation refuse and pronounced soil disturbance) and surface artefact patterning (indicating living, working and rubbish disposal areas).

2.3 Field and laboratory methods

Samples were collected using either a mild screw auger or a stainless steel garden trowel. After drying and chemical treatment metal contents were determined using conventional flame atomic absorption spectrophotometry.

2.4 Summary results

Inspection of the results (Fig. 3) indicates a general tendency for the lead, zinc and copper values from the specific archaeological sites to be greater than those from the regional transects, whereas the manganese values are smaller except at PP 17. Nickel values vary widely above and below the regional mean.

There was no evidence for consistent accumulations of nickel at the archaeological sites and this is consistent with the initial hypothesis that pollution by this metal

MEAN METAL VALUES OF INDIVIDUAL SITES AND THE REGIONAL SURVEY

| | METAL | | | | |
	Pb	Zn	Cu	Mn	Ni
	SITE MEAN SOIL METAL (mg/kg)				
REGION	6.6	6.6	5.7	761	192
THESPIAI	13*	18***	19***	239***	113
PP17	53***	7.5	13***	1019***	69***
PP27	11*	5.0	6.7	171***	89***
TPW2	23***	49***	23***	478***	446***
VM4	20***	17***	21***	70***	89***
VM64	16***	65***	26***	624*	232
VM89	19***	55***	28***	604***	473***
VM95	15***	55***	21***	532***	254

Values different from the regional mean are shown at the following significant levels: *** 0.1%,   ** 1%,   * 5%.

Fig. 3.

is essentially a modern phenomenon. As for manganese, the regional mean of 725 mg/kg is consistent with soil averages in the literature of ca 1000. Except for PP 17, site values are significantly below the regional mean. Whether the anomaly at farm PP 17 could be the result of stockpiling manure remains to be investigated. The zinc values are variable, with the means at Thespiae and VM 4 significantly higher than the regional mean, whereas at farm sites there can be both abnormally high as well as normal background values. This suggests that zinc may accumulate at village or urban sites where metal working and

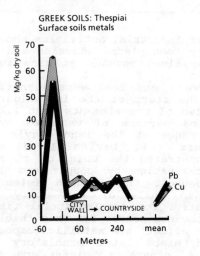

GREEK SOILS: Thespiai
Surface soils metals

Fig. 4.

161

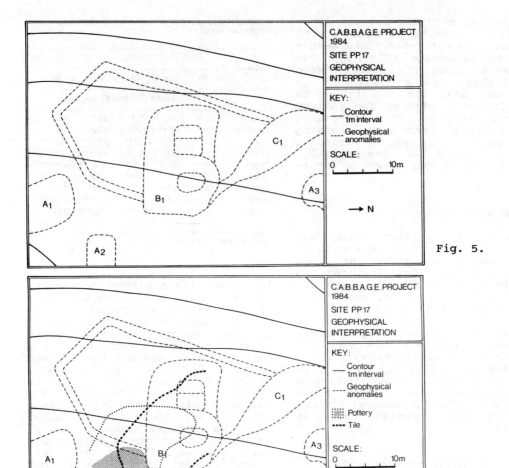

Fig. 5.

Fig. 6.

other industrial activities undoubtedly took place, but also and for
unexplained reasons at many rural
sites.

Copper and lead were identified
at the start of the investigation
as two of the elements most likely
to be markers of vanished human
occupance of the land. Davis and
others (cf. Davies 1978) have
demonstrated the ubiquity of soil
contamination by copper and lead
throughout the British Isles in
garden soils of both city and
country. For pre-Industrial times,
an obvious source for this 'habitation effect' are metallic compounds
used since later prehistory for
coins, ornaments, glazes and pig-
ments. However equally and possi-

bly more relevant in rural archaeological contexts is the evidence
from Classical written sources and
pottery disperal on and offsite
(cf. Bintliff and Snodgrass 1988b),
that long-occupied agricultural
landscapes and ancient farm and
village sites may have zones of
accumulation of human and animal
waste products, especially in the
form of manure, which may contain
abnormal concentrations of these
and other trace elements. Hence the
hypothesis that soils associated
with ancient habitation would contain residual accumulations of
these metals. Only at site PP 27
(where in any case we had low
sample numbers), was there no evidence of an excess of copper over

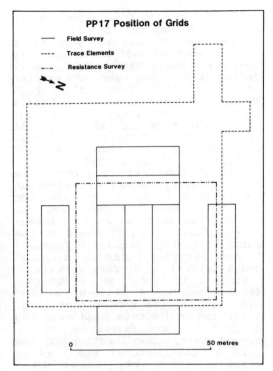

PP17 Position of Grids

— Field Survey
---- Trace Elements
-·-· Resistance Survey

N

0   50 metres

Fig. 7.

the regional background; lead was always elevated at the sites samples.

Perhaps the most dramatic illustration of these effects can be seen at the ancient city of Thespiae, where the sampling transect ran from the countryside across the ancient well into the former town enclosure (Fig. 4). Here metal values soar inside the walled area.

3 DETAILED ANALYSIS OF RURAL FARM/VILLA SITES

However the potential of the approach and its problems are best seen in smaller rural sites, typical for field survey, and where the activities involved anciently are much less understood compared with urban or large village sites.

3.1 PP 17

This site was located through surface finds of roof-tiles and potsherds and identified as a small farmstead of Late Hellenistic to Early Roman times. Possible outlines of the collapsed farmhouse came from resistivity survey (Fig. 5), together with additional features provisionally interpreted as farm enclosures and perhaps pits beyond. Contouring of the surface pottery (Fig. 6) showed the highest concentration left of the farmhouse, within and beyond the suspected yard; the roof-tile however was predictably focussed on the

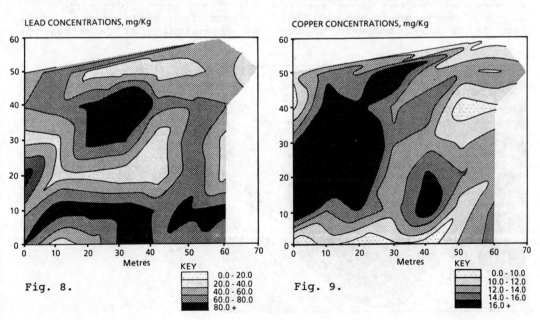

LEAD CONCENTRATIONS, mg/Kg

COPPER CONCENTRATIONS, mg/Kg

Fig. 8.

KEY
0.0 - 20.0
20.0 - 40.0
40.0 - 60.0
60.0 - 80.0
80.0 +

Fig. 9.

KEY
0.0 - 10.0
10.0 - 12.0
12.0 - 14.0
14.0 - 16.0
16.0 +

A TYPICAL BOEOTIAN DENSITY PLOT
In the northern sector, the ground slopes steadily from north to south; in the southern it is virtually level

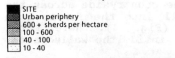

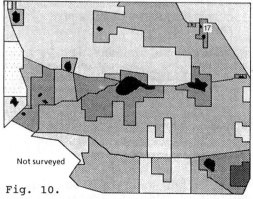

Fig. 10.

regional norm of 6.6, copper minimum is 8.4 compared to 5.7). Clearly the trace metals are picking up a wider area of past human activity than the habitation zone proper. Indeed a further set of samples taken in 1987 found that high values continue for both metals tens of metres beyond these diagrams away from the 'site'. Now if we look at PP 17 in terms of off-site pottery densities (Fig. 10) we can see at once that there is indeed what we call a strong site halo of high discard extending at least 100 m in all directions from the site focus. We interpret the combined evidence as showing intensive infield activity based at the farm, probably combining concentrated manuring, rubbish disposal and localisation of farm animals.

Further insights can be obtained if we look at a close-up of the site proper. The copper plot (Fig. 11) shows a discrete high over the query two-roomed farmhouse, with a second major concentration on the left of the picture; the lead in clear contrast (Fig. 12) forms a ring of high values around the farm but the actual structure is a pronounced trough of values. We seem to be picking up differential accumulation of the two metals across the site and in its halo, which should eventually shed light upon behavioural variations on this relatively short-lived site.

Apart from building-up a series of case-studies of farmsites like

dwelling structure. Interpretation here as elsewhere suggests that domestic rubbish disposal is associated with but not peaking within the living structure.

The trace metal sample grid covered a much larger area beyond these archaeological and geophysical features defined as 'site' (Fig. 7). The lead plot (Fig. 8) as the copper (Fig. 9) show values, even so, all well above the regional norm; all values shown are in excess of background (e.g. minimum lead is 22 mg/kg compared to the

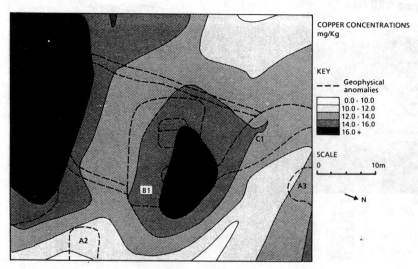

Fig. 11.

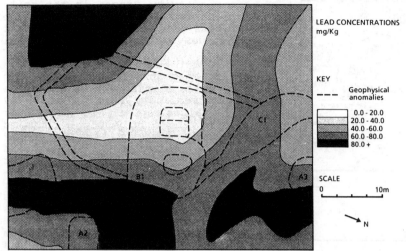

LEAD CONCENTRATIONS
mg/Kg

KEY

– – – Geophysical
anomalies

0.0 - 20.0
20.0 - 40.0
40.0 - 60.0
60.0 - 80.0
80.0 +

SCALE

0   10m

N

C1

B1

A3

A2

Fig. 12.

PP 17 to improve our understanding of such phenomena, a further avenue we hope to explore is taking comparable suites of samples from the extraordinarily well-preserved Classical farmsites in nearby Attica (Lohmann 1983, 1985), where the structural evidence is still free-standing together with contemporary field systems and agricultural installations.

3.2 VM 64

This is another small farm site (Fig. 13), this time of Imperial Roman date. The pottery contours identify a neat concentration with a northward tongue, and a fringe area to the south on a higher ter-

race. The tile counts (Fig. 14) identify essentially the same habitation focus, with a slight shift in peak values compared with the pottery peaks, yet also a northward tongue. For unexplained reasons at this site domestic discard broadly coincides with what seems to be the collapsed farmhouse. The geophysical interpretation (using an advanced Schlumberger array) (Fig. 15), compared with the tile and pot counts may be picking up one massive end and perhaps another boundary of this farmhouse, but also further unidentified features in the very top left and right sectors. Immediately adjacent to the query house is what could be an untiled yard or shed.

Magnetic viscosity measurements

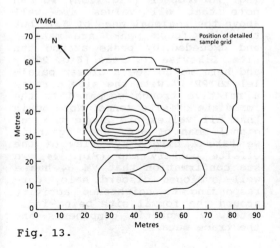

VM64

N

– – – Position of detailed
sample grid

Fig. 13.

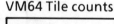

VM64 Tile counts

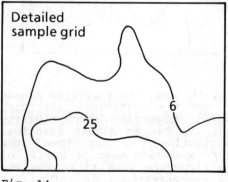

Detailed
sample grid

6

25

Fig. 14.

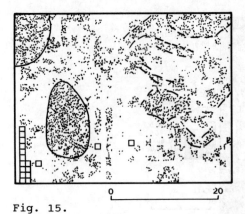

Fig. 15.

VM64 Mag. Vis.

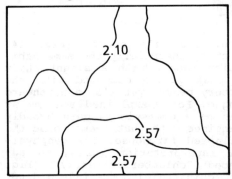

Fig. 16.

VM64 Mag. Sus.

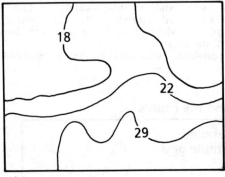

Fig. 17.

(Fig. 16) echo the roof-tile closely, and the mysterious northward
tongue. Magnetic susceptibility
(Fig. 17) has an almost identical
distribution. So far then, the
local separation seen at PP 17, of
main structure with tile from the
main concentrations of refuse and

human activity traces in the soil,
is contrasted at VM 64 where we see
a closer association. This contrast
continues with the trace metal
data.

Lead for example (Fig. 18) has a
strong concentration over the main
structure at this site, although we
note immediately that as at PP 17
high values appear in the upper
sectors where only the geophysics
had shown activity. As for copper
(Fig. 19) as at PP 17 one peak sits
discrete over the farmhouse, whilst
the other peaks are in more peripheral sectors, often where other
indicators apart from geophysics
are absent. The northward tongue is
a trace metal low in both cases.

Just as at PP 17 these hints from
the trace metals of a wider radius
of past human activity can be followed into a wider halo, beyond the
ostensible archaeological site with
ist structures and artefactual concentrations (Fig. 20). Four transects were set up running 50 m in
the cardinal directions away from
the site focus. Along each, soil
samples were taken for magnetic
susceptibility and trace metals.
The south-north pair (Fig. 20) for
magnetic susceptibility is here
placed against the tile counts
across the site proper; we see a
good agreement within the site, yet
the highest magnetic values are
just offsite to the south. Likewise
with the east-west pair of transects (Fig. 21), a very nice match
of tile counts and magnetic susceptibility on site, but the largest
peak is just offsite. The trace
metal results are even more striking: for copper (Fig. 23a) we can
note that all values are well
above the regional mean of 5.7, but
the site focus peaks are matched
and exceeded by peaks around the
site. Likewise for lead (Fig. 23b),
and here we do see a closer parallel to PP 17 with the site core as
a relative trough compared to the
immediate offsite zones. Note again
that all values are above the regional mean of 6.6. Once again if
we take a bird's eye view of the
offsite pottery map (Fig. 24) we
see confirmation that VM 64 has a
well-developed discard halo, corresponding to heightened activity
around the formal site being indicated by magnetic components and
the trace metals.

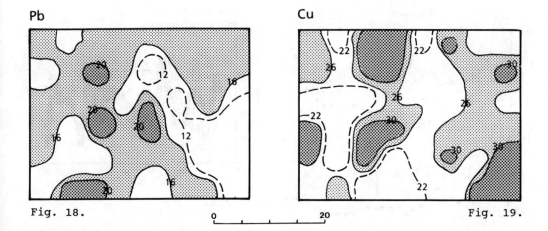

Pb

Cu

Fig. 18.

Fig. 19.

0   20

3.3 TPW 2

This is a much larger villa, typical for the Late Roman period. As may be seen from the regional sherd density map (Fig. 25) this 3.4 ha site lies in an area of extensive halo effects, in which its own substantial halo is merging with the gigantic halo effect of discard from the city of Thespiae nearby to the right of the picture.

Detailed analysis had only been made of a small hillock at the heart of the site. The tile count data for this sector of 60 by 40 m (Fig. 26) bring out two likely roofed structures and a lack of significant roofing to the left of the plot. The magnetic viscosity plot (Fig. 27) picks out the same two peaks but introduces a lesser accumulation in the far left. As for magnetic susceptibility (Fig. 28) we merely see the overall tendency mirroring the tile, to emphasize the right hand sectors versus the left on the sampled area. The resistivity plot (Fig. 29) is only available for the bottom limb of the L shape, but does give strong results: a massive east-west wall, a lesser north-south wall crossing it and what may be the corner of a structure in the upper right. If we overlay geophysics with tile (Fig. 30) it does ·look as if one roofed structure is defined by the lower enclosing walls, and the other roofed structure, seemingly larger, is defined by two walls running at right angles. It is quite likely that the

isolated wall stump on the right marks one corner of the upper farm building. The upper left sector seems well defined as a separate enclosure, with just a thin trail of tile above the wall maybe suggesting a shed or similar feature built up against the wall; interestingly the magnetic viscosity plot picks out this query feature as well.

Now for the trace metals. The copper plot (Fig. 31) picks out the lower roofed structure with a small peak, and larger ones for the upper roofed structure. But we also have a substantial accumulation in the neglected enclosure to the upper left. The lead plot (Fig. 32) is

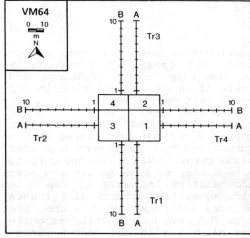

Fig. 20.

167

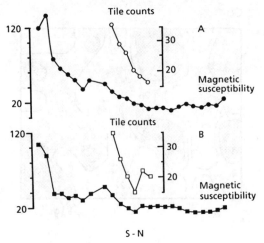

Fig. 21.

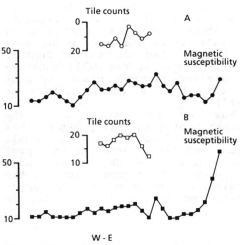

Fig. 22.

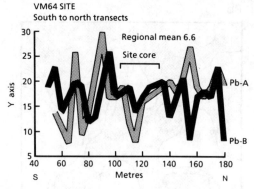

Fig. 23a.

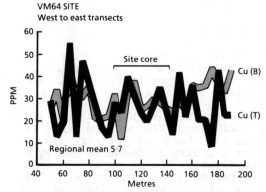

Fig. 23b.

peaking well over the lower structure, but peaks sit peripherally to the upper right structure and there is again accumulation in the upper left enclosure.

Comparing TPW 2 with our other rural sites we see once more that copper picks out the roofed structures, whereas lead overlies some structures whilst accumulating around others. Both metals are also accumulating in parts of the site lacking obvious structural evidence or artefact peaks. Within the site core the remnant magnetism associates closely with the roofed structures, but can be expected to ap-

pear in additional peaks peripheral to the habitation features identified by archaeology and geophysics.

4 CONCLUSIONS

We clearly have been able to demonstrate our initial hypothesis, that trace metals accumulate at very significant excess levels on and around ancient sites (even if as at PP 17 occupation may have lasted a mere 200 years), and furthermore that the patterning persists up to the present day. But is this going to be yet another example of the 'archaeometry paradox', where we produce scientifically satisfying analyses of archaeological data which nonetheless neither surprise the archaeologist, nor lead on to solve any important archaeological problems? No, in this case we would like to indicate some substantial

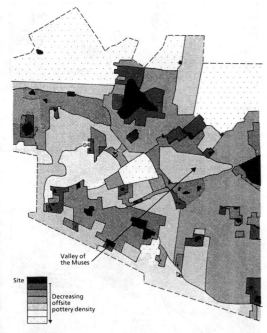

Fig. 24.

A TYPICAL BOEOTIAN DENSITY PLOT
In the northern sector, the ground slopes steadily from north to south; in the southern it is virtually level

■ SITE
Urban periphery
600 + sherds per hectare
100 - 600
40 - 100
10 - 40

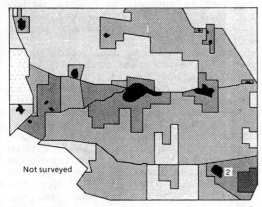

Fig. 25.

implications of the research results just outlined:
1) Firstly it has become clear that our concept of the 'site' should envisage on the one hand the traditional focus with buildings

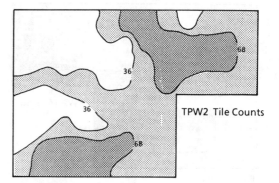

Fig. 26.

and peaks of artefactual refuse, but in addition a surrounding halo or infield of intense human activity, showing up from plateaux of offsite pottery discard and accumulations of magnetism and copper and lead that are often above site focus levels. Both zones have values all well in excess of the regional norm. The research frontier here will be to model ancient behaviour, and try to identify recurring suites of patterning, as well as to investigate accumulation patterns in modern farm contexts.

Site survey is a major archaeological tool. Only a tiny fraction of sites discovered will ever be excavated, so the application of this kind of battery of subsurface and surface approaches is a vital aid to interpretation of field survey data. In fact it is probable that excavation in the halo area would in any case find little or no structural evidence.

2) Secondly, these results shed unexpected light on a major issue in landscape archaeology, the

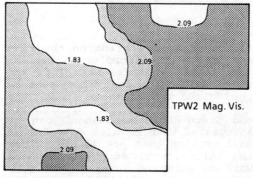

Fig. 27.

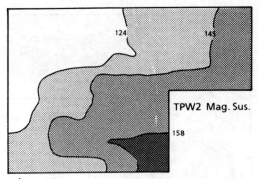

Fig. 28.

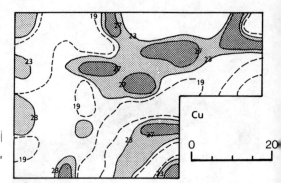

Fig. 31.

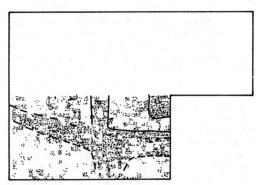

Fig. 29.

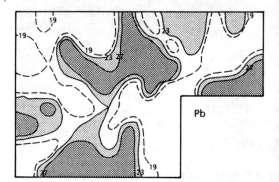

Fig. 32.

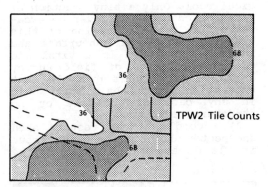

Fig. 30.

effect of soil erosion on the rise and fall of past complex societies. For Greece van Andel (cf. Pope and van Andel 1984) and other geomorphologists have shown that the cyclical collapse of prehistoric and Greco-Roman settlement can be associated with massive episodes of soil erosion that presumably ruined the agricultural economy. Our own work on relative densities of surface pottery (Bintliff and Snod-grass 1988b) shows a cline of ever greater amounts of surface pottery as one moves from England, through the Mediterranean, to Arabia, which we have interpreted as reflecting amongst other processes a cline of increased soil erosion.

Yet our Boeotian data allow us to set limits to the scale of these erosion processes. The pottery and tile peaks over site foci can of course remain even if the soil fines, their original context, have washed away, but the peak accumulations of remnant magnetic components and copper and lead within site foci and in the immediate halo can only be explained through the survival in situ of at least the original subsoil of the ancient sites. In support of this view Professor van Andel has estimated that the total depth of soil lost on average in the last 5000 years in the southern Greek landscape is less than 1 m (van Andel et al. 1986:111).

3) The trace metals programme may well prove vital in shedding new light on past intensity of land

170

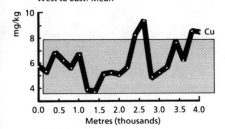

GREEK REGIONAL COPPER
West to East: Mean

Fig. 33.

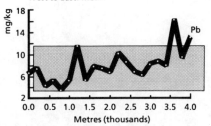

GREEK REGIONAL LEAD
West to East: Mean

Fig. 34.

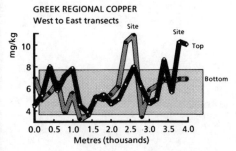

GREEK REGIONAL COPPER
West to East transects

Fig. 35.

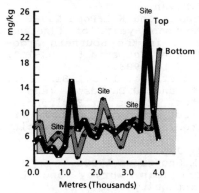

GREECE REGIONAL LEAD
West to East transects

Fig. 36.

use across the countryside. Already we have used the offsite pottery densities to suggest (cf. Bintliff 1988) that although field survey never finds all the ancient farm sites, the low numbers in the north of our survey area genuinely reflect less intensive land use. It should be possible (and we are already experimenting with area grid soil collection strategies in Yugoslavia and Greece to this purpose), to match trace metal accumulations with offsite pottery discard, if we are correct in our belief that much of the excess copper and lead reflect human and animal manure spread over the cultivated landscape.

Quite unintentionally our Boeotian regional trace metal transects, although designed as a control over anthropogenic accumulations at habitation sites, hint at the potential of offsite trace metal analysis for land-use history. We must point out that the sample collection design could not have been less suitable for obtaining a picture of local manuring patterns, with tiny soil samples gathered at 200 m intervals. Even so, if we note how the east-west transects run from lowish offsite discard into higher levels nearing the city of Thespiae, undoubtedly reflecting urban infield manuring, so on the mean plots for copper and lead (Figs. 33 and 34), we see a general trend of rising values towards the city. We can even say something about some of the peaks or hollows on these graphs, covering as they do 4 km of landscape: quite a few of the localised peaks mark sectors where soil samples were taken within site haloes (Figs. 35 and 36).

Clearly we need to take many more closely-spaced soil samples for an accurate comparison with field-by-field offsite pottery density values, in order to test the usefulness of trace metal assay for past land-use intensity. Trace metals should be much more firmly attached to the soil matrix than phosphates and their analysis could act as a complement and in many soils a replacement for phosphate analysis at the landscape level.

REFERENCES

Andel, T.H.van,
C.N.Runnels and K.O.Pope 1996.
Five thousand years of land use
and abuse in the Southern Argolid, Greece. Hesperia 55:103-128.

Bintliff, J.L. 1988.
Site patterning. In J.L.Bintliff,
E.Grant and D.Davidson (eds.),
Conceptual Issues in Environmen-
tal Archaeology, p.129-144.
Edinburgh, Edinburgh University
Press.

Bintliff, J.L.
and A.M.Snodgrass 1988a.
Mediterranean survey and the
city. Antiquity 62:57-71.

Bintliff, J.L.
and A.M.Snodgrass 1988b.
Offsite-pottery distributions.
Current Anthropology 29: 506-513.

Davies, B.E. 1978.
Plant available lead and other
metals in British garden soils.
Science of the Total Environment
9:243-262.

Lohmann, H. 1983.
Atene: eine attische Landgemeinde
klassischer Zeit. Hellenika Jahr-
buch:98-117.

Lohmann, H. 1985.
Landleben im klassischen Attika.
Jahrbuch Ruhr-Universität Bochum:
71-96.

Pope, K.O. and T.H.van Andel 1984.
Late Quaternary alluviation and
soil formation in the Southern
Argolid. Journal of Archaeological Science 11:281-306.

Man's Role in the Shaping of the Eastern Mediterranean Landscape, Bottema, Entjes-Nieborg & van Zeist (eds)
© *1990 Balkema, Rotterdam. ISBN 90 6191 138 9*

A Postglacial record from the Kopais Basin, Greece

14

Harriet Allen
Department of Geography, Homerton College, Cambridge, UK

ABSTRACT: Analysis of lake sediments from the Kopais Basin indicates that open water conditions gave way to marsh sometime between 5,000 and 3,500 years BP. The Postglacial pollen record is dominated by oak, until this declines from about 5,000 years BP. At the time of the decline there are peak values in the sediment record of frequency dependent susceptibility – a measure of the presence of magnetically enhanced minerals in the sediment. These are interpreted as being derived from inwash of eroded topsoil from the catchment. From this information it seems likely that a Mycenaean drainage attempt about 3,500 years ago occurred during a marsh rather than lake phase. A radiocarbon date from sediment close to one of the Mycenaean dikes provides possible further evidence for the date of the drainage attempt.

1 INTRODUCTION

This paper presents results of sediment analysis from the Kopais Basin, Greece, which can be interpreted in terms of human activity. As such, it is just part of a larger study of the basin sediment characteristics for approximately the last 27,000 years.

The Kopais Basin, in Boeotia, is about 80 km northwest of Athens. It has long been an area of archaeological interest because of a Mycenaean attempt to drain it about 3,500 years ago. Today it is dry and intensively farmed, but in the nineteenth century it was a large, seasonal marsh. The basin is a tectonic depression and the sediment record shows that a lake once occupied the lowest part of the catchment, fed by the Kephissos river which drains down from Mt. Parnassos, and the river Melas, which is spring-fed and rises in the northwest of the basin (Fig. 1). The catchment is predominantly limestone. Although there is no overland outflow from the basin, it is not hydrologically closed; sinkholes (katavothrae) border the northern and eastern sides and so

complicate the environmental interpretation of the sediments.

Two sediment cores were taken in metre lengths using a Livingstone corer. Core KA is 20.5 m long and core KB 16 m long. Both extend back approximately 25,000 to 27,000 years. From radiocarbon dates the uppermost material in core KB dates from soon after 12,500 years BP. The work presented here is therefore based on an analysis of core KA, which has a much younger finishing date, together with additional material from an exposure of lake sediment revealed for building purposes in May 1984 at Karditsa Farmstead (see Fig. 1 for location sites).

2 SEDIMENT ANALYSIS

Pollen analysis of core sediment was carried out by Professor J.C. Ritchie of the University of Toronto. Taxa were identified and counted at intervals of about 20 cm and both percentage and concentration diagrams were produced.

Radiocarbon dates were determined on organic material. There was relatively little datable material

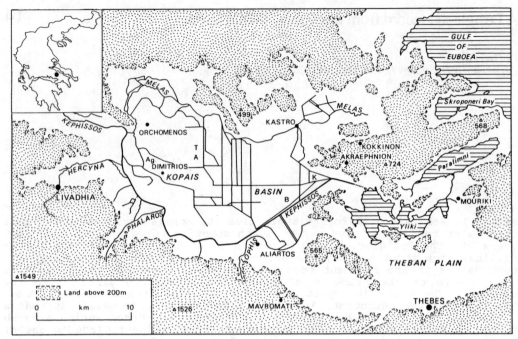

Fig. 1. The Kopais Basin. A and B mark the sites of cores KA and KB; T indicates the site of the Turner and Greig core; K is Karditsa Farmstead.

but two dates were obtained from core KA. The older date of 12,520± 150 years BP (Q-2487) matches a date of 12,300±150 years BP (Q-2488) from core KB, while the younger date of 9,900±110 years BP (Q-2486) matches a date of 9,970± 120 years BP (Q-2489) from the Karditsa Farmstead exposure. There were also two younger dates from Karditsa Farmstead of 4,620±150 years BP (Q-2490) and 3,480±150 years BP (Q-2491). Caution is needed with the calculation of sedimentation rates from extrapolation of these radiocarbon dates. Nevertheless this is the basis, together with the pollen record, for the estimate of the basal date of 25,000 to 27,000 years BP for both cores.

Mineral magnetic techniques were used to study the magnetic properties of the sediments. The basis of mineral magnetism is the fact that almost all rocks contain magnetic minerals, and that iron oxides are common in soils and, through erosion and deposition, in sediments. Iron oxides in soils are sensitive to the changing physical and chemical environment of the

soils. The application of such techniques has been most successful in areas where there is a source of primary magnetic material (from the underlying catchment geology, such as granite) or where a secondary magnetic component is present in the soils, resulting either from pedogenesis or fire (Thompson and Oldfield 1986). Thus magnetic parameters measured on sediments may be used to make inferences about some aspects of the environmental history of a lake catchment.

The magnetic parameters referred to in this paper are magnetic susceptibility (χ), frequency dependent susceptibility (χ_{fd}), isothermal remanent magnetization (IRM) and saturation isothermal remanent magnetization (SIRM). Magnetic susceptibility is the ratio of induced magnetization to applied field (Oldfield et al. 1978) and thus is a measure of how "magnetizable" a sample is. The susceptibility record can be used for correlation of two or more cores and can be interpreted in terms of the input of magnetic particles to the sediment. Frequency dependent susceptibility can be used as a measure of the presence of magnetically enhanced minerals in topsoils (Mullins and Tite 1973). It is calculated by measuring the initial low frequency susceptibility of a sample and then its high frequency susceptibility and is here expressed as the percentage ratio of frequency dependent susceptibility to low frequency dependent susceptibility (χ_{fd} / χ). High ratios in lake sediments may be associated with the inwash of eroded magnetically enhanced topsoil.

Magnetic enhancement is the formation of secondary ferrimagnetic oxides that occurs in the upper layers of soil (Le Borgne 1955). The pedogenic processes responsible for enhancement are poorly understood (Dearing et al. 1985) but it is thought that a major process may be via a redox cycle occurring under normal pedogenic conditions (Mullins 1977): microcrystalline maghemite or magnetite are formed from weakly magnetic iron oxides and hydroxides via reduction and oxidation cycles. Enhancement may also result from the burning of soils. It is best preserved in soils where gleying has not occurred. Tite and Linnington (1975) suggested that enhancement of soils on limestones in Italy, Greece, Turkey and Crete was largely a reflection of climate. A "fermentation" mechanism results from anaerobic soil conditions in the humid winters and oxidizing conditions in dry summers.

Isothermal remanent magnetization is the magnetic remanence grown by the application and subsequent removal of a magnetic field to a sample. The magnitude of the remanence depends on the strength of the steady field applied (Thompson and Oldfield 1986). Maximum remanence is known as saturation IRM. In the Kopais samples this was induced at a steady field of 1.0 Tesla which may in fact not be sufficient to produce saturation, which is dependent on composition and grain size of the magnetic material, but which is the highest field at which it was practical to produce remanence. IRM and SIRM are concentration dependent parameters and are used to differentiate types and sizes of magnetic minerals.

Loss on ignition at 1,000° C was used to estimate the carbonate content of the sediment. Because the Kopais sediments are rich in clay and silt sized particles the technique probably overestimates carbonate matter through loss of lattice water (Dean 1974).

X-ray diffraction and scanning electron microscopy were used to identify the dominant mineralogy of sediment samples.

3 RESULTS

The results of the sediment analysis are interpreted with respect to possible indications of human activity in the Kopais Basin and therefore only the Postglacial sedimentary phase is considered. For core KA this is represented by the top 9.5 m which date from the level of the 12,520±150 years BP radiocarbon date. The top of the core is interpreted as the end of the lake sediment phase. The reasons for this conclusion will be considered in more detail below, but this is dated to between 5,000 and 3,500 years BP.

The pollen stratigraphy for core KA (Fig. 2) is similar to those of other Greek pollen studies for the same period (van der Hammen et al. 1971; Bottema 1974, 1979; van Zeist and Bottema 1982) and indeed closely resembles a previous Kopais stratigraphy (Greig and Turner 1974; Turner and Greig 1975). One of the major characteristics of the KA record is the marked increase in Quercus pollen concentrations which occurs at the dated level of 12,520 ±150 years BP. At the same time total concentrations of all pollen taxa are rising to reach a peak at a depth of about 9.0 m and again at about 7.0 m just above the dated level of 9,900±100 years BP at 7.5 m. Thus the pollen spectra between 10.0 m and 7.0 m represent the period of climatic change from Pleistocene to Holocene conditions.

During the Postglacial, arboreal pollen predominates and herbaceous pollen declines. The most dramatic increase is in Quercus pollen. Concentrations and percentages of this remain high until it begins to decline at about 4.0 m. During the initial rise in Quercus pollen, Juniperus, Ephedra, Pistacia and Olea have relatively high percent-

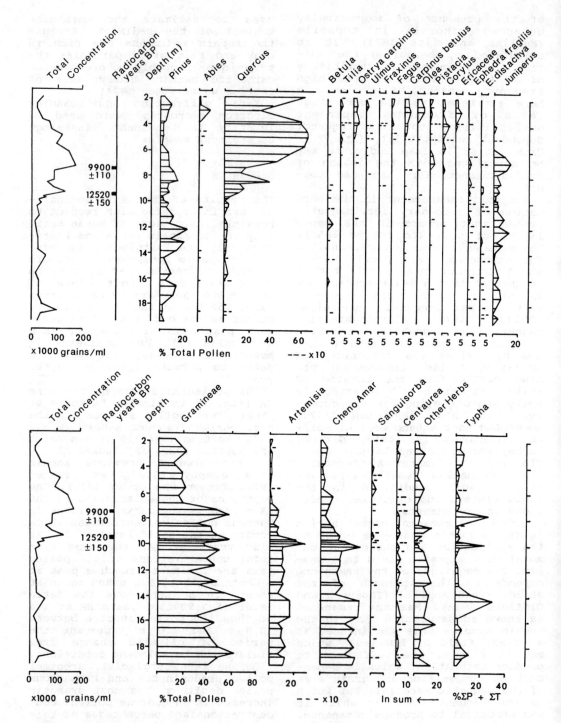

Fig. 2. Percentage pollen diagram for core KA.

ages but these decline in response to the continued rise in Quercus. Other trees now become important: Ostrya/Carpinus, Fagus and Carpinus betulus. Their relative importance increases above 4.0 m as Quercus percentages decline. At this point Gramineae pollen increases in both concentration and percentage values.

In the Greig and Turner (1974) pollen diagram the decline in Quercus pollen is associated with a radiocarbon date of 5,205±120 years BP. The dated material was peat and its formation was attributed to forest clearance and subsequent erosion of catchment slopes. It is argued that inwash of soil led to shallower, muddy conditions favourable for peat growth. If constant sedimentation rates can be assumed for core KA then the equivalent date in that core would be at a depth of 3.9 m. At this level Quercus concentrations are beginning to decline but the match position must remain tentative given that sedimentation rates need not have been constant. This, however, suggests that the top of core KA is younger than 5,000 years BP.

Throughout the Postglacial period, Olea pollen appears sporadically. It occurs earlier in core KA than in Greig and Turner's diagram but percentages are low; less than 0.5% between depths of 10.0 m and 5.0 m, i.e., well before the inferred date of about 5,000 years BP. However, in the last three pollen samples, above 3.2 m, percentages rise to between 3% and 5% as Quercus percentages decline. The presence of Olea need not be indicative of olive cultivation in the immediate area of Kopais because the pollen influx may have been derived from other areas of olive cultivation. In addition, the Olea pollen source may be the wild rather than domesticated olive. Nevertheless the relatively high percentages suggest a possibility of cultivation (Bottema and Woldring, this volume) and that this occurred sometime after about 5,200 years BP.

The record of specific magnetic susceptibility for core KA is shown in Fig. 3. Because calcite is diamagnetic and has a negative specific susceptibility, the KA values have been corrected for calcite

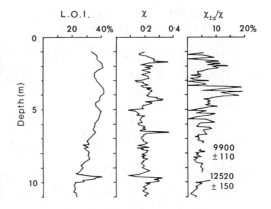

Fig. 3. Loss on ignition at 1,000° C, magnetic susceptibility (χ) in $\mu m^3 kg^{-1}$ and frequency dependent susceptibility (χ_{fd}/χ) for the top 11 m of core KA.

content on the basis of the estimated carbonate content. Not surprisingly given that the Kopais has a predominantly limestone catchment, specific susceptibility values are low. Limestone lacks a primary magnetic component. The corrected susceptibility profile shows peak values at depths of about 1.7 m to 2.0 m and 3.7 m to 4.2 m. By examining the profile together with that for frequency dependent susceptibility (Fig. 3) it is possible to suggest a reason for the peak values. Peaks occur at similar depths in the frequency dependent susceptibility profile. It must therefore be considered a possibility that the sediment at these levels comes from the inwash of magnetically enhanced eroded topsoil from catchment slopes. The older of these two events is coincident with the beginning of the decline of Quercus pollen.

The profile of the ratio of $IRM_{0.08T}$ to $IRM_{1.0T}$ is shown in Fig. 4. This can be used to identify the magnetic mineralogy of the sediment, distinguishing between antiferromagnetic material such as haematite and goethite and ferrimagnetic material such as magnetite and maghemite. Most ferrimagnetic material will saturate in fields below 0.1T, whereas antiferromagnetic minerals saturate at higher fields (Thompson and Oldfield 1986). Accordingly the higher ratios in core KA above 10.0 m

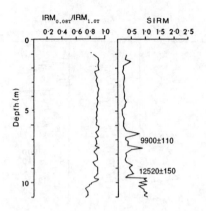

Fig. 4. The ratio of $IRM_{0.08T}$ to $IRM_{1.0T}$ and SIRM for the top 11 m of core KA.

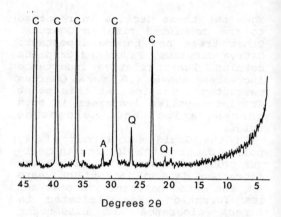

Fig. 5. X-ray diffraction trace of the less than 16 μm particle size fraction of the sediment from a depth of about 6.5 m in core KA. C: calcite; Q: quartz; A: apatite; I: illite.

indicate that the sediment is dominated by magnetite and/or maghemite. This mineralogy reflects the Holocene Mediterranean-style climate and its influence on soils. Tite and Linnington (1975) studied the effect of climate on soil magnetic mineralogy, especially susceptibility. In winter, anaerobic soil conditions promote the decay of organic matter and the reduction of iron oxides such as haematite. In summer, these are reoxidized to maghemite. The record of SIRM (Fig. 4) for the Postglacial is relatively constant suggesting little change in magnetic mineralogy during this period.

X-ray diffraction was used to identify the overall mineralogy of the sediments from core KA. Two bulk samples from the top 10.0 m of the core were split into particle size fractions. Fig. 5 is a diffractogram trace of the less than 16 μm size fraction from a depth of about 6.5 m. It is typical of the traces for other size fractions and of samples from a depth of about 2.0 m. Although no quantitative interpretation of the trace can be made, calcite is dominant with some quartz and a small amount of illite and apatite. Scanning electron microscopy of the same samples show that the calcite is in the form of rhomboid or elongated rhomboid crystals. This is indicative of authigenic carbonate precipitation. It contrasts with the calcite samples from the pre-Holocene sediments which are clastic and found together with quartz, dolomite, feldspar, kaolinite and chlorite, all of which are considered to be detrital in origin.

If a comparison is made of the carbonate and frequency dependent susceptibility profiles (Fig. 3) for the Postglacial period it can be seen that peaks in both occur at the same depths: around 2.0 m and 4.0 m. It is possible that at these levels there is the addition of detrital carbonate to the authigenic fraction as a result of topsoil erosion. However, this assertion needs to be confirmed.

4 DISCUSSION

From analysis of the sediment, indications of human activity in the Kopais Basin begin to appear around 5,500 to 5,000 years BP. The decrease in percentages of Quercus pollen, peaks in frequency dependent susceptibility and in carbonate content suggest that there was a decline in the Postglacial climax mixed oak woodland, and that this was accompanied by soil erosion. This state continued to the top of the core.

The dating of the top of the core is somewhat problematic. Extrapolation of sedimentation rates between the two radiocarbon dated levels places the top of the core at about 2,500 years BP. There are, however, no reasons to suppose that sedimentation rates remained constant through the Postglacial phase. The pollen record places the top of the core at post-5,200 years BP by comparison with the Turner and Greig (1975) record.

Further circumstantial evidence for a post-5,200 years BP date comes from a report that after modern drainage of the Kopais began in the 1880s, up to 3.5 m of peat wasted from the basin by the time of a second basin survey (Kenny 1935) in the 1930s. Various estimates can be made of the length of time needed for formation of this amount of peat. In Britain a study of Postglacial sedimentation rates for a variety of deposits including calcareous mud, fen/swamp mud, and fen and bog peats found that 63% of all accumulation rates ranged between 0.22 mmy^{-1} and 0.6 mmy^{-1} (Walker 1970). The rate for fen peat was between 0.11 mmy^{-1} and 1.0 mmy^{-1}. Although determination of accumulation rates in Britain is not necessarily valid for Greece, applying the slower rate of 0.2 mmy^{-1} to the 3.5 m of Kopais peat gives a period of between 16,500 and 17,000 years for formation. This is obviously too long and so too is the faster rate of 0.6 mmy^{-1} which gives a duration of about 5,800 years.

Evidence for the likelihood of peat existing below the Mycenaean drainage scheme comes from Knauss et al. (1984). A cross-section through one of the dikes near Stroviki at the northern edge of the basin (Fig. 6), reveals that the dikes were built of a double skin, with lake clay surrounding an interior of soil. Knauss's scheme suggests that the soil was removed from the site of a canal to form its banks. Lake clay underlying the soil was then placed on top of the soil to build up the banks. However, the drainage scheme by its very nature, was confined to the margins of the basin. Thus the presence of peat beneath the banks need not imply that peat had formed throughout the whole basin, but this must be considered as a possibility. Although the exact date of the construction of the ancient drainage scheme is still the subject of some debate, peat formation starting between 5,000 and 3,500 years would represent an accumula-

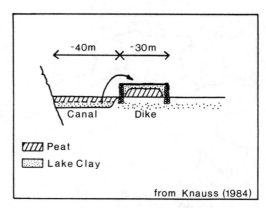

Fig. 6. Cross-section through a Minyan dike near Stroviki.

tion rate ranging from 0.7 mmy^{-1} to 1.0 mmy^{-1} which falls within the bounds of Walker's British results.

The Mycenaean drainage scheme (Fig. 7) is attributed to the Minyans of Orchomenos, a settlement in the northwest of the basin. Few remains of the scheme now exist for intensive cultivation of the Kopais Basin has destroyed many of the dikes, but there are several accounts of their nature (Kambanis 1892, 1893; Kenny 1935; Dean 1937; Knauss et al. 1984). The key to the success of the drainage scheme was the rock outcrop of Gla in the northeast of the basin. A Mycenaean fortress was built there during the Late Helladic IIIB period (Hope-Simpson and Lazenby 1970). Betancourt and Lawn (1984) place the LH IIIB period firmly in the thirteenth century BC, so suggesting a date for the construction of the scheme. However, Spyropoulos (1973) suggested that the scheme might date from an earlier period, the early phase of the Middle Helladic. He based this on the discovery of poorly preserved pottery of that age in one of the dike banks. The final stages of the Early Helladic are compressed into the third millennium BC and Betancourt and Lawn (1984) place the middle and late phases of the Middle Helladic period within the late third, or first half of the second millennium BC. This dates the pottery found in the Kopais by Spyropoulos to the end of the third millennium, in other words around 2,000 BC.

The location of the exposure of lake sediment at Karditsa Farmstead

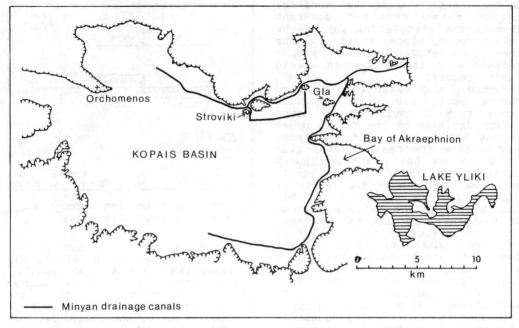

Fig. 7. The Minyan drainage scheme.

in 1984 was immediately to the east of the present road which crosses the entrance to Karditsa Bay (also known as the Bay of Akraephnion). The road follows the alignment of one of the Minyan dikes. One of the radiocarbon dates from organic matter at the exposure is 3,480±150 years BP. This can be calibrated to calendar years as 1750 cal. BC within the range 1980 cal. BC to 1670 cal. BC (Pearson and Stuiver 1986). The older of these range dates comes from the early phase of the Middle Helladic period (Betancourt and Lawn 1984) and is the time proposed by Spyropoulos (1973) for the construction of the Minyan dikes. It is therefore a possibility that the drainage scheme was either directly or indirectly responsible for the formation of the dated organic matter. The building of the dike would have locally changed the hydrological conditions. This association is only speculation. Contamination of the dated organic matter by roots growing through it could have introduced modern ^{14}C in which case the true age of the organic matter is older than its radiocarbon date. The sample was however treated for this possibility. In contrast, if the original age of the Minyan drainage scheme is LH IIIB then the date for the organic matter is too old.

The accumulation of peat in the Kopais Basin sometime after 5,000 years BP implies that water depths at the time must have been lower than during the previous sedimentary phase. Shallower water could have resulted from a number of different causes, including a change in the discharge of water into the basin, either from a reduction of inflowing water following climatic change or from a change in a river's course. Climatic change, in the form of hotter summers, might also increase rates of evaporation. An increase in the capacity of the katavothrae around the basin edge might also lower water levels. Finally, shallow water might result from the deposition and/or precipitation of minerogenic sediments and biogenic calcareous material, allowing the initiation of a hydrosere. Hydroseres cannot begin until water depth is shallow enough for floating-leaved macrophytes to become established. In addition, further shallowing is needed for progress to the next seral stage (Walker 1970).

180

It is virtually impossible to determine the cause of shallower lake levels at Kopais. Climatic change cannot be ruled out completely, but the existence of the katavothrae around the basin edge precludes a direct linkage between lake level change and climatic change. As already mentioned, the shape of the calcite grains is indicative of primary inorganic carbonate precipitation which could result from biogenic or physical processes. During the Postglacial period relatively high water temperatures could have reduced the solubility of calcium carbonate and favoured its precipitation.

5 CONCLUSIONS

There is a wealth of documentary and archaeological evidence for human activity in the Kopais area in the post-Mycenaean period; before that time archaeological remains are not so well preserved. There was some settlement during the Neolithic, more in the Early and Middle Helladic and settlement peaked during the Late Helladic (Hope-Simpson 1965). Complementary evidence for activity in the pre-Mycenaean period from other sources is needed. Some evidence is available from the sediment record of Lake Kopais: a decrease in Quercus pollen and the indications of the inwash of eroded topsoil from the catchment from around 5,500 years BP. However, this date does not necessarily mark the beginning of a period of increased human activity. There is inevitably a time lag between the initiation of such activity and its appearance in the sedimentary record.

This paper has not addressed the subject of possible climatic reasons for the changes in pollen percentages nor for the phases of soil erosion suggested by the magnetic susceptibility record. The possibility of a climatic cause exists, but the sediment of the Kopais Basin strongly suggests human rather than natural causes. These findings are in agreement with those of other workers in Greece and the Mediterranean region (for example, Pope and van Andel 1984).

6 ACKNOWLEDGEMENTS

This study was carried out while the author was a research student in the Department of Geography, University of Cambridge and was supported by a grant from the Natural Environment Research Council. The pollen analysis for this study was carried out by Prof. J.C. Ritchie of the University of Toronto, and the radiocarbon dates were supplied by Roy Switsur, Godwin Laboratory, University of Cambridge.

REFERENCES

Betancourt, P.P. and B.Lawn 1984.
The Cyclades and radiocarbon chronology. In J.A.McGillivray and R.N.L.Barber (eds.), The Prehistoric Cyclades, p.277-295. Edinburgh.

Bottema, S. 1974.
Late Quaternary vegetation history of Northwestern Greece. Thesis, Groningen University.

Bottema, S. 1979.
Pollen analytical investigations in Thessaly (Greece). Palaeohistoria 21:20-40.

Bottema, S. and H.Woldring (this volume). Anthropogenic indicators in the pollen record of the Eastern Mediterranean.

Dean, A.J. 1937.
The Lake Copais, Boeotia, Greece: Its drainage and development. J. Inst. Civil. Eng. 5:287-304 and 6:437-440.

Dean, W.E. 1974.
Determination of carbonate and organic matter in calcareous sediments and sedimentary rocks by loss on ignition: comparison with other methods. Journal Sedimentary Petrology 44:242-248.

Dearing, J.A.,
B.A.Maher and F.Oldfield 1985. Geomorphological linkages between soils and sediments: The role of magnetic measurements. In K.S. Richards, R.R.Arnett and S.Ellis (eds.), Geomorphology and Soils, p.245-266. London, Allen and Unwin.

Greig, J.R.A. and J.Turner 1974.
Some pollen diagrams from Greece and their archaeological significance. Journal of Archaeological Science 1:177-194.

Hammen, T. van der, T.A.Wijmstra and W.H.Zagwijn 1971. The floral record of the Late Cenozoic in Europe. In K.K.Turekian (ed.), The Late Cenozoic Glacial Ages, p.391-424. New Haven and London, Yale University Press.

Hope-Simpson, R. 1965. Gazeteer of Mycenaean Sites in Greece. London: Institute of Classical Studies.

Hope-Simpson, R. and J.F.Lazenby 1970. The Catalogue of Ships in Homer's Iliad. Oxford: Clarendon Press.

Kambanis, M.L. 1892. Le dessèchement du lac Copais par les anciens. Bull. Corr. Hellénique 16:121-137.

Kambanis, M.L. 1893. Le dessèchement du lac Copais par les anciens. Bull. Corr. Hellénique 17:322-343.

Kenny, E.J.A. 1935. Ancient drainage of the Copais. Ann. Arch. Anth. 22:189-206.

Knauss, J., B.Heinrich and H.Kalcyk 1984. Die Wasserbauten der Minyer in der Kopais - die älteste Flussregulierung Europas. Institut für Wasserbau und Wassermengenwirtschaft und Versuchsanstalt für Wasserbau, TU München, Bericht Nr. 50.

Le Borgne, E. 1955. Abnormal magnetic susceptibility of the topsoil. Annals Geophys. 11:399-419.

Mullins, C.E. 1977. Magnetic susceptibility of the soil and its significance in soil science: a review. Journal of Soil Science 28:223-246.

Mullins, C.E. and M.S.Tite 1973. Magnetic viscosity, quadrature susceptibility and frequency dependence of susceptibility in single-domain assemblies of magnetite and maghemite. Journal Geophys. Res. 78:804-809.

Oldfield, F., J.A.Dearing, R.Thompson and S.E.Garret-Jones 1978. Some magnetic properties of lake sediments and their links with erosion rates. Pol. Arch. Hydrobiol. 25:321-331.

Pearson, G.E. and M.Stuiver 1986. High precision calibration of the radiocarbon time scale 500-2500 BC. Radiocarbon 28B:839-852.

Pope, K.O. and T.H.van Andel 1984. Late Quaternary alluviation and soil formation in the southern Argolid: its history, causes and archaeological implications. Journal of Archaeological Science 11:281-306.

Spyropoulos, T.G. 1973. Introduction to the study of the Copaic area. Athens Annals of Archaeology 6:201-214.

Thompson, R. and F.Oldfield 1986. Environmental Magnetism. London: George Allen and Unwin.

Tite, M.S. and R.E.Linnington 1975. Effects of climate on the magnetic susceptibility of soils. Nature 256:565-566.

Turner, J. and J.R.A.Greig 1975. Some Holocene pollen diagrams from Greece. Review of Palaeobotany and Palynology 20:171-204.

Walker, D. 1970. Direction and rate in some British postglacial hydroseres. In D.Walker and R.G.West (eds.), Studies in the Vegetational History of the British Isles, p.117-139. London, Cambridge University Press.

Zeist, W. van and S.Bottema 1982. Vegetational history of the Eastern Mediterranean and the Near East during the last 20,000 years. In J.L.Bintliff and W.van Zeist (eds.), Palaeoclimates, Palaeoenvironments and Human Communities in the Eastern Mediterranean in Later Prehistory, p.277-321. BAR International Series 133.

Man's Role in the Shaping of the Eastern Mediterranean Landscape, Bottema, Entjes-Nieborg & van Zeist (eds)
© *1990 Balkema, Rotterdam. ISBN 90 6191 138 9*

Terraces and enclosure walls in the Cretan landscape 15

Jennifer Moody & A.T.Grove
Department of Geography, University of Cambridge, UK

ABSTRACT: Terraces and enclosure walls have probably been part of the Cretan landscape for over 3000 years. In this paper we present our observations on the relationships between terraces and enclosures on the one hand and their physical and human settings on the other. Factors that seem to influence the decision to terrace or not, to enclose or not are: slope, wind, bedrock, proximity to a habitation, dominant mode of subsistence (especially herding vs. cultivation), and crop type.

1 INTRODUCTION

Terraces and enclosure walls are among the most widespread influences of man on the landscape of the eastern Mediterranean (Plate 1). We are interested in how, why, where, and when these walls came to exist on Crete and what impact they have had on the local environment.

Sometimes it is difficult to distinguish terraces and enclosures. Two helpful rules of thumb are:

1. Terraces follow contour lines; enclosures cut across them.

2. Terraces usually have a single finished face; enclosures usually have two.

When we speak of terraces, we are referring to agricultural terraces unless otherwise specified.

2 PURPOSE AND CONFIGURATION

2.1 Terraces

Agricultural terraces serve at least four purposes:

1. They allow cultivation of steep slopes by creating narrow flat fields.

2. If they are walled, they help prevent soil loss.

3. They help retain moisture by providing deeper sediments for absorption.

4. They promote root penetration.

We also recognize three broad configurations of terraces in Crete (Fig. 1).

1. Traditional parallel terraces (Fig. 1:a). These can be found on any type of bedrock (hard and soft limestone, phyllites, quartzites and serpentines) and growing any of the major Cretan crops (vines, olives, grain, vegetable, fruit and nut trees).

2. Braided or switchback terraces (Fig. 1:b). These also occur in any type of bedrock and for most types of crops. The only crops we have

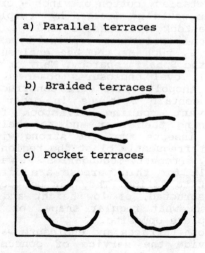

a) Parallel terraces

b) Braided terraces

c) Pocket terraces

Fig. 1. Terrace configurations.

not observed on braided terraces are vegetable gardens.

3. Pocket terraces (Fig. 1:c). This type of terrace is largely confined to hard limestone slopes and is usually planted with tree crops.

No other striking patterns have been noted with regard to terrace configuration, but we are in the early stages of this research. Further significant geographical distributions may yet emerge.

2.2 Enclosures

Enclosures can also be divided into three broad categories:

1. True enclosures - meant to keep something in. Almost without exception these are meant to contain livestock and are sturdily built. They are usually 1.5 m or more in height. If only one face is finished, it is the inside face, but they more frequently are double faced. Examples are livestock holding pens, which usually provide shade, are often irregular in shape, and sometimes contain water; or milking pens, which seldom have corners and usually have one narrow exit.

2. Exclosures - meant to keep something out, such as animals or wind. Like the previous type, these are well built but with even higher walls (2 m and more). If only one face is finished, it tends to be the exterior one. They usually contain tender crops such as maize, vegetables, cotton or vines - crops that would be damaged by trampling livestock or excessive wind.

Some enclosures combine types 1 and 2, such as the bee enclosures of the Sphakia eparchy. Many of the small oval enclosures observed in the Anopolis area were constructed to contain beehives in order to prevent roaming livestock from turning them over and to shelter the insects from the strong winds that frequently blast the region.

3. Property boundaries - walls built for this purpose are difficult to define. They can be poorly constructed, of low height and of a somewhat regular shape, or the complete opposite.

Both terraces and enclosure walls provide the service of consuming stones as they are cleared from nearby fields. This feature is especially pronounced around fields that grow crops that require plowing, like vineyards and vegetable gardens.

3 CONSTRUCTION

Casual interviews with locals in the Anopolis area indicate that terraces and enclosures were and are usually built by the landowner and his family. In a few cases, so-and-so-who-builds-walls is hired to do so, but this seems to be the exception rather than the rule. The situation could easily be different in less remote parts of the island.

All the walls considered in this study are dry-built, i.e. constructed without mortar.

3.1 Terraces

There are two basic ways to construct a terrace:

1. Excavate it into the hillside, filling-in behind the wall with the spoil. The steps are: clear the area of vegetation; dig out the larger boulders and rocks and use them to build a retaining wall; dig up the soil and much of the subsoil and bedrock (especially if it is marl) from the rear of each terrace; collect first-sized and smaller stones from the rubble and place them immediately behind the constructed wall blocking up holes between the larger stones in order to prevent soil from washing through the wall; push the remaining sediment forward to fill-in behind the retaining wall. It is important to realize that when this construction technique is used, the sediments behind the stone wall will be older than the wall itself - a fundamental point to remember when trying to date a terrace wall.

Excavated terraces are confined to areas with adequate soil cover or soft bedrocks such as marl sandstone, or phyllite. They rarely, if ever, occur as pocket terraces. Excavated terraces are instead parallel or braided. They are especially common in newly terraced areas; the advent of the bulldozer having increased their popularity many fold.

184

2. Build the wall on the surface and wait for it gradually to collect soil. For lack of a better term we call this construction a lynchet terrace or check dam. Lynchet terraces collect soil through plowing, while check dams collect it through sheet and gully erosion. These terraces tend to be constructed in places where the bedrock is too hard to excavate (e.g. crystalline limestone, marble, ophiolites) or where there is too little sediment to dig into. They are usually pocket or parallel terraces, not braided ones. Unlike excavated terraces, lynchets or check dams gradually build up sediment with a straight forward stratigraphy, i.e. the sediments behind these walls are younger than the wall.

We also note that terraces used for vines and olives tend to be better constructed than those used for grain and fodder, the extra value of the crop justifying the trouble of making stone walls.

3.2 Enclosures

Stone enclosures can be constructed in a variety of ways, but in Crete two styles predominate:
1. Two walls of large stones are built parallel to each other and the space between them is filled with rubble. Sometimes the top of the wall is capped with flat slabs.
2. A wall the thickness of a single large stone is built.

The building stone is usually cleared from the area to be enclosed. Sometimes so many small rocks are collected that huge stone piles grow up on the edges of cultivated areas or unnecessarily thick walls are constructed. This is particularly common in fields where vines are cultivated.

4 INFLUENCES

We compiled a list of eight factors we thought might influence a farmer's decision whether or not to enclose or terrace a piece of land. This list was made without consulting local farmers.
1. Slope. Although we have not made systematic slope measurements of terraced and unterraced slopes, it seems that most slopes between 5 and 40 degrees have been terraced with walls. Terraces on gentle slopes tend to be of the lynchet type.
2. Aspect. Aspect seems to have little direct bearing on whether a slope is terraced or a field is enclosed.
3. Wind. Wind is an important factor for enclosures, but does not seem to influence the decision to terrace or not.
4. Bedrock. a) Plattenkalk Limestones - terraced and walled; b) Mesozoic Limestones - usually walled and terraced, even on negligible slopes; c) Neogene deposits - almost 100% of the cultivated marl slopes are terraced, but only 50% of those terraces are walled; d) Phyllites dominant - less commonly walled or terraced than other bedrocks. The gentler slopes tend to be unterraced.
5. Depth of sediment. It is nearly impossible to determine the depth of soil at the time a terrace was constructed. Terrace traces can be seen in areas that today preserve little or no sediment, but we cannot quantify the amount of sediment that was lost because we do not know the original height of the wall.
6. Proximity to a habitation. Although most terrace systems are located near villages or hamlets, a number exist in places considered by the modern observer to be remote. Such terraces are often in poor repair and no longer cultivated. It is prudent, however, to remember that "remoteness" is largely a cultural term. Today we consider most places that cannot be reached by car to be remote, but in the past, when the dominant mode of transportation was by foot or mule, such places may not have been considered difficult to get to. Although travel-time (relative distance, not absolute distance) functions as the fundamental measurement of remoteness in both cases, it is the difference in the accepted mode of transportation (car vs. foot or mule) that changes the perception of an area's remoteness. Also important is that what one culture or individual considers a long journey, another may not. Such differences in perception of distance and time are not merely cultural but they can also be

sexual. In Crete, for example, males travel further from their home base than females do, marriage notwithstanding.

Enclosures in remote areas are usually associated with herding activities: holding pens, milking pens, etc.

7. Dominant mode of subsistence. In mixed economies with strong herding traditions the construction of exclosures near villages is encouraged in order to protect crops from roaming animals. It also results in isolated enclosures in remote areas, because of the necessity to move between summer and winter pastures.

8. Crop type. We considered only the major Cretan crops: grain, olives, vines, fruit and nut trees. We observed a tendency for crops to be planted towards the front of a terrace, probably because the soil is deeper there.

a. Grain. Grain terraces tend to be poorly constructed. From a distance many appeared unwalled, but on closer inspection most if not all proved to be constructed with insubstantial walls. They are occasionally enclosed for protection from livestock.

b. Olives. Olive terraces are usually well built. Sometimes they are enclosed for protection from livestock (especially if the grove is double cropped with grain, fodder or vines), but more often the enclosure represents a property boundary.

c. Vines. Vine terraces are well built. In particular they are very high (1.5 m+), retaining deeper soils and perhaps providing better root drainage. Vine terraces are usually enclosed for protection from wind and livestock.

d. Fruit and nut tree crops. Like vine terraces, these are usually well constructed and often enclosed for protection from wind and livestock.

5 THE MODERN STATE OF TERRACES AND ENCLOSURES

We have divided the current status of terraces and enclosures into three categories: New (built within the last 5 to 10 years); Old and still in use; Old and abandoned.

1. New. The Neogene, the Phyllite-Quartzite nappe, and the Pleistocene fluvial deposits are the areas of Crete that are being actively terraced today. All are cleared by bulldozers and all are of the excavated type of construction (Plate 2). Few of these terraces are walled, but they are nevertheless stable unless undermined by a 100 year deluge, such as occurred in the Pachyammos region of East Crete in September 1986 (Plate 3).

Walled terraces are still built, but they are few and tend to be on hard limestone. They are often filled in with soil brought in from elsewhere.

New enclosures are rarely built of stone. They are rapidly going over to wire fencing.

2. Old, still in use. These terraces are usually falling into disrepair. Maintenance is at best half-hearted.

Stone enclosures are in much the same state, repair being made with thorny brush, branches and wire instead of stone.

3. Old, abandoned. Among Crete's many striking features are its great flights of abandoned terraces. Many of these presently abandoned terraces were probably used for cereal cultivation as is suggested by nearby threshing-floors and water-mills. Such neglected terraces are especially found in arid parts of the island and in areas inaccessible by road. They have now turned into pasture or semi-natural woodland.

Terraces often go through a post-cultivation browsing phase before

Plate 1. Enclosed terraces in the Asterousia Mountains of South-Central Crete.

Plate 2. New terraces near Gra Ligia, Ierapetra.

Plate 3. "Melted" terraces near Pachyammos after the September 1986 deluge.

Plate 4. Hellenistic olive in Loutra, Sphakia.

Table 1. Terrace characteristics
(NS = not significant, NA = not available).

LANDUSE	Construction	Parallel terrace	Braided terrace	Pocket terrace	Excavated	Lynchet/Check	Abandoned
Crop							
Grain	poor-medium	x	x	x	x	x	many
Fodder	poor	x	x	x	x	x	many
Olives	medium-good	x	x	x	x	x	some
Vines	good	x	some	few	x	x	some
Fruit & Nut trees	medium-good	x	x	x	x	x	some
Garden vegetables	good	x	some	none	some	x	?
Strong herding							
tradition	good	x	x	x	x	x	many
Beekeeping	good	x	some	none	x	few	many
Remote	poor-medium	x	x	x	x	x	many
Near habitation	medium-good	x	x	x	x	x	some
CLIMATE							
Wind	NS	NS	NS	NS	NS	NS	NS
Aspect	NS	NS	NS	NS	NS	NS	NS
GEOMORPHOLOGY							
Bedrock							
Plattenkalk	medium-good	x	x	x	x	x	some
Mesozoic Limestone	poor-medium	x	x	x	some	x	many
Neogene	none-good	x	x	x	x	few	some
Phyllite	none-good	x	x	x	x	few	some
Deep soils	medium-good	x	x	some	x	none	NA
Steep slope	poor-good	x	x	few	x	few	many
Gentle slope	poor-medium	x	few	few	few	x	some
Ravine	medium-good	x	few	x	few	x	many

they are completely abandoned. We would estimate that at least one-third of the excultivated terraces on Crete are being systematically browsed by herded animals. Such activity tends to knock down terrace walls in a characteristic gapping pattern, a pattern that is preserved even when browsing stops. This process has been credited with phases of increased erosion in the Argolid (van Andel et al. 1986), but in most of Crete the breaching of terrace walls does not appear to be a major factor in promoting erosion. Much more important is the breaking up of the bryophyte and lichen surface crusts by trampling hooves or the construction of hairpin turns when building roads. Wind and trampling erosion seem to be particular problems along the south coast of Crete where herding is still pronounced, but this is true whether or not the slopes were terraced.

Completely abandoned terraces eventually grow up with semi-natural vegetation; the rate of closure depending on the climate and the nearby "wild" vegetation. In West Crete cypress (Cupressus sempervirens) and deciduous oak (Quercus brachyphyla) form the dominant invading woodland, while in East Crete it is the Cretan pine (Pinus brutia).

Some terraces that were abandoned long enough for woodland to become re-established are now being brows-

Table 2. Enclosures, exclosures, and property boundaries
(NS = not significant, NA = not available).

	Enclosure	Exclosure	Property boundary	Abandoned
LANDUSE				
Crops				
Grain	NS	often	often	many
Fodder	NS	rarely	rarely	NA
Olives	NS	some	usually	some
Vines	NS	usually	some	some
Fruit & Nut trees	NS	usually	some	some
Garden vegetables	NS	usually	usually	few
Strong herding				
tradition	many	many	rarely	some
Beekeeping	x	x	rarely	some
Remote	x	few	some	many
Near habitation	x	many	many	some
CLIMATE				
Wind	NS	x	NS	NS
Aspect	NS	NS	NS	NS
GEOMORPHOLOGY				
Bedrock				
Plattenkalk	NS	NS	NS	some
Mesozoic Limestone	NS	NS	NS	some
Neogene	NS	NS	NS	some
Phyllite	NS	NS	NS	some
Deep soils	NS	NS	NS	NS
Steep slope	x	x	x	many
Gentle slope	x	x	x	some
Ravine	NS	NS	NS	some

ed. This is probably due to a slight rise in herding over the last three years, a trend that is being encouraged by subsidies from the EEC (Kournas area, Gavdhos).

Abandoned enclosures become rock piles and among other things provide raw material for lime kilns and environments for specialized plants, e.g. Ricotia cretica.

The reduction in agricultural activity indicated by abandoned terraces and enclosures cannot be interpreted as desertification. With few exceptions, most abandoned terraces could be cultivated if it were considered worthwhile. These changes are probably part of a pattern familiar all over Europe: the retreat of cultivation from more difficult terrain. They are due to social and economic influences from outside the local system, such as the import of cereals from more easily mechanized areas like the Thessalian Plain in north-central Greece.

The recent history of vine terraces provides a good example of this change on Crete. Today the survival and expansion of viticulture seems to depend on the connectedness of an area. If a region is well connected by roads, vine cultivation, which is labor intensive and only moderately mechanizable, is considered worthwhile and flourishes (e.g. south of Ieraklieon or Kastelli Kissamos). It also hangs on in a small way in very poorly connected areas where the vine is cultivated for local consumption (e.g. the Asterousia, Anopolis). We have learned by chatting with people in Anopolis that the reason vines and grain are no longer grown in the enclosures and terraces constructed for them, is that it is now easier to buy their products (wine, bread) ready-made in Khora Sphakion than to make it themselves.

It is also possible that weather cycles may have encouraged the abandonment of some cultivation. For instance, a few bad harvests caused by short term drought may have induced a farmer to abandon

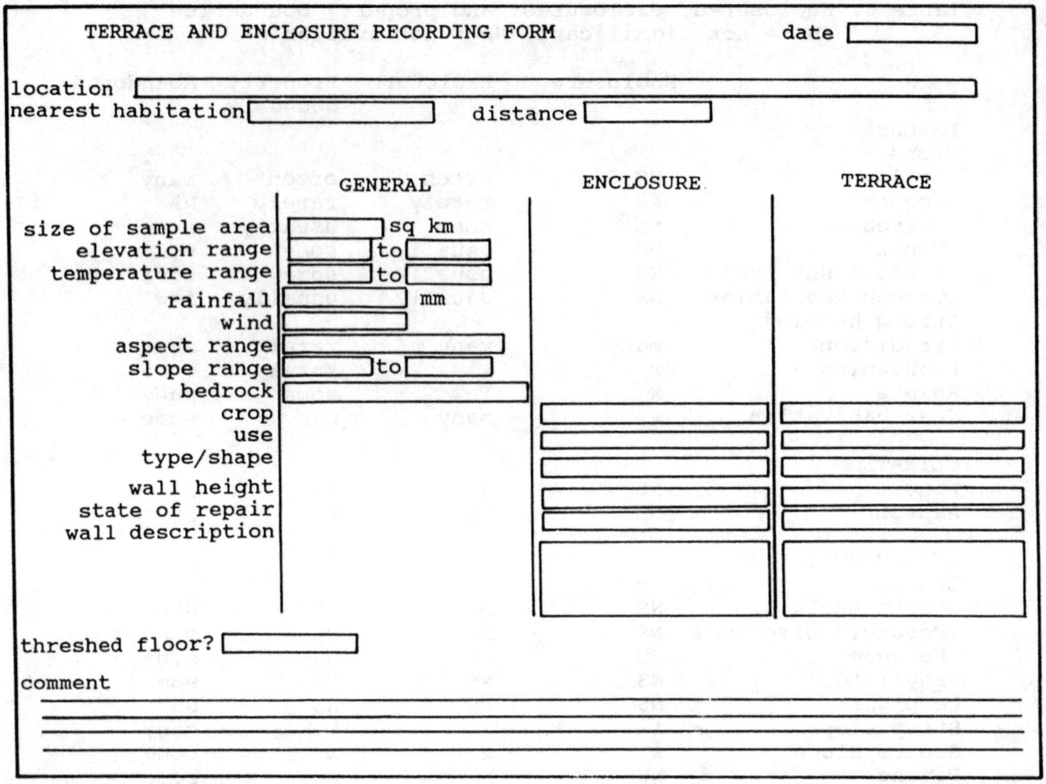
TERRACE AND ENCLOSURE RECORDING FORM date

location

nearest habitation distance

GENERAL ENCLOSURE TERRACE

size of sample area sq km

elevation range to

temperature range to

rainfall mm

wind

aspect range

slope range to

bedrock

crop

use

type/shape

wall height

state of repair

wall description

threshed floor?

comment

Fig. 2. Field recording form.

land that with better fortune might have continued to be cultivated.

6 CHRONOLOGY

It still remains to address the sticky question of chronology. Just how long has all this wall building been going on?

Terraces and enclosures have probably been part of the Cretan landscape for over 3000 years. The use of terrace walls for reinforcing part of a habitation dates back to the Middle Neolithic on Crete (ca 6000 BP), but the earliest documented use of walls as agricultural terraces is Middle Minoan (ca 3700 BP). This information is the result of recent research done by Prof. Richard Hope-Simpson and Ms. Julie Clark of Queens University on the island of Psiera, just off the NE coast of Crete. Similar dates for agricultural terraces have been proposed for the Greek Mainland (van Andel et al. 1986) and the Levant (Gophna 1979). Nevertheless, we do not know how extensive agricultural terraces were on Crete during the Bronze Age.

Terrace systems existed in the 8th century BC. In Homer's Odyssey, Odysseus is referred to as too lazy to lay a dry stone wall on a slope (1.357-59). Terrace systems also existed in the 5th century BC. Terraces are mentioned by a number of Ancient writers and in the Dyscolus a slave is even described as repairing a terrace wall. We also know there were terrace systems in the Hellenistic and Roman periods from walls we have been able to date, written records, and scenes in Roman wall paintings. There are also references to terrace systems in the Venetian (13th to 17th centuries AD) and Turkish records (17th to 20th centuries AD). Photographs from the turn of this century indicate that extensive terrace systems were in place and, in some cases, already abandoned. New terraces continue to be built.

This review of the chronology of terraces indicates that terrace systems have existed on Crete since the Bronze Age, but unfortunately it does not tell us which systems are Bronze Age and which are Medieval, much less how widespread they were in each period. It is unlikely that we will ever be able to answer such questions. The main obstacle is the difficulty of accurately dating the construction of individual walls. In some cases, we have been able to provide post quem dates for a terrace by the age of a tree growing over it (Plate 4), and ante quem dates for others by datable material found below the wall. A few walls can be dated by construction style and lichenometry hold some potential. For the most part, however, attempts to date the extensive visible terrace systems of Crete have met with frustration.

Enclosures are almost as difficult to date as terrace walls, but they have probably received less attention because they are not such prominent features in the landscape. They certainly date back to the Bronze Age, where enclosures are depicted in Minoan art. The history of enclosures built for herding purposes is poorly documented, but studies are in process (Chang and Koster 1986).

7 SUMMARY

Briefly, the decision to enclose or not seems to be more strongly influenced by climate and landuse than the decision to terrace. The decision to terrace seems to pivot more on geomorphology and topography. Once the decision has been made to terrace or enclose, another set of factors influences configuration and construction. These findings are summarized in Tables 1 and 2.

8 FUTURE WORK

This study is part of a larger project funded by the EEC on Desertification in the Eastern Mediterranean. We propose to include the following activities in our researches over the next two years:

1. Target a variety of walled areas and fill out a standard form (Fig. 2).

2. Interview farmers 50 years and older asking: "Why they terrace or enclose?", "Who builds them?", "How long does it take?", and "Why have so many been abandoned?"

3. With the aid of aerial photographs map out the terrace and enclosure systems of selected regions of Crete. Unfortunately, they cannot be seen on satellite images.

We would be remiss if we did not mention that the fascinating and complex Mediterranean landscape of terraces and enclosures is rapidly disappearing. This landscape is being bulldozed into flat fields, unwalled terraces and housing developments, as well as being overgrown by highly flammable - and in many cases - monospecies woodland.

REFERENCES

Chang, C. and H.Koster 1986.
Beyond Bones: Toward an Archaeology of Pastoralism. Advances in Archaeological Method and Theory 9:97-148.
Gophna, R. 1979.
Post-Neolithic Settlement Patterns. In A.Horowitz, The Quaternary of Israel, p.319-321. New York.
Van Andel, T.H.,
C.N.Runnels and K.O.Pope 1986.
Five Thousand Years of Land Use and Abuse in the Southern Argolid, Greece. Hesperia 55:103-128.

Zoology

Man's Role in the Shaping of the Eastern Mediterranean Landscape, Bottema, Entjes-Nieborg & van Zeist (eds)
© *1990 Balkema, Rotterdam. ISBN 90 6191 138 9*

Archaeozoological aspects of Late Holocene economy and environment in the Near East

16

Hijlke Buitenhuis
Biologisch-Archaeologisch Instituut, Rijksuniversiteit Groningen, Netherlands

ABSTRACT: Interpretation of the results of the analysis of animal remains from settlements in the Near East, dating to the Late Holocene, shows that economic motives were the major factor in the strategy for the acquirement of animal products. Ecological factors, which of course form the basis of this strategy, can only be studied indirectly. This duality is illustrated by four examples of archaeozoological data from the Middle Euphrates area.

For the Neolithic it is shown that the introduction of domestic animals, first sheep and goat and in a later phase also cattle and pig, caused a complete break with the earlier strategies as man became almost completely dependent on domestic animals. The influence on the ecology seems to have been very localized, however. In the Late Neolithic or Halaf period a developing semi-transhumance led to the exploitation of a less localized area. Specialized hunting again became of great importance.

At the beginning of the Bronze Age the declining importance of pig breeding seems to show that for the first time man's activity caused such irriversible changes in the ecology that man had to adapt his economy. In the Middle and Late Bronze Age the exploitation of the natural resources became very intensive and reached a high point in which also animals that were hunted never before, were now exploited.

From these examples it becomes clear that the introduction of animal husbandry had an enormous impact on man's economy, but that the effects on the ecology were slight and only became apparent in a much later period.

1 INTRODUCTION

Since his earliest beginnings, man as all other animals has needed to gather his food. Other animals became such a food source and provided man with much-needed fat and proteins. In the course of time animals became one of the major food sources of mankind, although not an exclusive one.

Archaeozoology studies the relationship between man and animals in the past, in particular the different uses man has made of animals. Since the beginning, this relationship has, by reason of man's developing technical knowledge, always been more favourable to man than to animals. However, while man was still a hunter-gatherer, he lived in close contact with his environment and any important environmental changes, caused either by himself or by nature, would cause him to adapt his survival strategies or suffer the consequences and in the final instance to disappear. In this phase of man's relationship with animals and nature the feedback of his actions would ultimately result in a strong check on his developing society. As long as man was dependent on hunting and gathering, no major environmental changes could therefore be caused by man unless his cultural achievements were also ready for major changes. Thus, archaeozoological studies of these periods will reveal the level of adaptation to the local environment and more or less reflect the natural fauna on which man preyed. Changes in faunal complexes from human occupation sites of these periods can be directly related to changes in the environment.

This relationship however changed drastically with the advance of the so-called 'Neolithic Revolution'. Apart from changes on the material and social plane, such as sedentary way of life, villages, the developing techniques of toolmaking, the discovery of ceramics and in a later phase the use of metal, one of the major, if not the most important facts of this revolution is the overall and all-including change in mankind's relation with his environment. This change is commonly described as: "Man becomes a food producer".

This short sentence describes an enormously complex process, which was of the utmost importance and still is the basic factor of human society. Archaeology, archaeozoology, palaeobotany and related fields of study can and do serve an important function, even for our own times, in reconstructing the developments caused by this process and laying bare the causes and effects of this revolution. Archaeozoological studies of these periods are mainly occupied with the analysis of faunal remains from human settlements, and result in a knowledge of which animals were killed, their relative importance, the age and sex of the slaughtered animals and sometimes of anatomical changes through time of the recovered species. The results must then be interpreted as to their origin and meaning. It is in this field that major problems arise as man's relationship with his animals is not a straightforward line of cause and effect as the two interact heavily.

2 THE STUDY AREA

I would like to discuss the problems in the light of four examples which are the result of an intensive study by myself and others of a number of sites along the Middle Euphrates in southeast Turkey and north Syria. As has been written:

"... rare are samples which come from well-dated sites and which are collected carefully and level by level, and are sufficiently large to permit the zoologist to draw reliable conclusions supported by significant statistical evidence. The small number of such samples is even more striking if one considers both the size of the region and the numbers of different environmental types and cultures represented..." (Bökönyi 1978).

This complaint which is now eleven years old and by no means new at that time is still valid for most of the Near East, even for the area to be discussed. The Euphrates valley has become a comparatively closely studied area because of the building of several dams in the river. This has resulted in several rescue projects in Turkey and Syria to salvage as much archaeological data as possible from the areas to be flooded. Thus a fairly large number of sites from different periods in a relatively small area were excavated, and the results of the analyses are now available for study (Fig. 1). But the complaint still stands as the total of archaeozoological studies of this area number only about fifteen, covering a period of some 10,000 years!

The region in which these sites lie consists of three zones; first the steeper mountains of the Taurus Mountains from which the Euphrates springs, with a mean annual precipitation of more than 400 mm and a varied terrain of steep hills, valleys and smaller floodplains. The second zone is made up of the foothills of these mountains, which form a zone of low hills and plains with a general decline to the south. The mean annual rainfall is 200-400 mm and the vegetation consists of small stands of Quercus and Pistachio within a grass-steppe (the so-called forest-steppe). The third zone consist of the dry wormwood (Artemisia) steppe of the Syrian Plain with a rainfall of less than 200 mm per year. Through these zones flows the river Euphrates, whose floodplain forms a separate ecological system regulated by the floodwaters and consists of clay, silt and gravel banks with a gallery forest of fast-growing trees such as Populus and Tamarix. Ac-

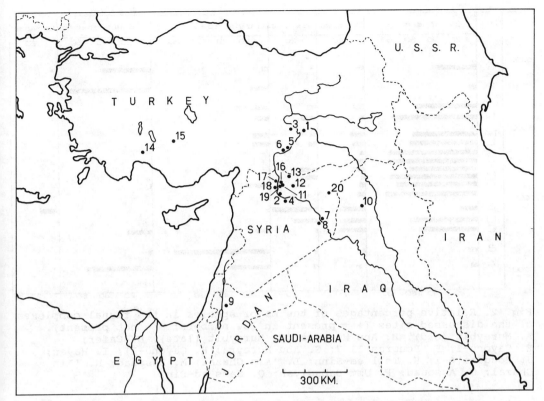

Fig. 1. Geographical position of the sites mentioned in this paper.
1: Çayönü; 2: Mureybet; 3: Çafer; 4: Abu Hureyra; 5: Gritille; 6: Hayaz
Höyük; 7: Tell es-Sinn; 8: Bouqras; 9: Ain Ghazal; 10: Umm Dabagiyah;
11: Shams ed-Din; 12: Sabi Abyad; 13: Tell Assouad; 14: Haçilar;
15: Çatal Höyük; 16: Tell es-Sweyhat; 17: El Qitar; 18: Hadidi;
19: Mumbaqa; 20: Sheikh Hamed.

cording to the palaeobotanists
(van Zeist pers.comm.) the climate
did not change appreciably in the
last 8000 years and the above-
mentioned conditions must have been
more or less the same during the
whole of the Later Holocene.

3 THE PRE-POTTERY NEOLITHIC A PERIOD

The advent of the Neolithic Revolution can perhaps already been seen
in the increased technological and
artistic developments of the Natufian period, which had its main
focus in the Levant, but whose influence extended into northern
Syria and southern Turkey. In this
period, ca 12,000 to 10,000 years
ago, an intensification and widen-
ing of the food-gathering strate-

gies can be observed.

The Natufian was followed by the
Prepottery Neolithic A period,
which can be found in these northern parts at villages such as
Çayönü, Cafer, Mureybet and Abu
Hureyra. Dating to the time of ca
8300-7500 BC, this period is characterized by the development of
increasingly complex dwellings
evolving into complete villages,
illustrating a sedentary lifestyle.
There is however no evidence yet of
food-production, and all animal and
plant remains seem to be of wild
species. The faunal assemblages
from these sites reflect the different ecological systems in which
these sites were located.

Although the Ergani region, in
which the village of Çayönü was
found, properly belongs to the
Tigris basin, Çayönü's situation

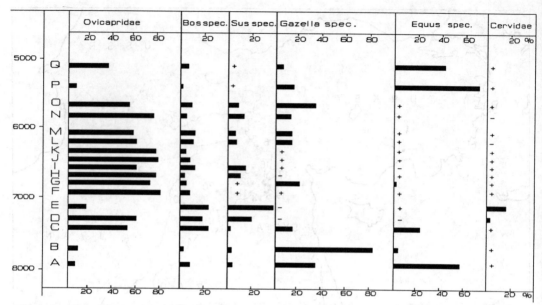

Fig. 2. Relative percentages of the major species in the faunal complexes of the discussed sites (+ = present in low numbers; - = not present).
A. Mureybit (old), B. Abu Hureyra; C. Mureybit (late); D. Cafer;
E. Çayönü-I; F. Bouqras 11-7; G. Abu Hureyra; H. Çayönü-II; I. Hayaz;
J. Bouqras 6-1; K. Tell es-Sinn; L. 'Ain Ghazal; M. Assouad; N. 'Ain
Ghazal; O. Assouad; P. Umm Dabagiyah; Q. Sams ed-Din.

must have been similar to that of sites in the nearby Euphrates valley at the same time. The major food animals found among the remains at Çayönü (Fig. 2) are wild sheep and goat (Ovis orientalis and Capra aegagrus), wild boar (Sus scrofa), aurochs (Bos primigenius) and deer (Cervus elaphus), while other species which must have been common around the site were also hunted (Lawrence 1980, 1982). Cafer Höyük lies near the area where the Euphrates leaves the steep mountains and enters the foothills of the Taurus. The characteristic fauna from this area, wild goat, wild boar, aurochs, wild sheep, red and fallow deer (Dama mesopotamica), are the major food animals recovered among the faunal remains (Helmer 1985a). Mureybet lies on the banks of the Euphrates in Syria near the 200 mm isohyet where the foothills change to the dry steppe. The major animals recognised among the remains are wild onager (Equus hemionus), Persian gazelle (Gazella subgutturosa), and far less important - aurochs, wild boar and wild sheep (Ducos 1978). The last site

to be discussed is Abu Hureyra, again on the banks of the Euphrates ca 30 km east of Mureybet, where up to 80% of the remains are of Persian gazelle and the remainder is equally divided among wild sheep, onager and aurochs (Legge 1975; Legge and Rowley-Conwy 1987). These Pre-Pottery Neolithic A sites show that although there are clear cultural affinities among them (Cauvin calls it the Taurus Prepottery) the "economy" is clearly based on the exploitation of the available natural resources and the analyses show as wide a variety as the different environments around the settlements.

4 THE PRE-POTTERY NEOLITHIC B PERIOD

The next cultural phase is called the Prepottery Neolithic B and is characterized by clear evidence of food production, in our case the appearance of remains of domesticated animals. Much has already been written on the possible causes of domestication and on the pro-

blems of recognising it in the faunal remains. It is not the purpose
of this discussion to go into this
problem, as we are discussing the
problems of interpretation and not
of analysis. However, in view of
the following discussion I would
like to say that, as evidence of
domestication seems to show itself
quite clearly and uniformly in
large parts of the Near East at
the same time, it seems unlikely to
have taken very long for animals
and plants to be domesticated, as
one would otherwise expect the evidence to occur at different times
in different regions and over a
much longer period.

Sites in the area under discussion that date from this period
are Hayaz Höyük (Buitenhuis 1988)
and Gritille in the foothills of
the Taurus Mountains, and Abu Hureyra, Tell es-Sinn (Clason 1979-
80) and Bouqras (Buitenhuis 1988)
along the Euphrates in eastern
Syria. The most remarkable fact
about the recovered faunal remains
from these sites is that they now
show an almost identical pattern
(Fig. 2). Domesticated sheep and
goat are the major food animals
forming up to 80% of the remains.
Other remains are of cattle and
pig, whose domestic status is uncertain, and even more rarely of
hunted species such as onager,
gazelle and deer. This change is
most clearly shown in the material
from Abu Hureyra where in the previous phase ca 80% of the remains
had become from Persian gazelle,
while in this phase more than 70%
are of domestic sheep and/or goat
and not even 20% of gazelle. Although the other mentioned sites
do not have earlier occupation
phases, the pattern of the faunal
composition is the same, showing
that this rapid change to an almost
complete dependence on domesticated
animals is universal in this region
and not an exception.

We have now come to the discussion of the impact of man on the
environment and the possibilities
of interpreting the analytical
results of faunal complexes from
settlements. It must be clear that
at this period we no longer can
interprete the results as evidence
of fluctuating environmental conditions. We can still see some regional differences among the scarce

remains of other animals such as
pig (Sus spec.), Persian gazelle
(Gazella subgutturosa) and deer
(Cervus elaphus and/or Dama mesopotamica). For example, pig remains
in Neolithic Hayaz Höyük form ca 5%
of the total remains (some 9100
fragments of which almost 2300
could be identified). The total
number of remains of pig in Bouqras
is seven, among 17,000 analysed
fragments (of which 5800 could be
identified). Gazelle however is
represented with one fragment in
Hayaz Höyük and with 72 fragments
in Bouqras, while deer show a different picture again with 32 fragments in Hayaz and 20 fragments in
Bouqras respectively. This clearly
shows the difference in environment
between the two sites, Bouqras lying in a rather desiccated area and
Hayaz in the foothills of the Taurus Mountains, where there is a
sufficient amount of rainfall for
a fairly lush vegetation. In Çayönü
we see quite a similar change in
the faunal complex of the later
phase of the occupation, although
the picture seems less clear because the change here is from wild
to domesticated animals, without a
clear change of preferred species.

Not only in the Euphrates valley
can we see this pattern. An almost
identical change can be seen among
the settlements of the coastal area
in the Levant and Israel from this
period. Here the major hunted animals in the Early Neolithic phase
(PPNA) were primarily deer, gazelle
and onager, while the domestic
species of the later phase (PPNB)
are sheep and goat and somewhat
later also cattle (Bar-Yosef 1981).

There are, however, exceptions to
this pattern, which may have been
the general rule. In the Prepottery
Neolithic site of Ain Ghazal in the
Jordan valley, Köhler-Rollefson
(Rollefson 1984; Köhler-Rollefson
1988) found that the introduction
of domestic goat, the first domestic species which appeared in this
area, did not lead to a sudden complete change, but to a more gradual
decline of other species over a
period of at least one thousand
years. This she ascribes to the
steady destruction of the natural
vegetation by the goat and the loss
of a variety of ecological niches,
through which species disappeared
(Fig. 2).

Thus, in some cases we have a pattern of sudden and complete change from a hunter-gatherer economy to an animal-breeding society, which can only be explained as a cultural choice of the people involved, albeit maybe forced by overexploitation of the areas surrounding the settlements. In other cases we see a pattern of much more gradual change which might be more of an exception, in which the introduction of domesticated animals led to a gradual change in the environment and in the economy.

Another aspect of this change is that there is no clear evidence that the major development of domestication took place at the centre of the geographical distribution of sheep and goat, in other words the Taurus Mountains. Most larger sites of this period found so far, are situated on the edge of the area where goat and sheep naturally occurred. It might very well be the necessity of introducing a "new" species into the somewhat impoverished environment around the settlements that was the reason for the sudden success of domesticated sheep and goat in the first place.

5 LATE NEOLITHIC AND HALAF PERIODS

The second example of problems in the interpretation of faunal material from human occupations dates to the Late Neolithic and Halaf periods. In the foregoing part of this article we discussed the Early Neolithic developments as the hunter-gatherer societies changed to a society in which animal husbandry was the major source of animal products. This period lasted well over a thousand years until the middle of the sixth millennium BC. A curious change then took place. All sites mentioned earlier were then abandoned and as far as we know there are no sites that show a continuous occupation from the Early Neolithic on into the Late Neolithic period. On the other hand, a number of new settlements have been found in north Syria and Iraq, the beginnings of which all date to the Late Neolithic. They lie in the same general area as their predecessors but not at the same actual locations. These sites are Tell Assouad, Sabi Abyad, Shams

ed-Din and Girikihacyan in north Syria and southeastern Anatolia, and Umm Dabagiyah in the Iraqi Jezireh. Except maybe for Umm Dabagiyah, none of the sites is of the size of the earlier Neolithic settlements. Their material remains such as architecture, tools and ceramics differ significantly from the remains of earlier periods.

The results of faunal analysis of these sites also show a marked difference from the earlier sites. All sites now show the presence of the four major domesticated food animals, sheep, goat, cattle and pig (Fig. 2). But although these animals were available and the tradition of animal husbandry was already well-established, we see that an important part of the faunal remains are of hunted, wild animals. In Tell Assouad (Helmer 1985b) up to 40% of the remains are of a subgutturosa (Persian gazelle) while in Umm Dabagiyah ca 70% came from wild onager (Equus hemionus) (Bökönyi 1973, 1986). In Shams ed-Din situated on the Euphrates north of Mureybet ca 40% of the identified remains came from wild onager, while also a considerable number of gazelle were hunted (Uerpmann 1982). On the other hand, sites as Sabi Abyad (van Wijngaarden-Bakker 1988) and Girikihacyan (Watson pers. comm.) do not have such large proportions of remains of wild animals. They differ from the earlier settlements mainly in the fact that domesticated cattle and pig now play an important part among the domesticated species beside sheep and goat.

At the same time, in other parts of the Near East, for example Central-Anatolia, other, dissimilar developments seem to have taken place, such as a preference for hunting and breeding cattle. It is, however, premature to compare the data from these early excavations with the more abundant remains from the above-mentioned sites. At settlements such as Hacilar and Çatal Höyük, often mentioned in the literature, excavations did not yield, or investigators failed to collect, sufficient numbers of animal remains to give a satisfactory picture of the existing economy. The many beautiful frescos, reliefs and figurines may not represent daily life practices, but an exceptional, maybe even an idealised picture of the philosophical and religious ideas of the people.

What we do have to ask ourselves is what the meaning of this renewed hunting is. The presence of these large amounts of remains from wild species once again demonstrates that in the earlier period it was a conscious decision to rely completely on domesticated animals for the production of proteins and animal fat. In this case, however, we see a reversal of that choice, although with the exception that is was not as general within the area as the previous one, and that important sites continued in the tradition of the earlier period. One of the factors that might have played a role, is the way society functioned in this period. In the Early Neolithic the settlements were very big with large populations. They must have been the centres of most activities for a large area. In the Late Neolithic or the Halaf period there was much more differentation in size and composition of the settlements. Akkermans (1987) supposes a developing semi-transhumance in which large settlements functioned as central pivots around which smaller groups moved. This much more mobile society moved within a larger area than before and could easily exploit the large herds of wild animals which they encountered. The bigger sites might have acted as market-places and/or production centres of goods such as ceramics and cereals, in exchange for which products of hunting were offered. The sites with the large number of remains from wild animals might then have been such market-places while sites such as Sabi Abyad and Girikihacyan might have been production centres, where the people were more sedentary and need not hunt. In Sabi Abyad a number of pottery-kilns were found as were large warehouses/stores, which might argue in favour of the above-mentioned hypothesis.

As we see, faunal analysis plays a major role in our understanding of the economy of the settlements in the area. However, indirectly it also gives us evidence of the existence of large areas still basically as the Near East was before the introduction of domestication. One can infer from this that although domestication had an enormous influence on man's way of life, nature and the environment had so far been only marginally changed.

The third case to be discussed is the part that pig, Sus (scrofa) domesticus, played in the economy of man in this area. Pig was probably the last of the major food animals to be domesticated. Although the earliest sites do not show much evidence of domestication of pig, it is clear that at the beginning of the sixth millennium BC the animal was domesticated and played an important role in the production of food.

The reasons for the later domestication of this animal might be twofold. First, the behaviour of pigs is different from the ruminants that were domesticated earlier. Sheep, goat and cattle live in large herds with a leading animal. Their behaviour is such that man can easily become part of their social pattern, and therefore their activities can be controlled by man, leading to domestication. Pigs, however, live in much smaller family groups, in which man cannot play such a role. Domestication of pigs is therefore a much more forced condition. Also, we have seen that domestication took place especially in the more marginal areas. Wild boar is an omnivorous browser and occurs only in areas with a richer vegetation. Especially in the southern part of the Euphrates region, wild boar could only be found in the river flood-plain, an area that was not exploited with any intensity, it seems (Buitenhuis 1988).

The importance of pig in this period is not yet fully studied, mainly because of the scarcity of well-excavated sites, but it does seem that at least in those settlements around which a reasonably lush vegetation existed, it forms a minor but important part of the faunal assemblage, reaching between 7-15% of the identified remains. The problems of interpretation come with the change of cultures at the end of the fourth millennium BC. At this time we see a small but clear decline in the relative number of pig remains from sites in this area. One can imagine that this decline is not because people did

Table 1. Wild species encountered in the faunal complexes from sites along the Euphrates from the Neolithic to the Early Bronze Age. (* also found in El Qitar, Hadidi and Mumbaqa; and in the late Early Bronze Age levels of Tell es-Sweyhat).

Vulpes vulpes	- fox*	Ardeidae	- herons*
Equus hemionus	- onager	Anser spec.	- goose*
Dama mesopotamica	- fallow deer*	Anatidae	- ducks*
Cervus elaphus	- red deer*	Anas platyrhynchos	- mallard*
Capreolus capreolus	- roe deer*	Falco tinnunculus	- kestrel*
Gazella subgutturosa	- Persian gazelle*	Tetraonidae	- grouse
Sus scrofa	- wild boar*	Alectoris chukar	- chukar*
Bos primigenius	- aurochs	Grus grus	- crane*
Capra aegagrus	- wild goat	Otis tarda	- bustard*
Ovis orientalis	- wild sheep	Rallidae	- rails
Lepus europaeus	- hare*	Fulica atra	- coot
Meles meles	- badger	Numenius arquata	- curlew
Erinacaeus europaeus	- hedgehog	Corvus frugilegus	- rook
		Struthio camelus	- ostrich

not want pig any more, but that circumstances forced them more or less to abandon pig breeding as a major occupation. The first reason that comes to mind is that the richer vegetational zones on which pig depended for its food were disappearing. And it is known that with the developing Bronze Age cultures more and more of the richer soils were taken under cultivation either for growing crops such as wheat, barley or pulses, or for the planting of orchards and vineyards. Indeed, the development of the "state" with its hierachical system also indicates the development of a market-economy in which people grew crops for a much larger population and therefore cultivated more land than was needed for their local needs. At the same time the developing metallurgy needed large amounts of fuel, and it has been suggested that this was a major factor in the deforestation which took place in this period (Bottema pers. comm.)

What we do see in this instance is a change in the recovered faunal complex that indicates an environmental change caused by man for its own sake. The effect was not that man changed his actions to allow him to continue in the traditional way but that he changed his economy. This might be considered one of the earliest instances of the destruction of man's environment that was not checked, and led to more intensive exploitation and therefore to further change of the environment.

6 MIDDLE BRONZE AGE

The last case of controversy between economic and environmental evidence within the faunal complexes of human settlements occurs in the Middle Bronze Age (2nd millennium BC) in settlements along the Euphrates in north Syria.

In these sites new developments can be observed. First there is the appearance of large amounts of equine remains. These species (Equus caballus - horse; Equus asinus - donkey and their crossbreeds, mule or hinny) were domesticated much earlier (late 4th millennium BC), but only with the increase in long-distance trade at the late Early Bronze Age and Middle Bronze Age do they become important, as reflected in the recovered remains. This change in the faunal complex occurred for purely economic reasons, as the species are not indigenous to the region and were purposely introduced by man in their domesticated state.

The second change in the faunal assemblage is much less clear. In this period the herds of sheep, goat and cattle are the main sources of animal products. Up to 90% of the remains are from these species. Hunting was of hardly any importance, it seems, and people hunted mainly for the species that were also hunted in earlier periods and must have been common, such as gazelle, onager, deer and hare. But in at least three settlements from the middle of the second millennium

Table 2. Wild species only encountered among the faunal remains from El Qitar, Hadid and Mumbaqa.

Ursus arctos	- brown bear	Ciconiidae	- stork
Elephas maximus	- indian elephant	Aythya nyroca	- ferrugineous duck
Castor fiber	- beaver	Circaëtus gallicus	- short-toed eagle
		Accipiter nisus	- sparrow hawk
		Coturnix coturnix	- quail
		Francolinus franc.	- francolin
Tatera indica)		Charadriidae	- plovers
Merines spec.) small rodents		Philomachus pugnax	- ruff
Gerbillus spec.)		Larus argentatus	- herring gull
		Columba spec.	- pigeon
		Asio otis	- long-eared owl
		Athene noctua	- little owl
		Turdus spec.	- thrush
		Fringillidae	- finches
		Pica pica	- magpie
		Corvus corax	- raven
		Corvus monedula	- jackdaw

BC along the Euphrates, Hadidi (Buitenhuis 1979), El Qitar (Buitenhuis 1988) and Mumbaqa (Boessneck and von den Driesch 1986), remains appear of many more species, a number of them never before encountered (Tables 1 and 2). The number of remains per species is very low, quite often just a single bone, and except for maybe elephant they could all be expected among remains from any period in this area. The surprising aspect is not that they were found at all, but that they were found all together at the same time. This variety of recovered species is totally new for any post-domestication settlement in this area, although in the Late Early Bronze Age settlements of Selenkahya (IJzereef unpubl.) and Tell es-Sweyhat (Buitenhuis 1986) there are already signs of this development.

The remains of bear (Ursus arctos syriacus) found at El Qitar may have been imported, but beaver (Castor fiber) found in Hadidi and El Qitar might very well have lived in the Euphrates floodplain. The only other recovered remains of this animal date from the Early Neolithic settlement at Abu Hureyra, more than 4000 years earlier (Legge and Rowley-Conwy 1986).

The remains of elephant (Elephas maximus dasyurus) found at El Qitar and Mumbaqa, but also at the Late Bronze Age levels of Sabi Abyad (I. Rossmeisl pers. comm.) in the Balikh valley and at Sheikh Hamed (Kühne pers. comm.) in the Khabur valley in eastern Syria, form something of an enigma. Although Syria is at this time known as a source of ivory, it is still a puzzle where these animals lived. Texts from several sources describe elephant hunts by pharaohs and kings in the second and first millennia BC, but no evidence of the existence of these animals in earlier periods was ever found. Considering the many paintings, figurines, theriomorphic vessels etc. one would expect at least some evidence of this imposing creature if it existed in this area. On the other hand, if these animals were imported, bred and released especially for their ivory, one wonders how they came to this region and could survive being hunted for at least a millennium, as they are not the most prolific breeders.

Their presence does on the other hand show a fairly rich vegetation and enough undisturbed terrain for them to live in. This rich vegetation is further illustrated by the remains of many different bird species that were found in this period (Tables 1 and 2). Although never in large quantities, we do find them all in the same period, indicating that they were not accidentally killed. The wide variety of species does show that the area was still rich enough for these animals to live there, but the reason for their occurrence in the archaeological material must be that it became economically feasible to hunt them.

7 CONCLUSION

Apart from our understanding of human society in the different periods, faunal analyses show us that human settlements depending on domesticated species for their animal products, give us a very lopsided picture of the available food sources, and that conclusions about the environment and changes therein can only be drawn with extreme caution. The very fact of the occurrence of many wild species in periods widely separated in time, but in the same area, shows us that the impact of man on the environment in the pre- and proto-historic period must have been much more local and less severe than is often assumed.

REFERENCES

Akkermans, P.M.M.G. 1987.
A Late Neolithic and Early Halaf village at Sabi Abyad, North Syria. Paléorient 13/1:23-40.
Bar-Yosef, O. 1981.
The Epi-palaeolithic complex in the Southern Levant. In Colloques Internationaux du CNRS, no 598: Préhistoire du Levant, p.389-408. Paris, CNRS.
Boessneck, J. and A.von den Driesch 1986. Tierknochen- und Mollusken-funde aus Mumbaqa. Mitteilungen des Deutschen Orient Gesellschaft 118:147-159.
Bökönyi, S. 1973.
The fauna of Umm Dabagiyah: a preliminary report. Iraq 35:9-11.
Bökönyi, S. 1978.
Environmental and cultural differences as reflected in the animal bone sample from five Early Neolithic sites in Southwest Asia. In R.H.Meadow and M.A. Zeder (eds.), Approaches to Faunal Analysis in the Middle East. Peabody Museum Bulletin 2: 57-62.
Bökönyi, S. 1986.
The equids of Umm Dabagiyah, Iraq. In H.-P.Uerpmann and R.H. Meadow (eds.), Equids in the Ancient World. Beihefte zum Tübinger Atlas des Vorderen Orients, Reihe A 19/1: 302-318.
Buitenhuis, H. 1979.
The faunal remains from Tell Hadidi. In M.Kubasiewicz (ed.), Archaeozoology I, p.164-175. Szczecin.

Buitenhuis, H. 1985.
The animal remains of Tell es-Sweyhat, Syria. Palaeohistoria 25:131-144.
Buitenhuis, H. 1988.
Archeozoölogisch onderzoek langs de Midden-Eufraat. Unpubl.diss., University of Groningen.
Clason, A.T. 1979-80.
The animal remains from Tell es-Sinn compared with those from Bouqras. Anatolica 7:35-53.
Ducos, P. 1978.
Tell Mureybet (Syrie IX-VII millénaires). Etude archéozoologique et problèmes d'écologie humaine I. Paris.
Helmer, D. 1985a.
Etude préliminaire de la faune de Çafer Höyük (Malatya, Turquie). Cahiers de l'Euphrate 4:117-120.
Helmer, D. 1985b.
Etude de la faune de Tell Assouad (Djézireh, Syrie) sondage J. Cauvin. Cahiers de l'Euphrate 4:275-286.
Köhler-Rollefson, I. 1988.
The Fauna from Neolithic Ain Ghazal. In A.Garrard and H.G. Gebel (eds.), The Prehistory of Jordan, p.423-430. BAR International Series 396.
Lawrence, B. 1980.
Evidences of animal domestication at Çayönü. In H.Çambel (ed.), The joint Istanbul-Chicago Universities prehistoric research in Southeastern Anatolia I, p.257-308. Istanbul.
Lawrence, B. 1982.
Principal food animals at Çayönü. In L.S. and R.J.Braidwood (eds.), The joint Istanbul-Chicago Universities prehistoric research in Southeastern Anatolia II, p. 285-308. Istanbul.
Legge, A.J. 1975.
The fauna of Tell Abu Hureyra: a preliminary analysis. Proceedings of the Prehistoric Society 41:74-77.
Legge, A.J. and P.A.Rowley-Conwy 1986. The beaver (Castor fiber L.) in the Tigris-Euphrates Basin. Journal of Archaeological Science 13:469-476.
Legge, A.J. and P.A.Rowley-Conwy 1987. Gazelle killing in Stone Age Syria. Scientific American 257:76-83.
Rollefson, G., 1984.
'Ain Ghazal': An Early Neolithic community in Highland Jordan, near Amman. Bulletin of the

American Schools of Oriental
Research 255:3-14.
Uerpmann, H.-P. 1982.
Faunal remains from Shams ed-Din
Tannira, a Halafian site in
Northern Syria. Berytus 30.
Wijngaarden-Bakker, L.H.van 1988.
The faunal remains from Tell
Sabi Abyad. In P.M.M.G.Akker-
mans (ed.), Excavations at Tell
Sabi Abyad. BAR International
Series 468.

Man's Role in the Shaping of the Eastern Mediterranean Landscape, Bottema, Entjes-Nieborg & van Zeist (eds)
© 1990 Balkema, Rotterdam. ISBN 90 6191 138 9

Herd management in the past and its impact on the landscape of the southern Levant

17

Eitan Tchernov & Liora Kolska Horwitz
Department of Zoology, The Hebrew University, Jerusalem, Israel

ABSTRACT: In order to assess the effect of herding practices on the Late Holocene landscape of the southern Levant, a method was developed using current carrying capacity of the region as a standard against which a diachronic series of faunal remains from archaeological sites in Israel was analysed. A trend of increasing frequencies of caprovines was found in two of the four regions studied and was considered to reflect lowered carrying capacities associated with overgrazing.

1 INTRODUCTION

The magnitude of environmental changes at the end of the last glacial in southwest Asia was great enough to affect the genetic configuration of species on the population level, but not sufficient to cause a sharp megafaunal turnover at the dawn of the Holocene, as is known from northern latitudes (Tchernov 1984). Yet, during the Holocene many of the large species of mammals became extinct in southwest Asia, not as a punctuated event but rather as a gradual process throughout this period. It is now generally accepted that the main cause for this decrease in biological diversity during the Holocene was anthropogenic. Likewise, human activities are considered to be the main cause for the degradation of the Mediterranean landscapes and the destruction of the southern Levantine ecosystems in the Holocene (Mikesell 1960; Naveh and Dan 1973; Pons and Quézel 1985). However, it is still not clear what kind of human action caused these changes: fires, deforestation, urbanization, agriculture, hunting, over-population, herding or a combination of several factors.

This preliminary study is an attempt to assess the effect of herding on the landscape of the southern Levant. For this purpose a method has been developed that uses data on the modern carrying capacity of the region, which has been applied to data from Holocene faunal assemblages from Israel spanning some 8000 years.

2 RATIONALE

The method outlined here is based on the assumption that the carrying capacity of a region reflects the quality and amount of suitable pasture available in a given region for a given animal species relative to its nutritional requirements. Sheep, goats and cattle have different nutritional adaptations and hence ecological requirements. Changes in the relative frequency of these species will therefore reflect changes in the carrying capacity of the region.

Sheep, goats and cattle are complementary in their feeding behaviour as they are adapted to exploiting different aspects of the same environment (Peters 1988). This feature enables the herder to fully utilise the available pasture areas; cattle are predominantly grass eaters; sheep, like cattle, are grazers and seldom browse bushes, mainly feeding on weeds and short grasses, while goats are mixed feeders which feed on weeds, grasses and herbs but spend most of their time browsing bushes and trees (van Dyne et al. 1980). Moreover, these three species differ in significant ways: goats and to a lesser extent sheep, have lower nutrient requirements, goats have a broader fodder-consumption spectrum as well as a better grazing ability making them preferable to cattle (and sheep) in regions of marginal vegetation (Noy-Meir and Seligman 1979; Peters 1988). Moreover, goats have significantly lower water requirements than cattle while still yielding quantities of milk and meat, while sheep fall somewhere between the two species in this respect (Schmidt-Nielsen 1979). Each species is adapted to different environmental conditions. Sheep are better adapted than goats to cold and to high elevations, cattle are best adapted to cool climates and goats are the best adapted of the three to arid-hot regions and are the best at surviving on poor pasture (MacFarlane 1968). These are generalities about the species, and it must be borne in mind that the different breeds of each species exhibit great variability in these respects, e.g. the Hejazi goat has an extremely low water consumption/turnover rate, making it ideally adapted to desertic conditions (Shkolnik 1988).

Given the differences in environmental and climatic adaptation among the three species, one would expect to find the highest frequency of each species in the region to which it is best adapted i.e. one would expect to find a higher frequency of sheep and goats in the more arid, southern regions of Israel or in those regions which have a low carrying capacity. In contrast, one would expect those regions which are cooler and/or have a higher carrying capacity to support a higher frequency of cattle relative to sheep and goats.

Admittedly, economic considerations related to the management goals of the herder (such as milk, meat or wool production), may be the crucial factor in explaining the relative proportions of these species in a herd. It has been noted (Marx 1967; Noy-Meir 1975), that though the Bedouins maintain mixed herds in a semi-arid ecosystem, these are usually dominated by sheep rather than goats, a factor probably related to cultural preferences. In most cases this is in regions where fodder is supplemented or areas with access to artificial water supplies.

However, economic considerations become secondary to environmental and physiological ones when it becomes impossible to maintain a herd in a hostile environment, e.g. large herds of cattle in a desert. In our modern world we have the ability to change our surroundings and hence the animals we keep, by providing fodder or water. However, it is highly unlikely that the level of technological ability required for doing this on a large scale was available to past populations in this region. Taking into account the amount of fodder needed per animal (Seligman et al. 1959), it was not feasible for past populations to maintain their herds entirely on grown or even collected fodder. This means that on the whole, herds were free ranging, possibly with access to harvested or fallow fields at certain times of the year. Domestic animals in the past, like their wild counterparts, were tightly bound to the carrying capacity of the environment, as it was only in exceptional instances that the animals were totally dependent upon man-supplied forage.

Given a particular fall-off point in the environment, carrying capacity drops to a point where it becomes uneconomic and impossible to maintain an animal that is unsuited to these conditions. Up to this point, cultural and other considerations may dominate in determining the herd structure. With a shift in the climatic regime of a region, we assume that a consequent shift in the frequency of sheep/goat relative to cattle will occur. Specifically, climatic amelioration will result in a lowered frequency of sheep/goat in regions with the lowest carrying capacity. This is because their carrying capacity will be increased, facilitating the herding of cattle. Conversely, under conditions of climatic decline, a rise in the frequency of sheep/goat is expected in the regions with medium to high carrying capacity, while in the more marginal regions the frequency of cattle should drop even more markedly. Likewise, overgrazing, which results in a lowering of a region's carrying capacity, will result in a shift in the relative frequencies of sheep/goat and cattle. The most marked effect of overgrazing, to be assessed from the archaeological record, will be visible in the regions with the highest carrying capacities or those with the most amenable climatic regime. These regions will usually be more densely populated than the marginal regions, and have a higher density of animals to begin with, especially cattle. Overgrazing in these regions will result in a raised frequency of sheep/goat and a lowering of the frequency of cattle as the carrying capacity of the region decreases. We should therefore expect that overgrazing will be more noticeable in the archaeological record of the optimal regions than in the more marginal ones. In the marginal regions overgrazing will be less evident as these areas are characterised by a high initial frequency of sheep/goat. We assume that overgrazing is distinguishable from deterioration due to climatic shift, in that climatic changes will affect the faunal composition of the region as a whole, whereas overgrazing will only be manifest in regions with a relatively high initial carrying capacity.

Thus, in the case of overgrazing the largest shift from sheep/goat to cattle frequencies will be observable in the regions with the medium and highest carrying capacities. The shift will be less marked in the optimal region as conditions there may never reach a point where the herding of cattle is altogether impossible. As a result, the most marked shift due to overgrazing is expected in the regions with medium carrying capacity, where the ratio of sheep/goat to cattle still favours cattle.

3 MATERIALS AND METHOD

The study of animal bones recovered from archaeological sites following animal domestication, provides us with information on man-animal relations in the past, pertaining especially to herd management and exploitation. An analysis was made of the relative frequencies of the main domestic grazing animals, sheep/goat and cattle, from various archaeological sites in Israel spanning the Pottery Neolithic to the Iron Age II (Appendix A). This was done in order to examine the possible impact of domestic animal herds on the southern Levantine environment in the past. Due to the paucity of data on the relative frequencies of sheep to goat, these two species were pooled into a combined caprovine category.

The data used here were derived only from habitation sites. All the available faunal reports from the relevant periods were utilized here, regardless of sample size. This, and the fact that the data were not obtained through a standardized analytical procedure, but from a variety of sources, and that in some instances data are missing for a particular period or region, will mean that the results reflect overall trends rather than closely defined changes.

The data set was based on numerical counts of bones per species (NSP) and not on counts of minimum numbers of individuals (MNI), as MNI counts can exhibit great variability depending upon the method used (Horton 1984). Most archaeozoological publications do not specify the method used in calculating MNI and in a few cases MNI counts are not given at all. Therefore the data used in this study are not yet well quantified and statistically tested. Rather, this study is an attempt to introduce a new method that may be used in assessing the impact of overgrazing in a region.

To our knowledge, in Israel all attempts to estimate herd size per site, region or period, so far have not been calculated from the faunal data directly. The most commonly used approach has been to apply data on herd size for present-day "traditional" pastoralists, nomads (Bedouins) and/or sedentary farmers to the archaeological record, assuming that the economic strategy was similar (Levy 1981; Dar 1986; Gophna et al. 1986-1987). A similar approach is based on herd numbers given in historical and literary sources, such as the

209

Bible or tax reports which are then used to estimate herd size in a given area (Dar 1986; Rosen 1986). Because of the problems inherent in each one of these approaches, we have developed an alternative technique which uses data generated from the faunal remains themselves rather than from extraneous sources. Though we have applied it here to a Near Eastern context, we feel it is suitable for application in any country/region where data on modern carrying capacity are known.

Carrying capacity of a region is a means of characterising a region's ability to support grazing animals, in this case domestic cattle and caprovines. It is an expression of several factors, including the type of vegetation, its density, spatial distribution, nutritional value and in some cases its seasonal availability; the topography of a region; the size of the area offering suitable grazing relative to the size of the region as a whole; and the nutritional needs of the animal expected to graze there; i.e. its main application is in determining the numbers of a specific animal (in terms of its nutritional needs) that may exploit a region for pasture.

The method that we have developed utilises values of modern carrying capacity of rangeland (pasture) for different regions in Israel, as a standard against which to compare changing rangeland usage in the past. The annual carrying capacity (A.C.C.) of Israeli pasture areas was calculated using data on modern rangeland presented in Seligman et al. (1959) which were collected during the 1950s for the 13 pasture regions they recognised (Fig. 1). The A.C.C. calculation was made according to methods used by Noy-Meir (1975). For each region the A.C.C. (in cow units per sq km), was calculated by dividing the total feed supply in the region (termed animal unit month, A.U.M. = amount of pasture needed to keep one adult cow for one month), by the total range area in the region, (in dunams). This was then multiplied by 12 (monthly data converted to annual amounts) and multiplied by 1000 (conversion from dunams to sq km) and provides an estimate of the A.C.C. of the region for cows. According to Seligman et al. (1959)

one cow is equivalent to about 5-6 caprovines. This is a simplistic model that assumes that nutritional requirements are balanced by the supply throughout the year, i.e. it compares the nutritional requirements of an animal (in this case an adult cow weighing 450 kg, needing 135 food units per month), with the nutritional supply of the utilised pasture on an annual basis (Noy-Meir 1975; Seligman et al. 1959).

The resultant A.C.C. is a measure of modern rangelands in Israel and reflects on the whole an optimal situation, as by the time Seligman's survey was carried out (in the 1950s) most of the forest and maquis had already been cleared for agriculture and grazing. By contrast, in the past certain areas would have been more forested and thus offered a lower carrying capacity as pasture. On the other hand it has been suggested that in the past there were fewer thorny and poisonous plants, a feature that would have increased the carrying capacity (Zohary 1983).

Data were collected on the numbers of caprovine and cattle bones found at each site, by period. Thus in multi-period sites, the numbers of bones of each species were added up separately for each period. The sites, by period, were then allotted to one of the 13 regions outlined in Seligman et al. (1959) as shown in the distribution map (Fig. 1a). Due to the small number of sites from the 13 regions outlined by Seligman et al., in this study the A.C.C. data from the different regions were compared and regions with similar carrying capacities pooled (Fig. 1b). In the end we only worked with four areas out of Seligman's original 13. For each of these four regions, the numbers of caprovine and cattle bones were added up. These totals were used to calculate the relative percentages of caprovines and cattle for each region per period. The small sample sizes did not allow the running of statistical tests.

If we want to assess the influence of climatic change on the landscape and hence on herd composition, it must have been quite severe and/or sustained for it to be visible in our faunal samples, as most of our samples cover long stretches of time (e.g. the Chalcolithic

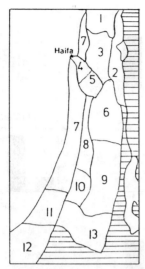

ARRANGED FROM HIGHEST TO LOWEST CARRYING CAPACITY

Map No.	Region	A.C.C.
2	Upper Jordan Valley	34.0
8	Foothills	28.2
5	Menashe	25.7
10	Bet Guvrin	25.6
7	Coastal Plain	23.2
11	Northern Negev	20.4
1	Upper Galilee	19.2
9	Jerusalem	15.2
3	Lower Carmel	14.5
12	Western Negev	13.4
6	Yiron	11.0
4	Carmel	10.1
13	Beersheva	4.4

Fig. 1a. Map of Israel showing areas (1-13) as defined by Seligman et al. (1959), showing the regions and Annual Carrying Capacity (A.C.C.) values.

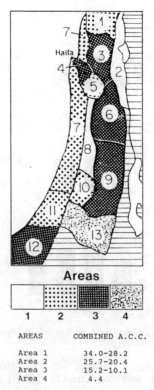

Areas

| 1 | 2 | 3 | 4 |

AREAS	COMBINED A.C.C.
Area 1	34.0-28.2
Area 2	25.7-20.4
Area 3	15.2-10.1
Area 4	4.4

Fig. 1b. Map of Israel showing the re-division of the original areas defined by Seligman et al. (1959), into the four areas used in this study.

spans some 1000 years: ca 4000-3150 BC). However, most sites were probably not occupied continuously throughout a period and our samples represent only a fraction of its duration.

Information on climatic change in Israel for the last 5000 years is still incomplete, and those data that we have are either inconclusive or contradictory (Goldberg and Rosen 1987; Horowitz 1974). However, it may generally be concluded that though minor climatic fluctuations occurred throughout the later Holocene (Horowitz 1974), current climatic conditions had set in by then (Danin 1985; Goldberg and Rosen 1987). The role of humans, rather than that of climate, in changing the vegetal landscape of Israel over the past 4000-odd years through agricultural activities has

been noted by researchers (Naveh and Dan 1973; Baruch 1983; Gophna et al. 1986-1987). However, here we have assumed a simplistic model that does not take into account shifts in management strategies, such as may occur given changing climatic conditions or shifts in the carrying capacity of a region. One of the obvious options open to herders is to move to areas of higher carrying capacity or those offering better climatic conditions in times of crisis. This, however, is not always possible, as it is dependent upon population density, as well as political and social factors. Unfortunately, in Israel demographic studies have not been carried out for all regions or archaeological periods, so that only selective data are available. The available data do reflect significant changes in population size and density of settlement (Shiloh 1980;

211

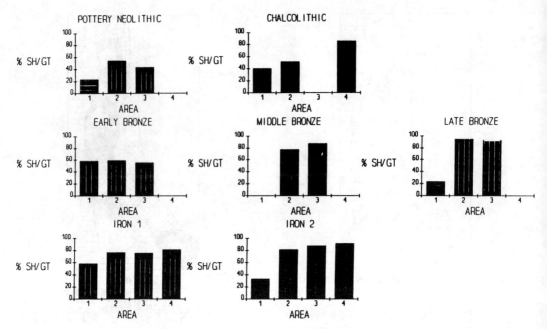

Fig. 2. Percentages of sheep/goat for the different areas by period.

Levy 1981; Gophna et al. 1986-1987; Gophna and Portugali 1988), a factor that certainly would have affected the distribution of herds and the management strategies practised in the past.

4 RESULTS

From the plots (Fig. 2) one can see a general trend in the ratio of caprovines to cattle in Israel, which follows a north-south gradient, with lower caprovine frequencies in the north of the country (roughly the Mediterranean region) and an increase in the more southern regions. This trend is especially visible in area 4 (our region of lowest carrying capacity and also the most southern) which consistently has the highest caprovine frequencies. We therefore conclude that the overall north-south gradient that is visible today in Israel was present in the periods under study. Hellwing (1986) reported that in a series of archaeological sites in Israel, the frequencies of goats increased from central to the southern regions of the country. This he ascribed to environmental factors that favour

goat herding in the more arid regions. A similar finding was found by Horwitz and Tchernov (in press) for a series of Early Bronze Age sites in Israel. In the present study, our data base of assemblages where sheep had been separated from goat, was too small to allow separate analysis.

Under a given climatic change, the largest shift in caprovine to cattle frequencies is expected to occur in the marginal zones or those with the lowest carrying capacity, because these (area 4) will be most visibly affected by a climatic change. In these regions, a few more (or less) millimetres of rain will make a significant difference in vegetation cover, which may be critical in allowing the survival of a species or making its presence in the region unviable. By contrast, in the optimal region or one with a high carrying capacity (area 1) such a climatic shift will make less of an impact on the vegetation and hence on the fauna, unless the climatic change is of some magnitude. The intermediate regions (areas 2 and 3) would have to be affected by a relatively dramatic climatic change for the relative species frequencies to be

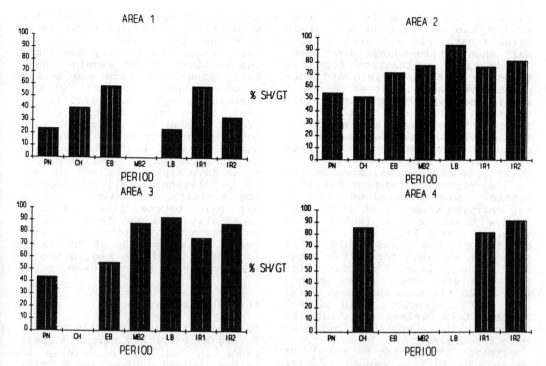

Fig. 3. Percentages of sheep/goat for the different periods for the four areas studied here.

significantly affected.

Looking at the plots in Fig. 3 we see that in area 1 (the region of highest carrying capacity) the caprovine frequencies are fairly constant, never exceeding 60%. It should be borne in mind that the sample, though derived from 9 sites, comprises only some 700 bones. In area 2, our next highest carrying capacity region, there is a trend, with some fluctuation in the Late Bronze Age, of increasing caprovine frequencies relative to cattle. In area 3, once again there is a trend of increasing caprovine frequencies. Area 4 shows a generally constant frequency of caprovines through time. The important point to note is that in this marginal region there is no major shift in time (admittedly the Bronze Age sequence is missing), a feature which we would expect if we were dealing with a climatic shift of any magnitude. Likewise, area 1, our area with the highest carrying capacity, also shows no major shift in caprovine frequencies over time. Even if some overgrazing should

have occurred, it is unlikely to manifest itself in the caprovine-cattle ratio, because an optimal region would have required an excessive degree of overgrazing. This would have resulted in dramatic population decrease in the region, a phenomenon for which there is no supporting evidence (Gophna and Portugali 1988; Shiloh 1980). More-over, this would have made the southern areas (area 4) totally unsuitable for human settlement. Areas 2 and 3 show the greatest change in the relative frequencies of caprovines to cattle, with a trend of increasing caprovine fre-quencies from the Pottery Neolithic to the Iron Age II. This same trend is not observable in areas 1 and 4 for the same period of time.

5 CONCLUSIONS

Despite the uneven nature of the data set used here, a definite trend towards increasing caprovine frequencies is observable in our areas of medium carrying capacity

213

(areas 2 and 3), while the areas at the two extremes of our scale (area 4-marginal, and area 1-optimal) show little change over time. One possible explanation for this trend is that the arable and more productive land in areas 2 and 3 was increasingly brought under cultivation. This would have excluded it from being used as rangeland. The remaining land available for pasture (such as rocky outcrops with scrub) would have been of lower productivity and more suited to the raising of caprovines than cattle. However, based on present-day carrying capacity of areas such as the Upper Galilee (which falls within our area 2), these less productive pasture areas would still have been suitable for cattle herding, though less productive for this activity than areas turned over to cultivation (Noy-Meir pers. comm.). Consequently, it is unlikely that this explanation would account for the changing faunal frequencies observed.

Climatic change can be ruled out as this would have caused a shift in faunal frequencies in all four areas examined. Moreover, the findings of geology, palynology and sedimentology all point to a fairly stable climate since the mid-Holocene. Admittedly, some minor fluctuations may have occurred, but their effect on the fauna was not sufficiently extensive to have left a permanent trace.

An alternative explanation for the shift in caprovine and cattle frequencies observed in areas 2 and 3, and one which is in accordance with our initial hypothesis (see section 1 above), is that such a pattern reflects lowered carrying capacity due to overgrazing. It has been proposed that the major source of the floral destruction and soil erosion is not the feeding habits of the herded animals, but the mismanagement of herds by their herders (Noy-Meir 1975). This refers to the maintenance of excessively large herds resulting in overcrowding and trampling which leads to overgrazing (Noy-Meir 1975; Pons and Quézel 1985). It is possible that disturbance and destruction of habitats through overgrazing occurred in the past because of the increased density and decreased mobility of animals kept under human control, a feature that accompanied increasing human sedentism and population density. Indeed, since the Pottery Neolithic, the earliest period examined here, human population size and density show an overall increase with an increasing degree of sedentism, especially in large urban agglomerations. Though the extent of agricultural activities must have expanded to meet increasing demands, so too must animal husbandry practices have expanded. Given increasing population density and decreasing mobility, extensive rangeland may have become less available, especially in areas favourable for settlement. Given time, this would result in a lowering of the carrying capacity of the region through overstocking and hence overgrazing.

ACKNOWLEDGEMENTS

Our special thanks are due to Prof. E. Noy-Meir for his valuable assistance in helping to develop the methodological approach used here.

REFERENCES

Baruch, U. 1983.
   The palynology of a late Holocene core from Lake Kinneret. Unpubl. M.A. Thesis, The Hebrew University.
Danin, A. 1985.
   Paleoclimates in Israel: evidence from weathering patterns of stones in and near archaeological sites. BASOR 259:33-43.
Dar, S. 1986.
   Landscape and Pattern: An archaeological survey of Samaria 800 BCE-636 CE. BAR International Series 308.
Dyne, G.M. van, N.R.Brockington, Z.Szocs, J.Duck and C.M.Ribie 1980. Large herbivore subsystems. In A.J.Breymeyer and G.M.van Dyne (eds.), Grasslands, System Analysis and Man, p.269-537. Cambridge, Cambridge University Press.
Goldberg, P. and A.Rosen 1987.
   Early Holocene palaeoenvironments of Israel. In T.E.Levy (ed.), Shiqmim I, p.23-33. BAR International Series 356.
Gophna, R. and J.Portugali 1988.
   Settlement and demographic pro-

cesses in Israel's coastal plain from the Chalcolithic to the Middle Bronze Age. BASOR 269:11-28.

Gophna, R., N.Lipschitz and S.Lev-Yadun 1986-1987.
Man's impact on the natural vegetation of the central coastal plain of Israel during the Chalcolithic period and the Bronze Age. Tel Aviv 13-14:71-84.

Hellwing, S. 1986.
Sheep or goats in archaeological deposits of Israel? Paper presented at 5th International ICAZ Conference, Bordeaux.

Horton, D.R. 1984.
Minimum numbers: a consideration. Journal of Archaeological Science 11:255-271.

Horowitz, A. 1974.
Preliminary palynological indications as to the climate of Israel during the last 6,000 years. Paléorient 2:407-414.

Horwitz, L.K. and E.Tchernov in press. Animal exploitation in the Early Bronze Age of the southern Levant: an overview. In P.de Miroschedji (ed.), The Urbanisation of Palestine in the Early Bronze Age. Paléorient.

MacFarlane, W.V. 1968.
Adaptations of ruminants to tropics and deserts. In E.S.Hafez (ed.), Adaptation of Domestic Animals. Philadelphia, Lea and Ferbiger.

Marx, E. 1967.
Bedouin of the Negev. Manchester: University Press.

Mikesell, M.W. 1960.
Deforestation in northern Morocco. Science 132:441-448.

Naveh, Z. and J.Dan 1973.
Human degradation of Mediterranean landscapes in Israel. In F.di Castri and H.A.Mooney(eds.), Mediterranean-Type Ecosystems, Origins and Structure, p.370-390. Heidelberg-Berlin-New York, Springer Verlag.

Noy-Meir, E. 1975.
Primary and secondary production in sedentary and nomadic grazing systems in the semi-arid region: analysis and modelling. Unpubl. research report submitted to the Ford Foundation.

Noy-Meir, E. and N.G.Seligman 1979.
Management of semi-arid ecosystem in Israel. In B.H.Walker (ed.), Management of Semi-Arid Ecosys-

tems, p.113-160. Amsterdam, Elsevier Publishing.

Peters, K.J. 1988.
The importance of small ruminants in rural development. Anim. Res. and Devel. 28:115-125.

Pons, A. and P.Quézel 1985.
The history of the flora and vegetation and past and present human disturbance in the Mediterranean region. In C.Gomez-Campo (ed.), Plant Conservation in the Mediterranean Area, p.25-43. Dordrecht, Dr. W. Junk Publishers.

Rosen, B. 1986.
Subsistence economy of stratum II. In I.Finkelstein (ed.), Izbet Sartah, p.156-185. BAR International Series 299.

Schmidt-Nielsen, K. 1979.
Desert Animals. 2nd ed. New York: Dover Publications.

Seligman, N.G., Z.Rosensaft, N.Tadmor, J.Katznelson and Z.Naveh 1959. Natural Pasture of Israel. Tel-Aviv: Workers Book Guild (in Hebrew).

Shiloh, Y. 1980.
The population of Iron Age Palestine in the light of a sample analysis of urban plans and population density. BASOR 239:25-35.

Shkolnik, A. 1988.
Physiological adaptations to the environment: the Israeli experience. In Y.Yom-Tov and E.Tchernov (eds.), The Zoogeography of Israel, p.487-496. Dordrecht, Dr. W.Junk Publishers.

Tchernov, E. 1984.
Faunal turnover and extinction rate in the Levant. In R.S.Martin and R.G. Klein (eds.), Pleistocene Extinctions: the search for a cause, p.528-552. Arizona, University of Arizona Press.

Zohary, M. 1983.
Man and vegetation in the Middle East. In W.Holzner, M.J.A.Werger and I.Ikusima (eds.), Man's Impact on Vegetation. The Hague.

APPENDIX A - List of sites by period used in this study.

POTTERY NEOLITHIC	EARLY BRONZE AGE	IRON AGE I
Tel Dan	Tel Dan	Tel Dan
Nahal Zehora	Gamla	Mount Ebal
Nahal Betzet	En Shahud	Tel Michal
Tel Eli II	Tel Dalit/Aphek	Tel Shiloh
Hagoshrim	Tel Erani	Izbet Sartah
Abou Zureiq	Tel Yarmouth	Miqne-Ekron
Munhatta 2	Arad	Tel Masos
Newe Yam		Tel Beersheba
Qatif Y3		Tel Arad
		Tel Jemmeh

CHALCOLITHIC	MIDDLE BRONZE AGE II	IRON AGE II
Tel Eli Ia-Ib	Tel Dan	Tel Dan
Munhatta 1	Tel Shiloh	Tel Shiloh
Metzer	Tel Dalit/Aphek	Tel Qasile
Tel-Aviv	Rafaim Valley	Hazorea
(Jabotinsky St.)	Tel Lachish	Miqne-Ekron
Gat Gurvin	Tel Nagila	Tel Lachish
Qatif Y2	Tel Haror	The Ophel
Grar B	Tel Jemmeh	Tel Masos
Grar C		Tel Arad
Tel Jemmeh		Tel Uza
Wadi Gazze		Tel Ira
Bir Abou Matar		Tel Jemmeh
Bir es-Safadi		
Gilat		
Shiqmim		
Horvat Beter		
Horvat Hor		

Botany

Man's Role in the Shaping of the Eastern Mediterranean Landscape, Bottema, Entjes-Nieborg & van Zeist (eds)
© 1990 Balkema, Rotterdam. ISBN 90 6191 138 9

Some reflections on anthropogenic indicators and the record of prehistoric occupation phases in pollen diagrams from the Near East

18

Karl-Ernst Behre
Niedersächsisches Institut für historische Küstenforschung, Wilhelmshaven, FR Germany

ABSTRACT: Difficulties in recording prehistoric occupation phases in pollen diagrams of the Near East are discussed. In order to present a more precise evaluation of the anthropogenic indicators, these were divided into two groups and new terms were introduced: primary and secondary anthropogenic indicators. An empiric approach of the fossil evidence was adopted to find out the indicator qualities of the various pollen types. For this purpose the Beyşehir occupation phase, which is very pronounced and clearly delimited in several SW Turkish pollen diagrams, was used as a key to evaluate the anthropogenic indicators. There are several reasons for the unsatisfactory record of archaeologically known habitation phases in pollen diagrams of the Near East: some of the anthropogenic indicators which are important in Europe, such as Cerealia and herbs of open habitats, present difficulties when used in the same way in the Near East, and on the other hand there is a lack of deposits suitable for pollen analysis in many areas of prehistoric occupation.

1 INTRODUCTION

During the decades after the Second World War fascinating results have been achieved in the prehistory of the Near East. In an interdisciplinary cooperation of archaeology and different branches of botany as well as zoology the origin of agriculture and the first farmer settlements could be traced. It turned out - in contrast to older ideas- that agriculture came into being not in the lowland river valleys of Euphrates and Tigris but on the slopes on the Zagros and other ranges bordering the so-called "Fertile Crescent" from Israel to Iran.

Important contributions as to the nature of the area, its vegetation and climate around 10,000 BP and later were expected from palynological investigations. Of special interest was the record of changes in vegetation and landscape caused by the introduction of farming as reflected in pollen diagrams. But also younger developments, such as

the establishment of irrigation cultures and the start of fruticulture as well as the environment of many sites well-known in prehistory, were and are important subjects for pollen analysis.

A great deal of excellent work on palaeo-ethnobotany and vegetation history has been done in the last decades in the Near East, most of it by W. van Zeist and S. Bottema of the Biologisch-Archaeologisch Instituut in Groningen. When they asked the present author to give his view on the difficult problem of how human impact can be observed in Near Eastern pollen diagrams, this was of course a delicate task. The authors of the original publications are most familiar with the area and the present vegetation of the sites investigated, and have their own views on their results. But they are also well acquainted with the difficulties and obstacles in tracing habitation periods in the Near East.

The following considerations from someone familiar with the European conditions and the empirical approach given below may be taken as an admission that the problem of anthropogenic indicators in the Near East is in several respects more complicated than in the formerly densely-forested areas of Europe.

2 GENERAL SURVEY AND PROBLEMS OF THE AREA WITH REGARD TO VEGETATION HISTORY

The Near East represents not much more than a geographical term that comprises various natural regions. The geological conditions and their geomorphological consequences range from extensive lowlands to large high plateaus and from hills to alpine mountains. The same applies to the climate, which varies from warm to cold and from arid to moist.

This great variety of basic facts leads to similar variety in the vegetation which is in parts arranged in zones, in other parts appears as sharply delimited local vegetation units as in oases, on single mountains etc. The natural plant cover ranges from xeric steppe vegetation and forest steppe, both in warm and cold varieties, to different types of forest and shrub vegetation such as cold-tolerant coniferous forests in the mountains and the Eu-Mediterranean coast.

Occupation in former times, in particular farming settlements, was dependent on certain climatic preconditions of which vegetation gives the best expression. This means that climatically induced changes in vegetation may have had severe consequences for the pattern of habitation areas.

The investigations of a number of pollen profiles in recent years (for location, see Fig. 1) gave new evidence as to the history of vegetation and climate. It turned out that during full and late-glacial conditions, the climate of most parts of the Near East was not moister but drier than it is today. The assumed pluvial period did not occur here. This dry climatic phase extended until early Postglacial time; then humidity increased, probably through a rise in precipitation. This is documented in several pollen diagrams, from Turkey (van Zeist et al. 1975) to Western Iran (van Zeist and Bottema 1977). During the early and middle postglacial phases the steppe vegetation in large parts of the Near East was replaced by forest. This transition took about 5000 years, from 10,600 BP to 5500 BP in Lake Zeribar, Western Iran, while in other places the date when modern AP values were reached, i.e. when present climatic conditions were established, was earlier: at Lake Urmia it occurred around 7300 BP, in Akgöl at about 8000 BP and the same date applies to several sites in SW Turkey (Bottema 1986; Bottema and Woldring 1984(1986)). The development shows a uniform general trend but considerable regional differences within the Near East.

This means that except in the early Neolithic, prehistoric people in most parts of the Near East encountered climatic conditions and vegetation patterns similar to those of today in so far as the latter had not been transformed by the activity of preceding cultures.

With regard to prehistory the general archaeological evidence across the Near East is not as good as most people believe. The history of habitation in such a large region is of course not uniform, but differs from area to area. A lot of archaeological work has been done in the Near East but apart from work on some farming settlements, mainly from the early Neolithic, many activities have concentrated in spectacular objects. Even today problems of architecture and history of art as well as the interest in ceramics and finds are much mnore important to some excavators than the simple questions of food production or other parts of the economy and the former environment. Our knowledge of farmer cultures and farming practices leaves much to be desired for several periods and several areas in the Near East.

A special drawback for most parts of the region is the lack of an archaeological survey as it is available in numerous European areas. This would be an important aid for the explanation of pollen diagrams and for prospecting new sites. At the moment one may find oneself in the peculiar situation of tracing a

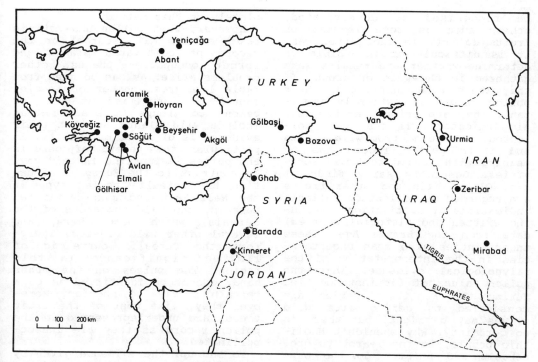

Fig. 1. Important pollen profiles in the Near East

pronounced occupation phase and having to explain its economy and even its area by pollen analysis only. This is the case with the Beyşehir occupation phase, where the evidence from pollen analysis is much better than the archaeological record (Bottema in press). If we realize all these special conditions of nature and knowledge we have the right starting point for finding a new way distinct from the conventional European one.

3 THE PRIMARY ANTHROPOGENIC INDICATORS IN POLLEN DIAGRAMS

The so-called anthropogenic indicators which are used for the interpretation of pollen diagrams include a wide range of species of quite different value for this purpose. To get a better impression of the reliability of these species they should be divided into different groups. This may give people outside the field of pollen analysis some help in the understanding of pollen diagrams. As primary anthropogenic indicators I define all

species which are cultivated in fields, orchards and gardens, which means that they are intensively grown in order to harvest them as crops, to use their fruits, nuts, fibres etc. They do not, however, include forest trees or meadow plants even if they have been planted or sown.

The best sources for finding out which species have to be regarded as primary anthropogenic indicators are the botanical macro-remains from archaeological excavations. Mainly due to the numerous papers by Helbaek and van Zeist there is a lot of evidence about cultivated plants in the early times of the Near East. Special attention was paid to the settlements of earliest agriculture, that is before 5000 BC, in the area of the Fertile Crescent. The results of these investigations in several cases pose the problem of whether to regard certain finds as primary anthropogenic indicators or not, as this is the period when the major cultivated plants were domesticated from their wild ancestors. While cereals often show clear characteristics to be recognized as domesticated, others such as some legumes or fruits do not. In the latter case it is difficult or impossible to determine whether the remains were gathered in the wild or grown. If the plants were cultivated, their pollen record is extremely important: they are primary anthropogenic indicators. If they were collected, they come from wild plants and their pollen record has no meaning with regard to human activities. Generally early finds of e.g. Olea, Vitis and other fruits are regarded as collected; reliable indications of cultivation (including written and pictorial sources) date from the Bronze Age. These uncertainties also mean uncertainties in the interpretation of the palynological evidence. That the pollen values of for instance Olea during the Neolithic period are considered to derive from wild olives may be right, but there is no certainty. Why shouldn't Neolithic people, having learnt to grow cereals and pulses, do the same with olives if these are not available in sufficient quantities in the natural landscape around their villages? This holds for other species too and makes it difficult to define certain anthropogenic indicators as primary ones for the earliest periods of agri- and fruticulture and thus to find out the share of gathering. A similar case is that of Fraxinus ornus, where the exudate is used. This certainly started with wild trees; latter additional ones were planted.

Another important problem that always has to be kept in mind with regard to the macro-botanical evidence as given in Table 1 is the chance of the remains becoming carbonized which varies between the species. While cereals in general have a good chance and pulses a moderate one, there always are only few fruit remains among the archaeological finds. As almost all fossil plant remains from the Near East are carbonized this severe selection within the basic material always has to be taken into consideration. This lack of information can for some species be compensated by pollen analysis, for instance for Juglans and Castanea, the history of which depends almost completely on this method.

However, when pollen analysis is taken as the main source for the record of cultivated plants and former occupation phases, other problems arise. As can be seen from Table 1 a great number of species cannot be identified at all, or belong to groups of species that include wild plants so that their evidence is of inferior quality. In particular the record of cereals and pulses is impaired in this way. In contrast to the European situation the Cerealia pollen type in the Near East includes cultivated cereals, the wild ancestors of the cereals, which occur here, and several other wild grasses. Therefore the Cerealia curve is of limited significance in this region. The pulses on the other hand, cannot be identified as to a certain cultivated species. Moreover they, like most of the fruit trees, are underrepresented in the pollen record as they are insect-pollinated.

To sum up: the evidence given by the primary anthropogenic indicators in the pollen diagrams is rather limited; this results in difficulties in tracing habitation phases by means of these species.

Table 1 presents a survey of the record of the major crop plants and fruits in the Near East. For the earliest, most important period, i.e. before 5000 BC, a subdivision into the main areas of the Near East is given. The figures show the numbers of excavations where the respective species were found (after Renfrew 1969; van Zeist 1976; Harlan 1977; van Zeist and Bakker-Heeres 1982(1985); Kislev 1985; van Zeist 1988). For the period of 5000 to 1000 BC only the occurrence (+) or frequent occurrence (++) of fossil finds within the whole area of the Near East is given (after Behre 1970; van Zeist and Bakker-Heeres 1985 (1988); van Zeist 1980, 1984; Kislev 1980; Costantini and Biasini 1984, 1985; Renfrew 1984; Kislev and Hopf 1985; Zohary and Hopf 1988). For the Greek and Roman period several excavations as well as written records were used. The last column of Table 1 shows the representation of the cultivated plants in the pollen diagrams, ignoring their differential

Table 1. The record of important crop plants and fruits in the Near East

	Before 5000 BC				5000 to 1000 BC Near East	Greek + Roman Near East	P = can be recorded by pollen analysis
	Turkey	Jordan Israel Syria	Iraq	Iran			
Cereals							
Triticum monococcum	3	6	2	1	++	+	
Triticum dicoccum	3	12	3	2	++	+	
Triticum durum/aestivum	2	5	1	1	++	+	
Hordeum distichon	1	8	2	4	++	+	
Hordeum vulgare	3	2	1	2	++	+	
Hordeum "nudum"	2	4	1	1	+	+	
Secale cereale	1					+	
Avena sativa					+	+	P
Panicum miliaceum					+	+	(Cerealia-type, includes several further wild grass species)
Wild cereals							
Triticum boeoticum	1	3	1	1	+		
Triticum dicoccoides	1	1					
Hordeum spontaneum	1	6	1	3			
Secale	1						
Avena	1		1		+		
Other crop plants							
Lens	3	8	1	2	++	+	
Pisum	5	6	1	1	+	+	P
Cicer	1	3			++	+	(included among different
Lathyrus (sativus + cicera)	4	3	2	1	++	+	types of Fabaceae; no
Vicia ervilia	1	2			+	+	species identification)
Vicia faba s.l.					+	+	
Trigonella foenum-graecum					+	+	
Linum usitatissimum	1	5	1	1	+	+	P
Camelina sativa					+	+	P (incl. in Brassicaceae)
Cannabis sativus						+	P (Cannabis + Humulus)
Wild, later cultivated, fruits and nuts							
Olea		1			+	+	P
Vitis	1	2			+	+	P
Ficus carica		4			−	+	
Punica granatum		1			+	+	P
Ceratonia		1					P
Citrus medica						+	P
Juglans	1					+	P
Castanea						+	P
Amygdalus	1	1		1	+	+	P (Prunus-type)
Prunus div. species					+	+	
Pistacia	2	5	1	1	+	+	P

The following species are excluded because they are rarely found in the the a analyses, are not recorded palynclogically, or occur in the wild only:

Allium porrum + sativum	Crataegus	Phoenix	Rubus
Capparis spinosa	Cucumis melo	Prosopis	Sesamum
Celtis	Cuminum	Pyrus	
Coriandrum sativum	Malus	Quercus	

representation in the pollen pre-cipitation.

4 THE SECONDARY ANTHROPOGENIC INDICATORS IN POLLEN DIAGRAMS

Agriculture as well as other ways of human activity and landscape transformation should normally be reflected in the pollen diagrams of the areas concerned. Apart from the primary anthropogenic indicators already mentioned there are a number of other species which can be used to trace different human activities in the past. This group I call secondary anthropogenic indicators, they are defined as species which are not intentionally grown by man but are favoured in various ways (apophytes) or un-intentionally introduced by man and his economy. They comprise weeds, ruderal and other adventive species as well as components of the mea-dows and pastures, briefly: all wild and synanthropic species that show a positive reponse to any form of human impact. As was shown by Behre (1981) most of these species occur in a variety of farming contexts and plant commu-nities; therefore the evaluation of their pollen curves has to be done carefully. As will be shown below the value of certain secondary anthropogenic indicators may vary considerably in different regions.

For the area in question mainly the following taxa which can be recorded in pollen diagrams have to be regarded as secondary anthropogenic indicators (see van Zeist et al. 1975; Bottema and Woldring 1984(1986); Bottema 1982(1985) and in press): the weeds of Chenopodiaceae, Polygonum aviculare-type, Brassica-type and Matricaria-type; species favoured by the establishment of pastureland such as Gramineae, Sanguisorba minor-type (including Sarcopoterium) and as a special case Plantago lanceolata-type which points to disturbed areas, but is sometimes taken as the most reliable indicator species for grazing. It is surprising that this plant, which is the most important secondary anthropogenic indicator in Central Europe, should show the same potential in this distant and different area. The spread of Plantago lanceolata is certainly favoured by pasture, though it may be due to other reasons too. The overestimation of Plantago lanceolata as a clear indicator of pastureland can also be seen in the interpretation of many European pollen diagrams (cf. Behre 1981:234 ff.).

Surface samples from the lower and upper Eu-Mediterranean zone as well as from the Oro-Mediterranean vegetation zone in SW Turkey (van Zeist et al. 1975) showed that in the open disturbed and/or grazed areas there is an increase of Plantago lanceolata-type pollen precipitation. This, however, is not a general picture as there are some grazed areas with quite high Plantago values and others with very low percentages. This indicates that grazing does not necessarily lead to a strong expansion of plantain and subsequently to a large share of Plantago in the local pollen precipitation (van Zeist et al. 1975:102). It is without doubt that Plantago lanceolata is a good and reliable anthropogenic indicator but it points in a far more general direction than merely to grazing. It has to be mentioned that the Plantago lanceo-

lata-type may to a certain degree contain other species of this genus too, for instance Plantago lagopus in Israel (Baruch this volume).

Apart from the herbs that are used as anthropogenic indicators a number of shrub and small trees took advantage of the destruction of the primary forests by man. These include Pistacia, Cercis, Phillyrea, Fontanesia as well as several Quercus species and Juniperus (Bottema in press). Of course there are many more species that belong to this category, but which cannot be recorded in pollen analysis.

A very important question is whether changes from forested areas to open forests or to the different steppe stages were caused by climate or man. Several pollen taxa such as Artemisia, Chenopodiaceae and in some areas also Gramineae are generally accepted as steppe indicators. With the help of these taxa the history of the full-, late- and early-Postglacial climate of the Near East could be elucidated. Difficulties arise, however, with the onset of farming. Grazing and other kinds of human activity lead to the destruction of forests, that is to shrub vegetation or to open pasture areas which at least in places resemble the adjoining steppe. Consequently the question is: to what extent are steppe indicators anthropogenic indicators? The answer should be: only in cases of anthropogenic origin of the steppe. It is evident that at this point there is great danger of circulation argumentation.

In most parts of Europe similar circumstances are much easier to explain: disappearance of forest vegetation and increase of herb pollen generally show human impact because the natural climax vegetation is formed by forests with very few exceptions only (Behre 1988). The changing natural pattern of forest, forest-steppe and steppe in the Near East is mainly caused by climatic factors. The marginal areas of open forests and forest-steppe were, however, most suitable for the earliest farmers, as we know for instance from the investigations in the Zagros mountains. In these sensitive areas farming activities, grazing in particular, may cause considerable changes in vegetation and landscape; unfortunately pollen diagrams from such places are lacking.

In the Near East the particular difficulties in distinguishing natural and anthropogenic changes in vegetation are evident. These include the problem of recording occupation phases. Though there are several publications on modern pollen precipitation (see for instance van Zeist et al. 1975; Bottema and Barkoudah 1979), only parts of them can be used for the interpretation of the fossil record. Additional help in this direction is provided in the empiric way by searching pollen diagrams for the reflection of definite occupation phases.

Up to now there are only few diagrams where distinct and clearly delimited habitation phases can be observed. The best known is the so-called Beyşehir occupation phase, which was first described by van Zeist el al. (1975) from a site south of Beyşehir Gölü in southern Anatolia, and was later reinvestigated by Bottema (in press). This pronounced phase lasted from 3500/3000 to 1500 BP and is represented in several pollen diagrams from the upper Eu-Mediterranean and the lower Oro-Mediterranean zone of SW Turkey which were compiled and evaluated by Bottema (in press). By comparing the primary and secondary anthropogenic indicators of these diagrams, the indicator value of the latter can be estimated. This is true of course, only with reference to this specific economy of the past, which up to now we can only deduce from pollen diagrams.

This empiric case study in order to find out the quality of secondary anthropogenic indicators covers the following pollen diagrams: Beyşehir (van Zeist et al. 1975; Bottema in press) (Fig. 2), Gölhisar, Pinarbaşi, Elmali (Bottema and Woldring 1984(1986)) and Söğüt Gölü (van Zeist et al. 1975).

Thus Plantago lanceolata-type turned out to be the most reliable secondary anthropogenic indicator. This must be due to the fact that this species is able to spread easily across soils disturbed in various ways by man's activities, including grazing.

The following taxa are well confined to the Beyşehir occupation phase and can be regarded as the best secondary anthropogenic indicators of the area in question:

Plantago lanceolata
Sanguisorba minor-type
Pistacia
Platanus
Quercus calliprinos-type
Juniperus

(the last one with the exception of Söğüt Gölü).

Another group of taxa shows a considerable increase in pollen percentages, but is present also outside the Beyşehir occupation phase (the order shows their decreasing value as anthropogenic indicators):

Quercus cerris-type
Brassicaceae
other Gramineae
and of minor significance:
Artemisia and
Polygonum aviculare.

It has to be kept in mind, however, that this evaluation of anthropogenic indicators is valid only for the Oro- and Eu-Mediterranean zone in the southeastern Mediterranean. Even in Greece the indicator species and the quality of their evidence differ markedly from southern Turkey as was demonstrated by Bottema (1982).

In comparing the anthropogenic indicators of Central Europe with those of the Near East there are considerable differences with regard to the value and the indicative direction of these species. This is the case even with primary indicators, of which Cerealia represent the most important group in Europe whereas this type can be used in the Near East with severe limitations only. Other primary anthropogenic indicators such as Juglans and Castanea can well be used in the Near East though their distribution also includes natural stands, but still the indicator quality of the pollen of these trees is better in Europe, as in this area both trees were introduced by man. They mainly reflect Roman and Medieval habitation phases, when they were extensively planted in suitable regions.

With respect to the secondary anthropogenic indicators it is striking that the most important one in Europe - Plantago lanceolata - plays the same role in the Near East. Others such as Brassicaceae, Chenopodiaceae etc. are of compa-

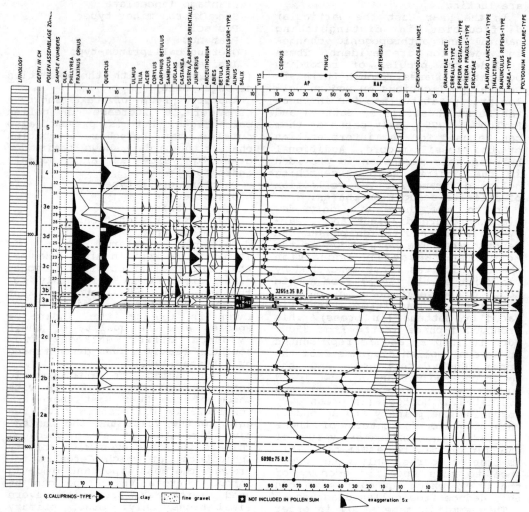

Fig. 2. Part of the pollen diagram of Beyşehir Gölü
(after van Zeist et al. 1975)

rable quality, whereas indicators of open vegetation (i.e. non or sparsely forested areas) such as Gramineae, Calluna and others, as well as the NAP sum, have to be evaluated in a different way. In European forests open areas were in general created by man, whereas in the Near East there are large steppe areas as well as open forests of natural origin, thus producing a pollen rain similar to that of anthropogenic pastures and fields. This concerns also the indicative quality of Artemisia,

which is quite a good anthropogenic indicator in inland areas of Europe but in the Near East it may also reflect natural steppe.

5 OCCUPATION PHASES IN NEAR EASTERN POLLEN DIAGRAMS: EVIDENCE AND PROBLEMS

The Beyşehir occupation phase, which was used in the preceding chapter to classify the secondary anthropogenic indicators, is the most pronounced one in the Near

East. This is due to several reasons: it covers an area that was forested, so that human impact can be seen already in the destruction and the changing composition of the forest. As the climate permitted the cultivation of fruit trees such as Olea, Juglans, Castanea and Vitis, as well as Fraxinus ornus for its exudate, we were provided with reliable primary anthropogenic indicators to record the occupation phase. Most of these indicators are lacking in the drier regions of the Near East, where arable farming and grazing were the main human activities. The chief crop plants, however, are difficult to identify in pollen analysis, as Cerealia pollen cannot be separated from the wild cereals and several other wild grasses that are common in the region. The other crop plants (legumes, linseed) distribute only very little pollen, which in most cases cannot be attributed to a particular crop plant (see Table 1).

Therefore it is very difficult to register the activities of the dry areas and to distinguish their impact from natural, climatically induced changes. An additional severe problem in these areas is the lack of suitable deposits, as there are no bogs and only very few lakes. In the eastern part of the area under consideration, several lakes have been investigated: the lakes Zeribar and Mirabad (van Zeist and Bottema 1977) as well as Urmia (Bottema 1986) in West Iran and Lake Van (van Zeist and Woldring 1978) in Eastern Anatolia. They provide the only good pollen diagram of that region and are very important for the history of climate since the full glacial period. The record of human impact is poor, however. Taxa such as Pistacia, Cerealia-type and Brassicaceae, which could be used as more or less reliable anthropogenic indicators in the westerly area as described above, lose their indicator value nearly completely, others are lacking altogether. The best indicator in this area also seems to be Plantago lanceolata, while Olea, which occurs too, cannot be distinguished from its wild progenitor. Distinct records of human activity can be shown in the youngest parts of the diagrams only, characterized

by Juglans, Platanus, and increase of Olea and by Plantago lanceolata. No occupation phases, or at least no hints of any human impact are registered in the older parts of the diagrams. It should be recalled, however, that according to well-documented archaeological and palaeo-ethnobotanical evidence, these sites are situated within the area of the Fertile Crescent, where the farmer cultures started in the early Neolithic.

The pollen diagram from Syria-Barada (Bottema 1977) and Ghab (van Zeist and Woldring 1980) - and from Israel - Lake Kinneret (Baruch this volume) - clearly show farming activities from about 4000 BP (Ghab), 3000 BP (Lake Kinneret) or the Middle Ages (Barada). In Lake Kinneret Ceratonia provides an additional curve of a primary anthropogenic indicator. The older part of the important Ghab diagram reaches back to late glacial times, but yields no evidence of early agriculture though it also is situated in the Fertile Crescent.

As shown above, a lot of work has been done to trace the earliest agriculture and its further development by means of pollen analysis. This work has focussed on the area where during the last three decades were excavated by archaeologists and confirmed by palaeo-ethnobotanists. Why is the evidence from pollen analysis with respect to this matter so disappointing, or is it not? The methodological problems concerning the anthropogenic indicators have already been discussed, but there are other facts that may have been overlooked.

A comparison with the habitation record in European pollen diagrams can be very useful. The first thing that should be mentioned here is that we know very little about ancient types of economy. In Europe we have learned that, for instance, in the middle Neolithic two types of farming existed side by side, the so-called landnam phase (after Iversen 1941) and the leaf-fodder economy (after Troels-Smith 1955) between which transitional forms occurred. The former phase is generally expressed very distinctly in the pollen diagrams, while the second one is reflected very poorly and only in the vicinity of the settlements. This was confirmed by

227

pollen analyses from burial mounds, a method that has been successfully practised mainly in the Netherlands (Waterbolk 1954; van Zeist 1967; Casparie and Groenman-van Waateringe 1980).

Other well-known prehistoric culture groups also are sometimes difficult to record in pollen diagrams. Another example from Europe may be the early Neolithic Bandkeramik culture which reached from France across Central Europe to southern Poland. There is excellent archaeological evidence from many Bandkeramik settlements and through palaeo-ethnobotanical investigations we have a good idea of the cultivated plants of that time. Also the domesticated animals are known through many bone finds. In contrast to this the record of the Bandkeramik culture the pollen diagrams is extremely bad. Up to now there are less than half a dozen diagrams where this period is distinctly registered, in some other faint hints are given by single grains of Cerealia pollen. These bad results can partly be explained by a lack of suitable deposits around the settlement sites which were generally situated on dry loess grounds. But even in most of the available diagrams of this loess area, traces of this culture are missing.

Another point that should be mentioned is the number of pollen diagrams available. The Near East as considered here is about as large as Europe from France to Poland and from the Alps to Sweden. There are now about 25 pollen diagrams of the necessary quality from the Near East compared with several hundred from the European area of the same size. Considering the much better methodological conditions with respect to anthropogenic indicators in Europe, the Near Eastern results are not too bad.

From inside a habitation area to the outside, there is a strong decrease of the pollen precipitation of most of the the anthropogenic indicators. At least in forested areas, the pollen record of an occupation phase may extend no farther than 3 km from the former fields, as was recently documented by Behre and Kucan (1986). The best way to detect former occupation and to separate different phases is to make borings small in lakes or kettle holes as close as possible to the supposed settlements. But even in Europe these requirements up to now could be fulfilled only in a few cases. The far less favourable conditions in the Near East will probably not offer such opportunities.

Reliable results for the history of habitation and vegetation in the Near East can be obtained only through a dense network of pollen diagrams and a good knowledge of the distribution of archaeological settlements. At the moment these requirements are not yet fulfilled.

ACKNOWLEDGEMENTS

The author appreciates very much the help of Professor W. van Zeist and Dr S. Bottema who provided him with all their published and unpublished material. Thanks are also due to Mrs A.C. Bardet, who cared for the linguistic improvement of the English text and to Mrs M. Janssen for typing.

REFERENCES

Baruch, U. this volume.
Palynological evidence for human impact on the vegetation as recorded in late Holocene lake sediments in Israel.

Behre. K.-E. 1970.
Kulturpflanzenreste aus Kamid el-Loz. Saarbrücker Beiträge zur Altertumskunde 4:59-69.

Behre, K.-E. 1981.
The interpretation of anthropogenic indicators in pollen diagrams. Pollen et Spores 23:225-245.

Behre, K.-E. 1988.
The rôle of man in European vegetation history. In B.Huntley and T.Webb III (eds.), Vegetation history, Handbook of vegetation science 7, p.633-672. Dordrecht.

Behre, K.-E. and D.Kucan 1986.
Die Reflektion archäologisch bekannter Siedlungen in Pollendiagrammen verschiedener Entfernung - Beispiele aus der Siedlungskammer Flögeln, Nordwestdeutschland. In K.-E. Behre (ed.), Anthropogenic indicators

in pollen diagrams, p.95-114. Rotterdam, Balkema.

Bottema, S. 1977.
A pollen diagram from the Syrian Anti Lebanon. Paléorient 3:259-268.

Bottema, S. 1982(1985).
Palynological investigations in Greece with special reference to pollen as an indicator of human activity. Palaeohistoria 24:257-289.

Bottema, S. 1986.
A Late Quaternary pollen diagram from Lake Urmia (Northwestern Iran). Review of Palaeobotany and Palynology 47:241-261.

Bottema, S. in press.
Palynological investigations on the relation between prehistoric man and vegetation in Turkey: the Beyşehir occupation phase. Proceedings of the 5th Optima Congress, September 1986, Istanbul.

Bottema, S. and Y.Barkoudah 1979.
Modern pollen precipitation in Syrian and Lebanon and its relation to vegetation. Pollen et Spores 21:427-480.

Bottema, S. and
H.Woldring 1984 (1986).
Late Quaternary vegetation and climate of southwestern Turkey. Part II. Palaeohistoria 26:123-149.

Casparie, W.A. and
W.Groenman-van Waateringe 1980.
Palynological analysis of Dutch barrows. Palaeohistoria 22:7-65.

Costantini, L. and L.Biasini 1984.
Resti vegetali dei saggi a Qal'eh Ismail Aqa e a Tappeh Gijlar. In P.E.Pecorella and M.Salvini (eds.), Tra lo Zagros e l'Urmia, p.397-402. Rom.

Costantini, L. and L.Biasini 1985.
Le piante di Yelkhi. In La Terra tra i due Fiumi, p.57-60. Turin.

Harlan, J.R. 1977.
The origins of cereal agriculture in the Old World. In C.A.Reed (ed.), Origins of Agriculture, p.357-383. Den Haag, Paris.

Iversen, J. 1941.
Landnam i Danmarks Stenalder. Danmarks Geologiske Undersøgelse, Raekke 2, Nr. 66.

Kislev, M. 1980.
Contenu d'un silo à blé de l'époque du fer ancien. Tell Keisan: 361-379.

Kislev, M. 1985.
Early Neolithic horsebean from Yiftah'el, Israel. Science 28: 319-320.

Kislev, M. and M.Hopf 1985.
Food remains from Tell Qasile. In A.Mazar (ed.), Excavations at tell Qasile, Part two, p.140-148. Jerusalem.

Renfrew, J.M. 1969.
The archaeological evidence for the domestication of plants: methods and problems. In P.J.Ucko and G.W. Dimbleby (eds.), The domestication and exploitation of plants and animals, p.149-172. London: Duckworth.

Renfrew, J.M. 1984.
Cereals cultivated in ancient Iraq. Bulletin Sumerian Agriculture 1:32-44.

Troels-Smith, J. 1955.
Pollen-analytische Untersuchungen zu einigen schweizerischen Pfahlbauproblemen. Das Pfahlbauproblem, Monograph Ur- und Frühgeschichte der Schweiz 11:11-58.

Waterbolk, H.T. 1954.
De praehistorische mens en zijn milieu. Thesis, University of Groningen.

Zeist, W. van 1967.
Archaeology and palynology in the Netherlands. Review of Palaeobotany and Palynology 4:45-65.

Zeist, W. van 1976.
On macroscopic traces of food plants in southwestern Asia (with some reference to pollen data). Philosophical Transactions of the Royal Society London B275:27-41.

Zeist, W. van 1980.
Plant remains from Girikihaciyan, Turkey. Anatolica 7:75-89.

Zeist, W. van 1984.
Palaeobotanical investigations of Tell ed-Der. In L. de Meyer (ed.), Tell ed-Der IV, p.119-143. Leuven.

Zeist, W. van 1988.
Some aspects of early Neolithic plant husbandry in the Near East. Anatolica 15: 49-67.

Zeist, W. van and
J.A.H.Bakker-Heeres 1975.
Prehistoric and early historic plant husbandry in the Altinova Plain, southeastern Turkey. In M.N. van Loon (ed.), Korucutepe, p.223-257. Amsterdam/Oxford, Elsevier.

Zeist, W. van and
J.A.H.Bakker-Heeres 1982(1985).
Archaeobotanical studies in the Levant. I. Neolithic sites in the Damascus Basin: Aswad, Ghoraifé, Ramad. Palaeohistoria 24:165-256.

Zeist, W. van and
J.A.H.Bakker-Heeres 1984(1986).
Archaeobotanical studies in the
Levant. IV. Bronze Age sites on
the north Syrian Euphrates.
Palaeohistoria 27:247-316.
Zeist, W. van and S.Bottema 1977.
Palynological investigations in
western Iran. Palaeohistoria 19:
19-85.
Zeist, W. van and H.Woldring 1978.
A postglacial pollen diagram from
Lake Van in East Anatolia. Review
of Palaeobotany and Palynology
26:249-276.
Zeist, W. van and H.Woldring 1980.
Holocene vegetation and climate
of northwestern Syria. Palaeohis-
toria 22:111-125.
Zeist, W. van,
H.Woldring and D.Stapert 1975.
Late Quaternary vegetation and
climate of southwestern Turkey.
Palaeohistoria 17:53-143.
Zohary, D. and M.Hopf 1988.
Domestication of plants in the
Old World. Oxford: Clarendon
Press.

Man's Role in the Shaping of the Eastern Mediterranean Landscape, Bottema, Entjes-Nieborg & van Zeist (eds)
© 1990 Balkema, Rotterdam. ISBN 90 6191 138 9

Anthropogenic indicators in the pollen record of the Eastern Mediterranean

19

Sytze Bottema, & Henk Woldring
Biologisch-Archaeologisch Instituut, Rijksuniversiteit Groningen, Netherlands

ABSTRACT: In this paper the role of primary and secondary anthropogenic indicators in the modern pollen rain of the Eastern Mediterranean is presented. Samples from degraded vegetations as well as from (semi-) natural vegetation, collected in various vegetation zones, are discussed. The presence of a species in the actuo-pollen record and spatial distribution in the area determine its indicative value. Besides, the modern pollen precipitation of a series of fruit-tree species is compared with the geographical distribution of the respective tree species.

The impact of man upon the forest vegetation is investigated by the values of the AP/NAP ratio. The study of the actuo-pollen precipitation by means of the contents of surface samples and the palaeo-pollen precipitation from cores taken in lakes or marshes cannot simply be compared. The information obtained from the modern pollen record is used to trace region-wide developments and especially human impact in the subfossil record which is derived from sites thoughout the area in the various vegetation zones.

In the Eastern Mediterranean it appears that solid evidence of human activity supported by indicative pollen types can be demonstrated for the first time at about 4000 BP. A period of very pronounced human activity, especially various aspects of farming, occurred towards the end of the fourth millennium. This period, which is described as the Beyşehir Occupation phase, is found in various forms over large parts of the investigated area. The pollen assemblages representing this phase point to an advanced form of agriculture, including fruit cultivation. The Beyşehir Occupation phase must be the palynological reflection of an important change in economy. It is suggested that climatic changes may have contributed to this conspicuous change.

1 INTRODUCTION

In this contribution the impact of prehistoric man upon the vegetation of the Eastern Mediterranean will be discussed on the basis of palynological evidence. Through palynological investigations we are reasonably well informed about the general late Quaternary vegetation development of the area concerned and the study of human impact upon the vegetation forms part of this research. The relation between man and his environment is not only of interest from the botanical point of view. Such studies were often instigated in relation to archaeol-

ogical problems. Human impact upon the vegetation has formed part of palynological investigations in Greece (Bottema 1974, 1982(1985)), Turkey (van Zeist et al. 1975, Bottema and Woldring 1984(1986)), Iran (van Zeist and Bottema 1977; Bottema 1986) and Israel (Baruch 1983).

Special attention has been paid to the impact of prehistoric man upon the vegetation of mainland Greece (Bottema 1982(1985)). The available Greek pollen diagrams were screened for possible indicator types. Attempts were made to analyse the role of pollen types that were likely to indicate crop farming, either as an agricultural product or as an accompanying weed, fruticulture or grazing, and to connect changes in the pollen record of the assumed natural forest vegetation with human activity.

The interpretation of the pollen record where human impact is concerned leans heavily on the results of studies from NW Europe (Behre 1981). For the area under study such results have to be applied with caution as the Eastern Mediterranean vegetation differs in many ways from the European temperate forest. A conspicuous difference between the pollen record of NW Europe and that of the Eastern Mediterranean is the presence of a group of anthropogenic types especially indicative for the former area. Pollen types ascribed to cereal crops and weeds, for instance, do not appear in the NW European Holocene until the beginning of the Neolithic. In the eastern part which we are dealing with here the same pollen types may be constantly present during the late Quaternary. Still the values of those types may significantly change in the course of time and such change may be a sign of human activity. Especially when changes in the relative values of several types take place at the same level in the pollen record, we should be alert.

One aspect of human activity stressed by Trabaud (1981) and Le Houérou (1981) is fire. Especially shrub vegetation is regularly burned down to produce grazing ground for sheep and cattle. Various species such as Quercus coccifera, Arbutus unedo and Buxus sempervirens act as active pyrophytes because of quick regeneration by shoots from roots or stem bases. The seed dispersal and germination of Pinus halepensis, P. brutia and Cistus species is greatly stimulated by fire. Some of these pyrophytes are very well represented in the pollen rain, for instance, Quercus coccifera-type. In the case of Pinus the problem remains which pine species we are dealing with. Arbutus is very much under-represented or absent in pollen samples. Buxus is scarce in Eastern Mediterranean pollen diagrams and forms a curve only in

the diagram of Edessa in Greek Macedonia (Bottema 1974). As this Buxus curve starts after ca 3200 BP it might be connected with intentional burning. Cistus displays high values in the Neolithic part of the Koiladha diagram (Peloponnese) where they accompany important values of anthropogenic indicators and a high charcoal content of the sediment. It is clear that anthropogenic indicators may be found among pyrophytes, especially in the Eastern Mediterranean vegetation zone. The authors could not define a consistent picture of this group of potential indicators. For that reason they will not form part of the discussion here.

Apart from the direct observation of the pollen record the archaeological evidence from the area concerned may inform us about human activity, at least if there is proof of Neolithic or younger habitation near a particular coring site. If radiocarbon dates for the pollen record as well as for the respective archaeological site are provided a correlation can be made to trace possible anthropogenic indicators.

One may question whether a large and diverse area as the Eastern Mediterranean can be treated as a whole where the impact of man on the vegetation is concerned. If changes in the various vegetation zones are to be studied in detail one should in fact subdivide the area. The initial Neolithic attack upon the natural vegetation, which from the archaeological evidence we know to have occurred, will not have taken place all over the area at the same time. Yet in those areas where early Neolithic activity has been demonstrated by archaeological investigations this could not be clearly traced in pollen diagrams (Fig. 1). Either human influence was still negligible or the distance between the coring sites and the nearest archaeological site was too large for the effect of such early human impact to be demonstrable.

The interpretation of anthropogenic pollen assemblages in terms of vegetation and agricultural practice remains difficult. Information on the modern pollen precipitation in (semi-)natural and contrasting disturbed vegetations will

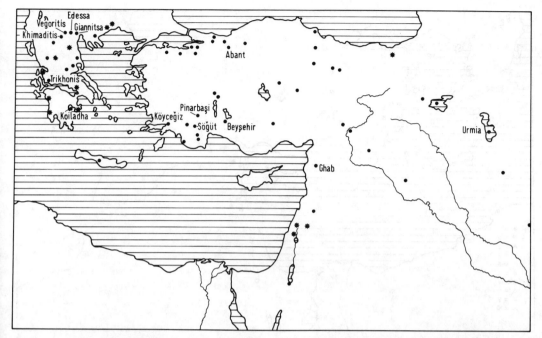

Fig. 1. Map of the area indicating the coring sites. Locations marked by black dots have been investigated by the palaeobotanical department of the Biologisch-Archaeologisch Instituut, Groningen. Those marked by asterisks by others.

be discussed here in this respect for the various zones. The geographical distribution of the actual deposition of a selection of pollen types possibly connected with human activity will be discussed in relation to the actual distribution of the present-day plant or tree species, in order to supply information on the (long-)distance effect of indicative pollen in fossil records.

The ratio of arboreal pollen values to the pollen values of herb vegetation gives an indication of the openess or density of the forest canopy. If dense forest is destroyed by man the arboreal/non-arboreal pollen ratio will be effected. Evidence on the AP/NAP ratio from modern situations will be compared here with that of the subfossil pollen record in order to trace human activity in the latter category.

2 THE EASTERN MEDITERRANEAN

The area defined in this contribu-

tion by the term Eastern Mediterranean is shown in Fig. 1. Its outline more or less follows the boundaries as given in the respective bioclimatic and vegetation maps of UNESCO-FAO (1963 and 1970) which are based upon the definition of the Mediterranean climate. The area includes a major part of what is geographically indicated as the Near East.

The delimitation of the area as treated in this paper is defined by the presence of suitable palynological information. This implies that steppe and desert are hardly or not included in the investigation. The geomorphology, geography, climate and vegetation of the Eastern Mediterranean will be briefly reviewed only for those pollen sites used in this paper (Section 5). For more detailed information on these subjects the reader is referred to the following relevant literature. For the Greek core locations information can be found in Athanasiades (1975), Bottema (1974, 1979, 1980). Information for Turkey is found in van Zeist et al.

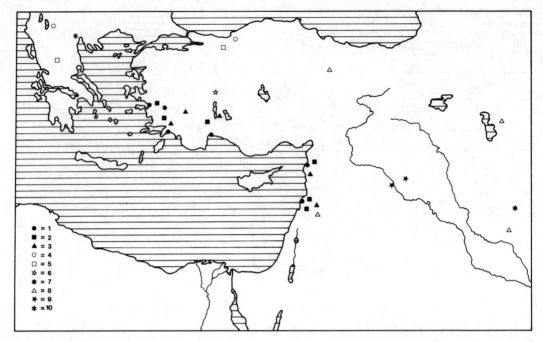

Fig. 2. Map showing the surface-sample transects chosen from the various vegetation zones. Information on the modern pollen rain is obtained from van Zeist et al. (1975), Bottema (1974), Bottema and Barkoudah (1979) and Wright et al. (1967).

(1968(1970), 1975); van Zeist and Woldring (1978); Bottema and Woldring (1984). For Iran the reader is referred to van Zeist and Bottema (1977) and Bottema (1986) and for Syria to Niklewski and van Zeist (1970), Bottema and Barkoudah (1979), van Zeist and Woldring (1980), Bottema (1975-1977). For general information on the vegetation we refer to Zohary (1973).

3 THE REPRESENTATION OF POTENTIAL ANTHROPOGENIC INDICATORS IN THE MODERN POLLEN RAIN

In this section the proportion in the modern pollen precipitation of some pollen types of which we assume that they indicate human activity will be dealt with. For the Eastern Mediterranean a reasonable amount of information on the modern pollen rain is available. From this evidence eleven pollen types and one spore have been selected and their role in various vegetation types in the Eastern Mediterranean will be discussed.

The average pollen values have been calculated for shorter or longer transects. Some transects include a large number of sampling sites, some represent only 1 or 2 samples. The location of the samples that have been studied is shown in Fig. 2. The average values of the selected types in the various zones, are shown in Fig. 3. The same has been done for some fruit-tree species and Platanus (see Table 2). The selected herb types are rather arbitrarily chosen. A detailed study of anthropogenic indicators in Greek pollen diagrams has shown that more potential types (Fig. 5) can be suggested (Bottema 1982 (1985)) than those shown here in Fig. 3. That the number of herb types discussed in this paper is restricted to twelve has practical reasons. The types must be present in most of the area in not too low values and preferably not be too much under-represented in the pollen rain. The twelve types listed in Fig. 3 will be briefly described.

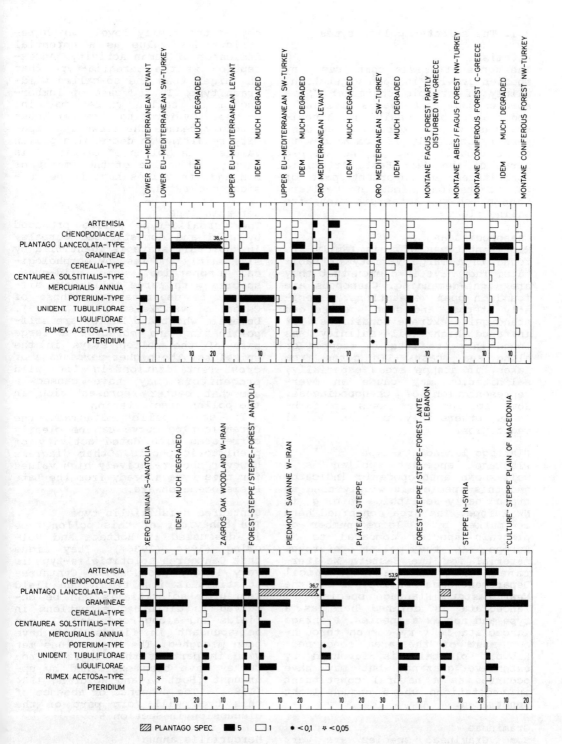

Fig. 3a,b. Modern pollen precipitation. Average pollen percentages for a selection of herb pollen types indicating human activity based upon surface samples from various vegetation zones in the Eastern Mediterranean.

3.1. The selected pollen types

Artemisia
The genus Artemisia comprises many species growing in open vegetation, mainly of steppic character. Some species show up as weeds especially under disturbed conditions. Artemisia has a very good pollen dispersal especially if compared with other Tubuliflorae. In the steppic parts of the Near East, Artemisia constitutes an important part of the vegetation. Along the Mediterranean coast Artemisia inhabits saline flats.

Chenopodiaceae
Representatives of this family are found in a large variety of habitats. They have in common that they are light-demanding. Chenopods are found in open vegetations, especially steppe, and some species can stand quite extreme conditions, for instance high soil salinity, as found in salt flats in steppes or along sea coasts. In cores from lakes, in steppe areas especially, salinization may cause an over-representation of Chenopodiaceae. Some species are pests in farmlands, others only occur in natural vegetation.

Plantago lanceolata-type
Plantago lanceolata pollen is a well-known anthropogenic indicator and this species is widely used to trace early-Neolithic farming in NW Europe. The area concerned here is marked by a large number of plantain species compared to NW Europe. As the pollen reference material for the Eastern Mediterranean in our Palaeobotanical Department does not include all the Near Eastern Plantago species, P. lanceolata is defined here as a type and not as a species. Plantago lanceolata is very common throughout most of the area concerned. Ribwort plantain is favoured by extensive grazing, but may have occurred as a natural constituent in vegetations where enough light penetrated.

Gramineae
Some Gramineae species are very probably connected with human activity, such as lumbering, herding, haying, meadow management. Grass pollen usually cannot be identified beyond the family level, which restricts its value as a potential indicator of human activity. An exception is the Cerealia-type that is larger than the so-called wild-grass type. In the case of lumbering grass pollen values may increase. Overgrazing however must strongly reduce the flowering capacity resulting in decreasing pollen values. The pollen of Gramineae is partly indicative of the impact of man and its values have to be considered carefully.

Cerealia-type
The Cerealia-type pollen produced by wild and domesticated cereals, in subfossil state is identified by size mainly and less by morphological properties. Some wild-grass species with large pollen are difficult to separate from those of Cerealia (van Zeist et al. 1975). Domestic wheat and barley are self-pollinating and moreover a large part of the pollen stays in the spikelets. The higher percentage of cross-fertilization in the wild progenitors may have caused a somewhat better representation in the pollen precipitation.

In some pollen diagrams the Cerealia-type curve can be clearly correlated with dated activity of prehistoric people. Other diagrams however show relatively high values for this type already from the Late Pleistocene onward.

Centaurea solstitialis-type
The behaviour of this pollen type is discussed in Bottema and Woldring (1984 (1986)). They argue that Centaurea solstitialis-type is very likely produced by Centaurea solstitialis itself. In the field Centaurea solstitialis can be observed in disturbed situations in fields and along roadsides. It can be abundant in fields that have been ploughed. The high values met with in part of the diagrams from Turkey have been explained by updraught (Bottema and Woldring 1984 (1986)). The presence or absence of this type will form part of the discussion in Section 6.

Mercurialis annua
Pollen of this Euphorbiaceous species is often met with in modern records from the coastal Mediterranean. It is also common in pre-

236

Holocene samples from the Huleh and especially in a young-Holocene core from the Bay of Koiladha (Argolid, Peloponnese) where Mercurialis strongly correlates with pollen types that indicate human activity. Its average values in the modern pollen rain for the various vegetation zones are presented here to assess its value as an anthropogenic indicator.

Poterium/Sanguisorba minor
Especially in the Mediterranean part of our area, pollen identified in surface samples and pollen cores will have been produced by Poterium spinosum, which forms part of the maquis or the phrygana. Poterium spreads after the degradation or destruction of Mediterranean forest or shrub. The spiny cushions of Poterium are hardly or not touched by herded herbivores, which moreover dislike the taste of this plant (Le Houérou 1981).

Farther inland pollen of this type will have been produced also by Sanguisorba minor, a light-demanding and more cold-tolerant species, which spreads after lumbering or extensive grazing. According to Le Houérou (1981) Sanguisorba minor is favoured by domestic animals.

Tubuliflorae and Liguliflorae
The majority of the Compositae is insect-pollinated. It is uncertain how indicative this group is for human impact. Their numbers are any rate favoured by the creation of open vegetations as caused by farming activity.

Rumex acetosa-type
In this paper the Rumex acetosa-type includes pollen grains that resemble those of Rumex acetosa and Rumex cyprius as well as Rumex acetosella. It must be stressed that Rumex acetosa does not occur in most of the area (Davis 1965-1988). In NW Europe pollen of this type is regularly encountered with prehistoric habitation from the Neolithic onward. In this paper the behaviour of this Rumex-type is studied to see how far its role extends to the east.

Pteridium
Increasing values for spores of Pteridium may be an indicator of human activity in certain forest types. Bracken is found in the vegetation of Greece and Turkey at higher elevations.

3.2 The representation of the indicator types in the pollen rain of the various vegetation zones

We will discuss the values of the twelve selected herb types in the various vegetations of the area considered (Fig. 3). From the ample evidence on the modern pollen precipitation in the Eastern Mediterranean we have selected samples taken in natural or semi-natural vegetations. In general even in quite natural-looking vegetations the influence of man was still present. If possible, samples were also selected from much-degraded vegetation to determine any differences with more natural counterparts. Experience has taught us that the pollen production of man-made habitats, such as arable land, is reflected even in the pollen samples taken in remnants of natural vegetation. On the other hand, the influence of tree pollen in deforested areas is greater than in the reverse case of herb pollen in dense forest.

Lower Eu-Mediterranean zone
Surface samples that were used to calculate average percentages for this zone originated from two areas (Fig. 3 and Table 1), viz. the Levant and SW Turkey. The results are more or less the same. Values of most types mentioned in Section 3.1 are less than 1%. Gramineae likewise are low, whereas Poterium-type score ca 3.5% in the Levant. There where the lower Eu-Mediterranean vegetation in SW Turkey is very much degraded, does Plantago lanceolata-type scores highly. Compositae and Rumex acetosa-type are better represented in the degraded part of the zone than in the comparatively natural part.

Upper Eu-Mediterranean zone
Average values of the herb types in the less disturbed parts of this zone very much resemble those of the lower Eu-Mediterranean zone. For the Levantine Upper Eu-Mediterranean, Poterium-type is very important. In the case of much-

degraded vegetation in SW Turkey, Gramineae and Plantago lanceolata demonstrate high values.

Oro-Mediterranean zone
In the Levant Artemisia, Gramineae and Poterium-type demonstrate quite high values. The values of Artemisia and Gramineae are 4-5 times higher in much-degraded parts than in less disturbed vegetation, and for the values of Cerealia-type and Compositae this ratio is even higher. Poterium-type does not increase in samples collected in disturbed vegetation.

In the Oro-Mediterranean cedar/juniper forest in SW Turkey herbs are unimportant. Some increase in the average percentages of the selected types is witnessed only if this forest is much disturbed.

Montane Fagus forest
The partly disturbed Fagus forest in NW Greece demonstrates high values of Plantago lanceolata-type, Gramineae, Cerealia-type, Poterium-type and especially Rumex acetosa-type and Pteridium. In this vegetation Poterium-type probably is represented by Sanguisorba minor.

The montane Fagus forest in the Yedigöller nature reserve in NW Turkey, often mixed with vast stands of Abies nordmanniana, looks very much undisturbed. Herb pollen values are very low.

Montane conifer forest
The effect of human activity in locally quite dense pine forest in Central Greece and NW Turkey is marginal judging by the percentages of indicative pollen types. Gramineae and Plantago lanceolata-type are fairly well represented in Central Greece.

In much-degraded pine forest in Central Greece high values of Plantago lanceolata-type have been recorded. It should be stressed that in surface samples from locations where all pine had been cut, Pinus pollen from stands further away still dominate the pollen rain.

Xero-Euxinian zone
This transitional zone of dry forest towards the steppe-forest or steppe of Central Anatolia shows high values for Artemisia while Chenopodiaceae are higher than in previous zones. The importance of cereal production in these parts is illustrated by ca 3% Cerealia-type pollen. Where the Xero-Euxinian vegetation is much degraded, especially the Artemisia value increases.

Zagros oak woodland
The amount of light that penetrates through the canopy of the Zagros oak woodland is considerable and enables much undergrowth. This is reflected in high herb pollen values including Artemisia, Chenopodiaceae, Plantago and Gramineae. For this area the value of all Plantago pollen is shown in Fig. 3, because types other than Plantago lanceolata are found. Compositae including Centaurea solstitialis-type are not important and neither is the value of the Cerealia-type. The latter fact would suggest that cereal growing and/or the presence of wild progenitors of crops do not play a role in this zone.

Forest-steppe/steppe-forest
The palynological picture of steppe-forest in Anatolia (Fig. 3) resembles that of the Zagros oak woodland but values of herb types are much lower.

The piedmont savanna is often changed into steppe by human interference. Very high Plantago (not P. lanceolata) values characterize the pollen assemblage of this zone.

The samples of the Iranian plateau steppe demonstrate high values for some pollen types produced by taxa which are characteristic of the natural vegetation. The same taxa are indicative as anthropogenic in other situations. The high values for Artemisia and Chenopodiaceae are produced by the steppe vegetation. The Plantago value of the plateau steppe is low compared to that of the lower piedmont savanna.

The open landscape of the Anti Lebanon with some scattered Juniperus excelsa being the remnant of the original steppe-forest, also produces quite high values for pollen of steppe plants such as Artemisia and Chenopodiaceae.

The steppe of N Syria displays about the same values for the herb types as the degraded steppe-forest of the Anti Lebanon. North Syria shares high values for Centaurea solstitialis-type with the Zagros piedmont.

"Cultural" steppe
As an example of the behaviour of the selected pollen types in the man-made steppe, the cultivated plain of Macedonia is shown here. The relatively high Artemisia and Chenopodiaceae values may have been caused by flooding of the river Axios, which brought about ruderal conditions. Plantago lanceolata-type and Gramineae are well represented. Cerealia-type is astonishingly low for an agricultural area. Contrasting with the steppe(forest) vegetations shown above, is the 3.2% Platanus. Plane tree pollen originates from trees planted in villages, but solitary trees or small groups do also occur in the plain.

3.3 The modern pollen precipitation and the geographical distribution of some fruit tree species

A wide variety of domestic fruit trees are grown in the Eastern Mediterranean. Only part of those species are reasonably well represented in the pollen rain. The insect-pollinating species, for instance members of the Rosaceae family such as apple, pear, cherry, prune and almond, are seldom met with in samples and even then identification to the genus level may be difficult. For this reason only a small group of fruit tree species could be used to investigate the activity of man.

The selection includes olive (Olea), sweet chestnut (Castanea sativa), walnut (Juglans regia), manna-ash (Fraxinus ornus) and grape (Vitis). The last one is in fact a liane but is often pruned to a low shrub when under cultivation. It must be stressed that we could not separate pollen of the wild ancestors from that of the cultivars. We include the plane tree (Platanus orientalis) in this selection because the pollen curve of Platanus correlates very conspicuously with those of the other five species.

The average pollen values of Olea, Castanea, Juglans, Vitis, Fraxinus ornus and Platanus for the various vegetation zones are shown in Table 2. The location of the area where the surface samples originate from is shown in Fig. 2.

In Figs. 7a-e the distribution of these species, except Vitis, has been drawn after Rikli (1943-1948) and Davis (1965-1988). The value of these maps is limited because in some cases natural distribution and cultivation area could not be separated. In the case of Olea the present area of cultivation is shown (Fig. 7a). For Castanea sativa, Fraxinus ornus and Platanus orientalis the modern distribution is given. This distribution undoubtedly includes former natural occurrences as well as escapes from cultivation. In the case of Juglans regia the map shows the present occurrence of the walnut. Walnuts have been planted in many places outside the assumed natural habitats. It is obvious that Juglans originally occurred in the wild somewhere in the Near East, possibly the Pontic and/or the Caucasic forest. There is no proof of any growth (natural or man-induced) of Juglans in Greece before the end of the fourth millennium BP and this is also true for most of Turkey.

Olea pollen is present all over the area as is shown by the various surface-sample studies. Within the distribution area Olea pollen scores up to 30%. Towards the interior, just out of the distribution area (Fig. 7a), olive pollen can be present in fairly high percentages but in the steppe or woodland area at some distance of the coast it drops to values of under 1%. In some samples of the steppe Olea pollen was missing altogether. The good representation can be explained by the fact that olive is wind-pollinated (Dafni in press). The presence of Olea in modern or in subfossil samples from locations situated outside the present distribution of the cultivated olive has to be explained by that phenomenon.

Castanea has a very low share in the present-day pollen precipitation whereas its percentages in the subfossil record can be much higher. It is rather surprising that its pollen was found in samples from the forest area in the northern Levant although sweet chestnut was not seen in the present vegetation there (Bottema and Barkoudah

1979). Percentages of ca 0.1% or higher point to the local occurrence of sweet chestnut or its presence in the vicinity.

Vitis occurs naturally in riverine forest from Greece to N Iran and has a predominantly northerly distribution in our area. A great deal of cultivated vine is grown outside its natural biotope and escapes do also occur. Its values in Table 2 are very low everywhere, rarely measuring 0.1%; mostly the average pollen percentage is lower than 0.1%. It should be stressed that this species never scores high in the pollen rain. Values of 0.1% or higher may point to Vitis growing nearby.

Fraxinus ornus is a tree that was used in the past for syrup-processing. In former times an exudate was collected that forms after the bark has been incised. Fraxinus ornus has a westerly distribution. Pollen is found in low numbers outside the present distribution area but it is lacking in the steppic areas. One may expect Fraxinus ornus to have been present in the vegetation where pollen values are at least 0.1% on average.

Platanus orientalis is encountered along streams and is often planted in villages. Present distribution includes a large part of the area (Fig. 7e). The plane tree is absent in the steppe and the very high montane zone. Platanus pollen demonstrates its highest values in the Eu-Mediterranean zone, Central Greece and the Plain of Macedonia. Platanus pollen scores low or is absent in the Oro-Mediterranean belt, the Xero-Euxinian zone, the steppe-forest and the steppe.

4 CHANGES IN ARBOREAL POLLEN VALUES AS AN INDICATOR OF HUMAN IMPACT

One may assume that people attacked the forest in a fairly organized way from the Neolithic onward. At a certain stage this must have been reflected in the pollen rain. The amount of tree pollen compared to pollen from light-demanding open vegetations may be a measure of human impact. Fig. 4 gives the present average AP/NAP ratios for the various vegetation zones; the legend for the numbers is given in

Fig. 4. Arboreal/non-arboreal pollen ratios. The arboreal parts have been calculated from surface samples and are shown as black bars. The numbers refer to Table 1.

Table 1. This ratio gives the relation between the regional tree pollen total and the total of regional herb pollen. We are informed about the density of forest or the openness of steppe if the AP/NAP ratio can be related to an extant vegetation.

If vegetations are properly described and their respective pollen spectra are compared with density of canopy or undergrowth, it is found that the relation between the two is less regular than would be expected. Small clearances in a dense forest may even increase the AP pollen production. This unexpected behaviour is explained by profuse flowering of lower branches of trees that did not flower before, because of the shade. If more forest is destroyed the AP percentages will eventually decrease. Surface samples demonstrate higher herb-pollen values than do core samples from the middle of lakes or even marshes. This is credible be-

Table 1. Origin of surface samples.

1a. Lower Eu-Mediterranean: Levant
Bottema and Barkoudah 1979
nos. 52, 75-85

1b. Lower Eu-Mediterranean:
SW Turkey
van Zeist et al. 1975
nos. 1, 6, 7, 9, 12, 13, 36,
37

1c. As 1b, but much degraded
nos. 20, 21

2a. Upper Eu-Mediterranean: Levant
Bottema and Barkoudah 1979
nos. 47-50, 54-56, 58-60, 62-73

2b. As 2a, but much degraded
no. 40, 51, 52, 57, 61, 72, 74

2c. Upper Eu-Mediterranean:
SW Turkey
van Zeist et al. 1975
no. 2-5, 11, 15, 16, 18, 32,
45-47, 50

2d. As 2c, but much degraded
nos. 17, 19, 22, 25, 51, 52

3a. Oro-Mediterranean: Levant
Bottema and Barkoudah 1979
nos. 30, 35, 41-43, 45, 63, 71

3b. As 3a, but much degraded
nos. 31-34, 36, 37, 46

3c. Oro-Mediterranean: SW Turkey
van Zeist et al. 1975
nos. 10, 23, 27, 30

3d. As 3c, but much degraded
nos. 26, 28, 28, 34, 35, 48, 49

4a. Montane Fagus forest, partly
disturbed: N Greece
Bottema 1974
nos. 64-72

4b. Montane Abies/Fagus forest:
NW Turkey
Bottema and Woldring (in prep.)
no. 32

5a. Montane coniferous forest:
Central Greece
Bottema 1974
nos. 88-90

5b. As 5a, but much degraded
nos. 85-87

5c. Montane coniferous forest:
NW Turkey
Bottema and Woldring (in prep.)
no. 37

6a. Xero-Euxinian: SW Turkey
van Zeist et al. 1975
nos. 58, 60

6b. As 6a, but much degraded
nos. 57, 59

7. Zagros oak woodland: W Iran
Wright et al. 1967:422, Fig. 3
26 samples

8. Forest-steppe/steppe-forest:
Anatolia
Bottema and Woldring (in prep.)
nos. 9, 10

9a. Piedmont savanne: W Iran
Wright et al. 1967:422, Fig. 3
6 samples

9b. Plateau steppe: W Iran
Wright et al. 1967:422, Fig. 3
10 samples

9c. Forest-steppe/steppe-forest:
Anti Lebanon
Bottema and Barkoudah 1979
nos. 7, 17, 29, 38, 38

9d. Steppe: N Syria
Bottema and Barkoudah 1979
nos. 1-6
Gremmen and Bottema in press
7 samples

10. "Cultural" steppe: Plain of
Macedonia
Bottema 1974
nos. 8-16, 40-42

cause a lot of herbs grow near the surface-samples which are collected in the field and not on the water. Tree pollen, being produced at a higher level, tends to travel further than a lot of herb pollen that is produced at ground level. Samples from a clearing may demon-strate rather high tree-pollen values deposited by nearby trees. Relatively high tree-pollen percentages may be caused by long-distance transport if the local herb-pollen production is low, for instance in deserts.

The effect of human impact by

changes in the AP/NAP ratio can be measured by comparing the average values for (semi-)natural forest or woodland with those of the same vegetation heavily degraded or destroyed by man. In much-degraded vegetations the AP values are generally half to three-quarters of those of their better preserved counterparts. Where pine forest is concerned (Fig. 4: 5a,b Central Greece) the difference between AP values taken within the forest and from the cleared parts is not important. This is explained by the good pollen production and dispersal of Pinus.

The AP/NAP ratio in the subfossil pollen record cannot be translated directly into amount of forest cover with the help of the surface-sample values. The last category will be only of indicative value. The course of the AP/NAP curve itself supplies useful information. The general tendency of Late Quaternary AP/NAP ratios for pollen diagrams from the Eastern Mediterranean is that of a steady to sometimes steep increase followed by a fairly stable part. In the upper Holocene the AP/NAP decreases again and this decrease was very likely caused by the impact of prehistoric people. In such diagrams the decrease of the AP percentages will be small compared to the difference between values from modern forest and clearances.

5 ANTHROPOGENIC INDICATIONS IN THE SUBFOSSIL POLLEN RECORD

5.1 Introduction

If we try to trace possible impact of the activity of prehistoric people upon the vegetation in the Eastern Mediterranean by means of indicative pollen types, several conditions have to be fulfilled.

As the area concerned is large and varied, a large number of pollen diagrams taken from the various vegetation zones should be available. In Fig. 1 it can be seen that, although quite many core locations are indicated, information is not distributed proportionally over the various zones. This is explained by the conditions required for the formation of sediments in which pollen is preserved.

Such sedimentation is highly dependent upon the local climate, geomorphology and hydrology.

When looking for possible signs of human impact upon the vegetation, proof of human habitation may be obtained from archaeological evidence. The simultaneous presence of archaeological and palynological information for a location however rarely occurs. Archaeology has informed us that the earliest proof of prehistoric agriculture is found in the so-called Fertile Crescent. Earliest indications have been traced by van Zeist and Bakker-Heeres (1982(1985)) and date back to the 10th millennium BP for the Damascus basin.

As the centres of early agriculture and the available pollen sites hardly coincide one may wonder whether we will be able to obtain much palynological evidence for early prehistoric impact upon the vegetation. Besides, as early Neolithic people seem to have settled by preference in open vegetation, alluvial plains, woodland or even steppe along rivers or lakes, the changes they caused in the vegetation may hardly have found expression in the pollen record.

The Akgöl diagram (Bottema and Woldring 1984(1986)) was prepared from a core taken at ca 100 km from Çatal Hüyük. The oldest date obtained for Çatal Hüyük so far is 6240±99 BC. Can Hasan III found ca 50 km from the Akgöl coring site is said to be ca 6500 BC.

At the level of the 7th millennium BC no decision about human impact can be made for the Akgöl pollen record because anthropogenic indicators are already present before 10,000 BP. In the record of the following, younger millennia no clear traces of farming activity are visible either.

The problem is and will be that potential weeds or other indicators are derived from wild plants that are found in smaller or larger numbers in natural vegetations. The pollen of weeds or crop plants may be found in subfossil assemblages, be it in small numbers, long before Neolithic activity appeared in the Near East.

From the early nucleus in the Fertile Crescent farming spread to the west. The routes it took are not yet precisely known. In the 9th or 8th millennium BP agriculture reached the alluvial plains in Greece. In W Turkey information on the development of agriculture is scarce. The settlement of Ilipinar, west of Iznik Gölü, so far has an earliest date of 7240 BP (written communication J.J. Roodenberg).

For part of the area treated in this paper, mainland Greece, an attempt was made to trace human impact by means of indicators in the pollen record (Bottema 1982 (1985)). In Fig. 5 a diagram of the palynological indications of human activity is given. From about 4000 BP (radiocarbon years) onward palynological evidence pointing to man-induced changes in the pollen record is present.

In diagrams from Turkey (van Zeist et al. 1975; Bottema and Woldring 1984(1986)) the first comparable indications that can be synchronized also appear around 4000 BP, where low but quite continuous curves of Plantago lanceolata-type, Cerealia-type, Olea and Quercus start.

Very distinctive is an occupation phase that starts towards the end of the 4th millennium, about 3200-3400 BP. Changes in the pollen diagram clearly indicating human activity, beginning at about 3200 BP, were first found in some parts of N Greece (Bottema 1974). Van Zeist et al. (1975) describe an event that correlates in time and palynological character with that found in N Greece. This conspicuous anthropogenic assemblage was most distinct in the pollen diagram of Beyşehir Gölü (Fig. 6a) where a combination of pollen types connected with various forms of agriculture and fruticulture appeared about 3400 BP. For that reason the occupation phase was given the name Beyşehir Occupation phase (B.O. phase).

5.2 The Beyşehir Occupation phase

The most illustrative pollen diagrams demonstrating the B.O. phase will be selected from the various parts of the area under discussion. From these diagrams only a selection of curves relevant to the discussion will be shown. A short description of the geographical location, climate and vegetation of the pollen sites follows here.

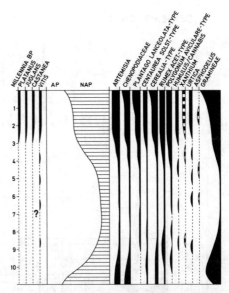

Fig. 5. Schematic pollen diagram showing a selection of pollen curves indicating human influence in Greece (Bottema 1982(1985)).

5.2.1 Beyşehir, SW Turkey

Lake Beyşehir lies at an altitude of ca 1120 m, to the west bordered by the Anamas Mts, which reach elevations of nearly 3000 m. Precipitation is ca 500 mm. The average January and August temperatures measure just below 0°C and ca 22°C respectively. The eastern part of the lake lies in the Xero-Euxinian zone but the south side where the cores were taken and the west side are in the Oro-Mediterranean belt.

Van Zeist et al. (1975) described a pollen assemblage zone found at a depth of 130-300 cm in which suddenly anthropogenic effects appeared (Fig. 6a). A much weaker influence of farmers' activities was visible in the pollen record even at ca 410 cm but at ca 300 cm Olea, Fraxinus ornus, deciduous Quercus, Juglans, Castanea make their appearance together with Plantago lanceolata-type, and Sanguisorba minor-type while Gramineae and Cerealia-type show · an increase. Values for unidentified Tubuliflorae, Liguliflorae and Centaurea solstitialis-type show a drastic reduction.

The original coring in Beyşehir covered ca 6000 years (van Zeist et

243

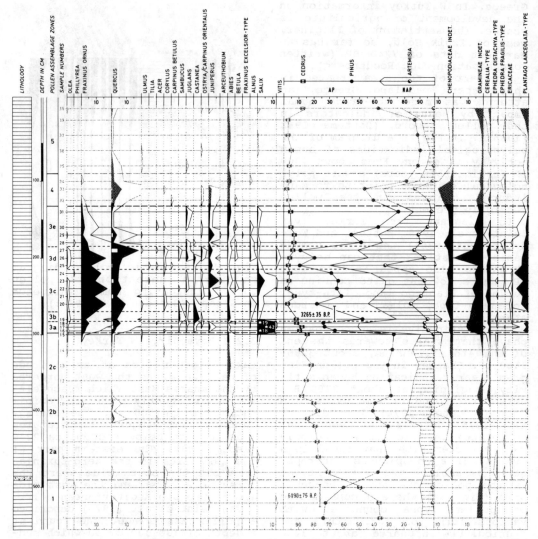

Figs. 6a-m. Selection of pollen diagrams demonstrating the Beyşehir Occupation (B.O.) phase (in black, the other parts shaded).
a. Beyşehir I (van Zeist et al. 1975)

al. 1975) and in 1977 a new coring was performed in the same marsh. The diagram prepared from that core extends the pollen record to ca 15,000 BP (Bottema and Woldring 1984(1986)). From this core Woldring prepared a detailed diagram (Fig. 6b) for the part that was described earlier by van Zeist et al. (1975) as zone 3. This diagram was discussed in 1986 at the OPTIMA

meeting in Istanbul and launched as the Beyşehir occupation phase (B.O. phase) because although comparable events were visible in many diagrams in the area under discussion, it was most clearly expressed in the Beyşehir diagrams. Van Zeist divided the B.O. phase into five subzones and this zonation is also applied to Fig. 6b. A discussion will follow in Section 6.

244

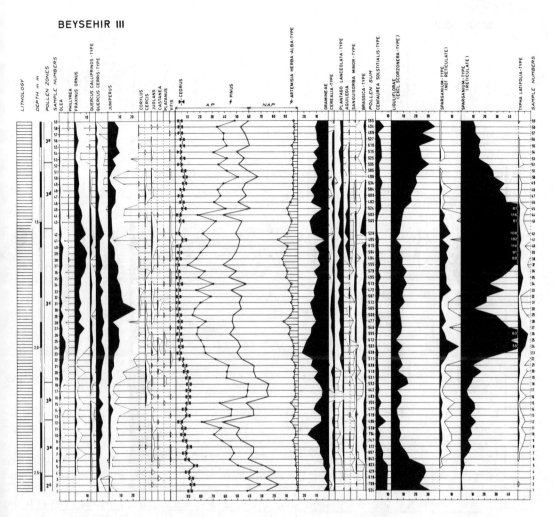

Fig 6b. Beyşehir III (Bottema and Woldring 1984(1986)).

5.2.2 Söğüt, SW Turkey

The Beyşehir occupation phase (B.O. phase) is thought to begin at a depth of 210 cm (Fig. 6c). The phase is characterized by the appearance or increase of the pollen percentages of Olea, Fraxinus ornus, Quercus calliprinos-type, Corylus, Juglans, Artemisia, Cerealia-type, Plantago lanceolata-type, Polygonum aviculare-type and spores of Pteridium. A marked decrease of Pinus, Juniperus, Centaurea solstitialis-type and other Tubuliflorae is visible. The beginning of the B.O. phase in Söğüt has been dated 2885±35 BP.

5.2.3 Pinarbaşi, SW Turkey

The B.O. phase starts at a depth of ca 150 cm (Fig. 6d). An increase of Quercus coccifera-type and Quercus cerris-type takes place at that level, together with Olea, Fraxinus ornus and Juglans. Pinus and Cedrus and many representatives of the composites decrease. Plantago lanceolata-type and Poterium/Sanguisorba appear.

5.2.4 Köycegiz Gölü, SW Turkey

The B.O. phase is located at a depth of 375-420 cm (Fig. 6e). At about 400 cm the phase is dated

245

SÖĞÜT GÖLÜ

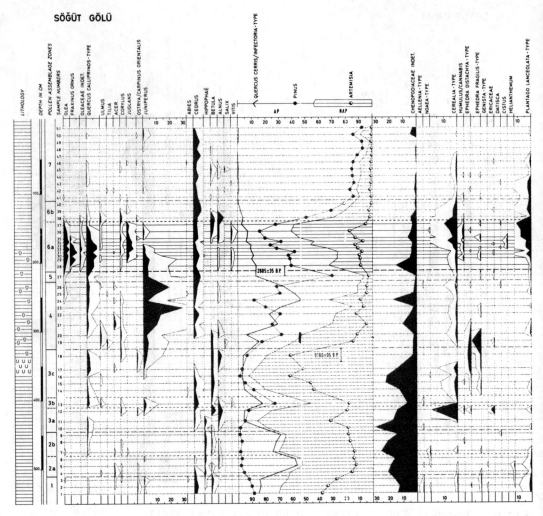

Fig 6c. Söğüt Gölü (van Zeist et al. 1975).

3070±55 BP. Just below the B.O. phase, which starts at about 420 cm depth, a volcanic ash layer is found. This layer was recognized by Sullivan (Denver) as having been deposited by the Santorini eruption. The B.O. phase is present only in the thin gyttja layer. This gyttja may however represent quite a long time.

Palynological characteristics are Olea, Vitis, Carpinus orientalis/Ostrya, deciduous Quercus, Plantago lanceolata-type, and Poterium/Sanguisorba minor. Pinus values sharply decrease.

5.2.5 Abant Gölü, NW Turkey

Abant Gölü is situated 30 km SW of Bolu at an elevation of ca 1300 m. Mountains to the west are up to 1760 m high. The meteorological station in Bolu (at an elevation of 753 m) gives an average precipitation of 523 mm. Average January and July temperatures are -5.3°C and ca 20°C respectively. Minimum winter temperature is -34°C. For Abant the Yeni Türkiye Atlasi (1977) gives a precipitation of more than 1000 mm, mostly falling in January. The Abant area has a very long-lasting

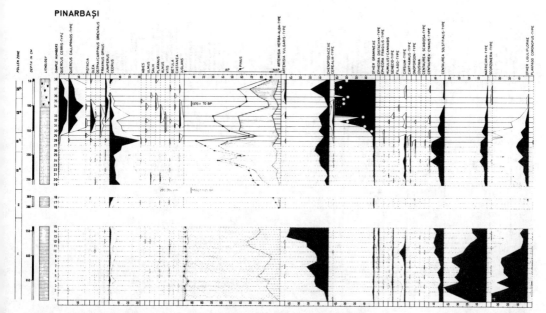

Fig 6d. Pinarbaşi (Bottema and Woldring 1984(1986)).

and deep snow cover during winter.

North slopes in Abant are mainly covered by Abies nordmanniana whereas south exposures are dominated by Pinus sylvestris. Deciduous species include Fagus orientalis, Carpinus betulus, Quercus robur, Q. virgiliana, Acer platanoides and Taxus baccata.

At a depth of about 480 cm (spectrum 43) up to about 320 cm (spectrum 50) curves for Olea, Juglans and Castanea suggest the presence of the B.O. phase (Fig. 6f). In the diagram of Yeniçağa (976 m), 35 km east of Bolu, the types so illustrative for the B.O. phase display much lower values. The Yeniçağa diagram is supplied with five radiocarbon dates which enable us to date the Abant record by correlation of the tree pollen curves. It is not clear why in Abant the values for Olea and Juglans are higher than in Yeniçağa where less extreme conditions are found. More to the east in a core from Ladik, which is still in preparation, a pollen assemblage is found that shows clear affinities with the B.O.phase.

5.2.6 Lake Khimaditis, NW Greece

An anthropogene phase in the younger Holocene pollen record, contemporaneous with the B.O. phase, has been described (Bottema 1974).

The Khimaditis III diagram shows important changes at a depth of 260 cm (Fig. 6g). Arboreal pollen composition rapidly changes. Pinus, Abies, Juniperus, Ulmus and Tilia sharply decrease, whereas Quercus and Fagus increase. A pronounced change in colour of the gyttja was visible at this level.

Secondly four tree-pollen types appear at this level, viz. Olea (not shown), Platanus, Juglans and Castanea. The level of this change in the pollen record has been dated 3135±70 BP.

5.2.7 Vegoritis, NW Greece

As was the case for nearby lake Khimaditis, two aspects are worth mentioning for the Vegoritis core. From 340-520 cm, high AP values are present. After 340 cm these values suddenly decrease, especially those of Pinus and Abies and to some extent Carpinus betulus.

At the same level curves for Quercus coccifera-type, Olea, Juglans, Vitis and Platanus appear. An increase of Juniperus takes place, often an indication of in-

247

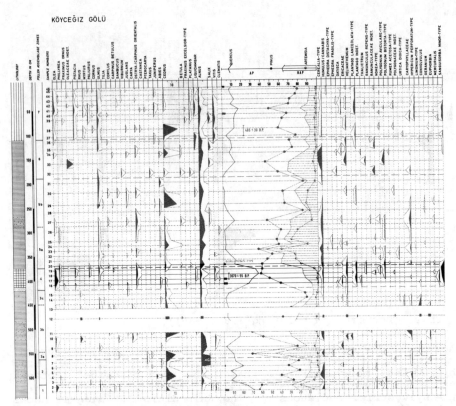

KÖYCEĞİZ GÖLÜ

Fig. 6e. Köyceğiz Gölü (van Zeist et al. 1975).

creasing human activity. In Fig. 6h a selection of curves is given that are illustrative for the B.O. phase.

The dating of the Vegoritis core and especially the B.O. phase is extensively discussed in Bottema (1982(1985)). The conclusion was that the Platanus and Juglans curves can be palynologically dated at ca 3200 BP, which agrees with the age suggested by the magnetic age-depth curve.

5.2.8 Edessa, NW Greece

The pollen diagram of Edessa (Bottema 1974) demonstrates a decrease for Pinus, Abies, Corylus, Carpinus betulus and Tilia at ca 300 cm. Quercus, Fagus and Juniperus show an increase at that level. Fig. 6i shows a selection of curves beginning or increasing at about 300 cm. This concerns Juglans, Castanea, Platanus, Vitis and a series of herb types that indicate human ac-

tivity. At the same time Olea (not shown) appears.

Below about 300-320 cm no pollen was found in the peaty sediment. It is assumed that pollen disappeared from this layer because the sediment was exposed to the air. This situation can only be explained by dry conditions. In Edessa the start of the B.O. phase is radiocarbon-dated to 3280±55 BP at 300 cm. A radiocarbon date at about 210 cm is difficult to explain as it seems to be too old.

5.2.9 Trikhonis, SW Greece

The beginning of the B.O. phase in this part of Greece is not easily dated. The curves of Juglans and Platanus start at a depth of 325 cm. This would suggest a date of ca 3200 BP. Creer et al. (1981) suggest the archaeomagnetic age to be AD 79 and linked with the volcanic ash layer of the Somma-Vesuvius that covered Pompei. The present

248

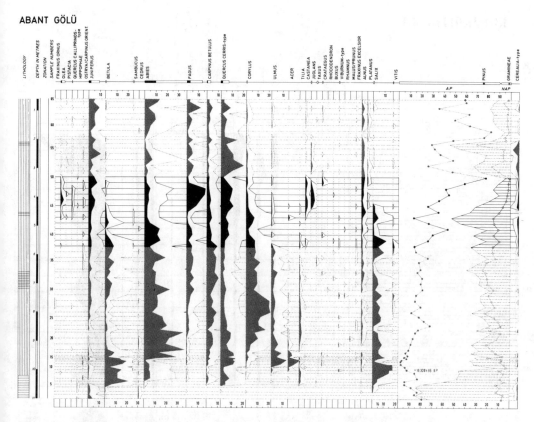

Fig. 6f. Abant Gölü (Bottema and Woldring in prep.).

author (1980) linked the ash layer with the Santorini eruption (now dated 1629 BC in calendar years; ca 3300 BP in conventional radiocarbon years). Sullivan (written communication) has good arguments however to suggest a connection with a volcanic eruption of the Somma-Vesuvius that took place ca 1200 BC.

If the beginning of the B.O. phase in Trikhonis is assumed to have started at a depth of ca 320 cm (Fig. 6j), the preceding period witnessed lower AP values than the upper part. Deciduous oak especially shows higher values. In contrast with the other Greek diagrams, Olea is present throughout the diagram, which covers ca 6000 years.

5.2.10 Koiladha, S Greece

The core was taken by J.Gifford, in the Bay of Koiladha at about 10 m water depth. The climate of the Argolid is typically Mediterranean. Precipitation amounts to 500 mm and mean January and July temperatures measure 10°C and 27°C respectively. The Argolid is mainly situated in the Eu-Mediterranean belt dominated by Quercus coccifera. On higher parts of the Peloponnese Oro-Mediterranean conifer forest with Abies cephalonica and Pinus is found.

The diagram of Koiladha, from which a selection of curves including those indicating human activity is shown in Fig. 6k, informs us about the vegetation history of the SE Peloponnese. From a core depth of about 425 cm up to 170 cm an open deciduous oak forest is postulated for the area. Values for Quercus coccifera are conspicuously low. At levels below 190 cm Pistacia was common together with Cistus and Umbelliferae. Types indicating human activity are very well represented. The lowest part of the diagram is dated about 6700 BP. Traces of Neolithic habitation

249

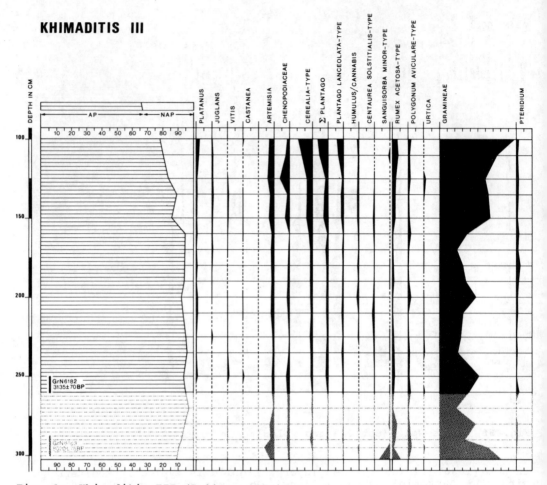

Fig. 6g. Khimaditis III (Bottema 1974).

have been found in the Koiladha area.

The palynological picture changes drastically at the level of 175 cm. Arboreal pollen values suddenly rise, predominantly caused by an increase of Pinus and Quercus coccifera-type and to a lesser extent by Abies. Ericaceae appear and establish a continuous curve. Very conspicuous is the decrease of the anthropogenic indicators except one type, Olea, which is found with very high values from 175 cm upward.

From about the same time, although not in a continuous curve, Platanus pollen is met with. Even today Juglans is not grown there and quite probably never was, at least this tree is not traced palynologically. Concluding from the

simultaneous abundance of the wind-pollinating Olea (Dafni, OPTIMA meeting Istanbul 1986) in many diagrams over a wide area, the level of 175 cm can be dated at ca 3200 BP.

5.2.11 Ghab, NW Syria

Among the pollen diagrams for this area that the Ghab III core (van Zeist and Woldring 1980) is of particular interest for our purpose (Fig. 61). Distinct human impact seems to begin in zone 8b with relatively low values for Fraxinus ornus, Castanea, Juglans and Plantago lanceolata-type. For the next zone, 9a, two dates have been obtained from the same level: 4460±40 and 3560±240 BP. At the beginning

250

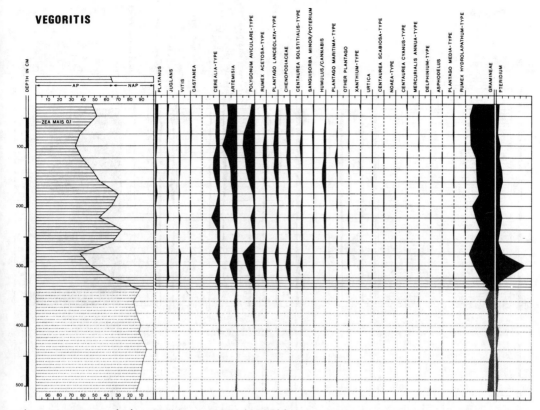

Fig. 6h. Vegoritis (Bottema 1982(1985)).

of zone 9b values for Olea, Fraxinus ornus, Vitis and Poterium/San-
guisorba minor increase distinctly.
The beginning of zone 9b is very
likely the beginning of the B.O.
phase. That Platanus does not show
its characteristic appearance or
increase at the beginning of zone
9b must be explained by the fact
that this tree has been a natural
constituent of the vegetation of
the Ghab valley for the last 50,000
years at least.

5.2.12 Lake Urmia, N Iran

The B.O. phase is postulated in the
Urmia diagram (Fig. 6m) to start
with zone 4 at ca 55 cm (core 20).
The levels of 205-210 cm and 295-
300 cm have been dated 7505±125 and
9540±130 BP respectively. If a constant sedimentation rate is assumed, the beginning of zone Z4 to
be dated to a mere ca 2000 years
BP. This would seem too young.
However, if core 21 is considered,

indicative types as Juglans and
Platanus are already present at a
depth of over 100 cm. The total
length of core 21 is not more than
that of core 20. No definite age
for the beginning of zone Z4 has
been obtained but the pollen assemblage very much resembles that
of the B.O. phase (Olea, Juglans,
Platanus and Plantago lanceolata-
type).

6 DISCUSSION OF THE POLLEN EVIDENCE

In Section 3 we have assumed that
12 selected herb types are indicative for human activity. This assumption, among others, was based
upon the work done by Behre (1981)
and the study of human activity in
Greece (Bottema 1982 (1985)). In
this section the nature of the B.O.
phase will be studied more closely
to test its validity as a record of
human impact.
Artemisia values increase in the
SW Anatolian records and rather

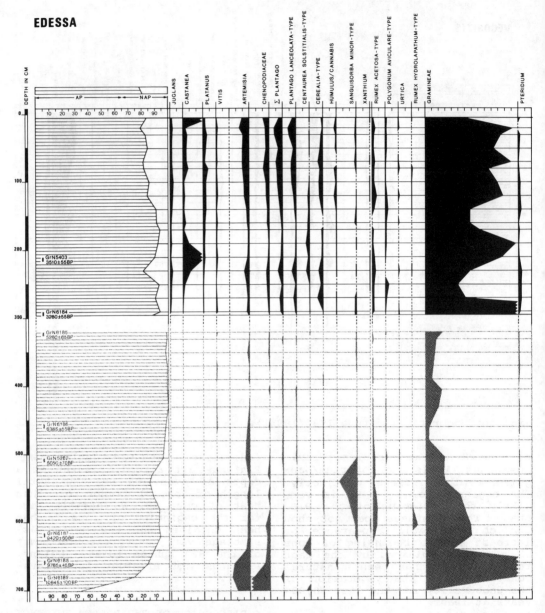

Fig. 6i. Edessa (Bottema 1974).

weakly in NW Greece. In the other sites no change has been recorded. On the Anatolian Plateau around Beyşehir and Söğüt destruction of forest may have favoured Artemisia, which forms a natural constituent of the vegetation towards the interior.

Chenopodiaceae are less indicative in our area than they are considered to be in NW Europe. The

record of the forest in NW Greece which somewhat resembles that of European temperate forest, demonstrates a slight increase in chenopod pollen. In the other parts Chenopodiaceae display high values even from Pleistocene times onwards.

Plantago lanceolata-type pollen, which in our studies very likely represents that species, reacts the

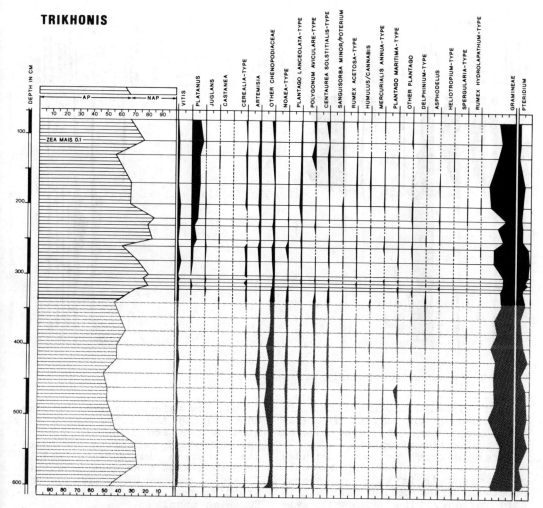

Fig. 6j. Trikhonis (Bottema 1982(1985)).

same way all over the area. It shows an increase in all the diagrams but one. Only in the diagram from Koiladha just off the Argolid coast (Peloponnese) was a decrease observed at the level where Olea together with tree pollen in general shows an important increase. The general increase of Plantago lanceolata-type is explained as increased activity of prehistoric man, especially stock breeding and consequently grazing. Either this grazing took place on abandoned fields and fallow land or on places where lumbering had taken place. Information from the surface samples (Fig. 3) indicates that in many places subfossil values for Plantago lanceolata-type were high-

er during the B.O. phase than at present. In NW Europe, conditions for the growth of ribwort plantain have deteriorated the last few decades, emphasizing that this plant thrives under certain forms of farming regime only.

Gramineae pollen values from the fossil record can be compared with those of the surface sample study only if cores taken in the middle of lakes are concerned. Gramineae pollen values from cores taken from marshes or lakesides are high and fluctuating. Non-local Gramineae pollen is merely 10-20%. At the beginning of the B.O. phase some curves show an increase in grass pollen that may have been caused by the destruction of forest.

KOILADHA

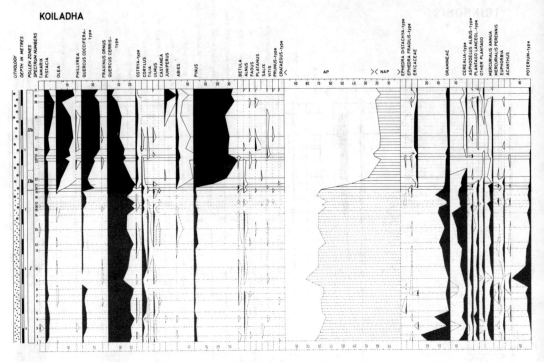

Fig. 6k. Koiladha (Bottema in press).

Either Gramineae increased in clearances or the effect is relative and caused by the lowered amount of arboreal pollen.

Cerealia-type pollen includes more than the pollen of domestic cereals and their wild ancestors. Some wild grass pollen fall within this category. The subfossil evidence is quite consistent not only in the values (2-10%) for the B.O. phase but especially in the course of the curves which show a clear increase at this level. In the modern pollen rain Cerealia-type values in the much degraded parts of the Upper-Mediterranean and Oro-Mediterranean or montane forest, especially in Greece and the Levant, are of the same order as those in the subfossil record. This suggests that a degradation of the natural vegetation, comparable to what can be seen nowadays in our area, occurred also during the B.O. phase.

The role of Centaurea solstitialis-type pollen will form part of a discussion that follows later in this contribution. This type behaves as an anthropogenic indicator in Greece. It is either absent or it has low values, increasing somewhat during the B.O. phase. Very high values are found in part of the subfossil record of SW Anatolia, whereas in surface samples from that area Centaurea solstitialis-type percentages are of some significance only in the Xero-Euxinian zone.

Mercurialis annua is mainly restricted to the pollen diagrams of the sites from the lower Eu-Mediterranean zone. A slightly positive correlation with other pollen types indicating human activity was already noticed for Greece (Bottema 1982(1985)) and this type correlates positively with anthropogenic indicators in the Koiladha diagram. In the modern pollen precipitation Mercurialis annua is restricted to the Eu-Mediterranean zone and parts of Syria.

The expansion of plants belonging to the Compositae, either Tubuliflorae or Liguliflorae, could have been favoured by the destruction of forest. Yet the pollen curves of neither of the taxa point to this. Values of Compositae before the time of the B.O. phase are often very high, especially in Turkey. At

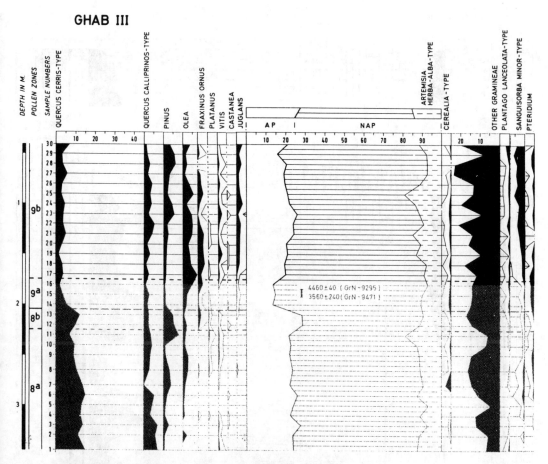

GHAB III

Fig. 61. Ghab III (van Zeist and Woldring 1980).

the beginning of the B.O. phase they show a distinct decrease and regain or partially regain their previous values after a considerable length of time in the order of 1500 years. The Compositae values in Greece are much lower and no clear reaction can be seen at the beginning of the B.O. phase. The modern values (Fig. 3) for Tubuliflorae and Liguliflorae range from less than 1% to ca 10%. This is considerably lower than the Compositae values in diagrams from Anatolia. An attempt will be made to explain this behaviour together with that of the Centaurea solstitialis-type.

Rumex acetosa-type was found to correlate with other anthropogenic indicators in Greece (Bottema 1982 (1985)). For Turkey this can only be observed in the more humid zone

of the northern, heavily forested, mountains. This tendency appears also from the surface-sample study. The only exception is a series of samples from much-degraded parts of the lower Eu-Mediterranean zone in SW Turkey where this pollen type scored much more highly than in other vegetation zones.

Especially in forested areas human activity may become visible by an increase in Pteridium spores. In the actual pollen rain this effect could only be found in partly disturbed beech forest in Greece.

A general conclusion is that in such a large and diverse area as the Eastern Mediterranean pollen types that are indicative for the whole area can hardly be found. It could be expected that steppic taxa are only indicative outside their natural range, for instance in

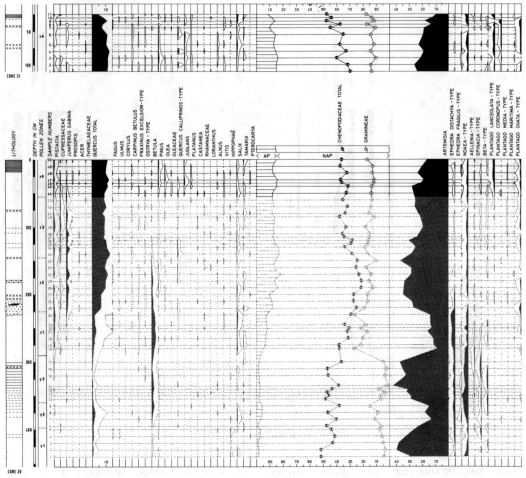

Fig. 6m. Urmia (Bottema 1986).

forested areas. The ecological diversity in Gramineae is so large that each diagram has to be weighed individually. Plantago lanceolata (-type) and Poterium-type are among the most useful indicators present in the major part of the area discussed. Cerealia-type pollen, if not specified in greater detail, is not very informative about prehistoric activity. Pollen of Rumex acetosa/acetosella and spores of Pteridium may be indicative in forested areas. Outside these vegetation zones they are not encountered. The large group of the Compositae follows the trend of Artemisia. In vegetations that are open by origin it is difficult to separate human activity from other potential causes where changes in their pollen curves are concerned.

It is stated above in Section 4 that a decrease in AP values could have been caused by prehistoric people who destroyed the forest for agricultural purposes or for the use of wood for various purposes. One would expect the AP percentages to decrease at the beginning of the B.O. phase. This takes place in some parts of the area, for instance in SW Turkey, where an important part of the forest must have been destroyed at that time. In N Greece destruction of the forest must have occurred as is concluded from the decreasing AP values.

Table 2. Average values of Olea, Castanea, Juglans, Vitis, Fraxinus ornus and Platanus in the modern pollen precipitation in various vegetation zones (see Table 1).

vegetation zone	Olea	Castanea	Juglans	Vitis	Fraxinus ornus	Platanus
1a	1.6	–	0.1	<0.1	–	0.1
1b	7.5	<0.1	0.8	0.1	<0.1	1.5
1c	8.4	0.1	0.2	–	–	0.1
2a	5.7	<0.1	0.1	<0.1	0.1	1.0
2b	5.5	–	0.1	<0.1	–	0.1
2c	6.3	0.1	0.1	<0.1	0.3	0.3
2d	3.4	<0.1	3.1	0.1	0.1	2.1
3a	1.5	<0.1	0.3	<0.1	0.1	0.2
3b	4.3	–	1.4	<0.1	–	0.1
3c	0.3	–	<0.1	<0.1	<0.1	–
3d	0.3	<0.1	0.6	–	0.1	0.3
4a	0.3	0.2	0.9	<0.1	0.1	0.3
4b	1.9	0.1	0.4	–	–	0.3
5a	0.6	0.1	0.5	<0.1	0.1	1.2
5b	1.4	0.1	0.5	<0.1	0.1	1.5
5c	0.7	–	0.1	0.1	–	–
6a	0.3	0.4	0.3	0.1	0.2	0.2
6b	0.2	<0.1	–	<0.1	–	0.1
7	–	–	<0.1	–	–	–
8	0.5	0.2	<0.1	0.1	–	<0.1
9a	–	–	0.4	–	–	–
9b	–	–	<0.1	–	–	–
9c	1.6	–	2.6	0.1	0.1	0.1
9d	0.1	–	<0.1	–	–	<0.1
10	0.3	0.2	0.2	<0.1	0.3	3.2

On the Greek Mediterranean coast (Trikhonis, Koiladha) AP values increase at the beginning of the B.O. phase. This is not easily explained by human activity but would sooner point to the absence of it.

The curves of Olea, Castanea and other fruit producing species testify to the rapid expansion of fruticulture during the B.O. phase. The curves of these six species in the subfossil record display values which may be even higher than those recorded at the moment. In Fig. 8 the maximum values in the B.O. phase for Olea, Castanea etc. are given for the various core locations. The location of the cores in the various vegetation zones can be found in Figs. 1 and 2. The values for the same species in the modern pollen rain are given in Table 2. The modern values are generally lower than their counterparts from the B.O. phase. But also within the same vegetation zone values can be quite different.

An important question remains to what extent presence of indicative pollen types in a site actually means impact of man on the spot. For instance, if Olea pollen is present with values of 1-5%, does that mean that the occupants of the area grew olives or that it is still possible that olive pollen originated somewhere else? Table 2 shows that Olea is very well represented in the modern pollen rain. The samples that produced those values are from transects indicated in Fig. 2. In Fig. 7a the area of cultivation of olive is mapped. If we compare the modern distribution of the olive with its pollen precipitation in various parts of the area, it becomes clear that Olea pollen indeed precipitates also outside the area where it is grown. One could expect the presence of Olea pollen outside the distribution area, because this tree is a windpollinator, but here some quantitative information is given. At present average percentages range from 1.6 to 8.4% within the distribution area. Outside the distribution area such values are generally under 1%. An exception

257

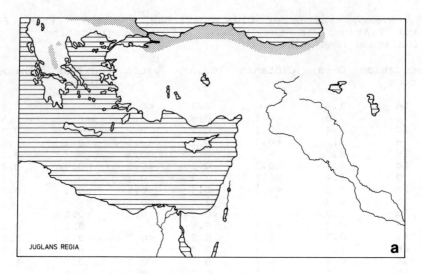

JUGLANS REGIA   a

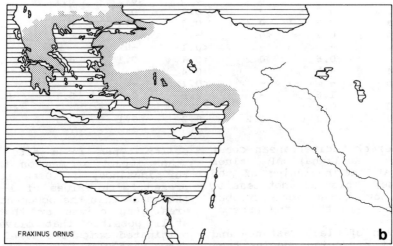

FRAXINUS ORNUS   b

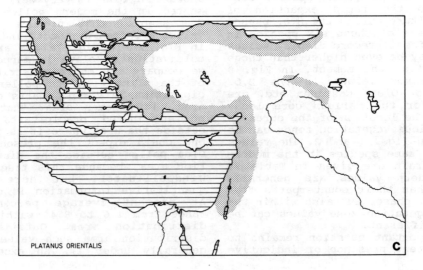

PLATANUS ORIENTALIS   c

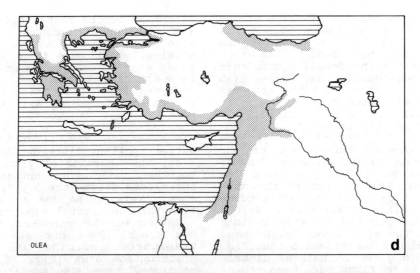

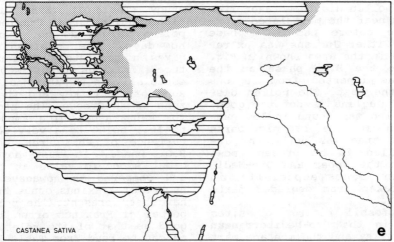

Fig. 7a. Present distribution of olive culture (after Rikli 1943-1948) and Davis Vol. 6, 1978).
Figs. 7b-e. Assumed natural distribution of b) Castanea sativa (after Rikli 1943-1948); c) Juglans regia (after Rikli 1943-1948); d) Fraxinus ornus (after Rikli 1943-1948 and Davis Vol. 6, 1978); e) Platanus orientalis (after Rikli 1943-1948 and Davis Vol. 7, 1982).

are those parts where Olea does not grow because of the high elevation, but that are close to the main cultivation area. This is found in the montane forest in NW Turkey where 1.9% Olea is found in a sample from dense Fagus/Abies forest, and in the Oro-Mediterranean zone in the Levant (1.5-4.3%). The high values may be caused by the short distance to the source as olive cultivation is very common in lower zones nearby. It is likely that updraught

caused up-slope transport of olive pollen from plantations in the valleys. Thus the high values for the olive during the B.O. phase do not necessarily point to the cultivation of olives in the Beyşehir area. The pollen influx may have been derived from olive groves more to the south.

The presence of Castanea, be it naturally or planted, cannot be easily concluded from its modern pollen precipitation when that is

259

compared to the distribution of the tree itself. Castanea pollen has very low values over most of the area, and is not found in the steppic part. In the fossil record this tree occasionally may have high values indicating that the tree was very common locally.

Nowadays Juglans is extensively planted and the pollen diagrams indicate that this started synchronously over a large part of our area, especially mainland Greece, Anatolia and probably N Iran. The map (Fig. 7c) only gives the supposed natural distribution according to Rikli (1943-1948). Walnut trees are planted in wide regions outside the area shown on the map. It is highly questionable that Fig. 7c should give the natural distribution as no finds have been registered in pollen diagrams taken from within or near the postulated growing range before the B.O. phase started. Either Juglans was extremely rare in the area shown in Fig. 7c before the B.O. phase or the walnut was imported from regions more to the east. The pollen dispersal of Juglans is not too good. Still pollen was found in low numbers even in the steppic parts where the tree was not seen. Juglans pollen is at present most common in the Upper and Oro-Mediterranean zones, especially in samples taken from degraded parts of the forest.

The subfossil records of sites situated in the Oro-Mediterranean part of Turkey and the montane part of N Greece show the highest Juglans percentages. Such environments seem to have witnessed the most intensive cultivation of the walnut during the B.O. phase.

There seems to be a certain discrepancy between the representation of Vitis in the modern pollen precipitation and in the subfossil record. Vitis percentages in the modern pollen precipitation are very low and the species is absent in samples from Iran and N Syria. In the subfossil record values can be up to 2% and Vitis pollen is fairly frequent in various zones from the Turkish and Greek coast up to the Oro-Mediterranean zone. One could expect Vitis pollen in lake sediments to have been produced by wild vine growing along small streams carrying its pollen to the

catchment basin. That would explain its abundant occurrence compared with the values in the surface samples, which were in general not taken near streams or moist places. In a surface sample taken from a vineyard in central Italy no Vitis pollen was found at all (Woldring pers. comm.). Van Zeist pointed to the fact that wild grape is dioecious, which may account for a better pollen distribution. However, the increase of Vitis pollen together with other anthropogenic indicators during the B.O. phase is more likely to be due to cultivation than to natural expansion.

Pollen of the manna-ash (Fraxinus ornus) does not seem to be transported outside its modern distribution area (Fig. 7d) as is concluded from the surface-sample study (Table 2). Even within its distribution area Fraxinus ornus pollen values do not exceed 0.3% nowadays. The subfossil record gives a completely different picture. Fraxinus ornus scores high especially in the Oro-Mediterranean zone of SW Turkey and the montane zone of NW Greece. The high values for manna-ash, which amount to up to 10%, point to a very common occurrence of that tree during the B.O. phase. It must have had a great economic value at that time and compared to nowadays a large number of Fraxinus ornus trees must have been present. The pollen dispersal of Fraxinus ornus is not so good as that of its relative Olea, as can be read from Table 2. On the other hand, the number of olives is much larger at present than the number of manna-ashes, a fact that influences the pollen values.

The modern distribution of Fraxinus ornus in SW Turkey stretches much further inland than that of Olea and it seems likely that Fraxinus ornus trees were planted in large numbers in the Oro-Mediterranean part.

The role and origin of Platanus are discussed in the study of the anthropogenic indicators in relation to Greek prehistory (Bottema 1982(1985)). Fig. 7e gives the present distribution of the plane tree. Undoubtedly this is not the natural distribution. Relatively high values for Platanus are present in pre-Holocene samples from the Huleh (Israel) (Baruch and

Bottema in prep.) and the Ghab (Niklewski and van Zeist 1970). During the B.O. phase Platanus must have spread or was planted over a large part of the Eastern Mediterranean. Its sudden appearance in many pollen diagrams from that region points to deliberate planting of plane trees. Platanus seems to have played a role especially in the Oro-Mediterranean part of SW Turkey, in various parts of Greece and even in N Iran. It cannot be excluded that Platanus profited from changes in habitat caused by human activity.

Summarizing we may state that the B.O. phase was a period during which agriculture and fruticulture in a broad sense strongly developed. All the crops in evidence during this period were not necessarily grown everywhere at the same time, limited mainly by environmental conditions.

So far we have focussed upon the B.O. phase as a period during which characteristic changes occurred in the pollen diagrams that were related to the impact of early-historical people upon the vegetation. However, in various diagrams characteristic palynological traits are visible that must be connected with other events. We have already mentioned that in some diagrams arboreal pollen increased after the onset of the occupation phase. It is difficult to correlate a rise in human activity with an increase in total tree pollen percentages as one would be inclined to think that in this period the reverse would take place.

In part of the area it was not so much the AP value that changed as the composition of the spectra. In N Greece Pinus and Abies pollen values sharply decreased and were replaced by deciduous oak pollen. Anatolia witnessed the same change be it that initial Pinus pollen values were not of the dimension of the Pinus values in N Greece and neither were the replacing Quercus values.

Van Zeist et al. (1975) explained the replacement of pine by oak by the difference in regenerating capacity. The oaks would have grown as low trees in the undercover of the pine forest. After cutting or burning of the forest, the formerly dominating pines would not recover

whereas the oaks would develop even from scrubwood. Here we are dealing with Pinus nigra or P. sylvestris and not with the pyrophyte P. halepensis. For NW Greece this means that most of the coniferous forest was destroyed by man and that the oaks took advantage of this destruction. However, it is unlikely that human activity should have resulted in destroying one type of forest without any visible interference with the secondary forest that developed. In Anatolia all this seems to have happened on a smaller scale as concluded from the lower pollen values of oak and pine compared with those found in NW Greece. Towards the end of the 4th millennium the production of iron will have demanded a lot of wood which in turn could be procured with iron axes. Still, it is not credible that iron production should have been practised everywhere at the same time, resulting in the destruction of so much montane conifer forest. Lumbering in connection with wood-trade must have occurred even if transport took place over large distances, for instance to Mesopotamia.

However, apart from changes in tree pollen composition, other changes in the pollen diagrams took place that merit attention. Especially the pollen diagrams from the Oro-Mediterranean and the Xero-Euxinian zone show very high values for composite pollen, predominantly Centaurea solstitialis-type, but also Liguliflorae and/or unidentified Tubuliflorae, before and after the B.O. phase. Surface samples from the Eastern Mediterranean do not show very high values for that group of pollen types as can be seen in Fig. 3. How can we explain Centaurea solstitialis-type values of 30-50% occurring before the B.O. phase, dropping to a few percent during this phase and increasing after the B.O. phase? It is clear that such high Centaurea solstitialis-type percentages do not reflect a vegetation dominated by this plant as even modern vegetations with much Centaurea solstitialis do not show such high pollen values for this type. Bottema and Woldring (1984(1986)) explained the anomalously high Centaurea solstitialis-type values as the result of strong upward air movement at the time of

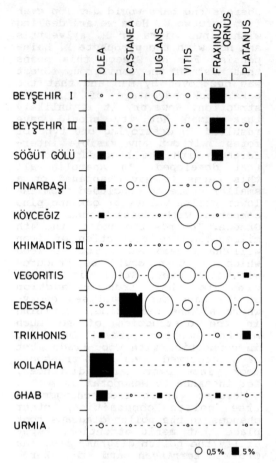

	OLEA	CASTANEA	JUGLANS	VITIS	FRAXINUS ORNUS	PLATANUS
BEYŞEHIR I	∘	∘	◯	∘	■	
BEYŞEHIR III	■	∘	◯	∘	■	∘
SÖĞÜT GÖLÜ	■		■	◯	■	
PINARBAŞI	■	∘	◯		◯	
KÖYCEĞIZ	■			◯	∘	
KHIMADITIS III	∘	∘	∘	∘	◯	◯
VEGORITIS	◯	◯	◯	◯		■
EDESSA	∘	■	◯	◯	◯	◯
TRIKHONIS	■		∘	◯	∘	■
KOILADHA	■			∘	∘	◯
GHAB	■	∘	■	◯	■	∘
URMIA	∘	∘	∘	∘		∘

◯ 0,5 % ■ 5%

Fig. 8. Maximum pollen percentages for Olea, Castanea, Juglans, Vitis, Fraxinus ornus and Platanus in 12 diagrams covering the period of the B.O. phase.

flowering. It was witnessed during fieldwork that a large amount of dust, pieces of straw and chaff precipitated into Thessalian lake Zirelia, in the middle of the day when the Thessalian plain was very hot. The debris had been collected by ascending hot air over the plain. The water of the lake was cooler than the surrounding land and the backflow of air caused a steady downpour of the same dust and pieces of organic material. The upper samples of this lake contained a large number of Liguliflorae pollen. These Liguliflorae very probably had been collected and concentrated by the airflow decribed above. A condition for this

phenomenon is the absence or scarcity of tree cover. In N Turkey where dense forest is found nowadays, no high composite pollen percentages are found in the Holocene record.

It is postulated here that strong heating effects occurred in the steppe, the Xero-Euxinian zone and on the edge of the Oro-Mediterranean zone. This took place during the summer, when composites are flowering. In this way Centaurea solstitialis-type pollen was gathered by the upward flow and concentrated, eventually to precipitate in locations with a lower temperature such as lakes. This would also explain the much lower composite pollen content of surface samples where the "normal" pollen precipitation is trapped and where no concentration takes place. It should be mentioned that selective preservation in the respective diagrams plays no role as the conservation was sufficient.

At the beginning of the B.O. phase, ca 3200 BP, values for Centaurea solstitialis-type and other composites suddenly decreased. It is assumed that the strong upward airflow somehow got blocked. Either summer temperatures became considerably lower or the presence of cloud cover prevented the heating of the Anatolian plateau. It is also possible that an increase in precipitation caused a dense vegetation cover to act as a buffer resulting in much lower temperatures. The increase in arboreal pollen that takes place in some pollen diagrams could be the result of moister conditions more favourable for tree growth developing ca 3200 BP.

It is striking that conditions very favourable for tree growth developed on the Peloponnese at the beginning of the B.O. phase together with definite human impact as demonstrated by an important increase in Olea percentages. If from this we infer a change in climate during the B.O. phase, the question arises if this resulted in a different distribution pattern of exploited species. Do the high Olea values during the B.O. phase in Beyşehir, a site that is situated outside the present-day olive cultivation, point to important local olive groves? If olive cultivation was important there at an elevation of 1120 m during the 3rd millennium BP, for instance winter temperature must have been higher. Calculating from the available radiocarbon dates and assuming a constant sedimentation rate, high values for Centaurea solstitialis-type and other composites return ca 1500 BP on the Anatolian Plateau. Climatic conditions of before 3200 BP seem to have returned, or the return to high Centaurea solstitialis-type values is to be explained by the rapid development of man-made steppe. Compared with the values of anthropogenic indicators during the B.O. phase much lower values are found for this group. We can conclude that the farming acreage in use had shrunk considerably.

Is there a link between an assumed change in climate and the wave of B.O. phase agro-fruticultural activities? Did farming possibilities increase because of more favourable conditions or is it pure coincidence that both events took place?

In the foregoing that part of the Eastern Mediterranean is discussed where the pollen record demonstrates clear traits ascribed to the B.O. phase. Still, there are pollen diagrams from other parts of the area under discussion where the B.O. phase pollen assemblage is represented very weakly or not at all. The explanation may be that local conditions were not suitable for such exploitation. It may have been too cold or too dry for agriculture and fruticulture. This is certainly the case for the Syrian steppe, where the available pollen evidence shows no signs of the B.O. phase. For East Turkey, in the Van area, a comparable occupation seems to have taken place later. In the Söğütlü core the first weak signs of human occupation are dated 2850 BP and significant values for Juglans and Plantago lanceolata start only after 1365 BP.

7 ACKNOWLEDGEMENTS

The authors express their thanks to Willem van Zeist for his suggestions and critical reading of the manuscript, to Petri Maas who made the drawings, to Wiebe Haajema and Geert Tamminga for the photowork, to Gertie Entjes-Nieborg for typing the manuscript and to Xandra Bardet for correcting the English.

REFERENCES

Athanasiades, N. 1975.
Zur postglazialen Vegetationsentwicklung von Litochoro Katerinis und Pertouli Trikalon (Griechenland). Flora 164:99-132.

Baruch, U. 1983.
The palynology of a Late Holocene core from Lake Kinneret. Master thesis, Hebrew University.

Behre, K.-E. 1981.
The interpretation of anthropogenic indicators in pollen diagrams. Pollen et Spores 23:225-245.

Bottema, S. 1974.
Late Quaternary vegetation history of northwestern Greece. Thesis, University of Groningen.

Bottema, S. 1975-1977.
A pollen diagram from the Syrian Anti Lebanon. Paléorient 3:259-268.

Bottema, S. 1979.
Pollen analytical investigation in Thessaly (Greece). Palaeohistoria 21:19-40.

Bottema, S. 1980.
Palynological investigations on Crete. Review of Palaeobotany and Palynology 31:193-217.

Bottema, S. 1982(1985).
Palynological investigations in Greece with special reference to pollen as an indicator of human activity. Palaeohistoria 24:257-289.

Bottema, S. 1986.
A Late Quaternary pollen diagram from Lake Urmia (northwestern Iran). Review of Palaeobotany and Palynology 47:241-261.

Bottema, S. in press.
Holocene Environment of the Southern Argolid. In T.W.Jacobsen and J.Gifford, Excavations at Franchthi Cave, Greece. Fascicule 4.

Bottema, S. and Y.Barkoudah 1979.
Modern pollen precipitation in Syria and Lebanon and its relation to vegetation. Pollen et Spores 21:427-480.

Bottema, S. and H.Woldring 1984 (1986). Late Quaternary vegetation and climate of southwestern Turkey. Part II. Palaeohistoria 26:123-149.

Bottema, S. and H.Woldring
in prep. Late Quaternary vegetation history and climate of
northern Turkey.

Creer, K.M., P.W.Readman
and S.Papamarinopoulos 1981.
Geomagnetic secular variations
in Greece through the last 6000
years obtained from lake sediment studies. Geophys. J.R. ast.
Soc. 66:193-219.

Dafni, A. in press.
The Mediterranean maquis as a
pollination environment. 5th
OPTIMA meeting, September 1986
Istanbul.

Davis, P.H. (ed.) 1965-1988.
Flora of Turkey and the East
Aegean Islands. 10 Vols. Edin-
burgh:Edinburgh University Press.

Gremmen, W.H.E. and S.Bottema
in press. Palynological investigations in the Syrian Jezireh.

Le Houérou, H.N. 1981.
Impacts of man and his animals on
Mediterranean vegetation. In: F.
di Castri, D.W.Goodall and R.L.
Specht (eds.), Mediterranean type
shrublands. Ecosystems of the
World 11, p.523-535. Amsterdam,
Elsevier.

Niklewski, J. and W.van Zeist 1970.
A Late Quaternary pollen diagram
from northwestern Syria. Acta
Botanica Neerlandica 19:737-754.

Rikli, M. 1943-1948.
Das Pflanzenkleid der Mittelmeer-
länder. Bern: Verlag Hans Huber.

Shahrabi, M. 1981.
Holocene lacustrine facies and
climatic cycles in the hyper-
saline lake Urmia Basin, Northwest Iran. ETH Zürich: Diplom-
arbeit Abt. Naturwiss.

Trabaud, L. 1981.
Man and fire: impacts on Mediterranean vegetation. In F.di Castri, D.W.Goodall and R.L.Specht
(eds.), Mediterranean type
shrublands. Ecosystems of the
World 11, p.479-517. Amsterdam,
Elsevier.

UNESCO-FAO 1963.
Carte bioclimatique de la zone
méditerranéenne. Note explicative. Recherches sur la zone
aride 21. Paris: UNESCO.

UNESCO-FAO 1970.
Carte de la végétation de la
région méditerranéenne. Note
explicative. Recherches sur la
zone aride 30. Paris: UNESCO.

Wright Jr., H.E., J.A.McAndrews
and W.van Zeist 1967.

Modern pollen rain in western
Iran, and its relation to plant
geography and Quaternary vegetation history. Journal of Ecology 55:415-443.

Yeni Türkiye Atlasi 1977.
M.S.B. Harita Genel Müdürlügü,
Ankara.

Zeist, W.van and H.Woldring 1978.
A Postglacial pollen diagram
from Lake Van in East Anatolia.
Review of Palaeobotany and
Palynology 26:249-276.

Zeist, W.van and H.Woldring 1980.
Holocene vegetation and climate
of northwestern Syria. Palaeohistoria 22:111-125.

Zeist, W. van, R.W.Timmers
and S.Bottema 1968(1970).
Studies of modern and Holocene
pollen precipitation in Southwestern Turkey. Palaeohistoria
14:19-39.

Zeist, W.van,
H.Woldring and D.Stapert 1975.
Late Quaternary vegetation and
climate of southwestern Turkey.
Palaeohistoria 17:53-143.

Zeist, W.van and
J.A.H.Bakker-Heeres 1982(1985).
Archaeobotanical studies in the
Levant. I. Neolithic sites in
the Damascus Basin: Aswad, Ghoraifé, Ramad. Palaeohistoria 24:
165-256.

Zeist, W.van and S.Bottema 1977.
Palynological investigations in
western Iran. Palaeohistoria 19:
19-85.

Zohary, M. 1973.
Geobotanical Foundations of the
Middle East. 2 Vols. Amsterdam-
Stuttgart: Gustav Fischer Verlag/
Swets and Zeitlinger.

Man's Role in the Shaping of the Eastern Mediterranean Landscape, Bottema, Entjes-Nieborg & van Zeist (eds)
© 1990 Balkema, Rotterdam. ISBN 90 6191 138 9

Vegetation and human occupation in the lowlands and foothills of eastern Georgia in the Middle Holocene

20

Liana K.Gogichaishvili
Institute of Botany, Academy of Sciences of the GSSR, Tbilisi, USSR

ABSTRACT: Palynological studies have been carried out on Middle Holocene sediments, including some archaeological excavations in eastern Georgia. Regional models of the evolution of vegetation and human occupation in this areas have been drawn up, using the local archaeological records. The Middle Holocene appears to have been a period of maximum forest cover of the foothills and valleys. Eastern Georgia was quite densely populated in the period, particularly in the Late Bronze Age and Iron Age, the human settlements evolving in accord with the environment.

1 INTRODUCTION

The vegetation cover of eastern Georgia underwent considerable changes in the Holocene, especially in the foothills and lowland areas where large forest stands had become comparatively wide-spread not long before. The principal stages of the development of the Holocene forest are related to general global climatic changes, but also depended on the local environment. As we know, the most significant changes of vegetation occurred in the Middle Holocene. Expansion of forest areas, displacement of the upper border of forests, differentiation of forest types, formation of the oak-hornbeam hemixerophyte piedmont belt and displacement of the beech to 300-400 m above its present-day lower limit occurred in the Caucasus. A model of the evolution of the Middle Holocene forest vegetation has been made on the basis of palynological records. The main investigated areas (Fig. 1) include the middle course of the rivers Kura, Aragvi, Iori, Alazani, the downstream course of the rivers Algeti and Khrami, and adjacent areas. The plant cover has since changed drastically under the influence of human activity (Ketskhoveli 1960).

2 MIDDLE HOLOCENE VEGETATION

Several sites illustrating the forest vegetation history were selected in the basin of the river Kura. For example, in the Middle Holocene the area from Tashiskari to Khashuri was predominantly covered with broad-leaved mixed forest which consisted of hornbeam, oak, maple, elm, occasional specimens of beech, chestnut, fir, pine, etc. Flood-plain forest formed narrow strips of woodland. Around Osiauri the area of lowland forest gradually expanded, the oak being predominant. Data collected from the neighbourhood of Gori show a predominance of open landscapes in the Middle Holocene. Patches of oak, elm and other lowland forests expanded while the area of flood-plain forest was reduced considerably.

A series of samples were collected from the bed of the river Narekvali. According to the results of sporo-pollen analysis the lowland oak forests predominated in the Middle Holocene.

A distinctly different situation was observed in the district of Shio Mgvime. In the early Middle Holocene the area of open woodland began to expand (until then this type of forest had not existed in any region). The proportion of

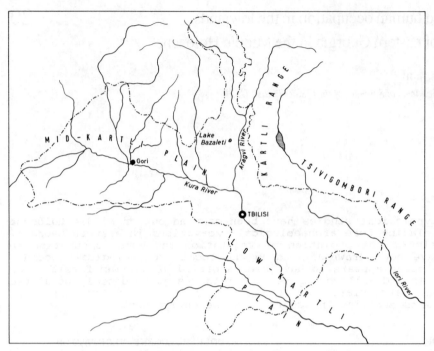

Fig. 1. General map of eastern Georgia.

grasses reached its maximum level. Higher mountain belts were covered with hornbeam-oak forests, the open woodland occurring below. Floodplain forests appear to have been fragmentary.

At an elevation of 800-850 m above sea level (Lake Bazaleti) the Middle Holocene spectra revealed 45% of oak pollen, 35% of hornbeam, 8% of elm and 10% of Zelkova. The last-named species is characterized by a rapid growth rate, high productivity and good quality timber. Nowadays, the area of this valuable species has become extremely small. Some specialists even believe it to be a regressing relict that is becoming extinct. However, Sharashidze (1967), who investigated the bioecology of Zelkova did not support this idea and he came to the conclusion that the present scarcity of the species is due to a rapacious use of the forests by man. The total spectrum composition shows that an area which is now the forestless Bazaleti valley basin, used to be covered with broad-leaved forests in the Middle Holocene.

In addition to peat, lake and alluvial deposits, sporo-pollen analyses included relict soils exposed locally in the river valleys. In the Aragvi basin the relict soils occur near Zhinvali at a depth of 3 m. The spectrum showed a predominance of tree species, with pollen of oak, hornbeam, maple and elm being the most common. A great variety of herbs were recorded. This is quite natural, as "the oak-grove flora is characterized by abundance and diversity of species, and also reflects comparatively well specific features of botanical-geographical regions" (Dolukhanov 1955).

The spectrum from the Kaishauri district (1750-1800 m above sea level) showed a high content of pine, fir and beech. As for the herbaceous pollen, sedges are dominant, grasses, Caryophyllaceae and Umbelliferae occurring in smaller quantities. In the Middle Holocene, beech forests with an admixture of fir expanded. Pine forests were comparatively restricted. The Middle Holocene deposits contained oak pollen, suggesting that oak became more common and grew at higher altitudes than it does today.

In Kvemo Kartli herbaceous and shrub formations remained prevalent in the Middle Holocene. However, at the same time the role of oak increased and the proportion of arid open woodland went up. The floodplain forest species were still scarce.

In Gare Kakheti (basin of the river Iori) the forest vegetation changed most significantly in the Middle Holocene. At that time the area of mixed lowland forest in humid habitats decreased. These forests lacked Pterocarya, walnut and plane-tree; meanwhile, the oak species became predominant. In this period the present-day oak-hornbeam hemixerophyte piedmont belt was formed. The pine was pushed back up to the eroded slopes of the Tsivigombori Range.

In Shida Kakheti (basin of the river Alazani) the area of mixed lowland forest expanded in the Middle Holocene. The foothills were covered with hornbeam forests. Beech forests of the early Middle Holocene formed a separate belt and only seldom extended down to the lowlands. In this particular case we were not able to isolate specific zones that might indicate changes in the forest composition, because the forest cover in these locations has not changed and only in the Early Holocene did beech forests descend to a level 200-300 m below their present border limit.

Thus, the Middle Holocene was a period of maximum forest cover in the territory of eastern Georgia. Most of this region was covered with oak forests, with occasional areas of arid open woodland combined with herb-shrubby vegetation. The riverside areas along the most important rivers of eastern Georgia were covered with flood-plain forests. At the end of the Middle Holocene the area of lowland and piedmont forests began to decline gradually.

3 LATE BRONZE AGE OCCUPATION

The relations between man and nature present one of the basic points in the study of the Holocene. We know that the environment played an important role in the life and activity of primitive man. But we also know that man himself has always played and is still playing an important part in the process of destruction and re-establishment of natural ecological systems. After the review of the Middle Holocene vegetation we shall present archaeological data on the density of the human population in eastern Georgia at that time in order to show where people settled and what was the basis of their livelihood and everyday activity.

The Middle Holocene period (8000-3000 BP) ranges from the early Eneolithic cultures to the Late Bronze Age. This has been confirmed by archaeological evidence and corresponding radiocarbon datings. The Early Eneolithic cultures in Georgia are generally dated to the 6th millennium BC and these cultures seem to be synchronous with the Early Chalcolithic cultures of West Asia (Kavtaradze 1981).

Omitting here datings for separate stages of the Middle and Late Eneolithic and the Early and Middle Bronze Age, we shall give only detailed datings for the Late Bronze Age, which coincided with the end of the Middle Holocene.

The Late Bronze Age in eastern Georgia had three phases. Phase I dates from the middle of the 16th century to the early 14th century BC. Phase II is dated back to 1297±274 BC, i.e. 13th/14th century BC. Phase III culture was found in Kakheti, in the basins of the rivers Iori and Alazani, and in Shida Kartli. The third phase begins in the 13th century BC (Kavtaradze 1981).

The territory of eastern Georgia was quite densely populated in the Middle Holocene, as confirmed by the numerous relics of the past. Farming and cattle breeding were the principle spheres of man's activity. It should be kept in mind that "in those times the standard of farming still depended on the environment. A great part of the territory of eastern Georgia (mountains and forest stands) seemed to be unsuitable for farming, while conditions were quite favourable in the valleys of the lowlands of Shida and Kvemo Kartli and in the Alazani valley" (Pitskhelauri 1979:45).

The material cultures in the territory of eastern Georgia were confined to the lowlands and the adjacent piedmont areas. In the Middle Holocene these lands were covered with lowland oak and piedmont broad-leaved forests. It is quite natural that people settled in the zone of oak forests since they "knew that these forests stood on the most fertile land which they needed so badly" (Fizhenko 1911:4).

It is noteworthy that the settlements arose in accord with the environment. In Kvemo Kartli cyclopean or simple stone structures were common. In Shida Kartli people occupied hills, terraces and plains, building earth structures there. In Gare Kakheti they settled on mountain slopes in unsheltered spots. In Shida Kakheti both the mountain slopes and the valleys were populated (Muskhelishvili 1960:40; Grigolia and Tatishvili 1960:70-80; Tskitishvili 1960:86; Berdzenishvili 1964:5-6; Chubinishvili 1965:8-9; Pitskhelauri 1979: 10).

The character of man's economic activity was quite an important factor in the distribution of human settlements. Numerous finds of farming tools, thick culture layers and multi-storeyed burials in various sites of eastern Georgia testify to the success of agriculture in the economy of the people. These witnesses of the past are Khovle, Kantlikhevi, Napargora, Tsikhiagora, Mochrili Gora, Rtskhilis Seri, Chaliankhevi-A. Multi-storeyed burials were discovered in Bakurtsikhe, Samtavro, Gulgula, Melaani, Chalianis Khevi, Khirsa, Kaspi and elsewehre (Pitskhelauri 1979). Farming tools were found in barrow no 2 in Ulyanovka (Lagodekhi district), in Bakurtsikhe, Melaani, Beshtasheni, Tsoisi, Churiekhevi, Uriatubani, Meligele, in Shida Kartli, where the so-called "Kokhi" stones of threshing boards were found, etc. (Nioradze 1934; Apakidze 1940; Japaridze 1961; Abramishvili 1965; Tskitishvili 1960, 1964; Muskhelishvili 1960; Kikvidze 1960; and others). It can be stated that all the lands suitable for farming were cultivated in the Early Bronze Age (Munchaev 1975:38) and in the later phases of the Bronze Age.

Besides agriculture, the native people were engaged in cattle breeding, "both of these branches of economy existing and developing simultaneously" (Japaridze 1961: 208).

4 HUMAN IMPACT

By the end of the Middle Holocene a gradual decline of the lowland forest areas began to show, due to the growing human impact. Owing to the changes in the vegetal landscape and to the rapacious exploitation of the fauna, the numbers and ranges of some mammals were reduced. "In the second half of the Middle Holocene the Caucasian aurochs became completely extinct in the territory of eastern Georgia, ... the numbers and range of beaver, wild horse, elk, chamois and many other large mammals inhabiting the territory of Georgia were also reduced" (Bendukizde 1979).

Thus man, whose economic activity had started already before the Middle Holocene, began to cultivate the comparatively extensive areas of Shida Kartli, Kvemo Kartli, Shida Kakheti and Gare Kakheti. Besides other factors, this process was made possible by a favourable environment: flat, open country with patches of forest biocoenoses, rich soils and herbage.

Developing further his economic activity, man went on destroying the forest stands, changing the landscape, rendering rare animals extinct. Palynological studies have revealed that this process was especially intensive in the Late Holocene.

REFERENCES

Abramishvili, R.M. 1964.
  Archaeological excavations in the Lagodekhi District. Tbilisi, OSIIAE and GKM 1.
Apakidze, A.M. 1940.
  Archaeological relics of Bakurtsikhe. Manuscript in the Library of the Tbilisi University.
Bendukidze, O.G. 1979.
  The Holocene vertebrate fauna in Georgia. Tbilisi: Metsniereba.
Berdzenishvili, D.K. 1964.
  Historical-geographical questions of Bolnisi. Tbilisi, SIGG 2.

Chubinishvili, T.N. 1965.
  Results of field studies of the
  Meskhet-Javakhetian archaeologi-
  cal expedition in 1964.
Dolukhanov, A.G. 1955.
  Typological characteristics of
  mountain forests of Georgian and
  Oriental oak. Transactions of the
  Tbilisi Institute of Botany 17.
Fizhenko, V.A. 1911.
  The fate of the oak forest in
  Transcaucasia, "Lesnoi Zhurnal".
Grigolia, G.K. and T.I.Tatishvili
  1960. The oldest relics of Kvemo
  Kartli. Tbilisi, SIGG 1.
Japaridze, O.M. 1961.
  On the history of Georgian tribes
  at the early stage of the Copper-
  Bronze culture. Tbilisi.
Kavtaradze, G.L. 1981.
  Chronology of archaeological cul-
  tures in Georgia in the Eneoli-
  thic and Bronze Ages, based on
  recent data. Tbilisi: Metsnie-
  reba.
Ketskhoveli, N.N. 1960.
  The plant cover of Georgia.
  Tbilisi: Metsniereba.
Kikvidze, J.A. 1976.
  Agriculture and agricultural cult
  in ancient Georgia. Tbilisi.
Munchaev, R.M. 1975.
  The Caucasus at the dawn of the
  Bronze Age. Moscow, Nauka.
Muskhelishvili, D.L. 1960.
  The results of field studies of a
  historical-geographical expedi-
  tion in Kvemo Kartli (1956-1958).
  Tbilisi, SIGG 1.
Nioradze, G.K. 1934.
  "The Glass-works" burial. Moscow-
  Leningrad, PIDO 3.
Pitskhelauri, K.N. 1979.
  Eastern Georgia in the end of the
  Bronze Age. Tbilisi: Metsniereba.
Sharashidze, R.V. 1967.
  Zelkova groves in Georgia. Tbili-
  si: Metsniereba.
Tskitishvili, G.G. 1960.
  Tsopi (a historical-geographical
  review). Tbilisi, SIGG 1.
Tsikitshvili, G.G. 1964.
  Everyday life and economy in
  Khovlegora. Tbilisi, NSOIIG 2.

Man's Role in the Shaping of the Eastern Mediterranean Landscape, Bottema, Entjes-Nieborg & van Zeist (eds)
© *1990 Balkema, Rotterdam. ISBN 90 6191 138 9*

Deforestation in Southern Jordan:
Evidence from fossil Hyrax middens

21

Patricia L. Fall
Department of Geography, Arizona State University, Tempe, Ariz., USA

ABSTRACT: Deposits formed by the Syrian rock hyrax have been preserved in the rock crevices of Petra, Jordan, for almost 2000 years. These deposits, or middens, contain pollen and plant macrofossils that characterize the surrounding vegetation. It is hypothesized that human disturbance degraded the Mediterranean forests of southern Jordan prior to the second century AD. A dramatic decline in arboreal pollen marks the end of imperial city life in Petra. This may be the legacy of several centuries of wood harvesting to supply the urban center of Petra with building material and fuel during the Roman and Byzantine periods. The drop in pollen from Olea, an important cultivated tree, may also implicate reduced maintenance and eventual abandonment of orchards and complex irrigation after the 4th century AD. Intensified browsing by livestock and continued human impact reduced the vegetation further to steppe following the collapse of Byzantine townlife at Petra.

1 INTRODUCTION

The beginning of plant and animal husbandry, and human population growth in the Neolithic Period began a long cycle of human impact on the natural environment. This is readily evident in the Middle East, where a deeply humanized landscape has evolved through millennia of clearing fields for farming, removal of woody vegetation by burning, harvesting of wood to fuel ovens and kilns, and intentional planting or encouragement of desired species. Probably the major impact of prehistoric man on the environment resulted from animal husbandry (Uerpmann pers. comm.). Clearing land for pasture and collecting fodder for livestock, as well as grazing and browsing by domestic animals have altered vegetation substantially. Some taxa may have become locally extinct; others may be more common than they were in the past. Still others have evolved techniques for defense against herbivores (e.g., by developing spines and barbs or poisons), or have utilized animals to distribute and

fertilize their seeds. Certainly the distribution of plants and relative abundance of taxa have changed through their coevolution with domestic animals.

The roles of direct human impact and mankind's indirect impact through domesticated animals on the environments of the Middle East, and their influence on the evolution of the modern landscape may best be determined through palaeobotanical studies. Isolated trees, often preserved intentionally or in places least accessible to animals and man, testify to the climatic potential for more extensive forests and woodlands. Although modern remnant vegetation offers a few tantalizing clues, it cannot reveal the distribution of plants and animals on the presettlement landscape. This paper introduces a new technique, hyrax midden analysis, as a means to illuminate past plant communities and the legacy of human exploitation in the Middle East. Preliminary results based on this technique demonstrate a reduction of woody vegetation in southern Jordan over the last 2000 years.

Palaeoecological studies in the Middle East are limited by the relatively few mesic depositional basins suitable for fossil plant preservation. In the deserts of North America, analyses of plant fragments and pollen in fossilized packrat middens have provided useful records of past plant ecology. Animals in other desert regions of the world create deposits that may be of comparable value in reconstructing past environments. Fossil middens of the stick nest rat, Leporillus, have been collected from Australia (Green et al. 1983). Middle Holocene age deposits made by Cricetidae or Chinchillidae rodents have been found in Argentina. Fossil nests from South Africa are attributed to dassie rat (Petromus) and hyrax (Procaviidae) (Scott in press). "Guano" from hyrax deposits in the Sahara was found to contain a rich pollen assemblage of Mediterranean flora, demonstrating that a different flora flourished in North Africa under wetter climatic conditions during the mid-Holocene (Pons and Quézel 1958). In 1985, fossilized deposits made by Procavia capensis syriaca were found in the sandstone outcrops of Petra (Fig. 1). Radiocarbon analyses confirmed their antiquity (Fall et al. in press).

Although middens made by animals from different desert regions of the world are being investigated for their palaeobotanical potential, thus far midden analysis has been utilized primarily in North America over the last 25 years for analysis of deposits made by packrats (Neotoma spp.). This technique is based on the assumption that the animals are nonmigratory and collect plants growing near their nests. In general, animals with non-discriminating tastes are most useful for obtaining samples of past vegetation. Plant fragments and fecal pellets become covered with the animal's urine that crystallizes, thereby forming rock-hard deposits or indurated middens.

Modern middens may be found in open settings, but fossilized remains are only preserved in arid rock crevices and caves. Each midden is radiocarbon dated and, generally, is treated as a single depositional unit, although there

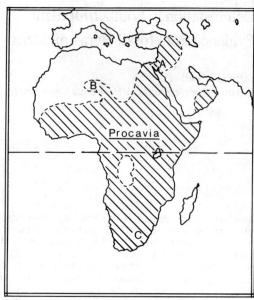

Fig. 1. Geographic distribution of Procavia. Fossil midden localities are reported from Petra (A), the Hoggar Mountains, North Africa (B), and South Africa (C).

are middens which have been formed over thousands of years. Over 1100 radiocarbon dates have been obtained from packrat middens, with the age of the deposits extending beyond the limits of radiocarbon (greater than 50,000 years BP) (Webb 1986; Webb and Betancourt in press). One additional advantage of midden research over palynological investigations is that the identification of plant fragments often can proceed to the level of species.

Packrat middens have been used to test anomalous plant associations [e.g., Sonoran desert taxa growing with woodland species (Van Devender et al. 1987); and limber pine and shadscale (Spaulding 1981)], and to test concepts of plants as communities or individuals (Cole 1981; Spaulding 1981). Holocene migration of plant species across several degrees of latitude over thousands of years has been documented through midden research (Thompson 1984). Fossil plant fragments in packrat middens have been used to record the dispersal of plants by animals, including man (e.g., Betancourt 1987), into new habitats. Destruction of woodland vegetation by the prehistoric inhabitants of Chaco Canyon, New Mexico, has been hypothesized from midden research (Betancourt and Van Devender 1981). Perhaps most significantly, midden analyses in the deserts and steppes of North America have demonstrated elevational displacement of plants and redistribution of species during the latest Pleistocene and throughout the Holocene in response to changing climates (Spaulding et al. 1983).

Based on this enormous potential, only now reaching fruition, midden research was initiated in the arid deserts and steppes of the Middle East (Fall et al. in press). Hyrax deposits were collected from Petra in southern Jordan because the region had a long and varied history of land use extending back to the beginnings of agriculture and animal domestication. It is assumed that changes in species composition documented by hyrax deposits reflect changes in the vegetation which, at least during the last few thousand years, were most likely influenced by human activities. Although climatic shifts may help explain some cultural changes in the Middle East, mankind's own impact on the environment has been a pervasive factor in changing settlement and economic patterns.

2 ENVIRONMENTAL SETTING

The ancient city of Petra, at approximately 1000 m elevation, lies in the southernmost mountains of Transjordan, along the eastern edge of the African rift system (Fig. 2). To the west, the Wadi Araba averages 100-200 m elevation, but drops to 396 m below sea level approximately 90 km to the north. The hills northeast of Petra climb to 1736 m before they give way to the Syrian Desert to the east.

2.1 Climate

The climate of southern Jordan is an arid Saharan variant of a Mediterranean climate characterized by mild, rainy winters and hot, dry summers. Winter temperatures usually fall below 0°C, with snow recorded almost every year, while

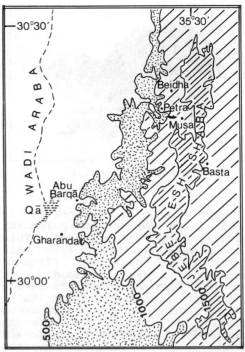

Fig. 2. Topographical map of the region around Petra, southern Jordan. Countour interval is 500 m.

summer temperatures reach 35°-40°C. Precipitation is concentrated between November and April. Mean annual precipitation measures 170 mm at the nearby town of Wadi Musa (Raikes 1966). Mean annual rainfall in the hills near Shobak at 1400 m elevation is 298 mm (Al-Eisawi 1984). The hill slopes above Petra to the east are estimated to receive 200-300 mm of rainfall per year. Zohary (1960) places Petra in the sub-Mediterranean vegetation belt which requires at least 200 mm rainfall per year.

2.2 Vegetation

The vegetation of southern Jordan includes floristic elements from the four major vegetation regions in southwestern Asia. Petra lies near the southern limit of the Mediterranean and Irano-Turanian vegetation territories, and at the northern edge of the Saharo-Arabian and Sudanian vegetation regions (Zohary 1973).

273

Fig. 3. Procavia capensis.

The highlands above Petra (1500-1700 m) are covered with a remnant Mediterranean type forest. This impoverished maquis of Quercus calliprinos with occasional Pistacia atlantica trees represents the southern terminus of Mediterranean vegetation in Southwestern Asia. Daphne linearifolia and Crataegus aronia are common Mediterranean shrubs in this forest type (Zohary 1973). Isolated trees of Cupressus sempervirens, Ceratonia siliqua, and Olea europaea survive in the maquis. Irano-Turanian elements form an understory dominated by the dwarf shrub Artemisia herba-alba. Centaurea damascena, Retama raetam, and Noaea mucronata are also common taxa (Zohary 1973). Artemisia herba-alba, which dominates the limestone slopes between 1100 and 1600 m elevation, "is the first (shrub) to penetrate into Mediterranean arboreal communities of the borderland affected by man and to make up the undergrowth in these cleared woods" (Zohary 1940:75).

Juniperus phoenicea and Artemisia herba-alba form an open steppe forest on sandstone between 800 and 1300 m elevation. Occasional trees of Pistacia atlantica and Crataegus aronia also can be found on these slopes. Thymelaea hirsuta, Ephedra campylopoda, and Ononis natrix are common elements of the semi-steppe batha. Steppe elements include Artemisia herba-alba, Hammada salicornia, and Anabasis articulata. Noaea mucronata and Peganum harmala invade ruined Artemisia steppe (Zohary 1973). Desert vegetation growing below 900 m elevation includes Zygophyllum dumosum, Ephedra alte, Salsola tetrandra, Suaeda asphaltica, S. aegyptiaca, and Heli-anthemum spp., with Retama raetam growing along wadi beds.

The vegetation in the Valley of Petra includes a diverse array of plants. Juniperus phoenicea, the most common tree in the valley, occurs with the Mediterranean maquis species Pistacia palaestina. In addition, the showy shrubs Nerium oleander and Capparis cartilaginea are common locally along drainages.

2.3 Ecology of the Syrian rock hyrax

The rock hyrax, Procavia capensis (order Hyracoidea) (Fig. 3), ranges throughout Africa, Arabia, Sinai and the Syrian Desert from sea level to 4500 m elevation (Walker 1975). The subspecies Procavia capensis syriaca (Schreber) lives in Sinai, Jordan, Palestine, Lebanon, and Syria (Olds and Shoshani 1982). The rock hyrax is a small, subungulate mammal, similar in size to a pika or a small marmot. Its closest evolutionary relative, however remote, is the elephant. It inhabits rocky terrain and favours steep mountains with numerous crevices and caves. The hyrax's unusual feet have naked elastic pads on the ends of each digit that contract into suction cups and permit climbing on precipitous exposures (Harrison 1968).

The gregarious rock hyrax lives in colonies that normally average about ten individuals but may include hundreds (Lynch 1983). The rock hyrax is primarily a diurnal browser or grazer that "will feed on almost any plant, preferring to feed near to the crevices" where it lives (Harrison 1968:320). Hyraxes need very little water to survive and can travel more than 600 m to drink (Dorst 1970). Their middens are made up of numerous plant parts, fecal pellets, and faunal remains, including snail shells. These deposits, which can be quite large (e.g., 64,000 cc), are hardened and preserved by hyracium, a substance in the animals' urine.

3 HISTORY OF HUMAN SETTLEMENT

The cultural history of the Petra area extends back to the Palaeolithic (Schyle and Uerpmann 1988), and is marked by dramatic fluctuations in human population and subsistence practices. Natufian settlement at the ancient village of Beidha, 8 km north of Petra, began in the eighth millennium bc (Kirkbride 1966; Byrd 1988). While experimentation with potential domesticates may have started at this time, the earliest evidence for local plant and animal domestication comes from subsequent Pre-Pottery Neolithic deposits (about 7000-6500 bc) (Helbaek 1966; Perkins 1966). Recent excavations at the site of Basta (Gebel et al. 1988) southeast of Petra augment this evidence from Beidha. Together these communities attest to a substantial local Neolithic population. Deforestation could have begun at this time. Use of fuelwood for plastered floor and walls at Beidha (Kirkbride 1966) and at Basta (Gebel et al. 1988), as well as reliance on sheep and goat husbandry, could have initiated a long-term process of deforestation and overgrazing in the greater Petra environment. Hyrax bones recovered from Neolithic Beidha suggest this animal's presence in the Petra area during the last nine thousand years of human settlement (Perkins 1966; Kirkbride 1984).

Evidence of settlement in the Petra area between the Neolithic and Nabataean periods is sporadic and poorly understood. Late Iron Age settlement (approximately 800-600 BC) at Tawilan and atop the hill of Umm al-Biyara relate to the Edomites of the Old Testament (Bennett 1964, 1966, 1971). Increasing local populations in this and subsequent periods most likely renewed the clearing of forests and grazing of livestock.

Petra (ancient Reqem), the Nabataean capital, emerged as a commercial trading center between the Mediterranean basin, Arabia, and the Orient by 312 BC (Negev 1986; Hammond 1973). The local economy was tethered to the larger exchange system of the Roman Empire. The Nabataean Kingdom was annexed formally by Rome to the province of Arabia in AD 106, and it remained under Roman administration until the establishment of the Byzantine Empire in AD 395. Under Byzantine imperial rule the lands of the eastern Mediterranean experienced population growth on a scale surpassed only in the twentieth century (Avi-Yonah 1958, 1966; Broshi 1979).

The city and its gardens and orchards were supported by elaborate water conservation methods (see Evenari et al. 1971 on Nabataean hydraulic engineering). Rock-cut channels and terra cotta pipes carried springwater and rain-fall runoff to cisterns chiseled out of the surrounding sandstone hills. Although Petra was a distant colonial city in both the Roman and Byzantine empires, the impact of its inhabitants on the natural environment would have been enormous.

Byzantine authority collapsed rapidly following the Battle of the Yarmouk in AD 636, and subsequent Muslim administration of the Levant was guided by very different commercial and political interests (Sharon 1969). Southern Jordan was no longer a nexus for trade with the Mediterranean, nor was it a border area worthy of government subsidy. Now denied larger imperial investment, Petra's inhabitants became increasingly reliant on sheep and goat pastoralism and local resources. From the seventh century to the present the Petra area has been characterized by a diminished, less sedentary population and intensive grazing with continued impact on the landscape. Modern technology induced a very pronounced episode of deforestation during the First World War when the Ottoman government decimated the remnant woodlands of southern Jordan for fuelwood to be used by the Hejaz Railway (Mousa 1982).

4 HYRAX MIDDENS

Over three days in 1985 eight hardened, or indurated, middens were collected from crevices in the mountain of Amm Seseban, and a modern midden (Petra 1) was found along the Siq, a narrow rock gorge that forms the eastern entrance to the valley (Fall et al. in press). Three of the middens (Petra 2, Petra 6, and Petra 9) have been radiocarbon dated. The unindurated midden (Petra 1) and pollen from a surface soil sample from Amm Sese-

275

Table 1. Radiocarbon ages of hyrax middens from southern Jordan.

Midden #	Radiocarbon Years BP	Calendar Years AD (1 Sigma)
Petra 2	1120 ± 110 (A-4529)	790-1020
Petra 9	1580 ± 65 (GX-13060)	420-550
Petra 6	1750 ± 60 (GX-13059)	160-390

ban provide modern analogs. The deposits from Petra are attributed to hyraxes for three reasons. First, Bedouin informants verified that the deposits were made by hyraxes. In addition, fecal pellets from the Jordanian middens were comparable in size and shape to modern fecal pellets from South African hyraxes (provided by Louis Scott). Finally, radionuclide analysis showed that proteins in crystallized urine from Petra 2 reacted with anti-hyrax serum (W. Rainey, pers. comm. 1987).

It is assumed that hyraxes sample the vegetation near their dens, and that plant fragments and pollen in the deposits characterize the vegetation near the den at the time the midden was created. In addition, some of the pollen is thought to be derived from the regional vegetation. Palynological analyses of packrat middens in North America show that pollen in packrat middens represents the surrounding vegetation in a broad sense even though it may be skewed by selective gathering by the animals. Pollen from packrat middens may be highly variable, but it may accurately reflect changes "of the magnitude of a shift from woodland to desert-scrub" (Thompson 1985:103). Similarly, pollen in hyrax middens comes both from the local and regional vegetation, and may reflect a preference for certain taxa by the hyrax.

4.1 Methods

The outer surfaces of the indurated hyrax middens were scraped and brushed to remove possible contamination. Samples of each midden, weighing 200-250 g, were soaked in a solution of water and dilute HCl to disaggregate the midden and free the plant fragments. After soaking, the plant fragments and sediments were washed through a 1-mm mesh screen. Material remaining on the screen was dried and sorted for plant fragments, seeds, faunal remains, and insects. Samples of fecal pellets (approximately 8.5 g each) were used for radiocarbon analyses.

Multiple pollen samples from each indurated midden (10-30 g) were soaked in water to dissolve the cementing matrix, sieved to remove larger plant fragments, washed thoroughly in distilled water to remove the hyrax urine, and then processed with HCl, HF, acetolysis mixture (Faegri and Iversen 1975) and KOH. The entire loose modern midden was soaked in water. The resulting liquid and sediment were concentrated and processed for pollen analysis. Unknown and unidentifiable pollen grains are included in the total pollen sums. Tablets of Lycopodium spores (Lund Batch no. 414831) added to each sample allowed calculation of pollen concentrations. Pollen concentrations range from 20,000 to 100,000 grains/g dry weight in the fossil middens, and are 4500 grains /g in the modern unindurated midden.

4.2 Radiocarbon dating

Radiocarbon ages ranging from 1750 BP to 1120 BP place the indurated middens in periods of distinctly different local economy and land use (Fall et al. in press) (Table 1).

Calibration to calendric years (based on Pearson 1983) suggests that Petra 6 and Petra 9 might date to the Roman and Byzantine periods, respectively. However, overlapping 95% confidence intervals show that the ages of these middens are not significantly different. Therefore, middens 6 and 9 are both interpreted with reference to Petra's

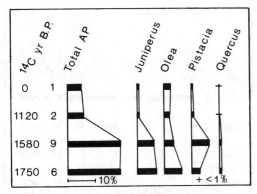

Fig. 4. Arboreal pollen frequencies for each of the four middens. Total arboreal pollen includes Juniperus, Pistacia, Olea, Quercus, Pinus, and Ziziphus.

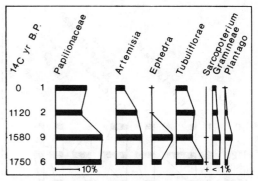

Fig. 5. Shrub and herb pollen frequencies. Papilionaceae includes three taxa.

Roman/Byzantine imperial affluence, while midden 2 reflects the city's post-imperial decline, and midden 1 serves as a modern analog for comparison of past and present plant material. Petra 1 is considered modern because it contains pollen from Eucalyptus, a tree introduced in the twentieth century.

5 DISCUSSION OF RESULTS

Changes in pollen frequencies in hyrax middens reveal past vegetation in the Petra area. Pollen taxa that vary significantly within a single midden, or have anomalously high frequencies in one midden are thought to be influenced, at least partially, by the collecting behaviour of the animals (Fall et al. in press). These types include Papilionaceae, Ephedra, Umbelliferae, Urticaceae, Boraginaceae, Liguliflorae, and Capparis. Pollen taxa which are more homogeneous within a midden include Juniperus, Olea, Pistacia, Quercus, Artemisia, Gramineae, Tubuliflorae, Chenopodiaceae/Amaranthaceae (Fall et al. in press). These taxa, constituting a "background signal," are the major types used in the following interpretation of past vegetation.

Total arboreal pollen (including Juniperus, Pistacia, Olea, Quercus, Pinus, and Ziziphus) occurs at very similar frequencies in the Roman/Byzantine middens (Petra 6 and Petra 9), and in the Islamic and modern middens (Petra 2 and Petra 1, respectively) (Fig. 4). However, a drastic decline in arboreal pollen marks the aftermath of imperial city life in Petra. When compared to Petra 6 or Petra 9, middens 2 and 1 reflect significant decreases in specific taxa: Pistacia, Juniperus, Olea and Quercus. This pervasive decrease in arboreal pollen may be the legacy of several centuries of Roman/Byzantine wood harvesting to supply a substantial urban population with building material and fuel. The drop in pollen from Olea, an important cultivated tree, also may implicate reduced maintenance and eventual abandonment of orchards and complex irrigation after the fourth century AD.

Pollen from shrubs and herbs also diminishes after the Roman/Byzantine Period in Petra (Fig. 5). This vegetation includes grasses, the woody shrubs Artemisia and Ephedra, and taxa in the subfamilies Papilionaceae and Tubuliflorae. Sarcopoterium and Plantago are also slightly more common prior to 1120 BP. Thus, a second component of Petra's natural vegetation was decimated over a span of centuries, probably by widespread foraging of domestic livestock. Pollen taxa that show significant increases after the Roman and Byzantine periods and may indicate disturbance are Thymelaeaceae, Chenopodiaceae/Amaranthaceae, Urticaceae, Umbelliferae, Liliaceae, and Cistaceae (Fig. 6). Capparis, Boraginaceae, and Liguliflorae flourished in the modern midden (Fig. 7). Unknown and indeterminant pollen

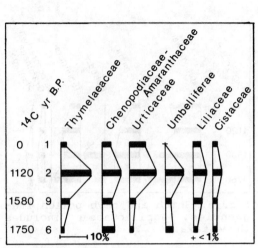

Fig. 6. Disturbance pollen taxa that show significant increases in middens 2 and 1.

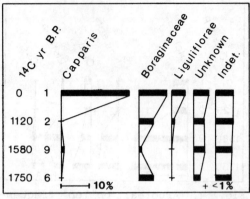

Fig. 7. Three pollen taxa that show significant increases in the modern midden. Frequencies of unknown and indeterminant taxa are relatively consistent in all four middens.

types are relatively consistent throughout the sequence.

5.1 Comparison of pollen from hyrax middens with modern surface samples

Pollen spectra from hyrax middens in southern Jordan are compared with modern pollen data from surface samples collected in Syria and Lebanon (Bottema and Barkoudah 1979) to broadly characterize the vegetation palynologically. Many of the same species and virtually all of the most abundant genera are common to both southern Jordan and Syria-Lebanon, enabling a very generalized comparison between pollen spectra from major plant zones (e.g., Mediterranean forest, steppe-forest, and steppe).

Bottema and Barkoudah (1979) present pollen data for 85 modern surface samples from several variations of Mediterranean forests, degraded Mediterranean forest, steppe-forest, foreststeppe, and steppe and desertsteppe. The most abundant arboreal pollen types in each of these broad zones include Quercus (two types), Pistacia, Olea, Pinus, and Juniperus. These are the same genera used to calculate the total arboreal pollen sums for the Petra hyrax middens. Average arboreal pollen frequencies in the modern surface samples from Syria and Lebanon are compared with

arboreal pollen percentages from the middens in southern Jordan.

Bottema and Barkoudah (1979) found that total arboreal pollen percentages ranged from 40 to 85% in the Mediterranean forest zones. (Unusually high Pinus pollen percentages in one of their zones account for the value of 85% arboreal pollen.) Average arboreal pollen is about 25% in "degraded" Mediterranean forests, and 22% and 18% in the steppe-forest and forest-steppe zones, respectively. Arboreal pollen averages 10% or less in the steppe and desert-steppe zones (Bottema and Barkoudah 1979).

Based on these modern analogs, total arboreal pollen percentages of 17% and 19% in hyrax middens 6 and 9 suggest that the vegetation during the Roman and Byzantine occupation of Petra was a degraded Mediterranean forest or forest-steppe. Total arboreal pollen drops to 6% in midden 2, dated approximately between AD 790 and AD 1020, and to 5% in the modern midden. Similarly, a modern surface pollen sample collected from Amm Seseban (1100 m) contains less than 9% arboreal pollen (Juniperus accounts for almost 7%). These middens, which postdate AD 550, are most analogous to surface samples from steppe or desert-steppe vegetation in Syria and Lebanon. It is suggested that intense utilization of the environment by the people of

278

Petra, and increased pastoralism (promoting intensive browsing by goats) following the collapse of Byzantine rule further reduced the vegetation around Petra to the denuded steppe or batha of today.

Modern vegetation on the hill slopes above Petra clearly represents a ruined Mediterranean oak-pistachio forest. Steppe elements have invaded and now form the understory of this batha. Closely trimmed lower tree branches suggest the continued heavy impact of browsing goats. Understory taxa are heavily grazed, permitting few seedlings to survive in this denuded environment. In Petra trees cling to cliffs and crevices, away from agile ungulates, while toxic species (Nerium oleander and Capparis cartilaginea) flourish along dry stream beds and in seeps in the sandstone walls.

5.2 Plant macrofossils

Although the analysis of plant macrofossils is not yet complete, a few points relevant to this discussion can be made. The most abundant plant macrofossils are Juniperus phoenicea, Ephedra spp., and Thymelaea hirsuta. Hyraxes probably favour these taxa for food or nest building. Ficus seeds are found in all middens and are particularly abundant in Petra 2 and Petra 1. Ficus carica, the domesticated fig, is cultivated widely in the region, and is a tree common in the canyons of Petra. An old Ficus tree grows about 100 m from the Petra 1 locality, which probably accounts for the abundance of Ficus seeds in this midden. A single Vitis vinifera seed was found in Petra 2. Grape also has been an important cultigen in the Middle East since the Early Bronze Age (Zohary and Spiegel-Roy 1975).

No plant fragments of Pinus, Quercus, or Ziziphus were found, and only one seed of Olea europaea and a few Anacardiaceae (cf. Pistacia) seeds were found in the analyzed hyrax middens. The majority of the pollen from these arboreal taxa most likely results from wind transport to the middens and does not directly reflect hyrax collecting behavior. As mentioned above, Juniperus macrofossils are common in the hyrax middens, and pollen deposition from this tree may be partially influenced by the hyrax.

6 CONCLUSIONS

Given a suitable environment for preservation, there is every reason to anticipate that hyrax middens can provide a fossil record of vegetation in the Middle East much as packrat middens have in the deserts of North America.

These data suggest a plausible explanation for the demise of arboreal vegetation in the Petra area. It is hypothesized that human disturbance degraded the Mediterranean forests of southern Jordan to a maquis or garique prior to the second century AD. Intensified browsing by livestock and continued human impact further reduced this vegetation to a Mediterranean batha or steppe following the collapse of Byzantine town life at Petra.

7 ACKNOWLEDGEMENTS

Many individuals have been instrumental in this study. I thank my co-authors on a previous publication, C.A. Lindquist and S.E. Falconer. Field assistance was provided by Dakhilallah Qublan, Harun Dakhilallah, S.E. Falconer, C.A. Lindquist, and H. Lindquist. The Department of Antiquities of Jordan issued a permit to collect middens in Petra, and the American Center of Oriental Research provided a jeep and research facilities in Amman. A. Long and C.A. Lindquist funded the radiocarbon dates, A. Linick calibrated the dates, and W. Rainey conducted the protein antiserum analysis. Pollen identifications were possible through the generous assistance of E. Van Campo and M. Van Campo at the Laboratoire de Palynologie, Montpellier, and R. Bonnefille and G. Riollet at the Laboratoire de Géologie du Quaternaire, Marseille. S.E. Falconer provided editorial comments.

REFERENCES

Al-Eisawi, D.M. 1984.
  Vegetation in Jordan. In A.Hadidi (ed.), Studies in the history and archaeology of Jordan, Vol. 2, p.

45-57. Amman, Department of Antiquities.

Avi-Yonah, M. 1958.
The economics of Byzantine Palestine. Israel Exploration Journal 8(1):39-51.

Avi-Yonah, M. 1966.
The Holy Land from the Persian to the Arab conquests (536 B.C. to A.D. 640). A historical geography. Grand Rapids, Michigan: Baker Book House.

Bennett, C.-M. 1964.
Chronique archéologique: Umm el-Biyara. Revue biblique 71:250-253.

Bennett, C.-M. 1966.
Fouilles d'Umm el-Biyara: rapport préliminaire. Revue biblique 73: 372-403.

Bennett, C.-M. 1971.
A brief note on excavations at Tawilan, Jordan, 1968-1970. Levant 3:v-vii.

Betancourt, J.L. 1987.
Paleoecology of pinyon-juniper woodlands: Summary. In R.Everett (ed.), Proceedings of the Pinyon-Juniper Conference. Ogden, Utah, U.S. Department of Agriculture General Technical Report INT-215: 129-139.

Betancourt, J.L.
and T.R.Van Devender 1981.
Holocene vegetation in Chaco Canyon, New Mexico. Science 214: 656-658.

Bottema, S. and Y.Barkoudah 1979.
Modern pollen precipitation in Syria and Lebanon and its relation to vegetation. Pollen et Spores 21/4:427-480.

Broshi, M. 1979.
The population of Western Palestine in the Roman-Byzantine Period. Bulletin of the American Schools of Oriental Research 236:1-10.

Byrd, B.F. 1988.
The Natufian of Beidha. Report on renewed field research. In A.Garrard and H.G. Gebel (eds.), The prehistory of Jordan. The state of research in 1986, p.175-197. BAR International Series 396.

Cole, K.L. 1981.
Late Quaternary environments in the eastern Grand Canyon: vegetational gradients over the last 25,000 years. PhD thesis, University of Arizona Tucson.

Dorst, J. 1970.
A field guide to arger mammals of Africa. Boston: Houghton Mifflin.

Evenari, M., L.Shanan,
N.Tadmor and Y.Itzhaki 1971.
The Negev: the challenge of a desert. Cambridge, Mass.: Harvard University Press.

Faegri, K. and J.Iversen 1975.
Textbook of pollen analysis, 3rd ed. New York: Hafner.

Fall, P.L., C.A.Lindquist
and S.E.Falconer in press.
Fossil hyrax middens from the Middle East: A record of paleovegetation and human disturbance. In J.Betancourt, T.Van Devender and P.Martin (eds.), Packrat middens: the last 40,000 years of biotic change. Tucson: University of Arizona Press.

Gebel, H.G., M.S.Muheisen,
H.J.Nissen, N.Qadi and J.M.Starck 1988. Preliminary report on the first season of excavations at the Late Aceramic Neolithic site of Basta. In A.Garrard and H.G. Gebel (eds.), The prehistory of Jordan. The state of research in 1986, p.101-134. BAR International Series 396.

Green, N., J.Caldwell,
J.Hope and J.Luly 1983.
Pollen from an 1,800 year old stick-nest rat (Leporillus sp.) midden from Gualta, Western New South Wales. Quaternary Australasia 1:31-41.

Hammond, P.C. 1973.
The Nabataeans - their history, culture and archaeology. Studies in Mediterranean Archaeology 37.

Harrison, D.L. 1968.
The mammals of Arabia, Vol. II. London: Ernest Benn.

Helbaek, H. 1966.
Pre-Pottery Neolithic farming at Beidha. Palestine Exploration Quarterly: 61-66.

Kirkbride, D. 1966.
Five seasons at the Pre-Pottery Neolithic village of Beidha in Jordan. Palestine Exploration Quarterly: 8-61.

Kirkbride, D. 1984.
The environment of the Petra Region during the Pre-Pottery Neolithic. In A.Hadidi (ed.), Studies in the history and archaeology of Jordan, Vol. 2, p. 117-124. Amman, Department of Antiquities.

Lynch, C.D. 1983.
The mammals of the Orange Free State. Memoirs Van Die Nasionale Museum Bloemfontein, No. 18.

Mousa, S. 1982.
Jordan: towards the end of the Ottoman Empire, 1841-1918. In A.Hadidi (ed.), Studies in the history and archaeology of Jordan, Vol. 1, p.385-391. Amman, Department of Antiquities.

Negev, A. 1986.
Nabatean archaeology today. New York: New York University Press.

Olds, N. and J.Shoshani 1982.
Procavia capensis. Mammalian Species 171:1-7.

Pearson, G.W. 1983.
The development of high precision ^{14}C measurement and its application to archaeological time scale problems. PhD thesis, Queen's University Belfast.

Perkins, D. 1966.
The fauna from Madamagh and Beidha. Palestine Exploration Quarterly:66-67.

Pons, A. and P.Quézel 1958.
Premières remarques sur l'étude palynologique d'un guano fossile du Hoggar. Comptes rendus des séances de l'Académie des Sciences 244:2290-2292.

Raikes, R.L. 1966.
Beidha, prehistoric climate and water supply. Palestine Exploration Quarterly:68-72.

Schyle, D. and H.-P.Uerpmann 1988.
Palaeolithic sites in the Petra area. In A.Garrard and H.G.Gebel (eds.), The prehistory of Jordan. The state of research in 1986, p. 39-65. BAR Int. Series 396.

Scott, L. in press.
Hyrax (Procaviidae) and dassie rat (Petromuridae) middens in paleoenvironmental studies in Africa. In J.Betancourt, T.Van Devender and P.Martin (eds.), Packrat middens: the last 40,000 years of biotic change. Tucson: University of Arizona Press.

Sharon, M. 1969.
The history of Palestine from the Arab Conquest until the Crusades (A.D.633-1099). In M.Avi-Yonah (ed.), A history of the Holy Land, p.185-222. Toronto, MacMillan.

Spaulding, W.G. 1981.
The late Quaternary vegetation of a southern Nevada mountain range. PhD thesis, University of Arizona Tucson.

Spaulding, W.G., E.B.Leopold and T.R.Van Devender 1983.
Late Wisconsin paleoecology of the American Southwest. In S.

Porter (ed.), The Late Pleistocene of the United States, p. 259-293. Minneapolis, University of Minnesota Press.

Thompson, R.S. 1984.
Late Pleistocene and Holocene environments in the Great Basin. PhD thesis, University of Arizona, Tucson.

Thompson, R.S. 1985.
Palynology and Neotoma middens. In B.Jacobs, P.Fall and O.Davis (eds.), Late Quaternary vegetation and climates of the American Southwest. American Association of Stratigraphic Palynologists, Contribution Series 16:89-112.

Van Devender, T.R., R.S.Thompson and J.L.Betancourt 1987.
Vegetation history of the deserts of southwestern North America: the nature and timing of the Late Wisconsin-Holocene transition. In W.Ruddiman and H.E.Wright (eds.), North America and adjacent oceans during the last deglaciation. The Geology of North America, Vol. K-3, p.323-352. Boulder, Geological Society of America.

Walker, E.P. 1975.
Mammals of the World, Vol II, 3rd ed. Baltimore: Johns Hopkins.

Webb, R.H. 1986.
Spatial and temporal distribution of radiocarbon ages on rodent middens from the southwestern United States. Radiocarbon 28:1-8.

Webb, R.H. and J.L.Betancourt in press.
Bias in the spatial and temporal distribution of radiocarbon ages from packrat middens. In J.Betancourt, T.Van Devender and P.Martin (eds.), Packrat middens: the last 40,000 years of biotic change. Tucson: University of Arizona Press.

Zohary, D. and P.Spiegel-Roy 1975.
Beginnings of fruit growing in the Old World. Science 187:319-327.

Zohary, M. 1940.
Geobotanical analysis of the Syrian Desert. Palestine Journal of Botany (Jerusalem) 2:46-96.

Zohary, M. 1960.
The maquis of Quercus calliprinos in Israel and Jordan. Bulletin of the Research Council of Israel 90:51-72.

Zohary, M. 1973.
Geobotanical foundations of the Middle East, 2 Vols. Stuttgart: Gustav Fischer.

Man's Role in the Shaping of the Eastern Mediterranean Landscape, Bottema, Entjes-Nieborg & van Zeist (eds)
© *1990 Balkema, Rotterdam. ISBN 90 6191 138 9*

Palynological evidence of human impact on the vegetation as recorded in Late Holocene lake sediments in Israel

22

Uri Baruch

Institute of Archaeology, The Hebrew University, Jerusalem, Israel

ABSTRACT: Three Late Holocene pollen diagrams (one from Lake Kinneret, two from the Dead Sea) are discussed. The vegetational changes reflected in these diagrams are interpreted in terms of the effects of human activity. Until the beginning of the 2nd millennium BC human impact on the vegetation seems to have been only limited. In the course of the 2nd and 1st millennia BC, large-scale forest-clearing activities took place and olive cultivation was practised over the entire region. The decline of agriculture from the second half of the 1st millennium AD onwards triggered a process of forest regeneration. However, as human interference with the vegetation continued in other, albeit limited, forms, those plant taxa which are pre-adapted to survive under anthropogenic pressure became dominant. The interpretation of the pollen record is supported by historical evidence.

1 INTRODUCTION

The present paper discusses the palynological evidence of the effects of human interference with the natural vegetation in the southern Levant, as reflected in Late Holocene pollen diagrams from Lake Kinneret and the Dead Sea (see Fig. 1 for locations). The Kinneret diagram has already been published in detail (Baruch 1986) and the following account is, in fact, an updated summarized version of the original publication. On the other hand, detailed publication of the Dead Sea study is still pending, as it has not yet been completed; the interpretation of the Dead Sea pollen record presented here should therefore be considered as tentative.

No description will be given here of the environmental conditions of the research areas, since this is beyond the scope of the present paper. For information on this subject the reader is referred to the relevant publications cited in the text.

2 LAKE KINNERET

A concise version of the Lake Kinneret diagram is shown in Fig. 2. The diagram is subdivided into 3 pollen assemblage zones, the lowest and the highest of which are further subdivided into 2 and 3 subzones respectively. The chronology of the diagram is based on four radiocarbon dates (shown in Fig. 2) calibrated and corrected for the reservoir effect (Thompson et al. 1985). The ages of the pollen-assemblage zones and subzones were interpolated from the radiocarbon-dated levels (Thompson et al. 1985: Fig. 7) and are given in rounded figures.

Subzone X1 (3550-1600 BC) is generally characterized by high arboreal pollen percentages (45-60%), mainly accounted for by the high values of oak species. A comparison of spectrum 1 with spectrum 21 indicates that in the 4th millennium BC the forest vegetation in the Lake Kinneret area was far denser than at present. The lower forest zone (0-500 m above sea level)

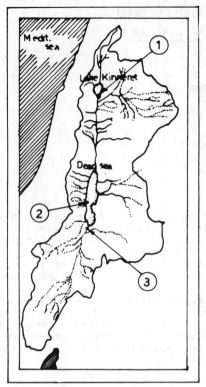

Fig. 1. Location map of the coring sites; (1) Lake Kinneret, (2) Ein-Gedi, (3) Sedom (adapted from Stiller et al. 1988).

must have been dominated by Tabor oak, while the higher zone (500-1200 m) was dominated by Kermes oak. In the highest reaches of the mountains (700-800 m and above) deciduous Cyprus oak (Quercus boissieri), which cannot be separated palynologically from Tabor oak, formed, no doubt, an important component of the maquis.

In the middle of subzone X1, oak values decrease rather markedly, while those of olive increase. Presumably this reflects a short-lasting, local episode of olive cultivation, practised by the lakeside population at the end of the EB (Early Bronze Age) II and the beginning of EB III period. At the top of this subzone the course of the AP curves is reversed, pointing to a decline of the olive and a re-expansion of the oaks. The presumed abandonment of olive cultivation at this stage may be related to the general collapse of the EB culture, which took place all over Palestine at the end of the 3rd millennium BC (Gofna 1982).

Subzone X2 (1600-350 BC) is characterized by a continuous decline of the AP values, from about 45% at the beginning to about 20% at the end of the subzone. This subzone corresponds chronologically to a period in which a marked rise in the settlement density took place in the Lake Kinneret area as well as in adjacent regions (Gal 1982; Kochavi 1972; Urman 1985). This contraction of the arboreal vegetation is therefore assumed to have been the result of forest-clearing activities, apparently aimed at providing space for new settlements as well as creating arable land. This interpretation is supported by the fact that at the top of subzone X2 a sharp rise takes place in the percentages of Plantago lagopus/ lanceolata pollen-type, which is considered an important anthropogenic indicator in European and Near Eastern pollen diagrams (see also Behre, and Bottema and Woldring this volume).

The archaeological record indicates that the increase in settlement density in Palestine started with the establishment of the large city-states of the Middle Bronze Age II (Gofna and Broshi 1984); this implies that the actual age of the beginning of subzone X2 should be raised by 200 years or so.

Zone Y (350 BC-AD 550) is marked by a sharp rise in the Olea percentages, pointing to extensive olive cultivation around Lake Kinneret during this period. This zone corresponds with the Hellenistic up to and including the Byzantine period, from which time-span there is abundant archaeological evidence indicating that the Galilee and the southern Golan Heights (the western and eastern flanks of the lake, respectively) had become major centres of olive-oil production (Frankel 1984; Urman 1985). This fact is also reflected in contemporary historical documents such as the writings of Josephus Flavius and the Talmudic literature (Felix 1982). The radiometric dates of the Lake Kinneret diagram suggest that olive cultivation in the area attained its apex during the early Roman period. Spectrum 10, where Olea

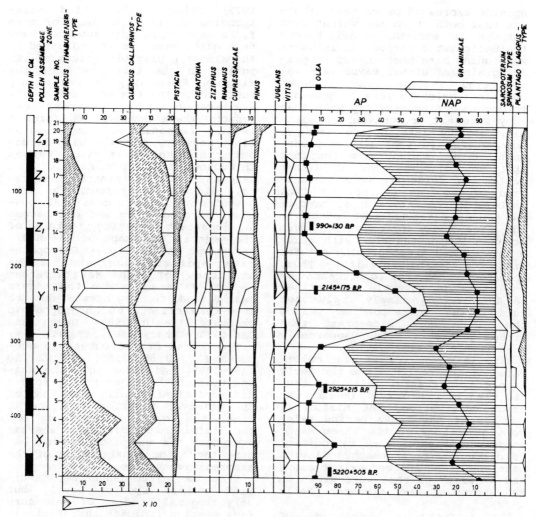

Fig. 2. Lake Kinneret pollen diagram (after Baruch 1986).

reaches its highest value (over 60% of the total pollen sum), is dated by interpolation to ca AD 10, but taking into account the standard deviation of the nearest radiocarbon date, the actual date should fall somewhere between the end of the 2nd century BC and the beginning of the 2nd century AD.

The upper part of zone Y is marked by a sharp decline in the percentages of Olea. This may be related to the more general decline in the standard of agriculture in ancient Israel which, as suggested by historical records, began in the second half of the 3rd century AD

as a result of the oppressive economic policy exerted by the Romans on the local population (Avi-Yona 1963; Felix 1982). Thus, the historical records seem, in general, to confirm the radiometric chronology of the Lake Kinneret diagram, as the chronological range of spectrum 11, which already reflects some decrease in the Olea values, centres on ca 250 BC.

The palynological evidence indicates that in addition to olive, walnut (Juglans), carob (Ceratonia) and grapevine (Vitis) were cultivated in the Lake Kinneret area during zone Y times. In view of the opinion expressed by certain scholars that both carob and walnut were unknown in ancient Israel before the Hellenistic period, it is worth mentioning here that indeed no pollen grains of either taxon were encountered in the Lake Kinneret sediments prior to zone Y. However, this does not necessarily mean that they were not present in the vicinity of the lake before zone Y. These taxa are poor pollen producers, as is evident from the fact that no pollen grains of either Juglans or Ceratonia were encountered in spectrum 21 (or, for that matter, in the entire upper part of the core) although both occur in the area today (carob trees even occur quite abundantly, with quite a few planted trees growing not far from the coring locality). Thus, the fact that the occurrence of both taxa is essentially confined to Zone Y, may simply imply that during the corresponding period they were more widespread than either before or after, apparently as a result of cultivation.

Vine is known to have been cultivated in the region since the Early Bronze Age (Frankel 1984) and thus its rise in zone Y may likewise reflect cultivation. The historical records of the Roman period refer to vine as one of the three major crops of ancient Israel in addition to olive and fig; Josephus Flavius mentions grapevine and walnut among the other crops that were grown on the shores of Lake Kinneret (Felix 1982).

The decrease in the values of olive pollen in the upper part of zone Y is matched by a rise in the percentages of Sarcopoterium spinosum-type, which is followed by an increase in the values of both types of oak and pistachio. These developments are taken here to reflect a process of forest regeneration, presumably triggered by the olive decline, and which apparently began with the invasion of Sarcopoterium spinosum into abandoned olive groves and other fields. The role of Sarcopoterium spinosum in the initial stages of the sere, which eventually leads to the establishment of climax arboreal associations, can still be observed today in climatically favourable parts of the Mediterranean region of Israel (Danin 1982; Zohary 1962,

1973). Prior to the period corresponding to the upper part of zone Y, Sarcopoterium spinosum must have been quite rare, as is indicated by the almost negligible values of its pollen in the lower half of the diagram. Presumably it was mainly confined to the semi-steppes on the borders of the Mediterranean region, where nowadays it forms a leading component of the vegetation. However, from the high Sarcopoterium spinosum-type values throughout the upper half of the diagram it may be inferred that its role did not end through the progression of the successional process. Sarcopoterium had now become an important, lasting feature of the vegetal landscape of the Mediterranean region. Today Sarcopoterium spinosum dominates large stretches of the Mediterranean region of Israel where the maquis has failed to regenerate due to long-term effects of anthropogenic pressure (Danin 1982; Naveh and Dan 1973; Zohary 1962, 1973).

The course of the curves in subzones Z1 (AD 550-1150) and Z2 (AD 1150-1800) indicates that the composition of the regenerating forest differed significantly from that of the primeval forest of subzone X1 time; the role of deciduous oak had diminished considerably whereas evergreen oak and pistachio had become the major constituents of the arboreal vegetation.

Pistacia pollen cannot be identified to the species level, but palynological studies of soil-surface samples indicate that Pistacia palaestina is the only one among the Near Eastern Pistacia species whose representation in the pollen precipitation reflects its actual share in the vegetation. Other species, such as P. lentiscus and P. atlantica, are usually underrepresented (Bottema and Barkoudah 1979; Wright et al. 1967). Thus, it may be assumed that during subzone Z1 and Z2 times, a vegetation type led by Quercus calliprinos and Pistacia palaestina (the leading components of present-day Mediterranean maquis) became established in the Lake Kinneret area, occupying - as one may judge from its present-day distribution - the higher forest zone. In the lower zone, however, Quercus ithaburensis could not regain its former extent (a fact which may also be true of Quercus boissieri in the highest reaches of the upper forest zone), and this area must have been invaded quite extensively by secondary vegetation such as is found there today, and whose leading components are usually not well recorded in pollen diagrams. The slight rise in the percentages of Ziziphus in subzone Z2 may be taken to reflect this development.

The history of the forest in the Lake Kinneret area from the middle of the 1st millennium AD onwards, as recorded in the pollen diagram, points to continuous human interference with the vegetation. According to our knowledge of the ecology of the arboreal taxa involved, this must have been mainly in the form of grazing and limited wood cutting, conditions under which the multiple-trunked, shrublike Quercus calliprinos and Pistacia palaestina survive far more successfully than the single-trunked deciduous oaks (Liphschitz 1982; Shmida 1980 and pers. comm.). As both taxa manage very well on rock exposures, it may be assumed that their considerable expansion during the time of zone Z was to some extent also due to the soil erosion that must have taken place in areas subject to prolonged agricultural activity.

As is evident from the diagram, towards the end of subzone Z2, and especially in subzone Z3 (roughly after AD 1800), the forest cover of the Lake Kinneret area diminished considerably. On the basis of historical records this recent decline of the arboreal vegetation may be attributed to renewed forest-clearing activities, which began in the 18th century, and which became more aggressive during the 19th century - with the growing needs of the developing charcoal industry (Felix 1968). The final death blow to the forest apparently was struck during the First World War, when large wood supplies were required for fuelling the military trains (Eig 1935).

The somewhat higher values of oak in spectrum 21 apparently reflect a slight re-expansion of the forest in the last few decades, as a result of the efforts made by the Israeli government to restore some of the country's former natural vegetation. At the same time afforestation programmes have also been carried out, as is well reflected in the conspicuous rise in Cupressaceae and Pinus.

3 THE DEAD SEA

Two pollen diagrams are at present available from the Dead Sea. One of them has been prepared by the present author for a 5-m-long core from near Ein-Gedi (Baruch in prep.). An 11-m-long core obtained from the Sedom salina was analysed by B. Lanjouw. As the prevailing winds in the region are westerlies and as both cores were taken near the western margins of the Dead Sea (Fig. 1), they are assumed to reflect in particular the area west of the lake, i.e. the Judean Mountains and the Judean Desert.

Figures 3 and 4 present concise versions of the Ein-Gedi and Sedom pollen diagrams, respectively. It may be seen that the two diagrams are similar, differing from one another mainly with respect to the much higher proportion of deciduous oak in the former. They also show much resemblance to the Kinneret diagram.

In the Dead Sea diagrams the deciduous oak pollen type was named Quercus boissieri, because in the Judean Mountains (as well as in the Moab highlands across the Jordan river) Tabor oak plays no role. As in the Lake Kinneret area, here too Cyprus oak joins the evergreen oak maquis at elevations of 700-800 m and above.

As the top of the Ein-Gedi core was truncated during recovery, another, short core (1-m-long) was taken from the same locality. In the uppermost sample of that core (a diagram of which has not yet been prepared), presumably reflecting the present situation, the percentages of the main arboreal taxa are somewhat lower than in the uppermost spectrum of the diagram of Fig 3.

3.1 Chronology

Two dates were published for the Ein-Gedi core (Stiller et al. 1988): 7700±570 BP for the level of 540-550 cm and 5100±180 BP for a

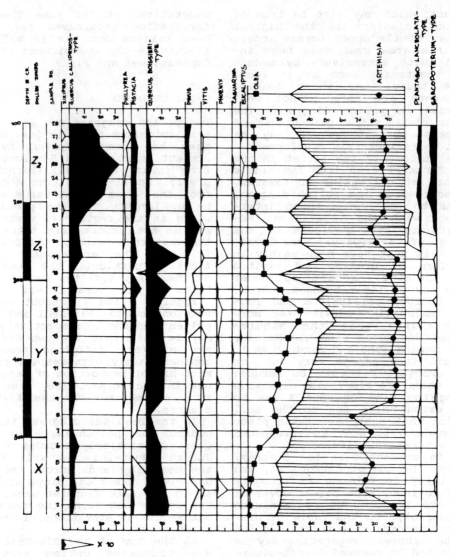

Fig. 3. Ein-Gedi pollen diagram (Baruch in prep.).

depth of 415-435 cm. Both dates were calibrated and corrected for the reservoir effect, resulting in ages of 8600 and 5900 BP, respectively. The chronological framework of the Ein-Gedi diagram, as suggested by these dates, implies a time lag of 2500-3000 years for corresponding vegetational developments between the Dead Sea and Lake Kinneret areas. For instance, the Olea peak of spectrum 15 in the Ein-Gedi diagram and spectrum 23 of the Sedom diagram would, on the basis of interpolation from the above-mentioned radiocarbon dates, be dated to ca 2300 BC, which is 2300-2400 years earlier than the corresponding Olea peak in the Lake Kinneret diagram. Such a time lag is very unlikely. The overall similarity of the three diagrams suggests that the Olea peak records a single, synchronous event which can only be interpreted in terms of large-scale olive cultivation. From a historical and archaeological point of view, the only period to which such a widespread cultivation of olive can be attributed, is the

288

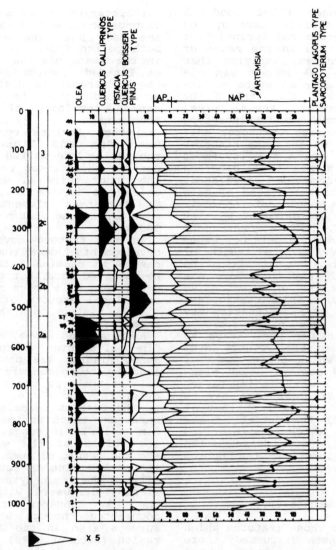

Fig. 4. A concise version of the Sedom pollen diagram (after S. Bottema, following a study by B. Lanjouw).

Roman-Byzantine period. A detailed discussion of this assumption is presented elsewhere (Baruch in prep.). The implication is that the radiocarbon dates of the Ein-Gedi diagram should be discarded, and that the chronological framework of the Kinneret diagram should be adopted also for the Dead Sea diagrams. Therefore, the following correlations are suggested here: zone X of the Ein-Gedi diagram and zone 1 of the Sedom diagram with subzone X2 of the Kinneret diagram

(see below); zone Y and subzone 2a of the Ein-Gedi and Sedom diagrams, respectively, with zone Y of the Kinneret diagram; and zone Z of the Ein-Gedi diagram and subzones 2b-2c and zone 3 of the Sedom diagram with zone Z of the Kinneret diagram. Accepting this view as a working hypothesis, at least until more radiocarbon dates will be available for the Dead Sea sediments, the problem which remains to be solved is that of dating the base of the Dead Sea cores.

The basal zones of both Dead Sea diagrams are characterized by low values of Quercus calliprinos-type pollen. These are in the range of present-day values, implying that the evergreen oak maquis was already in an advanced state of degradation even at the start of the period covered by these cores. Similar Quercus calliprinos-type values characterize the upper half of subzone X2 of the Lake Kinneret diagram, with which the lowermost zones of both Dead Sea diagrams should therefore be correlated. This implies that the base of both Dead Sea cores should date approximately to the beginning of the 1st millennium BC. Such a young date may seem somewhat surprising, especially in view of the length of the Sedom core, but it should be borne in mind that this core was taken from the edge of an extensive alluvial plain in which particularly high rates of sedimentation may be expected. This plain forms a terminal basin for Wadi Araba as well as for several other large wadi systems which drain the vast plains of the central Negev highlands. The lower sedimentation rate of the Ein-Gedi core may be accounted for by the fact that it was taken near the outlet of the Nahal 'Arugot, which is a relatively small wadi system draining the east-facing slopes of the Hebron mountains.

3.2 Vegetational history

In addition to those features which have already been discussed, there are several others which are common to the Dead Sea and Lake Kinneret diagrams.

The increase in Plantago lagopus-type values preceding the Olea rise and the rise of Sarcopoterium spinosum-type which follows the Olea decline in the Lake Kinneret diagram, may also be noted in both Dead Sea diagrams. The early stages of these events are less conspicuous in the Dead Sea diagrams than at Lake Kinneret, reflecting, as it seems, the fact that the area in which the expansion of the plant taxa involved took place, was quite far away from the Dead Sea. Even present-day distribution maps show that the main concentrations of Sarcopoterium spinosum and Plantago lagopus occur some 25-30 km west of the Dead Sea. The occurrence of both pollen types is less regular in the Sedom diagram than in that of Ein-Gedi, which fact reflects the difference in distance of the coring localities to the Mediterranean territory of the Judean Mountains.

Another feature common to the Dead Sea and Kinneret pollen records is the marked rise in the Quercus calliprinos percentages in the upper third of the diagrams, which, as is the case with other Mediterranean elements, is also more pronounced at Ein-Gedi than at Sedom.

As the factors governing these developments have already been discussed in section 2 they will not be repeated here, but the following paragraphs will focus mainly on the more local aspects of the vegetational history of the Dead Sea area.

As mentioned above, zone X of the Ein-Gedi diagram and zone 1 of the Sedom diagram are both characterized by conspicuously low Quercus calliprinos-type percentages; however, they do differ with respect to the Quercus boissieri-type percentages, which are much higher at Ein-Gedi. It is suggested that the low values of the evergreen oak are the result of human activities; the marked rise in settlement density in the Roman-Byzantine period, already discussed with regard to the Lake Kinneret area, is well documented through archaeological surveys also in the Judea-Samaria region (Kochavi 1972). Apparently, at this stage the anthropogenic pressure on the vegetation of the Judean Mountains was far more intensive in the lower forest zone than in the higher one, therefore affecting evergreen oak far more severely than deciduous oak. Comparison of the Quercus boissieri-type percentages in the lower half of the Ein-Gedi diagram with present-day values (as indicated in the uppermost sample of the short core) leads to the conclusion that during zone X (and zone Y) times deciduous oaks were far more common than today. However, they must have been confined largely to the northern parts of the Judean Mountains, where most of the remnants of Quer-

290

cus boissieri stands are still found today, and perhaps to Samaria. The much lower values of the deciduous oak pollen type in the Sedom diagram testify to the fact that towards the southern limit of the distribution area of Mediterranean arboreal vegetation in the Judean Mountains (coinciding in latitude with Ein-Gedi), Cyprus oak had become increasingly rare.

As already pointed out, zone Y of the Ein-Gedi diagram and subzone 2a of the Sedom diagram are characterized by a marked rise of Olea. At Ein-Gedi the Quercus boissieri-type values remain high throughout this period, which implies that olive cultivation concentrated mainly in the lower forest zone. This, in fact, is to be expected as olive is best adapted to moderate climatic conditions, and in particular cannot stand temperatures of below minus 4°C (Alon 1988). On the higher summits of the Judean hills, where Quercus boissieri is most common, such temperatures are not infrequent during wintertime. ·

Following the Olea decline (upper parts of zone Y and subzone 2a in the Ein-Gedi and Sedom diagrams, respectively) two developments take place: one is a drastic decrease in the deciduous oak values, and the other is a sharp rise in the percentages of Pinus.

The decrease in the percentages of the deciduous oak pollen-type, reflecting a most dramatic contraction of the Cyprus oak forests on the higher summits of the Judean Mountains, should, according to the chronological framework adopted here, be dated to the later part of the 1st millennium AD. There can be no doubt that the drastic decline of the deciduous oak forest was brought about by man. The low deciduous oak percentages from the upper part of subzone Z1 (Ein-Gedi diagram) onwards are in the order of present-day values and it is beyond doubt that the modern low share of deciduous oak in the arboreal vegetation of the Judean Mountains is due to human activity; the straight-trunked, tall oak trees have always formed a prime attraction for woodcutters (Avishai 1982). However, in historical sources no record has as yet been found of a specific event which would correspond to the initial, large-scale destruction of the deciduous oak forest, as reflected in subzone Z1 of the Ein-Gedi diagram; it may have been related to the Muslim conquest of Palestine, but this needs to be further investigated.

The short episode of pine expansion which took place immediately after the decline of deciduous oak - well reflected in both of the Dead Sea diagrams - may be explained by the peculiar ecology of this tree. Pinus halepensis (the only naturally occurring pine species in the southern Levant) is highly sensitive to competition; hence it usually thrives in habitats where competition with other arboreal taxa is lacking, due either to unfavourable edaphic conditions or to anthropogenic disturbance (Schiller 1985). The second possibility seems best to fit the case under discussion, because the pollen record clearly shows that pine expanded exactly during the short interval between the decline of deciduous oak and the rise of evergreen oak, when large openings, free of arboreal vegetation and hence free of competition, presumably became available in the Judean Mountains. As Aleppo pine is a fast-growing tree with a remarkable germinative capacity (Rabinowitch-Vin 1982), it could make use of these openings within a fairly short time. However, as it is also a short-living species, whose seedlings are very sensitive to shade, pine forest is quickly suppressed under a canopy of broad-leaved trees (Rabinowitch-Vin 1982). The steep decline of the pine curves at Ein-Gedi (upper part of subzone Z1) and Sedom (upper part of subzone 2b), which is matched by a marked increase in Quercus calliprinos-type values, no doubt reflects this process.

The fact that also in the Sedom diagram the rise of the Quercus calliprinos curve is quite conspicuous, is taken here as evidence of a considerable southward expansion of the evergreen oak maquis, probably as far south as the southern limit of the potential distribution area of Mediterranean arboreal vegetation. Today, however, no significant stands of Quercus calliprinos are encountered south of the latitude of Beit Lehem. The recent decline of the evergreen oak maquis is well reflected in the upper spectra of both Dead Sea diagrams, and, as has already been discussed, is ascribed to human activity.

4 SUMMARY AND CONCLUSIONS

The effects of man's impact on the vegetation in the southern Levant could be demonstrated through palynological studies of Late Holocene pollen cores from Lake Kinneret and the Dead Sea. Human activities, such as forest clearing, cultivation, grazing and burning, were inferred from the pollen record on the basis of the presence of anthropogenic indicators, first appearance or increase in pollen values of fruit trees, and changes in the composition of the vegetation. Similar results have been obtained from palynological studies carried out elsewhere in the Near East (see Bottema and Woldring this volume) which all indicate that man's interference with the natural vegetation of the Near East increased considerably from the middle of the 2nd millennium BC onwards. Apparently this was the result of intensification of agricultural activities and especially of the spread of fruit farming. As far as the studies presented in this paper are concerned, chronological correlation of the pollen diagrams with archaeological and historical records seem to indicate that the onset of these processes was associated with a marked increase in population density.

REFERENCES

Alon, A. 1988.
Olea europaea. In A.Alon (ed.), Plant and animals of the land of Israel, vol. 12 (ed. I.Arnon):114 (in Hebrew).
Avishai, M. 1982.
Quercus boissieri. In A.Alon (ed.), Plant and animals of the land of Israel, vol. 10 (eds. D. Heller and M.Livne), Flowering plants A:29 (in Hebrew).
Avi-Yona, M. 1963.
In the days of Rome and Byzantium. Jerusalem: Bialik Institute (in Hebrew).

Baruch, U. 1986.
The Late Holocene vegetational history of Lake Kinneret (Sea of Galilee), Israel. Paléorient 12/2:37-48.
Baruch, U. in prep.
The palynology of Late Holocene cores from the Dead Sea. PhD dissertation, The Hebrew University of Jerusalem.
Bottema, S. and Y.Barkoudah 1979.
Modern pollen precipitation in Syria and Lebanon and its relation to vegetation. Pollen et Spores 21/4:427-480.
Bottema, S. and H.Woldring this volume. Anthropogenic indicators in the pollen record of the Eastern Mediterranean.
Danin, A. 1982.
Sarcopoterium spinosum. In A.Alon (ed.), Plant and animals of the Land of Israel, vol. 10 (eds. D. Heller and M.Livne), Flowering plants A:133-134 (in Hebrew).
Eig, A. 1935.
A historical phyto-sociological study of Palestine forest of Quercus ithaburensis in past and present. Hateva veHa'aretz 3:115 ff. (in Hebrew, translated from the German).
Felix, Y. 1968.
The destruction of the maquis and the forest. Teva Va'arets 10:168-178 (in Hebrew).
Felix, Y. 1982.
The Jewish agriculture in the Land of Israel in the period of the Mishna and the Talmud. In Z. Baras, S.Safrai, Y.Tsafrir and M. Stern (eds.), Eretz Israel from the destruction of the Second Temple to the Muslim conquest, vol. I:420-441 (in Hebrew).
Frankel, R. 1984.
The history of the processing of wine and oil in Galilee in the period of the Bible, the Mishna and the Talmud. Unpublished PhD dissertation, Tel-Aviv University, Tel-Aviv (in Hebrew).
Gal, Z. 1982.
The Lower Galilee in the Iron Age. Unpublished PhD dissertation, Tel-Aviv University, Tel-Aviv (in Hebrew).
Gofna, R. 1982.
The Land of Israel in the dawn of history: the Early Bronze period and the Intermediate Bronze period (ca 3300-2000 B.C.). In Efal (ed.), The history of Eretz Israel, vol. 1. Keter Publishers

and Yad Itzhak Ben-Zvi (in Hebrew).

Gofna, R. and M.Broshi 1984.
Palestine in the Middle Bronze II: its settlement and Population. Cathedra: 3-26 (in Hebrew).

Kochavi, M. 1972.
Judea Samaria and the Golan, Archaeological Survey: 1967-1968. Jerusalem: The Archaeological Survey of Israel (in Hebrew).

Liphshitz, N. 1982.
Pistacia palaestina. In A.Alon (ed.), Plant and animals of the Land of Israel, vol 10 (eds. D. Heller and M.Livne), Flowering plants A:210-211 (in Hebrew).

Naveh, Z. and J.Dan 1973.
The human degradation of Mediterranean landscape in Israel. In F. di Castri and H.A.Mooney (eds.), Ecological Studies, Analysis and Systems, vol. 7:373-390.

Rabinowitch-Vin, A. 1982:
Pinus halepensis. In A.Alon (ed.), Plant and animals of the Land of Israel, vol. 10 (eds. D. Heller and M.Livne), Flowering plants A:17-18 (in Hebrew).

Shmida, A. 1980.
Kermes oak in the Land of Israel. Israel Land and Nature 6/1:9-16.

Schiller, G. 1985.
Natural occurrences and genetic relations between relicts of Pinus halepensis Mill. in Israel. Rotem 18:69-78 (in Hebrew).

Stiller, M., I.Carmi and A.Kaufman 1988. Organic and inorganic 14C concentrations in the sediments of Lake Kinneret and the Dead Sea (Israel) and the factors which control them. Chemical Geology (Isotope Geoscience Section) 73: 1-16.

Thompsom, R., G.M.Turner, M.Stiller and A.Kaufman 1985. Palaeoclimatic secular variations recorded in sediments from the Sea of Galilee (Lake Kinneret). Quaternary Research 23:175-188.

Urman, D. 1985.
The Golan. BAR International Series 289.

Wright, J.R., J.H.McAndrews and W.van Zeist 1967.
Modern pollen rain in western Iran, and its relation to plant geography and Quaternary vegetational history. Journal of Ecology 55:415-443.

Zohary, M. 1962.
Plant life of Palestine. New-York: The Ronald Press Company.

Zohary, M. 1973.
Geobotanical Foundations of the Middle East (2 vols.). Stuttgart: Gustav Fischer Verlag.

Zohary, M. 1980.
The vegetal landscape of Israel. Tel-Aviv: Am Oved.

Man's Role in the Shaping of the Eastern Mediterranean Landscape, Bottema, Entjes-Nieborg & van Zeist (eds)
© 1990 Balkema, Rotterdam. ISBN 90 6191 138 9

Introduction, development and environmental implications of olive culture: The evidence from Jordan

23

Reinder Neef
Biologisch-Archaeologisch Instituut, Rijksuniversiteit Groningen, Netherlands

ABSTRACT: The main crop plant assemblage in the Neolithic in the Near East consisted of annual species. In this area, a second wave of plant domestication, viz. the introduction of fruit-tree cultivation, occurred in the Chalcolithic. The earliest domesticates of horticulture include grape, date and especially olive. Olive cultivation probably started in the area of northern Palestine/southern Syria. Proof of early olive-tree cultivation is obtained from the plant macro-remains of three Chalcolithic sites in the Jordan valley, which reveal an economy largely based on the olive tree. There is evidence of olive cultivation in Jordan throughout the Bronze and Iron Ages. Possible effects of olive cultivation on the environment are discussed.

1 INTRODUCTION

For the past few years my work has mainly focussed on the study of the exploitation of wild and domesticated plant resources by prehistoric and early-historical man in Jordan. So far, comprehensive palaeoethnobotanical results were available only for a few sites in Jordan. Most notable are the investigations of Pre-Pottery Neolithic B Beidha (Helbaek 1966), Bronze and Iron-Age deposits at Deir 'Alla (van Zeist and Heeres 1973) and Bronze Age Bab edh Dhra and Numeira (McCreery 1980). For that reason a botanical sampling campaign was carried out at 15 archaeological sites ranging from the Neolithic to the Roman period. Although not every site provided well-preserved botanical material, a great deal of new data on the exploitation of plants came available for this area.

In this paper I will confine myself to the development of horticulture and especially to the cultivation of the olive. There are indications that olive cultivation was initiated in Jordan.

2 DISTRIBUTION AND CULTIVATION OF OLIVE

The olive tree, Olea europaea, is very well adapted to the Mediterranean climate. Nowadays, olive is cultivated around the whole of the Mediterranean basin. Of the olive tree usually two varieties are distinguished: Olea europaea var. oleaster (the wild olive tree) and var. europaea (the domesticated tree), the former being regarded as the ancestor of the latter. Olea europaea var, oleaster is distributed over large areas around Mediterranean basin, most notably as a constituent of maquis and garrigue formations (Zohary and Spiegel-Roy 1975). Sometimes it is very difficult to differentiate between wild and cultivated trees, because wild olive is fully interfertile with cultivated varieties. Oleaster types generally have smaller fruits and spincescent lower branches, but often these features are not clear. In fact, in a forest one may well be dealing with escaped cultivars or cross-breedings, because of the long and intensive

Fig. 1. A forest dominated by Quercus ithaburensis s.l. near Es-Sanma. Summer aspect.

Fig. 2. A forest dominated by Quercus ithaburensis s.l. near Es-Sanma. Winter aspect.

cultivation of this tree in the area.

In Jordan, except for riverine forests, forest vegetations are mainly limited to the Northern and Southern Highlands, where precipitation levels are high enough. It seems that in Jordan wild olive is a minor constituent of most of the forest associations dominated by the deciduous oak, Quercus ithaburensis s.l. (Figs. 1 and 2). Olive

is also present in associations of evergreen-oak forest at lower altitudes. In general, the tree grows between 300 and 800 m altitude, with an average annual rainfall of 300-500 mm and with a mean minimum temperature above +3°C during the coldest month (Polunin and Huxley 1965)(Fig. 3). Most of the Tabor oak associations grow on potentially good arable land, at least where the slopes are not too steep. In

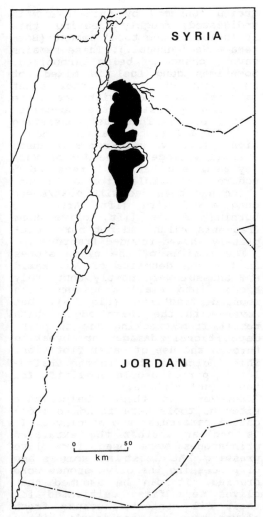

SYRIA

JORDAN

0   50
km

Fig. 3. Forests in which Olea occurs as a "natural" component (black).

Jordan these forest types therefore are mostly very degraded or have completely disappeared.

The introduction of horticulture is sometimes called the second wave of plant domestication. It took place a long time after the domestication of annual species, viz. cereals, flax and pulses, which started at the beginning of the Neolithic. Zohary & Spiegel-Roy (1975) already argued that horticulture started in the Chalcolithic. Olive is believed to be one of the first cultivated fruit trees, together with date palm, fig

and grape, probably because of their rather simple vegetatitave propagation.

The first definite signs of fruit-tree cultivation, around 3700-3500 BC, are from Teleilat Ghassul, a Chalcolithic site north of the Dead Sea. No forests with olive as a natural component are found in the vicinity of this site. Therefore the numerous olive stones and the charcoal preserved in the site are likely to be the result of cultivation (Zohary & Spiegel-Roy 1975).

Further data on olive-tree cultivation are now available from two other Chalcolithic sites in the Jordan Valley, namely Abu Hamid, in the centre, and Tell esh Shuna, in the north of the valley. Together with newly sampled botanical material from the upper occupation phases at Teleilat Ghassul (Hennessy 1969), this may give an answer to the question of how important fruit-tree cultivation, and that of the olive especially, may already have been for Chalcolithic communities. The environmental consequences of this early cultivation may also be reflected in pollen cores taken from nearby locations (Fig. 4).

Important for the discussion is the interpretation of the botanical macroremains, which, in the Near East, generally are preserved in a carbonized state. Carbonization of these remains is due to contact with fire and incomplete combustion. Thus, the sources of most of the botanical samples are the remainders of fires for heating, cooking, kilns and taboons. Only in exceptional cases (e.g. a house fire) is there a chance of finding storage supplies and wood constructions. At Teleilat Ghassul and Abu Hamid most of the samples originate from dung, which had been used for fuel. As I myself did not take samples at Tell esh Shuna North, it is difficult to judge the origin of this botanical material.

Dried dung, sometimes mixed with straw and other vegetable remains, formed into so-called dung cakes, is still an important fuel source in areas where wood is scarce. The earliest evidence of dung having been used for fuel comes from late PPNB layers at 'Ain Ghazal (Neef in prep.), where, among other things,

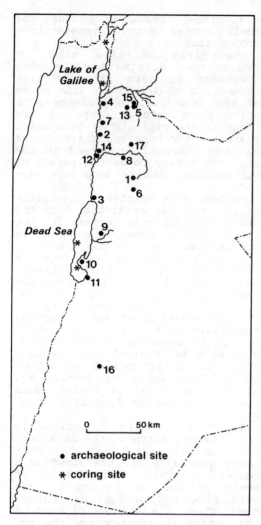

Fig. 4. Sites mentioned in the text. 1. Ain Ghazal, 2. Abu Hamid, 3. Teleilat Ghassul, 4. Tell esh Shuna North, 5. Zeraqun, 6. Sahab, 7. Tell el-Hayyat, 8. Abu Thawwab, 9. Khirbet Iskander, 10. Bab edh-Dhra, 11. Numeira, 12. Deir 'Alla, 13. Tell Irbid, 14. Mazar, 15. Mughayir, 16. Udruh, 17. Jerash.

limestone burning and goat husbandry led to a deterioration of the environment around the settlement (Köhler-Rollefson and Rollefson this volume). The importance of dung fuel as a source of botanical information was already stressed by Miller and Smart (1984) and Bottema (1984). Part of the seeds and grains consumed by animals remain undigested; roughly speaking, this is 10-15% of the total amount (Bottema & Neef unpubl.). These remains have a chance of being carbonized. Sometimes dung fuel is mixed not only with straw and other plant material, but also with the waste of olive pressing, the so-called jift (Fig. 5). This fuel consisting of pulp and stone fragments has a high caloric value. From Suleikhat, a small village in the Jordan Valley near Abu Hamid, I received a modern ash sample from a taboon, which had been fed with goat/sheep dung mixed with jift. After the burning of the jift, olive-stone fragments which had not burnt completely showed rounded fractures.

The remains of the olive stones in the ash deposits of Abu Hamid and Ghassul were mostly completely broken into small fragments with rounded fractures (Fig. 6), but never with the sharp edges which result from cracking due to post-depositional damage or breaking through the use of water flotation. This indicates that in the Chalcolithic period people used jift for their fuel mixture.

However, at these Chalcolithic sites no tools were found to indicate a particular use of olives. It is unclear whether the excavated grindstones were used for olive pressing. At least at some stage of processing the olive stones were cracked. It can be assumed that olives were first cultivated for their oil content, because fresh olives have an obnoxiously bitter taste. It seems that consumption of pickled olives was introduced in the Hellenistic or Roman period (Borowski 1979).

As Abu Hamid and Tell esh Shuna lay nearer to natural olive-tree occurrences than Teleilat Ghassul, one might speculate that the inhabitants of the first two had gathered the olives from the wild. Unfortunately, it is impossible to distinguish between the stones of wild and cultivated olive. Fruit setting in wild olives depends strictly on cross-pollination. The morphological features of seedlings can therefore differ widely in such a population. Cloning, however, leads to a uniform variety. Size and shape of the small number of whole, unbroken olive stones from

Fig. 5. Waste from olive pressing, the so-called "jift".
Fig. 6. Burned "jift".
Fig. 7. Olive stones (Tell esh Shuna E I, 13).

Table 1. Dimensions in mm of olive stones from prehistoric and early-historical sites in Jordan. L = length; B = breadth; T = thickness.

		L	B	T	100L/B
Tell esh Shuna EII 46	min.	7.0	5.5	5.3	114
Chalcolithic	aver.	9.4	6.2	6.0	151
N = 20	max.	12.2	7.2	7.0	189
	S.dev.	1.60	0.42	0.47	
Tell esh Shuna EI 12-3	min.	8.2	5.3	5.2	135
Chalcolithic	aver.	10.0	6.2	6.1	165
N = 50	max.	13.3	7.0	6.8	222
	S.dev.	0.99	0.43	0.41	
Teleilat Ghassul 1987 A	min.	8.2	4.3	5.2	144
Chalcolithic	aver.	10.2	6.2	6.1	165
N = 10	max.	13.3	6.5	6.8	273
	S.dev.	1.66	0.63	0.53	
Abu Hamid		8.3	5.3	5.5	156
Chalcolithic		10.0	6.7	6.7	150
4 stones		10.3	6.0	6.0	178
		10.8	6.3	6.2	171
Tell Irbid C4-248 (2nd floor)		11.0	5.7	5.8	194
LB/EI		12.0	6.0	5.8	200
3 stones		12.7	5.7	5.7	224
Tell Irbid C-ash floor (S)		9.7	5.7	6.0	177
LB/EI		10.5	7.0	7.0	150
3 STONES		10.8	5.8	6.0	186
Jerash AE 101-8		14.8	7.3	7.2	202
Late Byzantine		18.2	7.7	7.5	241
3 stones		15.8	7.8	7.7	202

Tell esh Shuna North and Teleilat Ghassul and Abu Hamid are not very uniform (Table 1, Fig. 7). This lack of uniformity can be explained by the presence of more than one variety in a sample, but one should keep in mind that uniformity of a cultivated product is a modern concept, not necessarily shared by ancient man (Spiegel-Roy 1986). Compared with modern reference material, especially the length of the olive stones is quite modest. Unfortunately not many measurable stones have been retrieved from Jordanian sites. Only the few stones from Late Byzantine levels at Jerash reach modern dimensions.

Additional evidence of cultivation comes from the charcoal remains. In all three sites, Teleilat Ghassul, Tell esh Shuna North and Abu Hamid, a relatively large amount of olive wood, compared to other wood species, was used for fuel (Table 2). Ash deposits mostly contain branches, which could point to pruning of the trees. Also beams of olive wood were used for construction in Teleilat Ghassul and Abu Hamid. It is very unlikely that from the natural forests only olive timber would have been cut, especially since it is a fruit tree. This evidence supports the view of Zohary and Spiegel-Roy (1975) that olive cultivation, and fruit-tree cultivation in general, started in the Chalcolithic period. The large amounts of wood and stone fragments also prove that olive played a substantial role in these Chalcolithic communities (Tables 2 and 3). It is well possible that a market economy based on an olive surplus already existed at these sites. However, the material remains provide no definite indication of trade (Dollfus et al. 1988).

Other indications for early olive cultivation come from Middle and Late Chalcolithic sites on the

Table 2. Olive wood from sites in Jordan. x = present.

Site	Period	Total number of samples	Flotation samples in litres	Number of samples with olivewood	olive wood in ml	olive wood percentage of the total amount of wood
Abu Hamid	Chalc.	58	710	28	96	71.5
Teleilat Ghassul	Chalc.	11	185	6	6.5	5
Tell esh Shuna North	Chalc.	45	211	7	100	99
Zeraqun	EB I,II	10	176	10	399	99
Tell el-Hayyat[1]	EB II,III				x	
Tell el-Hayyat[1]	MB V				x	
Sahab	EB				x	
Khirbet Iskander	EB	38	?	18	204	99
Deir 'Alla[2]	LB				x	
Tell Irbid	LB/E Iron	24	195	6	165	97
Deir 'Alla	E Iron	46	150	-	-	-
Deir 'Alla[2]	E Iron				x	
Mazar	E Iron				x	
Deir 'Alla	8-5th cent. BC	20	64	-	-	-
Deir 'Alla[2]	8-5th cent. BC				x	
Mazar	6-4th cent. BC				x	
Mughayir	5-4th cent. BC	8	120	3	183	96
Udruh	Nabatean	3	15	3	121	100
Udruh	Roman	4	18	4	36	97

[1] Falconer and Magness-Gardiner 1984
[2] van Zeist and Heeres 1973

Golan Heights (Epstein 1978 in Baruch 1985) and Palestine, viz. Tell Mashosh near Be'er Sheba (Liphschitz and Waisel in Zohary and Hopf 1988) and Tell Hreis, a coastal site near Haifa (Raban and Galili 1985).

For other Chalcolithic cultures in the area, such as the Halaf culture in Syria, it seems that olive was collected in the wild (viz. Ras Shamra, van Zeist and Bakker-Heeres 1984(1986)). For the contemporaneous Ubaid sites in southern Iraq there is some evidence of fruit-tree cultivation, viz. of date-palm, in El Oueili (Neef in press) and Eridu (Gillet 1976). One may wonder whether fruit-tree cultivation in general was an invention of the Sumerians, with their agrarian economy based on irrigation and with hardly any wild fruit trees in the floodplain of the rivers Tigris and Euphrates, except perhaps for the date-palm. From the archaeolo-

gical finds at Abu Hamid there is no evidence of Sumerian influence (Dollfus pers. comm.). Considering also the results from other Chalcolithic sites, it can be stated that olive cultivation most likely started in the north of Palestine and/or adjacent southern Syria.

In Table 4 radiocarbon dates are presented. Most of the dates were obtained from olive-tree remains. The outcome of the calibrated dates suggests a beginning of olive culture in the second half of the 5th millennium BC.

3 THE SPREAD OF OLIVE CULTIVATION

The next question to be raised is that of the overall impact of early olive cultivation on the environment. In principle, an answer could be gleaned from pollen cores from the area. However, Jordan offers hardly any possibilities for pollen

301

Table 3. Olive-stone remains from sites in Jordan (only samples with more than one identifiable plant remains part per litre are included).
x = present; * number estimated from fragments

Site	Period	Total number of samples	Flotation samples in litres	Number of samples with olive stones	Total number of olive stones
Abu Hamid	Chalc.	58	710	50	124*
Teleilat Ghassul	Chalc.	11	185	10	77*
Tell esh Shuna North (storage supply: 12495*)	Chalc.	45	211	25	151*
Zeraqun	EB I,II	10	176	8	61*
Tell el-Hayyat[1]	EB II,III				x
Tell el-Hayyat[1]	MB V				x
Abu Thawwab	EB I				x
Khirbet Iskander	EB	38	?	28	51.5*
Bab edh-Dhra[3]	EB II-IV				x
Numeira[3]	EB III				x
Deir 'Alla[2]	LB				x
Tell Irbid	LB/E Iron	24	195	16	30.5*
Deir 'Alla	E Iron	46	150	9	33
Mazar	E Iron	7	?	2	2
Deir 'Alla	8-5th cent. BC	20	64	–	–
Deir 'Alla[2]	7-5th cent. BC				x
Mazar	6-4th cent. BC	19	?	–	–
Mughayir	5-4th cent. BC	8	120	1	1
Udruh	Nabatean	3	15	2	2*
Udruh	Roman	4	18	3	1½*
Jerash	Roman to Umayyad				x

[1] Falconer and Magness-Gardiner 1984
[2] van Zeist and Heeres 1973
[3] McCreery 1980

Table 4. Radiocarbon dates from three Chalcolithic sites in the Jordan Valley. The calibrated dates are after Pearson et al. (1986).

Site/Locus Dated material	uncalibrated	calibrated (95.4% confidence level)
Abu Hamid A6b olivestone fragments	5745±35 BP (GrN-16358)	4720-4525 BC
Abu Hamid AJ1 emmer wheat	5670±40 BP (GrN-14263)	4670-4405 BC
Teleilat Ghassul BG 1 olive wood	5330±25 BP (GrN-15194)	4240-4045 BC
Teleilat Ghassul AA 1 olive wood	5270±100 BP (GrN-15195)	4350-3820 BC
Teleilat Ghassul BG 2 dung ash/twigs	5110±90 BP (GrN-15196)	4220-3700 BC
Tell esh Shuna North EI 12/3 olive wood	5115±25 BP (GrN-15199)	3990-3820 BC
Tell esh Shuna North EII 43 olive wood	5125±25 BP (GrN-15200)	3990-3820 BC

analysis, because of the lack of good pollen-bearing sediments. The closest information we can get is derived from the pollen diagrams of Lake Huleh (prepared by Tsukada in Bottema and van Zeist 1981), the Sea of Galilee (Baruch 1986) and the Dead Sea (Baruch this volume). However, there is no direct relation between coring localities and archaeological sites as the distance is relatively large.

As early as the Late Pleistocene, Olea played a role in the vegetation around the Huleh basin, although, according to the pollen percentages, not in large quantities (Bottema pers. comm.). After 7500 BP, the Lake Huleh diagram shows an increase in arboreal-pollen values, especially the values for oak (not specified as to deciduous or evergreen oak), olive and to a lesser extent pistachio. Bottema and van Zeist (1981) conclude that at that level precipitation increased and given the spread of Mediterranean xerophytic evergreens such as Olea and Pistacia, winter temperatures must have reached modern levels.

No olive stones or wood have been retrieved from Neolithic sites in Jordan. Consequently, one wonders whether wild olive was present at all in the country, and if so, in which type of forest it occurred and how numerous. Of much use for the younger periods is Baruch's (1986) pollen diagram from the Sea of Galilee. This diagram starts around 5250 BP, which unfortunately is too late for the initial stage of olive cultivation. The occupants of Middle- and Late-Chalcolithic sites on the Golan Heights must have laid out their orchards at the expense of the deciduous oak forests (Baruch 1986).

In the diagram of the Sea of Galilee, it is not until the Early Bronze Age that a sudden rise of the olive curve and decrease of the deciduous oak values is observed. In the Jordan Valley, the advent of olive cultivation in the Early- and Middle-Chalcolithic period was not necessarily at the expense of oak-dominated forest. That is to say, in the northern half of the Jordan Valley, in the vicinity of Abu Hamid and Tell esh Shuna North, it is possible to cultivate olives without irrigation on the lower escarpments of the Highlands. Provided that the water-storage capacity of the soil is sufficient, it is possible to grow olives if nursed through their juvenile stage. This cultivation would be at the higher elevations, where the Ziziphus (lotus/spina-christi) steppe zone is gradually replaced by Crataegus azarolus and Quercus ithaburensis s.l. This effect will hardly be visible in the pollen

Fig. 8. Ancient olive groves in the Wadi Kufrinji.

303

record because of the poor pollen
dispersal of insect-pollinated
Crataegus and Ziziphus. For Teleilat Ghassul irrigation is needed
for cultivation in the vicinity of
the site. As the three Chalcolithic
sites in the Jordan Valley, with an
economy substantially based on the
olive crop, are quite large (Abu
Hamid for instance covers 20 ha),
major olive cultivation may have
started in areas with rather open
forest. However, there is no botanical material available from
Chalcolithic sites in the Northern
Highlands to support this hypothesis.

Olive culture in the deciduous
oak forest zone was first attested
at Zeraqun. For this Early Bronze
Age city-state it seems that olive-
tree cultivation was important.
More irrigated olive orchards, as
at Khirbet Iskander, Babh ed Drah
and Numeira (McCreery 1980) near
the Dead Sea, then also appear.
Pollen diagrams from cores near the
Dead Sea give indications of olive
culture, but dating is a problem
(see Baruch this volume). From the
Early Bronze Age onwards, olive
cultivation was firmly established,
with several finds in Palestine.
Egyptian records mention olive oil
among the products imported from
Palestine (Stager 1985). According
to the decline in evergreen and
deciduous oak-pollen values, the
natural forest cover around the Sea
of Galilee diminished considerably
during that time (Baruch 1986).

A drop on the olive curve in the
Galilee pollen diagram is dated to
the Middle Bronze and Late Bronze
Age and relates to the decline of
the city-states at the end of the
Early Bronze Age (Baruch 1986).
From the macro-remains, it seems
that olive cultivation was still
important in Jordan from the Late
Bronze/Early Iron Age, until after
the Roman period, with sites such
as LB EI Irbid, Late Iron Mughayir,
Roman Udruh. Olive cultivation in
the Jordan Valley seems to have
declined. Olive stones and wood
were collected from EB and MB
layers at Tell el-Hayyat (Falconer
and Magness-Gardiner 1984). But
there is hardly any evidence of
local olive cultivation in the
botanically rich LB and Iron Age
layers at Deir 'Alla and in the
Iron Age layers at Tell Mazar. The

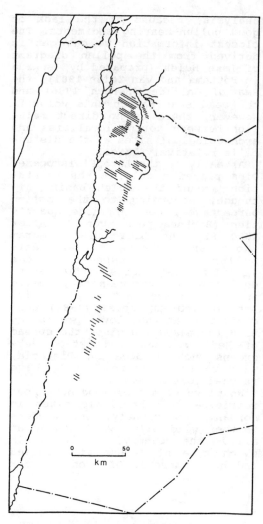

Fig. 9. Present area of olive cultivation in Jordan.

abandonment of olive cultivation in
the Jordan Valley could lie in the
fact that, like today, local people
appreciated the olive oil from the
valley less than that from the
mountains.

After the Roman period there was
a deterioration of irrigation-based
olive-cultivation in the south of
Jordan. This is clearly demonstrated by the decrease of Olea pollen
in fossil Hyrax middens in Petra
(Fall this volume) and by the decrease of olive macro-remains in
the neighbouring desert oasis of
Udruh. Neglect of olive plantations
will only in the case of irrigation

lead to a rapid deterioration of the trees. Olive orchards laid out in their ecological habitat zone will act as semi-natural forest, with a succession to oak-dominated forest or, depending on human-influence, a degradation to a Mediterranean batha type of vegetation.

A drastic decline of olive pollen values in the Galilee diagram during the post-Roman period points to a partial regeneration of the oak forest. It is difficult but not impossible to prove reforestation by olive in areas where the natural forest cover had disappeared through grazing and the exploitation of wood. An example of a complete replacement of the natural forest cover, in this case evergreen oak (Quercus calliprinos) forest, by olive groves is found in the valley of the Wadi Kufrin-ji, a tributary of the Jordan River. Extremely old olive trees are found in this valley, where massive olive cultivation dates back at least to the Roman/Byzantine period (Fig. 8). Nowadays olive cultivation in Jordan is mainly restricted to the foothills and highlands (Fig. 9).

4 CONCLUSION

The archaeobotanical evidence from Abu Hamid, Teleilat Ghassul and Tell esh Shuna North demonstrates that olive cultivation was practised in the Jordan Valley already during the Chalcolithic period. The start of this culture and of fruit-tree culture in general resulted in a wider variety of domestic plants available to farmers. It gave them better opportunities in exploiting the environment, especially in more differentiated landscapes; for instance, stony fields could now be planted with olive trees. The advantage of olive cultivation as a new oil source is obvious. At any rate in sparsely forested environments, such as the Jordan Valley, olive wood as a fuel and timber source seems to have been quite important.

Regarding soil conservation, the spread of the olive tree is a favourable development. Although nowadays the soil under the trees is mostly cultivated, it is preserved from erosion by the extensive root system. When the soil is bare during the early period of winter rain, when annual crops are sown, it is sheltered by the evergreen crown of the olive tree.

As it is at least six years before a tree bears fruit, olive culture demands a stable community (Zohary and Spiegel-Roy 1975) and if irrigation is applied a well-organized society is required. The laying-out of olive groves, whether or not involving terracing and irrigation systems, has definite implications for the livelihood of future generations. In an area where olive trees have been planted, people will not easily switch to a different farming economy.

ACKNOWLEDGEMENTS

I should like to thank Professor W. van Zeist and Dr S. Bottema for critically reading the manuscript, Dr G. Dollfus, Dr Z. Kafafi (Abu Hamid), Dr C. Gaube (Tell esh Shuna North) and Professor B. Hennessy (Teleilat Ghassul) for the opportunities offered for archaeobotanical research and Mrs Ohanessian-Charpin for the modern samples I received from Suleikat. I am indebted also to Professor W.G. Mook and Mr E. Taayke of the Centre for Isotope Research (Groningen) for the radiocarbon dates. Mrs G. Entjes-Nieborg typed the manuscript. The English text was improved by Ms A.C.Bardet. This study was made possible by a grant from the ARCHON foundation of the Netherlands Organization for the Advancement of Pure Research (NWO).

REFERENCES

Baruch, U. 1986.
The late Holocene vegetational history of Lake Kinneret (Sea of Galilee), Israel. Paléorient 12/2:37-47.
Baruch, U. (this volume)
Palynological evidence for human impact on the vegetation as recorded in Late Holocene lake sediments in Israel.
Borowski, O. 1979.
Agriculture in Iron Age Israel. Ann Arbor: University Microfilms Michigan.

Bottema, S. 1984.
The composition of modern charred seed assemblages. In W.van Zeist and W.A.Casparie (eds.), Plants and Ancient Man, p.207-212. Rotterdam, Balkema.

Bottema, S. and W.van Zeist 1981.
Palynological evidence for the climatic history of the Near East, 50,000-6,000 BP. In Préhistoire du Levant, chronologie et organisation de l'espace depuis les origines jusqu'au VIe millénaire, Lyon 1-14 juin 1980. Coll. intern. du C.N.R.S. no 598, p. 111-132. Paris, C.N.R.S.

Dollfus, G., Z.Kafafi, J.Rewerski, N.Vaillant, E.Coquengniot, J.Desse and R.Neef 1988.
Abu Hamid, an early fourth millennium site in the Jordan Valley. In A.N.Garrard and H.G. Gebel (eds.), The Prehistory of Jordan, p.567-601. BAR International Series 396.

Falconer, S.E. and B.Magness-Gardiner 1984.
Preliminary report of the first season of the Tell el-Hayyat Project. Bulletin of the American School of Oriental Research 255:49-74.

Fall, P.L. (this volume).
Deforestation in Southern Jordan: evidence from fossil Hyrax middens.

Gillet, J.B. 1976.
Botanical samples. In F.Safar et al. (eds.), Eridu, p.317-318. Baghdad, Ministry of Culture and Information.

Helbaek, H. 1966.
Pre-Pottery Neolithic farming at Beidha. Palestine Exploration Quaterly 98:61-66.

Hennessy, J.B. 1969.
Preliminary report on a first season of excavations at Teilelat Ghassul. Levant 1:1-24.

Köhler-Rollefson, I. and G.O.Rollefson (this volume).
The impact of Neolithic subsistence strategies on the environment: the case of 'Ain Ghazal, Jordan.

McCreery, D.W. 1980.
The nature and cultural implications of early Bronze Age agriculture in the southern Ghor of Jordan. Ann Arbor: University Microfilms Michigan.

Miller, N.F. and T.L.Smart 1984.
Intentional burning of dung as fuel: a mechanism for the incorporation of charred seeds into the archaeological record. Journal of Ethnobiology 4:15-28.

Neef, R. in press.
Plant remains from archaeological sites in Lowland Iraq. I. El 'Oueili (Ubaid). In J.L.Huot (ed.), El 'Oueili. Editions Recherche sur les civilisations.

Pearson, E.W., J.R.Pilcher, M.G.L. Baillie, D.M.Corbett and F.Qua 1986. High-precision 14C measurement of Irish oaks to show the natural 14C variations from AD 1840 to 5210 BC. Radiocarbon 28: 911-934.

Polunin, O. and A. Huxley 1965.
Flowers of the Mediterranean. London: Chatto and Windus.

Raban, A. and E.Galili 1985.
Recent maritime archaeological research in Israel - a preliminary report. The International Journal of Nautical Archaeology 14/4:321-356.

Spiegel-Roy, P. 1986.
Domestication of fruit trees. In C.Barigozzi (ed.), The origin and domestication of plants, p.201-212. Amsterdam, Elsevier.

Stager, L.E. 1985.
First fruits of civilization. In J.W.Tubb (ed.), Palestine in the Bronze and Iron Age. Papers in the honour of Olga Tufnell, p. 172-187. London, Institute of Archaeology.

Zeist, W. van and J.A.H.Heeres 1973.
Paleobotanical studies of Deir 'Alla, Jordan. Paléorient 1:21-37.

Zeist, W. van and J.A.H.Bakker-Heeres 1984(1986).
Archaeobotanical studies in the Levant. 2. Neolithic and Halaf levels at Ras Shamra. Palaeohistoria 26:151-170.

Zohary, D. and P.Spiegel-Roy 1975.
Beginnings of fruit growing in the Old World. Science 187:319-327.

Zohary, D. and M.Hopf 1988.
Domestication of plants in the Old World. Oxford: Clarendon Press.

Extinction of Acacia nilotica in Israel
A methodological approach

24

Mordechai E. Kislev
Department of Life Sciences, Bar-Ilan University, Ramat-Gan, Israel

ABSTRACT: Although remnants of Acacia nilotica were found at 3-4 sites in Israel, the tree does not grow in the country today. Archaeobotanical, archaeological and literary evidence as well as methodological principles are adduced to determine whether these remnants originated from plants native to the country. It is suggested that A. nilotica was native to Israel from the Miocene onward, but there is no conclusive evidence as to when it became extinct.

1 INTRODUCTION

Acacia nilotica is well recognized by its yellow flowering heads and its necklace-like, straight, indehiscent pod, which is narrowly and irregularly constricted between the seeds, forming numerous orbicular joints. The tree species, 2.5 to 14 m in height, is widespread in dry tropical and sub-tropical Africa and Asia and is divided into several subspecies characterized by differences in hairiness and pod form. Our attention will be focused on ssp. nilotica which is distinguished by its glabrous pods or almost so, and glabrous to shortly puberulous young branchlets (Fig. 1). It has a Sudanian distribution, from Senegal and Cameroon to the Nile Valley, with an extension into the Near East (SW Arabian peninsula) (Fig. 2). Its habitats are seasonally inundated clay pans, riverbanks and other moist areas (Wickens 1976: 107; Ross 1979:106-109). Apart from ssp. nilotica, few other subspecies rarely grow in Egypt, the Arabian Peninsula and Iran (Täckholm 1974:290; Heller and Heyn in press).

1.1 The introduction of Sudanian elements into Israel

There is no way to understand the

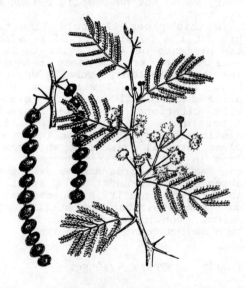

Fig. 1. Acacia nilotica: flowering and fruiting branches (from Täckholm 1974:288)

modern distribution of plants and animals without looking carefully into the past. The present configuration of Levantine biotas displays a temporary pattern and may only barely reflect the extremely dynamic past biogeographical events. Still in the early Miocene, closure of the Mediterranean-Indo Pacific seaway (the Tethys) triggered an interchange of terrestrial biotas between Africa (including Israel and the Arabian Peninsula) and Eurasia. The African elements which dominated the region witnessed a somewhat later invasion of North-Tethyan taxa (Tchernov 1988: 159ff.).

Acacia nilotica was probably abundant in Israel, Jordan and Sinai in ancient times. Contrary to the autochtonous view mentioned above, other scholars hold that African elements invaded the region during a period with a suitable climate. The tree could have grown there either following massive introduction of Sudanian flora during the Miocene, some 20 million years ago (e.g., Zohary 1962:61), or about 15,000 years ago, after the last glacial and together with the last introduction of elements of the Savana into the rift valley (cf. Bodenheimer 1935:38-40). However, we do not have solid evidence for that.

In this paper, I would like to present the possibility of proving the presence of A. nilotica in Israel and to provide some reasons for its extinction, probably during historical times. I will be mainly using macrofossil evidence, along with citations from the ancient literature. The difficulties in distinguishing native from imported plant material arise from shortcomings in our scientific methods. We can deduce the presence or even the absence of a product of a species in a region from its archaeobotanical remnants, but we still lack direct, convincing methods to determine its country of origin.

2 USES: LITERARY EVIDENCE

In Egypt, A. nilotica was apparently the main, or among the most abundant forest trees in the historical past (Täckholm 1954). The tree is economically important. Its foliage and green pods serve as fodder for camels, cattle and goats (Fig. 3). The pods and seeds are used for tanning. The flowering heads have a strong scent (Wickens 1976:107). The young bark yields a fibre. The wood is heavy, hard, durable and resistant to water and is superior to that of A. albida,

Fig. 2. Distribution map of A. nilotica ssp. nilotica (circles) and ssp. adansonii (triangles) (from Wickens 1976:map 69)

which is liable to insect attack. It has been exploited for house-beams, statues, panelling, boats, etc. The gum, although inferior to that of A. verek, is a commercial article (Theophrastus 4.2.8; Broun 1906:28-29; Uphof 1968).

2.1 Boats

There is literature evidence that A. nilotica timber was used for ship building for more than 4000 years.

2.1.1 Boats in ancient Egypt

The earliest document, perhaps, is the inscription of Uni which dates to the 6th dynasty (ca 2200 BC) and tells about an expedition to the alabaster quarry: "His majesty sent me to Hatnub to bring a huge offering-table of hard stone of Hatnub. I brought down this offering-table for him in only 17 days, it having been quarried in Hatnub, and I had it proceed down-stream in this cargo-boat. I hewed for him a cargo-boat of acacia wood of 60 cubits in its length, and 30 cubits

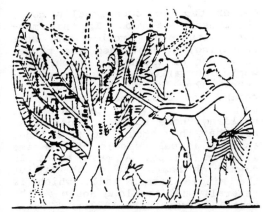

Fig. 3. A. nilotica broused and cut for wood (18th dynasty)(from Davies 1927:pl. XXX)

in its breadth, built in only 17 days, in the third month of the third season (eleventh month). Although there was no water on the -- I landed in safety at the pyramid (called): 'Mernere-Shines-and-is-Beautiful'" (Breasted 1906: I, 149).

A variety of boat types is mentioned among the offerings to Amon during the reign of Ramses III (20th dynasty, 12th century BC): towboats, (canal-)boats, cattle boats, warships, and Kara boats (Breasted 1906:IV,128).

2.1.2 Boats in classical Egypt

The classical description of a tow boat on the Nile is given by Herodotus (II,96) (5th century BC): "The boats in which they carry cargo are made of the acacia, which is in form most like to the lotus of Cyrene, and its sap is gum. Of this tree they cut logs of two cubits length and lay them like courses of bricks, and build the boat by making these two-cubit logs fast to long and close-set stakes; and having so built they setcrossbeams athwart and on the logs. They use no ribs. They caulk the seams with byblus (papyrus). There is one rudder, passing through a hole in the boat's keel. The mast is of acacia-wood and the sails of byblus. These boats cannot move upstream unless a brisk breeze continues; they are towed from the bank; but down-stream they are thus

managed: they have a raft made of tamarisk wood, fastened together with matting of reeds, and a pierced stone of about two talents' weight; the raft is let go to float down ahead of the boat, made fast to it by a rope, and the stone is made fast also by a rope to the after part of the boat. So, driven by the current, the raft floats swiftly and tows the `baris' (which is the name of these boats) and the stone dragging behind on the river bottom keeps the boat's course straight. There are many of these boats; some are of many thousand talants' burden" (Herodotus, Loeb Classical Library; translated by A.D. Godley 1920).

2.1.3 Traditional boats in modern Sudan

Special type of boat and its construction in the 19th century is described from Sudan by Schweinfurth in his "The Heart of Africa": "The boats which are used upon the upper waters of the Nile are called `negger'; their construction, I believe, is unlike what can be seen in any other country of the world. They are as strong as they are massive, being built so as to withstand the violent pushings of the hippopotamuses, as well as the collisions with the mussel banks, which are scattered in various directions. I am certain that one of these boats at any maritime exhibition would attract the attention of all who take any interest in such things. I am not aware that there is anything accurate to be found in any history of travel on this subject, and it may be permitted me therefore to insert a few particulars of the Khartoom shipbuilding.

There can be no question that the ship-building on the Red Sea, just like the architecture of the towns along its coast, is of Indian origin, all the timber required in Arabia being procured from India. At Khartoom, on the contrary, this art, although in many respects it has peculiarities of its own, has been derived from an Egyptian source. Taking their own special requirements into account, the boat-builders of Egypt have completely altered the structure and shape of their river boats. It must be borne in mind that the recurring cataracts, which interrupt the navigation of the Nubian Nile valley, rendered any ascent of the river a matter of difficulty, demanding indeed the most strenuous exertions. The cataracts are ten in number, and only recently have they been overcome by some small steam vessels of about 60-horse power. The only wood which is used in Khartoom for ship-building is that of the Sunt acacia (A. nilotica), which, though far heavier and harder than our oak, is the only wood which the soil of the Sudan supplies, which appears capable of being sawn into planks. But on account of the irregular texture and numerous branches of the trunk of this acacia, it is impossible to cut it into boards more than ten feet in length, and even these are rare. Masts and sail-yards, since those of deal seldom reach Khartoom, and then are of an exorbitant price, must be made by splicing together a number of small pieces. Externally these are bound with ox hide; but in violent gales they are extremely liable to start. Not only does the wood fail to be either straight or long, it is also so hard, that it requires to be sawn while it is green. The saw is an instrument so rarely employed throughout Nubia, that it is handled most unskillfully by the carpenters; as matter of course, there are neither steam-mills nor water-mills in Khartoom, and consequently the planks are cut without the faintest pretence to regularity.

All these defects are, however, cancelled by the unexampled toughness and indestructible nature of the wood; it might fairly be asked from what other material could boats 60 feet long and 20 feet broad be constructed without ribs or braces. The sides of the boat are a foot thick, and are formed of layers of different lengths, which acquire stability and firmness from their own support. An empty boat, seen from inside, has somewhat the appearance of an elongated shell of half a hazelnut. The planks, where they overlap or are dove-tailed together, are fastened by iron nails driven in perpendicularly, the necessary holes being bored from the outer to the inner surfaces in such a way that the same nail holds to-gether two, or occasionally more, thicknesses of wood. In this manner, with much trouble and more measuring, is obtained the proper curvature of the hull, which, as a whole, is marked by a complete symmetry. The cost of the stout iron nails, and the rapid wear of axe and saw, make the expenses of building these boats so considerable that they amount to five times as much as oak vessels of the same size in Europe. A mast about 20 feet high bears the giant-yard of the single lateen sail, which is generally half as long again as the boat" (Schweinfurth 1873:50-52).

2.1.4 Effects of wood consumption on the Egyptian landscape

The continuous use of timber required either for house or boat building, and for the industry of charcoal denuded both the land adjacent to the Nile and the wadis of the deserts. In the Eastern desert and Sinai, there are still many wadis which bear names of trees which once stocked these sites, though in most cases, none of the former trees are found there (Täckholm 1954).

2.2 Export of wood

There is also literary evidence of export of the wood. In Egypt, the tree is called, "Sant" or "Sont" in modern Arabic (Täckholm 1974:856) and "Shnd.t" by the ancient Egyptians which is linguistically allied to the Hebrew word "Shitta" (Loret 1892:84; Germer 1985:91). Therefore, the shittim wood, used by the children of Israel to build the Tabernacle, its ark, altars and table, is identified as that of A. nilotica (Celsius 1745:I,499). However, the Arabs in Israel (but not in Egypt) call a second species, A. albida, "Sont". This tree is also grown today in Egypt, though rather rarely (Keimer 1932), and its trunk can be quite broad and tall. It can reach a height of 30 m and its trunk the diameter of 2 m (Wickens 1969:181-182). It has also been identified with the shittim wood (Aaronsohn 1913:502). It is suggested here that the wood of the Tabernacle, sometimes 5 m long, plated with gold, was of A. albida whereas the bare pillars of the court, 2.5 m long, were made of A. nilotica (Kislev in prep.).

2.3 Pods for tanning

Theophrastus (4.2.8), already in the 4th century BC, mentions Acacia pods for use in tanning in Egypt: "The fruit is in a pod, like that of leguminous plants, and the natives use it for tanning hides instead of gall" (Fig. 4). Tannery as well as pods are known from the predynastic period (Table 1; Bravo 1933).

Today, the ripe, fallen pods are collected in April and May by old women in Sudan (Peake 1952). The tannins are concentrated in the pod tissue rather than in the seeds. When the seeds are eaten by insects their fraction of the total weight decreases and the percentage of tannins increases. One kg of ground fruits and seeds is necessary for tanning a single skin of goat or calf. Sometimes, skins of the Nile monitor lizard (Varanus niloticus) are also tanned with Acacia pods for use in high quality belts and purses. One kg represents about 6000 joints, or 1000 fruits when there are 6 joints per fruit on the average. This means that the crop of about one tree is needed for tanning a single skin.

3 ARCHAEOBOTANICAL EVIDENCE

Many archaeobotanical finds of Acacia nilotica are reported for Egypt from the predynastic period onwards (Table 1). It is almost certain that the actual finds are more numerous. There are several reasons for that:

1) The labels on some archaeological finds were lost and their dates and localities are not known (e.g., several dry pods in the Economic Museum, Kew, cat. no. 26555);

2) The wood of some of the objects was not identified;

3) Some wooden samples were not identified to the species level (e.g., Mond and Myers 1937:138; Emery 1939:70) although ancient wood objects of this species were recorded more than 100 years ago

Fig. 4. Tanning and sandal making in the 18th dynasty (from Davies 1943:pl. LIII)

(Braun 1879) and the specific anatomy of A. nilotica has already been described (Ribstein 1925);

4) Sometimes it is held that Acacia means A. nilotica, because it is the most common Acacia species in Egypt;

5) Some of the results are published in fairly obscure journals.

It will be interesting to identify precisely the pegs from the beautifully preserved royal ship of Cheops, 4th dynasty, which was buried in a pit near his pyramid, and is exhibited today in the Boat Museum by the Pyramids, Giza, as well as the wood of other ancient ships (Jenkins 1980:80,111).

In addition, there are many representations of the tree in reliefs and drawings, some of which are colourful and aesthetically beautiful, e.g., Beni Hasan, 12th dynasty. Some of them include birds such as pigeons, shrikes and hoopoe looking for shade or feeding on insects attracted by the flowers (Griffith 1900:IV,1).

Except for seeds and a branch fragment from Ukma West, N. Sudan, dated to 1800-1580 BC (van Zeist 1987 and pers. comm.), the only country in the Near East, outside Egypt, where remnants of A. nilotica were found, to my knowledge, is Israel, all of them from the Rift Valley, Mo'a on the Roman Petra-Gaza road (Table 2). The earliest finds, from Jericho, are reported as doubtful identifications (Western 1983:770-771). The charred material is stored today in the University Museum of Archaeology and Anthropology at Cambridge. The other remnants, are at my dis-

Table 1. Archaeobotanical finds of Acacia nilotica from Egypt

	Site	Context	Date	Wood and twigs	Flowering heads	Fruits and seeds
1.	Silsila	grave	predynastic	–	–	+
2.	Gabalein	tannery	predynastic	–	–	+
3.	Saqqara	grave	3rd dyn.	+	–	–
4.	–	beam	c. 3rd dyn.	+	–	–
5.	Abu Sir	grave	5th dyn.	+	–	–
6.	Abu Sir	graves	13th dyn.	+	–	–
7.	Deir el Bahari	garland	Amenophis I	–	+	–
8.	Deir el Bahari	garland	Ahmes I	–	+	–
9.	Tell el Amarna	pegs	Teje	+	–	–
10.	Gurna	–	18th dyn.	+	–	–
11.	Gurna	granary	18th dyn.	–	–	+
12.	Deir el Medine	grave	18th dyn.	–	–	+
13.	Thebes	–	18-19th dyn.	–	–	+
14.	Thebes	grave	18-19th dyn.	–	+	–
15.	Saqqara	dump	4-1st cent. BC	–	–	+
16.	Hawara	garland	3-2nd cent. BC	–	+	–
17.	Hawara	cemetery	3-1st cent. BC	–	+	+
18.	–	boning-rod	1st cent. BC(?)	+(?)	–	–
19.	–	mummy label	Roman	+	–	–
20.	Dachel	temple	Roman	+	–	–
21.	Roda island near Cairo	base of nilometer	c. AD 500	+	–	–

(?) = uncertain date or identification

References to Table 1

1. Germer 1988:47
2. Bravo 1933:86-87; Lucas and Harris 1962:34
3. Lauer et al. 1951:133-135 and figs. 39-40
4. Ribstein 1925:205,208; Lucas and Harris 1962:440
5. Borchardt 1909: 43; Lucas and Harris 1962: 440.
6. Schweinfurth 1908:158; Germer 1988:47. But cf. Lauer et al. 1951:135; Germer 1988:32
7-8. Schweinfurth 1884:363; Germer 1988:6
9. Borchardt 1911:11; Lucas and Harris 1962:440
10-12. Germer 1988:47
13. Germer 1988:47, fig. 60
14. Kunth 1826:422; Braun 1879:61-62
15. Hepper 1981:147; Germer 1985:90-91
16. Germer 1988:16
17. Newberry 1889:52; Germer 1985:90-91
18. Oakley 1932:159; Lucas and Harris 1962:440
19. Ribstein 1925:205,208; Lucas and Harris 1962:440
20. Braun 1879:61
21. Täckholm and Täckholm 1941:75; Lucas and Harris 1962:440

posal, all dry, from the Roman period (Fig. 5).

In addition, the species is recorded from Atranjikhera (Chowdhury et al. 1977) and apparently also from Inamgaon, India (Kajale 1988:765).

4 DISCUSSION

I would like to raise two questions here:

1) Leaving aside the uncertain identification of Acacia from the Jericho excavations, do the finds

Table 2. Finds of Acacia nilotica from Israel

Site	Locus and basket	Date	Wood	Fruit segments
Jericho	CS. 32	Early Bronze	+ (?)	-
Jericho	CS. 511	Early Bronze	many (?)	-
`En Rahel	15-186	1st cent. BC	-	8
`En Rahel	15-211	1st cent. BC	-	8
Masada	1035-9/1	1st cent. AD	-	32
Masada	1045-1646	1st cent. AD	-	1
Masada	1267-2079	1st cent. AD	-	3
Mo'a	3-248	2-3rd cent. AD	-	2

(?) = uncertain identification

from the Roman period produce satisfactory evidence that the tree grew near the sites, namely, in the Rift Valley, or were they imported from elsewhere?

2) And if it did grow there at the time, what were the reasons for its extinction?

To properly establish the extinction of a plant or animal species from a particular region, three facts must be made clear:

1) the species' presence in the area in ancient times;

2) its absence in more modern times; and

3) determination of the date of its disappearance. Sometimes, two of these factors can be used for extracting the third and reconstructing the history of the species.

A. nilotica is not recorded by Zohary (1972) in his Flora Palaestina for either Israel or Jordan, nor by Danin et al. (1985) for Sinai. However, it is mentioned in the region by several authors and travellers in the last and the present centuries. These include the distributional notes by E. Guest (Townsend 1974:50); a record from S. Sinai (Hart 1891:9,133; Post 1896:298); and a record from the Dead Sea area (Tristram 1884: 293). The most recent claim is by Al-Eisawi (1982:141) from Jordan, but without any details.

The extinction of A. nilotica can be established by proving its earlier existence in the wild. It seems that the "lists of rules" presented in Tables 3 and 4 produce one or two arguments in favour of its being native to the country. All the sites of A. nilotica finds are located in the Rift Valley, the main region in Israel which is occupied today by Sudanian elements. It is difficult to rationalize the import of A. nilotica fruits when there are other local plants which are known to be used, traditionally, for tanning (Bailey and Danin 1981; Table 5). Nevertheless, the arguments presented here are by no means conclusive. Apparently, with the desiccation of the ancient Lake Lisan, suitable, humid habitats for normal growing of A. nilotica became rare.

If one assumes that A. nilotica grew wild in Roman times, it is interesting to contemplate the possible factors which might have caused its extinction.

1) Wood consumption. Although the population in the region was not dense, several major events should be recalled here.

a) Continuous wood supply that was required for copper smelting in the Timna region in the S. Arava

Fig. 5. Pod segments of A. nilotica from Masada 1035 9/1 (1st century AD). Destruction of pod wall due to exit of bruchid beetles can be seen (x 3/4)

Table 3. Evidence in favour of plants being indigenous

1. Early finds
2. Numerous finds
3. Abrupt absence of finds in later periods
4. The organ is not likely to be transported
5. Abundance in a neighbouring country
6. Location of the find near the present distribution area
7. Linkage to the process of deforestation
8. The ability to become naturalized
9. Historical evidence
10. Change of climate
11. Pests, etc. which can be found only in the native country

Table 4. Evidence in favour of plants having beena newly introduced or imported

1. A useful plant
2. Large quantities of remnants
3. Ease of transporting the useful organ
4. Site located near trading routes
5. Site or locus of wealthy people
6. The plant is known to be grown as a cultivar
7. The finds are uniform

Valley during the 4th and 3rd millennia BC (Rothenberg 1988:14);

b) a similar situation at Punon, east of En Yahav as well as near Hazeva, N. Arava Valley (Israeli, pers. comm.); and

c) the building of a ramp, 200 m long, supported by wooden logs, during the siege of Masada by the Romans in AD 72 (Liphschitz et al. 1981:230).

2) Fruit and seed consumption for tanning.

3) Seed destruction by several species of bruchids. Sometimes the larva continues to eat the developing cotyledons without any apparent ill effect (Southgate 1978). In Sudan, A. nilotica is infested mainly by Bruchidius uberatus (= B. baudoni or Bruchus baudoni) (Decelle 1966). Apparently it is found throughout Africa, infesting also A. giraffae, A. Seyal, and Dolichos lablab (Luca 1965). Also A. sieberiana is a host plant of this beetle. The body of B. uberatus is 3.0-4.5 mm in length; elytra with 2 denticles at base of third and fourth striae; pronotum conical; eyes more strongly projected in male than in female; antennae serrate in female, strongly serrate in male (Prevett 1971). Attack occurs not only in ripe seeds but also in the green pods before these have fallen from the trees. In fact, several generations of insects infest the seeds throughout the year, starting in the green

pods, followed by further development in dry seeds. The total life span of these beetles amounts to about 40 days (Peake 1952). The pods collected at Luxor, S. Egypt, produced the same species, kindly identified by Dr. Halstead, Slough Laboratory, England (Fig. 6).

4.1 Interactions between acacias, bruchids and herbivores

It was found that, in Israel, bruchids infest the native species of Acacia, with more than 90% of the seeds of A. raddiana and A. tortilis, and above 60% of those of A. gerrardii suffering damage (Halevy 1974). Bruchidius uberatus, however, is not recorded from Israel. Above 70% damage is found in A. nilotica from Egypt, in pods collected in February. In pods attacked by B. uberatus more seeds are infested every generation. However, a large part of the embryo remains intact.

On the other hand, when there are sufficient gazelles (Gazella dorcas), mountain goats (Capra ibex) or domestic goats and camels to

Table 5. Plants utilized by the Bedouins for tanning in Sinai and the Negev (after Bailey and Danin 1981)

Acacia raddiana: bark
Ephedra alata: thin green stems
E. pachyclada: thin green stems
Helianthemum ventosum: root
Medicago laciniata: leaves
Pistacia atlantica: bark
Punica granatum: peel
Rhus tripartita: root

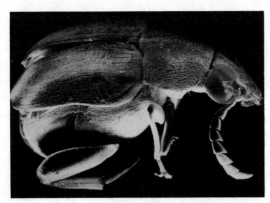

Fig. 6. Bruchidius uberatus, emerged from a pod of Acacia nilotica. Collected at Luxor, Egypt, 8 Febr. 1989 (x 16)

consume the fruits immediately after shedding, the development of bruchid larvae in the seed is halted, and the rate of germination is increased. The reason for that is the entry hole of the larva which allows the ingress of digestive juices during the passage through the alimentary canal. These seeds are diffused in wide areas, safe from attack by the beetles. Also the germination of the intact seeds is improved. When the population of large herbivore mammals decreases, less seedlings appear (Halevy 1974). A similar relationship was observed in Tanzania (Lamprey et al. 1974). The effect of the herbivores on the increase of viable Acacia seeds is more pronounced when the life of the bruchid involves several generations per year. Massive hunting of gazelles by "desert kites" (Meshel 1974) in ancient times might have considerably decreased the germination of new seedlings of Acacia species infested by bruchids. In fact, bruchids are one of the factors controlling the regeneration of leguminous trees in the semi-arid zones of Africa and north America. The interference of man in the biological complex could engender a serious break in the cycle, thus starting a decline in the forest ecosystem (Southgate 1979: 468).

Low percentage of infested seeds in charred, archaeobotanical samples may indicate using just after ripening, before further infesta-tion. If this is true, a native plant can be suggested because long distance transport would have taken some time, allowing for bruchid development. However, the Roman sites in Israel produced only insignificant numbers of dry pod fragments. In this case, infestation could have continued even after the destruction of the site.

At present, only a fragmentary picture can be presented. I hope that in the near future, with more and better identifications, more details will be available.

5 ACKNOWLEDGEMENTS

Thanks to Dr. R. Cohen and Mr. Y. Israeli of the Israel Department of Antiquities and Museums who kindly provided the botanical samples from `En Rahel and Moa', to Dr. E. Netzer and Dr. G. Foerster, The Institute of Archaeology, The Hebrew University, Jerusalem who gave me permission to publish the botanical finds from Masada. To Mr. F.N. Hepper, Royal Botanic Gardens, Kew, Dr. R. Germer, Hamburg, Dr. D.G.H. Halstead, Slough Laboratory, Slough, and Mrs A. Butler, Institute of Archaeology, London, for their valuable help. J. Langsam and T. Anker prepared the photographs, and Avrille Goldreich typed the manuscript.

REFERENCES

Aaronsohn, A. 1913.
  Notules de phytogéographie palestinienne (I). Une station peu connue de l'Acacia albida Del. Bull. Soc. Bot. France 60:495-502.
Al-Eisawi, D.M. 1982.
  List of Jordan vascular plants. Mitt. Bot. Staatssamml. München 18:79182.
Bailey, C. and A.Danin 1981.
  Bedouin plant utilization in Sinai and the Negev. Econ. Bot. 35:145-162.
Bodenheimer, F.S. 1935.
  Animal life in Palestine: an introduction to the problems of animal ecology and zoogeography. Jerusalem: Mayer.
Borchardt, L. 1909.
  Das Grabdenkmal des Königs Nefer-Ir-Ke-Re. Leipzig: Hinrichs.

Borchardt, L. 1911.
Der Porträtkopf der Königin Teje. Leipzig: Hinrichs.

Braun, A. 1879.
On the vegetable remains in the Egyptian museum at Berlin. Journal of Botany 8:19-23, 48-62, 91-92.

Bravo, G.A. 1933.
Leather in ancient Egypt. J. Int. Soc. Leather Trades Chem. 17:436-437.

Breasted, J.H. 1906.
Ancient records of Egypt: historical documents. Chicago, Illinois: University Press.

Broun, A.F. 1906.
Catalogue of Sudan flowering plants. Khartoum: El Sudan Printing Press.

Celsius, O. 1745.
Hierobotanicon: sive de plantis Sacrae Scripturae dissertationes breves. Uppsala: Sumtu Auctoris.

Chowdhury, K.A., K.S.Saraswat and G.M.Buth 1977.
Ancient Agriculture and Forestry in North India. Bombay: Asia Publishing House.

Danin, A.,
A.Shmida and A.Liston 1985.
Contributions to the flora of Sinai, III. checklist of the species collected and recorded by the Jerusalem team 1967-1982. Willdenowia 15:255-322.

Davies, N. de G. 1927.
Two Ramesside tombs at Thebes. New York: The Metropolitan Museum of Arts.

Davies, N. de G. 1943.
The tomb of Rekh-Mi-Re at Thebes. New York: The Metropolitan Museum of Arts.

Decelle, J. 1966.
La bruche sudaméricane des acacias: Pseudopachyremina spinipes (Erichson). Bull. Ann. Soc. R. Ent. Belg. 102:109-116.

Emery, W.B. 1939.
Excavations at Saqqara 1937-1938: Hor-Aha. Cairo: Government Press.

Germer, G. 1985.
Flora des pharaonischen Ägypten. Mainz: Philipp von Zabern.

Germer, G. 1988.
Katalog der altägyptischen Pflanzenreste der Berliner Museen. Wiesbaden: Otto Harrassowitz.

Griffith, F.Ll. 1900.
Beni Hasan. London: Gilbert and Rivington.

Halevy, G. 1974.
Effects of gazelles and seed beetles (Bruchidae) on germination and establishment of Acacia species. Israel Journal of Botany 23:120-126.

Hart, H.C. 1891.
Some account of the fauna and flora of Sinai, Petra and Wady Arabah. London: Committee of the Palestine Exploration Fund.

Heller, D. and C.C.Heyn in press.
Conspectus florae orientalis, Fasc. 5. Jerusalem: The Israel Academy of Sciences and Humanities.

Hepper, F.N. 1981.
Plant material. In G.T.Martin, Sacred animal necropolis at north Saqqara, p.146-151. London, Egypt Exploration Society.

Jenkins, N. 1980.
The Boat beneath the Pyramid: king Cheops' royal ship. London: Thames and Hudson.

Kajale, M.D. 1988.
Plant economy. In M.K.Dhavalikar, H.D.Sankalia and Z.D.Ansari, Excavations at Inamgaon, vol. 1, part II, p.727-821. Pune, Deccan College Postgraduate and Research Institute.

Keimer, L. 1932.
A propos d'un bosquet d'acacias situé aux environs des pyramides de Gizeh. Bull. Soc. R. Géogr. Egypte 18:85-95.

Kunth, C.S. 1826.
Recherches sur les plantes trouvées dans les tombeaux egyptiens par M.Passalacqua. Ann. Sci. Nat. (Paris) 8:418-423.

Lamprey, H.F.,
G.Halevy and S.Makacha 1974.
Interactions between Acacia, bruchid seed beetles and large herbivores. E. Afr. Wildl. Journal 12:81-85.

Lauer, J.P.,
V.L.Täckholm and E.Åberg 1951.
Les plantes découvertes dans les souterrains de l'enceinte du roi Zoser à Saqqarah (IIIe dynastie). Bull. Inst. Egypte 32:121-157.

Liphschitz, N.,
S.Lev-Yadun and Y.Waisel 1981.
Dendroarchaeological investigations in Israel (Masada). Israel Exploration Journal 31:230-234.

Loret, V. 1892.
La flore pharaonique: d'après les documents hiéroglyphiques et les spécimens découverts dans les tombs, deuxième édition. Paris: Leroux.

Luca, Y. de 1965.
Etude de la morphologie imaginale et remarques concernant Bruchidius baudoni Caillol (Col. Bruchidae). Bull. Inst. Franc. Afrique Noire 2:727-738.

Lucas, A. and J.R.Harris 1962.
Ancient Egyptian materials and industries, 4th ed. London: Arnold.

Meshel, Z. 1974.
New data about the "desert kites". Tel-Aviv 1:129-143.

Mond, Sir R. and O.H.Myers 1937.
Cemeteries of Armant, I. London: The Egypt Exploration Society.

Newberry, P.E. 1889.
On the vegetable remains discovered in the cemetery of Hawara. In W.M.F. Petrie, Hawara, Biahmu, and Arsinoe, p.46-53. London, Paul.

Oakley, K.P. 1932.
Woods used by the ancient Egyptians. Analyst 57:158-159.

Peake, F.G.G. 1952.
On a bruchid seed borer in Acacia arabica. Bull. Entomol. Res. 43: 317-324.

Post, G.E. 1896.
Flora of Syria, Palestine and Sinai. Beirut: Syrian Protestant College.

Prevett, P.F. 1971.
The larvae of some Nigerian Bruchidae (Coleoptera). Trans. R. ent. Soc. London 123:247-312.

Ribstein, W. 1925.
Zur Kenntnis der im alten Aegypten verwendeten Hölzer. Bot. Arch. 9:194-209.

Ross, J.H. 1979.
A conspectus of the African Acacia species. Mem. Bot. Surv. S. Afr. 44.

Rothenberg, B. 1988.
The Egyptian mining temple at Timna. London: Institute for Archaeo-Metallurgical Studies.

Schweinfurth, G. 1873.
The Heart of Africa, translated by E.E.Frewer. London: Sampson Low.

Schweinfurth, G. 1884.
Ueber Pflanzenreste aus altaegyptischen Gräbern. Berichte der Deutschen Botanischen Gesellschaft 2:351-371.

Schweinfurth, G. 1908.
Ueber die Pflanzenreste aus mR 29 und 30. In H.Schäfer, Priestergräber und andere Grabfunde vom Ende des alten Reiches bis zur griechischen Zeit vom Totentempel des Ne-User-Rê, p.152-164. Leipzig, Hinrichs.

Southgate, B.J. 1978.
Variation in the susceptibility of African Acacia (Leguminosae) to seed beetle attack. Kew Bull. 32:541-544.

Southgate, B.J. 1979.
Biology of the Bruchidae. Ann. Rev. Entomol. 24:449-473.

Täckholm, V. 1954.
The wood reserves of Egypt in the near past. In UNESCO, Symposium sur la Protection de la Nature dans le Proche-Orient. Beyrouth.

Täckholm, V. 1974.
Students' flora of Egypt, 2nd ed. Cairo: Cairo University.

Täckholm, V. and G.Täckholm 1941.
Flora of Egypt, Vol. 1. Cairo: Fouad University.

Tchernov, E. 1988.
The biogeographical history of the southern Levant. In Y.Yom-Tov and E.Tchernov (eds), The zoogeography of Israel: the distribution and abundance at a zoogeographical crossroad, p.159-250. Dordrecht, Junk.

Townsend, C.C. 1974.
Flora of Iraq, vol. 3: Leguminales. Baghdad: Ministry of Agriculture and Agrarian Reform.

Tristram, H.B. 1884.
The survey of western Palestine: the fauna and flora of Palestine. London: The Committee of the Palestine Exploration Fund.

Uphof, J.C.T. 1968.
Dictionary of Economic Plants. 2nd ed. New York and Codicote: Cramer.

Western, A.C. 1983.
Catalogue of identified charcoal samples. In K.M.Kenyon and T.A. Holland (eds.), Excavations at Jericho, vol. 5, p.770-773. London, British School of Archaeology in Jerusalem.

Wickens, G.E. 1969.
A study of Acacia albida Del. (Mimosoideae). Kew Bull. 23:181-202.

Wickens, G.E. 1976.
The flora of Jebel Marra (Sudanian republic) and its geographical affinities. Kew: Royal Botanic Gardens.

Zeist, W. van 1987.
The plant remains. In A.Vila, Le cimetière kermaïque d'Ukma ouest, p.247-255. Paris, Editions du CNRS.

Zohary, M. 1962.
  Plant life of Palestine: Israel
  and Jordan. New York: Ronald
  Press.
Zohary, M. 1972.
  Flora Palaestina, part 2. Jerusa-
  lem: The Israel Academy of Scien-
  ces and Humanities.

L'homme et l'environnement en Egypte durant la période prédynastique

25

Aline Emery-Barbier
Laboratoire de Palynologie, Musée de l'Homme, Paris, France

RESUME: Dans le site prédynastique de Nagada, l'analyse pollinique a mis en évidence une grande variété d'espèces végétales dont l'existence est confirmée par la détermination des graines. Les espèces arborescentes sont représentées principalement par l'Acacia, mais aussi par des espèces allochtones. Les résultats de l'analyse pollinique indiquent que les prélèvements ont été faits à proximité d'un champ ou dans une aire de conservation des grains de céréales. La présence de nombreuses espèces herbacées aux propriétés remarquables permet d'envisager que leur groupement n'était pas le fait du hasard, mais peut-être celui d'un jardin proche des champs de céréales. Ainsi, l'Homme a pu relativement tôt modifier son environnement, en développant les cultures et en introduisant des espèces étrangères.

ABSTRACT: Pollen analysis of soil samples from the pre-dynastic site of Nagada, on the Nile in Upper Egypt, revealed a great variety of species. The palynological results are confirmed by the examination of plant macro-remains. Acacia is predominant among the arboreal pollen. Pollen of Tilia and Cedrus, neither of them indigenous to Egypt, testifies to the importation of the timber of these species. High Cerealia-type pollen percentages point to cereal grain fields or a grain-processing or grain-storage area in the vicinity. The presence of the pollen of various herbaceous species with particular properties, e.g. medicinal plants, is very likely not accidental; the species concerned may have been cultivated locally. Already from an early date man has modified the environment by practising plant cultivation and introducing foreign species.

1 SITUATION DU SITE ET DATATION

L'analyse palynologique présentée ici a été réalisée dans le site prédynastique de Nagada, en Haute-Egypte, sur la rive gauche du Nil, en aval de Thèbes et des temples de Karnak et Louxor. Le site de Nagada a été étudié à la fin du XIXème siècle (1895) par l'égyptologue anglais Sir Flinder Petries, qui y découvrit une importante installation prédynastique. L'abondance du matériel trouvé dans la nécropole de Nagada fit de ce lieu le site éponyme d'une culture du IVème millénaire: le Nagadien. Différentes recherches ont fait apparaître que la région de Nagada avait été fréquentée ou occupée dès le Paléolithique; il semble que la ville ait pu être la capitale de l'Egypte méridionale durant la periode prédynastique. Le début de cette période est vraisemblablement lié aux premières tentatives d'utilisation du metal - la malachite - il y a environ 6000 ans (Michalowski 1968).

"L'utilisation du carbone radioactif C14, pour dater les objets de l'époque prédynastique n'a pas donné des résultats pleinement satisfaisants, mais nous permet néanmoins de situer la phase la plus ancienne de la culture de Nagada au cours des deux premiers siècles du IVème millénaire." (Michalowski 1968). La datation par la méthode du C14 des sites et villages prédynastiques en cours d'étude dans la région de Nagada donne un ensemble de valeurs comprises entre 5270 et 4600 années BP. Les charbons de bois prélevés dans le sud de la ville fournissent un ordre de grandeur entre 4920±90 et 4370-4600 années BP (Hassan, comm. pers.).

2 LES ECHANTILLONS

Les neuf échantillons analysées ont été prélevés par F.A. Hassan (Washington State University) en 1981. Les sédiments proviennent de quatre coupes différentes et recouvrent la stratigraphie d'ensemble du chantier. Les niveaux organiques ont livré un nombre de pollens important - de 400 à 750. Les grains de pollen se présentent la plupart du temps dans un état de conservation remarquable.

Les résultats interprétés et représentés graphiquement sont ceux des niveaux KH3 BI 54 E (East wall profile) et KH3 BI 54 3 (North wall profile). Le profil est comporte 4 échantillons, l'échantillon 1 étant l'échantillon inférieur, les graphiques représentent séparément les pollens des espèces arborescentes (AP) et non arborescentes (NAP) (Fig. 1). Un seul échantillon du profil nord a été figuré avec l'ensemble des pollens identifiés (Fig. 2). Les horizons de sable graveleux sous-jacents se sont révélés beaucoup moins riches en nombre de pollens et en taxons. La surface du chantier est stérile.

Les données de l'analyse palynologique seront comparées à l'étude des macro-restes réalisée par W. Wetterström (Massachusetts Institute of Technology) dans la région de Nagada-Khattara.

3 LES ESPECES ARBORESCENTES PRESENTES A NAGADA

Les arbres n'excéderont pas 15% dans les spectres polliniques observés, et les essences identifiées seront classées en deux catégories, selon qu'elles sont locales ou introduites.

3.1 Les espèces autochtones

L'Acacia est le plus représenté parmi les espèces autochtones. D'après Loret (1892), cet arbre a toujours vécu en Egypte, où il est encore fréquent de nos jours, dans la vallée et le delta du Nil, dans le désert lybique et ses oasis à l'ouest du Nil, et dans le Sinaï, au sud du désert d'El-Tih (Täckholm 1974). L'Acacia fournit un bois imperméable propre à la construction des bateaux et une résine aux nombreux usages: ces propriétés ont motivé son emploi lors des périodes dynastiques (Loret 1889). L'écriture démotique mentionne ses feuilles, ses résines, sa gomme, le charbon d'Acacia et son huile de première qualité (Charpentier 1981).

Ziziphus spina-christi (jujubier). Des grains de pollen de Ziziphus ont été mis en évidence. L'analyse des macro-restes témoigne de la présence de Ziziphus spina-christi (Wetterström 1980). Ce dernier, répandu sur tout le territoire égyptien actuel, produit un fruit comestible de la taille d'une cerise: la jujube (Täckholm 1974). L'écriture démotique des périodes dynastiques fait état du "bois de jujubier", de ses feuilles, de sa farine, de son pain et de sa bière (Charpentier 1981). Le nom de "jujubier" apparaît dans de nombreux toponymes, et le mot "jujube" dans les textes médicaux. Le jujubier était-il déjà utilisé lors des périodes prédynastiques? Wetterström (1980) note que les noyaux de Ziziphus identifiés, proches des noyaux actuels, pourraient représenter un stade intermédiaire dans le processus de mise en culture, de sélection et de domestication de l'espèce.

Capparis (câprier). Six espèces de Capparis sont présentes dans la flore égyptienne actuelle. Capparis decidua a la plus vaste répartition et occupe la vallée du Nil du Caire jusqu'au Wadi Halfa, au sud du pays (Täckholm 1974).

3.2 Les espèces allochtones: Cedrus et Tilia

Des pollens de Tilia ont été déterminés dans la momie de Ramsès II (Leroi-Gourhan 1985) et dans une momie datée du Ier siècle avant notre ère (Girard et Maley 1987); dans cette dernière, des pollens de

NAGADA 1981
KH3 BI54E

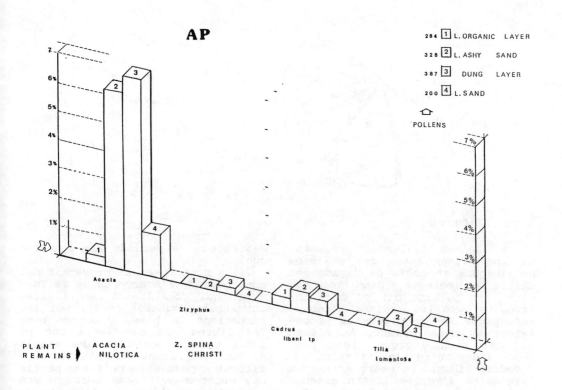

AP

284 1 L. ORGANIC LAYER
328 2 L. ASHY SAND
387 3 DUNG LAYER
200 4 L. SAND

⇧ POLLENS

Acacia

Zizyphus

Cadrus
libani tp

Tilia
tomentosa

PLANT REMAINS ▶ ACACIA NILOTICA   Z. SPINA CHRISTI

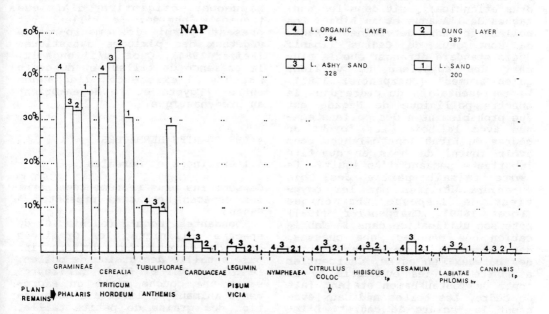

NAP

4 L. ORGANIC LAYER 284   2 DUNG LAYER 387
3 L. ASHY SAND 328   1 L. SAND 200

GRAMINEAE   CEREALIA   TUBULIFLORAE   CARDUACEAE   LEGUMIN.   NYMPHEAEA   CITRULLUS COLOC   HIBISCUS   SESAMUM   LABIATAE PHLOMIS hv   CANNABIS tp

PLANT REMAINS ▶ PHALARIS   TRITICUM HORDEUM   ANTHEMIS   PISUM VICIA

Figure 1.

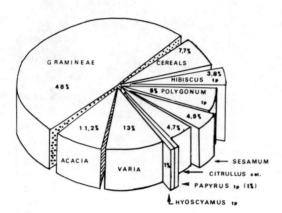

NAGADA 1981

K H3 B I 54—3

VARIA

BRYONIA. tp	0,5 %
ZIZYPHUS tp	0,5 %
LOTUS tp	0,25 %
GERANIACEAE	0,7 %
EPHEDRA	0,25 %
ACTINOPTERIS	1,5 %
CAPPARIS	1 %

NP 399

Figure 2.

cèdre étaient également présents. La comparaison entre ces analyses polliniques et celle de Nagada est difficile, puisque, dans les momies, les pollens ont pu être introduits avec les résines d'embaumement que les égyptiens se procuraient au Moyen-Orient. Au niveau du site archéologique, leur présence a une autre signification.

Cedrus libani. Le cèdre n'est pas originaire d'Egypte. Cette essence se trouvera soit dans l'Atlas (Cedrus atlantica), soit dans les montagnes de l'Amanus et au Liban. Les pollens de cèdre déterminés à Nagada sont ceux de Cedrus libani: "bois standard étranger que la plupart des égyptiens ne voyaient qu'en grumes" (Charpentier 1981). La représentation du cèdre dans le spectre pollinique de Nagada est due probablement à des pollens amenés avec le bois. Les forêts de cèdres du Liban sont célèbres pour avoir fourni du bois en quantité importante pendant l'Antiquité. Le cèdre faisait partie des bois étrangers utilisés par les égyptiens de l'époque pharaonique (Loret 1889). Charpentier (1981) note son utilisation dans la fabrication des meubles, des châsses, des pièges et de certaines parties des bateaux. En outre, Charpentier a montré que les oushabtis de la tombe de Toutankhamon étaient fait de cèdre. Les textes médicaux évoquent la "sciure de cèdre". L'importation du cèdre pourrait avoir

débuté dès la période pré-dynastique.

Tilia tomentosa. Il provenait des montagnes de l'Amanus ou de la Turquie, qui constituent ses limites actuelles (Mouterde 1947). Des importations de bois, d'écorce pour les fibres, ou de fleurs ont pu avoir lieu, à moins que des essais de culture aient été tentés. Le tilleul a peut-être pu faire partie des espèces cultivées hors de son contexte climatique, à l'instar de Mimusops, originaire d'Afrique tropicale humide. Le tilleul est présent parmi les macro-restes végétaux des périodes dynastiques (Keimer 1984). Quoi qu'il en soit, la présence du tilleul et du cèdre atteste l'existence d'échanges entre l'Egypte et le Moyen-Orient au prédynastique.

4 LES PLANTES HERBACEES

4.1 Graminées et Céréales

Ce sont les plus représentées parmi les espèces herbacées présentes à Nagada.

Abondantes jusqu'à fournir 70% du spectre pollinique, les Graminées sont de deux types, différenciés par la taille des grains de pollen. Le niveau KH3 BI 54 3, qui représente une couche riche en excréments animaux, a livré à l'observation des grains de petite taille. Les autres couches archéologiques contiennent une majorité de pollens ayant un diamètre de 50 μm, alors que celui des pores est de 5 à 6 μm pour l'extérieur de l'anneau.

Le niveau KH3 BI 54 3 contient 10% de pollens de Céréales. Dans les autres niveaux, la proportion varie entre 12 et 45%. Dans la pluie pollinique naturelle, les pollens de Céréales sont toujours faiblement représentés. Des mesures faites dans les champs cultivés et dans leur voisinage montrent que le pourcentages de pollens de Céréales est faible, inférieur à 3% à plus d'un kilomètre, compris entre 3 et 5% de la bordure des champs à un kilomètre; en limite des champs, le pourcentage n'excède jamais 12% (Bastin 1964). Les taux observés dans les niveaux organiques sont si élevés qu'il est possible de les interpréter comme un apport de paille le bétail, celle-ci étant utilisée comme nourriture ou comme litière. En ce qui concerne les autres niveaux, l'abondance des pollens de Céréales peut laisser supposer que les prélèvements ont été réalisés dans une aire de battage, de conservation ou d'utilisation des grains. Dans cette zone, l'analyse des macro-restes a fourni de nombreux grains et rachis de blé (Triticum dicoccum) et d'orge (Hordeum vulgare). Néanmoins, l'orge, supportant mieux l'aridité et l'alcalinité du terrain, est plus représentée que le blé. La dispersion des macro-restes suggère une utilisation de ces céréales comme litière (Wetterström 1980).

4.2 Les Anthémidées

Elles représentent 27% des pollens dans le niveau KH3 BI 54 E1. Le genre Matricaria dominait parmi les millions de pollens présents dans la momie de Ramsès II (Leroi-Gourhan 1985). Dans ce cas, il pourrait s'agir d'Anthemis, car des graines ont été identifiées. Anthemis est un nom grec désignant les plantes aromatiques utilisées en parfumerie et en médecine (Boulos et el-Hadidi 1984). Les Anthemis ont en commun de nombreuses vertus médicinales; elles sont fébrifuges, vermifuges, anti-spasmodiques, vulnéraires et anti-arthritiques. Les fleurs d'Anthemis pseudocotula, commune actuellement en Egypte, sont anti-sep-

tiques, anti-tumorales et anti-diabétiques (Boulos et el-Hadidi 1984). Malgré une large représentation pollinique des Anthémidées, la présence des graines est rare; les fleurs étaient-elles récoltées, comme à l'époque pharaonique, ou ont-elles été ramassées avec les Céréales lors des moissons?

4.3 La Coloquinte: Citrullus colocynthis

Selon Plu (1985), on la rencontre dans toutes les régions arides et désertiques de l'Afrique et de l'Orient. Elle occupe actuellement tout le territoire égyptien. Son fruit, une baie de la taille d'une petite orange, renferme une pulpe spongieuse et amère dans laquelle se trouvent de nombreuses graines. Elle est connue pour ses vertus médicinales, puisqu'elle soulage les maux d'estomac; sa pulpe est aussi purgative (Zohary 1982). Elle a été, semble-t-il, très utilisée en médecine humaine aux temps des pharaons. Leca (1971) cite de très nombreux remèdes où la coloquinte seule ou associée à d'autres produits a pu servir à soigner les maladies les plus diverses. Mélangée à des feuilles d'acacia, elle était utilisée contre le ver "hefet" - l'ascaris. L'ensemble acacia, coloquinte et dattes était anti-conceptionnel. L'application de résine d'acacia déséchée, de coloquinte et de papyrus guérissait les brûlures (Charpentier 1981).

4.4 Les Cucurbitacées: Bryonia tp.

Deux espèces de Bryonia sont présentes en Egypte: Bryonia syriaca et Bryonia cretica. Elles sont rares, et leur aire de répartition est peu étendue (Täckholm 1974).

Bryonia dioica est mentionnée dans les textes médicaux des périodes dynastiques et décrite dans les textes démotiques, où il est fait état de ses fruits, racines, vrilles et pousses de feuilles (Charpentier 1981).

4.5 La jusquiame: Hyoscyamus tp.

Les jusquiames sont des adventices

des cultures, produisant des petites baies qui referment un violent alcaloïde: la hyoscyamine. Actuellement, la plus commune en Egypte, la plus dangereuse aussi, est Hyoscyamus muticus, largement utilisée en médecine. Elle est également narcotique. Pour Bonnier (non daté), Hyoscyamus niger fournissait dans l'ancienne Egypte une huile pour les lampes.

4.6 Les Cypéracées:
Cyperus papyrus tp.

Si répandu en Egypte pharaonique, où d'après l'écriture démotique, il est "la plante réunifiant les deux Egypte" (Charpentier 1981), il n'est plus localisé que dans la Wadi Natrum (Täckholm 1974). En Egypte pharaonique, la base inférieure des tiges servait d'aliment à la classe pauvre, et il était utilisé dans la fabrication de charbon, de paniers, de cages, de bateaux et de papier.

4.7 Le chanvre

Un grain de pollen de type Cannabis a été identifié. Sa présence peut apporter une précision relative aux échanges qui avaient lieu entre l'Egypte et le continent voisin. Des recherches archéologiques dans le nord-est de l'Asie ont montré que le Cannabis était cultivé au Néolithique il y a à peu près 6000 ans. Des textes chinois vieux de 3000 ans indiquent, s'appuyant sur une longue tradition orale, ses capacités à fournir des fibres végétales (Hui-Lin-Li 1975). Si les égyptiens de la période prédynastique connaissaient le chanvre, on ne sait rien de son utilisation. Plus tard, des textes médicaux des périodes dynastiques citeront le Cannabis sativa. Cependant, sous les climats chauds, la teneur en résine du chanvre est beaucoup plus importante qu'en Europe, diminuant par la même la qualité de ses fibres; Mehemet Ali, vice-roi d'Egypte dans la première moitié du XIXème siècle, ne put obtenir, à partir du Cannabis européen cultivé en Egypte, les cordages nécessaires au gréement des navires engagés dans la guerre contre la Turquie (Touhami et Moussaoui 1985). Les analyses palynolgiques réalisées au Moyen-Orient n'ayant jamais encore révélé la présence du Cannabis, peut-on alors supposer que sa pénétration se serait effectuée par la péninsule arabique? Notons à cet effet une vague de migrations humaines venant de la péninsule arabique par la Mer Rouge aux environs de 5000 BP (Michalowski 1968). Le pollen de chanvre était présent dans les momies citées plus haut.

4.8 Le sésame

S'agit-il de Sesamum indicum, ou de Sesamum alatum? Sesamum indicum est signalé par Fournier (1961) comme le meilleur des oléagineux, et, comme tel, cultivé très tôt dans l'antiquité, notamment en Egypte (Darby et al. 1977; Keimer 1984). Son origine est polytopique: il est signalé d'abord en Inde (5500 BP), en Syrie et en Palestine (5000 BP), puis en Iran et en Egypte (4300 BP) (Mathon 1981).

Sesamum alatum, originaire des savanes africaines, est présent, bien que très rare, à l'est du Nil, de Louxor à l'actuelle frontière soudanaise.

4.9 Phlomis herba-vinti tp.

Quelques grains de pollen de type Phlomis herba-vinti ont été remarqués. La répartition actuelle de ce végétal est le Moyen-Orient et la région Méditerranéenne. Le duvet de la plante a pu servir à faire des mèches de lampes (Bonnier, non daté).

5 CONCLUSION

A Nagada, durant la période prédynastique, les céréales issues du Moyen-Orient sont cultivées sur les bords du Nil. Ceci est en accord avec les travaux de Clark (1965), qui situe dans la zone étudiée l'un des premiers établissements agricoles (6000-4800 BP). A la culture de l'orge, la plus ancienne culture africaine connue, vient s'ajouter celle du blé. Celle-ci est-elle liée à une amélioration des conditions climatiques, le blé nécessitant davantage d'humidité? Toutefois, les autres taxons, de même que les données sédimentologiques et géologiques, ne plaident pas en faveur de cette hypothèse (Hassan et Wendorf 1980). Cela correspond-il au début de l'irrigation, qui jouera un grand rôle dans la réunification des deux Egypte et dans l'installation de l'administration pharaonique (Michalowski 1968)?

D'autres végétaux allochtones font leur apparition, témoignant aussi de l'origine asiatique des plantes introduites. Ceci n'est pas sans relation avec le peuplement de l'Egypte: "au Pléistocène, le pays était situé dans la zone de climat subtropical et abondait en lacs. Le dessèchement climatique entraina l'exode de la population primitive en amont du fleuve vers les forêts tropicales. A sa place s'installeront des tribus chamites de la péninsule arabique." (Michalowski 1968). Les échanges entre Egypte et continent asiatique se sont perpétués.

Les autres taxons sont ceux de végétaux sauvages peut-être reconnus pour leurs propriétés. En effet, chacun des végétaux cités peut intervenir dans l'économie de l'Homme prédynastique, en entrant dans son régime alimentaire, en faisant partie de sa pharmacopée, ou encore en lui apportant une aide technique précieuse. Ainsi, tolérés et cueillis, ou propagés grâce à la création d'un milieu artificiel plus favorable à la formation des organes utilisés, ils pourraient justifier la grande représentation sur le site d'espèces qui n'apparaissaient pas dans le spectre pollinique des niveaux sous-jacents à l'habitat prédynastique.

BIBLIOGRAPHIE

Bastin B. 1964.
Recherches sur les relations entre la végétation actuelle et le spectre pollinique récent dans la forêt de Soignes (Belgique). Agricultura VII/2:341-373.

Bonnier, G. non daté.
Flore complète de France, Suisse et Belgique (12 vols.). Paris: Librairie Générale de l'Enseignement.

Charpentier, G. 1981.
Recueil de matériaux épigraphiques relatifs à la botanique de l'Egypte antique. Paris: Trismégiste.

Clark, G.D. 1965.
Les premiers établissements agricoles. In Cl.Ch.Mathon, Phytogéographie appliquée. L'origine des plantes cultivées, p.20. Paris 1981, Masson.

Darby, W.J., P.Ghalioungui and L.Grivetti 1977.
Food:the Gift of Osiris. London-New York-San Francisco: Academic Press.

Fournier, P. 1961.
Les quatre flores de France, 1er éd. Paris: Lechevallier.

Girard, M. et J.Maley 1987.
Etude palynologique. Nouv. Arch. Mus. Hist. Nat. 25:103-110.

Hassan, F.A. and F.Wendorf 1980.
Holocene ecology and prehistory in the Egyptian Sahara. In M.A.J. Williams and H.Faure (eds.), The Sahara and the Nile, p.407-419. Rotterdam, Balkema.

Hui-Lin-Li 1975.
The origin and use of Cannabis in Eastern Asia: their linguistic-cultural implications. Paris: Rubin.

Keimer, L. 1984.
Die Gartenpflanzen im alten Ägypten, I und II. Mainz am Rhein: Von Zabern Verlag.

Leca, A.P. 1971.
La médecine Egyptienne aux temps de Pharaons. Paris: Dacosta.

Leroi-Gourhan, Arl. 1985.
Les pollens et l'embaumement. In La momie de Ramsès II, p.162-165. Paris, E.R.C.

Loret, V. 1889.
L'Egypte aux temps des Pharaons, p.75-125. Paris: Baillère et Fils.

Loret, V. 1892.
La flore pharaonique d'après les documents hiéroglyphiques et les spécimens découverts dans les tombes, 2ème éd. Paris: Leroux.

L. Boulos and M.N. el-Hadidi 1984.
The weed flora of Egypt. The American University in Cairo Press.

Mathon, Cl.Ch. 1981.
Phytogéographie appliquée. L'origine des plantes cultivées. Paris: Masson.

Michalowski, K. 1968.
L'art de l'ancienne Egypte. Paris: Mazenod.

Mouterde, P. 1947.
La végétation arborescente des pays du Levant. Beyrouth: Ecole Française d'Ingénieurs.

Plu, A. 1985.
Bois et graines. In La momie de Ramsès II, p.166-174. Paris, E.R.C.

Täckholm, V. 1974.
Student's Flora of Egypt, 2ème éd. Cairo:Cairo University Press.

Touhami, M. et D.Moussaoui 1985.
Quelques données chimiques et botaniques: du Chanvre au Cannabis. L'univers du vivant 4.

Wetterström, W. 1980.
Predynastic agriculture in Upper Egypt: a note on palaeoethnobotanical studies in the Nagada-Khattara region. Bulletin de l'Association Internationale pour l'étude de la Préhistoire Egyptienne 2:20-32.

Zohary, D. and M.Hopf 1988.
Domestication of Plants in the Old World. Oxford: Clarendon Press.

Zohary, M. 1982.
Plants of the Bible. Cambridge: Cambridge University Press.

Man's Role in the Shaping of the Eastern Mediterranean Landscape, Bottema, Entjes-Nieborg & van Zeist (eds)
© 1990 Balkema, Rotterdam. ISBN 90 6191 138 9

The impact of man on the natural vegetation in Bulgaria from the Neolithic to the Middle Ages

26

Elizabeta D. Bozilova & Spassimir B. Tonkov
Department of Botany, University of Sofia, Bulgaria

ABSTRACT: The human impact on the natural vegetation is traced through the results of pollen analysis and palaeoethnobotanical research in different parts of Bulgaria.

1 INTRODUCTION

In order to establish the nature of the human influence and the degree of human impact on the vegetational cover in Bulgaria a great deal of pollen-analytical investigations have been carried out. The results obtained were corroborated by palaeoethnobotanical and archaeological data. The methodological problems concerning the anthropogenic indicators in pollen diagrams are discussed by Bottema (1982 (1985)) for the Mediterranean and Greece, but to a certain extent these indicators are of different value for Bulgaria. We accept the division of the anthropogenic elements into two groups - primary and secondary - put forward by Behre (this volume).

In the mountains of southwestern Bulgaria, characteristic secondary anthropogenic indicators include Juniperus, Plantago lanceolata, Rumex and Scleranthus. Special attention is paid to Plantago lanceolata, a species which follows different types of human activity such as livestock grazing in the mountain meadows. Very often some of the Poaceae, Artemisia, Chenopodiaceae, Polygonum aviculare, Urtica, Taraxacum, etc. could also be included in the group of the most common secondary anthropogenic indicators.

In this paper, graphs are given for most of the investigated sites under discussion (Fig. 1), showing both groups of anthropogenic indicators, extracted from the corresponding pollen diagrams.

2 INVESTIGATED LOCALITIES AND DISCUSSION

From the archaeological and palaeoethnobotanical evidence, and partly from the pollen analyses, it became evident that Thracia and southwestern Bulgaria were the first centres where agriculture had developed at the end of the seventh millennium BC. The first Neolithic cultures, Karanovo-I, Starcevo and Cavdar, arose here and displayed close relations with the settlements in southern Anatolia. It also became clear that at that time settlements existed with developed agriculture and stock-breeding with high productivity in the lower mountainous zone at ca 800 m above sea level.

2.1 South-Central Europe

The excavation of the Neolithic settlement Rakitovo (Fig. 1:1), located in the foothills of the northwestern Rhodopa Mountains, provided valuable information about the living conditions of the native population. The determination of the macro-remains (carbonized wood and seeds) from the cultural layer of 6000-5000 BC showed which tree species had been used for different purposes as well as the level of agricultural activity. The carbonized wood mainly consisted of Quer-

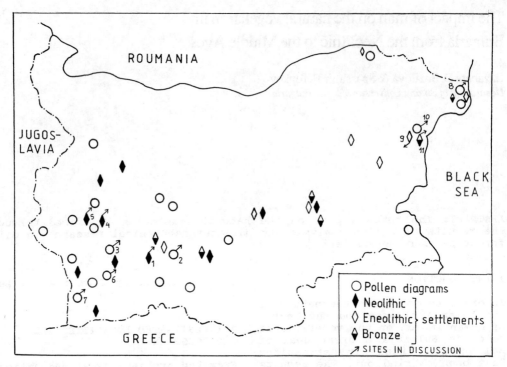

Fig. 1. Map of Bulgaria showing the distribution of the pollen sites. 1. Rakitovo; 2. Lake Sucho Ezero; 3. Rila Mountains; 4. Kremenik; 5. Galabnik; 6. Pirin Mountains; 7. Western frontier mountains; 8. Lake Durankulak; 9. Lake Varna.

cus, followed by Pinus sylvestris, Picea, Abies, Ulmus, Corylus and Fraxinus. It was the first find of coniferous wood in a Neolithic settlement, which proved the existence of such a type of forest in the close vicinity. The wood of Fraxinus could have been used for making tools and stakes; the branches of Corylus had been used for the construction of fences. The finds of these wooden remains implies that coniferous and deciduous forests had been present around the settlement.

The carbonized seeds of cereals, such as Hordeum vulgare and comparatively few Triticum dicoccum and Triticum monococcum seeds, suggest that these crops had been cultivated in almost pure cultures (Čakalova and Bozilova 1981).

The evidence from palaeoethnobotanical remains for early land occupation is confirmed by the pollen analysis of Lake Sucho Ezero (Fig. 1:2) in the southern Rila Mountains (Bozilova et al. in

press). The presentation of some selected pollen types (Fig. 2) starts at 9000 BP when the first Cerealia and Triticum pollen grains appeared. The relative abundance of the secondary anthropogenic indicators during Neolithic times is higher, with the considerable contribution of Artemisia, Poaceae and Chenopodiaceae pollen.

A slight increase in the proportion of cereals compared to the group of the secondary anthropophytes is observed for the Eneolithic period and this tendency is maintained in the subsequent millennia. In historical times the sharp increase in the pollen curves of the primary anthropophytes by no means testifies to well-developed and widely practised agriculture.

2.2 Southwest Bulgaria

Human impact on the natural vegetation of the Rila Mountains can be followed after the end of the Neolithic and the beginning of the Eneolithic period. In the higher parts of the Rila Mountains (Fig. 1:3) tree vegetation was periodically set on fire, most probably for new seasonal pasture during summertime. This supposition is supported by the appearance of ruderals and the short-term rises in the Juniperus and Corylus pollen curves. The quantity of pollen grains of Triticum and Hordeum increases in the Late Eneolithic (5600 BP) while Secale appears in the diagram after 3000 BP (Fig. 3) together with the rest of the anthropophytes. Later on, the Romans practised the smelting of iron and used timber for that purpose (Bozilova 1976; Bozilova and Smit 1979; Bozilova et al. in press).

Several sites were excavated in the foothills of the mountain slopes, belonging to the cultural periods Karanovo II-IV. The evidence collected from the palaeoeth-

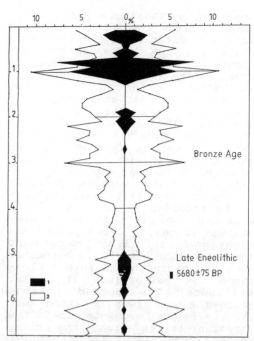

Fig. 3. Indicators of human activity in the diagram of "Dry Lake", Rila Mountains. 1: Hordeum, Triticum, Cerealia; 2: Artemisia, Rumex, Plantago lanceolata, Cirsium-type, Scleranthus.

nobotanical finds of the Neolithic settlement Kremenik (Fig. 1:4) suggested that since 6500 BP agricultural activity had been considerable and included the cultivation of Triticum monococcum, T. dicoccum and T. spelta (Čakalova and Sarbinska 1987). The increase of the group of secondary anthropogenic indicators, Chenopodiaceae, Artemisia, Polygonum aviculare and Convolvulus, is confirmed by their occurrence as weeds in the settlements Kremenik and Cavdar (Dennell 1978).

Carbonized wood of Quercus, Fraxinus, Acer and small pieces of Pinus and Fagus was determined from the cultural layer of the Neolithic settlement Galabnik (Fig. 1:5), located in a valley between the western Rila Mountains and some lower hills (Čakalova, unpubl. data). Between 8000-5000 BP the abovementioned taxa reach maximal values in almost all pollen diagrams from that part of the Rila Mountains.

The available pollen diagrams

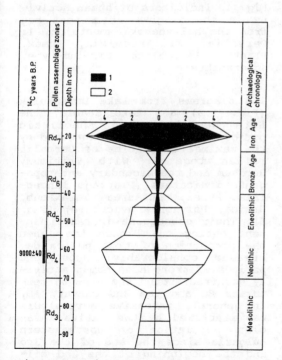

Fig. 2. Indicators of human activity (according to Berglund 1979) in the diagram of Kupena. 1: Hordeum, Triticum, Cerealia; 2: Rumex, Plantago lanceolata, P. major, Taraxacum-type, Cirsium-type, Scleranthus, Centaurea cyanus.

329

from the northeastern Pirin Mountains reflect the human influence upon the natural vegetation since the Bronze Age, concentrating particularly in the lower mountain zone. A high value of anthropogenic indicators in one of the pollen diagrams from that area (Fig. 1:6) coincides with the maximum of Cerealia. The decrease of these pollen taxa from the Bronze Age to the Iron Age is followed by two maxima in historical times (Bozilova and Stefanova, unpubl.).

In the lower western frontier mountains (Fig. 1:7) human influence is recorded at the end of the Neolithic, be it with lower percentage values of Cerealia and the anthropophytes. Their subsequent increase after 6000 BP is connected with the beginning of forest clearance for pastureland at higher altitudes. The second maximum follows around 2600 BP (Iron Age) when evidence suggests that the Thracian tribes along the river Struma moved higher up into these mountains (Fig. 4) (Tonkov and Bozilova, in press).

The investigations by Dennell (1978) are important for the reconstruction of the main tendencies of human impact in the lowlands and the mountainous areas for the period of 6000-3000 BC. For this period, the ratio between agriculture and stock-breeding remained unchanged. The economy of the settlements was based on the cultivation of cereals, seasonal pasture in the mountains and the use of leaf fodder for the animals. The later phases in the development of the settlements are connected with extension of the arable land and crop rotation.

2.3 Northeast Bulgaria

The Neolithic and Eneolithic periods started more than 1000 years later in northeastern Bulgaria than in the south and southwest of the country. The evidence of human impact was obtained from the complex investigation of several coastal lakes. In this area, herb vegetation is dominant, so that it is difficult to distinguish to any great extent the vegetational changes caused by climatic or anthropogenic factors. In the pol-

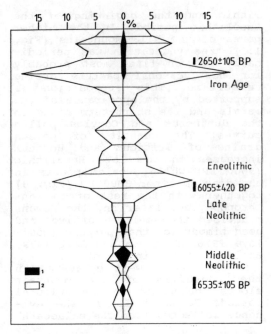

Fig. 4. Indicators of human activity in the diagram of a peat bog from the Maleshevska Mountains. 1: Cerealia; 2: Artemisia, Rumex, Plantago lanceolata, Cirsium-type, Scleranthus.

len diagrams from Lake Durankulak (Fig. 1:8) and Lake Shabla, the Late Neolithic and Eneolithic periods are quite well expressed by the maximal quantities of Cerealia pollen together with Triticum, Hordeum and the secondary anthropogenic indicators (Plantago lanceolata, Rumex, Centaurea, Taraxacum, Urtica, Polygonum aviculare) (Fig. 5). Their subsequent increase happens during the Bronze Age, when the proportion of tree pollen decreased considerably. Subsequent periods of pronounced human activity occurred around the 6th-5th centuries BC and the 2nd century AD. In general, intensive agriculture was practised by the native Thracian population of northeastern Bulgaria since the end of the 3rd and the beginning of the 2nd millennium BC (Bozilova and Filipova 1986).

The palaeoethnobotanical finds in the settlements of Durankulak and near Lake Varna of Neolithic and Eneolithic age are characterized by the presence of Triticum monococ-

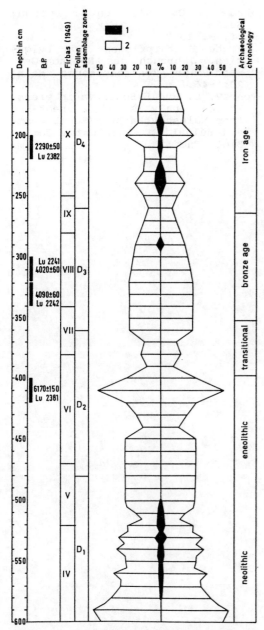

Fig. 5. Indicators of human activity in the diagram of Lake Duranku-lak. 1: Cerealia; 2: Artemisia, Urtica, Polygonum aviculare-type, Cirsium-type, Taraxacum-type, Centaurea jacea-type, Plantago lanceolata.

cum, T. dicoccum, T. aestivum, Hordeum vulgare var. nudum, Setaria, Rumex acetosella, etc. (Hopf 1973; Behre 1977; Boeva unpubl.). The Bronze Age botanical record is rich in seeds of T. monococcum, T. boeotium, Hordeum sp., Vicia ervilia, Setaria italica (Boeva, unpubl.). T. durum, T. spelta, Pisum and Vicia are determined for the Middle Ages.

In the area of Lake Varna (Fig. 1:9) numerous archaeological sites from the Eneolithic and Bronze Age are found. The pollen analyses demonstrate a considerable amount of cereals around 3400 BC, when all the deciduous trees decreased, together with a rise of Juniperus and the herbs up to 65%. The charred wood from the Bronze Age suggests that it was used for the construction of buildings and for other purposes. Charred seeds from Triticum monococcum, T. dicoccum, Hordeum, Setaria, etc. were also determined for this period (Čakalova and Bozilova 1984).

From the 1st century BC until the 3rd century AD, northeastern Bulgaria, the lower course of the Danube river, Dobrudza and Lower Mizia were occupied by the Romans. This is reflected in the pollen diagrams from that area by the abundance of anthropophytes and cereals.

The palynological and palaeoethnobotanical studies in various parts of Bulgaria provide distinct records of human activity. Future investigations are necessary to find more sites for pollen analysis closer to the archaeological settlements, in order to follow the separate phases of human occupation in full detail from every region.

ACKNOWLEDGEMENTS

The authors are indebted to Prof. W. van Zeist and Dr S. Bottema for the invitation to participate and present this paper at the symposium "The Impact of Ancient Man on the Landscape of the Eastern Mediterranean Region and the Near East". Thanks are due to Mrs G. Entjes-Nieborg for the typing of the manuscript.

REFERENCES

Behre, K.-E. 1977.
    Cereals from the Neolithic

settlement Sava near Varna (Bulgaria). Proc. Nat. Hist. Mus. Varna 13:214-215.

Behre, K.-E. (this volume).
Some reflections on the anthropogenic indicators and prehistoric occupation phases in the Near East.

Berglund, B. 1979.
Pollen analysis. In Paleohydrological changes in the temperate zone in the last 15000 years. Subproject B, Vol. II, p.133- 167.

Bottema, S. 1982(1985).
Palynological investigations in Greece with special reference to pollen as an indicator of human activity. Palaeohistoria 24:257-289.

Bozilova, E. 1976.
Pollenanalytical investigations in Eastern Rila Mountain. Ann. Univ. Sofia, Biol. Fac. 68/2:53-59.

Bozilova, E. and A.Smit 1979.
Palynology of Lake "Sucho Ezero" from South Rila Mountain (Bulgaria). Phytology 11:54-67.

Bozilova, E. and M.Filipova 1986.
Paleoecological environment in the northeastern Black Sea area during Neolithic, Eneolithic and Bronze periods. Studia Praehistorica 8:160-165.

Bozilova, E., S.Tonkov and D.Pavlova in press.
Pollen and plant macrofossil analysis of Lake "Sucho Ezero" in South Rila Mountain. Ann. Univ. Sofia, Biol. Fac. 80/2.

Bozilova, E., H.Panovska and S.Tonkov in press.
Pollenanalytical investigations in the National Reserve "Kupena", Western Rhodopes. Ann. Univ. Sofia, Biol. Fac. 81/2.

Čakalova, E. and E.Bozilova 1981.
Plant remains from the tell near the town Rakitovo. Interdisc. Res. Arch. Inst. VII-VIII:77-88.

Čakalova, E. and E.Bozilova 1984.
Pflanzenreste von der frühen Bronzezeit. Ann. Univ. Sofia, Biol. Fac. 74/2:18-28.

Čakalova, E. and E.Sorbinska 1987.
Untersuchungen von Pflanzenresten aus einer frühneolithischen Behausung in der neolithischen Siedlung Kremenik bei Sapareva Banja. Ann. Univ. Sofia, Biol. Fac. 78/2:3-16.

Dennell, R.W. 1978.
Early Farming in South Bulgaria from the Sixth to Third Millennia B.C. BAR International Series 45.

Hopf, M. 1973.
Frühe Kulturpflanzen aus Bulgarien. Jahrbuch des Römisch-Germanischen Zentralmuseums Mainz 20:1-46.

Tonkov, S. and E.Bozilova in press.
Pollen analysis of a peat-bog from Maleshevska Mt. (South-western Bulgaria). Ann. Univ. Sofia, Biol. Fac.

Preliminary note on human influence and the history of vegetation in southern Dalmatia and southern Greece

27

Susanne Jahns
Institut für Palynologie und Quartärwissenschaften, Göttingen, FR Germany

ABSTRACT: Cores from southern Dalmatia and southern Greece were investigated palynologically. The resulting diagrams show clear signs of human influence corresponding to the occupation history of in both areas. Attempts were made to gain additional information about the history of vegetation and human influence by pollen-morphological techniques.

1 SOUTH DALMATIA: MLJET

The core from southern Dalmatia was taken from the saltwater lake Malo Jezero on Mljet, the southernmost of the large Dalmatian islands (Fig. 1). In 1961 and 1962 Beug published pollen diagrams from Malo Jezero providing information about the vegetation history of this area for the first time (Beug 1961b, 1962, 1967). The cores, however, did not contain sediments of the last 2000 years and therefore new cores have been investigated. The new cores should enable us to examine man's interference with the vegetation in more recent periods.

In accordance with Beug's study, the new diagram also can be divided into four forest periods (Fig. 2). Period A saw a predominance of oaks. During period B the values of shrub vegetation were increasing, especially of the evergreen bushes Juniperus and Phillyrea. During period C evergreen oaks predominated (presumably Quercus ilex) and seem to have formed dense forests. Period C can be divided into subzones C1 (with the values of Juniperus still high), C2 (with high amounts of Erica) and C3 (with increasing values of Pinus).

In 1962 Beug stated that human influence during the Neolithic period and the Bronze Age is absent, which is in good agreement with the absence of settlements on

Fig. 1. Location of Mljet in South Dalmatia and of the Argive plain on the Peloponnese

Mljet during that time. Since about 400 BC Greek and Roman influence can be expected. In the new diagram too, no change in vegetation can be clearly attributed to human influence during the Neolithic and the Bronze Age (period A to subzone C3). In subzone C3 the increasing pine values and a continuous curve of Juglans are considered to indicate the time of Greek and Roman influence (Beug 1962; Bottema 1980; Brande 1973).

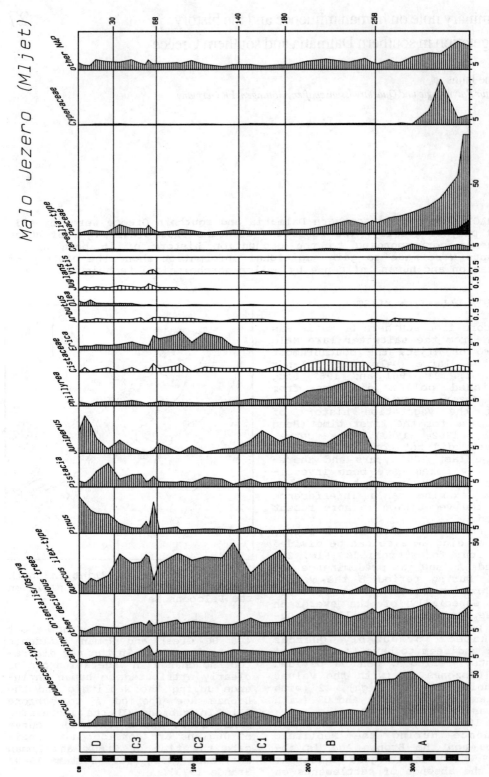

Fig. 2. AP percentage diagram of Malo Jezero, Mljet. The beginning of each pollen zone is dated after Beug (1961b): A: 7000 bc; B: 5600 bc; C1: 4300 bc; C2: 2200 bc; C3: 400 bc; D: 0 bc

Blatina Polje (Mljet)

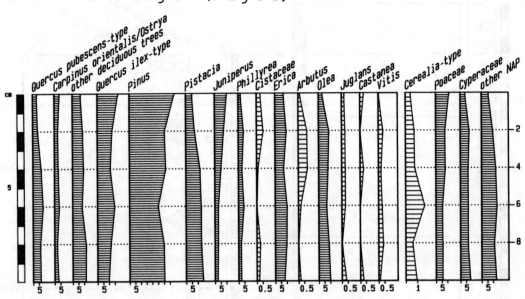

Fig. 3. AP percentage diagram of Blatina Polje, Mljet

In period D the oak forests were replaced by pine. During period D Pinus, Juniperus, Pistacia and Olea showed maximum values while those of the oaks decreased. The comparatively high Olea values together with maquis indicators, may be due to the spreading of wild olive or to farming activities.

Another diagram from Mljet, taken from the freshwater lake Blatina Polje, only covers a short part of period D (Fig. 3). It shows higher amounts of Olea and probably indicates olive cultivation better than the Malo Jezero diagram. At the same time there are high pine values and occurrences of Castanea, a tree which like Juglans did not grow in Dalmatia before the time of Greek and Roman influence (Beug 1961b, 1962, 1967; Brande 1973).

The upper part of the Malo Jezero diagram, which includes the Roman period, is still under study. Surface sediments show 52% Pinus which is twice as much as the uppermost sample of the core itself. So far, the deforestation of the Dalmatian coast during the last millennium does not seem to be represented in the diagram, because the ratio of AP and NAP remains almost constant in the upper part of the diagram (Fig. 4).

2 SOUTHERN GREECE: THE ARGIVE PLAIN

The diagram from southern Greece (Fig. 6) results from a 7-m-core, taken from the ancient Lake Lerna, in the Argive plain. The bottom of the lake was radiocarbon-dated to 6330 bc at a depth of 7 m (Finke 1988; Finke and Malz 1988). However, the sediments below 5.5 m do not contain pollen grains.

From the area under study, continuous settlements since the Neolithic period are known near to the coring point (Filip 1969; Hopf 1962). During the Bronze Age the cities of Argos and Lerna were situated close to the lake. Mycenae and Tiryns were not far away. Although they lost their importance at the end of the Helladic epoch, human influence in the Argive plain has never ceased.

The diagram can be divided into four forest periods. The oldest part of the diagram (period I) shows the predominance of deciduous oak, first with relatively high amounts of Mediterranean elements.

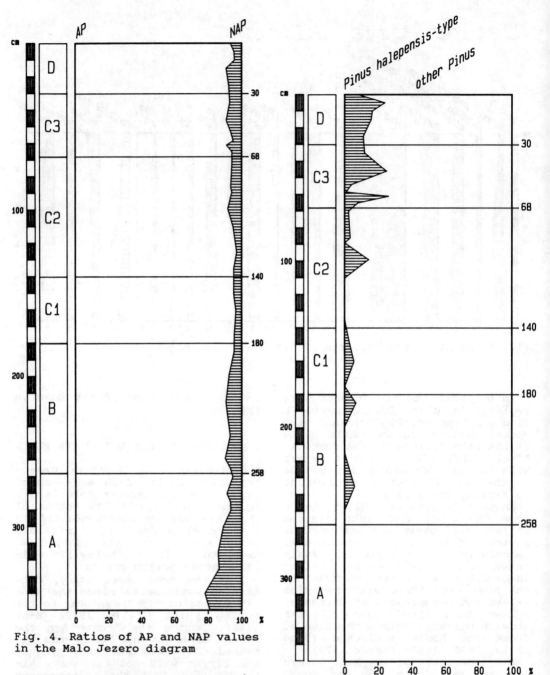

Fig. 4. Ratios of AP and NAP values in the Malo Jezero diagram

Fig. 5. Ratios of Pinus halepensis-type and other Pinus in the diagram from Malo Jezero

Later these elements decreased and the values of summergreen oak increased considerably.

Period II shows lower values of deciduous oak and a slight increase of the Carpinus orientalis/ Ostrya-type and of Pinus. During this period shrub and heath elements such as Erica and Cistaceae

spread slowly. Together with the decrease of Quercus this may be the result of deforestation, but it is remarkable that the curve of ever-

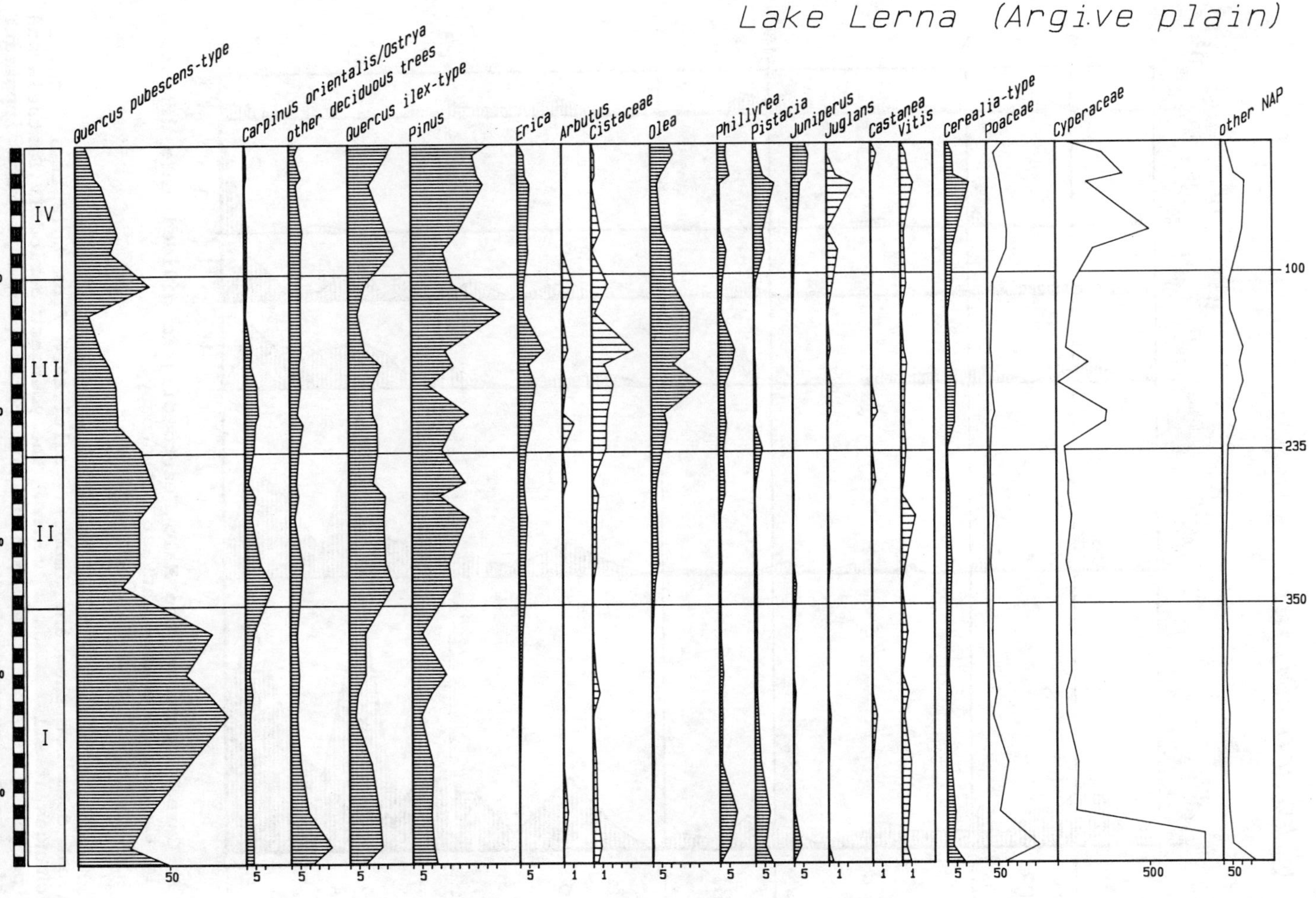

Fig. 6. AP percentage diagram of Lake Lerna, Argive plain

Malo Jezero (Mljet)

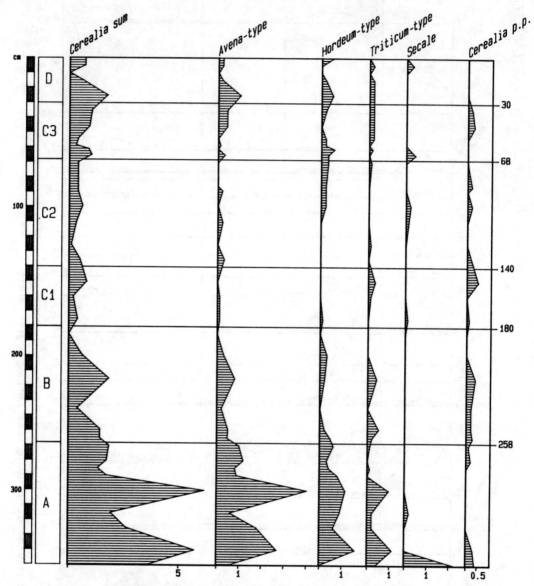

Fig. 7. Cereal curve of the Malo Jezero diagram divided into different types by the use of phase-contrast microscopy

green oak does not show any important changes at all.

In period III shrub vegetation was of great importance. Higher values are found for Erica, Phillyrea and Cistaceae. At the same time Olea and Juglans show a continuous curve. Possibly both were cultivated from this period on. In the youngest period IV Pistacia and Juniperus played a more important role.

More work needs to be done on the Lake Lerna core. Moreover, the dating of the periods distinguished is still uncertain.

3 PINUS HALEPENSIS

The rise of the Pinus curve in sub-zone C3 of the Malo Jezero diagram led Beug (1962) to suggest that Pinus halepensis, nowadays the most common tree on Mljet, might have been brought in by man, most probably during Greek or Roman times. Now an attempt has been made to check that interpretation. P. halepensis and P. nigra are the only pine species in South Dalmatia (Horvat et al. 1974). The pollen grains can be distinguished to a certain degree by their size (Agwu and Beug 1982). At least the larger P. halepensis pollen grains can be separated from those of P.nigra. In the Mljet diagram pine pollen grains from all four periods were measured. The results show a tendency to P. halepensis in the periods C3 and D, which are thought to be Greek or Roman in age (Fig. 5).

4 CULTIVATED GRASSES

Cereal pollen analysis in southern Europe is connected with many problems because Poaceae pollen morphology has never been thoroughly investigated here. In 1961 and 1962 Beug did not use the phase-contrast method (Beug 1961a) for his Mljet study. Therefore attempts have been made now to apply that method to the pollen grains of the so-called Cerealia-type.

In the Malo Jezero diagram cereal-type pollen can be divided into Avena, Hordeum and Triticum-type grains and Secale (Fig. 7). Because of its pre-Neolithic age, however, it is not likely that the high amounts of cereal-type grains in the older part of the diagram are due to farming activities.

One has to keep in mind that a large but unknown number of wild grasses have pollen types similar to the cultivated species. That may also hold for the Hordeum- and Avena-types. Wild rye is native in Dalmatia (Rikli 1948). It was expected that, as in Central Europe, the Triticum-type might be the best indicator of farming activities. However, this is not true. High values in Boreal times, for instance, must be attributed to certain wild grasses.

5 PISTACIA

Recently an attempt has been made to identify Pistacia grains to species level according to a method published by Ballouche (1986). For identification we used differential-interference contrast microscopy.

Mljet is situated in the northern Mediterranean area where Pistacia terebinthus is found, whereas southern Greece belongs to the area of the Oleo-Ceratonion of which the evergreen P. lentiscus is a typical constituent (Horvat et al. 1974).

However, so far we have found only P. terebinthus-type pollen grains, both on Mljet and at Lake Lerna.

ACKNOWLEDGEMENTS

The new investigation of the Malo Jezero sediments was made possible by Dr. Schulze from the Mondsee Institute of Limnology, Austria, who took cores with improved coring techniques. The core from the Argive plain was taken by Dr. E. Zangger, Cambridge.

REFERENCES

Agwu, C.O.C. and H.-J. Beug 1982. Palynological studies of marine sediments off the West African coast. "Meteor" Forsch. Ergebnisse, Reihe C 36:1-3.

Ballouche, A. 1986. Paléoenvironnements de l'Homme Fossile Holocène au Maroc. Thèse, Université de Bordeaux.

Beug, H.-J. 1961a. Leitfaden der Pollenbestimmung für Mitteleuropa und die angrenzenden Gebiete. Lieferung 1. Stuttgart: Gustav Fischer.

Beug, H.-J. 1961b. Beiträge zur postglazialen Floren- und Vegetationsgeschichte Süddalmatiens: Der See "Malo Jezero" auf Mljet, Teil 1: Vegetationsentwicklung. Flora 150:600-630.

Beug, H.-J. 1962. Über die ersten anthropogenen Vegetationsveränderungen in Süddalmatien an Hand eines neuen Pollendiagramms vom "Malo Jezero" auf Mljet. Veröff. Geobot. Inst. ETH Zürich 37:9-15.

Beug, H.-J. 1967.
On the forest history of the
Dalmatian coast. Review of
Palaeobotany and Palynology 2:
271-279.

Bottema, S. 1980.
On the history of the walnut
(Juglans regia L.) in Southeastern Europe. Acta Botanica Neerlandica 29(5/6):343-349.

Filip, J. 1969.
Enzyklopädisches Handbuch zur Ur-
und Frühgeschichte Europas.
Stuttgart-Berlin-Köln-Mainz:
Kohlhammer.

Finke, E. 1988.
Landscape evolution of the Argive
plain, Greece: Paleoecology,
Holocene depositional history and
coastline changes. Thesis, Stanford University.

Finke, E. and H.Malz 1988.
Der Lernäische See, Auswertung
von Satellitenbildern und Ostra-
codenfaunen zur Rekonstruktion
eines vergangenen Lebensraumes.
Natur und Museum 118:213-222.

Hopf, M. 1962.
Nutzpflanzen vom Lernäischen
Golf. Jahrbuch des Römisch-Germanischen Zentralmuseums Mainz:1-
19.

Horvat, I., V.Glavac
and H.Ellenberg 1974.
Vegetation Südosteuropas. Geo-
botanica Selecta 4. Stuttgart:
Gustav Fischer.

Rikli, M. 1948.
Das Pflanzenkleid der Mittelmeer-
länder. Bern: Hans Huber.

Man's Role in the Shaping of the Eastern Mediterranean Landscape, Bottema, Entjes-Nieborg & van Zeist (eds)
© *1990 Balkema, Rotterdam. ISBN 90 61 91 138 9*

The greening of Myrtos

28

Oliver Rackham
Corpus Christi College, Cambridge, UK

ABSTRACT: This paper compares observations made in 1968 in an arid part of Crete with the same scene 20 years later. Wild vegetation has responded very quickly to a decline in agriculture and the near-disappearance of pasturage. Trees and other plants, especially palatable species, have much increased; because the trees happen to be flammable, this introduces a fire risk. There is little effect on erosion. Similar changes will have happened in many places in the past.

1 THE IMPACT OF MAN ON THE LANDSCAPE?

Archaeologists tend to think in terms of Man and the Environment: to interpret the landscape in terms of human activities and of geological processes; to treat domestic plants and animals as a kind of artefact, and to relegate wild plants and animals to being part of the environment. It is often assumed that regions are deforested by cutting down trees; that trees, and only trees, protect the landscape from erosion: that there was no significant grazing or browsing before domestic animals; and that goats destroy all vegetation. All these are theories, not truisms, and need to be demonstrated, not assumed.

In reality, plants and animals are not passive parts of the scenery but actors in the play. They are not just part of the environment, but have their own lives to lead. They are all different from each other. Cutting down a pine is a different action from cutting down an oak: the pine dies, but the oak lives and recovers. Goats discourage trees that they are fond of, but encourage trees that they hate, such as cypress (Cupressus sempervirens).

The historical ecology of Mediterranean lands has been misunderstood for 200 years, because scholars have treated plants and animals as either artefacts or environment, and have not found out how each species behaves and how it interacts with soils and human activities.

2 THE DEFORESTATION OF GREECE

In Greece it has usually been assumed that the aboriginal pre-Neolithic vegetation was continuous forest. This forest has gradually been destroyed by human activities, and it is generally supposed that the destruction has been progressive: each century's destruction being added to the destruction accumulated in previous centuries. The theory has been eloquently restated, for example, by Thirgood (1981) and Hughes (1983). Is it true?

The pollen record leaves no doubt that, though aboriginal Greece was certainly more tree'd than today, much of it has never been continuously forested in this interglacial. We find not only the pollen of trees and of the wet-land plants that grew around the sites where pollen is preserved, but of a number of dry-land plants that do not flower in shade, for example asphodel, Caryophyllaceae, yellow-flowered Compositae, Centaurea-

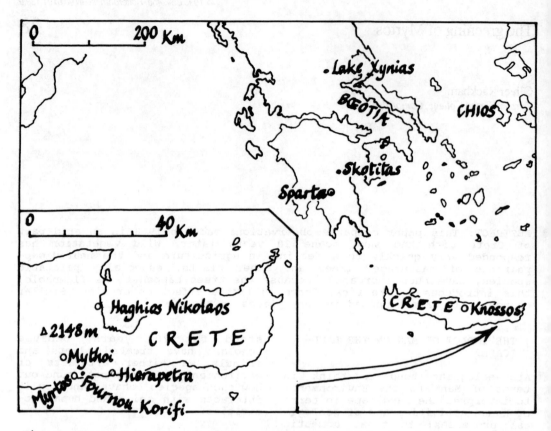

Fig. 1. Part of Greece, showing places mentioned in the text.

type, etc. Although not usually present in large quantities, they are very significant because plants in this category shed much less pollen than most trees. They prove that the canopies of the trees cannot have met each other continuously, but that there were large gaps in which such plants could flower.

There was therefore, in early prehistory, a mosaic of woodland and steppe not so very different from the mosaic of maquis and steppe which is common in Greece today. Indeed, as we shall see, the difference between woodland and maquis would not show up well in the pollen record. (It is quite possible than then, as sometimes today, the roots of the woody plants filled all the available space under the steppe as well as under the woodland.) The proportion of non-shade-bearing dry-land pollen is highest, as we would expect, in

what are now the more arid parts of Crete [in the pollen diagrams of Bottema (1980) and Moody et al. (in press)] and diminishes northwards into the less arid regions of middle Greece [e.g. at Lake Xynias (Bottema 1979)].

Historical documents and pictures refuse to support the theory of progressive deforestation. On the contrary, Greece 100-200 years ago was a much more arid-looking and less-vegetated land than today. This is shown by traveller's descriptions, early paintings and photographs, the sites of which can be identified and compared with what is there now. I have thus documented vegetation changes in Boeotia (Rackham 1983), in which there has been a consistent increase in woodland. The same is shown, often more dramatically, by the photographs of Trevor-Battye (1913) in Crete, photographs in early excavation reports such as

Fig. 2a. Fournou Korifi, looking west towards Myrtos, 11 July 1968. Steppe and very sparse phrygana with thinly-scattered Pistacia lentiscus bushes; less sparse phrygana with small pines on hill in middle distance.

Fig. 2b. The same, 10 September 1987. Phrygana in foreground has been replaced by a thicket of Atriplex halimus more than 1 m high; the Pistacia bushes are still there but are hidden. A pinewood is developing in middle distance.

Fig. 3a. Small coastal plain at Fournou Korifi, 11 July 1968. Former arable land, partly abandoned to steppe; some maize still grown; some young olive groves. Scattered big pines and carobs. Hill on left has phrygana with scattered lentisk bushes and a few trees.

Fig. 3b. The same, 10 September 1987. Most of plain is covered with plastic greenhouses (some of them disused); also young olive groves. Some steppe remains. Wild vegetation has increased on hill to left.

those of Sparta and Knossos, the sketches of Edward Lear from the 1860s, the travel diaries of Leake and Pouqueville in the 1800s, and many others. In very nearly every case there has either been an increase of vegetation, especially trees, or no change; I have only once or twice been able to document a decrease in trees. [See Rackham (in press); a full account must await a more extensive publication].

It is often possible, particularly in Boeotia, to compare the evidence of Classical authors, such as the guidebook of Pausanias in the second century AD, with what is there today. Often there is remarkably little change: for example Pausanias's oakwood called Skotitas in the Peloponnese still exists. It is possible to find forests today that seem not to have existed in Classical times, and vice versa (Rackham in press). The general impression is that Greece 2000 years ago was rather less vegetated than today, but rather more vegetated than 100 years ago.

3 MYRTOS

In July 1968 I visited Myrtos, at the invitation of Professor P.M. Warren, to make an ecological study in connexion with his excavation of the Bronze Age village called Fournou Korifi (Rackham 1972). I went back exactly twenty years later with my original photographs and notebooks to repeat the observations made then. An aerial photograph taken by the Germans in 1941 provides a further comparison.

Myrtos was not chosen with the intention of doing this kind of study. It is a middle-sized village on the mountainous south coast of Crete. In 1968 it seemed arid and impoverished, part of the 'European Sahara' in the rain-shadow that stretches along most of that coast. Tree growth was difficult except on north-facing slopes. Rainfall is not specially low - Myrtos lies between Hierapetra, with a mean annual rainfall in the 1960s and 70s of 420 mm, and Mythoi, with 620 mm (from figures kindly supplied by the Greek Agricultural Service) - but the rainfall is very variable, and the climate hot, windy and evaporative. I now appreciate that an important further limitation is the massive, compact marl rocks of the coastal belt, which retain moisture, but into which tree roots cannot easily penetrate to get at it.

At least half the area within 5 km of Myrtos was once cultivated, partly on small coastal plains and partly on terraced hillsides. The latter would probably have grown reasonable crops of barley (Moody and Grove, this volume). Cultivation had already declined before 1941, and by 1968 had shrunk to about one-third of the original area. Most of the terraces had by then gone out of use. Since 1968 the extent of cultivation has only slightly declined, but its character is now very different: it has changed from farming to market-gardening in plastic greenhouses. There has also been some extension of olive-growing, though less than in most of Crete.

Myrtos is now a prosperous seaside resort. Cultivation, though still important, is almost restricted to greenhouses and new olive-groves in the plains and to older olives in the hills. The remainder of the landscape consists of wild vegetation; some of it on terraces and other cultivated land abandoned for between 20 years and more than 50 years, and some on land which has never been cultivated. It is with wild vegetation that the rest of this paper is concerned.

4 CHANGES IN THE VEGETATION OF MYRTOS

Wild vegetation in the Myrtos area, as in most of Crete, consists of a mosaic of maquis, phrygana and steppe. I define maquis as consisting of low trees and shrubs. Most shrubs in Greece are trees bitten down into a shrubby form, for example prickly-oak, Quercus coccifera (known in Israel as Q. calliprinos), which can be either a tree or a shrub and produces abundant pollen and acorns when less than 1 m high. Phrygana (or garrigue) is a community of undershrubs, for example members of the Cistaceae, Labiatae and Leguminosae; these are mostly short-lived and never grow into trees. Steppe consists of grasses and herbaceous plants, especially bulbous plants and annuals. There are also stands of the Cretan pine, Pinus brutia, which forms woodland but cannot exist in the state of maquis.

Around Myrtos the predominant types of vegetation are phrygana and steppe. Maquis is very limited because of drought and poor root penetration. Most of the evergreen trees and shrubs, for example lentisk (Pistacia lentiscus), are deep-rooting. The marl shows no remains of tree roots having penetrated it in the past, which rules out any possibility that tree growth has ever been general.

There has been a modest increase in maquis since 1968. Then the chief shrub was lentisk, which is now almost unchanged: almost every bush photographed then is still there. There has been an increase in juniper (Juniperus phoenicea), which has overtaken lentisk in abundance. Prickly-oak is not abundant: the bushes of 1968 are slowly growing into trees but have not increased in numbers.

There has been a remarkable increase in undershrubs, which now cover wide areas which in 1968 were bare rock or tenuous steppe. Most undershrubs are short-lived; those alive in 1968 have now been replaced by a new generation, often of different species. Thyme (Thymus capitatus), spiny-broom (Calicotome spinosa) and Cistus salvifolius are still abundant, though not necessarily in the same places. Others, such as Erica manipuliflora and Anthyllis hermanniae, have much increased. The most dramatic increases are in Atriplex halimus (Chenopodiaceae) and Ebenus cretica (Leguminosae), both now widely dominant in places where there were only scattered individuals in 1968. These two, unlike other undershrubs, are long-lived and very palatable to goats and sheep. Ebenus is an endemic (that is, not found outside Crete).

In steppe there has not been much change. Ex-cultivated land at Myrtos is slow to be invaded by phrygana or maquis; many fields, recently abandoned in 1968, are still covered mainly by steppe. A remarkable increase is in Aristida adscensionis, an African grass which just extends into the driest parts of Europe. At Myrtos in 1968 it was rare, only in very dry rocky steppe; new road-making in the area has greatly extended its habitat.

Pinus brutia, though often shallow-rooted, can grow on marls and gypsum. If water is short it stays alive but grows very slowly.

In 1941 it formed small woods on north-facing slopes. By 1968 it had much increased. It has since at least doubled again, invading phrygana, steppe and ex-cultivated land; it has spread on to south-facing slopes. By the end of the century pines are likely to cover most of the entire Myrtos region, except for the remaining cultivated land.

5 THE DISAPPEARANCE OF BROWSING

There can be little doubt that the main cause of these changes is the decline of grazing. Crete has a history of browsing by sheep and goats. In many places browsing has declined since the last century, but at Myrtos this decline is unusually severe. In 1968 there was still some evidence of grazing. In 1988 there was virtually non except by wild hares; there was no difference between the vegetation inside and outside the fence around the archaeological site at Fournou Korifi.

In general, this agrees with the palatability of the plants that have increased. The shrub that has increased least is Pistacia lentiscus, which is very distasteful. Atriplex and Ebenus are the most palatable of all undershrubs, and the ones that have increased most.

It is somewhat surprising that other undershrubs, and pine, should also have increased, since none of them is very palatable. However, sheep and goats must have eaten something, and before 1968 they seem to have been reduced to eating undershrubs and pine for want of anything better.

These are the consequences of a big retreat of agriculture and the almost total disappearance of browsing. This may often have happened in the past, for a variety of social and economic reasons, but this time it is very severe. However, even when (as here) there has been a very clear change of land-use, the possibility cannot be quite excluded that a change of climate, or at least a run of wet seasons, may have contributed to the effect on wild vegetation. In a wet season the leading shoot of a tree may take less time to grow to the critical height at which a goat cannot reach it. There was, for example, a run of wet years in the mid-1940s, and 1964-5 was a wet season, in contrast to the dry 1950s.

In 1968 the plant communities were relatively simple: I then recognized only four kinds of phrygana. They were then probably determined largely by resistance to browsing, but now they are much more complex and depend on competition. Partly for this reason, Zohary and Orshan (1966) could describe the vegetation of all Crete in terms of only 17 plant associations, which would be a great oversimplification today.

6 THE COMING AGE OF FIRE

Another change is on its way. Pine is limited to about 5% of Crete, in four main areas. Its main distribution has not changed for at least 500 years, but in each of the four areas it is becoming more abundant. In these areas there have been four major fires in the 1980s, two of them in the Myrtos area. Pine is a fire-promoting tree, very combustible and with a loose flammable leaf-litter; in default of other ignition, it can be set on fire by lightning. Most big fires in Greece involve pines; other types of vegetation will burn but much less easily. Myrtos is therefore liable to change from the grazing-dominated landscape of the past to a fire-dominated landscape in the future, much as has happened in the island of Chios.

7 EROSION

Has the increase of trees, shrubs and undershrubs had any effect on erosion? Most of Crete, though often severely eroded in the Pleistocene, is not now actively eroding. I found some active erosion of marl slopes around Myrtos in 1968, but there is rather less now. In my experience, erosion in Greece has little to do with tree cover. Insofar as vegetation matters at all, the important cover is the crusts of bryophytes, lichens and blue-green algae which bind the soil surface. Before 1968 it was probably trampling by animals'

hooves, rather than lack of tall vegetation, that promoted erosion.

I have carefully looked for erosion after fires in Crete, and have found hardly even a trace, except locally where fire has been followed by extra browsing of the regrowth vegetation.

8 CONCLUSIONS

1. The retreat of agriculture and collapse of shepherding are common changes in the modern Mediterranean. There are now easier ways of making a living than growing barley on terraces.

2. Similar changes will often have occurred, for various reasons, in the past. Matters may have been made worse by the fact that in 1943 Hitler's soldiery sacked Myrtos and murdered twenty of the inhabitants. That, too, will have been an all-too-frequent event in the history of Crete.

3. Vegetation responds very quickly to changes in human affairs. Woodland comes back even in this very dry part of Europe, but it does not become continuous forest.

4. In Myrtos the invading trees happen to be pines, which bring in fire as the predominant ecological factor. Where similar changes occur in the 95% of Crete which is not piney, they set the landscape on a quite different course: the new woodland there is of juniper, cypress or oak, which are much less flammable.

5. There is no reason to think that the vegetation which develops through human activities declining will ever return to the state Myrtos would be in if these activities had never occurred.

6. There is nothing natural about a state with no grazing except hares. Crete had a native fauna including elephants, hippopotamuses and deer, but no carnivore more ferocious than a badger. Myrtos may now be less grazed than at any time, not merely since Crete had human inhabitants, but since it became an island.

ACKNOWLEDGEMENT

The 1988 visit to Myrtos was part

of one of the research projects on Desertification in Southern Europe, commissioned by the Directorate-General for Science, Research and Development of the Commission of the European Communities.

REFERENCES

Bottema, S. 1979.
  Pollen analytical investigations in Thessaly (Greece). Palaeohistoria 21:20-39.
Bottema, S. 1980.
  Palynological investigation on Crete. Review of Palaeobotany and Palynology 31: 193-217.
Hughes, J.D. 1983.
  How the ancients viewed deforestation. Journal of Field Archaeology 10:437-445.
Moody, J. and A.T.Grove
  (this volume). Terraces and enclosure walls in the Cretan landscape.
Moody, J., O.Rackham and G.Rapp
  in press. Paleoenvironmental studies of the Akrotiri peninsula, Crete: pollen cores from Tersana and Limnes. Journal of Archaeological Science.
Rackham, O. 1972.
  The vegetation of the Myrtos region. In P.M.Warren, Myrtos: an early Bronze Age settlement in Crete, p.283-298. London, Thames and Hudson.
Rackham, O. 1983.
  Observations on the historical ecology of Boeotia. Ann. British School of Archaeology at Athens 78:291-351.
Rackham, O. in press.
  Ancient landscapes. In O.Murray and S.Price (eds.), The Greek city.
Thirgood, J.V. 1981.
  Man and the Mediterranean forest. London: Academic Press.
Trevor-Battye, A. 1913.
  Camping in Crete. London: Witherby.
Zohary, D. and G.Orshan 1966.
  An outline of the geobotany of Crete. Israel Journal of Botany 14, Suppl.:1-49.

Author index